EUROPE BY TRAIN

Katie Wood was born and educated in Edinburgh. She read Communications then English at university, and worked as a freelance journalist before specializing in travel in 1981. Author of many guidebooks, she has made a name for herself both in Britain and internationally for her practical, down-to-earth approach, and the quality of her research.

Katie Wood continues to write freelance for numerous newspapers, including the *Scotsman* and contributes to television and radio travel programmes on a regular basis. She is a fellow of the Royal Geographical Society, undertakes specialist travel consultancy work for airlines and tourist boards, and is acknowledged as an expert on the impact of travel on the environment.

Married with two children, Katie Wood lives in Perth, Scotland. Train travel remains her first love, and she regularly takes to the rails to update *Europe by Train*. She has been the book's Chief Editor for the last seven years.

George McDonald was born in Dumfries, Galloway, and was educated at Fettes College and Edinburgh University. He developed a taste for train travel after a journey on the world's highest railway in Peru and a trip through the Soviet Union. Since 1981 he has been constantly on the move, and considers it unusual to be in one place for more than three weeks at a time.

GW00371318

KATIE WOOD AND GEORGE McDONALD

EUROPE BY TRAIN
THE COMPLETE GUIDE TO INTER-RAILING

Chief Editor: Katie Wood

Editorial Assistants: Vicky Lewis and Tim Cook
Head Researchers:
Tim Cook, Peter Ede and Alison Brown

This book is dedicated to
the memory of my mother,
without whose unstinting help and practical support
it could not have been written or continually updated.
With grateful thanks — K.W. 1992.

Fontana
An Imprint of HarperCollinsPublishers

Fontana
An Imprint of HarperCollins*Publishers*,
77–85 Fulham Palace Road,
Hammersmith, London W6 8JB

First published by Fontana 1983
This edition published by Fontana 1993

9 8 7 6 5 4 3 2 1

The maps, drawn by Illustra of Maidenhead,
are based on Thomas Cook's Rail Map of Europe

Whilst every attempt has been made to ensure accuracy
throughout this work, the turbulent nature of the international
travel industry is such that the authors and publishers
cannot be held liable for changes which occur after the time
of writing.

The Authors assert the moral right to
be identified as the authors of this work

ISBN 0 00 637924 9

Set in Times Roman

Printed in Great Britain by
HarperCollinsManufacturing Glasgow

CONTENTS

Northern Finland – Southern Finland – Russia (St Petersburg) – Estonia (Tallinn)

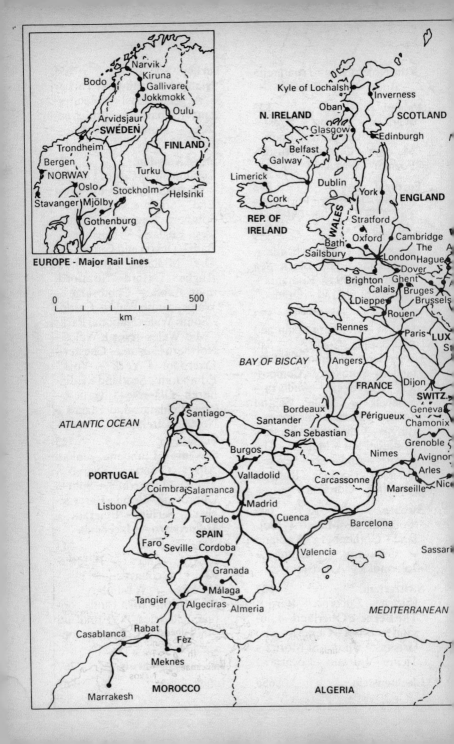

EUROPE - Major Rail Lines

0 ———————————— 500
km

FOREWORD

What makes this book different from other guidebooks on Europe is that it's train orientated and economy minded. Research for this guide stems from travel all over Europe. Thorough investigation and very tight budgets have been the basis of this work. This is the only guide of its kind giving train and station information, as well as information on accommodation and the sights. It was written because I, like thousands of others, needed a book like this and it didn't exist. Now it's here I hope you'll be able to learn from my mistakes and benefit from my experiences. The book tells you of the finds made when going round Europe in recent years (updated every year) and explains the different ways of using the various railpasses which offer an exceptional opportunity to see the sights, meet new people and broaden your horizons – all for an amazingly low price.

• **Prices and exchange rates:** Because these fluctuate, we can only give a rough guide. As a reference this book uses £1 = $1.80, but this rate and all the prices mentioned are subject to change. The costs in the former communist countries will be particularly vulnerable to inflation, as these countries move towards a market economy.

• **Any potential researchers or budding journalists out there?** Many of you write, asking if I need researchers to help update my guides. I do, but stringent rules apply. If, after reading this, you still feel you would suit, please send on a full typed CV, photo, list of where you've travelled and samples of any published writing or any travel writing care of the publishers. If you do not comply with these rules no reply will be sent. Sorry, but each year I'm inundated with enquiries and can only respond to those who have shown that they can follow instructions.

Criteria

1. You must have travelled very extensively.
2. You must be very interested in travel. And I mean manically interested, not just keen on going to foreign parts. Are you the type who never misses a travel programme; who immediately turns to

the travel sections of newspapers and magazines; who yearns for foreign travel more than anything else? Do you know, or are you prepared to learn, a lot about the travel industry?

3. Do you write well? Are you at least up to 'A' level English, preferably degree level, and are you competent with your language? You will have to be concise, yet interesting; you may have had to write it at 1 a.m., but it mustn't show. Can you read a booklet and translate it into a couple of sentences? This is what guidebook writing is all about. Could you instantly pick out the most salient points?

4. Can you work to deadlines? Publishing schedules wait for no man. If a guide isn't on the shelves by the holiday season, forget it. I work to very strict deadlines, and I am a hard task mistress! Could you deliver in time? You will be contractually bound to do so.

If you can do all of this, and want to travel, write to me now.

Katie Wood
c/o Fontana Paperbacks
HarperCollins Publishers
77–85 Fulham Palace Road
London W6 8JB

INTRODUCTION

For my part, I travel not to go anywhere, but to go. I travel for travel's sake.
The great affair is to move; to feel the needs and hitches of our life more
nearly; to come down off this feather-bed of civilization, and find the globe
granite underfoot and strewn with cutting flints.

ROBERT LOUIS STEVENSON, *Travels with a Donkey in the Cevennes*

Anything is possible on a train, a great meal, a binge, a visit from card
players, an intrigue, a good night's sleep, and strange monologues framed
like Russian short stories.

PAUL THEROUX, *The Great Railway Bazaar*

This 1993 edition of *Europe by Train* – the eleventh – contains a
wealth of new and even more detailed rail information. Given the
upheavals of 1992, it has to! Because accurate travel info is essential
to the smooth running of your holiday, I've really gone to town this
year to provide you with the kind of details you'll need: frequency of
services; length of journey; reliability of trains; attractive minor
routes, as well as details of the good long-distance trains to catch a
few winks on if you're short of money and need a night's sleep.

You'll find that the book is still very much geared towards those
on a tight budget. It's been great to hear how successful the new
'Over 26' Inter-Rail pass turned out to be last year. So many of you
wrote to me saying what a joy it is to be able to experience the
freedom of European train travel at a reasonable price once again!
It's obvious you're still keen to be as economical as possible when
travelling though, so I haven't skimped on the cheap recommendations or money-saving tips, despite the now-expanded older
readership. What I have done is add a few slightly more comfortable
recommendations here and there, which I'm sure European train
travellers of all ages will welcome – there's nothing worse than
roughing it too much or for too long. We all owe ourselves the
occasional treat – even if that's just a café meal instead of a
supermarket picnic, or a pension instead of a hostel . . .

As any seasoned eurorailer knows, one of the biggest headaches
of your trip is finding acceptable but cheap accommodation. When
my *Cheap Sleep Guide to Europe* (see p.15) was published in
January 1992, I'm glad to say it proved a runaway success. I wrote
the guide in the first place because space is restricted in *Europe by*

Train and I can, therefore, only list a few tried and tested places for cheap accommodation. The *Cheap Sleep Guide* is packed with literally hundreds of accommodation suggestions, so the chances of finding all of a given town's recommendations full – even in July and August – are really pretty slim. And you can't beat it for value: for the price of one booking fee, you get recommendations ranging from B&Bs, hostels (private and IYHF), hotels, campsites and Sleep-Ins, to where to sleep rough if it comes to the pinch – for all of Europe. You obviously found the *Cheap Sleep Guide* invaluable last year, so I've now added over forty more cities and towns (many of which are in Eastern Europe) for 1993 to make it even bigger and better. It should help prevent all those frustrating occasions when you arrive in a town to find the Tourist Office shut and just wish you'd found out about accommodation in advance!

Pre-planning should not, however, be regarded as a constriction on your flexibility. There's nothing to stop you changing your plans while you're away, but with a little careful forethought, you can ensure you see everything you'd ideally like to – without wasting precious time waiting in the long tourist and train-information queues. It's also a good idea to do a bit of background reading to keep the myriad sights in perspective. I recommend you get Kenneth Clarke's *Civilisation* from your local library, but most cultural histories will serve the same purpose.

And now to *Europe by Train* itself. In Part One, you'll find information on different aspects of eurorailing which will be of interest to everyone, regardless of your routes. Following this, in Part Two, there are individual chapters on the countries of Europe in alphabetical order; the destinations featured in these chapters follow the pattern you're best advised to take from the minute you step off the train at your chosen stop. I'll guide you to the accommodation service, the campsites, hostels and hotels, the Tourist Office, the eating places, and then the sights themselves.

Changes in Eastern Europe continue (notably in what used to be Yugoslavia and Czechoslovakia), and, although I've been able to expand the wealth of information given on the Eastern European countries, the fluctuating situation means that you'll have to be lenient if details have changed by the time this 1993 edition is in the shops. More than anything else, I can assure you that every single recommendation and suggestion throughout *Europe by Train 1993* has been thoroughly vetted, so that you'll be pushed to find a more accurate and up-to-date budget guide to Europe.

Another thing you won't find elsewhere is the kind of information contained in the factsheets (see p.13), which have also been updated and expanded, with a whole new section on Scenic Routes. One thing that hasn't changed is the price. Hope they help.

KATIE WOOD
Chief Editor, *Europe by Train*
December 1992

FACTSHEETS

Since 1990 I have been producing a series of factsheets in response to the great demand for itineraries tailored to suit your individual preferences when travelling. They have been an enormous success. Many of you wrote to say nice things about them and to tell me how useful they had been when planning your trip, and when away, so that makes it all worthwhile. The 1993 sheets have been totally updated, very much expanded and greatly improved – with much more information on off-the-beaten-track destinations.

For 1993 I have nine factsheets. Again they all incorporate the sections of The Sun Worshipper (where to find the best beaches); The Sightseer (where the most interesting sights are and what to look for); The Socialite (where best to people-watch; catch nightlife, and annual fiestas and events); The Nature Lover & Recluse (where to escape the crowds and head into the hills); Scenic Routes, and the Grand Tour (a taster itinerary, encompassing all the aspects above). Every type of traveller is therefore covered and will be directed towards the parts of Europe best suited to their needs.

Basic Accommodation suggestions are given for places not in *Europe by Train*, and sights and rail links are covered. Many places never before featured in the guidebook are in the factsheets (some of which are my personal favourites, which I've been keeping up my sleeve!)

Make your selection of factsheets from the choice below:

1. Europe – Grand Tour – a good run down on all 26 countries. This is ideal for planning your route. It also reads like an appendix to *Europe by Train*. This tends to be the most popular factsheet.

2. Italy

3. France

4. Germany – including eastern Germany

5. Greece

6. Netherlands

7. Spain

8. Eastern Europe – covering all eastern European countries

9. Scandinavia – covering four Scandinavian countries

Procedure

1. Send an A4 stamped self-addressed envelope, preferably self-adhesive, and ensure there is a first class stamp *per factsheet* on the envelope. Don't ask for seven factsheets and put on one stamp please!

   NB. If writing from abroad for factsheets, send an International Money Order for the price of the factsheets *in sterling*, plus £1.50 *per factsheet* for postage. If you're writing from Australia, or New Zealand or USA and would like the factsheets posted air mail (as opposed to surface), please send £3 *per factsheet* for postage (rather than £1.50).

2. Ensure your postal order/cheque really *is* inside the envelope before posting (you wouldn't believe how many I have had to return because of this!), and that it's made out to K. Wood for the correct amount.

Europe costs £5.00
Eastern Europe costs £4.50
Scandinavia, Italy, France, Spain, Greece, Germany and *Netherlands* cost £3.50 each

Send your postal order/cheque, stamped addressed envelope and a note of the countries you want to:

Katie Wood
c/o Fontana Paperbacks
HarperCollins
77–85 Fulham Palace Road
London W6 8JB

Please clearly mark your envelopes EUROPE BY TRAIN FACTSHEETS. Allow five weeks for delivery.

The Cheap Sleep Guide to Europe

Every year the most common question I am asked is how to make finding accommodation easier. From years of experience on the rails in Europe, I can sympathize, and can only agree that finding a bed is the one drawback of flexible Inter-Rail travelling. Booking too many beds ahead decidedly cramps your style, yet spending a night in a station or park leaves you vulnerable, exhausted all the next day, and is far from ideal.

There *are* enough hostels, pensions and campsites to go round in Europe. Supply does keep pace with the increasing demand – it's just a case of knowing where to go, and in which areas to look. Fine, when you have spent the last ten years doing this, but for many Inter-Railers, a little guidance is needed. That's the thinking behind my *Cheap Sleep Guide to Europe*, first brought out as a Fontana paperback last year and now thoroughly updated, with over forty new destinations, many in Eastern Europe.

Every major city and tourist location in Europe is covered – notably the destinations where you tell me you've had problems finding a bed. The idea is that this new guide, in conjunction with *Europe by Train* and any of the more detailed factsheets, will be all you will need, apart from the Thomas Cook *European Timetable*, to ensure a smooth-running European trip.

International Youth Hostels, privately run hostels, good pensions, campsites and Sleep-Ins are all covered. In certain cases, 'safe' sleeping rough suggestions are even given. Buying this guide will save you shelling out on the *Youth Hostels Handbook* or the *Campsite Directory*, and will save you a lot of time and money queueing up at Tourist Offices to get suggestions and pay for their booking services.

As with the guide, your input can help. To help keep this publication up to date I would value your comments. If you find any of these places are no longer worth recommending, or if you find new places that are, please write to me c/o the publishers, and tell me about them.

Be a Good Tourist

In 1991 *The Good Tourist* – A Worldwide Guide for the Green Traveller (Mandarin Paperbacks) was published, followed by the first three individual country guides in the series of which this was the launching book.

The theory behind this series is of relevance to all of us who travel, in any way, at any time. It addresses the issues of the impact of tourism on the environment and society. This may sound a bit heavy, but the reading of it is not. It's about what you are on the point of doing – travelling to a foreign country; any country. What you do; where you go; how you go; where you sleep; what you eat – it all has a great impact on that country. You can make this a positive or negative experience. For too many countries, for too many years now, the impact has been increasingly negative, and it's up to every one of us to take account of our actions.

Traditionally, travel has been seen as a good thing. Tourism generates valuable income for a country (indeed, more money is made through tourism and its related services than any other industry in the world!), and broadening the horizons and experiencing other cultures can only do good, can't it? Well, it can be good for the guest, but what of the host in this relationship? How much income goes back into the pockets of the waiters and taxi drivers in third world countries such as Thailand and Gambia from all the mass tourism in their country? How much land is given over to developments for wealthy tourists? What control do any of us as individuals have over the mass developments going on the world over in the name of tourism?

We are destroying the very things we set out to see. Europe is a classic case, and travelling through it by train is a good way to discover the truth about the tourist industry. Venice is sinking under the weight of tourists' feet; the Acropolis is being eroded by pollution and over-visiting; the once-beautiful beaches of the Spanish costas and the Med are polluted and ugly; the Alps are crumbling under the pressure of skiing.

Fortunately, the current wave of 'green thinking' is also percolating into tourism and travel. But is enough being done? Where is the mass industry going? Are you, as an Inter-Railer, leaving your conscience at home when you travel? Have you really questioned why you are making this trip? Do you truly respect the country you are visiting? What do you hope to gain from this trip? Do you make an effort to meet the locals and get to know the real culture of the place? Are you staying in appropriate accommodation; are you adding to the litter and pollution? The chances are that you, like most educated independent travellers, are among the few who try to be as 'green' as possible in your travel. The train is one of the best means of transport in terms of low pollution and energy efficiency. Staying in locals' houses, or hostels or camping makes sense, and having a caring and aware attitude, you will probably be contributing as little as possible to the deterioration of our world.

The series my husband (an ecologist) and I are writing looks at how to be a good tourist in various countries in detail, starting with the UK, France and Turkey; it looks at the impact of all different types of holidays; it tells you which companies to travel with (and which not to). Now that being green is so trendy, it's good to separate the wheat from the chaff. Reading *The Good Tourist* may make your European wanderings all the more pertinent and give you more of an idea of the overall plan of things.

The country guides (*The Good Tourist in France/the UK/Turkey*) are guides for people touring these countries who want to know more than the average where to stay, when to get information. They discuss what the locals feel about tourism, how to meet the locals, where to visit and where not to – where are the honeypots and what's genuinely worth seeing; when to go, how much revenue tourism brings to the region, what the controversial issues are surrounding the development of tourist sites – the sort of info only the locals can give you. Our researchers are local, and these books are as different from your conventional guide as you can get. They should appeal to you. Let me know.

Part One: EURORAILING

Every year the main roads of Europe become more and more congested and road improvements move at a slow pace, compared

The advantages of train travel

Besides the fact that eurorailing is a real bargain, there are many advantages to travelling by train which make your European travels more pleasurable. The train is without doubt the safest, most convenient and interesting means of transport to uncover some hidden corners of Europe that hitch-hiking can never show you. You can cover a lot of ground in a very short time – you leave from, and arrive at, stations which are invariably in city centres; and you don't lay yourself open to the vagaries of the weather – trains are very rarely cancelled due to fog or rain. You also cut out the inevitable traffic jams you would land in if you van round the roads of Europe in the high season. The advantages of eurorailing over hitching are numerous, but the main one is clear: you can rely on getting to your destination and can thus cram far more into your trip. All in all, there are virtually no tourist centres in Europe that cannot be conveniently reached by rail, and even if there were, there are always buses or bikes at the nearest station.

Believe it or not, the train (assuming you take a high-speed express and not a local shunt-about) can actually travel faster than a plane on a distance of under 400 miles, allowing for the time it takes to commute to and from airports. If you're on a long journey, the train allows you to walk about and stretch your legs, and to go for a meal or a snack when you please. You'll also find trains a wonderful meeting-place to chat to people, both the locals and other euro-railers. It's almost impossible to make a trip on one of the popular routes in a summer month and not end up swapping stories with groups of fellow travellers. On overnight journeys, the intimacy of the train compartment makes it *quite* impossible!

Almost all European trains are diesel- or electric-driven, and most are government-owned (the main exceptions being some lines in Switzerland). A long-distance international train may use rolling stock from several countries along its route, so it pays to discover quickly what each country's carriages look like, and head for the good ones (i.e. the Swiss, German or any of the Scandinavian ones) when the train rolls in.

Every year the main roads of Europe become more and more congested and road improvements move at a slow pace, compared to the investments continually being made on the European rail networks. In northern Europe, second-class seats today are comparable with the first-class ones of twenty years ago. Speeds of 125 m.p.h. and more are common now in France, Britain and Germany; as networks expand, new and simplified routes emerge, allowing you greater choice as to the particular part of the country you'd like to travel through in order to get to your final destination.

Anyone who has travelled by train in North America will notice the difference straight away. European trains are faster, more plentiful and more punctual, serving many more destinations. Historically the European networks have not been maintained on a profit-making basis – few networks actually 'make' any money. They are essentially a public service, and the Inter-Rail/Eurail pass is a good measure of this. For example, for the £180 the Inter-Rail ticket costs, you end up with an average saving of £200–400 off the fares you'd normally have to pay, and even these are subsidized at source so, economically, you can't go wrong.

From the environmentalist's point of view, trains are good news when you bear in mind they consume up to seventeen times less energy than aircraft, and five times less than cars, to transport the same volume. Per square foot, a train can carry more people than cars can – and without the same pollution problems.

One of the main beauties of eurorailing – and one of the main pleasures you'll look back on – is the immense feeling of freedom you enjoy. It's entirely up to you where you spend your time, when you move on to somewhere else, and how you choose to get there. It's quite a heady feeling, never really knowing where you'll be this time tomorrow. To preserve this, it's advisable not to book too many hotels, hostels or trains ahead of time – if you bother to book any. However, to counteract the negative side-effects of total flexibility, it's a good idea to arrive in the major cities as early in the morning as possible in order to get yourself a bed for the night. The best option is to buy Katie Wood's *Cheap Sleep Guide to Europe* (Fontana Paperbacks) or get to the tourist accommodation office (often on the station premises) before noon if you possibly can, otherwise you might end up having to spend precious sightseeing time searching for a room. Nearly every town has affordable places to stay within a few blocks of the station so don't worry, you'll not have to walk far.

Eurorailing: the options

Basically there are three schemes you can choose from: a BIJ (Billet International de Jeunesse) ticket or rover ticket covering a set route, an individual country pass or an Inter-Rail/Eurail, depending on where you live. BIJ operates under the auspices of the continental railways and offers reduced fares to the under 26s. Eurotrain is the largest company in this scheme in the UK, and Wasteels and now BR International are other operators in this market. They offer fares to over 2,000 destinations in Europe (including the CIS), Turkey and North Africa, with discounts of up to 40 per cent. As they allow you to break your journey anywhere you want on the route you've chosen, you have the flexibility to use your ticket as a sightseeing pass, so it's important to pick the route which takes in the places you most want to see. There are seven or eight routings to some cities, so it's possible to go one way and return another; for example, if your final destination is to be Rome, you could go out via Paris, Lyon and Turin, and on the return stop off in Florence, Lucerne, Luxembourg and Belgium. The extra cost in taking two singles is only £10–20 ($18–36), and it lets you see a lot more of Europe.

The price of 'add-on' fares (to get you to London from your home town) is another factor to consider. (Eurotrain and Wasteels tickets can be issued for travel from any British Rail station you nominate.) Before committing yourself, always check that British Rail aren't offering an even cheaper fare to London – but bear in mind that these concessions are usually only for restricted services, whereas BIJ tickets are good for all trains to London. The EuroYouth package from British Rail International is an option for the under-26 traveller, with optional 'add-ons' to London. Other tips: don't overlook the coach services to London offered by National Express, especially if you're travelling from Scotland. Also, if travelling from the North-east, consider the ferries from Newcastle or Hull.

At the end of the day, it all depends on where you want to go and how much distance you intend to cover: an Inter-Rail/Eurail would undoubtedly work out better value if you want to do the grand tour of Europe, from Copenhagen to Casablanca. The BIJ companies sell Inter-Rails through their offices anyway; their staff, who are generally very helpful, will advise you which scheme would work out cheapest. Before you rush out to buy any pass, do your research to find out if it will save you money. Add up the total second-class fares for the major routes you plan to cover (or get a travel agent to do it for you). If the sum comes near the price of the pass, the convenience of the pass is nearly always worth the extra.

• **Group travel:** Six or more constitute a group, as far as Eurotrain and Wasteels are concerned. This allows you all to travel at still further reductions. Further information from Eurotrain (071–823 5517), or Wasteels (071–834 7066). Wasteels offer a free place to a leader in a group of fifteen or more; Eurotrain include a free reservation facility. Phone for brochures.

INTER-RAIL – UNDER 26

• **Quick history:** The Inter-Rail scheme was thought up by the UIC (the Union of International Railways) in 1972. It was devised to commemorate fifty years of international transport law; its price is decided upon each year at a conference of all participating countries. The scheme was enlarged, to include those over 26, in May 1991 (details p.26). Around half a million Inter-Rails are sold each year.

In 1992 there were well-grounded fears that the Inter-Rail card, as we know it, was coming to an end. France, Italy, Portugal and Spain all voiced severe discontent with the share of the financial cake they were getting from the Inter-Rail scheme, compared with the number of seats that Inter-Railers occupied on their networks. To a degree, they have a case; we in Britain certainly have far fewer Inter-Railers than the French, Spanish, Portuguese and Italians on their trains, but it's rather ironic given '1992 and all that' that this excellent example of European unity should be threatened at this time.

Numerous meetings and countless arguments later, in October it was decided that the Inter-Rail ticket would be allowed to live on, in the short term anyway, in its current form, and all the countries who participated in 1992 are in it again for 1993. That's the good news.

The rub is that they have had to put the price up to appease the dissatisfied countries so that they get a larger share of the cake (and they've also scrapped the Inter-Rail +26 ticket, which is really bad news). But before you begin to feel decidedly less cordial about our neighbours over the Channel, read on . . . The plight of the pound, as I'm sure you all know, has been a sorry tale of late, and the Inter-Rail price is set in ECUs. The devaluation of the pound against the ECU meant that there was going to have to be a 20 per cent increase in the ticket's cost anyway to compensate for our devalued currency. The bottom line is that yes, the Inter-Rail ticket *has* gone up by a significant amount. But when you compare it to other holidays – *all* of which have had to be increased for '93 because of the devalued pound – it's still good value. And there is no equivalent holiday for flexibility, getting round the continent, and meeting other travellers. Bear that in mind when you're weighing up the pros and cons of Inter-Railing.

• **What is Inter-Rail Under 26?** It is a ticket anyone living in Europe under the age of 26 can buy; it allows you to travel an unlimited distance for one calendar month on the rail networks of the countries listed below, and in the country of purchase at discounts of up to 50 per cent (34 per cent in Britain, 50 per cent on boat trains). If you want to travel for more than a month, buy two or more tickets at a time, getting the dates to run consecutively. The price fluctuates each year, but for 1993 it is £249 ($423) and in April it is on special offer at £229.

With the standard Inter-Rail you can travel free in the following countries: Austria, Belgium, Bulgaria, Czechoslovakia, Denmark, Finland, France, Germany, Greece, Hungary, Italy, Luxembourg, Morocco, the Netherlands, Norway, Poland, Portugal, Republic of Ireland, Romania, Spain, Sweden, Switzerland, Turkey, the United Kingdom and Yugoslavia. It also includes the Brindisi–Patras ferry crossing. As you can see, this allows the Inter-Railer to visit the vast majority of European countries, either taking in as much as possible on a whistle-stop tour or concentrating on areas with particular appeal to the individual.

• **Who qualifies?** Anyone under the age of 26 on the first day the pass becomes valid – and it's up to you to decide when it will start and finish. You must hold a passport of a country participating in the scheme.

• **Rebates:** When you return home, take your Inter-Rail pass back to the station where you bought it and you'll get a rebate; it varies from year to year, but it's around £4 ($7.20). The train authorities use the information (where you travelled on your Inter-Rail, etc.) for market research. Take care not to lose your ticket as a refund is almost impossible to obtain, unless your holiday insurance can help.

• **Reductions:** An Inter-Rail pass bought in the UK entitles you to discounts of 34 per cent on British and Northern Ireland trains and 50 per cent on most Channel ferry services to the continental ports, including Hoverspeed, catamarans and hovercraft. Reductions on some of the private European railways are also granted, and these include most of the Swiss mountain railways. For real train buffs, the Inter-Rail gets you a reduction on admission into the various transport museums of Europe.

1. *Europabus* have an agreement with the Inter-Rail scheme by which they give a 25–30 per cent reduction on many of their runs. These tend to be slow but scenic and the best ones are mainly in France, the south of Italy, Sicily and Switzerland as they often cover areas not on the main rail network and go through small, out-of-the-way places. If you want further information, pick up a Europabus route-planner from British Rail International at Victoria Station – but don't forget: they get busy in summer, so reserve ahead.

2. *Ferries:* 30 per cent concessions are available on Sealink and P&O and 50 per cent on B&I ships; you can also obtain reduced rates on many continental services. The Irish Continental Line from Rosslare to Cherbourg or Le Havre offer 50 per cent reductions. See also the individual countries later in this book. See Appendix II for a complete list of Inter-Rail discounts.

If you need help with travel arrangements you should get in touch with the local station or tourist information.

NB In the UK, Inter-Rails can only be bought from appointed British Rail stations or through authorized BR agents. Do not attempt to get one on the black market as the railway authorities do very rigorous checks now, and you'll just end up being packed off home early, not to mention the local repercussions against you.

INTER-RAIL – +26

From May 1991 until late 1992, Inter-Rail +26 was great news for those not in the first flush of youth (like me). Once more we could don our backpacks and take to the rails at a bargain price. Unfortunately, being pretty inconsistent with the spirit of '1992', from 1993 this ticket will no longer exist. I'm sure many will join me in giving the thumbs down to the countries who have decided to pull out: France, Spain, Portugal and Italy (all of whom threatened to jeopardise the under 26s' Inter-Rail too, but at the last minute agreed to stay in if the price was hiked up).

British Rail International say that they will be introducing a new ticket for the over 26s, probably based on Euro Domino and which will 'allow the same flexibility for the traveller on a fixed budget as Inter-Rail has done in the past'. So, fingers crossed for that! It should be ready for the New Year but as we go to press things are still being discussed and decided upon – the best advice is to ask at your nearest main station or call BR International direct at Victoria (071–922 9874).

Wasteels (see page 33) are still running packages of accommodation to complement Euro Domino and their other tickets. For further information call them on 071–834 7066.

There is talk, as we go to press, about a new Northern European Inter-Rail being launched early in 1993, too. Again, call BR International for details.

EURAIL

• **Quick history:** Basically, Eurail came into existence because Europe had a new and expensive network of intercity trains that needed riders. Its purpose was to entice potential passengers from the other side of the Atlantic, by offering two months of unlimited second-class travel on any or all of the member rail systems. The first pass was issued in 1959 when 5,000 tickets were sold. Later developments were one- and three-month passes, 15-day passes, first-class passes and such fringe benefits as free access to many ferry and steamer connections and free or discounted bus transportation. In addition, the 21-day pass was developed in 1966 to complement air excursion fares.

The Eurail Youthpass was introduced for those under the age of 26. The value of eurorailing soon became apparent as Europe developed its own Youthpass system (Inter-Rail), followed closely by the individual country passes. If all goes to plan, the Eurail pass will also include four former Soviet Republics in 1993: Byelorussia, Latvia, Lithuania and Ukraine.

● **What is the Eurail Youthpass?** It is an unlimited-mileage pass available to anyone who can prove they are under 26 years old on the first day of travel. The price of one month's Youthpass is around $530 (£294), and for two months, around $691 (£384). The prices of Eurail passes may fluctuate according to exchange rates. The ticket may be purchased and used only if you reside outside Europe or North Africa.

Eurail Pass and Eurail Youthpass are personal and non-transfer-able. They are forfeited if presented by anyone other than the person for whom they were issued, or if they bear any evidence of alteration or mutilation. Presentation of a passport to European train personnel is compulsory. Therefore, if the issuing agent has made a mess-up with the spelling of your name, don't use it, but return it to the issuing office and get another. Your pass is valid until midnight of the last day of validity so be sure to take a train scheduled to arrive at your destination before midnight.

A Eurail Youthpass is valid in second class exclusively. This entitles you to unlimited travel on the national railways (except on special chartered trains) and many private rail lines, steamers and ferry crossings of the following countries: Austria, Belgium, Denmark, Finland, France, Germany, Greece, Hungary, Ireland (Republic of), Italy, Luxembourg, Netherlands, Norway, Portugal, Spain, Sweden and Switzerland. It also entitles you to free or reduced travel on buses run by the railway companies and some ferries. (For a full list of concessions granted to ticket holders, see Eurail Bonuses in the individual country sections.)

Reservation fees, meals, refreshments, sleeping accommodation and port taxes when using some steamers and ferries are not included in the price of the ticket and will have to be paid extra. It is sometimes obligatory to have a seat reservation (on Spanish express trains, for instance), so check first with station information. Also, a surcharge is required for travelling on some trains (IC, EuroCity/ICE/TGV, Rapidos).

The *Eurail Youth Flexipass Saver* is a second-class ticket, which allows 7 or 15 days' travel within two consecutive months. Three people under 26 years old must be travelling together. 7 days cost around $184 (£102) each, 15 days around $364 (£202) each.

From 1 June to 30 September, Adriatica di Navigazione and Hellenic Mediterranean Lines operating between Brindisi and Patras require $15.00 high season surcharge. During July and August advanced reservation ($7.00) is recommended.

Having a Eurail Youthpass does not guarantee a seat on a train nor space on ships unless a reservation has been secured in advance.

● **Refunds:** A Eurail Youthpass is not refundable if lost or stolen. It can only be replaced after having been validated, and provided the validation slip can be presented at time of replacement to a Eurail Aid Office. Any refund, if granted, is subject to a deduction of about 15 per cent from the price of the ticket.

● **What is the Eurail Pass?** It's the adult equivalent of the Youthpass, and has no age restrictions placed on it. It's a first-class go-as-you-please pass with prices of around $486 (£270) for 15 days, $616 (£342) for 21 days, $735 (£408) for one month, $1005 (£558) for two months and $1300 (£722) for three months. These are available from the same outlets as the Youthpass.

● **Eurail Saver Pass** (USA and Canada only): A 15-day Eurail Pass for two or more people travelling first-class off-season (1 October to 31 March) or a minimum of three people during the high season is now available at a cost of around $389 (£216) per person. This new pass represents a saving of around 25 per cent compared to the regular 15-day Eurail Pass and provides the same services, including free or reduced bus, ferry and steamer passage. The same conditions apply for the month-long pass, around $583 (£324) per person.

● **Eurail Flexipass:** This is a first-class Eurail Pass which allows a limited number of chosen days of travel inside a given time period.

The prices are around $302 (£168) for 5 days of travel in a 15-day period, $493 (£274) for 9 of 21 days, $659 (£366) for 15 days in 2 months.

• **Eurail Drive Pass:** A new pass for the adult market, it is a combination of first-class railpass and car rental. Cost from $300 (£166), with Hertz car rental with unlimited mileage.

• **Where to buy your Eurail:** Eurail Passes must be bought outside Europe. Nearly every travel agent in North America, Canada, Australia and New Zealand will be able to supply you with a pass. For more information contact CIEE (Council on International Educational Exchange), 205 East 42nd Street, New York, NY 10017 (Tel. 212-661 1450), or CUTS (Canadian Universities Travel Service), 187 College Street, Toronto, Ontario M5T 1P7 (Tel. 416-979 2406). If you are normally resident outside Europe and North America and arrived in Europe not more than six months ago, you can, as an exceptional measure, buy a pass in the UK through French Railways Ltd, 79 Piccadilly, London W1V 0BA (Tel. 071-493 9731).

• **Before you begin:** The pass must be used within six months of purchase, and must be validated before use by a railway official who will enter the first and last dates the pass can be used. It is important to get this done when buying the pass as validating it on board a train costs $6.23 extra. Rip out the counterfoil card from the pass as soon as you get it, and carry it separately and in a safe place. If you lose the pass you'll need this counterfoil as proof before a replacement can be issued, and if a railway official checks your Eurail during the trip this is considered your confirmation of ownership.
   Eurail Aid Offices are there to help you if you have any problems. They also stock timetables and maps free of charge; a list is given in Appendix V.

• **How to get the most out of your pass:** There are three basic ways you can use your Inter-Rail/Eurail Youthpass.

1. Cover as many countries as possible on a grand-scale European

tour, sampling each country (however sketchily), and deciding which ones you're most keen to return to on a later pass.

2. Head for a specific area or destination (the Greek islands, say, or the south of France or the art towns of Italy). Use the ticket to get you there by planning a route which takes in some of the European highspots, and come back by a different route. Often this can combine the best of both worlds since, if you stop off at three or four places en route and tire yourself out, you can relax, safe in the knowledge that you've still got two weeks' sunbathing on your Greek island before you have to set off, seeing more sights on your way home.

3. Concentrate on one specific country or area and tour it in depth by rail, stopping at every place that catches your eye.

Having carried out and enjoyed trips on all three principles, all we can say is that each is great fun in its own way – the choice is yours.

THE BRITRAIL PASS

To travel in Great Britain, which is not covered in the Eurail scheme, it is best to buy a BritRail Pass or BritRail Youthpass. These passes are valid for unlimited travel anywhere by rail in England, Scotland and Wales, excluding the London underground system; they do, however, include 50 per cent reductions on steamship cruises on Lake Windermere, in the north of England. Below is a table of current prices valid until the end of December 1992 in American dollars.

	Gold	*Silver*	*Senior 60+*		*Youth 16–25*
Consecutive days	1st	Standard	1st	Standard	Standard
8	$319	$209	$289	$189	$169
15	$479	$319	$429	$289	$255
22	$599	$399	$539	$359	$319
1 month	$689	$465	$619	$419	$375

Age 5–15 half price.

Since 1989 the BritRail Flexipass has been available. This more flexible pass allows you to travel for either 4 days in a given 8-day period, or 8 days in a 15-day period. The table below quotes current prices for 1992.

	Gold	*Silver*	*Senior 60+*		*Youth 16–25*
	1st	Standard	1st	Standard	Standard
Any 4 days in 8	$269	$179	$239	$159	$145
Any 8 days in 15	$379	$255	$339	$229	$199
Any 15 days in 1 month	$549	$369	$495	$329	—
Any 15 days in 2 months	—	—	—	—	$295

Age 5–15 half price.

For visitors to London, the 'London Extra' is of interest: 3-, 4- or 7-day passes for travel in and around London and the Home Counties cost $75, $90 and $135 for 2nd class; $95, $120 and $170 for 1st class. The London Visitor Travelcard (within London city) costs $18, $23 and $40 for 3, 4 and 7 days.

BritRail Passes can be purchased from over 22,000 travel agents throughout North America or by writing direct to BritRail Travel International, 10th floor, 1500 Broadway, New York, NY 10036. Don't forget that BritRail Passes cannot be purchased in Britain after you arrive.

● **The BritFrance Railpass:** This new pass can be used for either 5 days' unlimited travel during a 15-day period, or 10 days during a month, on both the British and French rail networks. It includes your hovercraft Channel crossing and prices for the under 26s are $199 for the 5-days-in-15 pass and $229 for the 10-days-in-a-month pass. There are also adult and first-class passes; all of these must be purchased in the USA or Canada.

EUROTRAIN

Eurotrain is the leading UK operator in continental rail travel for

94 JULY

11 MONDAY

neth   **A**   Amsterdam   Prague   Czech

Germany   Hamburg   Warsaw (visa)   Poland

       Berlin   Bucharest (visa)?

                                Romania

12 TUESDAY   Bank Holiday (Northern Ireland)

Greece   Athens   Patras --> Brindisi (Italy)

            ↓

        Milan - Paris   night train

13 WEDNESDAY

14 THURSDAY

15 FRIDAY

16 SATURDAY

17 SUNDAY

28

Independence Day (USA)   *MONDAY* **4**

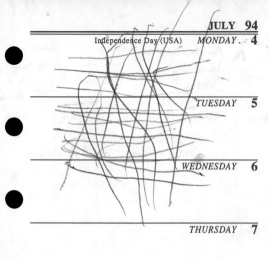

TUESDAY **5**

WEDNESDAY **6**

THURSDAY **7**

FRIDAY **8**

SATURDAY **9**

SUNDAY **10**

FACT SHEETS
TICKET
TIMETABLE
INSURANCE

students and young people. Generous discounts on normal rail fares are available to anyone under 26 to 2,000 destinations in Europe. Tickets are valid for up to 2 months (Turkey and Morocco returns for six months) and you can start your journey from any UK station. Fares to the CIS have recently been introduced, starting at £190 return London–St Petersburg.

Eurotrain fares allow great flexibility and freedom. You may choose your outward and return routes and stop off where and when you wish, and the ferry crossings are included. If you really want to see as much of Europe as possible then a Eurotrain Explorer ticket is the one for you. There are over a dozen super value explorers to choose from, each combining the major cities of Europe by the most interesting routing available. The Capital Explorer is particularly popular and allows you to experience the very best of four great capital cities – London, Paris, Brussels and Amsterdam. This summer it will cost around £90.

Explorer fares are valid for two months and you travel out by one route and return by another. You may stop off anywhere on your 'specified' route and stay for as long as you wish in the places you like best. They are introducing a scheme to allow passengers to book the first two nights' accommodation in Amsterdam, Dublin, or Paris. For full details contact: Eurotrain, 52 Grosvenor Gardens, London SW1W 0AG (Tel. 071–730 3402). A booth at Victoria Station operates 8 a.m.–8 p.m. daily.

The Eastern Explorer for £190 takes in Berlin, Prague and Budapest, as well as Amsterdam, Vienna, Zurich and Brussels. Other Explorer passes include the Venetian Explorer, Riviera Explorer and Spanish Explorer. Individual country passes include a Polish pass selling from £17.00, a Hungarian pass selling from £22.00, a Czechoslovakian pass for £23.00, a Portuguese pass for £47.00, and a Baltic States pass for £13.00. They are not only valid for under 26s, but are also for students with ISIC cards (any age), teachers/academics and accompanying spouses/children. They are valid for one week, offering unlimited travel throughout the country. The Polish pass includes all seat reservations and express train supplements.

WASTEELS

Wasteels UK is part of the International Wasteels group, Europe's largest rail operator. They operate their BIJ scheme in the UK under the name of Route-26 and it offers 1600 destinations. Wasteels sell rail tickets for all ages and on their Route-26 you get a free timetable – handy for stop-off information. As the name suggests these discounted tickets are valid for anyone under 26, and are available to similar destinations to Eurotrain. Valid for 2 months, or 6 months for Turkish and Moroccan destinations, they offer flexible routings. Wasteels also offer 8 Route-26 Mini-tour tickets, which combine major cities and places of interest.

Wasteels can also offer travel bargains for Italian nationals, from the UK to Italy, and are agents for Italian Railways. The 'Travel at Will Pass' covers the entire Italian network, and includes supplements and seat reservations. It is valid from 8 days to 30 days, costing £88 to £152. The Flexi Card is similar, but gives travel on 4 days in 9 (£66), 8 days in 21 (£94), or 12 days in 30 (£120).

Wasteels' Polrail Pass offers free travel (including seat reservations) on Poland's rail network for all ages, costing around £19 for 8 days, £22 for 15 days, £25 for 21 days and £28 for one month's unlimited travel. Wasteels also offer a two month Italian Kilometric Ticket, which allows the holder/s to make up to 20 journeys or travel a maximum of 3,000 kilometres within Italy. It can be issued for a maximum of 5 people; you can travel either as a group or as an individual on the pass, which costs £90.

Wasteels have around 200 local offices in 22 European countries, which will help you out if you have difficulties. They can also supply other international rail tickets, reservations, many individual country passes and Inter-Rail cards. They also provide an accommodation booking package as part of the new Inter-Rail +26 (see p.26). Wasteels also offer Euro-Domino cards for Hungary, Czechoslovakia and Austria for all ages.

Contact Wasteels at 121 Wilton Road, London SW1 (Tel. 071–834 7066).

THOMAS COOK

The Thomas Cook Rail Centre, which is located at the Thomas Cook shop at 5 Queen Street, Oxford OX1 1EJ, offers a personal, mail order, or telephone service for all rail travel, including most rail cards and passes in Europe. They sell a good value combined

Inter-Rail card, insurance and European Timetable package. For more details, and the latest prices phone 0865–240441.

EURO-DOMINO

Euro-Domino is a new flexible scheme from British Rail International, available from appointed BR stations including Victoria. Each pass is valid for three, five or ten days in a month, for second or first class. The prices include fast train supplements, e.g. on TGVs in France and Talgo in Spain. To get flexibility to travel in more than one country, you can purchase more than one Euro-Domino pass. More details from British Rail International (Tel. 071–834 2345).

New Euro-Domino cards – available for either 3, 5 or 10 days travel within one month

Country/ validity	2nd Class	1st Class	Youth
AUSTRIA			
3 day	£69	£102	£53
5 day	£76	£112	£58
10 day	£151	£224	£116
HUNGARY			
3 day	£40	£61	£31
5 day	£62	£95	£44
10 day	£111	£166	£83
CZECHOSLOVAKIA			
3 day	£37	£61	£28
5 day	£51	£76	£38
10 day	£87	£131	£66

EURO-DOMINO PRICES FROM 1 JANUARY 1993

Under 26s (2nd class)

Railway/ Shipping Company	3 days £	5 days £	10 days £
ADN/HML (Brindisi/Patras)	71	71	71
BR	–	–	–
CFL (Luxembourg)	7	11	19
CH (Greece)	26	29	44
CP (Portugal)	56	70	105
CSD (Czechoslovakia)	–	–	–
DB/IR (Germany)	81	90	134
DSB (Denmark)	37	55	74
FS (Italy)	68	85	142
HZ (Croatia)	–	–	–
JZ (Yugoslavia)	16	27	49
MAV (Hungary)	31	44	83
NS (Netherlands)	20	33	66
NSB (Norway)	–	–	–
ÖBB (Austria)	53	58	116
ONCPM (Morocco)	–	–	–
PKP (Poland)	–	22	
RENFE (Spain)	67	110	176
SBB/CFF (Switzerland)	47	68	90
SJ (Sweden)	58	84	111
SNCB (Belgium)	–	29	53
SNCF (France)	76	112	176
SZ (Slovenia)	–	–	–
TODD (Turkey)	–	–	–
VR (Finland)	42	59	79

EURO-DOMINO PRICES FROM 1 JANUARY 1993

Over 26s

| Railway/ | 3 days | | 5 days | | 10 days | |
Shipping Company	2nd £	1st £	2nd £	1st £	2nd £	1st £
ADN/HML (Brindisi/						
Patras)	141	167	141	167	141	167
BR	–	–	–	–	–	–
CFL (Luxembourg)	8	13	13	20	24	36
CH (Greece)	33	50	44	66	66	98
CP (Portugal)	73	108	91	134	137	202
CSP (Czechoslovakia)	–	–	–	–	–	–
DB/IR (Germany)	108	161	121	181	179	268
DSB (Denmark)	52	78	74	111	98	147
FS (Italy)	90	135	113	169	189	283
HZ (Croatia)	–	–	–	–	–	–
JZ (Yugoslavia)	22	33	37	55	66	98
MAV (Hungary)	40	61	62	95	111	166
NS (Netherlands)	26	40	44	66	87	131
NSB (Norway)	76	109	109	153	145	203
ÖBB (Austria)	69	102	76	112	151	224
ONCFM (Morocco)	–	–	–	–	–	–
PKP (Poland)	–	–	44	29	–	–
RENFE (Spain)	84	121	129	178	207	326
SBB/CFF (Switzerland)	62	92	90	135	119	172
SJ (Sweden)	79	107	111	153	149	203
SNCB (Belgium)	–	–	37	55	66	98
SNCF (France)	93	–	128	209	200	312
SZ (Slovenia)	–	–	–	–	–	–
TODD (Turkey)	–	–	–	–	–	–
VR (Finland)	55	83	79	118	105	157

EURO-YOUTH

Euro-Youth is British Rail International's entry into the BIJ market, available to the under 26s, with 200 destinations, and eight choices of sea routes to the continent. The tickets are available one-way or return, each valid for two months from date of departure, with stop-offs allowed anywhere on route. The prices include travel from London and the ferry crossing to the continent. Example prices are £38 single to Paris, £159 return to Vienna, £122 return to Berlin and £172 return to Moscow. Low price add-ons to London or ferry port are available when purchased. Again more details from British Rail International (Tel. 071–834 2345).

YOUTH HOSTEL PACKAGES

The youth hostel packages are extremely good value, based on rail travel and hostel accommodation, and operate in fifteen different countries, including Iceland, Israel, Japan, Australia and New Zealand. For further details write to YHA Travel, Trevelyan House, 8 St Stephen's Hill, St Albans, Herts AL1 2DY (Tel. 0727–55215).

INTER-RAIL CLUB

A club has been formed for Inter-Railers over 26 years. Based in Sweden, the Club +26's main purpose is to act as a network of contacts in different countries for Inter-Railers, and to help those no longer eligible for the traditional Inter-Rail card find out about the various passes available to them. Its Swedish members are also helpful towards Inter-Railers visiting their country. Monthly meetings take place in Stockholm, but postal membership (£5 p.a.) is possible too. Write to Club +26, Nybrogatan 51, 11440 Stockholm, Sweden.

OLD AGE DISCOUNTS

The Senior Railcard (£16) gives those over 60 at least one-third off fares on British Rail. Those with this card (or the equivalent from the following countries) can get discounts on rail and ferry travel of 30–50 per cent with the Rail Europe Senior Card (£7.50 from BR) on first- and second-class travel in Austria, Belgium, Denmark, Finland, France, Germany, Greece, Hungary, Ireland, Italy, Luxembourg, Netherlands, Norway, Portugal, Spain, Sweden, Switzerland (most lines), United Kingdom and Yugoslavia. Information on further discounts can be had from branches of Thomas Cook or in the US from the National Council of Senior Citizens, 925 15th St NW, Washington DC, 20005 (Tel. 202–347 8800).

PASSES FOR INDIVIDUAL COUNTRIES

Many countries offer their own touring passes which allow you the freedom of their individual rail networks. The disadvantage of these is that it's often more expensive to get to the country where the pass becomes valid than to buy a BIJ ticket or an Inter-Rail, which gets you out of Britain as well. Another point: even though you often get the use of ferries and coaches as well as trains, *you are still limited to just the one country*. It can be advantageous, though, if you're only interested in touring one country in depth, and don't want the route restrictions of a BIJ ticket. Many countries have passes with more flexible timescales, with tickets valid from four days to a month. There are no age restrictions on these go-as-you-please schemes so anyone, over or under 26, can still take advantage of them.

The Benelux countries, France and Switzerland offer a realistic alternative to continual touring: they make your ticket valid for travel on any of four, five or eight days of a holiday lasting 15–17 days, so you can spend a few days in each centre without worrying that you're missing out on the benefits of your rail pass.

The different deals range from 'very good value' to 'not worth your while', depending on currency fluctuations. Before committing yourself, decide how extensive and attractive the rail network of the country is and how much it'll cost you to get out there. A cheap flight to Greece, followed by one of their 'tourist cards' for the railways, can be an economical and effective way to see the country; conversely, by the time you've got yourself over to Austria and bought a touring card, you'll have spent well over the price of an Inter-Rail.

SNCF, the French railways, offers a 'youth railcard' for the under 26s called Carrissimo. This replaces the Carte Jeune and Carré Jeune, offering a 50 per cent reduction on off-peak and 20 per cent reduction on standard journeys on either four single trips (two returns) or eight singles (four returns), made within a period of one year. The 4-journey ticket costs around £20 and the 8-journey one around £35. They are valid on both first and second class. Apply in person with your passport and passport photo to SNCF, 179 Piccadilly, London W1V 0BA (Tel. 071–409 1224), or any other SNCF address.

The Nordturist Scanrail Pass is valid in Sweden, Denmark, Norway and Finland for 4 days rail travel within 15 days, 9 days within 21, and 14 days within 30. The four-day pass costs around £88 for second class and around £110 for first class; the nine-day pass costs £146 and £182 respectively; and the 14-day pass costs £212 for second class and £280 for first class. There is also a Nordturist Rail Rover Pass which offers 21 days of unlimited travel in the four Scandinavian countries. It costs £155 second class and £210 first class for adults; £115 and £155 respectively for 12–25-year-olds; and £78 and £105 for under 12s. If you want to extend your holiday, you can buy several tickets in succession. The ticket is also valid on the SJ and DSB ferries between Helsingborg and Helsingør, on all the domestic DSB ferries in Denmark and the routes Rødby Færge–Puttgarten Mitte See, Gedser–Warnemünde Mitte See and Trelleborg–Sassnitz Mitte See, on the boat-lines Stockholm–Åbo (Turku) (Silja Line), Göteborg–Frederikshavn (Stena Line) and Kristiansand–Hirtshals (Color Line), on the NSB bus service from Storlien to Trondheim, and on the combined boat and bus route between Halden/Sarpsborg and Strömstad (by Halden Turisttrafik A/S, SSV Bilselskap A/S, Swebus and AB Koster-Trafik).

A 50 per cent reduction on the normal fare is available on the following boat-lines: Stockholm–Helsinki (Silja Line), Copenhagen Havnegade–Malmö Skeppsbron (DSØ hovercraft), Copenhagen–Oslo (DFDS, deck seats), Copenhagen–Rønne (Bornholmstrafiken), Ystad–Rønne (Bornholmstrafiken), Umeå–Vasa (Vasaboats), Travemünde–Trelleborg (TT-Line), Nynäshamm–Visby (Gotland Line), Oskarshamm–Visby (Got-

land Line), Larvik–Frederikshavn (Larvik Line A/S), and Flåm–
Bergen (Fylkesbaatane). Bus lines offering 50 per cent reductions
are Bodö–Fauske–Narvik–Kirkenes (North Norway bus) and local
lines in Nordland. Private railways offering the same discount are
the Hirthals–Hörring line and the Växjö–Hultsfred–Västervik
line (VHVJ – seasonal traffic only).

Don't forget your 'Nordturist' railway ticket allows you free entry
to the railway museums in Gävle (Sweden), Hamar (Norway),
Hyvinge (Finland) and Odense (Denmark).

The Nordic Railpass is available from the Norwegian State
Railways Bureau, 21/24 Cockspur Street, London SW1Y 5DA
(Tel. 071–930 6666).

We've listed full details of *all* the available European touring
passes in their respective chapters. Many can be bought in Britain
from British Rail International, Victoria Station, London SW1V
1JY (Tel. 071–834 2345 for information; 071–828 0892 for credit
card bookings) or appointed BR stations. For further information,
write to the individual country's tourist authority (their addresses
appear on pages 64–67).

SPOIL YOURSELF

If you have the opportunity, there are some trains which are a
delight to travel on. They connect the major European cities and
are called:

LEONARDO DA VINCI	Milan–Innsbruck–Munich
LIGURE	Marseille–Nice–Genoa–Milan
ÉTOILE DU NORD	Paris–Brussels–Amsterdam
CATALAN-TALGO	Barcelona–Port Bou–Avignon–Geneva
L'ARBALETE	Zürich–Paris
MERKUR	Copenhagen–Frankfurt
FRANZ HALS	Amsterdam–Munich
BLAUER ENZIAN	Dortmund–Cologne–Stuttgart–Munich–Salzburg–Klagenfurt
CISALPIN	Paris (TGV)–Lausanne (EC)–Brig–Milan
COLOSSEUM	Basle–Lucerne–Milan–Florence–Rome
MONTEVERDI	Basle–Berne–Brig–Milan–Venice

NORDPILEN	Stockholm–Boden–Kiruna–Narvik
PERNILLE/BERGEN	
EXPRESS	Oslo–Bergen
REMBRANDT	Amsterdam–Cologne–Basle–Zurich–Chur
ROMULUS	Vienna–Klagenfurt–Venice–Florence–Rome
TRANSALPIN	Basle–Zurich–Innsbruck–Salzburg–Vienna

All are accessible with a first-class Eurail Pass (EuroCity etc.). The majority of intercity trains carry both first- and second-class passengers and are available to Inter-Rail, Eurail Pass and Eurail Youthpass holders, as are TGVs, the world's fastest, linking Paris to Lyon in two hours at 168 m.p.h. The two main TGV regions are known as TGV Sud-Est and TGV Atlantique. The former includes destinations in the South of France, the Alps and Switzerland, the latter Brittany and the Spanish border.

The German InterCity Expresses (ICE) started regular service during 1991, with initial problems, but now bring German train speeds in line with the French TGV. The Italian Pendolino trains are aiming to do the same in Italy.

Station information

The average major European city station will have most of the following facilities:

1. *Ticket desk:* At most large stations, tickets for domestic and international travel are purchased at different windows, so make sure you're in the right line.

2. *Train information office:* Marked with a blue letter *i*. Here you can find out the times and availability of trains from multilingual clerks. If the office is packed, see if large timetables are posted up on boards in the station. There are normally separate posters for arrivals (white background) and for departures (yellow background). Fast trains on both are given in red instead of black print, running chronologically from 0 hr to 24 hrs. Next to the time is the name or number of the train, together with its routeing, from point of origin to final destination, with the most important stops in between. Finally, the track and platform numbers, at which the train departs or arrives. Major stations provide this information on computerized boards. Train composition boards are always useful as they indicate where on the platform each coach stops. That way, you don't waste any time running to get your seat when the train rolls up.

3. *Left-luggage:* In the big stations, you'll find there'll be a manned depot (usually open until midnight – then it closes down till 5 or 6 a.m.) and automatic lockers. If you're catching a train before the manned depot opens again, get a locker, obviously. Note: Check that your rucksack will fit into the locker first.

4. *Lost property office:* Usually open 9 a.m.–5 p.m., from Mondays to Fridays only. If it's desperate (say, you've lost your ticket, rucksack, passport or money), go to the station master.

5. *Station master's office:* In theory he's in charge of the trains not the passengers, but as he's the 'king pin' in the station he's your best bet if it's a real emergency.

6. You can always count on there being *telephones* and *post boxes*. Some stations have an international telephone service on the spot, and in some you can even find a full post office operating.

7. Assorted *shops* and *news-stands*.

8. Often a *first-aid post:* In Germany and France there are travellers' aid organizations: 'Bahnhofsmissions' and 'Bureau accueil'. They'll help if you're ill, lost or generally in distress. If you're ill and there's no first-aid help, again go to the station master.

9. *Toilets:* Vary dramatically in degrees of cleanliness and are not always free.

10. *Waiting rooms:* Again, these range from quite OK to diabolic. Nevertheless, they are useful, obviously, to eurorailers. Many close at night, so you shouldn't count on them for spending the night in.

11. *Baths/showers:* Most large stations have these facilities where you can buy or rent towels, soap, shampoo, etc. They cost on average £1.50 ($2.70) a bath, £1 ($1.80) a shower.

12. *Foreign-exchange desk:* Unless you're really in need of the local currency, these tend to be a bad idea as their exchange rates are rarely competitive and there are usually long queues.

13. *Tourist information desk:* Extremely useful for eurorailers. Apart from handing out free maps and guides, they invariably run an accommodation service for a small charge, about 50p–£1.50 ($0.90–2.70). Watch out here as there can be long queues.

Obviously, the larger the station, the more facilities you can expect. If there are any outstanding facts relevant to a particular station, for instance, a cheap and good snack bar downstairs in Stockholm station, we mention that under 'Stockholm'.

PICTOGRAMS

Nearly every station is clearly marked with universal pictograms which overcome the language barrier very efficiently. Most of these are extremely straightforward and don't need explanation. There are some, however, which might cause confusion to first-timers:

Meeting Point

Lost and Found

Luggage and baggage store pictograms can even catch the old hands waiting in the wrong line, for example the self-service luggage-cart sign is:

Self-Service
Luggage-Cart

while that for a porter is:

Call for Porter

In some stations you will have enough trouble fighting the porters off without going out looking for them.

Confusion can also occur between the Luggage Registration Office (for sending luggage through to your next destination):

Luggage Registration
Office

and the left luggage or baggage check room:

Baggage
Check Room

You'll get a ticket which you have to present when you pick your
luggage up again.

Coin-operated lockers are different again:

Locker

Lockers are
also indicated by: CONSIGNE DES BAGAGES
GEPÄCKAUFBEWAHRUNG
CONSIGNA DE EQUIPAJES
DEPOSITO BAGAGLIO

RESERVATIONS

Unless you don't mind slouching in the corridor for hours on end, a
seat reservation can make a lot of sense on a busy route in summer.
On many services reservations are compulsory; these are marked
Ⓡ on timetables.

If you choose not to reserve, at least try to check how busy the train's going to be. For the equivalent of £1–£1.70 ($1.80–3.06) a reserved seat is worth it. If you suspect that your departure train's going to be mobbed, check up and reserve before leaving the station on your arrival. In many Western countries, reservations can be made up to two months in advance. Some countries have obligatory reservations, whilst in others you have to make your reservations at least two hours before departure (all this is noted in the chapters on individual countries). When making a reservation try going along at a time when the office should be quiet (generally 9–11 a.m., and 3–5 p.m., Monday to Friday). You'd be amazed how many people roll up at lunchtime and at weekends when all the locals are out in force trying to make their own reservations. In Sweden, if you board a train in which reserved seats are compulsory without having reserved a seat for yourself beforehand, you will be charged an extra fare in addition to the reservation fee on board the train.

If you find yourself on a train without having reserved a seat, quickly shoot down the corridors looking for free seats on the reservation notice located outside each compartment or on the actual seats themselves. If the train seems to be completely booked up, try asking the guard whether there are any other carriages being added on, or any cancellations.

When you're making a reservation, tell the clerk exactly what you want – unless you specify, say, a non-smoker, it will be presumed that you want a smoker! In southern Europe especially, you're rarely asked what you want, so make your wishes clearly known when booking. It often helps to write all the details down before getting to the counter. Bear in mind the following:

1. *Class:* Make sure you don't end up unintentionally in first class.

2. *Non-smoker/smoker.*

3. *Which side of the train* you want to sit. On some journeys this can be quite significant; for example, a seat on the south side of the train on a Riviera journey ensures you a good view, but you'd miss most of it by sitting on the north side.

4. *Facing/back* to the engine: Some people have a preference for looking either in the direction of travel or away from it.

5. *Aisle/window seat:* Often the window seat has a pull-out table which is useful for eating or writing, whereas the aisle seat allows more leg room.

SOME TIPS

Always check the name of the station if you're dealing with a city with more than one (see below). Don't assume that, as you're travelling north, you'll necessarily be leaving from the city's northernmost station – it doesn't always follow. The following towns and cities have more than one main station (the towns marked with an asterisk are those where the station used by trains connecting with ferry services is separate from the main station):

ANTWERP	*DOVER	LONDON	ROTTERDAM
ATHENS	DUBLIN	LYON	SAN SEBASTIÁN
BARCELONA	ESSEN	MADRID	SEVILLE
BASEL	EXETER	*MALMÖ	STOCKHOLM
BELFAST	*FOLKESTONE	MANCHESTER	*TILBURY
BELGRADE	GENEVA	MARSEILLE	TOURS
BERLIN	GLASGOW	MILAN	TURIN
BILBAO	HAMBURG	MUNICH	VENICE
*BOULOGNE	*HARWICH	NAPLES	VIENNA
BRUSSELS	*HELSINGBORG	*NEWHAVEN	WARSAW
BUCHAREST	HENDAYE	OPORTO	ZÜRICH
BUDAPEST	IRUN	PARIS	
*CALAIS	ISTANBUL	*PORTSMOUTH	
*CASABLANCA	LIÈGE	PRAGUE	
COMO	LISBON	ROME	

Refer to the city centre maps on the reverse of Thomas Cook's European Rail map to see which cities have more than one main line station.

Bear in mind the distances between stations in these cities are usually quite substantial (in London, between Paddington and Liverpool Street is about five miles; in Paris, between Gare de Lyon and Gare St Lazare is about four and a half). The moral is: don't count on split-second connections between stations.

Train information

NIGHT TRAVEL

Travelling at night has distinct advantages for the eurorailer who doesn't mind missing the scenery of a particular area or the fact that night trains invariably take longer to get to their destinations. The advantage of night travel is that in effect you add an extra day to your stay by arriving in the morning, ready to start your tour. How exactly you spend the night, and the consequent amount of sleep you manage to get in, depends largely on which of the sleeping arrangements you opt for, and how good a sleeper you are.

Basically there are four ways of travelling at night: sit up in the normal seats; get a seat which pulls down (as on the German and Italian trains) and allows you to lie down; buy a couchette; buy a sleeper. Taking each in turn, you can:

1. *Sit up all night* in a seat. It's free, but not guaranteed to find you fresh enough for a full day's sightseeing the next day. A neck air cushion is a good idea. Be careful, guards often get upset if they see your footwear on the seats.

2. *Pull-down seats*. These are great when you can find them, as they're free yet still allow you to stretch out, thus increasing the chances of sleep. Once all six seats are pulled down, they join together to form a massive 'bed'. How much room you end up with depends on how full the compartment was originally; if there are only two or three of you in the compartment, you're home and dry for a free sleep. Reserve one if you can.

3. *Couchettes*. This is a seat by daytime, which at night is converted into a proper full berth. In second class, there are six to a compartment (four in first class). There is no sex segregation but this is not normally a problem even for single girls as the couchettes are nearly always full. For your £8–10 ($14–18) (average cost, but see under individual countries) you get a sheet, blanket and pillow, and there's a bed-light. You can use the washroom next to the toilets for washing. Each couchette has a luggage rack, but it's always wise to take your valuables to bed with you. Standards of couchettes vary enormously as they're run by the individual national rail networks, so that in Germany they're very good, while in Spain and Italy they are not so good.

Reservations for couchettes are more or less essential in the summer. You are required to book at least five hours before the train leaves the station.

4. *Cabines*. French Railways operate Cabine 8, a compartment (in new air-conditioned coaches) with 8 semi-reclined bunks enabling you to stretch out in your own sleeping bag. They are completely free, but as they are very popular you will find it worthwhile reserving ahead.

5. *Sleepers*. Sleeping cars are a great step up in comfort from couchettes, but they're also a lot more expensive. As in Britain, European sleepers come in two classes and offer: a proper bed with all the trimmings, a sink with soap, towels and warm water, an electrical outlet and occasionally your own WC. The Thomas Cook European Sleeping Cars Book (£1.95) details the different types of cars in use, though it is now somewhat dated. There is also a brief description in their timetable.

Sleepers are operated either by the Wagons-Lits Company (an international concern) or by a subsidiary of the railway. Many of these are developing into combined groups, collectively calling themselves 'Trans Euro Nuit/Nacht/Notte'. The Scandinavian and East European countries operate their own sleepers, as does British Rail. The average two- or three-berth sleeper is £20–40 ($36–72) a person, but price is dependent on the distance you're covering.

A bit of general advice on travelling at night. Very often, your train gets into the station an hour before departure; if you've had a hard day, this is good to know as you can get yourself bedded down earlier. If you take the train right through to its final destination, you can often lie on for another half-hour or so in the morning, once it arrives, before getting ousted. If the train is packed, it might be worth asking the guard for permission to sleep in first class.

If you're reserving a couchette or sleeper, try for the top berths as they're roomier, there's more air and they afford you a slightly greater degree of privacy. Watch out when the train enters for the yellow stripe along the outside of the carriage, just below roof level. This indicates first-class coaches only.

If you're going by sleeper or couchette on an international trip (or even for some internal ones in Italy, for some strange reason), the attendant will take your passport, visa and ticket from you so that, in theory anyway, you won't need to be woken up at the border in the middle of the night. Don't worry, they will be returned the next morning.

Once you're all in, lock the door and hope you've not landed yourself – as I have so often in the past – with a collection of snorers! When you get into the couchette check for ticketless passengers hiding in the compartment (under the bunks).

The best trains for a good night's sleep are those that don't cross international borders (difficult to avoid) or stop every couple of hours at stations en route, otherwise you'll have customs officials coming in for a nose-around at 3 a.m., or train announcements blaring out all night long (you can bet it'll be your carriage that stops right beneath the loudspeaker). My advice to insomniacs is to have a heavy meal before the journey, take some ear plugs, and don't hold back on the local vino.

● **Warnings:** A few years ago, however, many travellers on Italian and Spanish trains accepted the 'hospitality' of their fellow travellers in the form of doped orange juice and other drinks, and woke up many hours later to find they had been robbed. Some copycat incidents occurred, but following arrests, this worrying trend seems to be over (but be warned). Thieves have also been known to use a knock-out spray, sprayed through compartment vents, to steal belongings, though such incidents are very rare.

Most night trains do not have a bar or eating facilities on board so if you're the type of person who enjoys a midnight feast or gets thirsty in the night, you had better bring your own supplies along or you'll wake up with an empty stomach and a throat like a vacuum cleaner.

● **Main night trains:** Below is a list of just some of the many good night trains in Europe. Remember you can save money by sleeping on these night trains and cover more ground during your vacation.

Amsterdam–Copenhagen	Madrid–Algeciras
Amsterdam–Munich	Madrid–Lisbon
Barcelona–Geneva	Madrid–Santander
Barcelona–Madrid	Milan–Paris
Barcelona–Nice	Nice–Geneva
Barcelona–Paris	Ostend–Munich
Barcelona–Pamplona	Paris–Amsterdam
Basel–Hamburg	Paris–Copenhagen
Belgrade–Thessaloniki	Paris–Munich
Brussels–Genoa	Paris–Nice
Brussels–Munich	Rome–Nice
Copenhagen–Hamburg	Vienna–Cologne
Hamburg–Munich	Vienna–Frankfurt
Heidelberg–Lugano	Vienna–Lindau
London–Edinburgh	Vienna–Venice
Malmö–Stockholm	

Don't forget that it is often preferable to sleep in a good compartment than in a crowded youth hostel. Try pretending you're sound asleep when the train pulls in to stations and you'll raise the chances of being left undisturbed.

EATING

Few eurorailers can afford to indulge in buffet or restaurant meals on the trains because they're never cheap. The majority of the dining services offered on European trains are run by the Wagons-Lits Company. However, the quality of the food and service varies from country to country, as it really depends on the staff and hygiene of the host country. Don't be fooled by the mobile mini-bars that wheel temptingly past you – they are extremely expensive, with coffee anything from £1. On top of that the food and drink is of very poor quality. As a general rule all EuroCity and most InterCity and long-distance express trains have a separate dining car with set-price meals from £5–15 ($9–27) or a bar/buffet car serving drinks, sandwiches and light snacks. It's a very satisfying experience having a leisurely meal along one of the scenic routes even if you can only afford it once.

Remember: You can't drink the water from the train washrooms anywhere in Europe. Buy your drink before you get aboard. The best bet is to stock up with food from the supermarkets before you leave and treat yourself to a good picnic on the train. 1987 saw the introduction of EuroCity, an international branding of high-speed and quality trains with first and second classes. EuroCity have absorbed International InterCity trains, and most former TEE trains, with the exception of those in France.

TRAIN SPLITTING

As the trains of Europe undertake some pretty complicated routes and use one another's rolling stock, trains on long international journeys often split into various sections at certain points, so obviously it's important to check that you get on the relevant part of the train. The best policy is to ask and make sure you're on the right segment before you settle down. If your coach is going to be shunted about on to another train, find out at which station it's due to happen and at what time. It's all made quite easy by the signs posted on the doors and windows at intervals along the train:

CALAIS

PARIS ———————— MILANO
(Nord) · VENEZIA (Centrale)

This shows that the coach starts at Calais, stops at Paris (Nord) and Milan (Centrale) and terminates in Venice. There will also be a '1' or '2' to tell you the class of the carriage; and often a symbol indicating smoking or non-smoking. Whatever happens, don't get out of a train which is due to split up, and then get back into another section of it with the intention of walking along to your seat – you could find you're no longer connected to that bit of the train! Just in case you do get separated from your fellow travellers, carry your own money, ticket and passport at all times. This advice is also relevant in case one of you gets mugged – that way you won't lose everything at once. In some stations, mainly termini, you'll find the train reversing and going back in the direction you've just come. This is often the case in Switzerland. Don't worry about it. It's just a standard shunting procedure. This often takes place on the last stop before, or first after, an international frontier, and is used to reduce the number of carriages or add on extra ones. If you're in any doubt about your train splitting, ask the ticket inspector as soon as you are on board.

SUPPLEMENTS

An Inter-Rail or BIJ ticket alone is not sufficient to travel on some of the express trains of Europe, or on many of the EuroCity services. If you want to use these trains, you'll have to pay a supplement, and this is calculated on the distance you're travelling and the type of express you've chosen (unless you have a regular Eurail).

Some countries, notably the Scandinavian ones, do not charge supplements as such, but make seat reservations compulsory on expresses. (Full details of all the supplements and surcharges are to be found below under the individual country chapters.)

It's often worth inquiring how much the additional first-class supplement is, particularly if you're feeling under the weather and the train's packed out. (As a survivor of the Spanish Olive Oil Epidemic of '81 trying to get home, I can vouch for it!)

TIMETABLES

One of the best timetables is Thomas Cook's European Timetable. This is published on the first day of each month. The June to September issues have a full summer schedule, and there are summer service forecasts from February to May. The full winter schedule appears in the October to May issues, with forecasts in August and September. In this book you'll find most of the trains that run in Europe and most ferry services. Although it seems expensive, the timetable is worth its weight in gold and can save you hours of queueing (particularly at Italian stations). It also has a table of airport city centre links. Back editions can be ordered for half price from Thomas Cook Publishing Office, PO Box 227, Peterborough PE3 6SB. If you do this, watch you buy one which has the appropriate summer or winter schedules. It is available from all Thomas Cook travel agents (price £7.30) or by post at £8.40 from Thomas Cook Publishing Office (£10.30 in Europe and £11.30 outside Europe). Also worth thinking about is the Thomas Cook Rail Map of Europe which costs £4.50 (£5.00 in Europe and £5.50 outside Europe) by post, published biennially. It's a good idea to check prices with Thomas Cook (Tel. 0733 505821/268943) before ordering. Visa/Mastercard taken. A new Thomas Cook guide in 1992 was the excellent *Guide to Greek Island Hopping*, price £8.99 (or by post from Thomas Cook Publishing for £9.95 UK, £10.50 Europe and £11.50 outside Europe). NB Check your UK Inter-Rail brochure for a voucher entitling the purchaser to £1.50 off the combined cost of the European Timetable and European Rail Map when purchased together at a Thomas Cook Travel Shop, providing you have bought an Inter-Rail card.

The best value is the free UIC international timetable on ABC lines, though copies are like gold in most travel agents. Also good to have is the Eurail timetable free from any Eurail issuing office.

If you want the more detailed national timetable and railmap for a particular country (often hard to find), contact the SBB Timetable Shop, Office 224, Hauptbahnhof, CH–9001 St Gallen, Switzerland, which runs a mail order service, though check first with Thomas

Cook Publishing, by sending them a self-addressed envelope and asking for their list.

Bear in mind the change from winter to summer schedules: all European rail networks start their summer schedules on the last Sunday in May and the winter schedules on the last Sunday in September, except in Britain. Check also the time zone the country's in, and keep an eye out for local and national holidays.

• **Public holidays affecting trains:** At public holiday times, you'll find services are amended, and those trains that are operating will be busier than usual and with more reservations. Check with stations for details and turn up earlier for the train. We list all the relevant holidays under the individual country chapters. In many countries the day, or at least the half-day, preceding an official public holiday is also regarded as a holiday. We give below a calendar of moving holidays for 1993:

Shrove Monday	22 February
Shrove Tuesday	23 February
Maundy Thursday	8 April
Good Friday	9 April
Holy Saturday	10 April
Easter Sunday	11 April
Easter Monday	12 April
Ascension Day	20 May
Whit Monday	31 May

Muslim holidays:

Ramadan begins	23 February
Id-ul-Fitr	5 April
Id-ul-Adha	10 July
New Year (1414)	21 June

HAZARDS

On those long hot runs in southern Europe, where temperatures are high and trains aren't air-conditioned, the temptation is to stick your head out of the window to cool off. Be warned: you may cool off more than you anticipated. When you feel that unexpected drop of rain upon your face, you may fear the worst . . . someone's been to the loo further up. Moreover, don't be reassured by the notices

announcing that it's illegal to throw rubbish out of the window.
Expect anything, and be on your guard, especially for cans and
bottles. Most importantly of all, always be on your guard for open
or unsecured doors; even the safety-conscious DB (Deutsche
Bundesbahn) estimate that nearly 225 people were killed in five
years by falling from trains. Always carry your valuables with you
when you go to the loo, and be extra careful on night trains as this is
where most theft occurs. Often a small padlock securing your bag to
a fixed point is enough to deter a thief. The importance of keeping
your passport on you at all times cannot be stressed enough.
Obtaining an emergency passport involves considerable red tape
and can restrict the options on your journey.

TRAINS IN EASTERN EUROPE

Train travel in Eastern Europe has improved immeasurably since
the overthrow of the various Communist regimes. Increasingly, the
Eastern European stations are being re-modelled on Western lines,
but until the mid 90s anyway, don't expect comparable standards.
The station facilities are basic, so don't expect luxuries like showers
or permanently staffed Tourist Information booths.

To avoid unbelievable anxiety and frustration while travelling in
Eastern Europe, it's useful to remember the following:

1. Tickets are often only valid for the specific date and class of the
   train stated on your ticket. To change your date is more trouble
   than it's worth, so always be sure of the exact date and time you
   wish to leave before buying your ticket or making a reservation.

2. Queueing is a fact of life, so try to buy tickets and make
   reservations at odd hours: one of the best times is late at night,
   since queues begin long before offices open in the morning.
   Whenever possible, try to buy your ticket/make your reservation
   from Western Europe (say, Vienna) at the appropriate student
   office.

3. For all international journeys, tickets and reservations are often
   obtained through the official government travel agents (listed
   under each country). Otherwise use the train stations where
   queues are slightly shorter.

4. Make sure you're in the right queue. There's often one queue for journeys over 100 kilometres, another for reservations, etc. These are not immediately obvious as often there are no signs and it's quite possible to stand for up to an hour in the wrong line.

5. When you reach the front of the queue try and get everything possible done in one go, so you don't have to queue again later: buy your ticket, make your reservation, ask what platform the train leaves from, etc. Write it all down first, in case the assistant doesn't speak English.

6. Try to view the whole exercise as an initiative test, and always be prepared for any eventuality. It's not uncommon to discover that all second-class seats are fully booked so, unless you fancy another hour's wait at the end of the queue, it's best to have considered alternative trains or routes, or whether you are prepared to pay the extra. Compared to the West, you'll find that train fares are cheaper, but this is changing. It can be worth the extra cost to go first class for the added comfort, space and – sometimes – cleanliness.

TRAIN AND BIKE TRAVEL

Those wishing to combine a cycling and train holiday will find the situation very different in the various countries. In some it is easy to arrange transport of your bike with you, in others almost impossible. Many railway systems publish leaflets giving details of trains on which cycles can be accommodated, with costs where relevant. You can take your bike free on Sealink Stena Ferries to France and Northern Ireland. For routes to Eire and Holland, and Hoverspeed services, there is a charge. In some countries it is also possible to hire a bike.

For advice and details contact the Cyclists' Touring Club, Cotterell House, 69 Meadrow, Goldalming, Surrey GU7 3HS. They publish Country Information Sheets, and have many other services, including cycle insurance.

Before you go

FLYING THE ATLANTIC

The basic rule is the more you pay then the greater your flexibility will be, or conversely the less you pay, the more restrictions you will have to face. As always, forward planning can not only save you money, but also buy you time in Europe. It is a good idea to spend time in countries not covered in the Eurail scheme (Great Britain or Eastern Europe, for example), either before your Eurail Pass becomes valid or when it has expired. Don't waste precious days of your pass in countries where you cannot use it. Consequently, it's important to choose the right city as your gateway to Europe.

Flying to London with Virgin Atlantic is one of the most popular starts and it's easy to see why, with return fares at only around £200 ($360) low season and £375 ($675) high season. To make a reservation, write or telephone Virgin Atlantic, 43 Perry Street, New York, NY 10014 (Tel. 212 242 1330) or Ashdown House, High Street, Crawley, West Sussex RH10 1DQ (Tel. 0293 38222). The take-over of the Pan Am and TWA routes to London by American and United means two powerful operators have entered the field.

Reservations can normally be cancelled or changed up to three days before departure: for some flights, there is no charge for this service; for others, it can cost up to £75 ($135). Virgin Atlantic work out slightly more expensive than some competitors but offer bonuses included in your ticket cost, such as in-flight snacks, a hot meal with wine, and a low-cost hotel scheme. During the peak season, June to September, all airlines are well booked up and unless you reserve well beforehand you may be forced to travel standby. If this happens, you stand a better chance midweek than at weekends. Also investigate the Icelandair route from New York to Frankfurt via Reykjavik, which might be worth considering if you intend to start your trip in continental Europe.

There is no shortage of airlines or types of tickets to get you over to Europe, but if money is the prime consideration set yourself the task of getting a really good, reliable travel agent. After briefing him on how much cash you have to spend and where you want to go, leave it to him to come up with a few ideas for you to think about. Do your own homework, too, and plan early as most reduced air fares are payable thirty days in advance. Scan the *New York Times* (especially Sunday's) and talk to as many other eurorailers as you can to pick up tips. Midweek days are usually the quietest for flying, so flexibility is an advantage, particularly if you're flying with Virgin Atlantic.

If you can't afford the luxury of being flexible, go for a charter flight which gives you a seat reservation but can involve you in backtracking to get back, for the return journey, to the airport you arrived at. If you've a bit more cash, an APEX (Advanced Booking Excursion Fare) allows you greater freedom as you can return from a different airport. Make sure you will land at an airport that has its own railway station: Amsterdam, Brussels, Frankfurt, Geneva, London LGW, Paris CDG, Zürich, etc.

• **APEX:** APEX flights represent one of the most flexible options on the reduced fares market, as they are not so restrictive as charters. With an APEX ticket it's possible to arrive at and depart from different cities (countries) and even on different airlines in some cases. If you decide to fly with a particular airline, ask if they operate a Super-APEX package which can mean an even cheaper deal.

• **Standby:** If you want to keep your options open until the last minute without committing yourself, a standby ticket is your best bet. Not all airlines offer standby, and your choice of both American and European gateways is limited. However, if you are flexible the rewards are high for apart from being the cheapest ticket around, it doesn't commit you to any particular time or place when returning to the US.

There are only a limited number of standby seats on each flight, so it's important to be well organized to improve your chances, particularly in peak season. A few days before you plan on leaving, phone up the airline's reservation desk and check out the seat availability on your optimum flight. Don't mention that you are planning to fly standby, as many officials are cagey about giving information away. Seats are always given out on a first come, first served basis, so be there in good time, and be prepared for a wait, even overnight if necessary. Most sales desks open at around 7 a.m. and it's not unusual for a queue to form before then. As soon as you've bought your ticket don't hang around, go straight to the check-in desk and get your name down on that list.

• **Budget fares:** Pricewise a budget fare is similar to a standby, yet it offers a confirmed seat reserved in advance. The only problem is that you must tell the airline which week you would like to fly out and return (if desired), and they will get back to you at least a week before your flight with the details. In this way, the airline gets to choose the exact day, at a time which is convenient to them, not you. In our opinion, it's only worth considering if you cannot find a suitable APEX flight, and don't want to take the risk of flying standby; even then, it only makes sense if you've got plenty of time on your hands before your rail pass begins.

• **Charter flights:** Charters are back and more competitive than ever. While most charter operators who have survived the last ten years in the hectic US marketplace can be considered reliable, you should still exercise care in booking a charter. Read the charter operator-participant contract to be fully aware of the rules governing a charter flight. Try CIEE's Council Charter (Tel. 800 223 7402) or Travac (Tel. 800 872 8800). Council Charter's brochure *Charter Europe* includes year-round low-cost flights to several European cities. Get a free copy from your nearest Council Travel Office or write to Council Charter, Charter Europe, 205 East 42nd Street, New York, NY 10017. Finally, try and keep an eye out for good deals in the Sunday papers.

• **Other options:** There are cheap scheduled flights from New York/California offered by Virgin Atlantic, World, Transamerica Capitol and Icelandic. Check with Council Charter for your best option, for apart from being the 'grand-daddy' of charter flight operators for students and young people, they also know what else is on offer.

Type of Air fare	Min/Max Stay Requirement	Advance Purchase Requirement	Cancellation Penalties	Stopover Possibilities
STANDBY	None	None	None	None
BUDGET	None	21 days	$50+	None
APEX	Varies from 7–180 days	Varies 21 days round trip only	10% of fare	Sometimes Check with airline
SUPER-APEX	Varies 7–180 days	Varies 21 days round trip only	10% of fare	None

• **Travel agents:** No special licence is required by travel agents in the US so anyone can set themselves up in business regardless of experience. At present, there are about 100,000 to choose from, so be selective. Only a small percentage are members of the American Society of Travel Agents (ASTA) which requires at least three years in business prior to membership. For a list of ASTA members in your area write to the American Society of Travel Agents, PR Dept, 711 Fifth Avenue, New York, NY 10022. They also produce free brochures giving general advice about travel overseas. Alternatively look out for the ASTA globe which is the symbol of membership.

Another good sign is the Institute of Travel Agents certificate which means that the agent must have worked in the industry for at least five years and have passed the relevant exams. For listings of CTAs in your area write to the Institute of Certified Travel Agents, 148 Linden Street, Wellesley, MA 02181 (Tel. 617 237 0280).

Always go to a travel agent after you've done your own research first to see if they can come up with a better deal than you were able to. Most travel agent services are free, so if it's necessary to make a transatlantic phone call let them make it. Never forget, the cheaper your ticket is, the less their commission will be, so the temptation will be for a travel agent to recommend APEX as opposed to standby unless they see you've done your homework beforehand.

CROSSING TO EUROPE

Most Inter-Railers setting off from Britain use the main ports of Dover and Folkestone, to Calais and Boulogne. However, there are many alternatives to these routes, which you might consider. Not all the ports are rail connected, so a less convenient bus service may have to be used. Sometimes this service is run by the ferry operator, and requires advance reservation; ask when booking your ticket. Also bear in mind that some services are seasonal, for instance the Truckline Poole to Cherbourg service only runs May–September.

P&O European Ferries, Sealink Stena and Hoverspeed operate frequent services to Calais and Boulogne all year round. Competition on this route increased in 1991 when Hoverspeed introduced the SeaCat service, cutting crossing times to under one hour. Also from Dover, P&O operate ships to Ostend and Zeebrugge, and a fast Jetfoil service to Ostend, connecting to direct train services to

Germany. Another option giving direct connections to Germany is the Harwich–Hoek van Holland route, by either the day or night crossing. Harwich also has boat connections to Hamburg, but this route, whilst giving direct entry to Germany, has no direct train connections.

Those wishing to start their travels in Scandinavia can also start at Harwich, by the Scandinavian Seaways service to Esberg. They also have services from Newcastle to Esberg and Goteborg. A competitor, Scandinavian Seaways, operates services from Newcastle to Bergen and Stavanger. All these routes are long, taking up to 24 hours, so bad sailors should stock up on seasickness cures.

A route often not considered by Inter-Railers is to go to Ireland, then onwards to France. There are many services to both Northern Ireland and the Republic, from Scotland and Wales. From Cairnryan P&O sail to Larne, but as Cairnryan has no rail connection you have to get a bus from Stranraer. Alternatively, from here you could get the Sealink Stena service to Larne. Services from Wales include Fishguard or Pembroke to Rosslare, and Holyhead to Dun Laoghaire. Once in Ireland there are ferry services from Cork and Rosslare to Le Havre and Cherbourg with Irish Ferries.

A summary of the main services to Europe is given in Appendix IV, with an indication of approximate crossing time and frequency. For more accurate times use Thomas Cook's timetable (tables 1001 onwards). When planning your journey remember that some services are very busy in summer, so advance booking is advisable, if not compulsory. Also check carefully that the timing is not affected by tides, which may result in an early sailing.

PRE-PLANNING

This can give great pleasure and add to the fun of the trip, as well as ensuring you get the very most out of your time abroad. After looking at the map of Europe, plan out a rough itinerary in your head and check its feasibility in your timetable (if using last year's, make sure it's the appropriate season's schedule – winter or summer); then write it down and roughly allocate days to it.

When planning a rail itinerary for a complete tour of Europe, there are three main considerations to take into account: the interesting destinations you'd like to go to; how many days you want to spend there; and the most scenic and enjoyable route to get there.

• **Time allocation:** Most cities require a minimum of two or three nights, though obviously you could mix a few 'one-nighters' into your schedule to make your time last out. Time allocation is a more serious consideration for those attempting a 'whistle-stop' tour, whereas those touring only a few countries can be more lax about it.

• **Time differences:** Bear in mind the different time-zones of the countries you'll be travelling in and allow for this when you're making connections. Remember: all these are based on GMT (Greenwich Mean Time).

Country	Summer	Winter	Country	Summer	Winter
AUSTRIA	+2(A)	+1	MOROCCO	+1(A)	GMT
BELGIUM	+2(A)	+1	NETHERLANDS	+2(A)	+1
BULGARIA	+3(A)	+2	NORWAY	+2(A)	+1
CZECHO-			POLAND	+2(A)	+1
SLOVAKIA	+2(A)	+1	PORTUGAL	+1(A)	GMT
DENMARK	+2(A)	+1	ROMANIA	+3(A)	+2
FINLAND	+3(A)	+2	SPAIN	+2(A)	+1
FRANCE	+2(A)	+1	SWEDEN	+2(A)	+1
GERMANY	+2(A)	+1	SWITZER-		
GREECE	+3(A)	+2	LAND	+2(A)	+1
HUNGARY	+2(A)	+1	TURKEY	+3(A)	+2
IRELAND	+1(B)	GMT	UNITED		
ITALY	+2(A)	+1	KINGDOM	+1(B)	GMT
LUXEMBOURG	+2(A)	+1	YUGOSLAVIA	+2(A)	+1

(A) = Summertime runs from end of March–end of September.
(B) = Summertime runs from end of March–end of October.

• **When to go:** Most eurorailers find themselves on the road (or rail) between June and September – for obvious reasons. Travelling in the high season gives you the advantages of encountering more people, getting better weather and being sure all the museums, hotels and places of interest are going to be open.

However, the counter-argument is obvious: prices are higher, the character of a place tends to get lost in the throngs of tourists, accommodation is difficult to find, people involved in the tourist industry have less time for you, and in general there are more hassles on the trains.

For the lucky few able to choose when to go, I'd personally

recommend spring to early summer – but whenever you go, you'll find it a fascinating experience.

● **Destination and routes:** Most eurorailers have a few special places in mind before they set off, maybe an urge to see Paris, Rome and Athens, and by using a timetable and the information given later in this guide you'll be able to work out the quickest and best routes between these places. Often there are two or three alternative routes to major cities, and there's bound to be one that appeals to you more than another. The *Europe by Train factsheets* aim to provide helpful information for those wishing to find the very best route for their particular needs (see p.13).

● **Advance tourist information:** If you know all the countries you're going to be visiting before you set off, write to their main Tourist Office in your own country and they'll gladly send you back free booklets and maps to whet your appetite for their country and give an idea as to what you'd like to see and what you can afford to miss out.

Addresses in the UK:
ANDORRA, 63 Westover Road, London SW18 (081–874 4806 – mornings only)
AUSTRIA, 30 St George Street, London W1R 0AL (071–629 0461)
BELGIUM, Premier House, 2 Gayton Road, Harrow, Middlesex HA1 2XU (081–861 3300)
BULGARIA, 18 Princes Street, London W1 (071–499 6988/9)
CZECHOSLOVAKIA, Čedok, 17–18 Old Bond Street, London W1 (071–629 6058)
DENMARK, 169–173 Regent Street, London W1 (071–734 2637/8)
FINLAND, 66 Haymarket, London SW1 (071–839 4048)
FRANCE, 178 Piccadilly, London W1 (071–491 7622)
GERMANY, 65 Curzon Street, London W1 (071–495 3990)
GREECE, 4 Conduit Street, London W1 (071–734 5997)
HUNGARY, Danube Travel Ltd, 6 Conduit Street, London W1 (071–388 5346)
IRELAND, 150 New Bond Street, London W1 (071–493 3201)
ITALY, 1 Princes Street, London W1 (071–408 1254)
LUXEMBOURG, 36/37 Piccadilly, London W1 (071–434 2800)
MALTA, 207 College House, Wrights Lane, London W8 (071–938 2668)

MONACO, 50 Upper Brook Street, London W1 (071–629 4712)
MOROCCO, 205 Regent Street, London W1 (071–437 0073)
NETHERLANDS, 25–28 Buckingham Gate, London SW1 (071–630 0451)
NORWAY, Charles House, 5–11 Lower Regent Street, London SW1 (071–839 2650)
POLAND, Polorbis, 82 Mortimer Street, London W1 (071–636 2217)
PORTUGAL, 22/25a Sackville Street, London W1 (071–494 1441)
ROMANIA, 17 Nottingham Street, London W1 (071–224 3692)
SPAIN, 57–58 St James's Street, London SW1 (071–499 0901/071–834 6667)
SWEDEN, 29–31 Oxford Street, London W1 (071–437 5816)
SWITZERLAND, Swiss Centre, 1 New Coventry Street, London W1 (071–734 1921)
TURKEY, 170–173 Piccadilly, London W1 (071–734 8681)

Addresses in the USA:
AUSTRIA, 500 Fifth Avenue, 20th Floor, New York, NY 10110 (212 944 6880)
11601 Wilshire Boulevard, Los Angeles, Ca. 90025 (213 477 3332)
BELGIUM, 745 Fifth Avenue, New York, NY 10151 (212 758 8130)
BULGARIA, 41 East 86th Street, New York, NY 10017 (212 573 5530)
CZECHOSLOVAKIA, 10 East 40th Street, Suite 1902, New York, NY 10016 (212 689 9720)
DENMARK, 655 Third Avenue, 18th Floor, New York, NY 10017 (212 949 2333)
FINLAND, 655 Third Avenue, 18th Floor, New York, NY 10017 (212 949 2333)
FRANCE, 610 Fifth Avenue, New York, NY 10020 (900 420 2003)
645 North Michigan Avenue, Chicago, Ill. 60611 (312 337 6301)
9401 Wilshire Boulevard, Beverly Hills, Ca. 90212 (213 271 6665)
GERMANY, 747 Third Avenue, New York, NY 10017 (212 308 3300)
444 South Flower Street, Suite 2230, Los Angeles, Ca. 90017 (213 688 7332)
GREECE, Olympic Tower, Fifth Floor, 645 Fifth Avenue, New York, NY 10022 (212 421 5777)
611 West Sixth Street, Suite 2198, Los Angeles, Ca. 90017 (213 626 6696)
168 North Michigan Avenue, Chicago, Ill. (312 782 1084)

HUNGARY, 1 Parker Plaza, 1104, Fort Lee, NJ 07024 (201 592 8585)

IRELAND, 757 Third Avenue, New York, NY 10017 (212 418 0800)

ITALY, 630 Fifth Avenue, Suite 1565, New York, NY 10111 (212 245 4822)

500 North Michigan Avenue, Suite 1046, Chicago, Ill. 60611 (312 644 0990)

360 Post Street, Suite 801, San Francisco, Ca. 94108 (415 392 5266)

LUXEMBOURG, 801 Second Avenue, New York, NY 10017 (212 370 9850)

MOROCCO, 20 East 46th Street, New York, NY 10017 (212 557 2520)

NETHERLANDS, 355 Lexington Avenue, 21st Floor, New York, NY 10020 (212 370 7367)

9 New Montgomery Street, Suite 305, San Francisco, Ca. 94105 (415 543 6772)

225 N. Michigan Avenue, Suite 326, Chicago, Ill. 60601 (312 819 0300)

NORWAY, 655 Third Avenue, 18th Floor, New York, NY 10017 (212 949 2333)

POLAND, 342 Madison Avenue, New York, NY 10173 (212 867 5011)

333 North Michigan Avenue, Ste 228 Chicago, IL 60601 (312 236 9031)

PORTUGAL, 590 Fifth Avenue, New York, NY 10036 (212 354 4403)

ROMANIA, 573 Third Avenue, New York, NY 10016 (212 697 6971)

SPAIN, 665 Fifth Avenue, New York, NY 10022 (212 759 8822)

845 North Michigan Avenue, Chicago, Ill. 60611 (312 944 0215)

1 Hallidie Plaza, San Francisco, Ca. 94102 (415 346 8100)

SWEDEN, 655 Third Avenue, 18th Floor, New York, NY 10017 (212 949 2333)

SWITZERLAND, 608 Fifth Avenue, New York, NY 10020 (212 757 5944)

250 Stockton Street, San Francisco, Ca. 94108 (415 362 2260)

TURKEY, 821 United Nations Plaza, New York, NY 10017 (212 687 2194)

UNITED KINGDOM, 40 West 57th Street, New York, NY 10019 (212 581 4700)

612 South Flower Street, Los Angeles, Ca. 90017 (213 623 8196)

John Hancock Center, Suite 3320, 875 North Michigan Avenue, Chicago, Ill. 60611 (312 787 0490)

Plaza of the Americas, North Tower Suite 750, Dallas, Texas 75201 (213 623 8196)

Addresses in Australia:

AUSTRIA, 36 Carrington Street, 1st Floor, Sydney NSW 2000 (02–299–3621)

CZECHOSLOVAKIA, c/o Czech Airlines, Tower Buildings, Australia Square, Sydney NSW (02–27–6196)

DENMARK, 60 Market Street, Melbourne, Victoria 3001 (03–62–33–63)

FRANCE, 12 Castlereagh Street, Sydney NSW 2000 (02–231–5244)

GERMANY, Lufthansa House, 143 Macquarie Street, Sydney NSW 2000 (02–221–1008)

GREECE, 51–57 Pitt Street, Sydney NSW 2000 (02–241–1663)

IRELAND, MLC Centre, Martin Place, Sydney NSW 2000 (02–232–7177)

MOROCCO, c/o Moroccan Consulate, 11 West Street North, Sydney NSW 2000 (9576717)

NETHERLANDS, 6th Floor, 5. Elizabeth Street, Sydney NSW 2000 (02–276–921)

SPAIN, 203 Castlereagh Street, Suite 21a, Sydney NSW 2000 (02–264–7966)

SWITZERLAND, 203–233 New South Head Road, Edgecliffe, Sydney NSW 2027 (02–326–1799)

UNITED KINGDOM, 171 Clarence Street, Sydney NSW 2000 (02–298–627)

Remember though, Tourist Offices are in the business of selling their country, so take some of their claims like having the 'most beautiful city in Europe' with a pinch of salt. However, as their brochures are nearly all free and usually very well produced, you've nothing to lose. Make sure you ask for country and city maps; often the tourist authority will send you free the same ones you might otherwise have to buy, once in the country.

• **Red tape:** Make sure your passport photo is up-to-date (i.e. looks like you) or there may be complications at borders in countries such as Romania or Poland.

• **UK red tape:** A valid passport, with the relevant visas for Poland, Bulgaria and Romania if you're going there, will get you in without problems. (Visas for Eastern Europe are in a great state of flux, and the best advice for the early 90s is to check with the London Embassy of the country concerned.) Likewise a British visitor's card is fine for many countries in Western Europe but no good for Eastern Europe. It costs £7.50 and is valid for twelve months. Apply at a post office in person with two recent passport-type photos and proof of ID, such as driving licence or National Health Service card and your birth certificate or certificate of naturalization.

For a full ten-year passport, get an application form at a main post office, complete it and send it on to your nearest passport office. This costs £15. Allow a month at least if you're posting off the form and at least three weeks if you take it in person.

• **North American red tape:** A valid US passport will get you into all Western European countries for up to three months without the need for a visa. The only Eastern European countries which still require a visa are Romania, Yugoslavia and some states of the former USSR. Apply to the nearest consulate/embassy of the country concerned (see under US visas).

If you're applying for the first time or your current passport was issued before your eighteenth birthday or if it's more than eight years old, you'll have to go along in person to any US Post Office or Passport Agency, otherwise you can send off a DSP 82 form by mail. Along with your application you should include two recent passport-type photos, signed on the back, plus around $40. If you have to go along in person, you'll need your US birth certificate and around $48 ($32 if you're under eighteen). Passports are valid for ten years if you're over eighteen, five if you're under. If you've any problems, contact the Passport Agency, Department of State, 1425 K Street NW Room 262, Washington, DC 20524, and ask them for their free booklet 'Your Trip Abroad'.

Canadian passports are valid for five years only and can be obtained by mail from the Passport Office, Department of External Affairs, 125 Sussex Drive, Ottawa, Ontario K1A 0G3 (or from your nearest Passport Office) for CDN $35. Allow four to six weeks' processing time from March to September, and two to four weeks from October to February.

• **Australasian red tape:** Australian nationals can obtain passports from post offices and passport offices. You need proof of nationality (birth certificate, nationality papers), proof of ID (driving licence etc.) and 2 photos. Cost is $88 for 32 pages or $124 for 64 pages; both are valid for 10 years. Visas may be required for Bulgaria, Czechoslovakia, France, Hungary, Poland, Romania, Spain and the CIS, so check with the relevant embassy well in advance.

New Zealanders should send passport applications to the NZ Passport Office, Documents of National Identity Division, Department of Internal Affairs, Box 10–526, Wellington. An adult passport costs NZ $56.25.

VISAS

Don't be put off from visiting a country because of the visa situation. The procedure is extremely straightforward and is invariably easier than most people imagine, especially with the increasing liberalization in Eastern Europe.

Where required, visas are best arranged in advance, by writing to the relevant embassy for their application form (see below). When you send off your application, don't forget to include two passport-type photos signed on the back, plus the relevant fee. Note that cheques are not always accepted, so use postal orders. Don't forget that you will still need visas for some countries, even though travel is valid with your ticket.

Allow up to four weeks for the processing of your application form, although it is usually turned round in a week or ten days. Get yourself organized early and do as much as possible by post as far in advance as possible (not too far in advance, as visas are only valid for certain periods). If you've left it until the last minute don't worry as you can normally pick up visas from the relevant embassy in London, Paris or Vienna. Bear in mind, though, that many embassy visa sections are only open for a few hours each day and that queues are inevitable. You may also find some countries insist you leave your passport overnight so don't count on obtaining more than one visa per day. Always take cash, as they often won't take cheques.

It goes without saying that you must be very careful not to lose your passport or visa; if this should happen, contact your embassy immediately (addresses are given under the individual countries). It is also important to have a recent passport photo.

• **UK visas:** For ROMANIA you can only get a visa in advance if you have prepaid accommodation, so it's best to buy your visa at the frontier, take dollars, and be prepared for the price to mysteriously increase. If you feel more comfortable with things arranged in advance, contact 4 Palace Green, London W8 (Tel. 071–937 9666). £20.

POLAND'S consulate, visa section, is at 47 Portland Place, London W1 (Tel. 071–580 4324). Apply in advance. £20.

BULGARIA requires a visa if you're travelling independently or if you're staying at private accommodation. Send for forms to the consular section of the embassy at 188 Queen's Gate, London SW7 (Tel. 071–584 9400). £20. You must change the equivalent of $15 per day.

UK passport holders now need a visa for TURKEY. This can be obtained upon arrival anywhere in Turkey for £5; take cash (sterling) with you to pay this. There is no need to obtain a Turkish visa in advance.

Contact the Visa Shop, 44 Chandos Place, London WC2 4HS (Tel. 071–379 0419) for the latest visa information in today's fast-changing world.

• **US visas:** A 30-day visa for ROMANIA will cost you around $15 at the border, and can be extended for up to 90 days for an extra $10. For further information contact the Romanian Tourist Office at 573 Third Avenue, New York, NY 10016.

When you cross the border into 'YUGOSLAVIA', a customs officer will take your passport and return it sometime later with a free 90-day visa. At smaller crossings, you may be asked to get off the train and follow him to the customs office while he does the paper work.

Because visa requirements can change quickly these days, it's worth contacting the Visa Center Inc., 507 Fifth Avenue, Suite 904, New York, NY 10017 (Tel. 212–986 0924).

• **Canadian visas:** A visa must be obtained for Bulgaria (Bulgarian Embassy, 325 Stewart Street, Ottawa, ON K1M 6K5 (613 232 3215)); Romania (Romanian Embassy, 655 Lidoau Street, Ottawa ON K1N 6A3 (613 232 3001)); and Poland (Polish Embassy, 443 Daly Avenue, Ottawa ON K1N 6H3 (613 236 0468)).

• **Australian visas:** A visa must be obtained for Bulgaria; Romania; Poland (Polish Embassy, 7 Turrana Street, Yarralumla, Canberra ACT 2600 (062 273 1211)); Czechoslovakia (Czech Embassy, 47 Culgoa Circuit, O'Malley, Canberra ACT 2029 (062 295 3713)); France (French Embassy, 6 Perth Avenue, Yarralumla, Canberra ACT 2600 (062 270 5111)); and Hungary (Hungarian Embassy, 79 Hopetown Circuit, Yarralumla, Canberra ACT 2600 (062 282 3226)).

• **New Zealand visas:** A visa must be obtained for Bulgaria; Romania; Poland (Polish Embassy, 196 The Terrace, Suite D, PO Box 10211, Wellington (04 712 456)); and Czechoslovakia (Czech Embassy, 12 Anne Street, Wadestown, PO Box 2843, Wellington (04 723 142)).

BUDGETING

Exactly how much money you have to spend will affect your 'lifestyle' on Inter-Rail in many ways. I'm making the general assumption that the average eurorailer is short of cash and won't ever be keen to spend more than he or she has to on basics such as accommodation and food. There's no shortage of information for those wishing to spend more – other 'budget' guides to Europe you can buy will list hotels for £30 ($54) a night, or restaurants for £20–25 ($36–45) meals. I'm not interested in that. After all, who needs advice on how to *spend* money in Europe? Also, you experience more of the real country when living like the locals on a budget.

It's a straight fact that £25 ($45) a day in Norway will just about get you a hostel bed and a cafeteria meal; the same £25 in Spain will give you a hotel bed and a restaurant meal, so take into consideration the countries you want to go to, and budget accordingly. The most expensive countries are: Norway, Sweden, Finland, Denmark, Switzerland and Austria; the intermediate ones are: West Germany, United Kingdom, Ireland, Netherlands, Belgium, Luxembourg, France, Italy and 'Yugoslavia'; and the cheap ones are: Spain, Greece, Portugal, Turkey, Eastern Europe and Morocco. The southern part of Europe remains much cheaper than the northern, but to take full advantage of this cheapness you have to be prepared to accept the local standards of hygiene, cuisine, etc. Eastern Europe is cheap for food, drink and entertainment, but hotel accommodation is expensive, so hostel or camp – though watch out for escalating camping prices in Hungary and Poland. The basic fact of the matter is: camping and hostelling are cheap all over Europe, and if you are prepared to do this and buy your food in the local shops and markets to make your own picnics, you can eurorail for very little money.

On average, for your bed and daily food, you'll need at least £25 ($45) a day for the expensive countries, £15 ($27) a day for the intermediate ones, and £12 ($21.50) a day for the cheap ones. Remember: if you're travelling on your own and you insist on a single bedroom in a cheap hotel, it can double your costs, so double up with fellow travellers where at all possible.

• **International Student Identity Card:** This saves you money all over Europe – often as much as 75 per cent on museums and art galleries, etc., or even free entry. It also entitles you to 10–15 per cent discount on rail travel, and up to 50 per cent reduction on some air fares. You need a certificate from your college or university, a photograph and £5. Remember to take the book of discount vouchers with you. The ID card when purchased in the USA even provides you with automatic accident/sickness insurance anywhere you travel (outside the US) for the entire validity period of the ID card. Apply to your local Student Travel Office or to one of these addresses:

UK: International Students' Travel Centre, BJC, c/o NUS Marketing, Old Co-operative House, 8 Ashton Street, Glossop, Derbyshire SK13 8JP or Campus Travel, 52 Grosvenor Gardens, London SW1N 0AG (Tel. 071–730 3402).

USA: CIEE, New York Student Center, Sloane House YMCA, 356 West 34th Street, New York, NY 10001 (Tel. 212–564 0142).

CANADA: Travel Cuts, 44 George Street, Toronto, Ontario M5S 2E4 (Tel. 416–979 2406).

AUSTRALIA: Australian Student Travel/STA, 220 Faraday Street, Carlton, Victoria 3053 (Tel. 03 3476911).

NEW ZEALAND: Student Travel Bureau, Students' Union, University of Auckland, Princes Street, Auckland (Tel. 375 265).

Ask for a copy of the ID discount guide for 1993.

• **International Youth Card (YIEE):** This is offered by the Federation of International Youth Travel Organizations (FIYTO) and is meant for young people who are not eligible for the ISIC card but wish to take advantage of travel concessions open to them; it is not necessary to possess both of these cards. The card is available at any student travel office. To get it you need proof that you are under 26 and £4. The card comes with a FIYTO booklet of discounts.

• **Discount Cards:** One way to save money in Europe is to take advantage of an expanding network of discount card schemes for those under 26. In Scotland, there's the *Young Scot* card, in

Belgium the *Cultureel Jonger en Passport*, in France the *Cartes Jeunes*, in Portugal the *Cartao Jovem* and so on. The cards cost about £5, can be bought from a variety of outlets, and offer literally thousands of discounts on meals, clothes, souvenirs and other goods. The cards can all be used interchangeably – so you can buy a Scottish card and use it to get discounts in France, for example.

• **Student travel offices:** There are about 60 STOs in the UK. The good thing about them is that they nearly all sell BIJ and Inter-Rail tickets, and the staff will work out the cheapest alternative for you. They also sell ISICs and are usually found in university or college complexes. Note: They offer their services to anyone under 26, not just students.

• **The Council on International Educational Exchange (CIEE):** The CIEE is a non-profit, membership organization based in the US, and is one of the foremost organizations concerned with budget travel.

They are there to help budget travellers of all ages with low-cost travel (air, train, etc.) as well as accommodation problems. In fact, they cover every aspect of your trip from your Student ID card to your airline ticket and reservations. Get hold of their 1993 Student Travel Catalogue which is a mine of information by writing to CIEE, 205 East 42nd Street, New York, NY 10017 (Tel. 212-661 1450). They also have offices in other US and European cities (see Appendix I). The catalogue provides information on Student ID cards, travel, study and work abroad. Use the Council's expertise as much as possible to get the lowest possible air fares, eurorail passes and other travel packages.

• A useful tip is to go to your local library and explore the world of travel grants to see what's available. It's amazing what funds are around, and it pays off to do your research well in advance.

Getting yourself together

WHAT TO TAKE WITH YOU

Obviously this very much depends on where you're going and at
what time of the year: if you're going to Scandinavia in the spring,
an extra jumper will certainly come in very useful. However, there
are various points to remember, irrespective of where you are going
or the time of the year. Unless you're visiting family or friends in
Europe and expect to be met at every station, we strongly advise
that you use an internal framed rucksack. Its advantages are
manifold: it gives one the feeling of membership of a eurorail club
and this stimulates conversation and communication which otherwise might not take place. Also – and more importantly – both your
hands will be left free to use, allowing you to produce your maps,
passport, etc., at the right moment. Shops specializing in outdoor
equipment are an invaluable source of information and help. They
will, in most cases, give free objective advice on what you really
need for your trip and which brand names to look out for to suit your
budget. If you're starting from scratch it'll take about £150 to get
together all the basic gear required to camp your way round
Europe, but once bought this will see you through future trips and
you'd easily spend that much on grotty accommodation in just one
Inter-Rail trip. Names to look out for in the UK are the Youth
Hostel Association shops, Field & Trek Equipment (catalogue
from 3 Waters Way, Brentwood, Essex CM15 9TB for £1.95 and
from many branches of W.H. Smith), and in the US write to L. L.
Bean Inc. at Freeport, ME 04033, USA for a catalogue. It's better,
though, for a novice to go to a shop and check out the equipment
first hand, and Blacks are best for this.

Daysacks, in which you can take all that's needed for a day's
sightseeing are handy, and if you're going to northern Europe it's a
good investment to go for a good duck-down sleeping bag.
Although the initial cost is steep you get back the value over the
years and if you can afford it it's well worth the extra cash.

Don't cut back on tents and bags unless you're only planning on
using your equipment for one or two seasons. Spend as much as you
can afford and take advice from the shop staff.

• **Packing:** Every summer, Europe is full of backpackers wishing they hadn't taken so much, so don't take more than you're prepared to carry with comfort. Before you set out, put out on the bed everything you want to take with you – then halve it. Before you finally make up your mind, try wearing your rucksack with everything you intend to take in it on a good walk. Remember, don't be overgenerous as you'll be returning with more than you left with in the way of presents and souvenirs, so leave room for them. All this is common sense really; however, we all need reminding from time to time, as it can make the difference between a relaxing and an exhausting holiday.

• **Essentials:** The rucksack: without doubt this will be your most important single piece of equipment, so it is essential to ensure that it is both comfortable and light. Beware of back-breakers and spine-grinders. The three most important features you should look out for are: that it sits just above your hips and, if possible, has a support belt for round your waist; that the shoulder-straps are well padded and that the tension can be adjusted; and (most important of all) that your pack is 'high' rather than 'wide', when packed to capacity. I wish I had a pound for every eurorailer I've seen creating havoc along the all-too-narrow train-corridors. If they're not pulling the door shut on someone's leg they're laying out the natives with swinging cameras and boots hanging from the rear.

A small daypack is also invaluable, especially when sightseeing, as it will hold your maps, guidebook, waterproof, camera, films, food, etc., all conveniently together. It will solve a lot of problems and saves you walking around all the time with a large rucksack. It's a good idea to put your name and address in the inside of your pack, just in case – something which many travellers overlook.

• **Valuables:** Keep an independent note of your ticket and passport numbers. If you do lose your passport, notify the police then get a copy of the report the police make out and go along with it to your country's nearest consulate or embassy. A photocopy of both, kept separately, may help your case. Also a photocopy of your birth certificate is another very useful thing to have with you, as are a couple of passport photos, which can come in handy for impromptu visas, replacement ISICs or passports.

One idea, very popular with the Scandinavians, is to buy a pouch that you hang round your neck with all your tickets in it. Keep cash separate – in a safe inside pocket, perhaps. Another good idea is a moneybelt. You can pick up one of these in Greece or Spain quite cheaply – assuming you can get that far without getting ripped off.

• **Sleeping bag:** Unless you plan to spend all your time staying with friends or in hotels you'll need a good bag. Hostels charge for bedding and many in northern Europe won't allow you to use your bag which is *very* frustrating – but the rule. Note: at some hostels you may find it compulsory to hire sheets, even if you do have your own. If taking a sheet sleeping bag ensure it is to YHA standards. Also at some stage in your travels it's likely you'll be a deck passenger on an overnight ferry somewhere. When you're shopping around for a sleeping bag, price is likely to be your main criterion, as it's not difficult to spend more on your sleeping bag than on your ticket. If you have no bag already, and can't borrow one from a friend, go along to your local camping shop and get the best you can afford. As with the other two basics, rucksack and shoes, the better the quality, the more money you can expect to spend. Do not make cutbacks in this direction: there are few things worse than a cold sleepless night before a hard day's sightseeing. Buying a cheap sleeping bag is a classic false economy. Shop assistants in camping shops are usually only too ready to help you out.

If you're taking a bag and plan to do a lot of camping or sleeping out on southern beaches, then a foam mattress is also advisable. Try and get one that is long enough but not too wide (remember those train corridors). Lie down on it in the shop to check it out. Print your name on it as you'll find mattresses disappear with remarkable frequency.

• **Comfortable walking shoes** (already broken in) are essential as you can expect to spend as much time walking as you will on trains. Don't go over the top and wear boots that would look better on Everest than strolling round the Vatican. If you're heading south, a pair of sandals is a necessity to give your feet a chance to breathe. If you don't have any, don't worry: they're cheap in southern Europe.

• **Camping gear:** If you're heading for northern Europe and plan to camp a lot, get a strongish tent with a fly-sheet; however, if you'll be mainly in the south, pick a light one, preferably of nylon. A small Calor gas stove can save you a lot of money, especially in places like Norway where buying a cup of tea or coffee can be expensive. Gas refills are widely available so don't bother carrying spares. Unless you're camping non-stop for about a month, don't carry food supplies and a lot of camping equipment with you, but do take cutlery. Shopping from the local supermarkets makes much more sense. Remember to take a torch for those late-night pitches.

• **Clothes:** Obviously it depends on where you're going and the time of year. Use your common sense, but don't take anything you don't absolutely need and remember: though you may look terrific in your white jeans when they're newly washed and ironed at home, you'll look terrible after you've sat up all night in them on an Italian train.

Take dark comfortable clothes that won't show the battering you're giving them. Laundries are often expensive, so take a little washing powder or liquid detergent and wash your own clothes. 'Washaway' tablets from Boots are particularly handy.

LAST-MINUTE REMINDERS

1. Women: take a scarf or shawl to cover your head and shoulders as often you'll be refused entry to churches and cathedrals if your arms and shoulders are bare. Shorts are also prohibited in many churches, so go prepared.
2. A travelling alarm clock is handy, especially if you have early trains to catch.
3. Don't forget toilet paper, soap, a universal plug and a small towel. You can never find a place to buy these, just when you need them most.
4. Plastic bags are essential for containing potentially leaky liquids, separating off dirty washing etc.
5. A Swiss Army penknife, with as many functions as possible (including a corkscrew and bottle opener), comes in handy.
6. A small padlock is often needed when hostelling (for the lockers) and for locking your bag to a fixed point if sleeping on a train. A cycle chain may also be useful to stop your bags wandering, and of course is essential if cycling.
7. A pre-filled water-bottle will save you cash on long thirsty journeys, as prices of drinks on trains are high.
8. A good book: take your reading supply from home as English-language books cost a lot abroad.

9. A notepad and pen. Get shopkeepers to write down prices before saying yes, if you don't have the lingo. This way, you'll know when you're being ripped off.
10. Postcards of your home town are a good ice-breaker and let foreigners see where you're from. It can even boost home town tourism!
11. A calculator for working out exchange rates. The cheapest one you can find will do.
12. A Walkman comes in handy if you get temporarily fed up with your travelling companions and want a bit of solitude. A pair of ear plugs can come in handy for the same reason, although you are more likely to find these useful in shutting out the escaping noise from *their* Walkman earphones!
13. Don't forget to take some camping cutlery (the type that clip together) and a sharp knife for cutting bread.
14. Insect repellant is a very good idea if you are visiting countries like Scotland or Scandinavia.
15. If you're taking the Algeciras–Tangier ferry, carry a photocopy of your Inter-Rail card as you need this for the crossing and to get it done at the other end is one big headache!
16. A length of string or cord can be useful as a washing line in youth hostels. A torch can also come in handy if you want to go to the toilet without waking everyone else in the dorm!
17. A small sewing kit and safety pins, very useful for mending those burst buttons.
18. Are you carrying sufficient information – factsheets/*Cheap Sleep Guide* (see Introduction)?
19. Photocopies of all documents (passport, visas, tickets etc.) may be useful, best packed separately, or with a friend.
20. A small first-aid kit; see p.82 for suggestions.
21. Take a warm sweater – for air-conditioned trains and ferry crossings.

MONEY

There's a 'Catch 22' situation with money in Europe. Undoubtedly, with violence and crime the way it is at present in Europe, especially the south, it's a big risk to carry around all your cash in ready notes on you, even in a moneybelt. To be weighed against this is the fact that by taking traveller's cheques you lay yourself open to continual queueing, especially in the summer, not to mention the problems trying to find a bank or travel agent to cash them. If you decide to play safe and take most of your money in traveller's cheques, then get them from one of the big banks or, even better, from Thomas Cook or American Express. Don't find yourself trying to cash an obscure brand of traveller's cheque.

When buying your traveller's cheques, always buy small denominations as this is more economical on a tight budget. Anyone from the USA or a major European country should buy cheques in their own currency – unless you're planning to spend 99 per cent of your time in one country. If you offer a £20 cheque and ask for £14 in French francs and £6 in Italian lire, most banks will charge you first to change into francs, then again into lire. It's better to get traveller's cheques in denominations of £10 ($20). In general, it's a good idea to take some bank notes of the countries you know you'll end up in, especially if there's a chance you will arrive late at night or at weekends. As a rule, I take £25 ($45) cash in four or five currencies in case there's no opportunity to change money on arrival and you have to pay for your room in advance. Again, it's best to order your currency from your bank at least two weeks in advance. However, banks do not always give the best rate. Shop around for the best rates. It's always worth while taking along a few US dollar notes as a standby as you will find them accepted almost everywhere, particularly in Eastern European countries where goods and services are often priced in US dollars.

Credit cards can be useful – if you're good at resisting temptation! Providing you keep them for emergencies only, credit cards may be able to get you out of a hole and are likely to be the only source of funds if you lose your traveller's cheques and are waiting for replacements. It is also becoming increasingly easy to find cashpoints from which you can withdraw cash using Visa/Master-card (if you know your PIN number!). It goes without saying that you should be very careful indeed and keep credit cards separate, so that if you are robbed you don't lose them as well. They are not as widely accepted abroad, particularly in Austria and Germany, as in the UK & US, but can help if you need to pay for something but don't want to use cash or change traveller's cheques. This can be important in Eastern European countries where you can't take the local currency out and lose on conversion deals at the border. Watch out for exchange rules. The maximum cash advance in

'Yugoslavia' on Access on any one day is £80, but you may find this is also the minimum you can change. When using cards you are at the mercy of fluctuating exchange rates. This can work to your benefit in a country with high inflation where the local currency is falling against your home currency – but it works both ways. Remember, if you use a credit card to buy your traveller's cheques from a bank before leaving, this is treated as a cash advance and you pay interest right away. If you have a Thomas Cook Credit Card and buy your cheques from them, you have up to 55 days to settle the bill before paying interest. This also applies to currency and tickets.

- **Money tips:**
1. Take a money belt or neck pouch.
2. Sending money abroad is expensive, so take ample with you.
3. Banks tend to offer better rates than station, hotel or 24-hour exchange bureaux, but check rates carefully. A similar rule applies to commission rates.
4. Check commission rates carefully, to see if it is a fixed amount per transaction, or a percentage, as this will affect you if you are changing small amounts. Also beware of places charging commission on traveller's cheques individually.
5. In some countries, notably in Eastern Europe and Italy, ripped or damaged notes may not be taken.
6. If taking your Eurocheque guarantee card or credit card, remember your PIN number; there are many cashpoints in Western Europe where you can get cash advances.
7. If you spot travellers arriving when you are leaving a country, offer your spare currency. It is a useful way of getting rid of that loose change, and gets you small change for another country. Be discreet in countries where currency control exists.

- **Money in Eastern Europe:** 'Hard' currency from the West helps strengthen the local stuff; as a result, some countries insist on a minimum exchange requirement. This is nearly always more than is strictly necessary, and in some cases you'll have difficulty trying to get rid of it. To discourage black-market dealings, you may have to declare all your hard currency and any valuables. This declaration is normally carried out on the train at the border.

If you're thinking of playing the black market you will have to 'forget' to declare some of your hard currency because if, on departure, you cannot account for the missing money or produce the required receipts, you will be in trouble. This still applies – even after 1990.

● **Black market:** The freeing up of exchange is starting to finish off the black market (as in Poland). The authorities in parts of Eastern Europe still come down with a heavy hand on those caught in the act (in some cases this means imprisonment). Hard currency is very much in demand, and many private citizens are prepared to pay far more than the official rate to get it. Some people are still prepared to pay high prices for jeans, pocket calculators, etc., though this is becoming less common. In general, never have any dealings with anyone who approaches you in the street; at best, you're likely to get poor rates and, at worst, they could be plain-clothes police or an informer. A final word: tipping is not general practice here, so hang on to your cash.

● **Banking:** You can cash a personal cheque of up to £100 in any European bank displaying the EC symbol if you've got a Euro-cheque Encashment Card and appropriate cheque book with you. Check the cheque book you've got, as the style changed in January 1989, and the old style is no longer usable. Eurocheques are normally written in the local currency (US dollars in parts of Eastern Europe) and no commission should be paid when cashing them (it's deducted from your account). Girobank plc runs a similar system to Eurocheques for its customers – these 'Postcheques' can get you up to £130 in foreign currency in 30 different countries and can be cashed at Post Offices (which often have longer opening hours than banks). In some countries, such as Germany, the post office changes money without taking as large a commission as the banks. In countries where there's a high service charge for cashing traveller's cheques, you're better off cashing your own personal cheques at Eurocheque banks using your banker's card. It is also possible to withdraw cash using a credit card. Banks in all countries open in the morning from Monday to Friday, but beware of the siestas in the Mediterranean countries (see the individual countries, for banking hours).

INSURANCE

Whether or not to get insurance cover depends very much on where you're going, and for how long. If you've a lot of expensive new camping gear and photographic equipment then undoubtedly it's worth it. Shop around for the best deal; call in at your local student travel centre and see what they have to offer. It could be you're already insured through your home policy (your parents' or your own), so check up first. Eurotrain offer a travel insurance scheme. It's worth bearing in mind that train travel is very safe indeed, and it's highly unlikely that you'll end up in hospital because of an accident, but your health and your valuables are a different matter. Still, after food poisoning in Morocco and with a doctor being called out at 2 a.m., the bill for one of us was less than the insurance premium would have been.

• **American and Canadian travellers:** If your personal policies don't provide adequate cover abroad, check with your travel agent or CIEE office to see what options are available.

• **Medical:** If you're only travelling in EC countries and you're British, go along to your local post office and get form E 111. This service is often neglected by eurorailers, which is surprising as it provides medical cover in EC countries to the same level that a national of that country enjoys. In theory it takes a few days to obtain, but usually can be granted there and then. Take your NI number with you. You may, however, have to pay part or all of your treatment and drugs. Keep receipts and claim back the cost from the DSS when you return home. Doctors in Europe can be very expensive, and often a chemist can give just as good advice – free! To find a 24-hour chemist, either ask at a police station or go to the nearest chemist's shop and look in the window, as there's often a notice saying where one is open.

Watch out girls, in Eastern Europe it's often impossible to get hold of tampons or sanitary towels, so take a supply along with you. Also, if you'll need contraceptives, take them from home.

If you've got to carry drugs or injection needles for medical reasons, take a doctor's note about them as you could otherwise be in for a hard time in Eastern Europe and Turkey.

Unless you've got an iron stomach, it's best to work on the theory that prevention is better than cure: take along some multivitamin pills to keep body and soul together during those long hauls, avoid the tap water in southern Europe, peel all fruit and make sure that meat is always well cooked. You'll be doing enough running for trains . . .

Whether or not you can drink the tap water depends a lot on where you are and how strong a stomach you have. It's really down to common sense. You should be OK in a city or large town, particularly in Scandinavia and near European countries, but in the more remote, hotter or less developed places be cautious and stick to bottled or boiled water. If you have an easily upset stomach play safe and stick to bottled water or water you have treated yourself with tablets, available from good chemists and camping stores.

In the event of your having problems with sangria, paella and the like, it's a good idea to keep some Alka-Seltzer and anti-diarrhoea tablets to hand. A mild laxative won't go amiss, in case all that foreign food and lack of fibre affects you the other way. The further south you go, the more mosquitoes and other undesirables you're likely to encounter, so if you're a big scratcher take along some soothing cream and a small pack of plasters and, should all else fail, some pain-killers.

To avoid sunstroke take a good sun-tan lotion; the fairer your skin the higher the screen factor you'll need. A good pair of sunglasses and a hat will also prove invaluable. Drinking plenty of liquid will help. Use your common sense, and stay out of strong midday sun.

A few weeks before you go, if possible, visit your GP to see if you need inoculations for cholera and typhoid if you are intending to go to places like Turkey or Morocco, or where sanitation is dubious. Check also if you need boosters for tetanus and polio. Also ask about anti-malaria tablets, which need to be taken before you go and after you return, as well as during the trip, if you need them at all. The chances are, you'll only need to take these if you're venturing as far as eastern Turkey. Make sure you get an International Certificate to prove you've been protected against these diseases or you may find you're not allowed to visit places where there are outbreaks of diseases such as cholera. A certificate costs about £3. You can also get advice and all the protection you need from the British Airways Medical Centre, 156 Regent Street, London (Tel. 071–439 9584). It is open office hours but tends to get busy around lunch time in summer, so expect delays of up to an hour. Free information is also available from the Robens Institute in Guildford, Surrey (Tel. 0483 68637/68673).

When you're there

ACCOMMODATION

As accommodation is the largest potential headache for eurorailers and I'm limited for space, I'm restricting suggestions to the main tourist centres. If you plan travelling off the beaten track or arriving late in peak season, I strongly recommend you buy my *Cheap Sleep Guide to Europe* (Fontana Paperbacks). For the price of a Tourist Board placing, it will save you a lot of time and trouble and money in the end. It is the only publication out to contain hundreds of recommendations in all categories, everything from where to sleep rough in safety, to cost of B&Bs. Remember that those travelling in July and August may end up paying more for accommodation, as prices often go up with demand.

My suggestions tend to be biased towards hostels, and to places located near stations. Basically there are four types of accommodation open to you: cheap hotels; youth or student hostels; camping and private accommodation. There is, theoretically, a fifth option for those with an open pass – and it will certainly ensure you get round Europe at a phenomenal rate – it is to sleep on the trains themselves, not just in the couchettes or sleepers which vary in price from £5 to £40 ($9–72) for a night's sleep, but for free in the seats. As we've discussed 'night travel' already and I do not really recommend you spending your eurorail doing this, we'll concentrate now on the other four.

• **Cheap hotels/pensions:** If you're travelling with your girlfriend/boyfriend, husband/wife and don't fancy camping and can't get into private accommodation, this is your only real alternative if you want to spend the night together. The advantages are obvious: relative comfort and convenience. If you're in a city and you haven't long to be there, it's best to try for one located near the centre, to save you bus journeys and hassles. The disadvantages are: it's more expensive than hostelling or camping, and if you're in a really cheap hotel, you often find a sort of 'skid row' atmosphere. The hotels I list under each country are the best compromise I could find between clean, pleasant surroundings and a fair price.

If there are two or more of you room-hunting, it's a good idea for one to wait in the tourist office queue with all the luggage, while the other goes looking for a room in one of the hotels you invariably find close to the stations. The rooms in these places are generally cheap and, of course, very convenient. Alternatively, if you all want to go off to hunt together, leave your heavy packs in left luggage. You won't regret the £1 ($1.80) you spend for the extra comfort and speed you'll get out of it.

Once you've found a suitable place and have been told the prices, ask the receptionist again if she has nothing cheaper. Often this works and you get a cheaper room tucked away near the top. The luxury of taking a room with a private bath or shower is bought at a high price, so you do best to use the communal one. Always ask how much a bath or shower costs. If you're travelling in a group it can be cheaper to have a room with a bath than to pay for four showers. In the vast majority of cheap hotels it's not included in the price, and it can come as a nasty shock when you get the bill.

Unfortunately the wonderful British institution of B&B does not really exist in Europe. Breakfast is often extra and rarely does it merit the name or the cost. Anyway, it's far cheaper and more entertaining to find a coffee bar or café where the locals go.

Pensions (guest houses) are often far more attractive and friendly than hotels. A double bed is usually cheaper than two singles. Remember to check all the following before deciding on a room in a hotel: the price of the room, including all taxes; whether breakfast is included; whether a bath/shower is included; whether there is nothing cheaper; whether the hotelier would mind if three or four people used a double room; and finally when you must check out the next day, to avoid paying for another night's accommodation.

● **Hostels:** Hostels run by the International Youth Hostel Federation are good value and an ideal place to meet up with other travellers. They're the next cheapest alternative to camping, ranging from £2 to £9 ($3.60–16.20) a night. You need to be a member of your own country's YHA or that of the country you're in, though often you can buy temporary membership on the spot. If you're already a member of the YHA, attach a photo of yourself to your YHA card to allow you to hostel in Europe.

Youth hostels offer simple basic accommodation for men and women in separate dormitory-style bedrooms, washing and toilet facilities, and a common room. Many hostels have their own communal kitchen, though, apart from odd exceptions like England, Scotland and Wales, you need your own utensils. In this way you can buy food at supermarket prices and cater for yourself for next to no cost at all. Economical meals (including vegetarian options) are laid on at many hostels (we list these below, under each country) and hostellers are expected to help with some domestic chores. Even if you bring your own sleeping bag, most hostels insist you hire their sheets – a pain, but nothing you can do about it. Some hostels will however accept standard YHA sheet sleeping bags. The general rule is that you can't stay more than three nights at any one hostel. Try phoning ahead, but often they will tell you they are full, even when they aren't.

If you've never hostelled before, it's a good idea to go round one or two at home so you get to know what it's like. If you're expecting room service or breakfast in bed, forget hostelling. (Actually, if you're strictly the breakfast-in-bed type, forget eurorailing!) Average cost is £6.50 ($12) a night and average meal £2–3.50 ($3.60–6.30).

• **Booking ahead:** During July and August it's a good idea to book your hostel bed ahead in the major tourist cities. If you're going to be doing a lot of hostelling in Europe, a useful system is International Multi-Lingual Booking Cards: they cost 5p each and allow one, two or more people to reserve beds and meals. You should be able to buy them at your local hostel or from your country's Youth Hostel Association head office. You post the cards on to the hostel concerned with an International Reply Coupon (60p at post offices). Beds reserved through this scheme are held until 6 p.m.

Hostels vary a tremendous amount; generally though, the further south you go, the less strict the rules tend to be, and also the more basic the accommodation becomes. Some hostels still insist on midnight curfews and lock you out between 10 a.m. and 4 p.m., while others are far more liberal. If in doubt, it's always a good move to phone ahead from the station and check out if there's space and what rules, if any, apply. Many hostels are open only in the summer.

Beware of the increasing number of unofficial hostels which are springing up, especially in southern Europe. Many call themselves 'Student Youth Hostels' and, though they impose no curfews or sex segregation, the facilities they offer are often very poor and the charges are more than those of official youth hostels.

If you intend staying in youth hostels a lot, you can either get a full list of all YHA hostels in Europe, or buy *The Cheap Sleep Guide to Europe* (Fontana Paperbacks) which lists the best ones, along with other accommodation options.

If you need more hostelling information, the London office of the YHA is: 14 Southampton Street, London WC2E 7HY (Tel. 071–836 1036). Go along in person. Written or telephone enquiries should be addressed to their head office: Trevelyan House, 8 St Stephen's Hill, St Albans, Herts AL1 2DY (Tel. 0727 55215).

• **Student hostels:** Student hostels are similar to youth hostels, but instead of a YHA card you need an International Student ID card. Many student hostels are unused student dorms and are only open during university vacations.

• **YMCA Interpoints:** YMCA Interpoint is a summer programme running throughout Europe between July and September. Offering cheap accommodation, Interpoints are run by young people, for young people and help also with the social needs of young travellers. Leaders organize activities (sightseeing, excursions, parties etc) and they are useful, cheap and very friendly places to stay. They are also good in a crisis, helping out when you lose your passport etc. Costs vary but about £5 a night is average. There are Interpoints available in '93 in the following cities: **Czechoslovakia** – Bratislava, Kremnica; **Denmark** – Copenhagen (2), Odense; **England** – Nottingham, St Leonards-on-Sea, Dover; **Finland** – Helsinki, Tampere; **France** – Toulouse; **Ireland** – Dublin (2), Newcastle (2); **Latvia** – Riga; **Netherlands** – Enschede, Utrecht; **Norway** – Bergen, Bodo, Oslo; **Scotland** – Aberdeen; **Sweden** – Gothenburg, Stockholm, Sundsvall; **Switzerland** – Geneva, Zurich; **Poland** – Gdynia.

For further info including directions from the stations, write to National Council of YMCAs in Ireland Ltd, St George's Building, 37–41 High St, Belfast. Most of them are listed in this guide, and all of them are in my book *Cheap Sleep Guide to Europe*.

To use the centres you need to buy a YMCA Interpoint Pass. These are available at any Interpoint and cost about £2. They can also be bought from the YMCA International Co-ordinator.

• **Camping:** If you're keen on the 'great outdoors', then camping in conjunction with a eurorail is ideal for you. There's no shortage of scenic sites, and even the major cities of Europe have campgrounds on their outskirts. But as a general rule we advise against it for big cities. The advantages of camping are obvious: it's cheap, if you're on a campsite you have all necessary facilities to hand, and it adds a dash of 'pioneering spirit' to your holiday. Prices on official campsites range from £2 to £6 ($3.60–10.80) a tent, and £2 to £7 ($3.60–12.60) per person.

The International Camping Carnet is useful only if you're doing a lot of camping at the various European campgrounds which insist on it, such as those in the state forests of France and Denmark. You can buy the Carnet at most sites.

The disadvantages of official camping that spring to mind are: other people, cars, radios, tents all around, queueing for showers, etc. Unofficial camping, however, removes all these problems and can be a memorable experience. Remember to check with the farmer or landowner before pitching tent for the night, and observe strict hygiene.

It's quite feasible to camp throughout your entire eurorail. A tent, gas stove, utensils, sleeping bag and foam mattress will solve all your accommodation problems at once. Don't skimp too much on equipment, however; a good tent is far and away the most important thing.

• **Private accommodation:** This is an interesting and, in many ways, preferable alternative to hotels. Pricewise, it's slightly cheaper than hotels, but more expensive than hostels or camping. Individuals arrange through local tourist authorities for tourists to come and stay at their houses for any period of time from a night to the whole summer. It's an excellent way to meet the locals and get a home-from-home atmosphere. It also provides the perfect opportunity to ask all the questions you want about the country, but otherwise could not. Understanding the locals gives you a much better insight into the country, and, for my money, this is the best form of accommodation. Ask at the tourist office and they will arrange the details for you. The only problem is that you may find all the places full in the high season as in many cities there are more prospective guests than recipient hosts.

• **Accommodation – Eastern Europe:** Since the collapse of the Communist regimes the accommodation problems in Eastern Europe have changed. Many of the former tourist-grade hotels have now gone beyond the budget traveller's price range, as the authorities take advantage of increased demand. This coupled with the lack of infrastructure has not made your accommodation problems any easier.

Your best choice is private accommodation. It is cheaper, gives you a better idea of Eastern European life, and can be arranged at tourist offices, or negotiated in the street. You will often find women meeting trains to offer their flats or rooms. This is common and perfectly acceptable, but use your own judgement if you are worried about the safety aspects of this. Camping is another good option, but as always, check how far out the site is, and check on the public transport situation.

At the official tourist offices expect long queues, especially in summer, as demand is increasing faster than the bureaucracy is improving. However, some of the old rules take a long time to go; for instance, you may still be told that all the youth hostels were booked up months ahead by large parties. In some places, such as Prague, several unofficial tourist offices have sprung up, which should help to relieve demand.

EATING

Whenever possible sample the local cuisine, for quite apart from being an extremely enjoyable way of learning about another culture, it's often a lot cheaper and more appetizing than eating the type of food one's accustomed to at home. If all the restaurants are expensive, don't despair; you'll find that nearly every supermarket has a section devoted to regional specialities where with a little bit of imagination you can prepare yourself a veritable feast. Like everything else, a little background knowledge can add greatly to one's enjoyment.

Here are the basic rules, accumulated over years of good and bad eating out:

1. Avoid expensive, pretentious-looking restaurants and cafés which display no prices.

2. Read the menu first, then add up the cost of your choices and all the taxes and service charges before ordering.

3. Go for 'menus of the day' or tourist menus with fixed prices wherever you can.

4. Serve yourself whenever you can.

5. Don't buy food or drink from vendors on the trains or from stalls in the stations. Buy in advance at supermarkets.

6. If you've an addiction to something like coffee in the morning, take your supplies with you in the form of a camping stove, a small pan and some instant coffee.

7. When it comes to cheeses, wines, meats, biscuits, etc., buy the local stuff. Imports are always more expensive and, anyway, it's good to sample the local produce.

8. Use fast-food chains if nothing else is available for cheap, reliable snacks. They're often far better and cheaper than local snack bars, especially in southern Europe where hygiene is often suspect.

9. Be adventurous, try something new. Ask for house wine: it's always cheaper than listed wine and there's a good chance it's the popular wine of the region.

10. Eat breakfast out when it's optional at your hotel as it's nearly always cheaper at a local café.

11. Make lunch your main meal of the day. Prepare yourself a big picnic whenever possible. Even when you eat at restaurants, it's at least 15 per cent cheaper than in the evening. Avoid tourist areas, where prices are nearly always higher. In large towns search out the university areas, where prices are generally more reasonable.

12. Look out in the stations for drinking water taps and fill your bottles for free when you get the chance.

13. Vegetarian travellers, and others with special dietary requirements, might need some advance organization. There are various specialist publications available. Try contacting the Vegetarian Society, Parkdale, Dunham Road, Cheshire WA14 4QG.

CITY TRANSPORT SYSTEMS

If you're going to stay in one place for more than a day or two, find out about the cheap travel passes on offer. Some cities offer day passes, others weekly ones and, if your accommodation is out of town, they can save you quite a bit. Before rushing off to buy one, however, check on a map for the location of the main sights you're interested in, as in many towns these are all within easy walking distance of one another and you won't need a bus pass. If you're not in a rush, using the buses as opposed to the underground lets you see a bit more of the city – which is worth bearing in mind. Tickets for the buses and underground can often be bought at tobacco kiosks, or from machines in central locations. Also beware of large on-the-spot fines for non-ticket holders. Thomas Cook's *Railpass Guide* is particularly good on local transport.

TELEPHONE AND TELEGRAM

You will usually find both these facilities at the general post office. Some countries also offer special telephone kiosks for international calls. Find out the international dialling code before you start: Britain, 44. USA and Canada, 1. Australia, 61. New Zealand, 64. Note that you will usually have to drop the leading zero from area codes.

Always try to dial direct as it's much cheaper. Direct dialling codes to and from the UK and US can be found in the basic information for each country. Never telephone via the switchboard at hotels or hostels as they invariably add on a whack – sometimes as much as the call itself – for themselves. Throughout Europe it's pretty standard that calls out of business hours (7 p.m.–8 a.m.) are charged at a cheaper rate. In nearly every country, dialling instructions in either English or pictograms are to be found inside telephone boxes.

Telegrams are expensive, and in almost every case you'll find it cheaper making a quick phone call; but if that's impossible, write out your message and hand it to the clerk to avoid spelling mistakes.

MAIL

Airmail letters from major West European cities to the USA and Britain arrive within a week or so. Letters from southern or Eastern Europe tend to take longer, so if you're on a eurorail lasting a month, it's hardly worthwhile writing. Postcards tend to be even worse. Use surface mail (by ship) for posting home any books or clothes you don't fancy carrying around. It's usually very cheap – but very slow too.

Trying to collect mail in Europe is more often than not a nerve-racking business. If you've no fixed address, the best method to use (and it's free or costs very little) is poste restante. This means your mail is sent to you c/o the main post office of any city or town. Depending on the vagaries of the country's domestic postal system, your mail should be at the poste restante office filed under your surname. Produce your passport or equivalent proof of identity and pick it up. If the clerk says there's nothing for you, get him to check under your first name too.

In Eastern Europe, get the sender to put a '1' after the city's name to ensure it goes to the main post office. American Express card holders or traveller's cheque holders can get mail sent on to AMEX offices to await collection.

SHOPPING

Unlike many other guidebooks, I don't include details on shopping. I take it for granted that most people won't have spare cash to blow in the shops, and if you do, you'll have enough common sense to head for the centre and find the main shopping areas for yourselves. In general, the studenty part of a city is cheaper, and for food the large supermarkets are your best bet.

Shopping hours vary from country to country but they're all based round the 8–6 routine, though lunch hours can range from none at all to three hours. As a basic rule, the further south you go, the longer the 'siesta', and you can only count on a half day on Saturday.

WOMEN TRAVELLERS

Each year I receive letters from women travellers who have encountered problems when travelling alone. It's a sickening fact of life that women are victims of harassment, verbal at best, physical all too often, so it makes sense to take certain precautions to help avoid problems.

The further south and east you get in Europe, the less emancipated women are, and the more men will look on you as a sophisticated Westerner, and easy game. The single most important thing to do is to *dress appropriately*. In Muslim countries especially, any large area of naked flesh (including arms, lower legs and shoulders) is read as the equivalent of a green light. Even a T-shirt and jeans can be construed as seductive clothing there. A cover-up shawl in light cotton is a good investment. Never mind that the other

European women don't seem to bother with this. If you are travelling alone, or could be in a situation where you are with just one or two other women and a lot of men, heed this advice.

No mini-skirts, wear a bra under T-shirts, and no shorts. Wear sloppy loose cotton trousers/skirts and a loose top. Clothes that don't show your shape are more comfortable for travelling anyway. Save showing off your curves (if you must) for the West, where it will be quietly appreciated, not read as an open invitation.

On trains, especially on the type with no corridor and with entrance from outside compartment doors, *do not necessarily choose an empty compartment*. Choose one with other women in it. It might be less private, but empty compartments can soon fill up with men, and then you've no control over the situation. It's good to meet other women travellers anyway.

Couchettes that are not allocated on a single sex or family basis are another potential headache. Always have a word with your attendant to ensure you're in with a family or other women. Simply *do not accept a couchette with a male majority* – it's unreasonable to expect you to. You'd be better spending the night sitting up in a public compartment.

Do not sleep in parks or stations, ever. Women on their own are at great risk if they do this. Who's going to know if anything happens to you? Throw yourself on the mercy of the station master, police, embassy, local church, but *don't sleep rough*. Plan ahead and get into town in time to find a room.

I have travelled in every continent as a woman on my own now, and I do understand the problems. These rules are the tip of the iceberg. I discuss more about the impact of clothing and how to act sensitively and sensibly when travelling in my latest book *The Good Tourist – a worldwide guide for the green traveller*, published by Mandarin Paperbacks. Before heading off to Europe, it could be well worth a read. See p. 16 for information.

LONE TRAVELLERS

Travelling alone in Europe is an adventure which some people would prefer to forgo, but it has its compensations, which make it worth considering. During a month travelling you could make many new friends, of many nationalities, quite easily. Staying in youth hostels is an excellent way of meeting people; it is easy to strike up a conversation whilst stringing up a makeshift washing line between bunks! During the summer it is easy to spot other lone travellers on the popular routes, who may wish to have a chat. Another great advantage of going alone is that you have more freedom to go where you want, when you want, with no arguing over the next destination.

The main problem of travelling alone is that you have to be even more careful with your belongings, as you have no one to fall back on. The same rules apply as to groups, but with more emphasis. A good policy is to leave an idea of your route with relatives or friends, even if it is only a rough idea.

DISABLED TRAVELLERS

The facilities available for disabled travellers vary widely across Europe, as you would expect. In general the best facilities are available in the north of Europe, with Italy being reportedly also fairly good. However, even the countries with well advertised facilities are not always up to scratch, relying as they do on the staff to be available to help.

In the UK wheelchairs can be accommodated on many trains, but to guarantee this it is advisable to contact the station first, to ensure that ramps and a place are available. In France a similar situation exists on TGV services. For other trains SNCF publish a booklet with the disabled traveller in mind. Elsewhere you may end up having to fold your wheelchair away. There are several important things to consider when travelling by train, the first being the platform access. In many places the access to platforms requires steps up to a bridge, or down to an underpass. Lifts are often hidden away from sight, and can only be operated by a member of staff, with the appropriate key. Another problem, especially at smaller continental stations, is the height of the train compared with the platform. Planning in advance, to ensure staff are available to help, is the only solution here.

Be familiar with your condition. Medical terms are precise and internationally understood whereas colloquialisms are not always meaningful to foreign medical personnel. The generic name of a medicine can be obtained from a GP or pharmacist: a particular brand name may not be available but the generic formulae will be.

Check the accessibility of sites with tourist information centres. It may be more expensive to join a tour but the guide may provide a helping hand or know of a more accessible route. Roads may be unpaved and unlit, pavements, if any, uneven and kerbstones steep: the wheelchair/pram pusher is rarely catered for away from main centres and should be physically able to cope with the terrain.

Certain foods may be unavailable in some countries. The Maltese use little fresh milk and foods for young babies are harder to find where prolonged breastfeeding is the norm e.g. southern Spain.

Attitudes to disability vary. The disabled may, on one hand, be treated as a normal part of society (which, of course, they are) or they may be closely questioned about their condition. This may seem impertinent but is often only genuine interest in the disabled person's welfare, and, in time, may lead to a greater understanding of the disabled traveller's needs.

Bathroom facilities may be unsuitable for the disabled in southern Europe: toilets are often of the Eastern 'squat' type in Turkey and parts of Greece – ask around – people are very understanding and will always direct one to Western style facilities. Hot water may be restricted to certain times of the day and, in times of drought, may be rationed and turned off for intervals.

Be flexible: alternatives may turn out better than the original plan. Try to meet obstructive people with charm and, above all, remember: Where there's a will there's a way!

Good sources of information on accessibility and services are provided by the British, French and Italian national tourist offices, but ask at the others as well – you may be lucky. Any of the disabled pressure groups will also be willing to help, with several of them producing guidebooks. Listen to Radio 4's programmes, such as 'Does He Take Sugar', which feature 'field tests' of accessibility.

TOURIST INFORMATION

At most stations you'll find a *Tourist Information Office*. When this isn't the case I give directions below on how to get there. These tourist offices are easily your best source of maps and detailed information. There seemed little point in reproducing their maps and rewriting the minuscule details of the sights for you here. My main aim in this book has been to direct you to the main things of interest, give you the basics, and let you fill in the rest from what you're given at tourist offices. Finally, so far as opening times are concerned, I've generally only listed irregular ones; take the rest as following the local norm.

Good eurorailing!

FREE BOOKS FOR MOST HELPFUL LETTERS

Please feel free to write in your comments and suggestions to me. If you've come across anywhere you think deserves more detailed treatment or come across a real 'find' you want to share with future eurorailers, give me as much detail as possible, like the full address, telephone number and how to get to it. Obviously in a book containing the amount of information that this does, facts and figures get out of date easily, and though I try to update as thoroughly as possible I would appreciate your help. While I enjoy reading about your experiences, please keep your letters brief and concise (2 × A4 sides *maximum*, preferably typed) and all letters *must* include relevant page references from this book. The writers of the six best letters of 1993 will receive a free copy of the updated 1994 guide. All correspondence should be addressed to: Katie Wood, *Europe by Train*, HarperCollins, 77–85 Fulham Palace Road, Hammersmith, London W6 8JB.

SOME INTERNATIONAL TIMETABLE SYMBOLS

R	Reservations compulsory	}	Trains running on certain days only
1,2	1st/2nd class		
	Couchette	◆	Trains subject to special regulations stated in the information notes of the relevant timetable
	Sleeping Car		
	Restaurant Car		
⊗	Buffet/Cafeteria		
	Drinks service and snacks		Frontier border station; customs and passport checks
ⅹ	Except Sundays and public holidays		Connection by bus
†	Sundays and public holidays only		Connection by boat
①,②	Mondays, Tuesdays, etc.		

Part Two: THE COUNTRIES

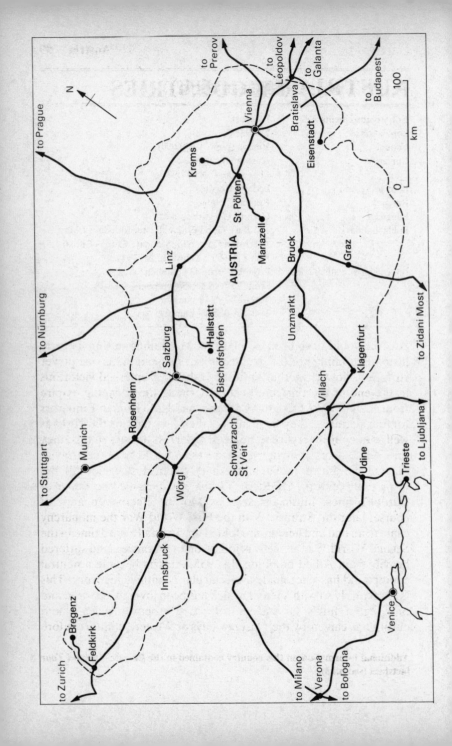

AUSTRIA (Österreich)

Entry requirements	Passport
Population	7,600,000
Capital	Vienna (pop.: 1,300,000)
Currency	Austrian Schilling
	£1 = approx. AS 17.90
Political system	Federal Republic
Religion	Roman Catholic
Language	German (English spoken)
Public holidays	1, 6 Jan.; Good Friday; Easter Monday; 1 May; Ascension Day; Whit Monday; Corpus Christi; 15 Aug.; 26 Oct.; 1 Nov.; 8, 25, 26 Dec.
International dialling codes	From UK 010+43+number
	From USA 011+43+number
	To UK 00+44+number
	To USA 00+1+number

Austria would have been no place for eurorailing during its early history, certainly not for sleeping out at the station, as one power struggle followed another until the Habsburgs emerged victorious at the end of the thirteenth century, ruling the changing empire from 1278 to 1918. As good Catholics and Holy Roman Emperors for four centuries, they spent most of their time fighting the Turks as well as keeping everyone at home in order. As a result of this, they provided a strong monarchy, but it was no fun to be in the army as Austria continued to be involved in political struggles till the eighteenth century. By then, Vienna had become the home of Europe's finest musicians such as Mozart, Beethoven and, of course, later on, Strauss. With the First World War the monarchy came to an end and her empire folded up. She had a hard time in the Second World War as she was joined on to Germany, and suffered heavily from Allied bombing. In 1955, Austria became a neutral country and has since made a spectacular economic recovery. This is particularly so with Vienna, which has been lovingly restored and once again fulfils its ancient role as a stopover place where eurorailers can enjoy their last few days of Western comfort before

Additional information on this country contained in the *Europe – Grand Tour* factsheet (see p.13).

heading into Eastern Europe. The Alpine scenery and distinctive villages in many provinces, including the well-known Tyrolean ones, make Austria one of Europe's most attractive countries and a perfect destination for those seeking the great outdoors.

AUSTRIAN FEDERAL RAILWAYS
(Österreichische Bundesbahnen, ÖBB)

As you might expect, trains run on time. They are clean and comfortable, as are the stations. However, there's generally a lot of queueing in summer, so be warned. Most intercities run two hours apart.

Train types are: long distance expresses (Expresszüge), expresses (Schnellzüge), semi-fast services (Eilzüge or Regionalzüge), and EuroCity trains. Apart from on some EuroCity trains, you can get by without supplements. Avoid local trains unless you have plenty of time as they tend to be slow, especially if you're on a mountainous route.

• **Inter-Rail bonuses:** See Appendix II for reductions.

• **Eurail bonuses:** The following services are free:
—Puchberg am Schneeberg–Hochschneeberg rack railway.
—St Wolfgang–Schafbergspitze rack railway.
—Steamers on Lake Wolfgang.
—Steamers operated by the Erste Donau–Dampfschiffahrts–Gesellschaft between Passau and Vienna.

Reduced fares:
—50 per cent reduction on steamers operated by steamship companies on Lake Constance.

TRAIN INFORMATION

Austrian Federal Railways main information for the whole country is at no. 9 Elisabethstrasse in Vienna.

Information officers are nearly all multilingual while most other rail staff speak at least a little English. You can easily tell the information officers: they wear yellow cap bands. Luggage lockers use ten-schilling pieces. Children under six travel free on ÖBB.

• **Reservations:** Are not necessary. If you want to make one, it can be done until two hours before your train leaves (cost: AS 40).

● **Night travel:** Austria's too small for an extensive service. Sleepers and couchettes are clean and comfortable. Reserve at least five hours beforehand. Couchettes cost from AS170–AS240. There are also compartments with pull-down seats which cost nothing.

● **Eating on trains:** For those with money, there are dining cars on all intercity trains. Mini-bars are to be found on all trains except locals. As always, we advise picnics, but if you don't have time to go to a supermarket before the train leaves, there are kiosks at most stations. Vienna's stations, in particular, have well-stocked deli-catessens which are open long hours, including Sundays.

● **Scenic tips:** The main Innsbruck–Zell am See–Salzburg line is one of the most scenic in the country. If you're going from Innsbruck to Italy, take the train to Brennero for beautiful mountainous scenery. If you're heading towards Yugoslavia, try Vienna–Trieste – this goes via Klagenfurt and Udine. If you're travelling from Innsbruck to Munich or vice versa, try the route via Garmisch – again the mountain scenery is beautiful. Bregenz, situated on the Bodensee in the west of Austria, is a good point of departure to sail across to Germany. From here you can go to Konstanz over the border (ask about reductions for train pass holders). Also at Bregenz you can take the Pfanderbahn up to the top for a wonderful view of the Alps and over the Bodensee. Go to the Vorarlberg Tourist Office in Bregenz on Jahnstrasse for information on Alpine villages and excursions. You can sail the Danube from the German–Austrian border (Passau) to Vienna or from Vienna to Passau. The trip lasts a day and a half, stopping overnight at Linz. Alternatively, there's the Linz–Vienna trip or vice versa. The prettiest part of the trip is from Krems to Melk. The train runs from both Melk and Krems. Further information from DDSG, Reisedienst 2, Handelskai 265. In Passau, go to DDSG-Schiffsstation, Im Ort 14A, Dreiflusseck. Get off the boat and take a look around as often as possible, as many of the stopping-off places are well-preserved medieval or baroque towns. If you're leaving Vienna for Salzburg, stop off at the village of Mariazell. It's beautiful. Surrounded by mountains, it was a religious pilgrimage site. Take the cable-car for the view. From Vienna take the train to St Pölten from the Westbahnhof, then change there to a train for Mariazell.

• **Bikes:** You can rent out a bike in nearly every important station in Austria – 'Fahrrad Am Bahnhof'. Take a quick look at the traffic situation before committing yourself. Prices are normally around AS 90, but your train ticket should get you half price.

• **Rover Tickets:** The Austrian Rail Pass (Bundesnetzkarte) is available to anyone. It gives unlimited first- or second-class travel for one month on ÖBB, the Schneeberg and Schafbergspitze rack railways and ÖBB ships. Also it gives 50 per cent reductions on Bodensee and DDSG ships, and a number of private railways. Cost AS 4650 first class, AS 3100 second class. There is also a one-year ticket. It is valid only on ÖBB, but does give reductions on some shipping services.

Also available are Regional Season Tickets (Regionalnetzkarte), giving unlimited travel for four days in ten, within any one of eighteen regions. The ticket also gives 50 per cent reductions on a number of private railways. Cost AS 400 second class, 50 per cent reduction for children. Another option is the national 'Rabbit' card, which allows travel on four out of ten days, for AS 660 (under 26), or AS 950 (over 26).

TOURIST INFORMATION

There's a local tourist office (Verkehrsverein) in every large town which will give you the addresses of the provincial tourist boards if required.

• **ISIC bonuses:** 50 per cent reductions on most art galleries and museums. For further information, contact Ökista at Türkenstrasse 4–6, Wien (Tel. 3475260).

• **Money matters:** 1 Austrian Schilling (AS) = 100 groschen (gr). Banking hours are Mon.–Wed., Fri.: 8 a.m.–12.30 p.m., 1.30 p.m.–3 p.m., Thurs.: 8 a.m.–12.30 p.m., 1.30 p.m.–5.30 p.m. The main banks in Vienna stay open over lunch. It's best to cash your traveller's cheques in large denominations as commission charges are high. You can cash Eurocheques without paying commission if you are staying at the Ruthensteiner hostel near the Westbahnhof.

• **Post offices:** Open Mon.–Fri.: 8 a.m.–12 noon, 2 p.m.–6 p.m., Sat.: 8 a.m.–10 a.m. Stamps can also be bought from Tabak-Trafik shops.

• **Shops:** Generally keep to the same hours as the post offices, closing on Saturday afternoons. Food shops usually open before 8 a.m., but close for lunch from 12.30–3 p.m.

• **Museums:** Tend to close on Mondays.

SLEEPING

• **Hostels:** To stay at any Austrian youth hostel, you need an International Youth Hostel Association membership card, though guest cards are always available. In general, they're open from about 6 a.m. till 10 p.m. and charge about AS 90–170 for bed and breakfast, from AS 60 for just bed, and about AS 60–120 for a meal, adding on an extra charge where cooking facilities are available. At many hostels breakfast is compulsory; check first. Provided space is available, you can stay more than three nights at most hostels unless you're travelling in a large group. If you are, write in advance to the warden and book your space.

• **Hotels:** Hotels are nearly always clean but wildly expensive, particularly in Vienna and Salzburg. If you travel off-season, prices are 20–40 per cent cheaper; also in May, June and September they can be 15–25 per cent cheaper than in July and August. You can expect to pay at least AS 350 for a double, from AS 500 in Vienna and other cities. Bear this in mind if you're approached by an Austrian hotelier trying to fill his hotel – he may be offering you a bargain. Don't be put off by this approach as it's a buyer's market; ask the price and location and what's included. You're under no obligation.

• **Private houses** (Privat Zimmer/Zimmer Frei): Rooms are around AS 160 per person and make an interesting alternative.

• **Camping:** The International Camping Carnet is not obligatory, but it'll get you preferential treatment on most sites. Generally, the sites are very good: clean, efficient and well laid out. Austrians are keen campers themselves, so in peak season you might find it advisable to get to the site and pitch as early in the day as you can. Charges are from AS 25 per person and AS 25 per tent, with Vienna at around AS 55 per person and per tent.

EATING AND NIGHTLIFE

Austrian food is wholesome stuff and great if you've a soft spot for pastries. In general, the pork (schwein) and fish dishes are better value than lamb and beef. Tafelspitz (boiled beef) is good and cheap, and this with a noodle or dumpling soup is a filling, inexpensive meal. The coffee-and-cakes scene is good news all round, except for the price. Strudel is excellent, as is Sachertorte. Having said all this, you may well end up eating from fast-food chains most of the time, owing to high restaurant prices. If so, try and eat the local dishes at least once, you won't regret it.

The nightlife is centred round coffee houses and the opera, rather than heavy-metal gigs and bars. You have to remember that discos and bars cost money in Austria and anyway they tend to be a bit smooth. The best advice is to head towards a wine tavern or beer cellar in the studenty areas where possible, as prices tend to be more realistic there. The east of the country is best for wine. However, if you're into opera, Vienna's the place. The season runs from September to June, but prices are very high.

Vienna (Wien)

Gateway between the East and West for over two thousand years, Vienna's middle-European flavour makes it unique among all capital cities. Its position as ruler of half of Europe for over six centuries has left behind a legacy of impressive buildings and an atmosphere of solid institutionalism. This is probably helped by the fact that a third of Vienna's 1.5 million population are pensioners.

The city is divided into twenty-three districts, with the 'Ring' in the city centre as No. 1. Vienna's not actually on the Danube – the river only runs through its suburbs – but the Danube Canal is part of the city.

If you want to sail on the Danube and are heading for Hungary it is a fraction of the price in Budapest.

Use this book, and do your sums carefully in Vienna to avoid its high costs during your stay. It's a great place, but at a price.

STATION FACILITIES

Vienna has two large main stations: the Westbahnhof and the Südbahnhof, with trains leaving daily from Westbahnhof at Europaplatz to France, Switzerland and Germany. Trains for Eastern European countries, southern Austria, Yugoslavia and Italy leave from Südbahnhof. Trains to Budapest leave from either Westbahnhof or Südbahnhof. Trains for Berlin and Prague leave from Franz Josef Bahnhof. For further info, telephone (1) 1717.

	SÜDBAHNHOF (South Station)	WESTBAHNHOF (West Station)	FRANZ JOSEF BAHNHOF
Train information	6.30 a.m.–9.20 p.m.	7 a.m.–8.30 p.m.	7 a.m.–8 p.m.
Reservations	7 a.m.–8.45 p.m.	7 a.m.–8.30 p.m.	7 a.m.–8 p.m.
Tourist information	6.30 a.m.–10 p.m.	6.15 a.m.–11 p.m.	none
Foreign exchange	6.30 a.m.–10 p.m.	7 a.m.–10 p.m.	none
Bar, Buffet	6 a.m.–10 p.m.	6 a.m.–10.30 p.m.	6 a.m.–10 p.m.
Snack bar	6 a.m.–7 p.m.	6.30 a.m.–11 p.m.	as above
Bath, Shower	4 a.m.–11.45 p.m.	Mon.–Sat.: 7 a.m.–10 p.m. Sun.: 8 a.m.–noon	none
Left-luggage lockers	Shut 12 midnight (AS10)	Shut 12.30 a.m.–4 a.m.	Shut 12 midnight–5 a.m.
Left-luggage store	4.30 a.m.–11.45 p.m.	4.30 a.m.–12 midnight	none
Shops	6 a.m.–10 p.m.	6 a.m.–11 p.m.	7 a.m.–10 p.m.
Waiting room	12 midnight–4 a.m.	1.15 a.m.–4 a.m.	As station
Station shuts	12 midnight–4 a.m.	1.15 a.m.–4 a.m.	12 midnight–5 a.m.

There are post office facilities at both main stations. Tram 18 connects the South and West stations. To get to the city centre from Südbahnhof take S-Bahn 1, 2 or 3 to Südtiroler Platz (1 stop), then U-Bahn 1. From Westbahnhof take Tram 58 or 52, or U-Bahn 3 (due for completion shortly). From Franz Josef, turn left down Althastrasse to Alserbachstrasse, turn left again, and walk to Friedensbrücke, on U-Bahn 4.

TOURIST INFORMATION

The main office is at Kärntnerstrasse 38, behind the Opera (Tel. 5138892). Open 9 a.m.–7 p.m. The travel agencies at Westbahnhof and Südbahnhof can also help out and provide an accommodation-finding service costing AS35. Pick up the city map, transport map and the students' magazine 'Jugend/Youth scene'. Tourist information for all of Austria is available at Margaretenstrasse 1 (Tel. 58 72 000). Open Mon.–Fri. 9 a.m.–5.30 p.m.

• **Addresses:**

POST OFFICE: Fleischmarkt 19. Poste restante. Open 24 hours.

AMEX: Kärtnerstrasse 21–23, Mon.–Fri.: 9 a.m.–5.30 p.m., Sat.: 9 a.m.–noon (Tel. 515400).

UK EMBASSY: Reisnerstrasse 40 (Tel. 7131575).

US EMBASSY: Gartenbaupromenade 2 (Tel. 315511).

CANADIAN EMBASSY: Karl-Lueger-Ring 10 (Tel. 5333691).

AUSTRALIAN EMBASSY: Mattiellistrasse 2–4 (Tel. 5128580).

POLICE EMERGENCY: Tel. 133.

MEDICAL EMERGENCY: Tel. 144/141.

ÖKISTA (Student Travel): Türkenstrasse 4–6, Mon.–Fri.: 9.30 a.m.–5 p.m. (Tel. 3475260). They help out with any accommodation problems you may have.

CITY PHONE CODE: 01.

• **Getting about:** Information on city transport is available at Karlsplatz U-Bahn Station. There are various passes on offer, but remember you can see most of Vienna on foot. Tickets for buses, trams, U-Bahn and S-Bahn (free on Inter-Rail) cost AS 20 each, AS 60 for blocks of four, and AS 75 for blocks of five if bought in advance at Tabak-Trafik. You can also buy three-day unlimited passes (Netzkarte 72 Stunden Wien) at Tabak-Trafik and the Karlplatz information office for AS 115. A one-week ticket for AS 125 (valid Mon.–Sun.) is also available from Tabak-Trafik (at stations and main subway stops). There is a 24 hr pass for AS 45 and an eight-day 'environment' pass which can be used by more than one person, if the ticket is punched for each person, for AS 235. Pick up a map of the city and transport system at the tourist office. Tickets can also be purchased from automatic machines in stations and on some trams, so have AS 5 and AS 10 coins to hand. Night buses, costing AS 25, radiate from Schwedenplatz. Forget the city tours, taxis, and 'Fiakers' (two-horse coaches at AS 400 a go) as they'll cripple your budget.

SEEING

Pick up leaflets from tourist information offices. These will give you all the history, details, opening times, etc.

At the heart of Vienna is St Stephan's Cathedral and its square, Stephansplatz, at the intersection of Graben and Kärntnerstrasse – it's a good place to sit and watch Viennese life go by. Rather than suggest a walking tour with everyone tramping round exactly the same treadmill like guinea pigs, we list the major sights and you can devise your own route by using the map.

ST STEPHAN'S CATHEDRAL: Built in the thirteenth and fourteenth centuries, it's the most important Gothic building in Vienna. Climb the 340 steps of the south steeple (or take the lift up the north steeple, AS 50) for a good view of Vienna, or descend to the catacombs and look at the Habsburgs' innards in the 'Old Prince's Vault' (AS 30).

THE HOFBURG: The old imperial winter palace sprawling all over the heart of the city and encompassing every architectural style from the thirteenth to the twentieth century; it includes the Spanish Riding School and the Hofburgkapelle where the Vienna Boys' Choir performs – though, crazily, both close down for periods in summer. Entry to the Hofburg is AS25 (reductions for ISIC holders).

SCHÖNBRUNN PALACE: This was the Habsburgs' summer palace. Situated at Schönbrunner Schloss-Strasse in the outskirts, south-west from Westbahnhof, U-bahn 4. There are a limited number of English tours for AS 50 (AS 25 ISIC) which are worth it. Also see the Gloriette, the gardens, and the butterfly collection.

THE BELVEDERE: Includes the Austrian gallery of modern art and a museum of medieval art.

THE KUNSTHISTORISCHES MUSEUM, Maria-Theresien Platz: One of the great art collections and the fourth largest gallery in the world. All the treasures the Habsburgs could get their imperial hands on are here. The Breughel room contains over half the artist's remaining pictures.

There's also the new KUNSTHAUSWIEN at Untere Weissgerber-strasse 13, open 9 a.m.–7 p.m. daily, which houses international art and interesting contemporary exhibitions.

The above are the main sights but, if you've any time left, take in the FREUD MUSEUM. Followers of the master can visit his house at Berggasse 19 (AS 30), small but well documented.

Of interest to musicians will be: HAYDN MUSEUM at Haydngasse 19; MOZART ERINNERUNGSRAUM, Domgasse 5; SCHUBERT MUSEUM, Nussdorferstrasse 54; and SCHUBERT STERBEZIMMER, Ketten-brückengasse 6; JOHANN STRAUSS MUSEUM, Praterstrasse 54. At all these addresses, the composers' original houses are still standing.

If museums are one of your passions, consider buying a general museum ticket (AS 150) which gives 14 coupons, each valid for one AS 15 museum entry. The charges for entrance seem to be constantly changing, but municipal museums should be free for all on Friday mornings, and national museums offer reductions for all students. But don't be surprised if the rules change – especially outside the high season. Pick up the leaflet 'Museums Wien' from the tourist office. Alternatively, as a break take a walk and a picnic in the Vienna woods which border the city on its southern and western sides. Take tram 38 to its terminus at Grinzing, then bus 38A to Kahlenberg.

SLEEPING

Write in advance if at all possible as cheap beds are few and far between in the summer. This is mainly due to the fact that they don't open their student hostels till July (making late June a particularly bad time); hotels are ridiculously expensive and the cheap pensions get full quickly. Use Katie Wood's *Cheap Sleep Guide* (see p. 15) or the ISTC accommodation booklet as these list all the best places.

There are two main accommodation-finding services in Vienna: the travel agencies at the stations, and the student organization Ökista. If you want to save the commission charge, try phoning yourself. Most hoteliers speak English, or you can try out your phrase-book German.

• **Student hostels:** Try the Internationales Studenthaus at Seiler-stätte 30 (Tel. 5128463). The location is very central, and they give 10 per cent reduction to ISIC holders, for stays of over one night. If they are full try Asylverein der Wiener Universität at Porzell-angasse 30 (Tel. 347282), tram D from Sudbahnhof or Franz Josefs Bahnhof (it is possible to walk from the latter), with doubles at around AS 140 per person (higher charge for one-night stays). Also try Pfeilheim on Pfeilgasse 6 (Tel. 4384762), a 15-minute walk from Westbahnhof: turn left outside station, and continue along main road, until you reach Pfeilgasse. Alternatively, take bus 13a from Südbahnhof, until it crosses Lerchenfelder Strasse. Costs AS 330 for double, including breakfast.

• **Youth hostels:** Ruthensteiner, Robert Hamerlinggasse 24 (Tel. 834693 and 8308265). 77 beds with all facilities, near Westbahnhof: turn right, cross Mariahilfer Strasse, next road parallel. Costs from

AS 114 for dormitory, to AS 169 for a single room. Free showers, but no lockers. They will store extra luggage free of charge (at your risk) if space permits. No curfew. Breakfast available at AS 22.

Myrthengasse, Myrthengasse 7 (Tel. 936316, 9394290). 221 beds and all facilities. All rooms have showers, near Centrum. Must be IYHF member and essential to book ahead. Walkable from Westbahnhof, or U-bahn 6 to Burgasse, then bus 48A to Neubaugasse, hostel nearby.

Brigittenau, Friedrich-Engels Platz 24 (Tel. 3382940). 334 beds, all facilities, curfew at 12.30 a.m. Near the Danube. Must be IYHF member. Tram N from Schwedenplatz (U-bahn 1 or 4) to Friedrich-Engels Platz.

Hütteldorf, Schlossberggasse 8 (Tel. 8771501). 277 beds and all facilities. Must be IYHF member. Take S-Bahn 50 or U-Bahn 4 from Westbahnhof to Hütteldorf, then a signposted ten-minute walk. AS 130 B&B, AS 70 for evening meal.

The YMCA, Kenyongasse 15 (Tel. 936304), mid-July to mid-August. Cost is around AS 110 (breakfast is compulsory). Other meals cost around AS 75. A rude lot, but at least the beds are cheap.

A novel hostel is in the bell tower of a church at Turmherberge Don Bosco, Lechnerstrasse 12 (Tel. 7131494). Take Tram 18 from Westbahnhof or Sudbahnhof to the end or U-Bahn 3. Men only. Costs AS 60. Don't confuse with hotel Don Bosco. No catering, and don't expect a long lie – the alarm bell is very loud and very close!

• **Hotels:** At the more expensive end, Graben, Dorotheergasse 3 (Tel. 5121531), near St Stephan's Cathedral, 46 rooms. Kärntnerhof, Grashofgasse 4 (Tel. 5121923). Doubles from AS 630, including breakfast.

• **Pensions:** Pension Columbia, Kochgasse 9 (Tel. 426757), quiet with doubles from AS 580 to AS 660, including breakfast. Tram 5 from outside Westbahnhof.

• **Private rooms:** Private rooms are available, owned by Hedwig Gally, near the Westbahnhof at Arnsteingasse 25/10 (Tel. 81 29073/83 04244). Prices start at AS 400 for a double, AS 500 for a double with shower. Try the rooms owned by Irmgard Launig at Kaiserstrasse 77/8, close to the Westbahnhof (Tel. 934152). Costs AS 200 including showers and cooking facilities.

Irene Hamminger, Turkenschanzstrasse 34 (Tel. 3450305) offers rooms in a Viennese villa for AS 400–500 for two people – 15 minutes from the city centre.

Frank Heberling runs an establishment at Siccardsburggasse 42 (Tel. 604 0229), phone first. Very friendly, walkable from Sudbahnhof.

• **Camping:** All grounds are located well out of the city with an average price of AS 52 per person and AS 50 per tent.

Wien West II, Hüttelbergstrasse 80 (Tel. 942314). Get off train at Hütteldorf, then bus 52B. Open throughout the year. Wien West I, just up the same street (Tel. 941449). Open mid-June–mid-Sept. But I've had terrible reports of declining standards in Wien West I and II, and despite promised improvement I would not advise them. Try Camping Süd (Tel. 869218), open June–early Sept., close to the Atzgersdorf-Mauer S-Bahn station. Quite near this site is the Rodaun-Schwimmbad site at An der Au 2 (Tel. 884154). Take tram 58 from Westbahnhof to Hietzing, then tram 60 to the end. Hot showers are AS 5, and there is a free swimming pool. Open end March–mid-Nov. If you are really desperate, sleep out at the Prater Park, but it is not to be recommended.

EATING AND NIGHTLIFE

There's no shortage of places to eat in Vienna – the only problem's the prices. As usual, though, if you know where to look you will be all right. The Hungarian and Turkish restaurants are usually good value.

The Schnell Imbiss counters (quick snacks) dotted all over the city serve cheap filling snacks (AS 40–80), and of course there's always McDonald's, one of them very convenient for the Westbahnhof on Mariahilferstrasse heading towards the city, on the left-hand side.

Cafés are a Viennese institution, serving up their delicious pastries and cakes, but they're expensive, so make your café visit on a wet afternoon when you can hang around reading the papers, playing cards and generally getting your money's worth.

For picnics, use the self-service supermarkets. There's no shortage of good breads, sausages, cheeses, fruits and wines, so picnicking is easy. Vienna's largest market, the NASCHMARKT, lying from the fourth to the sixth districts, has a few food bargains and plenty more besides. Get to it by the underground to Ketten-brückengasse.

• **Suggestions:** There is nowhere really cheap in the centre of Vienna to eat, but scrutinize any 'menu of the day' you see. Places worth trying include the Naschmarkt Restaurant chain, with one on Schwarzenberg Platz. The best place to head for is the seventh district around the Neustiftgasse where you will find the Phonixhof and Puppenstube restaurants. You can expect a good meal and wine for around AS 140 and if these are full there are other places in the vicinity. The student restaurant Mensa is at Universitätsstrasse 7. It's open for lunch and dinner, Mon.–Fri., and there's no problem getting in as long as you look like a student. Prices from AS 30 to AS 45 for a basic meal, good value for money.

Vegetarians should try Gasthaus Wrenkh, Hollergasse 9 (15th district) or at Bauernmarkt 10 (1st district).

The Viennese are happier at the opera or the theatre than engaged in active nightlife. Young people tend to congregate in the Kaffeekonditorei rather than in pubs or discos, but Vienna still has a few surprises up its sleeve. A good night out can be had at the Prater – Vienna's large amusement park on the outskirts of the city. Entrance is free and the rides average AS 15–25, although the big wheel, built in 1895 by British engineer Walter Bassett, costs AS 28. Open from Easter to October. Take tram 79A or 81, it's reasonably obvious where to get off, or U-bahn 1.

Bars and nightclubs can be sleazy and expensive, so watch out. Try U4 Disco, Schönbrunnerstrasse 222; it's very popular with the young Viennese and it's easy to get to, or look at the latest *Youth Scene*. In general, though, you're better off heading for a wine tavern or beer cellar. These represent best value by far. Try: Esterhazykeller, Haarhof, good studenty crowd with the best prices in town; or Zwölf-Apostelkeller, Sonnenfelsgasse 3, near St Stephan's, so low down from street level, the walls are covered with straw to diminish the dampness. Go down to the lowest level – it's liveliest. Open Sundays, but closed all July. There's a good atmosphere here. And for the connoisseur, Melkerkeller, Schottengasse 3, run by Benedictine monks, has excellent wine.

For enthusiasts, Europe's largest bowling alley is in Vienna. It's the Bowling-Brunswick at Hauptallee 124 and costs around AS 25 a line. Plenty of students congregate here.

If you're keen on opera and classical music, check with tourist information, but when buying tickets don't use an agency as they charge a 20 per cent commission. Sometimes standing room is available at the opera; queue and tie a scarf around the barrier to reserve your place.

Southern Austria

If you're travelling south on to Italy or Yugoslavia, you'll pass through the southern regions of BURGENLAND, STEIERMARK and KÄRNTEN.

Burgenland is the province next to the Hungarian border and is famous for its wines. EISENSTADT is its capital and between late August and early September this turns into a pretty lively place, thanks to its Weinwoche (wine week). Steiermark is in the south-eastern area of Austria, along the Yugoslavian border which the 'Weinstrasse' (wine road) runs through. The journey between Salzburg and Villach is particularly scenic and if you fancy visiting a typical alpine town you could do worse than to choose Badgastein. Although expensive, it is worth while spending a relaxing few hours here, taking in the wonderful views down the valley from the station and seeing the powerful waterfall at close range.

Kärnten (Carinthia) has as its capital KLAGENFURT. This is an attractive region with lakes, wildlife parks and rolling hills. Klagenfurt itself has two campsites, and a youth hostel in its centre, and is a good place to base yourself to explore the surrounding Naturpark Kreuzbergl.

Central Austria

South of the Linz–Salzburg line lies a region of Austria that the tourist hordes haven't as yet discovered or spoilt. It consists mainly of mountains, lakes and tiny old villages – the sort of Austria you'd optimistically imagined. Not being commercialized, prices are low, so it's really got everything going for it.

From Vienna or Salzburg catch a train to Attnang Puchheim, then take a local train going in the direction of Stainach Irdning, passing through Gmunden, Hallstatt and Obertraun.

GMUNDEN, a town at the northernmost end of the Traunsee by the largest lake of the region, is particularly lovely. Tourist information is at Am Graben 2. Traunsteinstrasse is one of the best streets in which to look for accommodation.

HALLSTATT is the third stop after Bad Goisern. It is a particularly beautiful village with lakes, cliffs and a waterfall as the backdrop to your views. The small youth hostel Lahn 50 (Tel. 06134 279) is open from May to September (only limited facilities), and there's camping at Campingplatz Höll (Tel. 06134 329). Tourist information is in the Prähistorisches Museum just off Seestrasse; they'll advise on accommodation. The oldest salt mines in the world (they claim) are here and can be visited. This area is rich in walks and sails; you can rent a small boat from AS 105 an hour. There's a ferry into the town from the station after each train arrives.

OBERTRAUN, the next stop along, has an interesting ice cave, and two other large caves, but the admission cost is quite high. Their youth hostel is at Winkl 26 (Tel. 06131 360) and opens at 5 p.m.; it is more pleasant than the hostel in Hallstatt, AS 100 for B&B.

Salzburg

Extremely expensive, touristy, but beautiful. The prince-archbishops who ruled over the town built many fine churches, palaces, mansions and gardens until it became known as the 'Rome of the North'. The town is famous for its festival (from late July to end of August), which attracts all the big international names in music and fills every hotel, hostel and campsite with the thousands who flock to this event.

Luckily, Salzburg is a university town, so this slightly eases some of the financial problems eurorailers may encounter. There are some student hostels and restaurants which are less than half the price of their commercial counterparts, but basically Salzburg is a town which caters for the middle-aged and middle-class.

Salzburg is 3¼ hours from Vienna, 2 hours from Munich in Germany, 2½ hours from Innsbruck and 5 hours from Zürich; there are daily trains to Cologne, Hamburg and Copenhagen. The tourist information office at the station will help you find a room for AS 25. It is to the left side of the building facing you as you come out of passport control.

STATION FACILITIES

Train information	Mon.–Fri.: 7 a.m.–8.30 p.m.,
	Sat. 7.45 a.m.–8.30 p.m. (Tel. 1717)
Reservations	Daily 8 a.m.–7 p.m. in train info office
Tourist information	Daily 8.30 a.m.–8 p.m. (Tel. 871712)
Foreign exchange	Daily 7.30 a.m.–8 p.m.
Buffet	Daily 8 a.m.–10 p.m.
Restaurant	Mon.–Fri.: 6 a.m.–11.30 p.m.
Left-luggage lockers	Always open
Waiting room	Always open
Food shops (or head towards centre for supermarkets)	Mon.–Sat.: 8 a.m.–6 p.m.

TOURIST INFORMATION AND ADDRESSES

The city's main tourist information offices are at Mozartplatz 5 (Tel. 847568, 88987330) (open all year Mon.–Sat.: 9 a.m.–6 p.m., Sun.: 9 a.m.–8 p.m.) and at the station. There is an information centre for young travellers, 'Jugend-Service-Stelle' at Hubert-Sattler-Gasse 7 (Tel. 8072–2592) open weekdays 9 a.m.–4.30 p.m., Tues. & Thurs., 2 p.m. Fri., and 7 p.m., Mon. & Wed. City transport information and free maps are obtained from the bus drivers. Single fares are AS18, with 24-hour and 72-hour passes available at AS48 and AS96. These passes give free entry to the railway for the castle, the Salzburg–Bergheim tramway and the lift to the Mönchsberg terrace. However, most sights are within walking distance of the centre.

POST OFFICE: Residenzplatz 9, Mon.–Fri.: 7 a.m.–7 p.m., Sat. 8 a.m.–10 a.m. or 24-hour service near main railway station.
AMEX: Mozartplatz 57 (Tel. 842501).
STUDENT TRAVEL SERVICE: Ökista, Wolf-Dietrich-Str 31 (Tel. 883252), Mon.–Fri.: 9.30 a.m.–5.30 p.m. Help out with travel problems.
CITY PHONE CODE: 662.

SEEING

Gone are the days when Salzburg depended on its salt; tourists now come in their thousands to see the impressive baroque legacy of the powerful archbishops. They weren't all good, though; they did their fair share of expelling the Jews, pillaging and persecuting the local Protestants – all the usual stuff. The HOHENSALZBURG FORTRESS (their main residence) shouldn't be missed. Take the funicular up 1,780 feet and kill two birds with one stone, as the view from the top over the city is tremendous. If you're getting fed up with your travelling companion, check out the torture section of the MUSEUM there.

The other four main sites are the RESIDENZ (seventeenth-century archbishops' palace), SCHLOSS MIRABELL, the CATHEDRAL and MOZART'S BIRTHPLACE at Getreidegasse 9. Slightly outside Salzburg is SCHLOSS HELLBRUNN, the baroque castle built by a prince-archbishop, surrounded by an Alpine zoo. Take bus 55 from the station, or the local train. If you've had enough of tourists, there are several escape routes: two of them a short bus or train ride away over the border in Bavaria. The first is a visit to Hitler's retreat, the 'EAGLE'S NEST', and the second is a visit to the salt mines. Organized excursions to the salt mines run several times a day from Mirabellplatz, although you can do both trips independently. The starting-off point for both trips is Berchtesgaden. You might find it more convenient to take the bus as it runs more frequently than the train, and since the journey is quite short the cost is reasonable at around AS 36. (Discount with Inter-Rail, free on Eurail.) Once you are at Berchtesgaden you need to take a bus to the mines where you can hire protective clothing for around 25 DM. Check to see if your bus passes the mine entrance on the way to Berchtesgaden. For the 'EAGLE'S NEST' you will need a local service bus to the entrance road, where you change to special buses for the trip up to the car park. Don't even think about going any further if you suffer from vertigo for the bus seems to be suspended in mid-air for most of the tortuous journey up the single-track mountain road. You then walk into the middle of the mountain before going up to the eyrie in a brass-panelled lift. Total cost about 20 DM. The view is quite spectacular, although you might be just as happy to take a cable car up to the top of the Untersberg (5,800 feet), which will give you fine views of the Alpine scenery without the same expense in time and money but even this is relatively expensive. Alternatively, take one of the regular 'Sound of Music' tours round the locations of this popular musical. Details from tourist information.

SLEEPING

Your best bet here is to go for private accommodation: ask at tourist information for their list of private rooms. Forget hotels and try one of the hostels or campsites. If you've no luck here, go to the tourist office and tell them the most you can afford, then wait and see what they can come up with. If all else fails, consider going out to one of the villages on the outskirts.

• **Youth hostels:** The Salzburg Nonntal youth hostel at Josef-Preis Allee 18 (Tel. 842670) has 390 beds and all facilities, but fills up quickly so go early or book in advance. It closes from 9 a.m. to 11 a.m. and at midnight. Reports on cleanliness vary. Take bus 5 to Justizgebäude then a short walk. The International Hostel at Paracelsusstrasse 9 (Tel. 73460) is only a few blocks away from the station and is a real 'find'. It is reasonably well kept, with a washing machine and drier on-site. Although showers and breakfast are extra, you can choose from Continental, British or American. There is also a cheap restaurant/bar which serves an excellent Wiener Schnitzel. Expect to pay around AS 100–130 for a bed. Near the centre of town is the Aigen hostel at Aigner Strasse 34 (Tel. 23248). Buses 5 or 6 and change to 49 at Zentrum. It can get very busy and noisy, however, and is open July and August only. The hostel at Glockengasse 8 (Tel. 876241) can be reached by bus 29: get off at Vogelweidestrasse. Open April to October only.

• **Pensions:** Zum Junger Fuchs, Linzer Gasse 54 (Tel. (8) 75496). Doubles about AS 340–380. Very good. Walk from the Staats-brücke bridge, along Linzer Gasse. Also try the Elizabeth at Vogelweiderstrasse (Tel. 871664).

• **Camping:** There are several campsites including City Camping (Tel. 71169–25) at Bayerhamerstrasse 14 (only a ten-minute walk from the station. Cross under the railway line, then walk behind the station). Most are open from 1 May to 30 September, and prices vary from AS 48–70 per person and tent. If visiting the sights near Berchtesgaden, try Camping Allwegehein on Untersalzberg mountain (Tel. 08652 2396).

EATING AND NIGHTLIFE

There are plenty of flash restaurants in Salzburg and no shortage of ways to blow your money if you have any. Try Pitterkeller, 6 Rainerstrasse (meals AS 90–140), near the station. The food's not bad and it's cheap by Salzburg standards. Recently renovated.

For picnic food, there's a good open-air market on Thursday mornings by St Andrew's Church, and there are two every weekday on Universitätsplatz and Franz-Josef Strasse. There is a cheap stand-up Imbiss place, with a larger range than most, at 10 Judengasse, where Wiener Schnitzel and chips can be had for around AS 80.

Beer Gardens: Salzburg is a bit more orientated towards beer than to wine, probably due to its proximity to the German border. The beer cellars invariably offer good value in eating, drinking and entertainment. Try Augustiner Bräustübl, Augustinergasse 4 – there are several small stalls in this building where you can treat yourself.

If it's just a drink you're after, try Stiegl Beer Cellar, Festungsgasse 10, which has a great atmosphere and views over the city to match (but closed during the winter), or Students' Centre, Gstättengasse 16, weekdays 9 a.m.–12 p.m. and 1 p.m.–6 p.m.

Western Austria

From Liechtenstein to the Arlberg Tunnel, the Vorarlberg Alps are particularly scenic: mountains, chalets, green fields, etc. The best towns to base yourself in to explore this region are FELDKIRCH and BREGENZ.

Feldkirch is an old town with many reminders of its Gothic heyday. The tourist office is at Herrengasse 12 (Mon.–Fri.: 8.30 a.m.–12 noon, 2 p.m.–6 p.m., Sat.: 9 a.m.–noon). They'll suggest walking tours. There's a youth hostel (Tel. 05522 73181) at Reichsstrasse 111 and a campsite.

Bregenz, on the shores of Lake Constance (or Bodensee), with its medieval old quarter, is the capital of the Vorarlberg region. It is well known for its festival in July and August. The information office is at Anton-Schneiderstrasse 4A. There's a youth hostel at Belruptstrasse 16A (Tel. 05574 42867) and four campsites.

Innsbruck

As capital of the Tyrol and the Austrian ski scene, Innsbruck is busy all the year round. It is beautifully situated and well worth a day or two of your time.

STATION FACILITIES

Train information	Daily 7 a.m.–9.30 p.m. (Tel. 1717)
Reservations	Daily 8 a.m.–7.30 p.m. (Tel. 1700)
Tourist information	Daily 9 a.m.–10.00 p.m.
Restaurant	Daily 6.30 a.m.–11.30 p.m.
Bar, Buffet	Daily 7 a.m.–7 p.m.
Left-luggage lockers	Always open

For food and provisions, head towards the Maria-Theresienstrasse area, two streets straight ahead from the station.

There are daily trains from Innsbruck to Cologne, Hamburg, Munich (2¼ hours), Salzburg (2¼ hours), Vienna (5½ hours), Milan, Rome, Venice and Zürich (4 hours).

There's a centre for young travellers at the station (opening times 9.00 a.m.–10.00 p.m.). It's wonderful. Seize this opportunity to be treated like a human being and use it.

TOURIST INFORMATION AND ADDRESSES

At the station, open daily 9 a.m.–10 p.m. They'll find you a room, change your cash and fill you in on what's happening. There's another office at Burggraben 3, in the city centre, open daily 8 a.m.–7 p.m. The post office is at Maximilianstrasse 2 (one block away from the Triumphal Arch). The AMEX office is at Brixner-strasse 3, and the student travel service, Ökista, is at Josef-Hirnstrasse 7/2. City phone code 0512.

• **Alpine information:** As you're in one of the best Alpine centres in Europe, you may feel inclined to head for the hills. Check up on conditions before setting off at Wilhelm-Greilstrasse 17 (Tel. 5320 171) or, if you prefer to take an organized hike, contact Verkehrsverein at Burggraben 3 (Tel. 59850). Some free hikes are available; persistence at the tourist office should get you information on these.

• **Mountain hut scheme:** There are over 700 huts up in the mountains surrounding Innsbruck. They belong to various local and national Alpine associations, and doing a tour of them, or even just staying the night in one, is very rewarding, cheap and provides a good memory of Austria. Many of the huts have some cooking facilities and some even serve up hot food. Prices range from about AS120 to AS250 for a night. Washing facilities tend to be basic.

Before setting out, make sure you have emergency food supplies, a waterproof and are wearing good climbing boots. The distress call in this neck of the woods is six visible or audible signals spaced evenly over one minute, followed by a minute's break, then the six signals again.

SEEING

The Nordkette mountains dominate the main shopping street – Maria-Theresienstrasse. At one end is the TRIUMPHAL ARCH and at the other the old Gothic town. The GOLDEN ROOF is the symbol of Innsbruck; it's an ornate Gothic balcony built in 1500 from 2,657 gilded copper tiles. The ski jump, on the hillside above the town, is a good viewpoint. You could also visit the rather small Olympic Museum here. The HOFBURG (Imperial Palace) is the other major sight.

For an all-round perspective, take the cable car up to HAFELE-KAR. At 7,500 feet, the view is quite spectacular. Take tram 1 to the Hungerburg funicular, then the cable car, but be warned, it is expensive to go all the way. There are also two other cable car routes. The 1964 and 1976 Winter Olympics were held at IGLS near Innsbruck, and if you're in the ski set you can still go and see the set-up (bus J from Innsbruck Station or tram 6). Enjoy the view but stay out of the cafés there. If you want to see a pretty Alpine village and travel on an open-sectioned train (highly recommended), go to the village of FULPMES, in good picnic country. Take tram 1 to Stubaitalbahnhof where the mountain train leaves. An alternative is to take the tram direct from the main station. Buy a hiking map (Wanderkarte) and try the rewarding walk from Fulpmes to the Pfarrachalm mountain inn.

SLEEPING

The Glockenhaus Hostel at Weiherburggasse 3 (Tel. 286515), is situated ten minutes' walk from the town centre and twenty minutes from the station, although there is a pick-up service from the station if you arrange in advance, or bus K. They also have a building at Innstrasse 95 (Tel. 86515) where they will send you if you want dormitory accommodation. Neither of these takes phone reservations, and there have been complaints about them. The owners lay on ski rental and organize skiing, hiking, river rafting and wind surfing excursions. A typical price is AS 310 for a double; there are also singles and larger rooms.

The Pension Tautermann, at Stamser Feld 5 (Tel. 281572) charges from AS 400–500 for a double room with shower *en suite* WC, and includes breakfast. Very comfortable. There is also a small hostel at Sillgasse 8a, although reports on the cleanliness vary. Only five minutes' walk from the station, it charges AS 190 for bed, breakfast and shower (Tel. 571311). Alternatively, there's the youth hostel at Reichenauerstrasse 147, which is a long way from the town centre, has a 10 p.m. curfew, is reportedly unfriendly, and has strict rules. Take bus O or R to Campingplatz or a 30-minute walk. Cost is around AS 120 (Tel. 46179). Also try the hostel, Torsten-Arneus Schnedenhaus, at 17b Rennweg (Tel. 585814). Open July and August only. Small rooms at AS 150 including breakfast.

The nearest campsite is Reichenau at Reichenauerstrasse (Tel. 46252), 30 minutes' walk from the station, follow river downstream, or take buses R, O or OA. It is expensive at AS 70 per person. Just before you reach the campsite is the cheap, clean, but highly regimented St Paulus youth hostel (Tel. 44291).

Avoid eating evening meals in the pensions. The meal may be 'fixed price', but the extras might be expensive.

EATING AND NIGHTLIFE

Head towards the university area. Try Gasthaus Gruber, Innrain 160 (between university and Old Town). Also, the Mensa (off Innrain) at Herzog-Siegmund Ufer 15, 2nd floor, offers cheap meals for ISIC holders, lunchtimes only. Good value meals are available in many old town restaurants, on the way from Maria-Theresien-strasse to the Golden Roof – and the bars/restaurants around here are lively in the evening.

There's a free Tyrolean evening in front of the Golden Roof most Thursday evenings in season at 8.30 p.m. Or try the St Nikolaus Kellerei, Innstrasse, open 8 a.m.–12 noon, 2 p.m.–8 p.m. Good wine, but no English spoken.

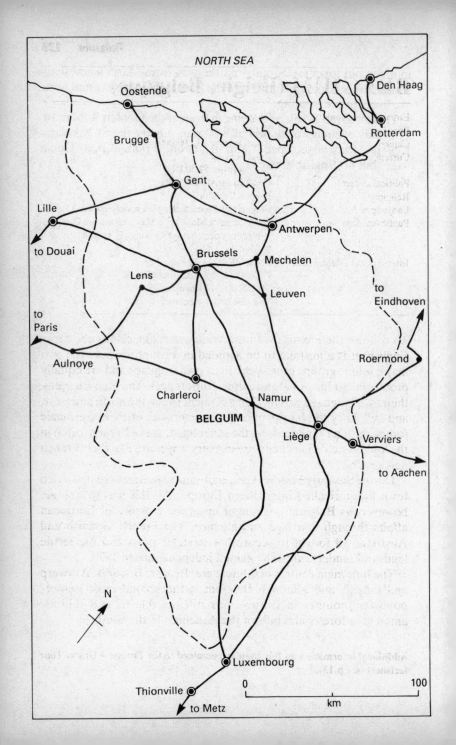

BELGIUM (Belgie; Belgique)

Entry requirements	Passport
Population	10,000,100
Capital	Brussels (pop.: 1,200,000)
Currency	Belgian Franc
	£1 = approx. 52.50 BF
Political system	Constitutional Monarchy
Religion	Roman Catholic
Languages	French and Flemish (English widely spoken)
Public holidays	1 Jan.; Easter Monday; 1 May; Ascension Day;
	Whit Monday; 21 July; 15 Aug.; 1, 11 Nov.;
	25 Dec.
International dialling codes	From UK 010 + 32 + number
	From USA 011 + 32 + number
	To UK 00 + 44 + number
	To USA 00 + 1 + number

To confuse the Flemish with the Walloons is like calling the Scots English; it is a mistake to be avoided in a country where the two major ethnic groups each speak their own language and are equally proud of their historical and cultural differences. The Flemish speak their own language closely akin to Dutch, live in the north and west, and still carry the hard-working characteristics of their Germanic forebears. The Walloons, on the other hand, speak French, often in the 'old French' dialect and are in every way more like their French neighbours.

During the early Middle Ages, trade and commerce created a rich town life unrivalled in northern Europe. All this was to change, however, as Belgium got caught up in the crossfire of European affairs through marriage and alliance. The French, Spanish and Austrians all fought to secure her strategic ports and the fertile lands of Flanders, until she gained independence in 1830.

The four main centres of interest are: Bruges, Brussels, Antwerp and Ghent, and although Belgium is the second most densely populated country in Europe, it's still possible to find solitude among the forests and hills of the Ardennes in the south.

Additional information on this country contained in the *Europe – Grand Tour* factsheet (see p.13).

BELGIAN NATIONAL RAILWAYS
(Nationale Maatschappij der Belgische Spoorwegen, NMBS)
(Société Nationale des Chemins de Fer Belges, SNCB)

Belgium's train network is one of the most reliable and extensive in Europe. The trains are frequent and go just about everywhere. To cross the country takes only 3½ hours, and trains leave for most internal destinations every hour. The fastest services are the EuroCity services and the Inter-City services (IC), and the semi-fast services are 'Inter-regional' (IR numbers). No supplements are charged for any trains running wholly within Belgium, but supplements are payable for travel by certain international trains. Inter-Railers and Eurail pass holders have an extra bonus as it's possible – and often advisable – to use one city as a base and tour the rest of the country from it (it only takes 1 hour from Bruges to Brussels).

● **Inter-Rail bonuses:** See Appendix II.

● **Eurail bonuses:** The following half-price reductions are granted by Europabus on transportation costs only and by local offices in Europe.
—Antwerp–Brussels–Menton
—Antwerp–Brussels–Barcelona
—Ostend–Brussels–Frankfurt (M.)
—Ostend–Lille
—Antwerp–Brussels–Le Havre–Lisieux

TRAIN INFORMATION

Information officers speak good English, other rail staff speak both Flemish and French. If you're spending any time in Belgium, ask for a copy of the official SNCB timetable ('indicateur'/'spoorboekje'), cost 150 BF, from any station. It has an introduction in English and explains all you need to know about schedules and supplements. There is also a free pocket-sized booklet giving details of the main services. If you don't get either, don't worry as there are large posters everywhere, giving departure and arrival information. Most stations have coin-operated lockers, or use the luggage offices, at 30 BF per item per day.

• **Reservations:** Are not necessary, or even possible, on inland routes. International reservations cost 80 BF and can be made up to two months in advance, if you're that highly organized. If you are, you'd probably also like to know that you can reserve seats on trains leaving for Austria, Denmark, France, Germany, Italy and Switzerland, at most large stations, as the SNCB's computer is linked up with these countries.

• **Night travel:** Belgium is too small to warrant inland services, but SNCB have couchettes and wagon-lit sleepers on international routes. (Look out for the German rolling stock with pull-down seats, to save a bit of money.)

• **Eating on trains:** There are not many services on inland trains; some have a mini-bar and a few have a buffet. Don't let that worry you, though, as Belgium's supermarkets are renowned for their food. International trains have all the usual expensive facilities, so either way prepare a picnic in advance, and don't count on station shops to supply it as there aren't any, except in major cities.

• **Bikes:** SNCB run a scheme called 'Train + Vélo' (Trein + Fiets in Flemish) which allows you to take advantage of Belgium's perfect cycling conditions. You can rent a bike for around 130 BF per day (with a rail pass) from 60 stations and hand it back at around 90. Most roads have cycle tracks and it's flat going all the way to explore the surrounding countryside. (Don't forget to ask for a free tour map.)

• **Rover Tickets:** There are three types of ticket which can be purchased for rover travel within Belgium. The 50% reduction card, for 550 BF, allows you to buy an unlimited number of single-journey tickets at half normal price. It is valid for one month on the whole of the Belgian network.

The 5-day Tourrail Card is valid for 5 days of your own choice within a 17-day period. For adults over 26 the second-class card is 1800 BF, juniors (12–25) pay 1350 BF. First class costs 50% extra. The Benelux Tourrail card, valid in Belgium, Netherlands and Luxembourg, works very much like the Tourrail card, costs 3080 BF for adults, and 2290 BF for under 26s. First class 50 per cent extra.

TOURIST INFORMATION

Local tourist offices are to be found in every large town. For any extra information on the provinces and the country, ask at the main office in Brussels. If you've any problems tourist information can't help out with, try the Info-Jeunes (Info-Jeugd) office. There are branches in most large towns.

● **ISIC bonuses:** 50 per cent off most museums. For further information, contact Connections, 13 rue Marche au Charbon, 1000 Brussels (also a Eurotrain office), or ACOTRA, rue de la Madeleine 51, 1000 Brussels.

● **Money matters:** 1 Belgian franc (BF) = 100 centimes.
Banking hours are Mon.–Fri.: 9 a.m.–12 p.m., 2 p.m.–4 p.m. Late opening, Friday till 4.30 p.m. AMEX are the only bank that do not charge high commissions on transactions involving traveller's cheques. Eurocheques are thus the preferred means of payment. The station exchanges take no commission, but their rate of exchange is about 10 per cent below the official one. The ferries give a good rate and their commission is considerably less.

● **Post offices:** Open Mon.–Fri.: 9 a.m.–5 p.m., tend to shut for lunch.

● **Shops and museums:** There are no hard-and-fast rules here, but museums tend to shut either on Mondays or Fridays, and some in the afternoons. Shops open from 9 a.m. to 6 p.m., Monday–Saturday, with lunch 12 noon–2 p.m. Bakers and newsagents open early in the morning, and you can also find a grocer open on Sunday somewhere. Many shops stay open till 8 p.m. Late night Friday.

SLEEPING

Apart from tourist information, the Info-Jeunes offices also give help with accommodation. Unmarried couples wanting to sleep together might find problems if they are under 18 as hoteliers can be imprisoned for up to three years under Belgian law for allowing this.

Hostels are your best bet – either the IYHF ones or those run by an organization called 'Amis de la Nature/Naturvrieden'. There are two IYHF organisations, one for the French region, one for the Flemish. There are a few unofficial ones, as well as student hostels which offer a more relaxed atmosphere. All of these are given in the Budget Holiday booklet which you can pick up at any tourist information office.

Hotels tend to be expensive (absolute minimum 1000 BF double) but clean, and offer an inclusive continental breakfast.

EATING AND NIGHTLIFE

The Belgians love their food and take eating very seriously, a fact which is borne out by the well-stocked supermarkets you will find even in the small towns. Always be prepared for an impromptu picnic. If you're eating out, go for your main meal at lunchtime as the fixed menu is not available at night, so making dinner a more expensive affair. Belgian cuisine is similar to French, both in quality and in price. If possible, try some local specialities: carbonnades flamandes (beef stewed in beer) and waterzooi (chicken and vegetables stewed in sauce). Don't miss the Belgian waffles served with fruit or cream, or the excellent pastry and cakes, and if you think the Swiss are the only Europeans who know how to make delicious chocolates, try the Belgian pralines (especially the fresh-cream-filled white chocolates, available from any branch of Leonidas). Apologies for making your mouth water if you're really broke, but there are always Belgian chips, which are small, thin and delicious and are served with mayonnaise. In fact, the 'friterie/frituur' is the cheapest and most prolific source of fast food in Belgium. There's always one near a station, and they serve kebabs, sausages, etc., too.

Belgium's selection of bars would satisfy the most demanding drinker. While wine is good and cheaper than at home, you'll do best to try what they're famous for: beer. In the cities, it's quite common to find pubs serving up to fifty varieties (La Houblonnière in Brussels boasts a hundred). Try one of the Trappist brews, a good nightcap, or for those willing to try anything once, kriek, a cherry-flavoured beer.

There is no shortage of theatres, cinemas or discos, and the set-up is very similar to at home. Don't waste your time looking for cheap seats or student discounts, as they do not exist.

Ostend (Oostende)

If you're coming from England by ferry or Jetfoil, chances are you will land here. There's not much to see, but if you want to stop overnight, the youth hostel 'de Ploate' at Langestraat 82 (Tel. 059 805297) is only five minutes from the docks and station and is very good. It is however difficult to get a bed during summer, so try to book in advance.

Bruges
(Brugge – Flemish, Bruges – French)

This beautifully preserved medieval town is more like an open-air museum than a twentieth-century city. If you're going to stop off anywhere in Belgium, make sure it's Bruges, as this is definitely one of the most attractive towns in Europe. For over 200 years, Bruges was one of the most important commercial centres in Western Europe, and the Counts of Flanders spent their money making the town's guildhalls, palaces and churches as impressive as they could. All this glory came to an end when their harbour silted up and made trade impossible. Bruges is known as the 'Venice of the North', and its network of canals, bridges (Brugge means bridge) and tall Gothic buildings reminds you very much of its Italian counterpart.

STATION FACILITIES

The station is on the southern edge of the town, one mile from the city centre. If you don't feel like a walk (although it is quite pleasant through the large park) get any of the buses going to the Markt, close to where the main tourist information is situated.

Train information	Mon.–Fri.: 7 a.m.–7 p.m.
	Sat.–Sun.: 9.30 a.m.–5.30 p.m.
	(Tel. 050 382382, multi-lingual)
Reservations	Same hours as above
Tourist information	Room reservation only, 2.45 p.m.–9 p.m.;
	Nov.–Feb.: 1.45 p.m.–8 p.m.; closed Sundays.
	Other services, Burg 11.
Foreign exchange	Mon., Wed., Thurs., Fri., Sat.,
	June–Sept.: 9 a.m.–6 p.m.
Left-luggage lockers	Closed 1 a.m.–3.30 a.m.
	No access 1.30 a.m.–3.30 a.m.
Buffet	6.30 a.m.–9 p.m.
Cycle hire	7.00 a.m.–8.30 p.m.
Station shuts	1.30 a.m.–4 a.m.

Daily trains to: Amsterdam, Cologne, Vienna, Koblenz, Berlin, Belgrade, London (via Dover), Munich, Salzburg, Basel, Brig, Milan, Brussels, Paris.

TOURIST INFORMATION AND ADDRESSES

The tourist office is at Burg 11 (Tel. 448686) and is open April to September, Mon.–Fri.: 9.30 a.m.–6.30 p.m. Sat. and Sun. 10 a.m.–12 p.m., 2 p.m.–6.30 p.m. and October to March, Mon.–Sat.: 9.30 a.m.–12.45 p.m., 2 p.m.–5.45 p.m. Closed Sunday. They will sell you a map for 20 BF, give you leaflets and fix up a bed for you. There is an exchange bureau in the building from April to October, daily except Wednesdays. The post office is nearby at the Markt.

CITY PHONE CODE 050.

SEEING

The main things to see are: THE BELFRY on the Markt, built from the thirteenth to the fifteenth century. Climb up for a good view of the layout of the old town and listen out for the CARILLON (bell concert). Two museums right next door to each other on the Dyver are GRUUTHUSE and GROENINGE (closed at lunchtime, and on Tuesdays in winter). Gruuthuse is a museum of applied arts, housed in a particularly beautiful fifteenth-century mansion, while Groeninge is devoted to Flemish Renaissance painting and contemporary art. Joined on to Gruuthuse is the thirteenth-century CHURCH OF OUR LADY, containing Michelangelo's 'Madonna and Child'. The BEGIJNHOF (a Belgian type of convent) is in a peaceful location off the Wijngaardplein. You can wander around the interior and the grounds for free or pay a few francs to visit the museum. The canal boat trips may seem a rip-off at around 130 BF a go, but they're actually quite good value as you get an added perspective on the town and they don't rush. Bus fares are 35 BF for any distance, but as you can see most of Bruges on foot, you shouldn't need to use them much. If you're wanting to see 'Alternative Flanders', try taking one of the cheap bus tours offered by Quasimodo's. They are very good, covering everything from beer tasting to the WWI and 2 cemeteries, expertly guided (Tel. 370470 or call at 52 Engelendalelaan, 8310 SWT–Kruis).

SLEEPING

Try and stay central as all the sights in Bruges are close together; bear in mind that the town gets its fair share of visitors in summer, so get there early. The Youth Hostel is at Baron Ruzettelaan 143 (Tel.

352679). It's not too central, but reasonable, although more expensive than some of the other hostels in town. There is an 11 p.m. curfew and you'll need an IYHF card and 380 BF for B&B. Closed 10 a.m.–5 p.m. Take bus 2 to Steenbrugge and get off shortly after the canal. The driver will point it out.

Camping St Michiel is at Tillegemstraat 55, St Michiels (Tel. 380819), 100 BF per person, 100 BF per tent. Quite a way out: take bus 7 from the station or 't Zand. Change traveller's cheques here free of commission.

The Snuffel Travellers Inn is good value, from 310 BF for B&B. It's at Ezelstraat 49 (Tel. 333133). Though not exactly luxurious, it is comfortable, central and friendly and has recently been renovated. There is a good choice of reasonably priced meals and the bar has a 'happy hour' each evening. Get there early as there are only 50 beds.

Bauhaus at Langestraat 135–137 has 105 beds (Tel. 341093). Cost from 950 BF for a double, B&B, five minutes from market place, near the windmills. Also Bruno's Passage Hostel, Dweersstraat 26 (Tel. 340232). Rooms booked per group, smallest group is four people, cost 1500 BF inc. breakfast. 10 minutes' walk from station, five minutes from market.

EATING AND NIGHTLIFE

As Bruges is not a university town, there's no specific cheap studenty area, but you can get by. The Lotus at Wapenmakers Straat does a good 'plat du jour' for lunch and serves vegetarian dishes. The Ganzespel at Ganzestraat 37 do a 'menu du jour' for about 220 BF. There are late-night cafés dotted around the old town; Vlissinge on Blekerstraat claims to be among the oldest in Europe.

Brussels (Brussel – Flemish, Bruxelles – French)

Brussels is a real patchwork of old and new: a city of extreme contrasts, from the seventeenth-century GRAND' PLACE to the modern skyscrapers of the multinationals, and the EC headquarters. The main part of this capital which is worth seeing is enclosed in quite a small area of the old town; don't waste your time on the new 'cement heap', as predictably there's nothing unique or particularly Belgian about it. The city revolves round 'the most beautiful square in Europe' – the Grand' Place. Try to view it in daytime, and then again when it's floodlit at night.

STATION FACILITIES

Brussels has three main stations: Gare du Nord, Gare du Midi and Gare Centrale. Though Centrale handles few international trains, it is conveniently located for the Grand' Place area, and there are interconnecting trains between the three stations every 15–20 minutes. Trains leave daily for Holland, Denmark, Germany, Switzerland, Italy and France. It takes less than 3 hours to get to Paris or Amsterdam from Brussels.

	NORTH (Nord/Noord) STATION	SOUTH (Midi/Zuid) STATION	CENTRAL (Centrale/Centraal) STATION
Train information	6.30 a.m.–9 p.m.	6 a.m.–10.15 p.m.	6.30 a.m.–9 p.m.
Reservations	8 a.m.–8 p.m.	Mon.–Fri.: 8 a.m.–8 p.m. Sat., Sun.: 9 a.m.–7 p.m.	8 a.m.–8 p.m.
Foreign exchange	7 a.m.–11 p.m.	6.45 a.m.–11 p.m.	8 a.m.–9 p.m.
Bar, Buffet	Mon.–Fri.: 6 a.m.–10 p.m. Sat., Sun.: 7 a.m.–9 p.m.	6.15 a.m.–9.45 p.m.	Mon.–Sat.: 6.10 a.m.–9.45 p.m. Sun.: 7 a.m.–9.45 p.m.
Restaurant	Mon.–Fri.: 7.30 a.m.–10 p.m. Sat.–Sun. 7.30 a.m.–7.30 p.m.	11.45 a.m.–4 p.m.	Temporarily closed
Left-luggage lockers	Not available	Always open	Closed 1.20 a.m.–3.50 a.m.
Left-luggage store	As per station	Closed 2 a.m.–4 a.m.	Closed 1 a.m.–3.50 a.m.
Waiting room	As per station	Always open	6 a.m.–10.30 p.m.
Duty officer (Sous-Chef de Gare)	As per station	Always open	Always open
Station shuts	Mon.–Fri.: 1.30 a.m.–4 a.m. Sat.–Sun.: 1.30 a.m.–4.45 a.m.	2 a.m.–4 a.m.	1.20 a.m.–3.50 a.m.

There are some booths near the South station selling food, and friteries in the nearby rue de France. For tourist information go to Gare Centrale and walk across Place de l'Europe for three blocks. There's a post office near Gare du Midi (open 24 hours) and at Centrale. You'll find social segregation at the Midi station in the form of the Brussels Tavern, which provides a snack bar, etc. Officially, these are only for the use of EuroCity or IC passengers, but in practice you can get in if reasonably dressed. Don't be tempted to buy anything as the prices are roughly double what you can pay elsewhere in the station. For information on city transport, head down to the metro station at Gare du Midi. Finally, if you arrive late at night when the tourist office is shut, head for the Gare du Nord, as there are several student hostels in this area.

TOURIST INFORMATION

The main office is at TIB on Grand' Place (Tel. 513 8940). Open 9 a.m.–6 p.m. daily (Sundays 9 a.m.–6 p.m., April to September, 10 a.m.–2 p.m. in October and November). They'll fix you up with accommodation and give you maps and all the usual handouts. Other organizations providing help with accommodation and what to see are: ACOTRA, rue de la Madeleine 51 (Tel. 512 8607 and 512 5540).

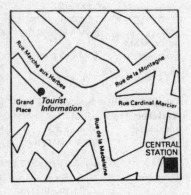

This youth organization provides a *free room-finding service.* They're open weekdays 10 a.m.–6 p.m., Thurs. to 7 p.m., Sat. to 1 p.m. INFO-JEUGD/JEUNES, in rue Marché-aux-Herbes 27 (Tel. 512 3274) is near the Grand' Place and is open Mon.–Fri.: 12 a.m.–6 p.m. National tourist information is available at rue du Marché-aux-Herbes 61 (Tel. 5540386 or 5540390), just behind Grand' Place.

● **Addresses:**

POST OFFICE: First floor of tall building at Place de la Monnaie, poste restante here.

AMEX: 2 Place Louise (Tel. 512 1740), open Mon.–Fri.: 9 a.m.–5 p.m., Sat.: 9.30 a.m.–noon.

UK EMBASSY: Britannia House, 28 rue Joseph II (Tel. 217 9000).
US EMBASSY: 27 Boulevard du Régent (Tel. 513 3830).
CANADIAN EMBASSY: 2 Ave. de Tervuren (Tel. 735 6040).
AUSTRALIAN EMBASSY: 6 rue Guimard (Tel. 231 0516).
AMBULANCE: (Tel. 100)
POLICE: (Tel. 101)
24-HOUR CHEMIST: Tel. 479 1818, Ave. Houba.
CITY PHONE CODE: 02

• **Getting about:** Basically, there's a flat rate of around 40 BF within the city which is valid for transfers between metro, bus and tram, for 1 hour. There's also a tourist pass which gives unlimited travel for one day, costing 160 BF. You can also buy a ten-trip pass from metro stations for 275 BF, or a five-trip pass for 180 BF. For information on city transport, there are offices under the Place Rogier, Porte de Namur and Gare Midi.

One tip – if using the metro take a map with you, there is limited information posted, and it is hard to understand.

SEEING

If you have only a single day, a bus tour is the best bet. But try to avoid the traditional ones in luxury coaches, six languages and which end your tour at a lace shop where the driver gets a backhander – there's usually a much better alternative with Chatterbus. It's run by the former manager of one of the city's youth hostels and aimed at the young eurorail type of customer. Chatterbus takes in all the places you want to see in Brussels – and a few of the ones the city authorities would rather you didn't. You'll get a good tour of the city and an honest assessment of the places not worth exploring further. The cost is around 650 BF, or 500 BF if you are staying at one of the youth hostels. The same group also runs Brussels on Foot tours during the summer at around 250 BF each. If you're in a group they will arrange off-beat tours such as hijacking a tram, or a beer-tasting night, including beer-flavoured food and they also have lists of ordinary Brussels residents who are prepared to act as guides for the price of the telephone call to book them. Book through youth hostels, or call Chatterbus directly (Tel. 673 1835). As Chatterbus is more of an informal service than a profit-making business, you may find it only runs on certain days and at certain times. But it is well worth making the effort to try to catch one of these tours.

If you've a bit more time or like to be independent, head for the GRAND' PLACE which is *the* sight of Brussels – a well-preserved collection of Gothic guildhalls and public buildings from the seventeenth century. In the mornings, except Mondays, a flower market is held there and at night it's floodlit. Opposite the MAISON DU ROI (the city museum) is the Gothic TOWN HALL, considered Brussels' most elegant building. MANNEKEN-PIS (a small statue of a boy having a pee) is the symbol of Brussels and is situated behind the Town Hall on rue l'Etuve. There are several stories as to his origin, the main one being that he saved the city by damping down some dynamite – in a natural and effective fashion.

The MUSÉE DES BEAUX ARTS has a good collection of early Flemish masters, including Rubens (free; closed Monday). In contrast, next door is the modern art gallery: the MUSEUM OF ART AND HISTORY, one of the largest in Europe, covering absolutely everything (closed Monday). It is situated at the Parc du Cinquantenaire. The MUSICAL INSTRUMENT MUSEUM has the largest collection in the world (over 4,000).

If you've any time left, try and see the PALAIS DE JUSTICE, closed weekends, ST MICHAEL'S CATHEDRAL and ERASMUS' HOUSE.

Paris has the Eiffel Tower and London Big Ben, but Brussels' big monument (apart from Manneken-Pis) is the ATOMIUM, an immense model of an iron molecule, which was built to celebrate the 1958 International Exhibition at Heysel. At the foot of the Atomium is MINI-EUROPE, a collection of 350 models of well known European sights. Spot the places you have seen, but at a price, 350 BF. Open April–December. Also in the same area, known as Bruparck, there are a water theme park, a planetarium, an IMAX cinema and a 27-screen cinema, claimed to be the world's biggest.

A few interesting day-trips from Brussels are: LEUVEN, a medieval university town (20 minutes by train); WATERLOO, site of the battle, now with museums; and BOKRIJK, the largest open-air museum in Europe with over a hundred reconstructions of medieval buildings (April–October). Trains from any Brussels station (90 minutes). Note that it is quite a walk from the Waterloo station to the Wellington Museum – and too far to walk to the battlefield (though a bus runs in peak season).

There is a good amusement park at BIERGES – a half-hour journey from Gare du Nord. Called ·WALIBI·, it costs around 490 BF (all-in ticket).

SLEEPING

Unless you're prepared to go a long way out of town, your choice is limited to hostelling or hotelling (the campsites are a long way out). There's not much difficulty getting a bed in Brussels, even in summer, and things are getting easier. The best area to concentrate your efforts on is round the Gare du Nord. If you have any trouble ACOTRA (see under tourist info) will find a bed for you.

● **Student hostels:** Sleep Well at rue de la Blanchisserie 27 (Tel. 218 5050) is the best value in the city. It's clean, central (near Gare du Nord, in the direction of Place Rogier), cheap and has a good atmosphere. It makes an effort to be different, and in fact the piped background music is all classical. Dormitory beds are around 300 BF, singles 480 BF and doubles 820 BF. Closes 10 a.m.–5 p.m. Try to reserve ahead as it's popular. In summer, it arranges city tours by local students. Due to move a short distance away during 1993.

Another student hostel which offers good value is CHAB at 8 rue Traversière (Tel. 217 0158) close to the Botanique metro station, or 10 minutes' walk from the Gare du Nord. It has 180 beds in dorms (290 BF), 3/4 bedded rooms (400 BF), twins (480 BF) and singles (580 BF). Although school groups are accepted in low season, the preferred age range in summer is 18–35. Open from 7.30 a.m.–2 a.m. This hostel also has kitchen, laundry and locker facilities. They organize walking tours of Brussels and free, or cheap, music and art events, plus, there is an open-air cinema at the nearby Botanique Culture Centre.

● **Youth hostels:** There's a hostel at Heilige Geeststraat 2 (Tel. 5110 436) near the Kappelle Kerk/Église de la Chapelle, head down Keizerslaan from the Central station. It's known as the Breugel and costs from 360 BF to 590 BF including breakfast. You'll need an IYHF card. Also try Maison Internationale, Chaussée de Wavre 205 (Tel. 648 9787). From the Central Station take metro to Porte de Namur or bus 38 or 60 to Trône. Open June–Sept. Costs 300 BF to 350 BF including breakfast and shower.

The International Accommodation Centre 'Jacques Brel' is at rue de la Sablonnière 30 (Tel. 218 0187). It has 134 beds and charges between 350 BF and 590 BF including breakfast. It is open all year round, but booking is essential in summer. Has a cafeteria, information and TV room; Metro Botanique or Madou. Hostel 'Jean Nihon', at 4 rue de l'Eléphant, has 130 beds, and charges 560 BF to 590 BF (Tel. 410 3858). Take metro to Comtes de Flandres.

• **Pensions/hotels:** There are a few at Avenue Fonsny (opposite Gare du Midi): the Merlo is OK and reasonably priced by Brussels standards. Hôtel Sabina at 78 rue du Nord (Tel. 218 2637) and Hôtel De L'Yser, 9–13 rue d'Edinbourg (Tel. 511 7459) are worth investigating. The Hotel Du Grand Colombier at rue du Colombier 10 (Tel. 217 9622 or 219 5136) charges around 1100 BF for a double, with shower, including breakfast. Ask at TIB for other suggestions.

• **Camping:** Try Beersel, Steenweg op Ukkel 75 (Tel. 331 0561 or 378 1977), 9 km south of the city, or Paul Rosmant, at Warandeberg 52 (Tel. 782 1009) although the latter, while nearer town, is only open between April and the end of September. Metro to Kraainem, then bus 30 to Place St Pierre. Also Grimbergen at Veldkanstraat 64 (Tel. 269 2597), open Jan. to Oct., bus G from Gare du Nord to terminus, then walk.

EATING AND NIGHTLIFE

It's easy to eat cheaply and well in Brussels. Use the stalls on the main shopping streets for waffles. There are plenty of fast-food chains and no shortage of cheap restaurants with fixed-price meals. For a splash out, go along the rue des Bouchers, trying the varieties of moules marinières (360–400 BF). The department stores offer good food at reasonable prices and the shopping centre, City 2, located off Place Rogier (5 minutes from Gare du Nord), has several cafés; the one on the top floor does soup and as much salad as you can get on your plate for around 100 BF. Open 9 a.m.–8.30 p.m. The Vietnamese and African restaurants are also good value and Le Breton, 59 rue des Drapiers, offers authentic Belgian food, beer and wines in a studenty atmosphere.

Head for the Gare du Midi – the student quarter – for pubs, clubs, etc. Discos are expensive, so make do with a lively pub if you can. Try Le Dolle Mol, 52 rue des Eperonniers, for the young crowd. To meet the locals go to La Mort Subite at rue Montagne aux Herbes Potagères or Bierodrome, Place Fernand Cocq 21. Films are good value (usually 180 BF for students), and the Styx, 72 rue de l'Arbre Bénit, shows revival films with midnight meals, which usually attract an interesting crowd.

Southern Belgium

The main line to Luxembourg passes through Namur and the Ardennes. To explore the area, it's best to base yourself at NAMUR; the regional tourist office is at rue Notre Dame 3 (Tel. 081 22 29 98). For information on the city, go to the pavilion next to the station or the Info-Jeunes at the belfry in the town (Tel. 081 71 47 40). Namur has one of the friendliest youth hostels in Europe at Rue Félicien Rops, 8 La Plante (Tel. 081 22 36 88, bus 3 or 4 from the station).

Antwerp (Antwerpen – Flemish, Anvers – French)

Belgium's second city is famous for its flourishing diamond trade, its shipping and fine art. For 1993, Antwerp is the European City of Culture, and several events will stress this. There are two stations: Berchem and Central. International trains stop only at Berchem, except for those coming from Paris and Amsterdam. The tourist office is at Grote Markt 15, open Mon.–Sat.: 9 a.m.–6 p.m.; Sun. and holidays: 9 a.m.–5 p.m. Most sights are concentrated in the old town: OUR LADY'S CATHEDRAL, PETER PAUL RUBENS HOUSE, the ROYAL MUSEUM OF FINE ART with over 2,500 paintings and an excellent exhibition of eight centuries of northern painting, the GROTE MARKT, ST CHARLES BORROMEO'S CHURCH, the PLANTIN-MORETUS MUSEUM of sixteenth-century printing, and CASTLE STEEN – a maritime museum. Most of the museums are shut on Mondays. There are free diamond-cutting exhibitions and tours of diamond works – ask at tourist information.

The student hostel 'Boomerang' at Volkstraat 58 (Tel. 2384782) is centrally located and reasonably priced, though reports of standards vary. Take bus 23 from Central Station to the museum stop, or tram 8 from Berchem Station. Hôtel Florida, at De Keyserlei 59, is right in front of Central Station. The New International Youth Pension at 256 Provinciestraat (Tel. 2300522) is clean, friendly and near the station, down Pelikaanstraat, 20 minutes to Provinciestraat. There is a campsite at Vogelzanglaan (Tel. 2385717), bus 17 to the Holiday Inn Crowne Plaza hotel, which is cheap. Another site is located at St-Annastrand, on the left bank of the river (Tel. 2196090). The youth hostel (IYHF) is at Eric Sasselaan 2 (Tel. 2380273). Tram 2 or bus 27 from Central Station, to just after bridge across main road. Don't be taken in by the 'rooms for tourists' advertised in cafés around the station – they're brothels.

For food, the Prinsstraat area (round the university) has several cafés doing fixed-price menus. The docks area is lively in the evenings and round the Grote Markt there are bars and restaurants – but they're rather expensive.

CITY PHONE CODE: 03.

Ghent
(Gent – Flemish, Gand – French)

Renowned for its art and flowers and a glut of historic buildings. Day-trippers from Antwerp should get off at Dampoort Station which is nearer the centre, but from all other destinations you go on to St Pieter's Station.

Train information	Daily 7 a.m.–9 p.m. (Tel. 091 214444/224444)
Reservations	Daily 7 a.m.–8 p.m.
Tourist information	In centre
Foreign exchange	Hours variable, generally 9.00 a.m.–4 p.m., closed lunchtimes and Sundays
Left-luggage lockers	Always access
Buffet	Mon.–Sat.: 6.30 a.m.–10 p.m.; Sun. 7.30 a.m.–11 p.m.
Cycle hire	7 a.m.–8.30 p.m.
Station shuts	Always open

Daily trains to: Cologne, Vienna, Koblenz, Berlin, Belgrade, Munich, Salzburg, Basel, Brig, Milan, Brussels, Paris.

Tram 1 will take you to the centre, Korenmarkt. Tourist information is at Botermarkt Crypt, Town Hall (Tel. 091 253641 and 241555) April to 8 November: Mon.–Sun.: 9.30 a.m.–6.30 p.m. 9 November to March: Mon.–Sun.: 9.30 a.m.–4.30 p.m.

All the sights are central and within easy walking distance of one another. The main sights are: the CATHEDRAL OF ST BAVO, containing Van Eyck's, 'The Mystic Lamb'; next door is the BELFRY, 'S'GRAVENSTEEN' – the twelfth-century FLEMISH COUNTS' CASTLE – and the guildhouses by Graslei. As the youth hostel closed down you are limited to pensions or the university halls of residence during holidays which are at Stalhof 6 (Tel. 220911), just off Overpoortstraat (open 24 hours, all single rooms). The university at Overpoortstraat is also your best bet for eats and nightlife, and has the added advantage of being near the station – take bus 9, 70, 71 or 90. There is camping at Camping Blaarmeersen, Zuiderlaan 12 (Tel. 215399), bus 51, 52 or 53 to the Europaburg, then bus 38, or a 30-minute walk from St Pieter's Station.

CITY PHONE CODE: 091.

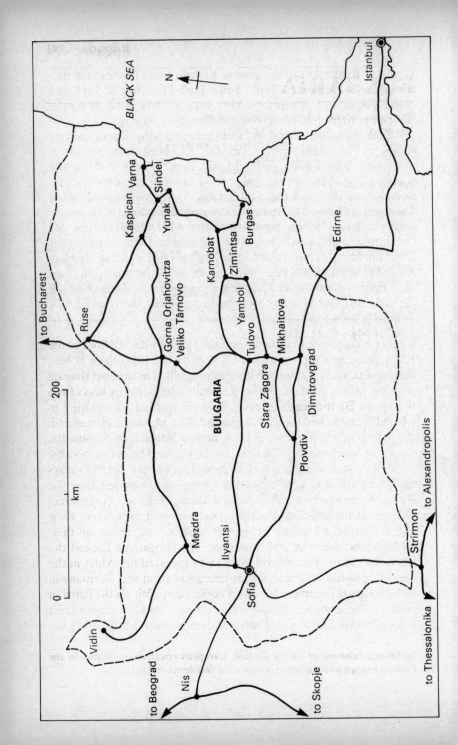

BULGARIA

Entry requirements	Passport and visa
Population	9,300,000
Capital	Sofia (pop.: 1,000,000+)
Currency	Leva
	£1 = approx. 43 leva
Political system	Republic
Religion	Eastern Orthodox
Language	Bulgarian (Russian widely spoken; some German, French and English understood)
Public holidays	1 Jan.; 1, 2 May; 9, 10 Sept.
International dialling codes	From UK 010 + 359 + number
	From USA 011 + 359 + number
	To UK 00 + 44 + number
	To USA 00 + 1 + number

Every year, swarms of tourists from East and West alike flock to the Black Sea coast for the sun. Few venture far from their hotels, leaving much of the country's interior unspoilt. The original Bulgars were an Asiatic tribe who were eventually conquered by Slavs from the north. By the tenth century, Bulgaria had her own empire in which literature and the arts flourished. This process continued till the fourteenth century, when trade helped Bulgaria to become the leader in south-eastern Europe. In 1396, the Ottomans became worried at what was going on and moved in. For the next 500 years they hung about to keep a check on things, and only left after the Russo-Turkish war of 1877 obliged them to do so. Fortunately during this long period the Bulgarians managed to preserve their native culture by giving refuge to writers and artists in their monasteries, many of which survive. The Bulgarians backed the losing side in the First World War, and supported the Allies in the Second. Shortly after the Soviet liberation from the Germans in 1944, Bulgaria became a Socialist People's Republic, in the Russian mould. The ousting, during 1989, of the hard-line communist leader, Todor Zhivkov, led towards democratic reforms. With the

Additional information on all Eastern European countries contained in the *Eastern Europe* and *Europe – Grand Tour* factsheets (see p.13).

emergence of political parties and the free elections of summer 1990, Bulgaria followed the trend in other Eastern European countries, but with the reformed and renamed communists holding power. With new freedoms, ethnic tension between the Bulgarians and the formerly repressed Turkish Muslim minority occurred. Prices here are still relatively low but rising fast, and hard currency buys the traveller less each month.

BULGARIAN STATE RAILWAYS (BDZ)

Trains tend to be overcrowded and slow in Bulgaria. Occasionally things come together and they run on time, but this is the exception rather than the rule. There are three types of trains: express (Ekspresen), fast (Brzi), and slow (Putnichki). Avoid the latter at all costs. Unfortunately, BIJ only run as far as Sofia. In theory, it should be possible to cross the country to the Black Sea coast and return again late the same day – trains leave Sofia early every morning, arriving at Burgas in the early afternoon. In practice, there are often delays at intermediate stations. Whenever possible, buy your ticket at least a day before setting off, reservations are compulsory on most expresses, or arrive early at the station to be sure of a seat. An alternative would be to take the overnight sleeper trains. Fortunately for eurorailers, Sofia is not too far across the Yugoslavian border: take an express from Belgrade to Dimitrovgrad, at the border, then the normal fare to Sofia. During 1992, many of the services between Bulgaria and Yugoslavia were suspended due to the civil war. The situation in 1993 will affect the services. Try to buy the ticket before getting the train, if possible elsewhere in other Eastern countries, as the fare charged on board is higher. Bulgaria is now part of Inter-Rail.

TRAIN INFORMATION

Few of the staff speak English, so you might find German and French more helpful. Timetables are given in the Cyrillic alphabet, but there is a Latin equivalent shown against international trains. If you're stuck, try: 'Ot koi peron zaminava vlaka za . . . ?' (From which platform does the train to . . . leave?) Depend on your Thomas Cook European Timetable for most of the time.

• **Reservations:** To be sure of a seat you'll have to reserve at least one day in advance. Reservations are obligatory on international expresses, but are not available on the Sofia–Istanbul leg of the Munich express. They can be made through Balkantourist or RILA offices. They may be available for foreign travellers at stations by this year.

• **Night travel:** All couchettes and sleepers are operated by the state railways and fall well short of Western standards.

• **Eating on trains:** There's either a buffet car or mini-bar on all fast trains.

TOURIST INFORMATION

There are Balkantourist offices in nearly every large town. They answer all your travel and accommodation problems as well as giving out tourist information. With the recent political upheaval some street names have changed.

• **ISIC bonuses:** With an ISIC card (obtainable from ORBITA Youth Travel Bureau, 45a Boulevard Stambolijski, Sofia), cheap entrance charges to many museums and galleries are available.

• **Money matters:** 1 leva = 100 stotinki.
Banking hours are 8 a.m.–12 noon. Visitors to Bulgaria receive a bonus when they change cash or traveller's cheques at Balkantourist exchange bureaux. As usual, forget the blackmarketeers; you risk being ripped off.

• **Shops:** Open 9 a.m.–8 p.m. with a siesta on Monday from 1 p.m.–2 p.m. Corecom are the hard currency shops; some Bulgarian goods can be bought here.

• **Museums:** Tend to shut on Mondays, but there's no fixed pattern; opening times also tend to vary.

• **Language:** Like the Russian language, Bulgarian is written with the Cyrillic alphabet, with some variations.

CYRILLIC ALPHABET	ENGLISH EQUIVALENT	SOUND VALUE	CYRILLIC ALPHABET	ENGLISH EQUIVALENT	SOUND VALUE
А а	A	for **Anglia**	П п	P	for **Park**
Б б	B	for **Bed**	Р р	R	for **Road**
В в	V	for **Vault**	С с	S	for **Soft**
Г г	G	for **Garage**	Т т	T	for **Trail**
Д д	D	for **Day**	У у	Ou	for **Cool**
Е е	E	for **Engine**	Ф ф	F	for **Fair**
Ж ж	Zh	for **Azure**	Х х	H	for **Hot**
З з	Z	for **Zebra**	Ц ц	Ts	for **Tsar**
И и	I	for **In**	Ч ч	Ch	for **Cheese**
Й й	Y	for **Yes**	Ш ш	Sh	for **Ship**
К к	K	for **Kerb**	Щ щ	Sht	for **Ashtray**
Л л	L	for **Lip**	Ъ ъ	U	for **Under**
М м	M	for **Morris**	Ь ь	J	for **Yodel**
Н н	N	for **Nut**	Ю ю	Yu	for **You**
О о	O	for **Austin**	Я я	Ya	for **Yard**

It is also useful to remember that in Bulgaria a nod means 'No' (Ne), and that a horizontal shake means 'Yes' (Da).

SLEEPING

When dealing with Balkantourist offices, bear in mind that they always try to fill up their own hotels first. Ask for a room in a private home whenever possible, as they're always a lot cheaper and more interesting. If you decide to bypass the tourist office and take up a local on the offer of a room, you're still supposed to register this with the police. There's no real need to do this if you've already got a couple of official stamps on the card you were given at the border. Be careful here, for if you cannot account for several nights, you could still face a fine. As time goes on, this bureaucracy is diminishing, and you probably will not be bothered. ORBITA, the student travel service, will find you a cheap bed in one of their hostels any time between mid-July and mid-September. For advance bookings write to International Tourist Relations, ORBITA Youth Travel Office, 45a Boulevard Stambolijski, Sofia. Camping costs about £1.50/$2.70 per tent and similar per person on any of the hundred or so official campsites. Freelance camping is illegal, with a fine if caught. Most accommodation still has to be paid for in hard currency.

EATING AND NIGHTLIFE

Eat as much as you can in Bulgaria as food is tasty and cheap. National dishes have a strong Turkish influence, with lamb and pork as the most common meats. Try haiduchki kebab (lamb cooked with onions, white wine and pepper) or one of their wonderful meat and vegetable dishes, slowly cooked in an earthenware pot, known as gyuvech. You cannot go wrong with any of the charcoal-roasted meat dishes with fresh salad. Yoghurt originated here and the Bulgarians are addicted to it, the thick sheep's milk type is particularly good, but not always available. Their ice cream is excellent, too. Vegetarian travellers should try shopska salad, vegetarian versions of gyuvech, or one of several aubergine dishes, including iman bayaldu. For drinks try any slivova, a spirit made from plums. Bulgarian wine has become well known in the West, and can be enjoyed cheaply here. Avoid the Bulgarian beer, it has little to recommend it. Upset stomachs are not uncommon when in Bulgaria and very few loos supply paper, so bring plenty with you!

Most Bulgarian towns have at least one theatre, several cities having open-air ones. A range of plays, operas and ballet can be seen. See the local Balkantourist office for details and tickets. They will also give information on arranged folklore events. Also look out for occasional rock concerts with local bands.

Sofia

The 5,000-year-old city of Sofia lies in the middle of the Balkan peninsula. It's got a lot going for it: it's the 'greenest city in Europe', has skiing (from December to April) less than half an hour away, and has some fascinating buildings – mosques, museums and churches which range from Byzantine to Roman, Turkish and Greek architecture. There are also many communist-inspired concrete piles around the city.

STATION INFORMATION

Sofia has one of the most modern and impressive stations you are ever likely to find with all facilities except showers. It is open from 4 a.m. to 1 a.m. and the Balkantourist money exchange office is open from 6 a.m.–10 p.m.

TOURIST INFORMATION

There is a Balkantourist office at the station with limited services, open 7 a.m.–10 p.m. The main office is on Dondukov Ulica 37 (open 7 a.m.–10 p.m. daily); they will find you a private room and general information, and guided tours at good rates. Take tram 1, 7 or 15 from the station and get off after four stops. The Balkantourist office is a short walk away, down the side of the large Central Department Store (TSUM). For train information telephone 311111.

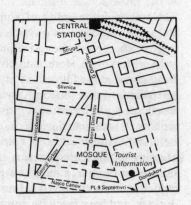

- **Addresses:**

CENTRAL POST OFFICE: Gurko Ulica 2, open daily 7 a.m.–8.30 p.m. Also poste restante here.

ORBITA – STUDENT TRAVEL OFFICE: Will grudgingly find you a room in a student hostel. 45a Boulevard Stambolijski (Tel. 879552), continue along Georgi Dimitrov to Pl. Lenin, then head down Stambolijski away from Balkan-Sheraton hotel. Open daily 9 a.m.–12 p.m. and 1 p.m.–5 p.m., but times unreliable.

RILA: International Railway Bureau, Gurko Ulica 5 (Tel. 870777). All tickets for international journeys, except those wanted for today's date, can be bought here. Open daily 8 a.m.–11.30 a.m., 12 noon–4 p.m. Make sure you have your exchange forms with you.

UK EMBASSY: 65 Boulevard Tolbuhin (Tel. 885361).

US EMBASSY: 1a Boulevard Stambolijski (Tel. 884801).

24-HOUR CHEMIST: Alabin Ulica 29 (Tel. 879029).

CITY TELEPHONE CODE: 02.

• **Getting about:** The city buses and trams are reasonably priced. Buy your tickets in advance from the special kiosks, and also grocery stalls. The main area worth seeing, however, is easily walked around. A metro system is under construction, expect changes to bus/tram routes as more sections are opened.

SEEING

The two main churches of Sofia are the twentieth-century, neo-Byzantine ALEXANDER NEVSKY, and the sixth-century, early Byzantine ST SOPHIA on Nevski Square. The former, topped with its golden domes, is dedicated to the Russians who fell liberating Bulgaria from the Ottoman Empire. The fascinating crypt is stuffed full of beautiful icons from all over the country (closed Tues.). Also worth seeing is the BOYANA CHURCH, at the foot of Mount Vitosha, with its restored medieval frescos. In the courtyard of the Sheraton hotel is the fourth-century ST GEORGE ROTUNDA, the oldest standing building in Sofia. Built during the late Roman period, it has been used as both church amd mosque. The St George and St Sophia churches are both closed for restoration, for an unspecified length of time, and have been for some time.

The church of SAINT PETKA SAMARDZHIYSKA is situated below street level, built in the fourteenth century, in a plain style, so as not to upset the Ottoman conquerors.

The NATIONAL ARCHAEOLOGICAL MUSEUM, 2 Boulevard Stambolijski (closed Mondays) is in the former Buyuk mosque, with Roman, Greek, Thracian and Turkish finds. The NATIONAL HISTORY MUSEUM at 2 Boulevard Vitosha, in the former Palace of Justice, contains the national treasures, including Thracian gold and ecclesiastical art plus much more. Probably the best one to visit, open 10.30 a.m.–6 p.m., Friday 2.30 p.m.–6.30 p.m., closed Mondays. This may move if the building regains its former function.

At one end of Boulevard Russki is the September 9th Square, with, on the South side, the MAUSOLEUM of GEORGI DIMITROV, the first leader of the former People's Republic. His body has now been buried elsewhere, and the building is due to be re-used or demolished. On the opposite side of the square is the former royal palace, built during the Ottoman empire. This now houses the NATIONAL ETHNOLOGICAL MUSEUM. The NATIONAL GALLERY OF

PAINTING AND SCULPTURE, also here, is due to be relocated to Alexander Nevski Square, open 9 a.m.–6 p.m., closed Monday.

On Georgi Dimitrov Boulevard there is the sixteenth-century BANYA BASHI MOSQUE, behind which is the run-down mineral baths building. Both of these have been recently undergoing renovation, and will be opened in the next few years. Opposite the mosque is the HALI market hall, built in the National Revival style in 1910; due to 'restoration' the inside has been spoilt.

SLEEPING

Use either Balkantourist on Dondukov Ulica 37 or ORBITA for private accommodation and expect to pay 100 leva for a double through Balkantourist, and less through ORBITA. Do not be surprised if Balkantourist give you the keys of the house, and there is no one there, and be aware that your host will probably not speak English. If you're arriving late and these offices are shut, stay in the station and 'look lost'. You'll find locals coming up to you and offering a place in their house for about 50 leva a person. People do halve the price by *discreetly* paying them in hard currency (sterling, dollars, marks, francs). If you want hotel accommodation, and Balkantourist is closed, go to the hotels directly. If the trend in Bulgaria follows that in other Eastern European countries, expect the cost of accommodation to soar.

ORBITA Student Hostel, Anton Ivanov 76 (Tel. 652952). This official students' residence (you'll need ISIC) is OK and not too far out from the centre, tram 2 or 9 to road junction of Anton Ivanov and Georgi Trajkov. There are several hostels in the Vitosha National Park. Book via the PIRIN agency at 30 Stambolijska Boulevard, who will give you directions.

Worth a try is Hotel Bulgaria at 4 Boulevard Ruski, near the Dimitrov Mausoleum (Tel. 871977) or Hotel Slavia at Ulica Sofijski Geroi 2 (Tel. 525551), tram 13 from station, about three stops down General Totleben. Be warned, prices are rising rapidly, and former cheap hotels suddenly become four-star ones.

If things look desperate, make your way to the university, set in a park off Boulevard Lenin (trams 1, 2, 7, 9, 14 and 18, then change to 4 or 10) and ask around for a student to let you share.

Camping Vrana (Tel. 781213) is on Boulevard Lenin and offers campsites and bungalows. Bus 313, 213 or 305 from station and then bus 5 or 6. Another site is Cherniya Kos (Tel. 571129); take tram 5 from the city to the end of the route, then bus 58 or 59. Bungalows are also available and the site is at the base of the mountains. Both sites open May–October.

EATING AND NIGHTLIFE

Food's cheap and good, and eating out in Sofia can cost far less than picnicking in Western Europe, although the price is expected to rise rapidly. Count on around 40 leva for a full and excellent meal. For Bulgarian specialities, try Koprivshtitsa, on 3 Boulevard Vitosha; for Russian food, try Krim, 2 Dobroudja St; and for German food, Berlin on 2 Boulevard V. Zaimor. There are new 'European' restaurants too, Forum and Havana – both centrally located. If you're really cutting corners, there are plenty of self-service places and an open-air market on Georgi Kirkov Ulica near the station. There are also Bulgarian-style fast food places on Vitosha.

Balkantourist fill you in on what shows and concerts are on. These tend to be more classical than popular, but the National Folk Ensemble put on some good things.

EXCURSIONS

If your long journey to Sofia has filled your lungs with smoke, hike up to the VITOSHA MOUNTAINS NATIONAL PARK, five miles from Sofia. Take tram 5 to its last stop, in the Kinyazevo district, then a short uphill walk to the cable car. Alternatively there are several bus routes up to Vitosha, ask at Balkantourist. The mountain air will do you good, and if you're feeling energetic ZLATNIY MOSTOVE, the glacial moraine, should provide the necessary challenge.

As Bulgaria is known for its monasteries another possible excursion from Sofia is to the RILA MONASTERY, around 75 miles south. Balkantourist arrange day trips; alternatively you can get yourself there, with difficulty, by bus from the Ouchna Koucha terminus, or by train to Kocherinovo station, then bus. Camping Bor is within walking distance of Rila. Ask at Balkantourist or the bus station for the services, and book accommodation in advance.

Plovdiv

Plovdiv is only two-and-a-half hours from Sofia by train and is Bulgaria's second largest city. Whilst much of this city is now industrialized, with many modern grey apartments, there is much worth seeing in the old town.

The main Balkantourist office is at 34 Moska Boulevard (Tel. 55 51 42), trolley-bus 2 from the railway station, to just over the river. Pick up a map here, but they are of little help with accommodation. Try Hotel Bulgaria, 13 Ul. Patriarch Eutimii (Tel. 22 60 64/22 55 64), upwards of 15 leva, or Hotel Leipzig (Tel. 23 22 50), 76 Rousski Blvd, similarly priced. The nearest campsite is Trakiya (Tel. 55 13 60), 4 km west, bus 4 or 23.

For food try the cafes around the 19 Noemvri Square, restaurants in the old town, or in the cheaper hotels. If you are really cutting cost there is also a self-service canteen on Maksim Gorki, and another opposite the railway station.

The main attractions are in the old town, located on the three hills which gave rise to Plovdiv's Roman name of Trimontium. Around the maze of cobbled streets rise houses of the National Revival Period and the remains of the old fortress walls. A restored portion of a ROMAN AMPHITHEATRE is situated in this area, and is now used for theatrical performances. Also in the old town is the ETHNOGRA-PHICAL MUSEUM and an Icon Exhibition. The partial remains of a Roman stadium may be seen in 19 Noemvri Square and other ROMAN REMAINS in the Tsentralen Square. Also in 19 Noemvri Square is the fifteenth-century DJOUMAYA MOSQUE. The ARCHAEO-LOGICAL MUSEUM, in Saedinenie Square has many relics of ancient Plovdiv. However much of its excellent collection of Thracian gold has recently been moved to the National History Museum in Sofia, and replaced with mock-ups.

Veliko Târnovo

The capital of Bulgaria until the Ottoman invasion of 1396, this old city on the Jantra river is stunning, and well worth the trouble of getting there. Take the train from Sofia towards Varna, and change at Gorna-Orjahovitza, use table 963 of Thomas Cook's timetable. You will arrive at the station, on the southern outskirts, at the foot of the Sveta Gora hill. Use one of the many buses to the centre.

Balkantourist is at 1 Vasil Levski (Tel. 2 18 36). Try Motel-camping Sveta Gora for tents and chalets, bus 14 from Balkan-tourist, or bus 15 from the station. A moderate price hotel in the old town is Hotel Jantra, 1 Velohova Zavera Square (Tel. 2 03 91).

The two main areas of interest are VAROSHA and TSAREVETS. Walk around these to get the best from them, but prepare for tired legs – it is not exactly flat. From Balkantourist head into Varosha, the old Ottoman town, armed with your map. The National Revival Museum is on the site of the Ottoman town hall, or Konak, with the Revolutionary Museum nearby, in a former Turkish prison. All museums are shut on Monday. Tsarevets, almost completely enclosed in a loop of the river, is approached by a stone causeway. The continuing digs turn up more each year. Parts of the impressive ramparts are on view, as are the Palace ruins. The views from Tsarevets make the uphill struggle, literally, well worthwhile, even for those not interested in old stones. One of the views, in an adjacent loop of the river is the Trapezica Hill. Here excavations of several of the old Bulgarian rulers' churches and other buildings is in progress.

Black Sea Coast – Varna and Bourgas

The two main cities are Varna and Bourgas, each reachable by around six trains a day from Sofia. Along the whole coast accommodation is difficult, if not impossible, to find during the summer, due to the increasing popularity of the area, both to eastern and western tourists. Varna has more going for it, with Roman remains, an early Christian basilica, and several reasonable museums. Buses can be taken from either Varna or Bourgas along the coast. If you are along the coast at the Sunny Beach resort and get bored of soaking up the rays, visit the Nessebur museum town. This is a UNESCO listed heritage centre, with ruins of over 40 medieval churches.

In Varna there is a Balkantourist office, open all year, opposite the railway station, at Ul Avram Gachev (Tel. 222389), open 8 a.m.–9 p.m. A hotel that is worth trying is the Mussala, 3 Ul Mussala (Tel. 223925). The nearest campsite is Galata, bus 17 to the end, then a short walk. Bourgas has a Balkantourist office at 2 Ul Purvi Mai (Tel. 45553). The cheapest hotel is probably Primonets at 1 Liliana Dimitrova (Tel. 44117).

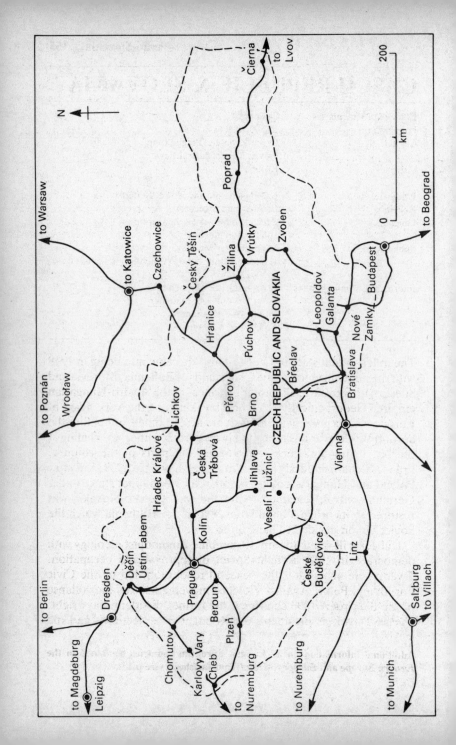

CZECH REPUBLIC & SLOVAKIA

Entry requirements	Passport
Population	15,500,000
Capital	Czech Republic: Prague (pop.: 1,500,000); Slovak Republic: Bratislava
Currency	Koruna £1 = 45.24 Kčs.
Political system	Czech Republic and Slovak Republic
Religions	Catholic and Protestant
Languages	Czech and Slovak (some German and English understood)
Public holidays	1 Jan.; Easter Monday; 1, 8 May; 5 July; 6 July (Czech Republic only); 25, 26, 31 Dec.
International dialling codes	From UK 010 + 42 + number From USA 01 + 42 + number To UK 00 + 44 + number To USA 00 + 1 + number

The independent state of Czecho-Slovakia came into being in 1918 with the political union of the Czech lands of Bohemia, Moravia and Silesia with Slovakia, all former provinces of the Austro-Hungarian empire. Geographically, Czecho-Slovakia is at the very heart of Europe – not a good place to be at the best of times, but before the Second World War it was positively disastrous. Hitler was chafing at the bit, demanding the German-speaking parts of the country. France, Britain and Italy agreed to let him have it in 1939, and after Poland and Hungary took parts too, a Slovak puppet state, under German control, remained. After the war, Czecho-Slovakia was restored to its original boundaries, except for Ruthenia which the Soviet Union decided to hang on to.

Dubček's ill-fated attempt to combine Communist ideology with democracy in 1968 brought Soviet disapproval and occupation. Twenty-one years later the peaceful revolution, led by the Civic Forum and Public Against Violence movements, saw the collapse of the old order. 1990 confirmed the former dissident playwright, Vaclav Havel, as president, and brought free elections, and the

Additional information on all Eastern European countries contained in the *Eastern Europe* and *Europe – Grand Tour* factsheets (see p.13).

departure of Soviet troops followed by June 1991. The slow and painful course of the country to a market-led economy was given a jolt in June 1992, when the election result prompted the Slovaks to form their own government in Bratislava, and to declare Slovakia an independent nation. This will have considerable economic repercussions, so expect the exchange rate and other facilities to be constantly changing.

CZECHOSLOVAK STATE RAILWAYS
(Československé státní dráhy, ČSD)

The service is a hot contender for the title of slowest in Europe. Like Britain, they have their own 125 – the only trouble is it's 12.5 m.p.h. However, the system is relatively dense, and so most places can be reached by rail. Trains are frequent and tickets are sold according to the speed of the train. Don't cut corners here as it's generally recognized that even buses are faster than the expresses. Go for the fastest possible (Expresní or Rychlík). Unfortunately, these require seat reservations and supplements, and that may mean queues. Generally avoid travel on Friday and Sunday afternoons. Price rises in the last years mean that rail travel is not as cheap as it once was. However, since 1990 Inter-Rail has included Czecho-Slovakia.

TRAIN INFORMATION

Take it for granted that the staff will be friendly but won't speak English at information offices so have the German vocabulary at the ready. If you still have no success, try: 'Z kterého nástupiště odjíždí . . . vlak do . . . ?' (From which platform does the train to . . . leave?). However, there are generally plenty of timetable boards available, if a bit confusing. Express trains are marked in bold or red letters, Arrival – Příjezd/Prichod, Departure – Odjezd/Odchod (Czech/Slovak languages). A lot of the left-luggage lockers in the main towns are vandalized – it's not that you've got the combination wrong. The left-luggage offices normally cost between 5–10 Kčs.

• **Reservations:** Try to reserve well ahead of time to be sure of a seat, as trains are always busy. This is obligatory on some expresses marked with an R in a box, or míst. Use the ARES office located at

120 stations. If you are going on to Hungary, it is essential to specify which of the routes you are taking and get your ticket from the appropriate counter. The crossing points are Štúrovo and Komárom.

• **Night travel:** Sleepers and couchettes are operated by the state railways and run on all long journeys. Avoid sleepers as they tend to be expensive. Beware, numerous thefts from couchette compartments on International routes have been reported in recent years.

• **Eating on trains:** There's either a restaurant car or buffet on a few selected fast trains.

• **Rover tickets:** The European East pass is available in North America from several outlets; this is also valid here.

• **Scenic trips:** The lines in and around the High Tatras; between Margecany and Brezno; along the Hailec and Hron rivers; along the Labe river between Lovosice and Děčín; and along the Berounka river south-west of Prague.

TOURIST INFORMATION

The official agency is Čedok. They suggest tours and supply local information. The student travel offices (CKM) are staffed by students and issue ISIC and IYHF cards. They are normally very good.

• **ISIC bonuses:** 25 per cent off East European train fares, discounts at some museums.

• **Money matters:** 1 koruna (Kčs) = 100 hellers (hal).
Banking hours are Mon.–Fri.: 8 a.m.–3 or 4 p.m. There is no longer any minimum currency exchange and the black market has died down. Avoid the remains of the black market; you will be ripped off, and are likely to be given worthless Polish Zloties, not Koruna. Private exchange offices are now flourishing, permitted under new laws.

• **Post offices:** Open from 8 a.m. to 6 p.m.

• **Shops:** Follow the usual pattern, opening at 9 a.m. and shutting at 6 p.m. on weekdays and at noon on Saturdays.

• **Museums:** Open Tues.–Sun.: 10 a.m.–5 p.m. Generally closed Mondays.

SLEEPING

Despite the revolution, the accommodation situation has not really improved. This is due to increased demand and lack of infrastructure; however, the situation will improve as new developments are financed. The prices below are likely to be subject to inflation during 1993. If booking advance accommodation through Čedok in London (address in introduction), expect it to take 14 days, minimum. They also will not book student hostel and budget accommodation. For these, advance booking use CKM (address in Prague section, p.165), but allow for a long wait and a booking fee. In Vienna, their office is at Parkring 12 (Tel. 513 2609). Hotels are graded from C (one-star) to deluxe A (five-star). The rare 2-star doubles should cost about 400 Kčs per night, though bargains can still be found outside the main towns. Make sure you have agreed beforehand on the cost. In a country where the main languages are Czech and Slovak, the second Russian and the third German, your chances of winning an argument in English are somewhat minimal. The Czechs and Slovaks are keen campers. There are over 400 sites in the country and they average 150 Kčs.

Staying at a private home also works out a lot cheaper than hotels, though you may have to commit to a minimum of three nights, but this practice is ending. In Prague, Pragotur are the main official agency for this form of accommodation. New private agencies are coming forward to supplement Pragotur and Čedok.

Apart from Čedok offices, it's also possible to find accommodation through the student travel offices (CKM) during July and August. In Prague avoid the AVE accommodation service in the station as they charge a hefty commission. It is now possible to arrange private accommodation privately at the stations; this can be a bargain; but take the usual precautions. Payment in this case is still usually required in Deutsch Marks or US dollars.

Dormitories (internáty or koleje) are converted into youth hostels (střediska), many of which have good two-bedded rooms from only 90 Kčs to 250 Kčs per person on an IYHF card, more without.

There has been an increase in the numbers of independent hostels in the main centres. Finding out about these may be a problem, as Čedok, and other agencies will direct you to their own hostels. Look in the stations for notices, or ask fellow travellers.

EATING AND NIGHTLIFE

Food is generally pretty uninspiring: lots of pork and few salads and veggies. Dinner is eaten early. If you go after 8.30 p.m. you're likely to have very little choice. Specialities include zeleninová (a vegetable and cream soup) and any dish made from pork (vepřové). For cheap meals, try any of the self-service stand-up restaurants (automaty). A lot of the grade-one and -two restaurants have dancing, but apart from this things are very quiet by Western standards. Cedok should be able to help out on what open-air concerts, etc., there might be. The best way to find out what's happening is to ask any young locals. They will probably advise you to head towards a wine bar (vinárna) or beer hall (pivnice) where most young people meet. Try Budvar, Prazdroj or any other beer you're recommended, for not only is Czecho-Slovak beer among the best in Europe, it's also the cheapest.

Slovakia

The eastern republic of Slovakia occupies around 40 per cent of former Czechoslovakia. The people have their own strong personality, quite different from the Czech's. Much of the region is unspoilt mountains and forests, and ideal for hiking, with many castles scattered around, as well as for visiting the many small towns. From Bratislava head up into the Lesser Carpathian Mountains, an area with many vineyards. To the north of Slovakia are the Low Tatras, with the High Tatras further east. These make up the second highest mountain range in Europe, after the Alps. Take the train from Prague to Poprad-Tatry, a mainly industrialized town, then the local trains up into the hills. Trains go to Starý Smokovec, where there is a Youth Hostel, and to Tatranska Lomnica, where there is a camping site to base yourself at. Use Thomas Cook's Tables 885 to 887, to get around the region.

Bratislava

The largest city and capital of Slovakia was also, for three centuries, the capital of the Hungarian Kingdom, when it was known as Pozsony. Situated on the Danube, close to both the Austrian and Hungarian borders, and influenced by all three countries, Bratislava may be reached by train and boat from both Budapest and Vienna, the journey from Vienna taking around an hour by either means. Despite being an essentially modern city, it still has over 400 historically interesting buildings.

TOURIST INFORMATION

Čedok is at Jesenského 1–7 (Tel. 499 613), open Mon.–Fri., 9 a.m.–5 p.m., Sat. 9 a.m.–12 p.m. The student agency, CKM, is at Hviezdoslavovo námesti 16 (Tel. 331 607), open Mon.–Fri., 9 a.m.–4.30 p.m. The Bratislava Information Service (BIS), is at Laurinská 1, in the old town centre (Tel. 333 715/334 325), open Mon.–Fri. 8 a.m.–4.30 p.m., Sat. 8 a.m.–1 p.m. BIS publish a leaflet Kam v Bratislave (Where to Go), with English information sections. They also speak some English here. Tram 13 from the station gets you into the area of all three agencies. There are boards around town, with maps on to help you out, although street names sometimes differ from those printed.

- **Addresses:**

US CONSULATE: Hviezdoslavovo námesti 4 (Tel. 330 861).
EXCHANGE OFFICES: Several banks in námesti SNP, also at post office in town centre.

SLEEPING

Try Čedok or CKM for accommodation suggestions, or look at the station for posters on private accommodation and hostels. The CKM hostel Sputnik is at Drieňová 14 (Tel. 234 340/238 065). Take tram 8 from the centre to the lake on the outskirts. There is a YMCA Interpoint hostel at Karpatska 2 (Tel. 493 267), open from mid-July to mid-August. Walk from the station to Malinovskeho Street, then turn left. The hostel is five minutes' walk from here and costs 150 Kčs. Two other hostels to try are the Belojansova and the

Bernolak. For camping, take trams 2 or 4 to the last stop at Zlaté Piesky (Tel. 65170/60578). These are pleasant lakeside sites, which also offer bungalows for rent.

FOOD AND DRINK

As with the rest of Czecho-Slovakia, try the wine bars or beer halls for food. Reputedly the largest beer hall in Central Europe is Stará Sladouňa, on Cintorinska. The wine bar, Velki Frantiskani at Dibrivova is in an old cellar, offering good local food and occasional folk music. The local Slovakian wine is worth a try. For cheap fast-food and drink, try Gurrian at Poštova Str, in the city centre.

SEEING

The city is dominated by the thirteenth-century BRATISLAVA CASTLE, burnt out in 1811 by Napoleon, and rebuilt after the war. Now the home of the Slovak parliament, and the SLOVAK NATIONAL MUSEUM, featuring Slovakian history and archaeology. ST MARTIN'S CATHEDRAL, with a distinctive golden crown on its tower, dates from the fourteenth century and is the resting place of several Austro-Hungarian kings and queens. The OLD TOWN HALL, fifteenth-century, now houses the CITY MUSEUM, with an interesting torture hall. A museum of viniculture is nearby. The SLOVAK NATIONAL MUSEUM with geological and natural history collections is at Vajanského nábr, near the Danube. The TOWN GALLERY in the Mirbachov Palace at Franiškánske námestie, has seventeenth- to nineteenth-century art on display. The MUSEUM OF ARMS AND FORTI-FICATION is in the St Michael's Tower, the only remaining tower of four original medieval ones. Close by is the PHARMACY MUSEUM and the Palaces where Mozart and Liszt played their early concerts. A complete contrast is the ultra-modern SNP bridge, spanning the river below the castle. A good view can be had from the restaurant at the top, but do not eat there.

• **Excursions from Bratislava:** There are boat trips to the DEVIN CASTLE ruins, dating from the ninth century, once an impressive fortress of the Holy Roman Empire. The castle is near the border point of Austria, Slovakia and Moravia. Take the boat from Osobne pristavisko, on the river bank, running on Saturdays and Sundays in summer. Trips by boat are also available in summer to Vienna and Budapest.

Czech Republic

The western Czech republic comprises the regions of Bohemia and Moravia, and includes the capital Prague, as well as the two beer towns of Pilsen and České Budéjovice.

Brno

The capital of Moravia and Czecho-Slovakia's third city has quite a lot to offer. A royal city, founded in the thirteenth century, on the rail line between Prague and Bratislava.

The Čedok office at Divadelní 3 (Tel. 23166), and CKM at Česká 11 (Tel. 23641), are your best bets for accommodation suggestions. The city gets filled up, with several exhibitions during the year. The summer student hostels are at Purkyňova 93 and Kohontova 55; apply to the CKM office. The nearest camping site is the Obora, 15 km from Brno (Tel. 791105), not easily reached by public transport. Private accommodation may be your best bet.

The ŠPILBERK CASTLE, founded 1277, and rebuilt in the eighteenth century, houses the MUNICIPAL MUSEUM, and ART GALLERY. The whole of the castle is now closed for restoration, for several years. See the display of torture instruments in the museum. Dominating the city and castle is the CATHEDRAL OF ST PETER AND ST PAUL. Also worth seeing is the OLD TOWN HALL and the CAPUCHIN MONASTERY, complete with mummified monks on display. Also see the colourful outdoor CABBAGE MARKET.

České Budéjovice

Like Pilsen, this town is renowned for its beer – Budvar or Budweiser – and its salt trade, and is located in the beautiful region of south Bohemia. It may be reached from Prague by a couple of trains a day, taking around two hours. The more frequent buses from Prague may be a better bet. Budéjovice was founded in 1265 as a Royal Borough, at the strategic meeting point of the Vltava and Malše rivers.

The town is centred on the large Zizkova nàm square, surrounded by painted baroque buildings. The TOWN HALL, dating from 1555, was modified in the early eighteenth century, to give its current frontage. The 72-metre high BLACK TOWER, also on this square, dates from the sixteenth century, built as a watch tower and belfry, for the ST NICHOLAS church. The tower is a good viewpoint, open Tues.–Sun., 10 a.m.–4 p.m. Close to the Malše river bank are the remains of the original gothic city defences.

Čedok is based on the Zizkova Square, but they may not prove to be too helpful with accommodation suggestions, so during the summer try CKM at Osvobození 14. The Stromovka campsite (Tel. 38308) is on Na Dlouché lovka, open April–October. The large Masné Krámy beer hall is lively and is an ideal place for trying the local beer, and to get some basic food if hungry.

Pilsen (Plzeň)

Basically, this is an ugly, uninspiring place, the regional centre of western Bohemia, but if you're a beer-fan it's pilgrimage country, for this is the birthplace of Pilsner Urquell beer. See the BURGHER'S BREWERY, the BREWING MUSEUM on Roosevelt St. The ABBEY OF THE VIRGIN MARY and ST BARTHOLOMEW'S CHURCH are the town's other saving graces.

Čedok is close to the town centre, on the corner of Sedláckova and Prešková, open Mon.–Fri., 9 a.m.–6 p.m. (shuts for lunch). No IYHF hostel, the nearest campsite is Bílá Hora (Tel. 35611/62850), also lets chalets; take bus 20 from the centre. For hotels ask at Čedok.

Prague (Praha)

Prague, the fourteenth-century capital of the Holy Roman Empire, is where to go if you want to step back into medieval life and have all your preconceptions of an Eastern European city shattered. As far as sights are concerned, many consider Prague to be on a par with, if not better than, Paris, London or Rome. It lies in western Bohemia and is a riot of bridges, parks, hills and a fascinating array of architectural styles. Prague is the capital of Bohemia, the Czech Republic and the Czecho-Slovak Federative Republic.

STATION FACILITIES

There are three main stations in Prague: Praha–Wilson (or Hlavní), Masarykovo and Holešovice. The first two are located close to the centre, with the latter to the north, across the Vltava river. Wilson (Hlavní) is used by domestic services and international trains to Germany, Poland, the Soviet Union and Hungary; Masarykovo is mainly for domestic services. Holešovice has international trains for Germany, the Soviet Union and Hungary. Some trains from Germany call at Holešovice before getting to Wilson (Hlavní). All these stations are served by the metro system, and have the usual facilities, including an influx of exchange offices. The left luggage facilities at Holešovice are available 24 hours. Take care when setting locker combinations and with left luggage receipts: theft at stations is increasingly common.

TOURIST INFORMATION

There is a tourist information office in the main concourse at Wilson (Hlavní) station, which hands out basic information. The AVE office, also at the station, will also help out with accommodation, but charge a hefty commission.

Alternatively, from the main station (Praha–Wilson) or Praha–Masarykovo, walk up Hybernská to the centre. The Prague Information Service is at Na Příkopě 20 (Tel. 54 4444). They'll give you maps, 'what's on' and general information (open Mon.–Fri.: 8 a.m.–8 p.m., Sat.: 8 a.m.–noon). Čedok, the Czecho-Slovak national travel organization has two main offices: Na Příkopě 18

(Tel. 2127111) change money and operate a room-finding service round the corner at Panská 5 (open Mon.–Fri.: 8 a.m.–10 p.m., Sat.: 8 a.m.–8 p.m., Sun.: 8 a.m.–5 p.m.), Tel. 227004 or 225657.

There are also a number of privately run 'tourist offices' set up around the city. AVE Agency will book accommodation ahead.

● **Addresses:**
POST OFFICE: Jindřišská 14, 24-hour service. Also poste restante here. International phone calls from here.
CKM (the student agency): Žitná ulice 12, 12105 Prague 2. Open Mon.–Fri.: 8 a.m.–10 a.m., 1 p.m.–5 p.m. (Tel. 299941).
FIRST AID: Jungmannová 14 (Tel. 247771).
POLYCLINIC FOR FOREIGNERS: Karlovo náměstí 32 (Tel. 299381).
UK EMBASSY: Thunovská Ulice 14, Malá Strana.
US EMBASSY: Tržiště 15, Malá Strana (Tel. 536641).
CANADIAN EMBASSY: Hradčany, Mickiewiczova 6 (Tel. 326941).
PRAGOTUR: U Obecního domu 2; also operate a room-finding service. Open Mon.–Fri.: 8 a.m.–8.30 p.m., Sat.: 9.15 a.m.–6 p.m., Sun.: 8.30 a.m.–3 p.m. (Tel. 231700).
INFORMATION SERVICES: Na Příkopě 20 (Tel. 544444); Panská 4 (Tel. 223411).

● **Getting about:** The underground is efficient and cheap, and the bus and tram network covers every corner of the city. Buy tickets in advance from news-stands, hotels, machines and tobacconists and stamp them on the buses. There is a special tourist ticket valid for 24 hours and giving unlimited travel on trams, buses, metro and Petőíu funicular for 25 Kčs. Two-, three-, four- and five-day passes are also available; the one-day one can be purchased from the red ticket machines at metro stations in the city centre. The yellow machines sell single tickets for 8 Kčs. Be warned, the on-the-spot fine for having the wrong ticket is high – 100 Kčs – and ignorance of the rules tends not to be accepted. Forget taxis altogether.

SEEING

Don't judge the city by its station. I nearly boarded the first train out again on my first visit, but it is in two halves – the platforms ancient, crowded and dirty, and the rest of it like an airport terminal. Had I done so, I'd have missed a city with as much to see and do in as Paris. Prague started off as five separate towns, and each one of them merits a visit: the New Town (Nové Město), the nineteenth-century commercial centre; the Old Town (Staré Město), medieval buildings and fascinating Jewish Quarter; the Lesser Town (Malá Strana), the baroque area of palaces and churches; Hradčany, the area round Prague Castle; and Vyšehrad, the ninth-century fortress-town opposite the castle. A good way to get your bearings is to take a boat trip on the Vltava. Leave from Vltava Quay in the New Town and rather than return by boat take metro line 3 from Palacky Bridge (Most Palackého).

● **Nové Město:** The main sights are WENCESLAS SQUARE, locally known as Václavské náměstí, the main boulevard, the NATIONAL MUSEUM and CHARLES SQUARE (Karlovo náměstí), the largest square in Prague with a park in its centre and the NEW TOWN HALL on its north side. Also DVOŘÁK'S MUSEUM, Ke Karlovu 20, is in this vicinity.

● **Staré Město:** The Old Town dates back to 1120 – and you can feel it. The POWDER TOWER, used to store gunpowder in the fifteenth century, gives a good view from the top, while the OLD TOWN SQUARE was at the centre of medieval Prague. Here is to be found the 1490 Astronomical Clock of the OLD TOWN HALL which performs every hour. Tour round the Town Hall, and then see the TÝN CHURCH on the east side of the square. This twin-Gothic-spired church has a baroque interior and dates from 1365.

The JEWISH QUARTER houses the oldest synagogue in Europe (1270) and the fifteenth-century JEWISH CEMETERY with its 12,000 tombstones piled on top of one another. The museum in KLAUS SYNAGOGUE tells of the extermination of Jews in the Second World War.

Bordering the New Town is the BETHLEHEM CHAPEL where the Czech hero John Hus preached, and the baroque CHARLES BRIDGE has superb views of the castle, the island of Kampa and the River Vltava.

● **Malá Strana:** The rich seventeenth- and eighteenth-century merchants spent their money on this town. The LESSER TOWN SQUARE and NERUDA ST are testament to that. ST NICHOLAS' CHURCH is the finest baroque building in Prague, and just north of it is the palace of the Habsburg general, Albrecht Wallenstein. Much of this area is undergoing restoration; scaffolding is everywhere.

• **Hradčany:** PRAGUE CASTLE today houses the Czech government, but it used to be the palace of the kings of Bohemia. Try to get on a tour round it. A good view over the city can be had from the adjacent terrace. Also in this 'royal city' is ST VITUS' CATHEDRAL which is quite incredible, and is certainly the most detailed Gothic church in central Europe, with amazing stained glass windows. The National Gallery is in the ŠTERNBERK PALACE in the castle square and has an excellent collection of French impressionists.

A charming walk can be taken down the GOLDEN LANE where the alchemists tried to turn their lead into gold. The STRAHOV MONASTERY, west of the castle, houses the Museum of Czech Literature and offers a good view over the whole of Prague.

• **Vyšehrad:** The VYŠEHRAD FORTRESS has in its grounds the eleventh-century Rotunda of St Martin, and in its cemetery Dvořák, Smetana, and other Czech 'greats' are buried.

If you have a couple of hours to spend, the Zoo in the north of the city at Troja (Tel. 84 14 41) is well worth a visit.

• **River Vltava:** Sightseeing trips on the river Vltava leave from the Jiraskuv Most quay and are well worth taking.

SLEEPING

This is your main headache in Prague. As the number of tourists has increased drastically, the situation has got worse. Čedok, Pragotur, AVE, KMC or a private arrangement are your best bets for finding a room (see above). Prepare yourself for the inevitable long queues and insist on somewhere central and cheap. They often charge a hefty commission. Private accommodation is cheaper, so ask for this or, better still, the student hostels. You will probably do best contacting the campsites yourself; you will be pleasantly surprised by the sites' quantity and quality. Get a list from Prague Information Service.

• **Hostels:** Student hostels charge from 500 Kčs a night. Go in person as official offices often charge hefty commissions. The Junior Hotel, at Žitná 12, charges less if you have an IYHF card. This hostel is often fully booked, and the staff unhelpful (Tel. 299941 or 292984). Also try the Sleep-In at Žitná 42. Čedok's hostels are booked through Panská 5 where there is a clean hostel serving breakfast and snacks. They don't make waves about unmarried couples, but cost more than the others.

Strahov, Spartakiádní Station. Reception opens at 10 a.m. (be there at about 8.30 a.m.).

Hotel Jarov, Kovĕvova 196 (Tel. 824641) is not terribly central (next to the Economics Institute), but pleasant. Tram 9 or 21. Try Intermat Sov, Vrbova 12333, metro to Smichovske nadrazi, the bus 198/196 for five stops. Not central but cheap.

• **Student Rooms:** Try Rooslieltova Kolej, Stonjnika 7, take tram 12, 5 or 7 from Holeservice Metro Station, to the Universal Exhibition site. This is a cheap stopover, and includes showers, bars and a night club.

• **1-star hotels:** Every year they get thinner on the ground, and those which are left all charge about the same rate. The cost of these has risen significantly over the last year. Hotel Balkan, Svornosti 28 (Tel. 540777) from 650 Kčs, offers good pub grub. The three botels moored on the River Vltava, which runs through Prague, are now expensive, and cramped. They are the Admiral (Tel. 548685), Albatros (Tel. 2316996) and the Racek (Tel. 759513 and 723241).

• **Private rooms:** Try Vĕra Hlaváčová Na Balkáně 126/2116 (Tel. 821008). Take tram 9 from Hlávni for the 15-minute ride to Stojovačí. Comfortable rooms with kitchen facilities and English-speaking hostess. NB: Don't be reluctant to accept offers from those selling rooms at the stations. Settle a price and go for it!

• **Camping:** There are several sites around Prague, try: Sokol Troja at Trojská 171 (Tel. 842 833), Sokol Dolní Počěrnice at Dolní Počernice Nár. hrdinu (Tel. 718 034) and Kotva at V ledáren 55 (Tel. 466085/461397). Ask for a full list and tram/bus details from Pragotur.

EATING AND NIGHTLIFE

Beer halls (pivnice) and wine cellars (vinárny) are dotted all over the city. These are safe bets for cheap food and drink, as are the stand-up snack places. Don't expect a huge menu, but what there is is usually OK. There are plenty of 'Automats' – self-service restaurants – in the Wenceslas Square area, which are good and cheap. On Wenceslas Square, try the Staropraška Rychta or the Halaligrill. Take advantage of the Czech beer while you can. Recommended are: U Prince, Old Town Square, opposite the

Town Hall: good but pricey in a wonderful setting; closed Thursdays. U. Fleku, Křemenova II, is much akin to a Munich beer hall, and comparatively cheap. Also, on Panská Street, the Free Press Jazz Club (very trendy), or U Kalicha on Na Bojišti 12, the local of author Jaroslav Hasek of 'The Good Soldier' fame. Berjozka Bistro, Na příkopě: a good Russian restaurant next to the Prague information service. Homesick Westerners could head for the pizzas, MTV and endless coffee of the American Hospitality Centre, off Wenceslas Square, at Malé hám. 14, open daily 10 a.m.–10 p.m.

The Prague Spring Festival (12 May–4 June) is a big draw for music- and drama-lovers. The monthly 'What's On' can be had from PIS, Na příkopě 20. The Laterna Magika, Národní 40, is a review of films, ballet and drama which deserves a mention, but you usually need reservations of up to a month.

The citizens of Prague love their ice-cream (zmrzlina), and everybody seems to be licking furiously away. One of the best ice-cream places we have found outside Italy is in Prague, on Vodičkova, in the shadow of the New Town Hall. You can join the queue outside on the pavement to buy one to enjoy in the nearby Charles Square (Karlovo náměstí) or queue up inside for a seat in this popular café.

Beer halls or wine cellars are the most likely places to meet Czech students. Try: U Malvaze, Karlova 10, big student dive, U Zelené Žáby or U Kalicha on Na Bojišti 12. The strongest beer can be found at U Supa at Celetná 22. At night, the places to be are the Old Town Square and Charles Bridge – both have illuminations and street entertainment.

• **Excursions from Prague:** Half an hour in the train is all it takes to get to the amazing fourteenth-century castle of KARLŠTEJN – Bohemia's finest example. Take the train from Smíchov Station – on the Metro. Visit Karlštejn as a day trip from Prague. The famous spa of KARLOVY VARY (Karlsbad) also makes an interesting trip. Trains to get there take about three hours. Čedok is at Tržiste 23. Another castle of note is KŘIVOKLÁT, medieval seat of Bohemia's kings, located above the Berountia river, a worthwhile sight in its own right. Take the train from Prague–Smíchov, change at Beroun, then on to Křivoklát.

Olomouc

Czecho-Slovakia boasts many beautiful historic towns, and Olomouc is one which you might consider visiting. The town is on the direct line from Praha–Hlavní, the journey taking around three-and-a-half hours. Olomouc became an important city in Moravia as early as the eleventh century, and today is a tourist's delight.

From the station, the centre is a 15-minute walk, and on several tram routes. Tourist information, Čedok is at Horní náměstí 2 (Tel. 28831), located in the city central square, providing the usual facilities. CKM is at Denisova 4 (Tel. 29009). Try these for accommodation suggestions, or in July and August the Studencentrum, at Křížkovského 14, may help to find a room. There is no campsite in the town, but half an hour away by train, in Šternberk, there is a site. If really stuck try sleeping out at the Smetanovy sady park. There are plenty of beer halls, wine cellars and restaurants, so there should be no problems. To meet local students try Mikulovská vinárna and U Trojice wine cellars, in the city centre.

The town is a protected urban reservation. The main sight is the superb twelfth-century ST WENCESLAW CATHEDRAL, with the PRZEMYSL CASTLE, ST ANN'S CHAPEL and CHAPTER DEANERY nearby. The Renaissance TOWN HALL is also worth a look, as are some of the buildings of the University, the second oldest in Czechoslovakia. A trip on bus 11 from the railway station will bring you to the Kopeček hill, with a good view of the town, and site of the seventeenth-century VIRGIN MARY CHURCH and MONASTERY.

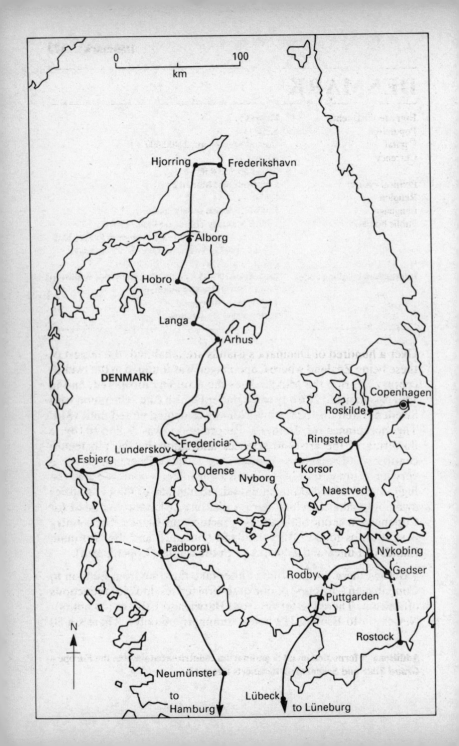

DENMARK

Entry requirements	Passport
Population	5,200,000
Capital	Copenhagen (pop.: 1,400,000 +)
Currency	Kroner
	£1 = approx. 9.89 kr.
Political system	Constitutional Monarchy
Religion	Lutheran
Language	Danish (English widely spoken)
Public holidays	1 Jan.; Maundy Thursday; Good Friday;
	Easter Sunday and Monday; Common Prayer Day
	(7 May, 1993); Ascension Day; Whit Monday;
	Constitution Day (5 Jun); 25, 26 Dec.
International dialling codes	From UK 010 + 45 + number (no area code required)
	From USA 011 + 45 + number
	To UK 009 + 44 + number
	To USA 009 + 1 + number

Over a hundred of Denmark's islands are inhabited, the largest of these being Zealand where Copenhagen was founded in the twelfth century. During the Middle Ages the economy prospered, and in 1397 Sweden and Norway came under Danish rule. The union with Sweden lasted till 1523, while Norway remained united until 1814. The acceptance of Luther's Reformation was followed by a flowering of the arts and sciences and culturally the nineteenth century was Denmark's 'Golden Age'. Today Denmark enjoys a very high standard of living; from a eurorailer's point of view, the high degree of social planning and the number of public facilities available make travelling here a pleasure, whether you head for Copenhagen or one of the smaller, picturesque islands. The country is split up as follows: the mainland (Jutland); and the two main islands of Funen and Zealand (with the capital, Copenhagen).

• **Getting there:** From Britain either take the train from London to Copenhagen (26 hours) or one of several ferries; look for reductions off-season. There are ferries from Harwich to Esbjerg (20 hours), Newcastle to Esbjerg (19 hours, summertime only). There's a 50

Additional information on all Scandinavian countries contained in the *Europe – Grand Tour* and *Scandinavia* factsheets (see p.13).

per cent reduction with an Inter-Rail on the Scandinavian Seaways DFDS ships.

DANISH STATE RAILWAYS
(Danske Statsbaner, DSB)

In Denmark you spend as much time on water as you do on land, when entire trains clamp down on to specially adapted ferries which connect the islands with one another and with mainland Sweden and Germany. With hourly intercity trains, they've had plenty of practice and have got the whole operation down to a fine art. There's a great feeling of camaraderie once you're on board. Passengers are free to get out and wander about. This is particularly the case on the Kalundborg–Århus crossing (3 hours); a more leisurely affair than the Great Belt (Storebaelt) crossing (1 hour). Work is underway on a fixed link for the Great Belt, with a combined motorway and rail bridge and tunnel. The rail link will open in 1993, cutting the crossing time to 10 minutes. The whole system runs efficiently with trains rarely running late.

The rail network is divided into four categories:

1. Lyntog (Lightning trains) L. Almost as luxurious as Eurocity and used on long hauls, such as Copenhagen to Frederikshavn. The new DSB IC3 intercity trains are now in service; they serve all major cities.

2. Intercity IC. Equally fast, serving the shorter distances between large towns.

3. Regionaltoget. Slower regional trains, connecting up the smaller towns with the main network.

4. S-tog. Copenhagen's underground, connecting up the city with the suburbs.

• **Inter-Rail bonuses:** See Appendix II.

• **Eurail bonuses:** The following services are free:

—Ferry crossings Århus to Kalundborg, Knudshoved to Halskov, Nyborg to Korsør, Fynshavn to Bøjden.

—Ferry crossings Rødby Faerge to Puttgarden (Germany).

—Ferry crossings operated by the Danish and Swedish State Railways between Helsingør and Helsingborg (Sweden).

—Ferry crossings operated by Stena Sessan Line between Frederikshavn and Gothenburg (Sweden).

Reduced fares:

—50 per cent reduction on the Danish Navigation Company, 'Øresund', on the hydrofoil between Copenhagen and Malmö.

—20 per cent reduction on the normal fares of the Steamship Company DFDS between Esbjerg–Harwich, Esbjerg–Newcastle, Esbjerg–Faroe Islands, Copenhagen–Oslo.

—30 per cent reduction on the normal fares of the Steamship Company KDS between Hirtshals and Kristiansand (Norway).

—50 per cent reduction on couchettes.

TRAIN INFORMATION

Timetables are dotted everywhere around the stations, and all the staff seem to speak fluent English. If you're spending some time in Denmark ask for the Køreplan, a timetable for all the ferries, trains and buses.

• **Reservations:** Are only compulsory on any IC or Lyntog train crossing the Great Belt between Sjaelland and Fyn (that is, from Korsør to Nyborg). The cost is 15 kr. on IC and 30 kr. on Lyntog trains. Reservations can also be made for other Lyntog and IC trains.

• **Night travel:** Couchettes/sleepers cost *relatively* less in Scandinavia than elsewhere in Europe. A couchette costs around 65 kr. and a bed in a two-berth sleeper approximately 165 kr. Within Denmark, they operate between Copenhagen and Esbjerg as well as to Struer and Frederikshavn and cost less than on international journeys.

• **Eating on trains:** There are no dining cars, even if you could afford them, though on L and IC trains there are buffets and trolleys selling snacks. The coffee is reasonably priced but the sandwiches are as expensive here as they are everywhere else. If you're starving, try to survive till you get aboard the ferries as they have self-service cafeterias. The Puttgarden-Rødby service usually does a good choice at reasonable prices.

If you're on an international crossing, don't forget to check out the duty-free shops. They have good prices for cheese, wine, cigarettes and chocolates. Don't forget that in Scandinavia, and especially in Norway, normal prices are high.

• **Scenic tips:** There's good coastline scenery if you're on your way to Frederikshavn from Copenhagen or vice versa. Take the route which goes via Odense and Fredericia. If you're heading for Stockholm from Copenhagen, your best route is to train it to Helsingør (1 hour) then take the ferry to Helsingborg (free on Inter-Rail).

• **Bikes:** You can rent out a bike in the summer at most of the larger stations, with the exception of Copenhagen, for 30 to 50 kr. per day, plus deposit between 100–200 kr. Ask at stations for leaflet 'Take a Train – Rent a Bike'.

• **Rover tickets:** The best ticket to go for is the Nordturist 'Scanrail' pass, which is valid in Denmark, Norway, Sweden and Finland for 21 days. It covers all rail services and the major ferry services between the countries, with reductions on some other inter-Island sailings. It costs about £151 second class and £203 first class. These tickets are available to people under 26 at a discount of 25 per cent. If you are travelling with at least three paying passengers (adults and children) there are discounts of between 20–40 per cent available on the Nordic Family Ticket. Available from Norwegian State Railways Bureau, 21 Cockspur Street, London (Tel. 071–930 6666). Monthly tickets for unlimited travel on Danish domestic rail and ferry services cost 1,340 kr. In Denmark children under 4 travel free and those between 4 and 12 at half price.

TOURIST INFORMATION

In Denmark the tourist offices are the best in Europe, particularly for the under 26s. They are both friendly and efficient, and if every tourist board was like them we would be out of a job.

If you tune in a radio to Radio Denmark programme 1 on 90.8 MHz at 8.10 a.m., Mondays–Fridays, you'll hear news in English, and information about exhibitions and other events in Copenhagen for that day.

• **ISIC bonuses:** 50 per cent reductions on films, theatres and museums. For further information, contact DIS Skindergade 28, Copenhagen.

• **Money matters:** 1 kroner (kr.) = 100 øre.
Banking hours are Mon., Tues., Wed., Fri.: 9.30 a.m.–4 p.m., Thurs.: 9.30 a.m.–6 p.m. Bank commission varies from 10–18 kr. For late-night service there are facilities at Central Station and Tivoli Park in Copenhagen. Some tourist offices may exchange money out of banking hours. Those with credit cards can use Cash Dispensers labelled 'Kontanten', coloured red – valid for Mastercard and Visa.

• **Post office:** Opens Mon.–Fri.: 9 a.m.–5 p.m., Sat.: 9 a.m.–12 noon, with variations out of large towns.

• **Telephones:** Either fully automatic or through the operator if the number starts with letters. Insert 1 kr. for local calls or 2 kr. for long-distance. You do not get change from 25 øre coins, and with older machines get no change at all.

• **Shops:** Hours vary from town to town; in general: Mon.–Thurs.: 9 a.m.–5.30 p.m., Friday to 7 or 8 p.m., Saturday to 1 p.m. or 2 p.m. First Saturday of each month to 5 p.m. in larger towns.

SLEEPING

Youth hostels require you to register before 9 p.m. and have IYHF membership. An average charge is 53–79 kr. per night and outside Copenhagen an 11 p.m. curfew is the norm. A free booklet listing all of Denmark's hostels and many campsites is available from the tourist office. There are over 500 campsites and the Camping Carnet is required. An average overnight stay will cost 32 kr. Town mission hostels are excellent, clean and cheap. If you can't get into a hostel and don't want to be bothered with camping stay in a private home (anything but a hotel, as these really are very expensive). Tourist information will put you in touch with a Danish family who'll put you up.

EATING AND NIGHTLIFE

Danish food is expensive, but don't despair: shop at the well-stocked supermarkets and prepare your own smørrebrød (open sandwiches). Pølser (hot dog) stands are on most street corners, and the famous Danish brews round off picnics in style. Look out for cafés with signs 'Madkurve kan Medbringes' (literally, 'bring your own food'), so just buy a coffee.

ISIC gives you 50 per cent off films, theatres, etc., and there's no shortage of pubs in Denmark. For Copenhagen, 'Use It' have leaflets which give you a rundown on what's on, and if that's not enough they also have special information sheets on entertainment.

Copenhagen (København)

The largest city in Scandinavia, situated on the north-eastern shore of Zealand, Copenhagen is a well-run, exciting place with lots going for it and an almost Parisian *joie de vivre*. The Danes are known to be a socially-minded lot, and this shows particularly in their capital where they operate two free services for young travellers which are almost too good to be true. The YMCA and YWCA get together and open two centres for eurorailers in high summer where you can go for advice on what to see and where to go, and for help with problems. They're at Store Kannikestraede 19 (Tel. 33113031). Open 8 a.m.–12 p.m. and 2.30 p.m.–12.30 a.m.; 1 July–14 August. Also at Valdemarsgade 15 (Tel. 31311574). Open 8 a.m.–12 noon and 2 p.m.–12.30 a.m.; 15 July–15 August.

The second organization, called 'Use It', is much larger, is open all year, and is sponsored by the city youth organization. It offers countless free or non-profit-making services: free maps, tourist information and advice, a series of leaflets on cheap restaurants and hostels, free luggage storage, and at its centre at Rådhusstraede 13 (Tel. 33156518), 10 minutes' walk from Central Station along Tietgensgade, down one side of the Tivoli, on into Stormgade, then left into Rådhusstraede. There is a restaurant, jazz club, rock/folk club and cinema where you can meet fellow travellers and young Danes. 'Use It' will also find you a bed you can afford, or help you out if you've an emergency or crisis. They're open in summer from 10 a.m.–7 p.m. and off-season from 10 a.m.–4 p.m.

Bear in mind: the YMCA/YWCA set-up is a Christian organization and can be quite strict – even in Copenhagen – so if you're after advice on the hottest places for evening entertainment, etc., go to 'Use It'.

These sort of facilities are unique in Europe, so make the most of them whilst you're there, and don't expect anything remotely like it in southern Europe.

STATION FACILITIES

Train information	8 a.m.–10 p.m.
	(Tel. 33 14 17 01)
Reservations	8 a.m.–9 p.m.
Left-luggage lockers	Shut 1.30 a.m.–4.30 a.m.
Left-luggage store	6.30 a.m.–12.15 a.m.
Duty officer 'Inspektion'	All hours
Chemist	7 a.m.–11 p.m.
Waiting room (in cafeteria)	6.30 a.m.–11.45 p.m.
Restaurant	7.30 a.m.–10.30 p.m.
Cafeteria	6.30 a.m.–11.45 p.m.
Bar, Buffet	7 a.m.–11 p.m.
Snack bar	7 a.m.–11.45 p.m.
Shopping	Supermarket by station open 8 a.m.–12 midnight
Foreign exchange	7 a.m.–10 p.m.
Station shuts	1.30 a.m.–4.30 a.m.

There are post office, banking and telephone facilities.
Copenhagen–Malmö 40 minutes, to Gothenburg 4½ hours, to Hamburg 5 hours.

Copenhagen's 'Hovedbanegård' is the terminus for all main-line trains. It's a particularly fine station with many facilities. The platforms are below ground level. The 'S' trains (suburban electrics) also use the station. Look out for drunks, however.

Note: These S-togs are free to Inter-Rail or Eurail card holders. The nearest room finding service is at Bernstoffsgade 1. As their commission is 15 kr., it is best to go to 'Use It' who offer this service free.

• **Inter-Rail Centre:** DSB's Inter-Rail Centre was opened on 1 July 1984 and was the first of its kind in the world. Anyone with a youth Inter-Rail, Eurail Youthpass or BIJ ticket can use its excellent facilities from mid-June through till mid-September. (Open 7 a.m.–midnight.) These facilities include a common room and a dining room where everyone meets up, as well as toilets and washing facilities. Throughout the day, there are news bulletins in English, German and French, and tape-recorded tourist information in the same languages. There are also vending machines with hot and cold beverages and sandwiches, music and a large collection of folders. Use the showers at odd times of the day to avoid queues. The centre is usually very full.

TOURIST INFORMATION

At the Town Hall Square, by Tivoli entrance, is Danmarks Turistråd – tourist information, H. C. Andersens Boulevard 22 (Tel. 33111325). Open May: Mon.–Fri.: 9 a.m.–5 p.m., Sat.: 9 a.m.–2 p.m., Sun. and holidays: 9 a.m.–1 p.m. June to mid-Sept.: daily 9 a.m.–6 p.m. Off season Mon.–Fri.: 9 a.m.–5 p.m., Sat.: 9 a.m.–noon. Their service is excellent and helpful and there are leaflets on everything you could possibly need to know. Be specific and ask for everything you might need, for instance camping, walking, other parts of Denmark, etc. Don't forget to pick up their free map and a copy of 'Copenhagen This Week'.

If you want to hire a bike, ask at tourist information for details of the 'City Bikes' scheme. This scheme uses 5,000 bikes, with 750 racks distributed around the city. To use insert a 20 kr. coin in the rack.

● **Addresses:**
USE IT: Rådhusstraede 13 (Tel. 33156518). They help out euro-railers with everything and will even hold your mail and find you a bed for the night. Not always over-friendly, but useful!
POST OFFICE: Tietgensgade 37 (behind Central Station). Poste restante here too. 9 a.m.–6 p.m., to 1 p.m. on Saturday.
AMEX: Amagertorv 18 (Tel. 33122301).
UK EMBASSY: Kastelsvej 36–40 (Tel. 31264600).
US EMBASSY: Dag Hammarskjölds Allé 24 (Tel. 31423144).
CANADIAN EMBASSY: Kristen Bernikowsgade 1 (Tel. 33122299).
AUSTRALIAN EMBASSY: Kristianiasgade 21 (Tel. 31262244).
24-HOUR CHEMIST: Steno Apotek, Vesterbrogade 6c (Tel. 33148266).

• **Getting about:** The S-tog is free with any rail pass. If you haven't got one, the buses are a better bet at 9 kr. a ride, although they are cheaper if you buy a nine-ride pass from the driver for 70 kr. All tickets are interchangeable between buses and trains providing they are used within the hour. The best way of all, however, is to invest in a 'Copenhagen Card' which gives you unlimited travel by bus and rail in the whole of the metropolitan area and includes North Sealand. It also gives free admission to many sights, attractions and museums. If you don't have a pass which gives free or reduced ferry crossings to Sweden, the Copenhagen Card allows a 50 per cent reduction. It is valid for one, two or three days and costs about 120 kr., 200 kr. and 250 kr. respectively. Children aged 5 to 11 pay half-price.

If you're thinking of going to Malmö in Sweden, carefully compare the ferry lines on offer. Prices vary considerably; bonuses for Inter-Rail may be available. The jetfoil saves you 45 minutes' travelling with an Inter-Rail reduction, otherwise the trip takes 1½ hours.

SEEING

Copenhagen is a great walking city and most of the sights can easily be negotiated on foot. There are six well-planned city walking tours which last about two hours (ask tourist information or Use It).

TIVOLI (the famous amusement park) is in the centre across from the station and has, over the years, become rather too commercial for our liking. Entrance 33 kr., with rides from 8 kr. but generally overpriced; a Tour Pass ticket at 140 kr. allows unlimited rides. Avoid eating here. Open May–mid-September, 10 a.m.–midnight. An alternative is the free entry amusement park of BAKKEN. Take the S-tog to KLAMPENBERG (free on Inter-Rail and Eurail) and walk through the park. Open April – end August, 12 noon–12 midnight. The CARLSBERG and TUBORG breweries run a good deal (a classic favourite for thirsty eurorailers): tours of the breweries with free samples afterwards (beware of the time limit on your sampling), closed weekends. Carlsberg tours at 11 a.m. and 2 p.m. Take bus 6 or 18. Tuborg tours at 10 a.m., 12.30 p.m. and 2.30 p.m. S-tog line A to Svanemøllen or Hellrup, or bus 6, 21, or 23. Tuborg brewery have opened the EKSPERIMENTARIUM in an old bottling hall, an interactive science museum, entrance fee around 50 kr.

As you will be on foot, you will not miss STRØGET, a series of streets throbbing with life. The area around the university is host to a multitude of bookshops, bric-a-brac and a good selection of cafés. See also the RUNDETÅRN, the summit of which affords a great view of the old town and is curiously reached by a continuous spiral ramp.

Another good view of the town can be obtained by climbing the unusual tower of VOR FRELSERS KIRKE on Prinsessegade and Torvegade. The spiral staircase is on the outside of the church's spire and gets progressively steeper and more uneven. Not recommended in high winds or rain! It costs 10 kr. to climb it. The tower is undergoing renovation and will be shut during 1993.

'Alternative' Copenhagen can be experienced at CHRISTIANA on Prinsessegade. Occupied in 1971 by a group of hippies who enjoyed the free Danish attitudes to pot, drinking and nudism, it makes an interesting visit! The veggie cafe and craft stalls are worthwhile and it is safe to look round. Restaurants, bars and shops are cheaper than in the rest of the town. Avoid taking photographs of the inhabitants to avoid any unpleasantness.

Copenhagen has a multitude of museums and perhaps the best are the WORKERS MUSEUM and the NATIONAL MUSEUM which is best on Danish history and the Vikings. Also worth a look are the THORVALDSENS MUSEUM for the work of Denmark's famous sculptor. NY CARLSBERG GLYPTOTEK (free entry on Wed. and Sun.) for classical art and the interesting RESISTANCE MUSEUM, tracing the growth of opposition to the German occupation during the Second World War.

The Bellevue is a beach between Copenhagen and Helsingør, known locally as 'Fluepapiret' (fly-paper) for its ability to draw the bikini-clad blondes and the local likely lads.

The walk to the little mermaid, along the LANGELINIE, is the best part of the trip, as the statue's nothing special. Look out for the nearby Gefion Fountain. The comprehensive leaflet provided with the 'Copenhagen Card' gives full details on opening times, locations and other facilities. Most of the sights, including the Little Mermaid, can be seen during the good 16 kr. boat trips round the harbour and canals.

Your best day trip from Copenhagen is 40 km north to Frederiksborg Castle at Hillerød (35 minutes by S-tog, leaving from the main station).

SLEEPING

Hotels in Copenhagen are busy all year round, with prices starting at 380 kr.; you are better investigating the city hostels, private house schemes and campsites. If you are organized in advance try the 'Living Rooms' flat agency, at Knabrostraede 5, 1210 Copenhagen K, to book a flat.

• **Hostels:** These are busy in summer, so don't waste time touring round them yourself. 'Use It' will help you find a bed (when their office is shut, they often post up the latest bed situation outside their office). The main youth hostel (you'll need an IYHF card), Bellahøj at Herbergvejen 8 (Tel. 31289715), is very good and situated in a park in a nice suburb about 15–20 minutes from the city centre. The cost is around 55 kr. with and 75 kr. without an IYHF card. Take bus 2 from the station almost to the end of the route. Security can be a problem, so use the lockers in the basement. The Copenhagen Youth Hostel (IYHF) at Sjaellandsbroen 55 is very clean and modern. Book in after 1 p.m. (Tel. 32522908). Take bus 13 or train to Valby Station, changing to bus 37. Vesterbro Ungdomsgård, Absalonsgade 8 (Tel. 31312070) is more expensive than the other hostels, due to its good location. Take bus 16 from the station, or a 10-minute walk along Vesterbrogade. Cost 85 kr. Active University, Olfert Fischersgade 40 (Tel. 31156175) is still very cheap (40 kr. per night) but very busy during the summer. There are two YMCA hostels in Copenhagen, both costing 50 kr. You'll need a map from the station to get to the one at Valdemarsgade 15 (Tel. 31311574; open mid-July to mid-August). The other is at St Kannikestraede 19 (Tel. 33113031; open 1 July–22 August, 10 minutes' walk from station). Finally, there's 'Sleep-In' which is permanently based at Per Henrik Lings Allé 6 (Tel. 31262946). Very few restrictions; IYHF cards are not required; co-ed dorms; bring your own sleeping bag. The cost is 75 kr., including breakfast. Take bus 1, 6 or 14 to Idraetsparken; Per Henrik cuts through this park. Open from end June to end August.

• **Private accommodation:** Use Kiosk P at Bernstorffsgade 1 to find yourself a room in a private house, and expect to pay up to 250 kr. for a single, 350 kr. a double. They also take about 15 kr. commission per person.

• **Hotels:** If you have no alternative and want to stay in an hotel try the Amager in Amagerbrogade (Tel. 31544008) or the Carlton on Halmtorvert (Tel. 31212551). You will also find places in the area behind the Central Station on Helgolandsgade and Colbjørn-sensgade.

• **Camping:** There are seven sites costing around 36 kr. per person with Danish camping pass. The all-year site is at Absalon Camping, 132 Korsdalsvej (Tel. 31410600): take the S-tog, line B or H, to Brøndyøster Station. Cabins are available for up to five people, but the shop here is expensive.

EATING AND NIGHTLIFE

This is varied, interesting and there is no shortage of places to choose from. For meals, you can't do much better than the set menus at Chinese restaurants. To keep you going there are pølser (hot dog) stalls, fast-food chains, daily specials (dagens ret) and smørrebrød. (See the 'Use It' brochure, 'Where to Eat'.) One of the most popular places for smørrebrød is Smørrebrødforretning at Gothersgade 10, open 8 a.m.–10 p.m.

Universitetspoppen (university refectory), 52 Kobmagergade, charge 40–50 kr. for huge lunchtime meals. You'll need an ISIC, but they are closed July and August. At Pasta Basta, Valkendorfsgade 22, eat as much spaghetti as you can for a fixed price. There are good 'eat as much as you can' places, at reasonable prices. Try Alexander's Pizza House: pizza and salad for around 50 kr., at Lille Kannikestraede 5.

Spisehuset, Rådhusstraede 13 (part of 'Use It'). All you can eat reasonably cheaply (noon–3 p.m.). In the evenings it's a pub (serving food).

There are hundreds of pubs, clubs and discos in Copenhagen. NYHAVN (the dock district) makes an interesting nocturnal wander – but it is not advisable for girls to go there alone. The 'Use It' house is as good and cheap a place for a drink as any, and Frederiksberg-gade comes alive at night. Good jazz can normally be found on Norregade. Basically, in Copenhagen you don't need to look hard for nightlife.

Århus

Denmark's second city is a busy industrial and commercial centre.
See the old town (den gamle by) OPEN AIR MUSEUM, a reconstructed
sixteenth-century village, the CITY PREHISTORIC MUSEUM with the
amazing red-headed mummy of the Grauballe man, the twelfth-
century CATHEDRAL and the VIKING MUSEUM.

Tourist information is in the Town Hall, one block from the
station, and is open 9 a.m.–8 p.m. Shorter hours out of season,
small charge to book accommodation (Tel. 86121600). It's a
university town and the student centre is at 84 Niels Juelsgade. The
IYHA hostel is Vandrerhjemmet Pavillonen (Tel. 86167298);
closed 12 noon–4 p.m. It's good and well situated in a forest, near
beaches. Take bus or tram nos. 1, 6 or 8 to the terminus, then follow
signs. Hotel Århus Sømandshjêm at 20 Havnegade, near the port
(Tel. 86121599), has single and double rooms which are quite
cheap. There is a Sleep-In, Kulturgyngen, at Mejlgade 53, with 75
places. There is also a nightclub and café here. The campsite (Tel.
8627 0207) is 7 km out at Blommehavn, Ørneredevej 35, bus 6.

Your cheapest lunch is at the Matematiske Fakultet (University)
off Langelandsgade; closed after 1 p.m. and all July. Even better is
the 'Use It' Youth Centre at 15 Vester Allé. They also give free
concerts and plays. Musik café at Mejlgade 53 is worth a try in the
evenings.

Odense

En route from Copenhagen to Jutland, Odense is one of Denmark's
oldest towns. It's the home town of Hans Christian Andersen; you
can visit his house at Hans Jensens Straede 39–43 (17 kr., no
reductions).

Tourist information is in the Town Hall, south of the station (Tel.
66127520). Open in summer 9 a.m.–7 p.m., Sundays 11 a.m.–7 p.m.
Odense has an YWCA/Inter-Rail point at Rødegårdsvej 91 (Tel.
66142314), open mid-July to mid-August and costing 50 kr. The

'Odense Fairy Tale Card', gives free admission to museums and other sights, costs 70kr. for 2 days: good value, if a tacky name. ST CANUTE'S thirteenth-century cathedral and the OPEN AIR FOLK MUSEUM and operating farm on the outskirts of Odense are interesting. At Ladby (20 km north-east of Odense) is the coffin ship of a tenth-century Viking chief.

The youth hostel is at 121 Kragsbjergvej (Tel. 66130425). It has 230 beds, and is on bus route 6 from the station. There is a campsite at Odensevej 102 (Tel. 66114702), bus 1. There is a YMCA/YWCA centre offering accommodation at 50kr. per night, breakfast at 20kr. See the detailed map at the train station.

Aalborg

The 1,000-year-old centre of north Jutland. The main sights include the remains of a Viking village and mass grave (at Nørresundby, just outside Aalborg), the well-preserved OLD TOWN, the fifteenth-century MONASTERY OF THE HOLY GHOST, ALBORGHUS CASTLE, ST BOTOLPH'S CATHEDRAL and the baby brother of Tivoli, TIVOLILAND. There is a new museum at the Viking site, with many artifacts from the area. All Americans in Aalborg on 4 July should make their way to the Rebild National Park, 30 km south of the city, for the most extensive Independence Day celebrations outside the USA.

The Aalborg Vandrerhjem hostel is at Skydebanevej 50 (Tel. 98116044), with a campsite (Tel. 98127629), Strandparken, nearby. Bus 2 or 178 from centre or railway station, to terminus.

Legoland

One of Denmark's most famous exports is Lego, the children's plastic building brick. At BILLUND in mid-Jutland there is a mini-town of houses, railway, harbour, boats and cars – all made out of the stuff. Legoland is open from May to mid-September, with some indoor exhibitions from Easter to mid-December.

Take the train to Vejle and then bus 912 from the station to Billund (28 kr. each way). Journey takes about one hour.

Entrance fees cheapen during the day, costing from 45 kr. It stays open until 8 p.m.–9 p.m., dependent on season, closed for winter.

There are also aviation and motor vehicle museums close by, open daily 10 a.m.–8 p.m.

There is a campsite very near Legoland, at Nordmarksvej 2 (Tel. 75331521).

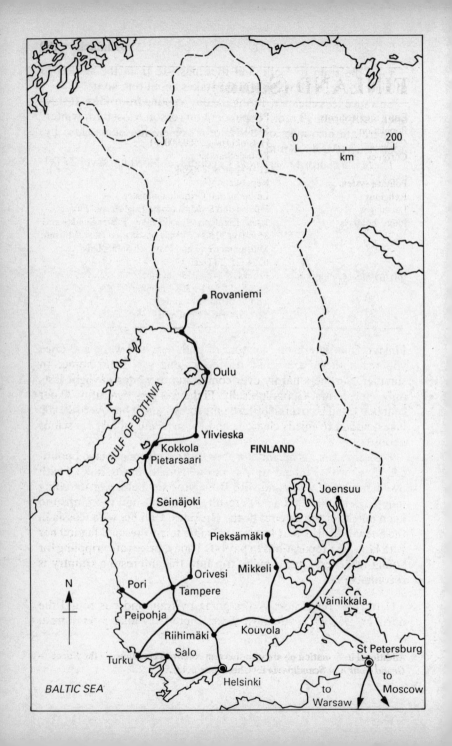

FINLAND (Suomi)

Entry requirements	Passport
Population	5,000,000
Capital	Helsinki (pop.: 500,000 +)
Currency	Finnish Markka
	£1 = approx. 7.87 mk.
Political system	Republic
Religions	Lutheran and Orthodox ministry
Languages	Finnish and Swedish (some English spoken)
Public holidays	1 Jan. Epiphany; Good Friday; Easter Sunday and Monday; 30 Apr.; 1 May; Ascension Day; Whitsun; Midsummer Eve and Day; All Saints Day; 6, 24, 25, 26 Dec.
International dialling codes	From UK 010 + 358 + number
	From USA 011 + 358 + number
	To UK 990 + 44 + number
	To USA 990 + 1 + number

Finland is an interesting mixture of both east and west, and once you reach there you really do feel a long way from home. In summer, darkness hardly ever comes and in winter daylight lasts only a few hours. Geographically, Finland is very beautiful: 70 per cent of its land is covered by lush pine forests and it has over 188,000 lakes; added to this is clear air and an environmentally conscious people.

For centuries, its neighbours, Sweden and Russia, played political chess with Finland as the pawn. (Finland was linked with Sweden for 650 years and with Russia for 100 before proclaiming independence in 1917.) As a result, you won't find the Finns too keen on either the Swedes or the Russians. Conflict with Russia in the Second World War lost her valuable territories and landed her with large war reparations to pay off. Today, prices are crippling for young travellers, but a quick trip into this interesting country is recommended.

• **Getting there:** Unless you're going by train and bus round the north of Sweden, your most direct route is to take a ferry from

Additional information on all Scandinavian countries contained in the *Europe – Grand Tour* and *Scandinavia* factsheets (see p.13).

Stockholm to either Turku or Helsinki. It's a beautiful cruise (10–11 hours and 14–16 hours respectively). The main shipping lines are Silja and Viking. An Inter-Rail gets you a 50 per cent reduction on both lines, while Eurail holders travel free with Silja and on a 50 per cent reduction with Viking. Facilities on both lines are excellent. Cabins are expensive, so get your sleeping bag down on deck somewhere, or, better still, head for the free 'sleep-in'. On the older ships these have 60 beds, but the excellent new ships on the Silja Lines Turku–Stockholm route have 200 places available on all sailings. It is worthwhile taking a day sailing as the route is very scenic and you pass many small islands on the way, with the ship constantly zig-zagging to keep in deep water. Snacks and coffee on the ship are reasonably priced as are the duty-free goods – by Scandinavian standards. There are several services each day with prices varying depending on the crossing. The Helsinki ferries leave at 6 p.m. or 7 p.m. and cost a minimum 84 mk. on Viking Line, or 235 mk. on Silja Line. The Turku ferries leave at 10 a.m. and 8 p.m. during high season, and cost a minimum of 69 mk. on Viking Line, and 110 mk. on Silja Line.

FINNISH STATE RAILWAYS
(Valtionrautatiet, VR)

Big, solid and reliable (like the Finns!), the majority of the rolling stock is new. There are four types of trains: IC-trains (IC-juna), special expresses (Erikoispikajuna), regular expresses (Pikajuna) and locals (Henkilöjuna). Their service extends as far north as Lapland and includes nearly 6,000 km of line.

• **Inter-Rail bonuses:** See Appendix II, plus free entry to the VR Railway Museum in Hyvinkää, and Narrow Gauge Railway Museum in Jokioinen (Gare Minkio).

• **Eurail bonuses:** Free services:
—Ferry service of the Silja Line between Helsinki and Stockholm and between Turku–Aland Islands–Stockholm. Full fare is charged for cabin space.

TRAIN INFORMATION

At the major stations you'll find the staff speak English. Contact the 'Neuvonta' at the station if you've problems.

• **Reservations:** Obligatory on the IC-trains and special expresses (marked EP in timetable); optional on other trains. Oddly, reserved seats are not marked, making it difficult to tell if a seat is free. Costs are 18 mk. on the special expresses, 25 mk. on IC-trains (2nd class), and 15 mk. on other trains.

• **Night travel:** There are no couchettes, only sleepers which are reasonably priced, 90 mk. in 3-berth compartment or 180 mk. in 2-berth. Reductions off-peak. During the peak periods (Easter and July/August) try and reserve sleepers as far ahead as possible.

• **Rover Tickets:** There are two tickets offering unlimited travel, either the Finnrail Pass which is limited to Finland, or the Nordic Tourist Ticket, which is valid for all the Scandinavian countries plus major connecting sailings, rover tickets valid in Denmark. The Finnrail Pass is valid for 8, 15 or 22 days and costs 470 mk., 730 mk. and 920 mk. respectively for second-class travel, 50 per cent higher for first-class.

TOURIST INFORMATION

City offices, Matkailutoimistot, provide excellent maps and leaflets on their locality. For Finland as a whole the national tourist board, 'MEK', has its base in Helsinki. Museums tend to close on Mondays.

• **ISIC bonuses:** Student discounts on museums, art galleries and theatres.

• **Money matters:** 1 Finnish markka (mk.) = 100 penni (p).
Banking hours are: Mon.–Fri.: 9 a.m.–4 p.m., but varies by locality. Banks give the best rate of exchange. All banks and exchange bureaux close over the mid-summer weekend holiday.

• **Post offices:** Open 9 a.m. to 5 p.m., Monday to Friday. Stamps are also sold at bookshops, newsagents and stations. Post boxes are yellow.

• **Shops:** Monday to Friday 9 a.m.–5 p.m. or 6 p.m. (with department stores staying open to 8 p.m. summer weekdays). Saturday hours 9 a.m.–2 p.m. or 3 p.m. (department stores to 6 p.m.).

• **Telephones:** Accept one and five mk. coins only, returned if no reply.

SLEEPING

Youth hostels and campsites are graded on a star basis with four grades. There's no age limit to Finland's 160 hostels and you don't need IYHF membership, except in the most expensive category, which often have saunas. Prices range from 30–150 mk., though most cost around 50 mk. For further information about youth hostels in Finland contact Suomen Retkeilymajajärjestö, (SRM), Yrjönkatu 38 B SF-, 00100 Helsinki (Tel. 6931347/6940377). There are something like 340 campsites, varying in price from 27–75 mk. per tent. For more details on hostelling and camping, ask at tourist information for the current leaflet 'Finland Budget Accommodation'.

Private accommodation and small boarding houses are also available. Summer hotels are often made out of student dorms, and they're usually clean, modern and reasonably priced. The cheapest you'll get for a hotel room (double) with breakfast is 100–150 mk. per person.

If organized in advance, and you have a preference for hotels, ask at the Finnish Tourist Office in your country about the FinnCheque advance booking system.

EATING AND NIGHTLIFE

The baaris, grillis, krouvis or kahvilas are a mixture of cafés and fast-food chains. They're OK but vary dramatically in quality. The student-run cafés are your best bet. Finnish specialities include salted Baltic herring, rye bread, crayfish and fruit-filled pancakes. Various fish dishes are common, and if you eat meat, watch out for dried reindeer.

Nearly all restaurants have set lunch and dinner menus but you're better advised to starve yourself and look out for a Voileipäpöytä or Smörgåsbord (Scandinavian cold table) for a set price, usually available at lunchtime. This often includes hot dishes as well, and you work on the basis of eating as much as you like for a set price. Heavy tax on alcohol means consequently high prices e.g. a pint of beer 15–25 mk. Alcohol sales are controlled by a state organization, and only beer and non-alcoholic drinks are available elsewhere.

Finns are keen on dancing and there's plenty of that going on on Vappu Night (30 April). This is the students' spring festival which is a good excuse for Helsinki's 20,000 students to let rip and have a knees-up after the long winter. Whether you've been sleeping on deck or going by train and bus round the north, there's nothing like a real Finnish sauna to relax you. Most hotels welcome non-residents. (Rub birch-leaves with the Finns – it's cheaper to take a sauna in a group but do not expect mixed saunas!)

Helsinki

A clean, bright, modern capital city. Your first impression will probably be of the colourful harbourside market, a daily event in front of the City Hall and President's Palace. Helsinki particularly reminds one visually of its geographical location: the solid eastern-looking buildings contrast with the modern department stores selling endless well-designed consumer goods. In some ways, you feel closer to Russia in Helsinki than you do in Budapest.

STATION FACILITIES

There are daily trains from Helsinki to Turku, Tampere, Kontio-mäki, Oulu, Kemi and Rovaniemi (10–13 hours). If you have a Russian visa, there are also daily trains (a more frequent service is planned) to St Petersburg (formerly Leningrad). Helsinki Central is one of the world's few architecturally famous stations. It's a classic example of *art nouveau*, designed by Eliel Saarinen.

Train information	Mon.–Sat.: 7 a.m.–10 p.m., Sun.: 9 a.m.–10 p.m.
	(Tel. 1010115, International queries Tel. 627804)
Reservations	Times as above (Tel. 1010116)
Tourist information	Mon.–Fri.: 7 a.m.–8 p.m., Sat.: 7.30 a.m.–5 p.m.
	Sun. 9 a.m.–6 p.m.
Cafeteria	Mon.–Sat.: 6.30 a.m.–12 midnight
	Sun. 8 a.m.–12 midnight
Restaurant	Daily 9 a.m.–1 a.m.
Left-luggage lockers	Shut Mon.–Fri.: 1.30 a.m.–4.40 a.m.
	(Sat., Sun.: 1.40 a.m.–5 a.m.)
Left-luggage store	Open 7 a.m.–10 p.m.
Shops	Mon.–Sat.: 10 a.m.–10 p.m., Sun.: 12 noon–10 p.m.
	Shopping gallery in underground passage
Station shuts	Mon.–Fri. 1.35 a.m.–4.40 a.m.
	Sat.–Sun.: 12 midnight–5.25 a.m.

There are left-luggage lockers on both the lower and upper floors. The small ones on the lower level are too small for packs and cost 15 mk. You may get a pack in the larger ones on the upper level.

'Hotellikeskus' is the accommodation-finding service in a building between the station and the nearby post office, at Asema-aukio 3 (Tel. 171133). They take 10 mk. commission per find. Summer hours: weekdays open 9 a.m.–9 p.m., Sat.: 9 a.m.–7 p.m., Sun.: 10 a.m.–6 p.m.; off-season Mon.–Fri.: 9 a.m.–6 p.m. They also have a list of all the IYHF youth hostels in Finland.

TOURIST INFORMATION

The main city tourist office is west of the market at Pohjoisesplanadi 19 (Tel. 169 3757). Open mid-May to mid-Sept., Mon.–Fri. 8.30 a.m.–6 p.m., Sat. 8.30 a.m.–1 p.m., mid-Sept. to mid-May, Mon. 8.30 a.m.–4.30 p.m., Tues.–Fri., 8.30 a.m.–4 p.m. They produce very comprehensive leaflets and are incredibly helpful. Pick up a tourist map, 'Helsinki This Week', 'Helsinki Guide', 'Helsinki Today', and

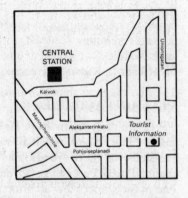

'Helsinki on Foot', which includes six self-guiding tours. They have a free phone here which you can use to ring up your accommodation. If you're staying for a while, ask them about the city transport passes. Another possibility is the Helsinki Card which is valid for either one day at 75 mk., two days at 105 mk. or three days at 125 mk. Not only does it allow you free travel on all public transport, but it also entitles you to free entry to various museums, and other discounts.

If it's a wet day or you're fed up with walking, tram 3T does an excellent round trip from the station. It takes about an hour and all the main sights are pointed out. (Weekdays 10 a.m.–3 p.m. and 6 p.m.–8 p.m., weekends 9 a.m.–8 p.m.)

● **Addresses:**

FINNISH TOURIST BOARD: Eteläesplanadi 4 (Tel. 40301300 or

403011) for information on all of Finland. Open Mon.–Fri.: 9 a.m.–5 p.m., Sat.: 9 a.m. to 1 p.m. during the summer.

POST OFFICE: Mannerheimintie 116, open Mon.–Fri.: 9 a.m.–5 p.m. Poste restante is here.

AMEX: Pohjoisesplanadi 2, open Mon.–Fri.: 8.30 a.m.–5 p.m.

UK EMBASSY: Itäinen Puistotie 17 (Tel. 661293).

US EMBASSY: Itäinen Puistotie 14a (Tel. 171 931).

CANADIAN EMBASSY: Pohjoisesplanadi 25B (Tel. 171 141).

24-HOUR CHEMIST: Yliopiston Apteekki, Mannerheimintie 5.

STUDENT TRAVEL AGENCY: Travela, Mannerheimintie 5c (Tel. 624 101). Near the train station.

HELSINKI TODAY: Tel. 058 for information and events in English, 040 for news and weather.

CITY DIALLING CODE: 90.

SEEING

The neo-classical centre of town, around the Senate Square, built after a fire which devastated Helsinki, makes a good starting point. On the Square stand the Lutheran CATHEDRAL, UNIVERSITY and GOVERNMENT PALACE, all built in the early nineteenth century. Heading down towards the sea front, the PRESIDENT'S PALACE, CITY HALL and ORTHODOX CATHEDRAL can be seen. The tourist office's walking tours take you around the sights. The NATIONAL MUSEUM, north of Mannerheimintie from the station, is worth a visit on route to the ROCK or TEMPPELIAUKIO CHURCH. From the museum head down Aurorankatu, then along Temppelikatu. Two island locations of note are the SEURASAARI OPEN-AIR MUSEUM, bus 24 to its terminus, and the SUOMENLINNA FORTRESS ISLAND, reached by ferry from near the tourist information. Finland is also rightly acclaimed for being a world leader in manufacturing design, and the MUSEUM OF APPLIED ARTS at Korkeavuorenkatu 23 brings together all the best the country has to offer.

SLEEPING

Hotels are expensive in Helsinki and are often fully booked in summer. The hostelling news is good and there are always Matkustajakoti (rooms for travellers) advertised around the station if you're desperate.

• **Hostels:** Try Youth Hostel Stadionin Maja, Pohjoinen Stadiontie 3B (Tel. 496071), from 40–100 mk. with IYHF card. Located in the Olympic Stadium complex and reached by tram 3T or 7A from Mannerheimintie, just out of the station. Eurohostel, at Linnan-katu 9 (Tel. 664 452), is open all year, price 130–160 mk. There's a YMCA Interpoint Hostel at Raumantie 5 (Tel. 90 557 849; open 1 July–15 Aug., bus No.18 from station). It costs 45 mk. Also try the Academica, Hietaniemenkatu 14 (Tel. 4020206), head across Mannerheimintie from the station, and down Arkadiankatu, then Pohjoinen Rautatiekatu to the junction with Hietaniemenkatu. During the summer the Hotelli Satakuntatlo, Lapinrinne 1A (Tel. 695851) has dorm facilities, and single rooms. Near the station.

• **Camping:** The nearest campsite is Rastila (Tel. 316551), take the metro from the station to Östra centrum, then bus 90, 90a, 96 or 98, first stop after the bridge. Open May to September, around 25 mk. per person.

EATING AND NIGHTLIFE

There are plenty of stalls, takeaways and cafés, as well as the excellent markets, so eating is no problem. If you're really down on your luck, wait till the end of the markets and fight for the pickings of the stall-holders' leftovers. Stockmann's department store have a good basement food hall, and if you're going for a restaurant meal you've the usual choice of Chinese, Indian, etc., or Russian.

Vanhan Kellari, Mannerheimintie 3. Good self-service, popular with students. Open till 1 a.m. Try Kasvisravintola, Korkeavuoren-katu 3, for good vegetarian food. Open Mon.–Fri. 11 a.m.–6 p.m., Sat.–Sun. 12 p.m.–6 p.m. Closes at 5 p.m. in summer.

Finns really come to life in the pub, of which Helsinki has no shortage. You don't have to look far for them. Try the following pubs: Hamlet at Vilhonkatu 6; Konig at Mikonkatu 4; or Kaarle XII on Kasarmikatu. KY Exit at Pohjoinen Rautatiekatu 21 is popular with students; also worth trying is the Café Adlon at Fabianinkatu 14.

If you're in Helsinki on 30 April or Midsummer's Eve, prepare yourself for a late night as they stay up all night dancing and drinking.

Turku (Åbo)

The oldest town and former capital of Finland. If arriving on the ferry from Sweden, take the train or bus to the city centre, from outside the terminus.

TOURIST INFORMATION

Käsityöläiskatu 3, open Mon.–Fri. 8 a.m.–4 p.m., from 8.30 a.m. in winter. Also at Aurakatu 4, open June to mid-Sept., Mon.–Fri. 8.30 a.m.–7.30 p.m., Sat.–Sun. 10 a.m.–5 p.m. Mid-Sept. to end May, Mon.–Fri. 8.30 a.m.–6 p.m., Sat.–Sun. 10 a.m.–5 p.m.

Telephone code 21.

The main sights are the twelfth-century CASTLE, originally a Swedish stronghold, which now houses part of the PROVINCIAL MUSEUM. Entry is 15 mk., but get off the train at the harbour station to see it and save a 25-minute walk. TURKU CATHEDRAL, dating from the thirteenth century, the SIBELIUS MUSEUM containing his instruments and personal possessions, and the LUOSTARINMÄKI MUSEUM where craftsmen put on live demonstrations of their skills in an old style street. SUOMEN JOUTSEN, a sailing vessel open to the public, is anchored in the Aura River and worth a look, as is the Museum ship Sigya nearby. Also, there are boat excursions through the archipelago to the neighbouring town of NAANTALI.

SLEEPING

• **Hostel:** Kaupungin Retkeilymaja at Linnankatu 39 (Tel. 921 316578). 128 beds in dorms and small rooms. Take Bus 10 or 20 from the station to the Market Square; from here or the ferry terminus, take Bus 1, getting off at the Marinsitta bridge. Reception open 3 p.m. to midnight, 30–50 mk. and 20 mk. for sheets.

Turisti-Aula (Tel. 334484) is central and very good. One block north of city tourist office at Käsityöläiskatu 11, from 170 mk. single, to 290 mk. double.

• **Camp:** Island of Ruissalo (Tel. 589249), bus 8 from Market Square. Buses are not too frequent and it is a 20-minute ride.

Facilities are good with a worthwhile restaurant and beach nearby, also has sauna facilities.

EATING

Go to MARKETPLACE (8 a.m.–2 p.m.) where the food's good, as cheap as you can expect to find, and is a sight in itself. There is also an evening market in summer until 8 p.m.

Just up the road is the KAUPPAHALLI (covered market). It's open 8 a.m.–5 p.m. and Saturday morning, and is full of delights.

There are several pizza places and the department stores have good cafés.

Tampere

Located on the isthmus between two lakes, Tampere is Finland's second city. Although an industrial centre, it has plenty going for it to make it worth a visit.

TOURIST INFORMATION

At Verkatehtaankatu 2. Open weekdays 8.30 a.m.–8 p.m., Saturdays 8.30 a.m.–6 p.m., Sundays 11.30 a.m.–6 p.m., weekdays only off season, 8.30 a.m.–5 p.m.

Telephone code 31.

SEEING

SÄRKÄNNIEMI not only has an amusement park, but also an aquarium, dolphinarium, planetarium, children's zoo and the NÄSINNEULA OBSERVATION TOWER, which affords a good view of Tampere and its surroundings. The SARA HILDÉN modern art museum is also nearby (open 11 a.m.–6 p.m. daily, closed Mon.).

The LENIN MUSEUM at Hämeenpuisto 28 (open Mon.–Fri. 9 a.m.–5 p.m., Sat. & Sun. 11 a.m.–4 p.m.) is possibly unique as the only museum outside Eastern Europe dedicated to the life of V. I. Lenin.

The CATHEDRAL, built 1907, is worth a look for its altar piece and frescos, as is the ORTHODOX CHURCH at Tuomiokirkonkatu 27, which although it is the only neo-Byzantine church in the Nordic countries, has the largest bells in Finland.

SLEEPING

• **Hostels:** Uimahallin Maja at Pirkankatu 10–12 (Tel. 229460) is central for most of the sights and about 1 km from the railway station. Head down Hämeenkatu and bear right at the end. An alternative is the hostel and summer hotel Domus, at Pellervonkatu 9 (Tel. 550 000), take bus 25 from the station, only open 1 June to 31 August. The YWCA at Hameenpuisto 14 is also fairly central and nearer the station, head down Hämeenkatu and Hameenpuis, but only open from 15 June to 15 August. It costs 35 mk.

• **Campsites:** Härmälä camping has 400 beds in cabins for 3 to 5 persons, open early May to late Aug. only (Tel. 651250), take bus 1 from outside tourist office.

Northern Finland

If you want to sail in the midnight sun and walk in the forests of Europe's remotest northern land, prepare yourself for a minimum of twenty hours' train travel from Helsinki and buses and ferries which don't always connect up as smoothly as one would like.

The end goal is a unique experience, but to be honest it's easier to get up to the Arctic tundra through Norway or Sweden. OULU is the most attractive of the northern towns. The trip from Helsinki to Rovaniemi isn't too bad – a direct 12-hour train journey – and this takes you to a convenient starting point for your Lapland excursions. The tourist offices at Oulu and Rovaniemi will supply you with all you need to know and suggest accommodation. The Rovaniemi youth hostel, at Hallituskatu 16 (Tel. (960) 344644) is good and clean and costs 37 to 50 mk. Turn right outside the station and follow the signs.

Southern Finland

The lakes and woods of the south make this area an outdoor recreation paradise and one of Europe's last wildernesses. SAVON-LINNA is a good centre to base yourself at. In this neck of the woods you really ought to camp to get the feel of Finland. The tourist office can arrange canoes and bikes for you.

Savonlinna, near the Russian border, 6 hours from Helsinki, has more charm than the other towns in the Lake Region.

Don't wait on the train for the main station at Savonlinna, get off at the stop near the centre, Savonlinna–Kauppatori, as you're nearer the tourist office there. It's at Puistokatu 1 and is open in early June and late August 8 a.m.–6 p.m. every day, late June–late August to 10 p.m. every day, and 9 a.m.–4 p.m. Mon—Fri. on other dates.

At the heart of the town is Olavinlinna, on a small island, the medieval castle with the old wooden houses of Linnankatu surrounding it. Take the English guided tour of the castle.

During most of July, the Opera Festival takes place, and it fills up beds at an incredible rate and is expensive to participate in. Use the open-air markets to picnic from, and try to stay at the excellent Malakius Youth Hostel at Pihlajavedenkuja 6 (Tel. 23283), 55 mk., either a 15-minute walk along Tulliportinkatu and Savonkatu, or by bus 2 or 3 from centre. Camp at Unolimaki (Tel. 537353), 6 km from the centre, take bus 3.

Almost on the Russian border, and on the route to Savonlinna, is the small town of Imatra, on the Vuoksi river. The youth hostel and campsite are on the sandy shore of a lake in the forest. Despite the 2½ mile walk, or bus, it is a great place to relax.

Russia – St Petersburg

As there is a daily train from Helsinki to St Petersburg (formerly Leningrad) which only takes seven hours, you may feel the urge to visit Russia. Unfortunately, due to the timetable an overnight stay in St Petersburg is essential and likely to be relatively expensive, but services are scheduled to improve. Full details from Intourist, 219 Marsh Wall, London E14, or 71 Deansgate, Manchester M3 2PW, or 8 Belmont Crescent, Glasgow G12 8EV.

Intourist will be able to arrange the necessary visa and accommodation. Allow at least two to three weeks. Intourist will probably only offer you expensive first-class hotel accommodation, unless you insist on cheaper.

A ticket from Helsinki to St Petersburg is likely to cost around 238 mk. single, 480 mk. return.

Despite the relatively high cost, you may feel this is more than worth it for a glimpse at one of the most historic cities of Russia.

Estonia – Tallinn

There are ferries five or six days a week from Helsinki to Tallinn, run by Tallink and Saimaa Lines, which cost from around 180 mk. single. Again contact Intourist, or Estonia's successor to this, for details of current Visa/currency requirements.

ENGLISH CHANNEL

Rotterdam

Dunkirk

Calais

Brussels

Cherbourg

Liège

to
Cologne

Le
Havre

Dieppe

Lille

Arras

Brest

Quimper

Mont St.
Michel

Bayeux

Pontorson

Rouen

Amiens

Aulnoye

Charleville

Mezieres

Lorient

Rennes

Argentan

Compiegne

Paris

Luxembourg

Redon

Angers

Le Mans

Fontainebleau

Reims

Epernay

Thionville

Nantes

Tours

Orleans

Lerouville

Nancy

La Rochelle

Vierzon

Poitiérs

FRANCE

Nevers

Dijon

Culmont-
Chalindrey

St Germain
des Fosses

Belfort

Coutras

Périgueux

Mâcon

Dole

Basle

Bordeaux

Clermont-
Ferrand

Frasne

Bern

Lausanne

Dax

Puyôo

St
Etienne

Lyon

Aix-les-
Bains

Geneva

Culoz

Annecy

Lourdes

Montauban

Valence

Chambery

Milan

Toulouse

Grenoble

Carcassonne

Nimes

Avignon

Narbonne

Tarascon

Genoa

Perpignan

Arles

Marseille

Port Bou

Toulon

Nice

Pisa

Barcelona

N

to Venice

to Valencia

0   200

km

MEDITERRANEAN SEA

to
Rome

FRANCE

Entry requirements	Passport
Population	53,500,000
Capital	Paris (pop.: 10,825,000)
Currency	Franc
	£1 = approx. 8.66 F
Political system	Republic
Religion	Mainly Roman Catholic
Language	French (English spoken in cities)
Public holidays	1 Jan.; Easter Monday; 1 May; 8 May; Ascension Day; Whit Monday; 14 July; 15 Aug.; 1, 11 Nov.; 25 Dec.
International dialling codes	From UK 010 + 33 + number (no area code required)
	From USA 011 + 33 + number
	To UK 19 + 44 + number
	To USA 19 + 1 + number

France is a country of great diversity whose long and eventful history has left behind a wealth of attractions and pleasures to experience. Because of the efficient rail network, you can make as much or as little of France as you want: it's just as possible to explore each region in depth as it is to take an overnight express straight to the Riviera, if time and tanning are of the essence.

France (Gaul) was part of the Roman Empire till the Germanic Franks moved in during the fifth century. Charlemagne was crowned by the Pope on Christmas Day 800, but after his death the French nobles tried to go it alone. More successful than most were the Dukes of Burgundy and Normandy. In 987 the Capetian dynasty began to centralize power which led to a period of prosperity and trade, and the eventual growth of Paris as the intellectual centre of Europe in the thirteenth century. England's Norman kings held vast estates in France till the Hundred Years War sent them packing. This further strengthened the French

Additional information on this country contained in the *France* and *Europe – Grand Tour* factsheets (see p.13).

monarchy; a process which continued under the Valois and Bourbon kings, till Louis XIV said it all – 'L'état, c'est moi' ('I am the state').

Under the 'Sun King' (Louis XIV), literature and the arts flourished and all the stylish people in Europe wanted to speak French. From this high point things gradually turned sour, and heads began to roll with the revolution in 1789. The First Republic didn't last long; then out of the chaos emerged Napoleon and dictatorship. During the nineteenth century the French Empire continued to grow, with power constantly changing hands between democracy and dictatorship. The revolution of 1848 brought about the Second Republic, which was followed by a coup d'état and the dictatorship of Napoleon III (nephew of the first). The Third Republic of 1870 survived until the German occupation of France in 1940. After Liberation the Fourth was created, and de Gaulle got the Fifth off the ground in 1958.

FRENCH NATIONAL RAILWAYS
(Société Nationale des Chemins de Fer Français, SNCF)

Arguably, Europe's best railway with the most luxurious carriages travelling at the fastest speeds on the most extensive rail network. On the Sud-Est and Atlantique routes the TGVs (train à grande vitesse) offer the only convenient services (Paris–Lyon–Marseille–Toulon and Nice), and are well worth the supplement. In general, though, supplements are only required on about 40 per cent of journeys. The high speed network is being expanded with huge investment, not only within France but to neighbouring countries, and includes the Channel link with England. The existing ferry connections will be supplemented, and possibly superseded, by the Channel Tunnel, and associated rail connections, during 1994. Strasbourg is only four hours away from Paris, with Berne only four-and-a-half hours and Nice under seven hours. Planned extensions to the Atlantic coast will mean that in the future Bordeaux will be three hours away and Hendaye, on the Spanish border, just over five hours (cutting two hours off current journey times). Further improvements to the TGV will give more powerful units, and will include sleepers. The non-supplement Corail trains are almost indistinguishable from the Eurocity in comfort and in many cases run at the same speed. The network serves over 5,500 destinations using four different types of trains: TGV; Eurocity; Corail; and Turbo-train.

There are two special overnight trains from Calais to the French Riviera. Depending on the season they may call at Paris Nord, but no change is required, see Thomas Cook 12, 12a and 12b. These trains have no seating accommodation so you will have to go for either a sleeper or a couchette at about £8.20.

As with most other aspects of French life, the train network is centred round Paris, so if your route is via Paris, generally you're OK, but if you're crossing France from east to west, your impression of SNCF will be somewhat less glowing.

• **Carrissimo:** The Carrissimo card scheme for the under 26s now replaces the old Carte and Carré Jeune. It offers 50 per cent reduction on all off-peak ('blue period' – see below) travel, and 20 per cent reduction in the white period. Valid for one year from the date of the first journey, a four-journey card costs £20 and an eight-journey card costs £35. The card is valid in first or second class, for up to four people travelling together. Similar schemes, called Carte Kiwi and Carte 'Vermeil', are available for those under 16 and over 60 respectively, ask at SNCF offices.

• **The 'blue, white and red' tariff calendar:** The French Railways tariff calendar is colour coded as follows:

'Blue' (off-peak) period: generally from 12 noon Monday to 12 noon Friday and from 12 noon Saturday to 3 p.m. Sunday.

'White' (standard) period: generally from 12 noon Friday to 12 noon Saturday and from 3 p.m. Sunday to 12 noon Monday plus some French public holidays.

'Red' (peak) period: approximately 60 days in the year when no reduction is available.

To help you plan your trip(s), you are supplied with a copy of the tariff calendar when you buy your Carrissimo.

● **Where to buy your railcard:** You can buy your Carrissimo at French Railways, 179 Piccadilly, London W1, upon presentation of your passport, as proof of your age, accompanied by a passport-size photograph. The four-journey card can be bought at any railway station in France for 190 F.

● **Family Trains:** Another novel idea from SNCF is the Family Train which runs on 11 long-distance routes, mainly from Paris, but also from Nice and Nantes. Each train has fully-equipped play areas where young children can while away the journey as their parents look on. Special menus are available for family groups and there are even power points for baby's bottle-warmer. There is no additional cost, and children under four travel free if they don't occupy a seat. If they do, quarter-price fares are charged – but this only applies to Family Trains. Provided at least four full fare paying passengers, including at least one under 12, are in a group, a whole compartment may be reserved.

● **Rover Tickets:** Those resident outside France and Britain could consider the new BritFrance Railpass (details p.33). As of January 1993 France Vacances passes have been replaced by Euro-Domino (details pp.35–37).

● **Air France Rail Tickets:** The Air France Rail Ticket offers direct flights from 15 UK and Irish airports to Paris and rail travel for nine days within one month and four days within 15 days. A further discount is the free rail travel from Paris Charles de Gaulle airport to the city centre.

From London a four-day ticket costs £168 for second class and £199 for first class. A nine-day ticket costs £224 and £285 respectively. From Manchester a four-day ticket costs £215 for second class and £246 for first class, £271 and £332 respectively for a nine-day pass. From airports in Scotland the cost of a four-day ticket is £245 for second class and £276 for first class, £301 and £362 respectively for a nine-day ticket.

Further details can be obtained from travel agents, Air France or French Railways.

● **Liberté:** Introduced in 1990, this is a four-day pass with accommodation and meals booked in a countrywide network of over 140 hotels. Optional extras include single rooms, first class rail, B&B or half board, and a nine-day pass. The basic cost is £199, but

with supplements depending on number of persons and class of
hotel.

• **Eurail bonuses:** Free:
—Digne–Nice or vice versa on the Chemins de Fer de la Provence.
—Ferry crossing on the Irish Continental Line between Le Havre
  (France) and Rosslare (Ireland) 21 hours, or Cork (Ireland) 21½
  hours, and between Cherbourg (France) and Rosslare (Ireland)
  17 hours. If cabin accommodation is requested, an extra charge
  will be made. Port taxes are extra and payable in French francs.
  During July and August advance reservation is recommended. It
  is compulsory if cabin accommodation is requested. Check the
  sailing schedule always.

The following half-price reductions are granted by Europabus on
transportation costs only and by local offices in Europe.
253 Besançon–Lausanne
254 Chamonix–Evian–Geneva
255 Geneva–Nice
256 Grenoble–Nice
257 Grenoble–Briançon
258 Thonon–Evian–Stresa
446 Best of Brittany

TRAIN INFORMATION

English is spoken by rail staff at the major stations. Agents d'accueil
('welcome officers') wear orange caps and armbands and are in the
stations to help with travel queries and any problems you've
encountered on your journey, i.e. if you've had your rucksack
stolen. They tour round as opposed to sitting in the information
offices. At the ticket barriers in all French stations you'll see a bright
orange machine. Use this to validate your ticket only if you've
bought it in France. Otherwise ignore it. But if you have a
French-purchased ticket, including Résa reservation/supplement
cards, you must validate it, or face a fine.

• **Reservations:** Obligatory on all Eurocity and TGVs as well as a
few of the Rapide trains. If you are taking a Eurocity you'll find the
reservation charge is included in the supplement you'll have to pay.
The supplement depends on distance – between 45F and 61F.
Other optional reservations cost about 14 F. Reservations can be

made up to noon, for trains between 5 p.m. and midnight on that day, and up to 8 p.m. for trains from midnight to 5 p.m. the following day. For trains to or from Paris, give yourself 2–3 days if possible. If you are very well prepared you can reserve up to four months in advance. Eurocity are reservable up to one hour before departure. Generally, it's a good idea to reserve on international trains and on days before public holidays. On some services the reservation ticket is known as 'Résa'. Note that on these services you must validate the reservation ticket along with the main ticket.

• **Night travel:** A sleeper or couchette in France will cost you more than anywhere else in Europe. Granted the service is good, but at a price. SNCF offer both first- and second-class couchettes with four and six berths respectively. Couchettes cost about 80 F and must be reserved in advance, not later than 8 p.m. French Railways introduced a super new concept in budget night travel, the Cabine 8. This is a second-class air-conditioned coach with compartments containing eight semi-reclined bunks which are completely free of charge to use. Needless to say, it was an instant success and SNCF are considering increasing the number of routes from last year's eight. If you are contemplating a long-haul overnight journey in France, check to see if Cabine 8 coaches have been added to the train you intend to use (check this in the Thomas Cook timetable, in the French section). In view of their success, it is advisable to reserve your bunk, for the standard seat reservation fee. Unless you're loaded with cash, avoid the TEN (Trans Euro Nuit) sleepers. Second-class sleepers are either (T3) three beds or (T2) two beds.

• **Eating on trains:** Surprisingly, few stations have tempting delicatessen selling fresh croissants, pâtés and cheeses, so you must come prepared if you want to picnic. There are restaurants and bars at stations which are good but pricey. If you're going to have a blow out, you'd do far better going for a meal which you can at least be sure will be good, rather than for a snack from the ridiculously priced mini-bar trolleys, from which a coffee, for example, will cost about 12 F.

• **Scenic tips:** Take a train anywhere in southern France and you won't be disappointed. Not surprisingly the Alps provide a spectacular backdrop on any run. If you just want to breeze through, consider the Paris to Turin route (10 hours) which goes via the Mont Cenis tunnel (8½ miles long). For those who aren't happy with anything but the best, change at Culoz or Aix-les-Bains, for Chamonix. If you want to head down to the coast, we recommend the run from Grenoble to Marseille (5 hours), then Marseille–Genoa (be sure to sit on the right-hand side of the train on the Riviera stretch). All this journey along the Côte d'Azur is beautiful.

On the other side of the country: the lines between Clermont-Ferrand and Béziers, and Limoges and Toulouse, provide fine upland scenery. The Perpignan to La Tour de Carol is another favourite, as is Valence to Briançon.

● **Bikes:** The scheme's called 'Train et Vélo', and bikes can be hired at any of 283 stations from 50 F a day, plus 500 F deposit. Note, it is not easy to transport bikes with you on SNCF.

● **Advance tickets:** Tickets to and for within France can be purchased at British Rail Travel Centres and at Continental Shipping and Travel Ltd (CSTL), first floor, French Railways House, 179 Piccadilly, London. CSTL also provides a timetable information service by telephone 071–491 1573. French Railways, at the same address, supplies the various passes.

TOURIST INFORMATION

There are over 5,000 tourist information offices in France. They're called Syndicats d'Initiative or Offices de Tourisme. Those designated 'Accueil de France' will help you out with your travel and accommodation problems, as well as booking a bed for you for a small fee. The French tourist literature is good and generally free. Always ask for a map. If you're touring a whole region in depth and require further information, look up the address and phone number of the Comité Régional de Tourisme, and contact them.

● **ISIC bonuses:** Up to 40 per cent reduction on long-distance coach journeys. 50 per cent off all state museums and galleries, museums and theatres.

● **Money matters:** 1 franc (F) = 100 centimes.
Banking hours are 9 a.m.–12 noon, 2 p.m.–4 p.m. weekdays. Closed Saturdays (main towns) or Mondays, and closed early on

day before bank holiday. Shop around before exchanging currency, as banks vary with their commission charges. The best I could find was the Crédit Agricole. Not every bank now changes currency, so if you're arriving on a Sunday night you won't be able to get any anywhere except the main station in the larger cities, where commission charges average 10 F and credit cards and some traveller's cheques are not accepted. French traveller's cheques are much more useful than those in sterling or dollars. Also, if relying on EuroCheques, note that not all banks take them.

● **Post offices:** Open 8 a.m.–7 p.m. weekdays, and 8 a.m.–12 noon on Saturday. The larger railway stations have post offices which keep these, or longer, hours.

● **Shops:** Tend to shut from around 12 noon to 2 p.m., and even longer in the south. They generally stay open till 7.30 p.m. Some food shops, especially bakeries, are open Sunday mornings.

● **Museums:** Follow the same pattern as shops; you'll find many of the state-owned ones closed on Tuesdays, with municipal ones shutting Mondays.

SLEEPING

Your best bet is to use the facilities offered in the various Foyers des Jeunes Travailleurs which are in all major centres. These studenty hostels are usually more central and less strictly run than youth hostels (they don't make a fuss about unmarried couples, etc.). The Acceuil des Jeunes en France (AJF) has numerous hostels throughout France (5,000 beds in Paris alone). Another organization, Union des Centres de Rencontres Internationales de France (UCRIF), operates several hostels throughout France, with sixteen in Paris.

France is well supplied with official youth hostels (auberges de jeunesse) which charge 38–59 F per person. They do ask for IYHF cards, so membership is obligatory. You can join up in France either at the head office at 10 Rue Notre Dame de Lorette, Paris, or at major hostels.

Hotels run on a one- to four-star system with the government fixing prices; these are posted on the back of hotel room doors. So always check you've been quoted the right price. One-stars start at about 90 F and are perfectly adequate so long as you don't expect the luxury of a bath. In France a shower or bath (and often breakfast, too) will almost always cost extra. Try to reduce your costs if you're travelling in a group by getting a third bed put in the room – this'll cost an extra 30 per cent or so and is cheaper than another room.

Camping should present no problems in France as nearly every major town has at least one site. They also operate on a star system. The International Camping Carnet is advisable at most sites – you can buy it at site offices on the spot.

EATING AND NIGHTLIFE

Eating and drinking are about the only things in France not centred on Paris. Each region has its own specialities based on the local produce. There's no such thing as a hurried snack – the midday lunch break is at least a 12-to-2 affair. The French take their food very seriously and like to think themselves connoisseurs. Cafés are for sitting and watching the world go by, not for cheap eating. If you're desperate for a coffee, check the price and size of cup first, make it last and drink in the atmosphere as long as possible. Also try the chain self-service restaurants, often cheap and cheerful, but do not expect the best in French dining. Vegetarians be warned, some chain restaurants (e.g. 'Quick') will often refuse to serve beer if you do not order a meat main course! It's far better, though, to get a baguette under your arm and head for the corner charcuterie and crémerie, where you can choose from a huge selection of cheeses (watch out: chèvre is goat). Fortunately, supermarkets are reasonable and still maintain a high standard. Look out for branches of Prisunic, Monoprix, Uniprix, or Codec.

The wines are cheap and the parks free. Unless you're really broke, it's well worth eating out in the evenings with the fixed-price menus always a safe bet. Try where possible to sample the local dishes, as they give an added interest to touring.

Rouen

It is a pity that many Inter-Railers en route to Paris pass through the fascinating and historic region of Normandy without stopping. Situated on the Seine, Rouen is the capital of Normandy and is perhaps best known for its links with Joan of Arc.

TOURIST INFORMATION

At 25 Place de là Cathédrale (Tel. 35 71 41 77); during summer open Mon.–Sat. 9 a.m.–7 p.m., Sun. 9.30 a.m.–12.30 p.m., 2.30 p.m.–6 p.m.; winter, shut Sundays. They will hand out useful leaflets and help you find a cheap room.

SEEING

The OLD TOWN dates from the twelfth century and boasts a fine collection of beautiful half-timbered houses. A circular walking tour enables you to appreciate the main sites. Unmissable is the RUE DU GROS-HORLOGE, as it connects the OLD MARKET PLACE to the CATHEDRAL (and is adjacent to Tourist Information).

The OLD MARKET PLACE was where JOAN OF ARC was burnt at the stake in 1431 and now contains the STE JEANNE D'ARC national monument, a church and a small covered market, all designed by Arretche.

NOTRE DAME CATHEDRALE dates from the twelfth century and is a fine example of Gothic architecture.

Rouen has many fine churches; perhaps the most notable is ST MACLOU for its large five-panelled porch. The nearby ST MACLOU CLOISTER at 184–186 rue Martainville should also not be missed. This tranquil cloister is one of the last examples of a medieval plague cemetery and was used as a charnel-house until the eighteenth century.

SLEEPING

Cheap rooms are plentiful and many are in the heart of the old city. Tourist Information will assist.

• **Hostel:** Centre de Séjour at 17 rue Diderot (Tel. 35 72 06 45), bus 12, direction Diderot, from the railway station. Alternatively cross over the river, turn left and walk along the river bank.

EATING AND NIGHTLIFE

All the Normandy culinary specialities can be found. The seafood, Rouen duck, calvados and cider are all recommended. Most restaurants are good value and offer fixed menus. The many small bars offer cheaper snacks or just one course and the universal burgers are also available.

A cheap meal can be had at the Maison des Jeunes, 114 ave. de Bretagne, close to the Centre de Séjour, weekday lunchtimes for about 35 F.

Bayeux

An impressive town, Bayeux deserves at least a few hours' sightseeing. It is most notable for its connections with William the Conqueror and the world famous Bayeux Tapestry, graphically telling the story of the Norman Conquest of Britain.

Tourist Information is in the centre of town on corner of rue St Martin and rue des Cuisiniers (Tel. 31 92 16 26), and will provide the usual assistance and information. Open 9 a.m.–6.30 p.m., shutting for lunch, and Sundays off season.

SEEING

QUEEN MATILDA'S TAPESTRY, also known as the BAYEUX TAPESTRY is now magnificently displayed in the Cultural Centre on rue de Nesmond. Open mid-May–mid-September 9 a.m.–7 p.m., otherwise closed over lunchtime and slightly shorter hours; last admission one hour before closure. The BARON-GERARD MUSEUM has fine displays of old paintings, lace, porcelain and tapestries. A combined ticket for four museums can be obtained.

The CATHEDRAL was originally completed in 1077 and is now an impressive mixture of Norman and Gothic architecture. Also worth a look is the MUSEUM OF THE BATTLE OF NORMANDY 1944 in boulevard Fabian Ware. Open 9 a.m.–7 p.m. in the summer, the museum recounts the Allied invasion of France June–August 1944 and is near a British military cemetery.

• **Hostels:** Should you feel inclined to stay, there is no IYHF affiliated hostel, but you could try the Centre d'Accueil Municipal, 21 rue des Marettes (Tel. 31 92 08 19), situated about 1½ miles from the station, ask at tourist information. The Family Home Hostel on rue Général de Dais 39 (Tel. 31 92 15 22) is good value, follow the signs from the station. Reservations recommended. There is also a campsite at Boulevard d'Eindhoven (Tel. 3192 0843), open March–Oct.

Mont St Michel

Although not on a direct railway line, the extra difficulties are well worth it to see the 'marvel of the western world'. Mont St Michel is a solitary village and abbey dramatically perched on a small island linked to the mainland by a causeway which occasionally floods completely at high tide. A tide table is available from the local tourist office, located in the town hall. There is another office on the island as well.

• **Getting there:** Mont St Michel is actually on the boundary between Normandy and Brittany. Take the train from Caen to Rennes and get off at Pontorson. Mont St Michel is about 6 miles away and reached by STN bus, from opposite station, about seven buses a day during summer.

   A further disadvantage is the hordes of tourists, but if you make the trip, you will be rewarded by an unforgettable sight and experience.

SEEING

The splendid ABBEY dominates the island and is open 9.30 a.m.–11.30 p.m. and 1.30 p.m.–4 p.m. (6 p.m. May–Sept., all day during high season), closed on holidays. The guided tour lasts around ¾ hour, at about one-hour intervals. The MERVEILLE or 'marvel' is the group of superb early-thirteenth-century buildings and is aptly named. The VILLAGE is a steep labyrinth surrounding the abbey and is itself encased in RAMPARTS which have good views of the bay.

SLEEPING

The nearest hostel is at the Centre Duguesclin, rue Patten, Pontorson (Tel. 33 60 00 18), open June–Sept., ½ mile from Pontorson Station. Camping sites are better situated but do not be tempted to sleep rough on the causeway or beach as the tides are very unpredictable and dangerous. The nearest is Camping du Mont-St-Michel (Tel. 33 60 09 33), with 350 sites.

Brittany

You'll curse the rail network if you want to visit this region in depth. Local trains all connect up to the main Paris–Brest line rather than other nearby towns. On the new TGV line from Paris it now only takes just over two hours to Nantes and around two hours to Rennes. For accommodation and general information on the area, visit the Centre Information Jeunesse Bretagne in the Maison du Champ de Mars at 6 Cours des Alliés, Rennes. There is a campsite (Tel. 99 36 91 22), open April–Oct., and a youth hostel at 10–12 Canal St-Martin (Tel. 99 33 22 33).

From RENNES it's possible to make a day trip to the impressive walled port of ST MALO, formerly a pirates' stronghold, and preserved almost intact. Pushing south, NANTES has a majestic fifteenth-century ducal palace, as well as a very good museum devoted to Breton folklore. The youth hostel in Nantes is at 2 Place de la Manu (Tel. 40 20 57 25), open July and August only, there is also a campsite (Tel. 40 74 47 94), open all year.

Also consider a trip to CONCARNEAU. Take the train to ROSPORDEN and then a railway bus (free on Eurail) to Concarneau. Check your timetable first, because the bus doesn't connect with every train.

The Loire Valley

This pastoral region contains many of France's most elegant and impressive buildings. To do justice to the area would take at least a week. Fortunately for the eurorailer, most of the châteaux and palaces lie between Angers and Blois, a distance of about 80 miles. Where to base yourself depends on your style. Perhaps the most impressive châteaux are CHAMBORD and CHENONCEAU. There are campsites everywhere, and youth hostels at Saumur, Tours, and Blois.

BLOIS is typical of the Loire: THE BISHOPS' PALACE, the CHÂTEAU, the OLD QUARTER – all set in a picturesque location among fine churches and gardens. The campsite at Blois is good. About three miles out of town, by bus or taxi from the station (about 0.40 F and 35 F respectively) or take the metro to Port Maillot and then the campsite bus. The last bus from Blois leaves at 6.15 p.m. For those who prefer a cheap hotel, it's best to base yourself at TOURS, where rooms are plentiful around the station. Try the Olympic opposite the station at 74 rue Bernard–Palissy (Tel. 47 05 10 17), or Hôtel Comté behind the station, at 51 rue Auguste Comté (Tel. 47 05 53 16). If you're out of luck, the tourist office is just in front of the station at Place Maréchal Leclerc (Tel. 47 05 58 08) (open Mon.–Sat.: 9 a.m.–12.30 p.m., 2 p.m.–9 p.m., Sun.: 10 a.m.–12.30 p.m., 4 p.m.–9 p.m.). For a fee of about 5 F they will fix you up with a room and give free advice on bus tours, etc., to the châteaux. If you can't afford the bus, don't worry as they rent out bikes at the station for around 50 F a day plus a hefty deposit. Most of the châteaux are easily accessible, all shutting around 6 p.m. The town itself, like Blois, has a charming OLD QUARTER and a former BISHOPS' PALACE which now hosts the MUSÉE DES BEAUX ARTS. Further down the line, SAUMUR and ANGERS both have very impressive castles perched on high, overlooking the Loire and Maine respectively. If you prefer to stay at this end of château country, the Syndicat d'Initiative, opposite the station at Angers, will find you a room for a small charge.

Wherever you end up, it's a good idea to go along to any train information desk in the area and pick up one of the local timetables giving all the smaller stops.

Paris

Everyone has his or her own impressions and expectations of Paris – so much has been said and written about it, and it all seems a cliché, yet Paris is everything you've probably ever heard, and more. It's a fabulous city and you can't help but enjoy a few days there.

Paris has twenty 'arrondissements' (districts) with the Louvre as No. 1. The city is divided into the Left Bank (Rive Gauche) and Right Bank (Rive Droite), with the River Seine dividing them. Generally speaking, the Left Bank is the trendy, studenty and less expensive area, and the Right Bank is more classy.

STATION FACILITIES

There are five international stations in the city: Austerlitz serves southern France, Spain and Portugal; Est serves Germany, Switzerland and Austria; Lyon serves the south-east of France, Italy and Switzerland. Nord serves Belgium, Holland, Scandinavia, Germany, the north of France, and Britain's ferry entry ports of Calais and Boulogne. St Lazare serves Britain's entry ports of Dieppe and Le Havre.

		AUSTERLITZ	EST
Train information	Mon.–Sun.:	All hours (Tel. 45 82 50 50)	All hours (Tel. 45 82 50 50)
Reservations	Mon.–Sun.:	8 a.m.–7 p.m. (Tel. 45 65 60 60)	8 a.m.–7 p.m. (Tel. 45 65 60 60)
Tourist information	Mon.–Sat.:	8 a.m.–3 p.m. (Tel. 45 84 91 70)	8 a.m.–9 p.m. (8 p.m. in low season) (Tel. 46 07 17 73)
Foreign exchange	Mon.–Fri.:	8.45 a.m.–5 p.m.	7.30 a.m.–8 p.m.
Bar, Snacks	Daily	6 a.m.–12 midnight	7 a.m.–11 p.m.
Bath, Shower	Daily	5.30 a.m.–8.30 p.m.	6.15 a.m.–10 p.m.
Left-luggage lockers	No access:	0.30 a.m.–5.30 a.m.	1.15 a.m.–5.45 a.m.
Left-luggage store	Daily	6 a.m.–0.30 a.m.	6 a.m.–12 midnight
Shops		7 a.m.–11 p.m. Lower level and at Blvd de l'Hôpital	Mon.–Sat.: 8 a.m.–12.45 p.m. 2.30 p.m.–7.30 p.m. Sun.: 8 a.m.– 12.45 p.m. Rue du 8 Mai and Faubourg St Denis
Waiting room		As station	As station
Toilets		As station	As station
Station shuts		0.30 a.m.–5.30 a.m.	1.15 a.m.–5.45 a.m.

There are post office facilities at both these stations (8 a.m.–7 p.m., half day Saturdays). SNCF run buses for 14 F which connect most of the stations, or metro line 5 connects Paris Est and Paris Nord and Austerlitz. Paris Lyon is reached by buses 61 and 65 from Austerlitz, and bus 65 from Est.

	PARIS LYON	PARIS NORD
Train information	All hours (Tel. 45 82 50 50)	All hours Office: 6 a.m.–10 p.m. (platform no. 19) (Tel. 45 82 50 50)
Reservations	8 a.m.–7 p.m. (Tel. 45 65 60 60)	8 a.m.–7 p.m. (Tel. 45 65 60 60)
Tourist information	Mon.–Sat.: 8 a.m.–9 p.m. (Tel. 43 43 33 24)	Mon.–Sat.: 8 a.m.–9 p.m. (Tel. 45 26 94 82)
Foreign exchange	6.30 a.m.–10 p.m.	6.30 a.m.–10 p.m. Also opp. station, Mon.–Fri.: 9 a.m.–4.30 p.m. Sat.: 9 a.m.–1 p.m. at BNP (smaller queues and better rates)
Bar, Buffet	5.40 a.m.–11.30 p.m.	6 a.m.–11 p.m.
Restaurant	5.40 a.m.–11.30 p.m. (ground level) 11 a.m.–2 p.m. 6 p.m.–9.15 p.m. (upstairs)	11.30 a.m.–2 p.m. 6.30 p.m.–9.45 p.m.
Bath, Showers	6 a.m.–8.30 p.m.	6 a.m.–8.30 p.m.
Left-luggage lockers	No access 1 a.m.– 4 a.m.	All hours. (Use the ones upstairs beside the left-luggage store)
Left-luggage store	All hours	6 a.m.–12 midnight
Shops	Rue Hector Malot	Mon.–Sat.: 8 a.m.–12.45 p.m. 2.30 p.m.–7.30 p.m. Sun.: 8 a.m.–12.45 p.m.
Waiting room	As station	As station
Toilets	As station	As station
Station shuts	1 a.m.–4 a.m.	2 a.m.–5.45 a.m.

Post office facilities at both stations, Mon.–Fri.: 8 a.m.–7 p.m., Sat.: 8 a.m.–12 noon (rue Diderot for Paris Lyon). SNCF buses will get you from one station to another, or from Paris Lyon you can get to all the other stations by metro line 1 to Bastille then change to line 5. From Paris Nord, line 5 takes you to Austerlitz, Est and Lyon (change on to line 1 at Bastille). An additional route from Nord to Lyon is to take RER line B to Châtelet les Halles, then RER line A to Lyon (much faster). With six stations in Paris it's important to get the right one. Plan well ahead, and wherever possible use your timetables, as train information queues can be up to two hours long in the summer. At Gare du Nord reservations for the TGV to Lyons are now made at an automated machine.

	ST LAZARE	MONTPARNASSE
Information	Tel. 45 82 50 50	Tel. 45 82 50 50
Reservations	Tel. 45 65 60 60	Tel. 45 65 60 60
Tourist Information		Mon.–Sat.:
		8 a.m.–9 p.m. (high season)
		8 a.m.–8 p.m. (low season)
		(Tel. 43 22 19 19)

FROM	TRAINS GO TO:
Gare de l'Est	Eastern France
	Germany
	Switzerland
	Eastern Europe
Gare de Lyon	Riviera
	Italy
	South-east France
Gare d'Austerlitz	Central France
	Southern Atlantic coast
	Spain
Gare Montparnasse	Western France
	(Chartres, Loire Valley by TGV, and Brittany)
	Spain
Gare St Lazare	Normandy
Gare du Nord	North coast
	Belgium
	Holland
	Germany (Hamburg)
	Britain

TOURIST INFORMATION

The main office of the Paris Convention and Visitors Bureau is at 127 Avenue des Champs Elysées (Tel. 47 23 61 72) (metro to Charles de Gaulle–Etoile). Open Mon.–Sun.: 9 a.m.–8 p.m. They'll give you information on Paris and the Ile de France. They also run a wide-ranging accommodation-finding service on a commission basis. For recorded tourist information in English phone 47 20 88 98.

• **Accueil des Jeunes en France (AJF):** This non-profit-making office for the young is at 119 rue St Martin (Tel. 42 77 87 80), across from the Pompidou Centre (Beaubourg) (Metro Les Halles or Rambuteau.) Open Mon.–Sat.: 9 a.m.–5.30 p.m. They'll find you a bed or a place in a Foyer for 90 F and upwards. They also have offices at Gare du Nord, 139 boulevard Saint Michel, open June and July only (RER Port Royal) and 16 rue du Pont Louis-Philippe (métro Hôtel de Ville). The policy these days seems to be to pay the full accommodation price over to AJF when booking, so remember to change money before joining the queue. To get the best rooms be in the queue by 8 a.m.

• **Union des Centres de Rencontres Internationales de France (UCRIF):** This centre for young tourists is at 4 Jean-Jacques Rousseau, near their hostel (Tel. 42 60 42 40), can arrange reservations, and gives advice on travel.

• **Usit Voyages:** 6, rue Vaugirard (Tel. 43 29 85 00), Mon.–Fri.: 9.30 a.m.–6 p.m., Sat.: 1 p.m.–5 p.m. They will help you out with all travel requirements, and fix you up with an ISIC (métro Odéon or Luxembourg).

• **Federation Unie des Auberges de Jeunesse (FUAJ):** The central booking facility for IYHF hostels in Paris, France and also for some European destinations. Operates from the hostel at 8 bd Jules Ferry (Tel. 43 57 02 60, métro République). They also can arrange sightseeing coaches and various other services.

• **Addresses:**
POST OFFICE AND POSTE RESTANTE: 52 rue du Louvre (Tel. 40 28 20 00), open 24 hours a day (métro Louvre).
AMEX: 11 rue Scribe, Mon.–Fri.: 9 a.m.–5.30 p.m., Sat.: 9 a.m.–5 p.m. (Tel. 47 77 77 07) (métro Opera).
UK EMBASSY: 35 rue du Faubourg St Honoré (Tel. 42 66 91 42). The Emergency Consulate is at 9 Avenue Hoche (Tel. 42 66 91 42) (métro Charles de Gaule–Etoile).
US EMBASSY: 2 Avenue Gabriel (Tel. 42 96 12 02), Mon.–Fri.: 9 a.m.–6 p.m. (métro Concorde), visa section open 8.45 a.m.–11 a.m.
CANADIAN EMBASSY: 35 Avenue Montaigne (Tel. 47 23 01 01) (métro Franklin-Roosevelt).

AUSTRALIAN EMBASSY: 4 rue Jean Rey (Tel. 45 75 62 00) (métro Bir-Hakeim).

24-HOUR CHEMIST: Pharmacie Dhéry, 84 Avenue des Champs Elysées (Tel. 45 62 02 41) (métro George V).

SOS HELP LINE: English speakers to help you with personal problems, etc. 3 p.m.–11 p.m. (Tel. 47 23 80 80).

● **Getting about:** the métro in Paris is one of the world's best underground systems and you're bound to use it at some point to get you quickly round this incredibly large and sprawling city. The system is open from 5 a.m. to after midnight. The lines are designated by the terminal station. It's a cheap as well as efficient way of getting about. Buy tickets in 'carnets' of 10 for around 35 F, and hold on to them till the end of your journey. The same tickets can also be used on the buses – validate them in the machine on the bus, using two if crossing a zone – and central Paris RER trains.

Tourist passes, known as Paris Visite, valid on both métro and buses, are available for three or five days, over three or four zones. Available from Tourist Offices, in main métro and RER stations, SNCF stations and at Paris airports, the three-day pass costs 80 F, the five-day 130 F, for three zones. A one-day pass, Formule 1, is also available for 23 F.

Recently there has been an increasing number of reports of crime on the métro, including drug users and dealers causing problems for the authorities. Be especially careful of trouble late at night. Also beware of buying a ticket at anywhere other than an official booth: you are only asking to be ripped off.

SEEING

● **The Champs Elysées:** The ÉTOILE is the great circle at the western end of the Champs Elysées with twelve avenues radiating out from it, literally a 'star'. In its centre is the massive ARC DE TRIOMPHE, Napoleon's thank-you to his army; note the sculpture of 'the Marseillaise' by Rude. At the other end of the long and elegant Champs Elysées is the PLACE DE LA CONCORDE, regarded as the most beautiful square in the world. This is where Louis XVI, Marie-Antoinette and some 1,300 others met their death in the French Revolution.

● **The Left Bank:** ST GERMAIN-DES-PRÉS, the oldest church in Paris, is surrounded by open-air restaurants and cafés and quiet little streets like PLACE FURSTEMBERG which make a pleasant stroll.

BOULEVARD ST MICHEL, the centre of Bohemian student life of the 1960s, still makes an interesting excursion. Sitting in one of the cafés along the 'Boul Mich' in the Latin Quarter (so called because the Sorbonne students were lectured to in Latin in the Middle Ages), you're bound to make new friends. The TOUR MAINE-MONTPARNASSE (690 feet), gives you a great view over the city. (The lift up is advertised as the fastest one in Europe.)

Also on the Rive Gauche is the beautiful church of LES INVALIDES with its golden dome and the mortal remains of Napoleon. A good view of NOTRE DAME CATHEDRAL can be seen from SQUARE RENÉ VIVIANI.

• **The Right Bank:** Opposite the LOUVRE is Richelieu's PALAIS ROYAL where the Comédie Française is based, and not far from here is the oldest square in Paris – PLACE DES VOSGES – the beautiful Renaissance square built by Henry IV early in the seventeenth century; VICTOR HUGO'S HOUSE at No. 6 is now a museum. The GEORGES POMPIDOU CENTRE (known as the Beaubourg) is a good place to meet trendy young Parisians and see interesting exhibitions. Closed Tuesdays, it's open 10 a.m.–10 p.m.

The SACRÉ-COEUR is the white dome that dominates all of Paris, built on the hill at MONTMARTRE, the artists' quarter that flourished in the late nineteenth century when many of the Impressionist painters lived and worked there. The artists' quarter is more than the touristy PLACE DU TERTRE. Stroll along rue Norvins into rue des Saules and check out the LAPIN AGILE, a meeting point for writers and artists and very atmospheric. A climb to the dome of the Sacré-Coeur gives you a fifty-mile view over Paris, and is cheaper than climbing the Eiffel Tower. This is a great place to be in the evening, but watch out for pickpockets in this area. Even someone asking the time might be after your watch.

• **Île de la Cité and Île St-Louis:** The tiny island where Paris began in pre-Roman times is the Île de la Cité. The oldest bridge in Paris, the PONT NEUF, leads you to the statue of Henry IV and on to the PALAIS DE JUSTICE (law courts). The SAINTE CHAPELLE is a Gothic church built to house Holy relics, dating from 1248. The relics have now been moved to Notre Dame, but the stained glass windows here can be viewed.

NOTRE DAME is only a short walk from here; this thirteenth-century cathedral is the first church of Paris, where Napoleon was crowned and all national celebrations are staged.

The other main sights are the OPÉRA GARNIER, 1875 (the new opera built in 1989 is located at Place de la Bastille) and, of course, the EIFFEL TOWER, which looks its best floodlit at night. A five-year renovation scheme costing millions of francs has made great improvements, but it is still expensive to ride to the top. There are three stages of lifts, getting progressively more expensive the higher you go. It is possible to walk up the first two stages to save on the cost (8 F), but if you use the lifts all the way there is a 49 F charge. The queues can be long, even with all lifts in action, also check you're in the right queue. The view from SACRÉ-COEUR is just as impressive. If you are visiting it on 14 July (National Day), make sure you go at night and catch the spectacular hour-long fireworks display. If you want to tour the famous PARIS SEWERS, call in at place de la Résistance, 7e.

There are various city tours: ParisVision buses with prerecorded commentary, and Cityrama tours, or the famous bateaux-mouches which sail down the Seine (go for the evening one when the illuminations are on). Shop about, as they vary from reasonably priced to extortionate. Still, if you've only a day or two, the three-hour Parisvision tour gives you a pretty comprehensive idea of the city.

By far the best-value way to see the city is on a Bateaux Mouche trip. Leaving from Pont de L'Alma on the right bank, 30 F will buy you a 1½-hr cruise with recorded commentary. (Don't take one of the over-priced lunch/dinner cruises – they're 300 F and decidedly not worth it!)

● **Museums:** All state-owned museums in Paris are shut on Tuesdays and those owned by the city close on Mondays. An ISIC will get you into most places for half price. There are over 100 interesting museums in the city; pick up a leaflet on them from tourist information.

The MUSEUM AND MONUMENT CARD, available from metro stations, tourist office and major museums, permits direct entry to 63 museums and monuments in the Paris region. Valid for one day (cost 55 F), three consecutive days (cost 110 F) or five consecutive days (cost 160 F); unlimited visits are permitted and access is immediate, avoiding the often lengthy queues. The card can be bought in advance, but your name and the date must be written on it on your first visit in order to validate it.

THE LOUVRE: Pyramide, Cour Napoléon. Treasures include the Venus de Milo, and the Mona Lisa. Open 9 a.m.–6 p.m., except Wednesday, 9 a.m.–9.45 p.m., on Mondays only certain rooms are open, and many departments close at 5 p.m. or 5.30 p.m. every day. Entry is 31 F, all under-26s half price, half price on Sundays. Remember, you *must* leave your hand luggage at the entrance. Queues are very long on Saturdays and Sundays.

As it now houses the underground entrance, it is impossible to miss the controversial 71-foot-high GLASS PYRAMID in the courtyard of the Louvre. Designed by Pei, it not only houses the reception area, including a complex of restaurants and shops, but has greatly expanded gallery and exhibition space.

The Jeu de Paume collection is now included in the wonderful new MUSÉE D'ORSAY, which has also absorbed the contents of a few other museums. It is situated on the Left (south) Bank, near the Tuileries. Closed Mondays. Admission 31 F, open 10 a.m. to 6 p.m., from 9 a.m. on Sundays, open to 9.45 p.m. on Thursdays. Reduced entry for 18–24 year olds and ISIC holders. You can spend all day in the Louvre or Musée d'Orsay.

POMPIDOU CENTRE: A modern multi-cultural art centre conceived by Georges Pompidou and opened in 1977, this eccentric building is home to just about every modern art-form you can think of. It also includes an excellent library with hundreds of daily newspapers, including most English and American ones. Although entrance is free, special exhibitions and the cinema usually incur a charge of 16 F. A special one-day pass is available at 50 F. There's usually plenty of free entertainment in the form of fire-eaters and street artists outside. Also known as the 'Beaubourg'.

For button-pushers, the CITÉ DES SCIENCES ET DE INDUSTRIE, at 30 Avenue Corentin-Cariou, will keep you occupied all day. A combination of science exhibitions, computer games, practical demonstrations and videos are all included in the 35 F admission. The Planetarium is included, but entry to the giant movie theatre is extra. Take buses 150, 152 or 250.

MUSÉE DE CLUNY: 6 Place Paul-Painlevé (corner of Boulevard St Michel and Boulevard St Germain). Open 9.30 a.m.–12.30 p.m., 2 p.m.–5.15 p.m. Medieval art housed in a fifteenth-century mansion next to the Roman baths of Paris.

MUSÉE DE L'HOMME: Palais de Chaillot, Place du Trocadéro. Open 9.45 a.m.–5.15 p.m. Very good anthropological museum – documentary films are shown daily.

• **Parks:** There is no shortage of attractive parks and gardens in Paris, and they make good picnic venues.

The BOIS DE BOULOGNE is the wood at the western edge of the city with seven lakes, a waterfall, various sports facilities and a campsite. The BOIS DE VINCENNES is the wood on the south-eastern edge. There's a zoo, a racetrack and a couple of museums out here too. The two most central picnic parks are the JARDIN DES TUILERIES and the JARDIN DES CHAMPS ELYSÉES; the LUXEMBOURG, off Boulevard St Michel, is a very picturesque, formally laid-out garden in French style.

SLEEPING

Campsites are not central, and with so much to see in Paris the commuting may be a waste of valuable time. Private accommodation is hardly heard of in Paris so your choice is between a cheap hotel, a student hostel or a Foyer. Your choice will be dictated not just by your pocket but also by how many you are. Paris really is a city for lovers – it's often virtually the same price for a single or a double bed so couples are on to a good deal, but singles are better off in a Foyer.

The average night in a hotel double room is anything upwards from 150 F, for one star, and a single Foyer stay will be about 90 F. Always ask hoteliers if there's nothing cheaper and get as many as possible into a room to bring the cost down. If you have any problems try the UCRIF/AJF information office at Gare du Nord, but don't try sleeping there or you'll be ejected about 1 a.m. or mugged. Also try the UCRIF/AJF and FUAJ offices listed under **Tourist Information**.

• **IYHF Hostels:** The main youth hostel is at 8 Boulevard Jules Ferry, near place de la République (Tel. 43 57 55 60). Take the métro to République.

A 411-bed hostel called Auberge de Jeunesse d'Artagnan is at 80 rue Vitruve (Tel. 43 61 08 75). The nearest métro is Porte de Bagnolet. Open 24 hours. There is also a temporary hostel, open July–15 Sept., book through the Jules Ferry hostel.

• **Hotels:** The best districts to concentrate your attention on for cheap hotels and basic B&B-type accommodation are around the Place de la Bastille, Nation, St Paul, Gare de Lyon, Place de Clichy and Pigalle. Try: Sorbonne, 6 rue Victor Cousin (Tel. 43 54 58 08); Hôtel Notre Dame, 1 Quai St Michel (Tel. 43 54 20 43). Also worth a try are Dacia, 41 Boulevard St Michel (Tel. 43 25 34 53), Hôtel Henri IV at 25 Place Dauphine (Tel. 43 54 44 53), and the hotel at 13 rue de Malte. The Hôtel Speria at 1 rue de la Bastille is also worth checking out, as are Hotel Bel-Air, 5 rue Rampon, and Hôtel Keppler, 12 rue Keppler (Tel. 47 20 65 05).

• **Foyers and student hostels:** CIS Léo Lagrange, 107 rue Martre Clichy (Tel. 42 70 03 22), métro Mairie de Clichy; Maison des Clubs UNESCO, 43 rue de la Glacière (Tel. 43 36 00 63, métro Glacière); Hôtels des Jeunes (AJF), at four locations in the city at 11 rue du Fauconnier, 6 rue de Fourcy (both Tel. 42 74 23 45, métro St-Paul), 12 rue des Barres (Tel. 42 72 72 09, métro Hôtel de Ville), and 151 av. Lédri Rollin (Tel. 43 79 53 86, métro Voltaire); Centres International de Paris (BVJ), also with four locations, 20 rue Jean-Jacques Rousseau (Tel. 42 36 88 18, métro Châtelet or Louvre), 44 rue des Bernardins (Tel. 43 29 34 80, métro Maubert), 11 rue Thérèse (Tel. 42 60 77 23, métro Pyramides or Opéra) and 5 rue du Pélican (Tel. 40 26 92 45, métro Louvre or Châtelet). BVJ International at 11 rue Thérèse is excellent. Open all day but with a 2 a.m. curfew. Foyer International d'Accueil de Paris, 30 rue Cabanis (Tel. 45 89 89 15, métro Glacière). The two CISP (Centre International de Séjour de Paris) hostels may also be worth a try, but do not get good reports. They are at 6 ave. M. Ravel (Tel. 43 43 19 01, métro Porte de Vincennes) and at 17 boulevard Kellerman (Tel. 45 80 70 76, métro Porte d'Italie). Two Foyers normally for women only: 234 rue de Tolbiac (Tel. 45 89 06 42), short stays only allowed during July and August, otherwise one month minimum (Métro Tolbiac); 93 bd St-Michel (Tel. 43 54 49 63), normally women only, but allows men during July to Sept. (Métro Luxembourg).

• **Camping:** Camping du Bois de Boulogne, allée du Bord de l'Eau (Tel. 45 24 30 00), take the metro to Porte Maillot, then bus 244, then a short walk. Shower facilities are limited, and it costs around 55 F per night, get there early in summer. Also, south of Paris, try

'Paris Sud' at 125 Avenue de Villeneuve, Choisy le Roi (Tel. 48 90 92 30), some way out.

• **Stuck in Paris with no money for a bed?:** There are good overnight trains to Madrid (from Austerlitz), Salzburg (from Est); Venice (from Lyon), and Copenhagen (from Nord).

EATING AND NIGHTLIFE

Both are a great pleasure in Paris and can be afforded, in one category or another, by everyone. The French seem to have invented the picnic and you'd have to be completely blind or stupid not to be able to make yourself a delicious picnic of baguette, pâté, cheese, wine and fruits. There are several open-air markets and boulangeries (bakers) in every district while the épiceries (grocers) stay open till 7.30 p.m.

If you want a change from French food, there are plenty of alternatives provided by the numerous immigrants from France's ex-colonies. The centre of the North African (Algerian, Tunisian, Moroccan, etc.) restaurant area is between rue St Jacques and Boulevard St Michel; there are also many Greek and Italian restaurants here.

There are fast-food chains and self-service cafés too in Paris, but you're better – and it's often just as cheap – to look for a French restaurant which offers a 'menu du jour', and eat real French cuisine – for once at a price you can afford. The areas round rue de la Huchette and rue Mouffetard in the Latin Quarter will prove fruitful for reasonably priced restaurants. Around the La Huchette area watch out for the plate throwing, it gets excessive at times. For good cheap French restaurants try the street Gregorie de Tours.

Often the best value set menus are in Chinese restaurants. Try the Palais de Chine for especially good value. It's at 31 rue St Jacques, off the Boulevard St Germain.

For those wanting to eat at student restaurants on their ISIC, call at CROUS, 39 avenue Georges Bernano (métro Port Royal), open Mon.–Fri. 9 a.m.–5 p.m. for a list of all the places you can eat for under 20 F in this scheme. CROUS is shut during June and July.

A few suggestions: Crêperie St Germain, 27 rue St André des Arts; Chartier, 7 rue du Faubourg Montmartre – about 60 F for three courses and a drink – very traditional restaurant; Restaurant des Beaux Arts, 11 rue Bonaparte – good cheap set menus – expect a really good set meal with wine from 65 F; Country Life vegetarian restaurant, 6 rue Daumou, Mon.–Fri. 11.30 a.m.–2.30 p.m.; Crêperie de la Houff, 9 rue Mouffetard; Au Grain Folie, 24 rue de la Vieuville, Montmartre, 7 p.m.–10 p.m., small but good vegetarian.

For current events in Paris, buy *Pariscope*, or contact tourist information.

If you were thinking of the stereotyped trip to the Moulin Rouge, Lido or Folies Bergère, you might as well forget the rest of your European itinerary, as a night out in one of these places will cost you about 500 F minimum. It's actually more of a spectacle walking round the Blanche and Pigalle areas, just down from Montmartre, or Montparnasse, but watch out for drug-pushers and pickpockets around here. For the serious red-light seekers, the place is rue St Denis.

Slightly more sedate a time can be had watching the fountains at the Trocadéro and admiring the view of the Eiffel Tower, or wandering down by the Seine; often there are buskers in the area round Place du Vert Galant. On a fine evening, wandering around the Place de Tertre, Montmartre, is also a great experience.

There's an active theatre and cinema scene in Paris – for details of what's on, see *Pariscope*. The area along the Seine on the Left Bank is best for affordable jazz and rock clubs. Le Caveau de la Huchette, 5 rue de la Huchette, is known to all Parisian students as their informal club, but they ask 50 F (60 F on Friday and Saturday nights) on nights when there's jazz or dancing. For clubs try Le Palace on rue de Faubourg-Montmartre. Closed Monday and Tuesday. Entrance 120 F or free if you eat in the restaurant (130 F minimum). Les Bains on rue du Bourg-L'Abbé is the ultimate rowdy club in an old Turkish bathhouse. Live music is good at Gilbus, 18 rue du Faubourg (métro Republique). Another good jazz club worth trying is New Morning, 10 rue des Petites Ecuries (10e). The cafés at Montparnasse remain a typically Parisian vantage point from which to watch life go by, but watch out for the prices. In August, when many French restaurants are closed, these are often the only places open.

EXCURSIONS FROM PARIS

VERSAILLES, the elaborate palace of Louis XIV, is the main attraction near to Paris. Entrance to the palace costs 30 F. Get there early, or you'll be queueing all day instead of viewing. The gardens cost 17 F, but go there after seeing inside, as the fountains usually aren't switched on until after 3.30 p.m. Take RER C5 from St Lazare or Invalides out to Versailles RG. The palace is open Tues.–Sun.: 9.45 a.m.–5 p.m. (free under 18, half price on ISIC, half price on Sundays). Also within striking distance is the palace of FONTAINEBLEAU with its beautiful park-forest. Take the train from Gare de Lyon. Open 10 a.m.–12.30 p.m., 2 p.m.–6 p.m., except Tues. Fill in your Inter-Rail and take it to the ticket office: you'll be given a free ticket for Fontainebleau or Versailles on the suburban railway. CHANTILLY is an attractive small château, reached by train from Gare du Nord, but it's open only on Sundays and holidays. CHARTRES, home of the world's most famous Gothic cathedral, is an hour away from Gare Montparnasse. If you really want to make a day of it, take the hour-long train ride to Epernay where Moët et Chandon, on Avenue de Champagne, play hosts for another enjoyable tour with free samples.

Of course, the most publicized excursion from the French capital now is to see Mickey and his pals at EURO DISNEY. Fans of theme parks will love the place, though it is appreciably more expensive than its Florida counterpart. £25 for a day pass for an adult and you're not allowed to take in your own food (as Disney makes as much profit on its food outlets as on entrances), while the food on offer is nothing to write home about and pricey. Despite that though, if you can cope with queues, you'll love the place, it really is a great day out.

You can get there on the RER. Take Route A from Charles de Gaulle/Etoile to Marne la Vallee/Chessy. Journey time, around 45 mins.

Alsace and Lorraine

After many years of occupation, the German influence is strongly felt in this region, especially in the cuisine: choucroute (sauerkraut with ham and sausage) and backaoffe (casserole with lamb, pork, beef and potatoes) are our favourites; swallowed down with some pression (local draught lager), they make a meal you won't forget.

Strasbourg

Apart from being the seat of the European parliament and the capital of Alsace, it is one of France's most attractive cities. The tourist office is opposite the station when you arrive. They will supply you with a map (2 F) and information on the city, as well as provide a room-finding service. Alternatively there is another office at 10 Place Gutenberg (Tel. 88 32 57 07). Both youth hostels are quite far away, so it's best to try somewhere more central like Hôtel de l'Ill, 8 rue des Bateliers (Tel. 88 36 20 01). There are several hotels near the station, and the tourist office by the station puts up a board with suggestions when closed.

STATION FACILITIES

	STRASBOURG GARE
Train information	Mon.–Sat.: 7.30 a.m.–8 p.m.
	Sun.: 8 a.m.–8 p.m. (Tel. 88 22 50 50)
Reservations	Mon.–Sat.: 7.30 a.m.–8 p.m.
	Sun.: 9 a.m.–5.30 p.m.
Tourist information	Mon.–Fri.: 9 a.m.–12.30 p.m., 1.45 p.m.–6 p.m.
	Sat.: 8 a.m.–7 p.m. Shorter hours out of season
	Outside in front of station
Foreign exchange	8 a.m.–8 p.m.
Left-luggage lockers	All hours
Left-luggage store	6.30 a.m.–9.15 p.m.
Showers	6 a.m.–10 p.m.
Cafeteria	6 a.m.–11 p.m.
Restaurant	11 a.m.–2.30 p.m. and 6 p.m.–10.30 p.m.
Waiting room	All hours
Post office	Mon.–Fri.: 8 a.m.–7 p.m.
	Sat.: 8 a.m.–12 noon

Daily trains to: Luxembourg (2 hours), Brussels (4 hours), Munich, Stuttgart (2½ hours), Basel (1½ hours), Zürich (2½ hours), Milan, Lyon, Paris (4 hours). (The main tourist office is at 10 Place Gutenberg, open till 7.30 p.m. in summer.)

From the station, walk down to LITTLE FRANCE (well-preserved old houses bordering the canal) and wind your way through the covered bridges and narrow medieval streets to the Gothic CATHEDRAL. Try and arrive for 12.30 p.m. when the astronomical clock comes into action or see the sound and light show in the evenings (24 F or 14 F for students). If you fancy a climb up for a good view – the entrance fee is 4 F. South of the cathedral, the CHÂTEAU DES ROHAN contains a fine museum of archaeology, ceramics and paintings. Closed Tuesday, 15 F. Boat trips are available around the city; try the early evening, it's too busy during the day. For eating, try the areas around Place du Marché aux Cochons de Lait and Place du Corbeau. For cheap and well-prepared Alsacian specialities, go to 9 Porte de Kehl. If you like to eat in a crowd try Au Pont St Martin at 13–15 rue des Moulins (Tel. 88 32 45 13) overlooking the river. In early June there is an International Music Festival.

• **Hostel:** The youth hostel, René Cassin, at 9 rue de l'Auberge de Jeunesse, Montagne Verte (Tel. 88 30 26 46) about 1½ miles from the station on bus 3, 13, 23 from Marché Ste Marguerite to Auberge de Jeunesse. IYHF is obligatory here, and there is also a campsite. The hostel is good, with friendly staff, cost 59 F for B&B; the campsite costs 33 F per person. There is another hostel at rue des Cavaliers, Parc du Rhin (Tel. 88 60 10 20), but this is further out. Take bus 21 from central station to Parc du Rhin; the nearest station is, however, Kehl in Germany, about half a mile away. Alternatively, stay at the hostel at Kehl.

The Alps

In our opinion, CHAMONIX is one of the best places to visit in the Alps by train. The mountain railway which winds its way through picture-book villages is an unforgettable experience; sit on the right-hand side for the best view. Another unforgettable experience is the cable car to the Aiguille du Midi. When you get to Chamonix, the tourist office at Place de l'Eglise (open till 7.30 p.m., in summer) will help you out on accommodation, etc. (prices are expensive), or you could try camping; the tourist office can supply a list of eighteen sites in the area, four are fifteen minutes' walk from the centre. Check out the price of 'Le Chamoniard' chalets, with the tourist office. The Youth Hostel is at Les Pélenus (Tel. 50 53 14 52). It does dinners and packed lunches, and you can also get discounts on cable cars here. It is about a forty-minute walk from town and only a few hundred metres from the nearest station, called Les Pèlerins.

If you have only a day and want to head for the hills, ask tourist information for the list of 'Promenades à Pied' (walking tours), state how long you want to walk and ask what their suggestions are, as the possibilities are endless. If you take your walking seriously, contact the *Club Alpin Français* on Avenue Michel Croz (Tel. 50 53 16 03) for information on mountain refuges and conditions.

Even if you don't make it up the mountains, go and rub shoulders with the climbing set and have a beer with them in the Nationale, rue Paccard. Local Alpine food specialities include smoked sausage, various cheeses and, of course, fondue.

Two other very beautiful spots are AIX-LES-BAINS and ANNECY. Aix-Les-Bains is a pretty spa town on a lake, with good walks in the surrounding hills and around the lakeside which afford panoramas of the deep blue lake and of the town. The hostel at Promenade du Sierroz (Tel. 79 88 32 88) is very good. Take bus 2 towards Plage-Piscine and the Grand Port if you don't fancy the walk of about 1¾ miles. Annecy is another picturesque lakeside town. The old town with its narrow streets and fortress is well worth seeing. The campsite, Le Belvédère, is good value and gives a great view of the lake (Tel. 50 45 48 30). The hostel is 'La Grande Jeanne' at 16 route du Semnoz (Tel. 50 45 33 19). Take bus 1 towards 'Paradis'!

Burgundy

If wine is what takes you to Burgundy, be sure to visit the MUSÉE DU VIN in the Hôtel des Ducs de Bourgogne at BEAUNE and take the tour at MAISON PATRIARCHE, rue du Collège, where they even give you a little bottle for the train. Apart from wine, Burgundy possesses some of the finest abbeys in France, the most spectacular one being at VÉZELAY, and though this isn't on the rail, there's a bus from AVALLON which is. From Paris or Dijon, change at Laroche-Migennes. You could also visit the ornate monastery and other historic buildings of CLUNY, which is on the SNCF bus route between Mâcon and Chalon-sur-Saône.

Dijon

Capital of Burgundy and an important centre in the fourteenth and fifteenth centuries, Dijon went into a decline for about 400 years until the railway brought commerce and industry back in the 1850s. Now it is known for its edible specialities such as mustard, cassis (blackcurrant liqueur), spiced bread (pain d'epices) and snails, and is a thriving commercial and industrial centre.

STATION FACILITIES

	DIJON GARE DE VILLE
Train information	Mon.–Sat.: 8 a.m.–7.30 p.m.
	Sun.: 9 a.m.–12 noon, 2 p.m.–6.30 p.m.
	(Tel. 80 41 50 50)
Reservations	As above
Tourist information	Mon.–Sat.: 9 a.m.–12 noon, 2 p.m.–7 p.m. (winter)
	or 9 p.m. (summer)
	In Place Darcy, three blocks away
Foreign exchange	As 'tourist information'
Bar, Buffet	7.30 a.m.–10 p.m.
Left-luggage lockers	No access 1 a.m.–4 a.m.
Left-luggage store	All hours
Shops	Regular hours. In Place Darcy
Station shuts	1 a.m.–4 a.m.

Daily trains to: Paris (2½ hours, 1 hour 40 min by TGV), Strasbourg (4 hours), Venice, Genoa, Lyon (1½ hours) and Marseille–Nice.

TOURIST INFORMATION AND ADDRESSES

Place Darcy (Tel. 80 43 42 12), near city centre; open daily 9 a.m.–12 noon, 2 p.m.–9 p.m. (until 7 p.m. in winter). Room-finding service.

● **Addresses:**
POST OFFICE: Place Grangier, Mon.–Fri.: 8 a.m.–7 p.m., Sat. and Sun.: 8 a.m.–12 noon.
24-HOUR CHEMIST: Tel. 80 41 28 28.

CENTRE INFORMATION JEUNESSE DE BOURGOGNE: 22 rue Audra (Tel. 80 30 35 56).

SEEING AND SLEEPING

The best way to see Dijon's well-preserved past is on foot; the tourist office gives out a free brochure on walking tours. Recorded commentaries for walkmans can also be hired here.

The former ducal palace, which houses an art museum, deserves a visit, as do the streets of the old town surrounding it. The archaeological museum has artefacts dating back to the ninth century BC (closed Tuesdays).

The youth hostel at 1 Boulevard Champollion (Tel. 80 71 32 12) is good but a long way from the station. Bus 6 from station to Place de la Republic, change to bus 5, to Epirey. The Foyer International d'Etudiants at Avenue Maréchal Leclerc (Tel. 80 71 51 01) requires an ISIC and is also quite far out of town. Hôtel Confort Lamartine, 12 rue Jules Mercier (Tel. 80 30 37 47) has rooms for around 100 F. The campsite is at Avenue Albertler (Tel. 80 43 54 72), overlooking the lake. It's clean, and in the summer it fills up early, so phone first.

Restaurants can be an expensive luxury in Dijon, so buy from the market stalls not far from rue de la Liberté. One of the least expensive restaurants is Moulin à Vent at 8 Place Françoise-Rude. For a jar of the famous mustard, go to 'Maille' on rue de la Liberté.

Lyon

This red-roofed city enjoys a spectacular location, where the Saône and Rhône rivers meet, with impressive Roman ruins and a gastronomic reputation.

STATION FACILITIES

There are two stations of importance; Part-Dieu on the TGV line, and Perrache, for other trains. Daily trains to Paris (2 hours by TGV), Marseille (3 hours by TGV), Turin (4 hours) and Geneva (2 hours). Both stations have the usual facilities: Part-Dieu has no tourist office; Perrache's office is towards the métro interchange. Both stations are open long hours, from around 5 a.m. to 12 midnight.

TOURIST INFORMATION AND ADDRESSES

Place Bellecour (Tel. 78 42 25 75), with a smaller branch at the Perrache station. Open Mon.–Fri. 9 a.m.–7 p.m., Sat. 9 a.m.–6 p.m., Sun. 10 a.m.–6 p.m., shorter hours off-season.

● **Addresses:**
POST OFFICE: Place Antonin-Poncet, close to the Tourist Office.
MEDICAL EMERGENCY: SOS Medecins (Tel. 78 83 51 51).

SEEING

The city is split neatly into three sections: Vieux Lyon the Saône side (west); the Presqu'Ile, which is the tongue of land between the Saône and Rhône; and the Modern City, on the Rhône side (east).

To the west of the old town is the FOURVIÈRE HILL, the site of important Gallo-Roman remains. The hill is reached by the steep streets and steps known as the MONTÉES. The PARC ARCHÉOLOGIQUE DE FOURVIÈRE contains an impressive first century BC ROMAN AMPHITHEATRE, a smaller ODEAN, a TEMPLE and other Roman remains. There is also a museum of finds from the site.

The Old Town itself is a protected area, with well-preserved Renaissance houses. Between and under these run little alleyways called TRABOULES, originally used for carrying silk around, but exploited by the Resistance in the war. The gothic ST-JEAN CATHEDRAL, on rue St-Jean, has an astronomical clock and a treasury, which are worth a visit.

The CROIX ROUSSE district, to the north of the Presqu'Ile, is where the silk and weaving trade was based. Today the traditional methods have been revived at the MAISON DES CANUTS, 10–12 rue d'Ivry. The TERREAUX quarter, with its lead fountain, and the HOTEL DE VILLE complex are also worth a visit.

Museums of note include the FINE ARTS museum, housed in the seventeenth/eighteenth century PALAIS ST-PIERRE, once a Benedictine Abbey. The Museum of PRINTING AND BANKING is also worthwhile, looking at the influence these trades had on Lyon. Probably the most important is the MUSEE HISTORIQUE DES TISSUS, with fabrics and silks from around the world.

SLEEPING

The youth hostel is at rue Roger Salengro (Tel. 78 76 39 23), about three miles from the city centre. From Perrache station bus 53 to Etats-Unis/Viviani, or bus 35 from Place Bellecour to George Levy (last bus 9 p.m.)

The campsites are all about six miles from the centre; try Dardilly, at Porte de Lyon (Tel. 78 69 80 07), bus 19 from Hotel de Ville to Parc d'Affaires.

Cheap hotels worth trying: Alexandra, 49 rue Victor-Hugo (Tel. 78 37 75 79); Croix-Pâquet, 1 place Croix-Pâquet (Tel. 78 28 51 49); Des Marronniers, 5 rue Marronniers (Tel. 78 37 04 82).

EATING

Whilst there are many gastronomic delights well beyond the price of the budget traveller, there should be no trouble in picking up a reasonable meal. Vegetarians can try the L'Eau Vive, 65 rue Victor-Hugo. Le Vivarais, at 1 place Gailleton, serves local specialities.

The Riviera (Côte d'Azur)

EXCURSIONS

In the past you would have had to be crazy to try and base yourself anywhere but Nice on the Côte d'Azur, but that doesn't apply any more should you want to visit the swanky resorts such as Cannes, Monte Carlo, Juan-les-Pins and St Tropez. A day's sunbathing will cost you nothing and you'll find prices only slightly more expensive. The beautiful people of St Trop have not permitted such vulgar inventions as public trains to spoil their paradise, so you'll have to bus it from St Raphael to get there. Still, if you want an all-over tan – or to scrutinize other people's – it's the only place to be.

If you hit a cloudy day, go through to Monaco and put on your best bib and tucker and brave it out in the famous casino at Monte Carlo: you must be able to prove you're 21 or over. The cheapest slot machine is 1 F, and minimum bet at roulette 20 F. The palace is also worth seeing, but is expensive. The Oceanographic Museum, where Jacques Cousteau was director for many years, has all things aquatic, including 450 species of fish. Open all year 9.30 a.m.–7 p.m., except during the Monaco Grand Prix, but it is expensive.

If you're staying overnight, try and get into the Relais International de Jeunesse in Cap d'Ail (Tel. 93 78 18 58) just outside Monte Carlo. The excellent Princess Stephanie Youth Centre is at 24 av. Prince Pierre, and has an age limit of 26. No advance reservations allowed here, registrations start at 10.30 a.m., 60 places in mixed rooms. Another good place to base yourself is at the Saint Michel Ment (Tel. 93 35 81 23) campsite at Menton near the Italian border. A tent for two people a night costs from 29 F, depending on season. Look out for bogus lifts from the station to the campsites as we've had reports of drivers taking money and leaving people at the site entrance knowing it to be full. The Menton youth hostel offers fabulous views over the bay – as well as what is reputed to be the best Youth Hostel evening meal in France. For windsurfing, sailing and other water sports, make for St Raphael, as prices are cheaper here and there's more likely to be wind than further up the coast.

A reasonably cheap place to base yourself is Biot. Look hard for the station between Nice and Cannes as it's easy to miss. Biot has a particularly good campsite opposite the station. Le Logis de la Brague is cheap and close to the beach.

Another good spot is Villeneuve Loubet Plage, between Antibes and Nice. It is a small pleasant town with several campsites. A friendly and cheap campsite is Savoy (Tel. 93 20 16 06) which is right on the beach. Easy access to other resorts by train which runs frequently along the coast.

A good campsite just outside Toulon is Camping Bureguard, which is reached by bus 27 or 9.

The island of CORSICA can be reached from either Nice or Marseille. The cheapest fare is on a night ferry travelling fourth class (sleeping on deck) from Nice, Marseille or Toulon, one way. Corsica is very beautiful. Bonifacio, Ajaccio (Napoleon's hometown) and Bastia are the three most attractive centres on the island. Basically though, you'll need to be really keen to go to

Corsica to make it worth while as rail fares are expensive and rail passes aren't valid here, though Inter-Railers get a reduction. Eurotrain have reduced fares from Nice to Corsica, available from USIT.

Nice

This is without doubt your best base for a spell on the Riviera; it's cheaper than the more pretentious resorts along the Côte d'Azur and has more facilities suited to the eurorailer's lifestyle. It gets very busy, especially in August, and you might have to fight hard for your space on the pebbly beach, but at least there's the reassurance that you're only a few minutes by train from other small Riviera resorts with less crowded beaches like Villefranche, Beaulieu and Menton.

STATION FACILITIES

	NICE GARE DE VILLE
Train information	Daily 6 a.m.–10 p.m. (Tel. 93 87 50 50)
Reservations	Mon.–Sat.: 8 a.m.–7 p.m. Sun.: 8 a.m.–12 noon, 2 p.m.–7 p.m.
Tourist information	Mon.–Sat.: 8.45 a.m.–12.30 p.m., 2 p.m.–6 p.m. In summer, daily 7 a.m.–6.45 p.m. (Hotel reservations from 10 a.m.)
Foreign exchange	Mon.–Fri.: 7.30 a.m.–8 p.m. Sat., Sun. and holidays: 9 a.m.–7 p.m.
Café	7.30 a.m.–10 p.m.
Left-luggage lockers	No access 1.15 a.m.–5.30 a.m.
Left-luggage store	5.30 a.m.–12 midnight
Bath, Shower	8 a.m.–9 p.m.
Station shuts	1.15 a.m.–5.30 a.m.

Daily trains to: Paris, Strasbourg, Genoa, Milan, Rome, Marseille.

TOURIST INFORMATION AND ADDRESSES

The main office is to your left, coming out the station, at Avenue Thiers (Tel. 93 87 07 07). Youth Information CIJ, 19 rue Gioffrédo (Tel. 93 80 93 93).

● **Addresses:**

POST OFFICE: 23 Avenue Thiers. Daily 6 a.m.–10 p.m.

POSTE RESTANTE: Rue des Postes.

AMEX: 11 Promenade des Anglais, Mon.–Fri.: 9 a.m.–12 noon, 2 p.m.–6 p.m., Sat.: 9 a.m.–12 noon.

NIGHT CHEMIST: 7 rue Masséna. 7.30 p.m.–8.30 a.m.

DOCTOR AND AMBULANCE: SOS Médecins (Tel. 93 83 01 01).

SNCM: 3 Avenue Gustave V, for boats to Corsica.

USIT VOYAGES: 10 rue des Belgiques, 06000 Nice (Tel. 87 33 34 96). Also Eurotrain office.

SEEING

The old town of Nice with its street markets and Italian atmosphere has some typically Mediterranean walks through narrow winding alleys, which come as a sharp contrast to the commercial, touristy feeling on the main streets of Nice. To get a view over Nice and the Mediterranean, climb the 300 feet up to the château. If you've only an hour or two in Nice, spend it walking the length of the Promenade des Anglais. Eating in the cafés is prohibitive but the manwatching scope is great.

Among the main things to see are: the PALAIS LASCARIS at 15 rue Droite (former residence of the Count of Ventimiglia), the RUSSIAN ORTHODOX CATHEDRAL, the old PORT of Nice where the beautiful people keep their beautiful yachts, the MATISSE MUSEUM at Avenue des Arènes with some of the artist's works and personal possessions, and the MUSÉE NATIONAL MARC CHAGALL, Avenue du Dr Ménard.

SLEEPING

During the Jazz Parade each July beds become very scarce, and at any other time beds are still hard to find, so come early and phone around. Most of the cheap hotels are located round the station. The IYHF youth hostel is 4 km away at route Forestière du Mont Alban (Tel. 93 89 23 64), bus 14. Use les Collinettes, the university accommodation, at 3 avenue de Robert Schuman (Tel. 93 97 06 64) bus 17, girls only. Price is around 50 F. The Relais International de Jeunesse (Tel. 93 81 27 63), Avenue Scuderi, is OK, but could mean a long wait to be checked in. There is a Foyer, with a good cafeteria,

two minutes from the beach at Espace Magnan, Rue Louis de
Coppet (Tel. 93 86 28 75). Costs around 60 F, varied reports. Hotels
in the following streets are central, clean(ish) and affordable: rue
d'Angleterre, Avenue Durante, rue Alsace Lorraine, rue de
Belgique, Avenue Thiers. The Hotel Ideal Bristol in rue de
Belgique (Tel. 93 88 60 72) charges 100 F for a double – which
includes a fridge! Try Madame Garstandt, 55b rue Gambetta next
to the station. Meublé Let's Go, 26 blvd Raimbaldi, 2nd floor (Tel.
93 80 98 00), five minutes from station. 51 F a night in dorms
including shower. Hotel Central in Rue de la Suisse offers good,
cheap accommodation and has friendly staff. The beaches are
closed from midnight to 6 a.m. so it is impossible to use them for a
cheap sleep. You may be lucky and find one open, but it will be very
crowded and a bit of a bearpit. There are lots of campsites at
Villeneuve–Loubet, 8 km from Nice and on the line from Nice to
Cannes. Although expensive, facilities are good. A map of the sites
is available from the Tourist Information Centre at Nice Station. If
stuck, go to the hostel in Menton.

EATING AND NIGHTLIFE

Food in Nice is among the best in France; the proximity of Italy (30
minutes away) is clear in the cuisine, so the pizzas in Nice are better
than many you'll find in Italy, and there's plenty of fresh seafood
from the Mediterranean. Sitting in an outside restaurant in one of
the pedestrianized streets watching life go by is one of life's great
pleasures, and Nice abounds with good set menus at prices from
45–80 F. Try Le Felix Fauvre, 12 avenue Felix Fauvre; Chez Davis,
11b rue Grimaldi; Chez Nino, 50 rue Trachel (100 beers). For
self-service try the Café de Paris at one of 3 locations – 42 rue
Pastorelli, rue Massena or in the Old Town. Try the Café Casino,
almost opposite the station. For those cutting corners there are
some good supermarkets in the centre.
    Discos and clubs are expensive, and anyway a walk down the
Promenade des Anglais is just as entertaining.

Marseille

Marseille lacks the charm and finesse of the Riviera resorts but it does have character. It's France's oldest city (dating back to 600 BC) and one of the world's major ports, but it tends to cater more for businessmen than tourists.

STATION FACILITIES

	MARSEILLE ST CHARLES
Train information	Mon.–Sat. 9 a.m.–7 p.m., closed Suns. and hols. (Tel. 91 08 50 50)
Reservations	9 a.m.–7 p.m. Mon.–Sat.
Tourist information	Winter: Mon.–Fri.; 9 a.m.–12.30 p.m., 2 p.m.–6.30 p.m. Summer: 8 a.m.–8 p.m. Otherwise main office
Foreign exchange	6 a.m.–8 p.m.
Bar, Buffet	5 a.m.–12 midnight
Restaurant	11 a.m.–2 p.m., 6 p.m.–9.30 p.m.
Left-luggage lockers	No access 1.30 a.m.–4 a.m.
Left-luggage store	All hours
Shower	4 a.m.–12 midnight
Station shuts	1.30 a.m.–4 a.m.

Daily trains to: Paris, Strasbourg, Lyon (4 hours), Nice (2¼ hours), Milan, Bordeaux, Nantes, Amsterdam, Brussels, Rome, Barcelona.

TOURIST INFORMATION AND ADDRESSES

To be found at the station, otherwise at 4 La Canebière (near the Old Port) (Tel. 91 54 91 11), open 9 a.m.–7.30 p.m., 8 a.m.–8.30 p.m. during high season. They have an accommodation-finding service. Youth Information is at rue de la Visitation (Tel. 91 49 91 55).

• **Addresses:**
POST OFFICE: Place de l'Hôtel-des-Postes (metro Colbert).
24-HOUR CHEMIST AND DOCTOR: Tel. 91 52 84 85.

SEEING

Marseille's most famous street is the Canebière (can-o-beer to generations of British and American sailors) which leads up from the Old Port to the REFORMIES CHURCH. This gets quite lively at night, but you're safer walking round here than in the slums of the North African quarter. The Bar du Téléphone was the scene of the biggest gangland massacre ever. Having said that, there is a lot to see of interest.

The MUSÉE DES BEAUX ARTS in the Palais de Longchamp is the city's art gallery. The MUSÉE DES DOCKS ROMAINS (Roman docks), 12 place Vivaux, was the unexpected result of a 1943 German bomb, which revealed the ancient storage depots, with giant storage jars.

ST VICTOR'S ABBEY, a fortified church, built between the eleventh and fourteenth centuries, has a CRYPTE and CATACOMBS. The CATHEDRALE SAINTE-MAIRIE-MAJEURE, is a nineteenth-century, neo-Byzantine building. Off the coast, served by a regular boat shuttle service, is the CHATEAU D'IF. This old fortress, once also a prison, is associated with Alexandre Dumas's, the COUNT OF MONTE CRISTO. Slightly further from the centre is the PARK AND CHÂTEAU BORLEY, built in the eighteenth century. The BASILICA OF NOTRE-DAME DE LA GARDE, in Romano-Byzantine style, was built in the nineteenth century and is surmounted with a gilded statue of Mary. Has a great view over the city, open 7 a.m.–7.30 p.m., bus 60. By complete contrast visit Le Corbusier's 17-storey CITÉ RADIEUSE, a study in concrete.

SLEEPING

The two youth hostels are a long way from the centre but are all right once you get there: Marseille-BoisLuzy (FUAJ), at Avenue de Bois-Luzy (Tel. 91 49 06 18) bus 8 from Bourse (near Canebière), and Auberge de Bonneveine (FUAJ), at 47 Avenue J. Vidal (Tel. 91 73 21 81), métro to RD–PT du Prado, then bus 44.

Beware when looking round for a cheap hotel, especially near the docks – many of them are 'multi-purpose' establishments. Try Camping de Bonneveine, on the beach and cheap (Tel. 91 73 26 99).

EATING AND NIGHTLIFE

Bouillabaisse, the famous French fish stew, comes from Marseille, and is at its best here. There's no shortage of restaurants-cafés and fixed-price menus can be found. The Tunisian and Moroccan restaurants are cheap, though not always good – but it's not wise for unaccompanied girls to head into the North African quarter at night. Chez Papa down by the port does a spectacular ice-cream sundae for less than 30 F.

Nightlife more or less finds you in Marseille: there are plenty of discos around. Just watch out you don't go into too low a dive as, if things get nasty, we've heard the police don't lose too much sleep over the odd mugged eurorailer.

Provence

Renowned for its cloudless skies and Roman remains, Provence's rich countryside has acted like a magnet to artists and eurorailers alike for years. The best time to go is May or September as Aix-en-Provence and Avignon have Arts festivals in July and August, and rooms are hard to find.

If you're going to or from the south or west and have plenty of time, consider breaking your journey at VALENCE. Valence is a pretty, peaceful town with a good youth hostel/campsite near the station called Centre L'Eperviere. Costs are around 14 F a night and the centre also has a swimming pool and bar/restaurant.

Avignon

If you're coming from Lyon, consider getting off the train half an hour before Avignon at ORANGE to see one of the finest Roman theatres in the world.

After a fracas between the Vatican and Philip IV of France, Boniface VII moved to Avignon. The inner walled city is still dominated by his palace, the PALAIS DES PAPES, which is most impressive from the outside; they are restoring it and English tours are available. Be sure to visit the park above the palace for a superb view of the River Rhône.

Sleeping will be your greatest problem in Avignon, but there is an accommodation service inside the station, which you're advised to use to save yourself hassle. If you don't mind large dormitories, try the Youth hotel at Camping Bagatelle (Tel. 90 86 30 39), located on the Ile de la Barthelasse in the middle of the Rhone. Prices are good and there is a superb view of the palace. Centre Pierre Louis Loisil, on the avenue Pierre Sémard (Tel. 90 25 07 92), costs around 52–65 F, plus 5 F membership. Also try the YMCA foyer, 7 Chemin de la Justice (Tel. 90 25 46 20), 90 F. Finally, there's a hostel, called the Squash Club, at 32 Boulevard Limbert (Tel. 90 85 27 78), from the station, walk around the city walls to the right. The tourist information office is at 41 Cours Jean-Jaurés. Open 9 a.m.–1 p.m., 2 p.m.–6 p.m., Sat. 9 a.m.–1 p.m., 2 p.m.–5 p.m., closed Sundays. During the festival in July the tourist office is open Mon.–Sat. 9 a.m.–6 p.m.

If you're camping, Avignon has several sites near each other on the Ile de Barthelasse, Camping municipal (Tel. 90 82 63 50), Camping Bagatelle (Tel. 90 86 30 39), Parc des Libertés (Tel. 90 85 17 73) and Camping des deux Rhônes (Tel. 90 85 49 70). Although they are all within walking distance of the station, the rather infrequent No. 10 bus from by the Post Office (6 F) will take you there.

Arles

An important centre in Roman and medieval times with an impressive amphitheatre which today has reverted to its function as a blood bath, imported Spanish bulls having replaced the gladiators. The MUSEUM OF CHRISTIAN ART is well worth a visit, as is the ROMAN THEATRE from the first century BC and the ROMAN CEMETERY.

Tourist information is on Boulevard des Lices (Tel. 90 96 29 35): they'll supply a ticket for 20 F (14 F on ISIC) for entry to all the museums and monuments as well as help you out with accommodation if necessary. The youth hostel is on rue Foch (Tel. 90 96 18 25), a block behind the tourist office. If you want to venture into the Camargue, Arles is about the nearest you'll get by rail (they rent out bikes at the station and the going is flat).

Nîmes

Some of the best Roman remains in France are here, with the MAISON CARRÉE and the AMPHITHEATRE stealing the show. Tourist information is at 6 rue Auguste (Tel. 66 67 29 11), open Mon.–Sat., 9 a.m.–7 p.m., Sun., 10 a.m.–3 p.m., and they run a similar system to Arles: ticket for the monuments, ISIC reduction. They'll also give you the best route to the PONT DU GARD, a 2,000-year-old Roman aqueduct which is almost intact, and the old Crusaders' port of AIGUES-MORTES, now well inland through silting up. Both are well worth visiting. There are also several castles in the area; the best is at UZES, open all year, ask again at Nîmes tourist office for route.

The hostel is about two miles out at Chemin de la Cigale (Tel. 66 23 25 04). Either bus 6 or 20 – note the last bus is at 8 p.m.

Aix-en-Provence

Birthplace of Cézanne and intellectual and cultural centre of the region, Aix fancies itself somewhat and gives off an air of sophistication that is lacking elsewhere. Sit in any café and you'll feel a strange air of self-importance. The MUSEUM OF TAPESTRIES in the former Archbishop's Palace, is particularly interesting. Avoid their festival, as prices and crowds increase dramatically. Tourist information is at 2 Place du Général de Gaulle (Tel. 42 26 02 93). Try Hôtel du Casino, 38 rue Victor-Leydet (Tel. 42 26 06 88), or the Auberge de Jeunesse at 3 Avenue Marcel Pagnol (Tel. 42 20 15 99) – take bus number 8 to Estienne d'Orves or 12 to Vasarely from the Place de Gaulle, as it's 2 km from the station. Look out for the Vasarely building.

Central/South-west France

The Auvergne, Dordogne and Languedoc regions are sparsely populated and consequently trains are few and far between;

however, if you have the time and patience for the local trains, the rewards are great.

CARCASSONNE, the medieval gem of the Languedoc region, is on the main line and services are good. This is arguably Europe's best-preserved relic of the Middle Ages, and certainly the most interesting walled city in France. After centuries of building and fortifying the town, it was left to rot in the sixteenth century and it wasn't till the nineteenth that restoration began. The tourist office is on Boulevard Camille Pelleton; they find rooms and are generally helpful. Arrive early as Carcassonne is not a well-kept secret and in summer rooms get scarce.

CLERMONT-FERRAND and PÉRIGUEUX are not particularly interesting towns in themselves but they make excellent bases for touring the Auvergne and Dordogne. The tourist board at Clermont is at 69 Boulevard Gergovia, and Périgueux's is in Avenue de l'Aquitaine. They'll provide you with details on the surrounding area and how best to reach the places of interest. Accommodation should be no problem in either town: most of the cheap hotels surround the stations.

LES EYZIES DE TAYAC (the prehistoric capital of Europe) is about 40 minutes south-east of Périgueux by train and its cave paintings are within easy walking distance of the station, as is the tourist information office (Tel. 53 06 97 05). There are plenty of hotels to choose from in the village and there's camping on the other side of the river.

Bordeaux

Famed for the many quality wines it produces, Bordeaux is a good place to head for if your money's running out and you fancy a week or two working on the grape harvest which is picked in September. A short stay here will give you a totally different perspective on French life from your few days in Paris: whilst Paris is very Parisian, Bordeaux is terribly French.

STATION FACILITIES

	ST JEAN STATION
Train information	8 a.m.–9 p.m. (Tel. 56 92 50 50)
Reservations	Mon.–Fri. 9 a.m.–8 p.m., Sat. 9 a.m.–7 p.m., Sun. 10 a.m.–12 noon, 2 p.m.–7 p.m. (Tel. 56 92 60 60)
Tourist information	9 a.m.–7 p.m. (weekdays) 10 a.m.–7 p.m. (Sunday) (Tel. 56 91 64 70)
Foreign exchange	8 a.m.–8 p.m.
Bar, Buffet	5 a.m.–12 midnight
Restaurant	Daily 7 a.m.–9.30 p.m.
Shower	5 a.m.–11 p.m.
Left-luggage lockers	No access 12 midnight–5 a.m.
Left-luggage store	4 a.m.–11 p.m. (some days from 6 p.m.)
Shops	5 a.m.–11 p.m. In Cours de la Marne
Waiting room	All hours
Post office	Mon.–Fri.: 8 a.m.–6.30 p.m. Sat.: 8 a.m.–12 noon
Station shuts	12 midnight–5 a.m.

Daily trains to: Paris, Lyon, Nantes, Toulouse, Marseille, Nice, Biarritz, Madrid and Lisbon.

TOURIST INFORMATION AND ADDRESSES

The main tourist information office is at 12 Cours du 30 Juillet (Tel. 56 44 28 41), just off the Esplanade des Quinconces. The main post office is at 52 rue Georges Bonnac. For a 24-hour chemist or doctor, telephone 56 90 92 75. The Centre Information Jeunesse Aquitaine is at 5, rue Duffour-Dubergier (Tel. 56 48 55 50), and will help with accommodation. The walk into town takes about 30 minutes.

SEEING

Explore Bordeaux on foot, starting your tour at the GRAND THÉÂTRE on the Place de la Comédie. From here you can work out the best route on the map to take you to the other sights: the ESPLANADE DE QUINCONCES, the largest square in France, the PLACE

DE LA BOURSE with its eighteenth-century façades, the CATHÉDRALE ST ANDRÉ, the MUSÉE DES BEAUX ARTS, the MUSÉE DES ARTS DÉCORATIFS, and the smart shopping streets round RUE BOUFFARD. Also worth a visit is the interesting MUSEUM OF THE RESISTANCE, and MUSEUM OF AQUITAINE. In the ESPLANADE DE QUINCONCES see the Monument aux Girondins, erected to commemorate the Deputies of the Revolution.

To get the feel of things, take a 'wine tour'; the tourist office arrange these daily. The cost is around 100 F per person, high season, Saturdays only during low season.

SLEEPING

A bed is no problem in Bordeaux, even though many places close down in August. The basic FUAJ youth hostel is close to the station at 22 Cours Barbey (Tel. 56 91 59 51). Head down Cours de la Marne, fifth turning on left. There are 247 beds, a bar, kitchen and a great atmosphere. Costs 39 F with IYHF card, 44 F with passport. Open 7 a.m.–10 a.m. and 6 p.m.–11 p.m., but rucksacks can be left at reception. There are several cheap hotels in the area; ask at the tourist office on arrival. For camping check out the site at Lorréjean, a half-hour bus ride on route 'B', leaving from the bus station at Quai Richelieu, down by the river. The site is a few minutes' walk from the terminus.

EATING AND NIGHTLIFE

Predictably enough, the local cuisine makes good use of the regional wines and there are all sorts of dishes using the delicious bordelaise sauce. Set menus at affordable prices can be found in restaurants on rue des Augustins, Place Général Carvail, and rue du Maréchal-Joffre.

The main shopping street is rue St Catherine, where there are plenty of good supermarkets and eating places.

Ask tourist information for a 'What's On' and try sampling the regional wines at bistros.

Cerbère

If you are heading for Spain along the Mediterranean coast and decide to break your journey for the night at the border, give the station and the beach a body swerve. Instead walk back along the main road towards France for a few hundred yards and take the foot-path up the cliff. Both the scenery and sleeping potential here are much better.

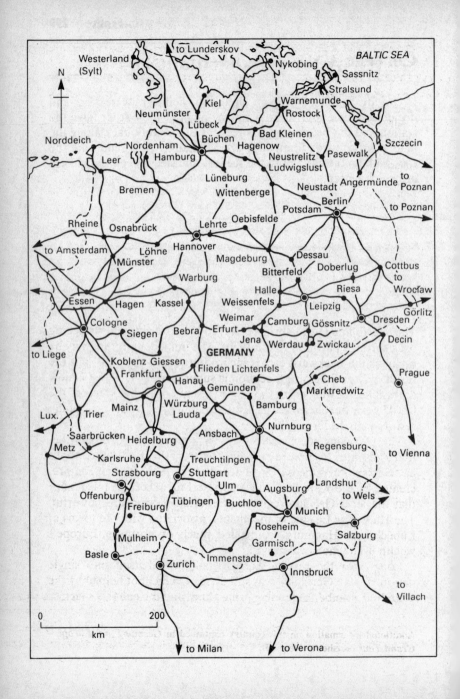

GERMANY (Deutschland)

Entry requirements	Passport
Population	78,000,000
Capital	Berlin (pop.: 2,960,000)
Currency	Deutschmark
	£1 = approx. 2.53 DM
Political system	Federal Republic
Religions	Protestant and Catholic
Language	German (English spoken in major cities)
Public holidays	1 Jan.; Good Friday; Easter Monday;
	1 May; Ascension Day; Whit Monday;
	3 Oct.; 22 Nov.; 25, 26 Dec.
International dialling codes	From UK: 010 + 49 + number
	From USA: 011 + 49 + number
	To UK: 00 + 44 + number
	To USA: 00 + 1 + number

The new united Germany has emerged from a nightmare stretching back through partition to the 1930s. The immediate future may be rocky as the backward east is incorporated into the west, but the result may well be a new economic super-power. The east is now accessible and well worth the visit to see not only the effects of the last 45 years but also to see its history, exemplified by the beautifully restored city of Dresden.

The Germans are a restless lot. Wherever you go in Europe, there they are. It's always been like this from the days of the Franks and Saxons. Most people have heard of the Holy Roman Empire, created by Otto I in 962, which survived till 1806, but few realize that the local German regimes were often much more powerful. The Hanseatic League of merchants, associated with the towns of Lübeck and Hamburg, controlled much of northern Europe's wealth in the medieval period.

Long after the rest of Europe had formed itself into single nation-states, 'Germany' was still divided, a fact not helped by the incredible number of feuding princedoms and the country's lack of

Additional information on this country contained in *Germany* and *Europe – Grand Tour* factsheets (see p.13).

natural boundaries. These divisions came to a head in the Thirty Years War of 1618–48 when the Catholic south defending the Habsburg emperors and Protestant north, inspired by men such as Luther and the Reformation movement, fought it out between themselves. In 1871 Bismarck was the force bringing the German nation into being. The autocratic rule, attempts to conquer an empire, and rapid industrialization led to discontent, and topped with Kaiser Bill's blunderings, this ended up as the First World War. After the failure of the liberal Weimar Republic, Hitler started stirring things up again, and we all know what Nazism led to . . .

The end of the Second World War saw Germany occupied by the Allies. Cold-war tensions caused the division into two states. Germany has survived all these trials. The Wall is down and, despite the chaos, we have a united Germany again.

GERMAN FEDERAL RAILWAYS
(Deutsche Bundesbahn, DB)

DB offer one of the best deals in Europe. They're fast, clean and efficiently run. Unlike Britain and France where all the main lines radiate out from the capital, the Germans have an excellent series of interconnecting cross-country lines which serve all the principal cities and the smaller towns throughout the country. The Inter City Expresses (ICE) offer 175 m.p.h. travel with an hourly service between Hamburg and Munich. Apart from the speed, other facilities include built-in radios and coat cabinets; the ultimate in comfort for a bit extra.

The number of trains crossing the old border has been doubled to approximately 200 a day. This year, a single timetable is being produced for east and west.

There are several types of train, apart from EuroCity: the ICE trains; fast Inter City trains (IC) which require a 6 or 7 DM supplement – supplements for journeys across a frontier vary; the InterRegio (IR) trains are nearly as fast and connect to smaller cities and the IC network (require a 3 DM supplement); Schnellzüge (D) and Fern-Express (FD) are similar to IRs but are older, commanding the same supplement; the Eilzüge (E) serving the regional areas; Personenzüge or Nahverkehrszüge, which are slow local trains. The new generation of German trains – the 150 m.p.h. plus electric intercity expresses (ICE) mentioned above – are excellent but charge a supplement of around 28 DM.

The German Rail Pass is becoming more popular each year at £99 for five days' unlimited travel, £149 for 10 days and £179 for 15 days second class (all within a month). The card frees you from paying most supplements. If you are under 26 there is also a Youth Pass, which is valid for second class only. It costs £69 for five days, £89 for 10 days and £109 for 15 days. The Rail Pass also includes the Deutsche Reichsbahn. Cards are available from BR-appointed travel agents, BR continental booking offices or German Rail Sales, DER, 18 Conduit Street, London W1 (Tel. 071–499 0577). In the United States write to German Railways for further information at 747 Third Avenue, 33rd Floor, New York NY 10017 (Tel. 212–308 3100).

When in Germany anyone under 23 (students, 27) can buy a one-month, go-as-you-please Tramper-Monat ticket for 246 DM at any of the larger stations. You can also buy it from DER before you go for £90. You need evidence of age, such as a passport or IUS card. If you plan on spending a long time in Germany, look out for the DB Junior Rail Pass available for anyone aged between 12 and 22 (students, 27). It's valid for a year and gets you 50 per cent reduction on all rail tickets, although you still have to pay EuroCity and IC supplements. It costs 110 DM and can be purchased from BR travel centres at Liverpool Street and the International Rail Centre at Victoria Stations in London and DER Travel.

DB also have Regional Rail Rovers which are available in 30 regions and are valid for unlimited second-class travel for 10 days out of 21. A single ticket costs £33, a ticket for two is £44 and a family ticket including any number of unmarried children under 26 is £55. For families travelling throughout Germany a minigroup ticket can be purchased. The first two adults pay full fare, additional adults pay half price and children quarter price. The maximum group size is 5½ (children count as ½).

● **Inter-Rail bonuses:**
NB Inter-Rail tickets are now valid on the Berliner S-Bahn as well as in other German cities, but not on the U-Bahn. Free entrance to Transport Museum, Lessingstrasse 6, Nürnberg. For further Inter-Rail reductions, see Appendix II.

• **Eurail bonuses:** Free:
—Ferry crossings from Puttgarden to Rødby (Denmark).
—Steamers operated by the Köln-Düsseldorfer Deutsche Rhein-schiffahrt (KD) making regular runs on the Rhine between Cologne and Frankfurt (Main) and on the Moselle between Trier and Koblenz (except on ships making cruises of several days between Basel and Rotterdam and vice versa). For the use of Express-steamers, an extra charge will have to be paid by Eurail Youthpass holders, and for the use of hydrofoils by Eurail Pass as well as by Eurail Youthpass holders.
—Most of the bus lines of the integrated bus transport Post/Railway bus union.
—Europabus line 189 – Burgenstrasse (Castle Road) from Mannheim–Heidelberg–Heilbronn–Rothenburg ob der Tauber–Ansbach–Nürnberg.
—Europabus line 190 – Romantische Strasse (Romantic Road) from Wiesbaden–Frankfurt (Main)–Rothenburg ob der Tauber–Füssen/Munich.

Reduced fares:
—50 per cent reduction on hydrofoil service between Cologne and Mainz.
—50 per cent reduction to Eurail Pass and Eurail Youthpass holders on the normal fares of the ferry crossing operated by TT-Saga-Line between Lübeck–Travemünde and Malmö (Sweden).
—50 per cent reduction on regular steamer services operated by the German Federal Railways on Lake Constance.
—Eurail Pass and Eurail Youthpass are not valid on private railways in the Federal Republic of Germany. However, the following mountain railways grant reduced fares:
  1. Garmisch-Partenkirchen–Grainau–Zugspitze   (Schneefernerhaus).
  2. Freiburg (Breisgau)–Schauinsland: 50 per cent on ordinary tickets, for Eurail Pass and Eurail Youthpass.
—25 per cent reduction for students producing a valid student ID card on the round-trip bus fare Braunschweig–Berlin or vice versa operated by Bayern Express and P. Kuhn Berlin GmbH.
—20 per cent reduction on some half-day or full-day excursions out of Munich operated by the Oberbayern GmbH.
—10 per cent on Munich city sightseeing tours operated by the Oberbayern GmbH.

• **Deutsche Reichsbahn, DR:** It is expected that the eastern and western systems will be combined, but this will inevitably take time. The former East German DR system is efficient and frequent compared to that in other east European countries, but slower than the western system. The faster trains – special diesel express (Ex), expresses (D) and semi-fast (E) trains – require some supplements. Avoid the local (Personenzug) at all costs, as they stop at nearly every station.

• **Rover tickets:** The East European Explorer, offered by Eurotrain, also covers East Germany (see p.33). The DB Railpasses are valid over DR lines, and offer excellent value. They cover an area, such as Rhineland, Bavaria or the Black Forest, and range in price from £42 for one to £114 for a family for 10 days' unlimited travel within 21 days.

TRAIN INFORMATION

Information officers wear yellow capbands and generally speak good English, though you may have problems in smaller towns in eastern Germany. Left-luggage lockers take 1 DM and 50 Pfennig pieces.

• **Reservations:** Can be made up to two hours before departing, but not after 10 p.m. They are included in the price of the supplement for ICs (5 DM from an automatic ticket machine or 6 DM if you buy it on the train) and EuroCity (10 DM). On all other trains, it's optional and costs 3.5 DM. Reservations on DR cost 1 DM, first class, 0.5 DM second. German Rail Pass holders are exempt from the IC supplement.

• **Night travel:** Some German compartments have pull-down seats which make excellent free beds. Couchettes have six berths and cost around £8.20. Tourist-class sleepers (four-berth) cost £10.90 and three-berth compartments are more expensive at around £20.60, but it's often possible to get one between two out of season, as they're usually underbooked. DB has extended the special couchette service introduced in 1984 between Dortmund and Munich which it called 'Rollende Jugendherberge' (Rolling Youth Hostel). It is now called 'Twen-Nachttramper' (Night Tramper) and the services last year ran between Aachen to Copenhagen via Hamburg, Hamburg to Munich and Dortmund to Munich. It allows you to have a couchette for only 4 DM and all you need is a sleeping bag or blankets. If you don't have either, you can buy a paper blanket on board for 6 DM from the conductor. You don't have to worry about reservations either as you can pay the 4 DM on board, although the number of places is limited and the service has proved to be very popular. Look out for extra services being laid on and check with DB before booking couchettes for an overnight journey in case your route has come into the scheme.

• **Eating on trains:** Prices are lower than British Rail, while the quality is higher. So if you've the money, it's worth considering a meal on the ICs. Other trains (except E-trains) have mini-bars which are pricey for what you get.

• **Scenic routes:** The Rhine valley, Black Forest, Romantic and Castle roads, as well as the Alps, all provide scenic routes within Germany. If you've always wanted to go cruising down the Rhine, it's best to do it between Koblenz and Rüdesheim or Mainz as this gives you magnificent views of both sides of the valley. If you're coming from the opposite direction and want to stay with rivers, then head to Giessen from Koblenz. To see the Black Forest, there are a variety of options. The Romantic and Castle roads are arguably best seen by Europabus, which are nearly always busy and require advance reservations. The Munich–Nürnberg, Heilbronn–Heidelberg train follows more or less the same route as the bus at no extra cost. For the Alps, try the line to Salzburg or Innsbruck from Munich – both are equally attractive. If you're going to Switzerland, try Freiburg–Basel or Würzburg–Zürich.

• **Bikes:** Can be hired from around 300 stations throughout Germany at half the normal rate (5 DM) to anyone with a valid ticket or rail pass. You can either do a circular tour of the region or merely cycle from A to B and return the bike to another station.

TOURIST INFORMATION

Tourist offices are usually called Verkehrsamt or Verkehrsverein. Many towns in eastern Germany have an office, simply described as an information office. Also expect most east German Reiseburos to be open. Many cities have free pamphlets specially prepared for the under 26s.

• **ISIC bonuses:** Museum discount, with varying reductions at some sports centres. For further information, contact Europa Sprach Club, Amalienstrasse 67, Munich 40. There are branches in all main cities. In Berlin also try the Jugendtourist office at Alexanderplatz 5, 1026 Berlin.

• **Money matters:** 1 Deutschmark (DM) = 100 Pfennig.
Banking hours vary, but generally are Mon.–Fri.: 8.30 a.m.–1 p.m., 2.30 p.m.–4 p.m.; Thurs.: until 5.30 p.m. It's also possible to change money at some post offices; they often give a better rate, because they make mistakes.

• **Post offices:** Open Mon.–Fri.: 8 a.m.–6 p.m., Sat.: 8 a.m.–1 p.m.

• **Shops:** Open Mon.–Fri.: 9 a.m.–6/6.30 p.m. In smaller towns they shut for lunch, 12 noon–3 p.m. On Sat. they only open till 2 p.m., and until 4 p.m. on the first Sat. of each month.

• **Museums:** Hours vary depending on locality. Check with tourist information.

SLEEPING

Youth hostels cost 12–21 DM a night and there are over 600 scattered throughout Germany. Tourist information have a free map and brochure showing their locations. In Bavaria there is an age limit of 27 in hostels. Youth guest houses (Jugendgasthäuser) are in nearly all the large towns, but they tend to be stuffed with groups, so always phone first. There's no uniform system of classification for Germany's hostels and hotels, so you'll find they vary dramatically. The accommodation side of tourist information, however, is usually very obliging and you need never feel really stuck as in the end they'll fix you up with something in your price range. As in many other countries, the towns are ideally laid out for eurorailers and many of the cheap hotels are near the stations. In smaller places, look out for signs hanging up saying 'Zimmer frei' (room to let) or 'Gasthof' (inn), and for private accommodation turn to tourist information for lists. With over 2,000 campsites in Germany, you shouldn't find any problems. Again, tourist information have a free map and brochure showing where they are. Facilities are generally very good and prices usually fair.

There is still a problem in eastern Germany, due to the demand and lack of infrastructure. This is despite the fact that private citizens are now able to offer B&B, and formerly east Germans-only establishments are now available. Inter hotel prices have now risen beyond the budget traveller's range – upwards from £80. This effectively leaves Jugendtourist hostels and campsites, but even here the demand will mean overcrowding. Ask at local tourist information offices and Reiseburo for suggestions, including Verband Christlicher Hospize which has hostels in Berlin, Leipzig and Weimar.

EATING AND NIGHTLIFE

German cuisine is as varied as French – the only difference is that the former like to eat more of it. There are countless types of beer and Würste (sausages), but it's unfair to think that's all there is, as so many do. The food halls of the large department stores (e.g. Hertie, Kaufhof) are real showpieces, and the quality and quantity of the produce means there's no excuse for not living off picnics and saving your Marks that way. Fast food's also available in the major cities, and Schnell Imbiss stalls with Würste and beer also crop up. Note that if you drink at one of the beer gardens, it is not unusual to be charged a deposit for your glass – remember to claim it back. Alcoholic drinks can be very expensive in Germany.

As far as regional specialities go, try some of the following: Grünkohl mit Pinkel (green cabbage with bacon sausage) from the north, Sauerbraten (braised beef in sour sauce) from the west, and for your picnics sample Westphalian Pumpernickel (black bread) or Vollkornbrot (bread made of whole unground grains of wheat). Many of the Würste look revolting, but don't let that put you off. Vegetarians tend not to be well catered for here.

The Germans are keen on large-scale celebrations: some of their festivals resemble Wagnerian opera sets, and no expense is spared. If you get a chance to join in, do. As far as music goes, the classics are always well represented and there's an active jazz and disco scene in all the major cities.

Berlin

There is literally no other city in Europe, or elsewhere, like Berlin. It was once as beautiful and cosmopolitan as Paris or London, but was reduced to rubble in the Second World War. Then in August 1961 the city was cut in two by the notorious Wall which split life on either side between the two political polarities. Recent events are obvious, and very little of the Wall remains. Now the capital of the united Germany, this is undoubtedly one of *the* great cities of the world. With a background as dramatic as this, it's only to be expected that Berlin is a city of extremes and contradictions. This was the city at the heart of the Cold War of the mid-twentieth century, and that alone makes it significant enough for a visit – it's not so much the sights that are worth coming for, as the atmosphere, the world-famous 'Berliner Luft'. The tremendous changes have made Berlin, once again, a vibrant and exciting city. Even so the two halves still have their obvious differences.

STATION FACILITIES

The three main stations are Bahnhofzoo, Hauptbahnhof (formerly Ostbahnhof) and Lichtenberg. Bahnhofzoo and Hauptbahnhof currently serve international destinations, and Lichtenberg domestic and eastbound trains, but check timetable carefully. Hauptbahnhof has been undergoing massive rebuilding of its platforms, so watch your feet. The formerly important border station, Friedrichstrasse, has lost its importance, and its steel dividing wall. When arriving use Bahnhofzoo.

	BERLIN– HAUPTBAHNHOF	BERLIN– LICHTENBERG
Train information	8 a.m.–10 p.m.	6 a.m.–10 p.m.
Reservations	6 a.m.–8 p.m., weekdays 8 a.m.–6 p.m., weekends	6 a.m.–8 p.m., weekdays 8 a.m.–10 p.m., weekends
Tourist information	None	None, S-Bahn to Alexanderplatz
International tickets	6.30 a.m.–9 p.m., weekdays 8 a.m.–6 p.m., weekends	6 a.m.–9 p.m., weekdays 8 a.m.–6 p.m., weekends
Shop	6 a.m.–10 p.m., to 8 p.m. at weekends	6 a.m.–10 p.m.
Snacks/Buffet	6 a.m.–6.30 p.m.	6 a.m.–10 p.m.
Restaurant	6 a.m.–9 p.m.	6 a.m.–10 a.m. and 11 a.m.–10 p.m.
Left-luggage lockers	As station	As station
Left-luggage store	As station	As station
Station shuts	12 a.m.–4 a.m.	12 a.m.–4 a.m.

Luggage lockers also available at Alexanderplatz and Friedrichstrasse S-Bahn stations. Daily trains from Hauptbahnhof to the west of Germany, from Lichtenberg to Copenhagen, Dresden, Leipzig, Malmö and Prague, from Bahnhofzoo to Copenhagen, Cologne, Hamburg and Malmö.

BERLIN BAHNHOFZOO

Train information	6 a.m.–10 p.m.
Reservations	Mon.–Fri.: 6 a.m.–9 p.m.
	Sat. and Sun.:
	8 a.m.–4 p.m.
Tourist information	In the main hall, 8 a.m.–11 p.m. (Tel. 313 9063)
Foreign exchange	Mon.–Sat.: 8 a.m.–9 p.m., Sun.: 10 a.m.–6 p.m.
Left-luggage lockers	Available, but quite small
Restaurant	6 a.m.–12 midnight
Post office	Always open
Station shuts	12 midnight–5 a.m.

• **Getting around:** A variety of tickets covering different parts of the transport network are available so consider the options carefully. A single ticket covering the whole BVG network for two hours costs 2.70 DM (Multiple tickets, Sammelkarten, allow five journeys for 11.50 DM). A day ticket valid for 24 hours costs 9 DM. If you're staying for longer, then the six-day or month Umweltkarte costs 26 DM or 65 DM. All multiple tickets must be obtained from the machines at S-Bahn and U-Bahn stations or from the BVG office in front of Zoo station. Individual and multiple tickets must be validated before use.

Currently the BVG controls all of the system, except the U-bahn, trams and buses in the eastern portion, which are controlled by the BVB. Tickets purchased on the western side are valid everywhere, but only eastern citizens can use BVB tickets in the west. So if heading to the eastern side, take sufficient tickets to get back. When the BVB subsidy is removed this restriction will not apply.

TOURIST INFORMATION AND ADDRESSES

TOURIST OFFICE: On the Budapesterstrasse side of the Europa Centre, open daily 7.30 a.m.–10.30 p.m. (Tel. 262 6031). Accommodation service for 3 DM. The free book 'Berlin For Young People' is excellent. Among other bits of interesting information, it lists 20 or so cheap pensions. Berlin–Information on Alexanderplatz (Tel. 212 4675) under the TV tower. Open Tues.–Fri., 8 a.m.–6 p.m., Mon. from 1 p.m., Sat. and Sun., 10 a.m.–6 p.m. Also on Friedrichstrasse at the Berlin Bahnhofzoo (Tel. 313 9063), open 8 a.m.–11 p.m.

POST OFFICE: Bahnhofzoo. Twenty-four hours. Also poste restante here. Most offices are open 8 a.m.–6 p.m. weekdays.

AMEX: Kurfürstendamm 11 (2nd floor) (Tel. 882 7575), Mon.–Fri.: 9 a.m.–5.30 p.m., Sat.: 9 a.m.–12 noon.

CURRENCY EXCHANGE: Alexanderplatz, Bahnhofzoo, Friedrich- strasse, Hauptbahnhof, also major hotels.

ARTU REISEBÜRO: Hardenbergstrasse 9. Student Travel office selling BIJ tickets and IUS card. Open Mon., Tue., Thur., Fri.: 10 a.m.–6 p.m. Wed.: 11 a.m.–6 p.m., Sat.: 10 a.m.–1 p.m.

UK CONSULATE: Uhlandstrasse 7 (Tel. 309 5292)/Unter den Linden 32–34 (Tel. 220 2431).

US CONSULATE: Clayallee 170 (Tel. 832 4087)/Neustädtische Kirch- strasse 4/5 (Tel. 220 2741).

CANADIAN CONSULATE: Europa Centre (12th floor) Tel. 261 1161.

AUSTRALIAN CONSULATE: Europa Centre (Tel. 261 8030).

TELEPHONE CODE: 030 (East Berlin: 2), subject to change as system becomes integrated. Check all numbers with tourist information.

SEEING

The scant remains of the WALL (Die Mauer) where so many people died not so long ago, are the tourist attraction of today. You should cross through the site of the old Checkpoint Charlie (now a lorry park) to compare the development of the two sides of the city separated for so long. The actual hut is now in a nearby museum. Near the checkpoint is the MUSEUM OF THE WALL which tells its story. Not far outside the main exit of the Hauptbahnhof is the EAST-SIDE GALLERY: just over a mile of wall has been transformed into an open-air art gallery celebrating freedom.

KURFÜRSTENDAMM (Ku'damm) pulsates with life late into the night and is the city's preferred promenade and thoroughfare. The famous Berlin institution CAFÉ KRANZLER is found on the junction with Joachimstaler Strasse, but eat elsewhere as it is expensive. The ruined KAISER-WILHELM GEDÄCHTNISKIRCHE is unmissable and the focal point of the Ku'damm and a popular meeting place. The church itself reflects the city's story – it has been built, bombed, partly rebuilt and preserved, and mirrors Berlin's present mixture of old and new. A few yards away beyond an elaborate fountain complex stands the massive EUROPA CENTRE, twenty-two floors of pubs, shops, discos, boutiques and a cinema which shows a useful introductory film on Berlin's history. The rooftop café affords an excellent view of the city, or watch time go by on the water clock. Berlin's premier department store, KaDeWe at Tauenzienstrasse, is well worth a look, especially for its food halls. The SIEGESSÄULE, celebrating Prussian victories in the 1860s and 1870s, can be climbed for an impressive view towards the eighteenth-century BRANDEN-BURG GATE. TIERGARTEN is a beautiful park, next to the city zoo, which has more species than any other in the world. Next to the zoo is the world's most extensive collection of fish and reptiles in the AQUARIUM on Budapesterstrasse. The OLYMPIC STADIUM conjures up images of Jesse Owens and Hitler and is worth the 1 DM entrance fee. Take U-Bahn 1.

SCHLOSS CHARLOTTENBURG lies a few miles north-west of Berlin, bus 54 or 74. This seventeenth-century palace houses several galleries and museums and is the best example of Prussian architecture you'll find around Berlin (closed Mondays, students half price). The EGYPTIAN MUSEUM opposite has a fine collection including the fabulous bust of Queen Nefertiti. The DAHLEM MUSEUM, near U-Bahn Dahlem-Dorf, is a complex of seven museums (closed Mondays), so you're bound to find something to interest you. The BAUHAUS MUSEUM with exhibits of the school's designs (closed Tuesdays), is at Klingelhöferstrasse. The photographic story of German nineteenth- and twentieth-century history at the REICHSTAG BUILDING also makes an interesting visit. Another chilling reminder of the past are the crosses to those shot trying to go over the wall close by.

For a good view over the city climb the Berlin Radio Mast, FUNKTURM (4 DM) or the FERNSEHTURM TV Tower at Alexanderplatz. Also see the TEUFELBERG not far away in the GRUNEWALD. At 380 feet high, it is the highest hill between Warsaw and the Netherlands. It is made of an enormous mound of rubble from the ruins of Berlin after the Second World War. It now has a ski and toboggan run, whilst the very peak is an American radar station.

The 1390-metre long UNTER DEN LINDEN is the most impressive street of eastern Berlin and is at its very centre. From here you can see the Brandenburg Gate, refurbished during summer 1990, and the east's city centre. The BERLINER DOM, closed for many years, is close to the east's old parliament building, now without a function. Not far from here is MUSEUM ISLAND where the main eastern Berlin museums are located. Avoid Mondays, when most are shut.

General hours 10 a.m.–5 p.m., but various exhibits only certain days.

On Museum Island are: the PERGAMON (stunning collections of Eastern and Roman artefacts), the BODEMUSEUM with its Egyptian works; the twentieth-century art gallery, the ALTES MUSEUM and the NATIONAL GALERIE of nineteenth-century art. Another museum, undergoing reconstruction, on Museum Island is the NEVNES MUSEUM. The work on this is disrupting the whole area. The MUSEUM FÜR DEUTSCHE GESCHICHTE in the Arsenal (Zeughaus), the oldest building on Unter den Linden, has German history from prehistory onwards. The MÄRKISCHES MUSEUM traces Berlin's history, at Am Köllnischen Park, closed Monday/Tuesday. MARIENKIRCHE is Berlin's oldest church dating from the thirteenth century, just off Alexanderplatz.

Old Berlin lives again in the NIKOLAIVIERTEL QUARTER, a veritable cat's cradle of narrow streets and alleys around the ST NICOLAS CHURCH. It is interesting for the reconstructed half-timbered buildings, mullioned windows and the odd quaint corner.

For signs of the past, try a walk to the SYNAGOGUE on Oranienburgerstrasse. This was burnt on the infamous Kristall-nacht 1938, and in recent years has been undergoing restoration. The MONUMENT TO THE VICTIMS OF FASCISM AND MILITARISM on Unter den Linden and the SOVIET WAR MEMORIAL in Treptower Park, which is reached on the S-Bahn, will set you thinking.

The Spree River flows through the city and it's possible to take a boat ride on one of the white excursion boats (Weisse Flotte) from April to September. You can get off at various points; the best is the MECKLENBURGER DORF – a reconstruction of a nineteenth-century German village. Boats leave eight times a day from Treptower Park S-Bahn Station. (The commentary is usually given in German only.) An alternative is 'Bus 100', which takes in many sights, from the zoo or Alexanderplatz.

SLEEPING

Finding a bed isn't easy and this is one city where you would be really wise to book ahead; write about two to three weeks in advance, to the Tourist Board: Verkehrsamt Berlin, Europa Centre, 1000 Berlin 30 (Tel. 262 6031), or DJH Berlin, Tempel-hofer Ufer 32, 1000 Berlin 61, for hostels, stating how much you can pay. You will probably have better luck in the old West Berlin, due to lack of established facilities on the eastern side. But here try desk 13 of Reiseburo on Alexanderplatz or Jugendtourist, also here. If you aren't organized enough to plan ahead, don't worry; ask at tourist information for their map of Berlin with all the hotel and hostel listings. For hotels look at the board at Bahnhofzoo, though they tend to be expensive.

If you are organized in advance, try booking flats through Zeitraum, who charge from 25 DM per day, discounts for students. Open 9 a.m.–1 p.m. and 3 p.m.–8 p.m., Sat. 12 noon–4 p.m., at Horstweg 7, 1000 Berlin 19 (Tel. 030 325 6181).

• **Youth hostels:** Ernst Reuter (IYHA) at Hermsdorfer Damm 48, Berlin 28 (Tel. 404 1610) is good, though well out of the town centre, in a leafy suburb, by a lake, 16.90 DM per night plus 4.90 DM for breakfast, U-Bahn 6 to Tegel then bus 125. Jugendgästehaus Berlin (IYHA) at Kluckstrasse 3, Berlin 30 (Tel. 261 1097) is the most central, 21 DM plus 4.90 DM for breakfast. It is 10 minutes from Ku'damm by bus 29 or U-Bahn to Potsdammer Strasse. Being central, it gets very busy, so don't count on getting in. Although it is 20 minutes on the S-Bahn to Nikolassee, try also at Jugendgästehause Wannsee (IYHA) Badeweg 1, Ecke Kronprinzess-Innenweg (Tel. 803 2034). It is clean, cheap and very modern, price as above. The Studentenhotel is at Meininger Strasse 10, Berlin 62 (Tel. 784 6720), a way out at Schöneberg. Take bus 73; cost for two-bed room 30 DM. The eastern Berlin Jugendtourist hostel is the Egon Schultz at Franz-Mett Strasse 7, U-Bahn to Tierpark (Tel. 510 0114).

• **Pensions:** The area round Fasanenstrasse and Uhlandstrasse is your best bet. Also on Carmerstrasse, Grolmannstrasse and Knesebeckstrasse. Try Pension Savoy (Tel. 881 3700) at Meinekestrasse 4; just next door are Pension Zeinert (Tel. 881 3319) at No. 5 and Pension Witzleben (Tel. 881 6395) at No. 6. For good doubles try Pension Fischer at Nürnbergerstrasse 24A (Tel. 246 808), near the station (50–60 DM). Also ask at tourist information for B&B, now opening up on the eastern side of the city.

• **Camping:** International Youth Camp is very good, and costs 8 DM a night; blankets and mattresses free. Open 1700–0900 daily

June–Sept. (Tel. 433 8640) Waidmannsluster Dam, Ziekowstrasse (subway station Tegel/bus 222). Maximum stay: three nights. Ages 14–23. Zeltplatz Kladow 1 and 11, Krampnitzer Weg 111/117, bus 35, then 35E (Tel. 365 2797). Zeltplatz Dreilinden, Albrechts Teerofen (Tel. 805 1201) bus 18. Kohlhasenbruck Neue Kreisstrasse – U-Bahn Oskar-Helene-Heim, bus 18 (Tel. 805 1737). Also try the former Intercamping Krossinsee site, tram 86 to end, then walk across bridge, and take the third turning on the right. If you're desperate, the Bahnhof Mission in the station will help out, or go out to the Grünewald and sleep there.

EATING AND NIGHTLIFE

The department stores have good cafeterias and there are fast-food chains and sausage stands. There are many good authentic Turkish restaurants on Oranienstrasse in Kreuzberg.

Berlin's a big cultural centre and there's always plenty happening in the evenings. Festival follows festival and the student community is large and active. Head off to the area round Konstanzerstrasse, Düsseldorferstrasse, Joachimstaler Strasse and Lietzenburgerstrasse. With literally thousands of pubs, clubs and discos you should find something to occupy you. Many of the bars in the former East Berlin are north of the river from Friedrichstrasse station. Try the 'Kleine Melodie', Friedrichstrasse 127, for a disco. For a taste of the 1930s Berlin atmosphere try Zum Trichler on Schiffbauerdamm, only a stone's throw from the Brecht Ensemble Theatre. A very atmospheric place to have a drink as the walls are lined with old photos of Brechtian productions, murals and clocks. There is even a small stage for cabaret performances. In the Irish Pub on Eisenacherstrasse (and also in the Europa Centre) you're guaranteed to meet a fellow Brit, most of the staff speak English, and in Leierkasten on Zossenerstrasse you'll bump into the local students. The Jungle, 53 Nuernbergstrasse, is the hottest club in Berlin. 'Tip' – the bi-weekly listing of what's on, and 'Zitty' are worth buying if you're staying a while.

If you miss a hostel curfew don't despair as many bars begin to serve breakfast at 2 a.m. and Berlin is literally open all night. The cafés here are an institution, try Schlander on Olivaer Platz.

For tickets for classical music and drama try Zentral/besucherdienst below the Palast Hotel, Karl-Liebnechtstrasse, or desk 1 of

Reiseburo on Alexanderplatz. The Haus der Jungen Talente, Klosterstrasse, has young musicians' concerts with cheap tickets.

Potsdam

In 1744, Frederick the Great chose this town as his permanent seat, and from then on Potsdam flourished to become one of the main imperial centres of Europe. As Potsdam is less than one hour from the centre of Berlin, it can be treated as a day trip, but, be warned, there is a lot to see.

The impressive SANS SOUCI PARK and surroundings contain baroque palaces and elaborate pavilions. The SANS SOUCI SCHLOSS, the large NEUES PALAIS, SCHLOSS CHARLOTTENHOF, the ORANGERIE and gold-plated CHINESE TEAHOUSE, are all here. The Orangerie houses forty-seven very good fake Raphaels, with nearby the SICILIAN GARDEN. Another large park, the NEUER GARTEN, on the shores of a lake, includes the SCHLOSS CECILIENHOF, scene of the three-powers agreement to divide Germany. Part of this complex is now an expensive hotel. Most palaces are open 9 a.m.–5 p.m., closing at lunchtime; some also close on Mondays, and out of season. The city centre has been extensively rebuilt, but the Dutch quarter retains its charm and elegance. Just outside the town is the incredible EINSTEIN OBSERVATORY TOWER. Make the effort to see it if you can.

The Tourist Office is at Friedrich-Ebert Strasse 5 (Tel. 21100), take one of several trams to the city centre from the Potsdam-Stadt station. Ask at tourist information for the usual leaflets, maps and accommodation suggestions. There is an IYHF hostel, 'Am Neven', at Eisenhartstrasse 5 (Tel. 22515). Take bus F from Hauptbahnhof to Neven Garten. It is advisable to phone or ask tourist information first though. There are several campsites, but some distance away. With its proximity to Berlin, it might be better to commute. While in Potsdam eat out at a Schnell Imbiss and have a beer at the Froschkasten on Kiezstrasse.

City phone code 0331.

Dresden

Two hours from Berlin, Dresden is the cultural centre of eastern
Germany and, though the old city was devastated by saturation
bombing in February 1945, what was left was carefully restored.
The new city is green and well laid out.

STATION FACILITIES

There are two main stations, Hauptbahnhof and Bahnhof–
Neustadt. Many trains call at both, eastbound ones tend to use
Neustadt only. The facilities at Neustadt are similar to those at
Hauptbahnhof. There is a post office near Hauptbahnhof (on
Prager Strasse).

	HAUPTBAHNHOF
Train information	6.30 a.m.–9.45 p.m.
Reservations	6.30 a.m.–8 p.m.; to 6 p.m. on Sat. and Sun.
Tourist information	None – at Pragerstrasse
Restaurant, buffet	7.30 a.m.–10 p.m.
Shops	Mon.–Fri., 7.30 a.m.–9 p.m.
	Sat.–Sun., 9 a.m.–4 p.m.
Left-luggage lockers	As station
Left-luggage store	As station
Station shuts	Train departures 24 hrs, but do not rely on all facilities being open

Through trains use the elevated platforms on each side, terminating ones the central
platforms.
Daily departures to Berlin (Lichenberg), Leipzig, Munich, Prague, Warsaw.

TOURIST INFORMATION

Dresden information centre is at Pragerstrasse 10/11 (Tel. 4955025)
(five minutes from station). Open Mon.–Fri.: 9 a.m.–8 p.m.; Sat.: 9
a.m.–2 p.m.; Sun.: 9 a.m.–1 p.m. You can change money here
Mon.–Sat. only. 'What's On' leaflet from here: 'Dresden-
Information'. Bus and tram tickets have to be bought in advance,
but most of the worthwhile area is walkable from Hauptbahnhof,
along pedestrianized Pragerstrasse.

City phone code 051.

SEEING

Head down Pragerstrasse, then bear left towards the river where most of the sights are located. Starting at the ALBERTINUM, one of Dresden's great museum complexes, you will find included the GRUNES GEWOLBE (Green Vault), containing a fabulous collection of the treasures of the Saxon dukes. Opens 9 a.m. most days, closed Thursdays. Walk further down the Bruhlschen Terasse above the River Elbe, where you will pass down the Munzgasse. Down here are the remains of the devastated FRAUENKIRCHE, which is surrounded by rubble, but is now being rebuilt. Further along the river is the Catholic CATHEDRAL and the immense RESIDENZSCHLOSS, the palace of the Saxon electors and dukes. It is being rebuilt from the ruins and is hoped to be finished by 2006 for the city's 800th anniversary. Next comes the magnificent OPERA-HOUSE. Close by is the old Augustinerbrucke, leading to the New Town across the river, which holds little of interest except a statue of the GOLDEN RIDER, Augustus the Strong, so-named because he fathered 300 children.

Back on this side of the river, close to the opera, is the unmissable ZWINGER PALACE, an incredible piece of Baroque architecture containing half of Dresden's impressive museums: the magnificent GEMÄLDEGALERIE ALTE MEISTER (closed Mondays); the HISTORIS-CHES MUSEUM of weapons (closed Wednesdays); the MATHEMATI-SCH PHYSIKALISCHER SALON (maths and physics, closed Thursdays); and both the ZINNSAMMLUNG and the PORZELLANSAMMLUNG display the famous Dresden porcelain (closed Fridays).

SLEEPING

The youth hostel at Hübnerstrasse 11 (Tel. 470667), a few blocks from the station, down Wincklemannstrasse, then into Schnorr Strasse, which leads into Hübnerstrasse, is one possibility. The other hostel is the Oberloschwitz at Sierksstrasse 33 (Tel. 36672), take tram 5 to Nurnburger Platz, change to bus 61 or 93, get off two stops after crossing the Elbe. Then it is only a short walk away. The campsites are far flung; ask at the Tourist Information Centre for full details. A series of sites are located to the north, in a wooded area; take bus 81 to the terminus, then a 15-minute walk. The tourist office will also find rooms in private houses.

EATING

Restaurants in the 'Am Zwinger' complex on Wilsdruffer Strasse are worth trying for cheap meals. Also try the Kulturpalast, reasonably priced, if not spectacular. The cafés on the cobbled Munzgasse are worth a try.

Leipzig

The second city in eastern Germany is only 1½ hours from Dresden, and though it is more a commercial and industrial centre, there are still enough points of interest to make it worth a stop-off. It makes a fascinating contrast to some of the more opulent western towns: bullet holes in walls, crumbling facades of buildings, the old-fashioned feel of the tram service. The atmosphere of Second World War damage and post-1945 neglect is still tangible. The Hauptbahnhof is reputedly Europe's largest terminus, with 26 platforms. Tourist information is at Sachsenplatz 1 (Tel. 79590), open weekdays 9 a.m.–7 p.m., Sat. 9.30 a.m. to 2 p.m.

City phone code 41.

STATION FACILITIES

	HAUPTBAHNHOF
Train information	6 a.m.–10.15 p.m.
Reservations	Mon.–Fri.: 6.30 a.m.–8 p.m.;
	Sat.–Sun.: 9.30 a.m.–5 p.m.
Tourist information	Mon.–Fri.: 9 a.m.–6 p.m.
Foreign exchange	6.30 a.m.–9 p.m.; to 12 p.m. Sunday
International tickets	6.30 a.m.–8 p.m.
Restaurant/buffet	6.30 a.m.–10 p.m.
Left-luggage lockers	Always accessible
Left-luggage store	As station
Post office	6 a.m.–10 p.m., Mon.–Fri.:
	9 a.m.–12 midnight; Sat.–Sun.: 10 a.m.–1 p.m.
Station shuts	Train departures 24 hrs, but do not rely on all facilities being open.

This is Europe's largest terminus and many facilities are duplicated, so if one is shut, look around. Leipzig's small S-Bahn system departures are also from here (platforms 6 and 7). Daily departures to Berlin (Lichtenberg), Cologne, Dresden, Hannover, Frankfurt am Main, Munich and Warsaw.

SEEING

The main part of Leipzig that is worth seeing is within the Ring promenade, a partly pedestrianized area, starting opposite the station. Bach spent his last 27 creative years working as the Kantor (Choirmaster) in ST THOMAS' CHURCH, and is buried here. The boys' choir, once conducted by Bach, can be heard on most Friday evenings and Saturday afternoons. Dating from 1212 and 1496, St Thomas' is currently being restored. The old, sixteenth-century ALTES RATHUS (town hall) now houses the city history museum. The NIKOLAIKIRCHE, located nearby, and a focal point of opposition in autumn 1989, is also worth a visit.

As well as having associations with Bach, Leipzig has other musical connections, with Mendelssohn, for example, who conducted the Gewandhaus Orchestra, Europe's oldest, and financed a monument to Bach. The city also has strong literary connections, with large numbers of bookshops and libraries. Goethe set the scene between Faust and the devil in the AUERBACHS KELLER in Mädler-passage, the decorations of which are now based on the book.

• **Excursion:** Near Leipzig is the small town of Colditz, location of the famous castle which was used as an officers' POW camp in the Second World War, the story of which was made into a TV series of the same name. Much of the castle (now a hospital), is inaccessible to the public, but the trip is worthwhile, and the beer brewed here is excellent. Ask at the tourist information centre for details, particularly important if you wish to see the cellars and church escape sections, as this must be arranged with the appropriate museum authorities.

SLEEPING AND EATING

As with the rest of what was East Germany, hotels formerly in the budget pocket are now well outside it. The Jugendherberge hostel is at Käthe-Kollwitz Strasse 62/66, take tram 1 or 2, to just before the Klingebruche bridge. A second hostel, Am Auensee, is at Gustav-Esche-Strasse 4 (Tel. 57189); take the S-Bahn to Wahren, or tram 10, 11 or 28 from the Hauptbahnhof. Trams 10 and 28 terminate at Wahren, then walk down Linkel-Strasse, continue into Strasse der Jungen Pioniere. There are also some signs to the nearby Auensee campsite, at Gustav-Esche-Strasse 5 (Tel. 52648). For private house accommodation ring 795934.

There are plenty of reasonably priced restaurants and pubs, but expect the costs to be approaching West German levels. There are cheap self-service restaurants at Grimmaische Strasse. Opposite the station's Wintergartenstrasse exit and in the Horfeu department store there is a well-stocked supermarket.

Weimar

Homeland of Cranach, Bach, Liszt, Schiller, Goethe and Nietzsche, and the Buchenwald concentration camp, this town was also the site of the first German Republic (the Weimar Republic) which fell in the 1930s, just before Nazism rose to power. It is only one hour from Leipzig and makes a good day-trip from there if you're in a rush and can't spare the time to stay.

TOURIST INFORMATION

Weimar-Information, Marktstrasse 4 (Tel. 21 73), open Mon.: 10 a.m.–6 p.m., Tues.–Fri.: 9 a.m.–6 p.m., Sat.: 9 a.m.–4 p.m. Take bus 11 or 71 from the station to Goetheplatz and walk to Theaterplatz, then along Schillerstrasse to the Marktplatz. Tourist Information is off the square, to the right of the Rathaus. They can arrange the usual bus tickets, accommodation and a museum pass.

SEEING

The LUCAS-CRANACH HAUS is the richly decorated Renaissance building in the Marktplatz. Close by is the SCHLOSSMUSEUM, with its collection of German Renaissance works, and the Gothic church, HERDERKIRCHE. The KIRMS-KRACKHOW HAUS has displays on the philosopher Herder and poets Schiller and Goethe, among others. There are museums devoted to Schiller and Goethe, also within walking distance. Another famous son of Weimar, Liszt, also has a museum here.

• **Excursions:** the Rococo SCHLOSS BELVEDERE, a former Royal summer palace, can be reached by bus from Goetheplatz – ask at the information office for details, as this was closed during 1990 for restoration; check that it has reopened at the same time. The Nazi concentration camp of BUCHENWALD can also be reached by bus, leaving from stop No.31, near the Hauptbahnhof. Now a grim memorial to the more than 56,000 Jews, communists and others killed between 1937 and 1945. An excellent English guidebook is available from the Memorial bookshop.

SLEEPING AND EATING

There is no convenient campsite, the nearest is listed under Erfurt, and is some distance from there. The Am Poseckschen Garten hostel, at Humboldtstrasse 17 (Tel. 64021), charges 20 DM per person for B&B, including linen. It's around 1½ miles from the station.

The Germania Youth Hostel, at Carl-August-Allee 13 (Tel. 2076), has 72 beds and charges 20 DM. Ask at Tourist Information for details of private B&B.

People eat early in Weimar and you'll find places closing from 8 p.m., and all weekend, so get some supplies in. Try Alt Weimar, Steubenstrasse 27, or the Elephantkeller on the Markt.

Erfurt

The capital of the forested and mountainous region of Thuringia, a short journey from Weimar. The very well-preserved medieval centre of the 'City of Flowers' makes the trip well worthwhile.

The Tourist Information Centre is on the road to the railway station, at Bahnhofstrasse 37 (Tel. 26267) and near the City Hall at Krämerbrücke 3. Open at Bahnhofstrasse Mon.-Fri.: 9 a.m.–6 p.m., Sat.: 10 a.m.–3 p.m., at Krämerbrücke Mon.–Fri.: 9 a.m.–5 p.m., Sat.–Sun.: 10 a.m.–4 p.m.

The twin towers of the Gothic CATHEDRAL and the thirteenth-century ST SERVERUS CHURCH, on the Domberg, dominate Erfurt's skyline. The unusual bridge, KRÄMERBRÜCKE, is lined with a collection of restored fourteenth-century houses. Not far away is the Anger, a restored street of Renaissance and Art Nouveau buildings.

Erfurt boasts several monastic buildings, including the Gothic AUGUSTINERKLOSTER, a thirteenth-century complex, restored after war damage. Martin Luther, who was briefly a monk in Erfurt, has an exhibition here.

The youth hostel is at Hochheimer Strasse 12, about 5 km from the centre, take line 5 from Hofbahnhof to Hochheimer Strasse (Tel. 26705). Cost per person 17 DM per night. Otherwise ask at the Tourist Office for private accommodation or for the scarce cheap hotels. If stuck, try commuting from Weimar, 20 minutes away by train.

Northern Germany

Northern Germany – the area between Schleswig and Bremen – is comparatively unspoilt by tourism. The main centres of interest are: Bremen, Hamburg, and Lübeck, and also you could take in the little towns of Hameln (of Pied Piper fame) and Celle, if you've enough time left.

Bremen

Bremen with its port, Bremerhaven, is the oldest seaport in Germany. The tourist information office is right in front of the station, open Mon.–Fri.: 8 a.m.–8 p.m.; Sat.: 8 a.m.–6 p.m.; Sun.: 9.30 a.m.–3.30 p.m. Tackle Bremen on foot and take in the old medieval section round the MARKTPLATZ, the RATHAUS, the STATUE OF ROLAND and ST PETER'S eleventh-century CATHEDRAL with its cellar full of mummified bodies. The old section of the town called the SCHNOORVIERTEL is particularly attractive, with its narrow winding streets dating back to the 1500s and its half-timbered houses. Take a stroll down the WALLANLAGEN (Rampart Walk) with its windmill, and have a look in the craft shops round there.

The youth hostel is at Kalkstrasse 6 (Tel. 0421–1713 69), about 20 minutes' walk from the station, or bus 26 or tram 6 from the station to Brill.

The campsite at Am Stadtwaldsee 1 is excellent. Take tram 5 outside station. At the terminus, change to the bus for the Universität and then it's a 1-km walk. Clean, friendly – with a good cheap restaurant. It's only open from April to October and costs 6.50 DM per person and 4–8 DM per tent.

Hamburg

Germany's second largest city, after Berlin, and largest seaport. Unlike many of Germany's cities, Hamburg does not lack character or things to see.

STATION FACILITIES

	HAUPTBAHNHOF
Train information	All hours (Tel. 19419)
Reservations	7 a.m.–8 p.m.
Tourist information	7 a.m.–11 p.m.
Foreign exchange	7.30 a.m.–10 p.m.
Left-luggage lockers	No access 2 a.m.–5 a.m.
Left-luggage store	6 a.m.–11.30 p.m.
Bar, Buffet	All hours
Restaurant	6 a.m.–12 midnight (intercity)
Waiting room	All hours
Post office	All hours

Daily trains to: Copenhagen (5 hours), Hanover (1½ hours), Frankfurt (5 hours), Vienna, Munich, Basel, Zürich, Milan, Bremen, Düsseldorf (4 hours), Cologne (4½ hours), Brussels, Paris.

The Hamburg Metro, particularly around the Hauptbahnhof, is unsavoury at night, so be careful.

TOURIST INFORMATION AND ADDRESSES

There is a tourist information office inside the station, and the head office is just around the corner on Hachmann Platz, open Mon.–

Fri.: 7.30 a.m.–6 p.m.; Sat.: 8 a.m.–3 p.m. They'll supply you with maps, a fortnightly programme of local events 'Where to go in Hamburg', and the 'Hamburg Guide'. Ask for 'Muzikszene', 'Tango' or 'Oxmox' for entertainment.

A cheap suggestion for those wishing to see several of the sights: try the 'Hamburg – Card', available from any tourist office. Valid for one day at 9.50 DM, it covers the city transport systems, as well as eleven museums.

There's a separate information office (Hotelnachweis) also at the station and they'll find you a bed for a fee.

Rail pass holders go free on Hamburg's S-Bahn.

US CONSULATE: Alsterufer 27 (Tel. 41171 213).

POST OFFICE: Münzstrasse 1, near the station. Poste restante and 24-hour telephone service is here also. There is a post office within the station.

AMEX: Rathaus Markt 5 (Tel. 331 141).

STUDENT TRAVEL OFFICE: Rothenbaumchaussee 61 (Tel. 410 2081).

24-HOUR CHEMIST: Tel. 228 022.

TELEPHONE CODE: 040.

SEEING

The PORT dominates the city and is difficult to ignore. It's also quite interesting to watch what goes on and there are tours of it available. The best leave from Landungsbrucken. ST MICHAEL'S, the eighteenth-century baroque brick church, affords a good view from its tower, currently under renovation. If there at 10 a.m. or 9 p.m. listen out for the tower herald playing his trumpet. Lift up the tower costs 3.50 DM. Of the many museums in Hamburg the best are: the HAMBURG ART GALLERY; the DECORATIVE ARTS AND CRAFTS MUSEUM; the MILLERS VETERAN CAR MUSEUM; and the HAMBURG HISTORY MUSEUM. Take a day trip to the nearby open-air museums: the VIERLANDE MUSEUM (S-Bahn to Bergedorf) and the MUSEUM VILLAGE in Volksdorf (U-Bahn). All museums are closed on Mondays.

SLEEPING

There are plenty of cheap pensions north of the station along Steindamm and Bremer Reihe so you shouldn't have any problems.

Consider spending 1 DM for the Hotelführer list available from the tourist office. Try Pension Nord at 22 Bremer Reihe (Tel. 244 693).

The Auf dem Stintfang Hostel overlooking the harbour is excellent though the evening meal is poor value. It is at Alfred-Wegener-Weg 5. (Tel. 313 488). Always use the lockers provided as security has recently been a problem. Nearby Landungsbrucken station is on both S-Bahn (free to Inter-Rail) and U-Bahn. Less central is the Horner-Rennbahn hostel at Rennbahn Strasse 100 (Tel. 6511671). Take the U-Bahn to Horner-Rennbahn. Also try Pension Terminus (Tel. 2803 144), Steindamm 5 – 70 DM for a twin room including breakfast and shower and helpful English-speaking staff. Pension Sternschanze (Tel. 43 33 89), Schanzenstrasse 101, located close to the Congress Centre and the student area, has double rooms for 75 DM, including breakfast. The best of the campsites is at Kielerstrasse 374 (Tel. 540 4532), open summer.

For cheap hotels – and there are plenty – head for the commercial area or, if you don't mind the noise of squeaking bedsprings, the red-light district.

EATING AND NIGHTLIFE

The university Mensa is at Schlüterstrasse 7 and represents your best bet. Being a port, seafood and fish restaurants are plentiful and good in Hamburg. Try the ones along Landungsbrücken or the Fischerhaus at the St Pauli fish market, however, Landungsbrücken has recently become more expensive. Try also near the station.

One thing Hamburg's not short of is nightlife. The famous Reeperbahn and St Pauli area is one of the liveliest in Europe with the trendiest clubs, discos and bars in the town. The sex shops and porn movie-houses, which made the area's name, are also obvious, but this should not put you off. Use your judgement to avoid falling into the tourist rip-off traps; also do not look for beds in the Palais d'Amour as it offers more than beds for the night . . . Before leaving Hamburg be sure to visit DIE FABRIK on Barnerstrasse, one of Germany's first and best-known youth centres for music and student hangouts. Also try the Front Club, 32 Heidenkamps Weg.

Lübeck

Only 40 minutes away from Hamburg is the attractive old town of Lübeck, former headquarters of the medieval trading group, the Hanseatic League. Since 1987 Lübeck has been a UNESCO World Heritage Site. You'll see as many Scandinavians as Germans here as this is one of their favourite holiday destinations. Tourist information is in the station. Open Mon.–Sat.: 9 a.m.–1 p.m., 3 p.m.–7 p.m., Sun.: closed. The office on the Markt is open Mon.–Fri.: 9.30 a.m.–6 p.m., Sat.–Sun.: 10 a.m.–2 p.m. There is also an office at Beckergrube 95, closed weekends.

Lübeck is known as the 'City of Seven Spires' because the skyline is dominated by the spires of five imposing churches, including the cathedral. Extensively bombed during the war, you can see the shattered bells at the foot of the former belfry in the MARIENKIRCHE where they have lain undisturbed since being blasted free of their fastenings in 1942. For a good view of the city the lift up the tower of the PETRIKIRCHE is good value at 2 DM (1 DM for students).

Lübeck is renowned for its brickwork, so take a close look at the gabled houses, particularly BUDDENBROOKHAUS – the house Thomas Mann (a Lübecker) used as the background to his novel *Buddenbrooks*. The actual city centre is quite small and it's possible to walk round all the sights there: the thirteenth-century RATHAUS with its original black glazed tiles, the Romanesque ST MARIEN DOM, the HOLSTEN GATE and the old city walls and MUSEUM.

The youth hostel, 'Folke-Bernadotte-Heim', is at Am Gertrudenkirchhof 4 (Tel. 0451–33433), 14 DM per night. A second, more expensive, hostel is at Mengstrasse 33 (Tel. 0451 70399). A good campsite at Steinrader Damm 12 is reached by bus 7 or 8 from the station towards Dornbreite. The buses stop near the site entrance. Tourist information will find rooms for you.

Hannover

Primarily known as a centre for trade fairs, Hannover is nevertheless deserving of a visit. Hannover will host the world exhibition 'Expo 2000'.

The Tourist Information office is opposite the station at Ernst August Platz 8 (Tel. 0511–1682319). Open 8.30 a.m.–6 p.m., 7.30 p.m. on Fridays, 12 noon Saturdays. Ask for the booklet 'The Red Thread' which takes you around the main sights of the city by following a red line painted on the pavements.

Get around by following the red line. Sights worthy of special mention are the 300-year-old ROYAL GARDENS, BAROQUE GARDEN, BERGGARDEN and GEORGE GARDEN. The gardens are linked to the city by the mile-long Herrenhausen Avenue lined by 1300 lime trees. The gardens are often the venue for Music and Theatre, and Festivals of Light are often held. Check with Tourist Information for details.

Look out for the Marksmen Festival and Old Town Festival during the summer. The Flea Market on Hohes Ufer every Saturday is an interesting diversion. The KESTNER MUSEUM, the MUSEUM OF HISTORY and LOWER SAXONY REGIONAL MUSEUM are also worth a look.

The hostel is at Ferdinand-Wilhelm-Fricke-Weg 1 (Tel. 0511–322941), 20 minutes from the station on tram 7 or 3 to Fischerhof. A more expensive youth guest house operates at the same address. There is also the Naturfreundehaus at Hermann-Bahlsen-Allee 8 (Tel. 0511–691493), 30 minutes from the station by tram 3 or 7 to Spannhagen Strasse.

Eurotrain has an office at Karl-Wiechert-Allee 23 (Tel. 0511–5670). The German ICE links Hannover to the southern part of Germany, with Munich 6 hours away, Frankfurt 2½ hours.

The Central Belt and the Harz Mountains

Frankfurt, Düsseldorf and Bonn are all fairly modern industrial centres which have little to offer that is worth breaking your journey for. You do far better to head for centres like Marburg, Göttingen, Hannoversch-Münden, Karlshafen, Goslar or the resorts round Münster: Attendorn, Alt-Astenburg and Berleburg. These have far more of the aspects of German life you're probably looking for.

Baden-Württemberg – the Black Forest

The south-western region of Germany from Karlsruhe to Basel is considered by many travellers its most enchanting. The pace of life is slower and the villages and towns dotted round the forests really are as attractive as the tourist brochures make them look. The main towns of this region are Heidelberg, Freiburg, Tübingen, Baden-Baden and Stuttgart. The first three are picturesque old university towns and worth a day or two; unless you've time, forget Baden-Baden as it's very expensive; Stuttgart is an interesting industrial city. A day trip from Heidelberg to Freiburg, Donaueschingen and Offenburg is a good 'pushed for time' introduction to this area.

Heidelberg

Famous for its university and magnificent castle, most of Heidelberg's sights can be seen in a day, but are nevertheless well worth seeing. Start your tour (get a bus or taxi as it's a 40-minute walk into town) at the MARKTPLATZ and take in the HEILIG-GEIST KIRCHE and HAUS ZUM RITTER, a Renaissance mansion house, now a hotel and restaurant. The OLD UNIVERSITY has an interesting STUDENTS' JAIL (STUDENTENKARZER) which proves that graffiti weren't a twentieth-century invention. From here cross the Karl-Theodor Bridge or Old Bridge over the River Neckar and take the hour-long PHILOSO-PHER'S WALK to the 1,400-foot Heiligenberg. Apart from a good view of the town, there are reconstructed Roman ruins and the twelfth-century ST STEPHEN'S CLOISTER. Back across the river, inside the amazing SCHLOSS (castle), 4 DM admission, 2 DM for students, is the GERMAN APOTHECARY MUSEUM with interesting reconstructions of laboratories of the seventeenth century. You can get up to it by funicular railway from Kornmarkt if you don't fancy the climb (3.5 DM).

The tourist information office, just outside the station, is open Mon.–Sat.: 9 a.m.–7 p.m., Sun. 10 a.m.–6 p.m. March–Dec., closed Sundays Jan. and Feb. They run an accommodation-finding service for a small fee and supply you with leaflets and maps. Ask for 'All Around Heidelberg', 'Heidelberg This Week', and the official town map, which includes a picture map and a walking tour of the main sights. AMEX is at Friedrich-Ebert Anlage 16. HS Reisebüro, who do student travel deals, are at Bismarckplatz (Tel. 06221–27151). Try to get around town by bus and streetcar. There is a special Tourist Ticket available; ask at the Tourist Office.

Hotels tend to be expensive as Heidelberg gets its fair share of middle-class, middle-aged tourists, so they don't exactly cater for eurorailers in a big way. Still, there's a youth hostel at Tiergartenstrasse (Tel. 06221–412066), on bus routes 33 or 330 with connecting tram at night. The Neckertal campsite is in Schlierbach (Tel. 06221–802506). You are not allowed to leave the campsite before 8 a.m., so don't pitch your tent there if you have an early start the next morning. Your passport is kept as security. There is a train station nearby, but services are limited to two trains at night, and one in the morning. The Haide campsite is between Heidelberg–Ziegelhausen and Kleingemünd. Take bus 35 to Orthopädische Klinik, then across the bridge and 10 minutes further along the river (Tel. 06223–2111).

Use the Mensa restaurants for meals: there's one off Universitätsplatz and another in Marstallhof – or a student inn. These are dotted all round the city. The station restaurant is reasonably priced, providing you pick carefully from the menu. A filling meal with beer can be had for around 14DM.

Freiburg-im-Breisgau

An attractive city of 189,300 people which has fully recovered from its heavy wartime destruction and is restored and as picturesque as ever. Though the university is the source of most young Freiburgers' social life, the summer schools based there make sure things don't grind to a halt outside term-time.

Two blocks down Eisenbahnstrasse from the station is the tourist information at Rotteckring 14. They can arrange accommodation for you, or if you're staying more than two days, you can get into private accommodation (Privatzimmer). Also ask for details of the 24-hour, 48-hour and 72-hour passes. These will save you money if you find yourself staying out of the centre.

The Altstadt (Old Town) has at its centre the MÜNSTER – the beautiful medieval cathedral with its intricate carvings and gargoyles. Climbing the Münster spire is a rewarding and exhilarating experience (cost 1.50 DM). Opposite the cathedral to the south is the sixteenth-century KAUFHAUS (merchants' hall), and nearby is the RATHAUS (town hall) made out of two old patrician houses. Medieval and baroque art of the Upper Rhine can be seen in the AUGUSTINER MUSEUM.

There's a youth hostel and a campsite in Kartäuserstrasse at 151 and 99 respectively (Tel. 0761–67656 and 0761–35054). Take tram 1 from the station to Römerhof. With woods and forests all around, you shouldn't be stuck for a place to pitch your tent, but if things are desperate see the Bahnhofmission at the station.

The last week of June sees the Wine Festival; Baden white wine is well worth trying, and Freiburg has many wine bars and cheap (by German standards) eating places. Concentrate on the university area and Augustinerplatz.

Tübingen

The University of Tübingen, founded in 1477, still makes use of the town's Renaissance castle (SCHLOSS HOHENTÜBINGEN) and though you only visit it at weekends from April to October, you can get a good view over the Old Town and the Neckar from its gardens. In the centre there are old gabled houses and a fifteenth-century church, STIFTSKIRCHE. In the Neckar on a man-made island is the PLATANENALLEE – an avenue of plane trees which makes a good walk. Reach it via the Eberhard Bridge.

The youth hostel is at Gartenstrasse 22/2 (Tel. 07071–23002), ten minutes from the station, and there's a campsite on the banks of the Neckar (Tel. 07071–43145). The university Mensa is on the corner of Wilhelmstrasse and Keplerstrasse and is open for lunches and dinners.

Stuttgart

Described as 'one of the most interesting cities in Europe' by one reader, Stuttgart has got to be worth visiting. Stuttgart is the capital of Baden–Württemberg and despite being an industrial centre, boasts that over 50 per cent of the city is woods, vineyards and parks. It is also the largest wine growing city in Germany.

TOURIST INFORMATION

Tourist Centre 'i-Punkt', Königstrasse 1A, near the station (Tel. 0711–222 8240). Open 8.30 a.m.–10 p.m. (Sundays and holidays 11 a.m. to 6 p.m., Sundays Nov.–April 1 p.m.–6 p.m.). In addition to providing details of walking tours and maps, they will also provide details of budget accommodation.

Also try JIZ (Jugend-Informationszentrum) at Hohestrasse 9 (Tel. 0711–293058), specifically for forthcoming events and where the action is.

SEEING

As the centre of Stuttgart is largely pedestrianized, it is best seen on foot.

SCHLOSSPLATZ and SCHILLERPLATZ are typical of Stuttgart and are surrounded by most of the major sights. The SCHLOSSGARTEN stretches northwards to the River Neckar and here you can enjoy landscaped woods, lakes and a zoo. Stuttgart boasts the most abundant mineral water springs in western Europe, and the mineral baths make an interesting diversion from the Schlossgarten. Alternatively take U14 to Mineral-bäder. LEUZE mineral baths has both an outdoor swimming pool and a heated indoor pool.

Museums especially worth a visit include the imposing extension of the STAATSGALERIE (built by a British architect) on Konrad Adenauer Strasse and the MERCEDES BENZ AUTOMOBILE MUSEUM just outside the main city, open Tues.–Sun.: 9 a.m.–5 p.m. Take S-Bahn 1 to Neckarstadion or bus 56. All city-owned museums are free of charge.

SLEEPING

Should be no problem as 'i-Punkt' will help.

The DJH Hostel at Haussmannstrasse 27 (entrance on the corner of Werastrasse and Kernerstrasse) is central and modern and is only ten minutes from the station. Take S-Bahn 15 to Eugensplatz (Tel. 0711–241583).

The campsite at Cannstatter Wasen (Tel. 0711–556696 or 561503) is less central, on the banks of the River Neckar.

EATING AND NIGHTLIFE

It should be easy to find a decent place to eat. Follow the locals to a nearby 'Kneipe' for a popular meeting place and refreshment. They normally fill up very quickly and become quite lively. Wine is varied and excellent, whilst local culinary specialities include 'Maultaschen' – lentils with Weiner sausages, and hand-made noodles or roast beef with sauerkraut.

Stuttgart has a lively youth scene and the many jazz clubs are popular. Ask at 'i-Punkt', JIZ or any young resident for the latest details.

Not to be missed in summer/early autumn are the variety of street fairs and 'happenings'. Equally, the WINE FESTIVAL in late August–September at Schillerplatz and Marktplatz is lively, whilst the CANSTATT VOLKSFEST in late September–October, should not be missed as it is only equalled in scale by the Munich Oktoberfest.

Harz Mountains

QUEDLINGBURG has some 1,600 protected buildings which provide a unique opportunity to see the development of half-timber construction through the centuries. The historical value of the town has been recognized by UNESCO. Tourist information is at Markt 12 (Tel. 2866 or 2633). WERNIGERODE has half-timbered houses, a fine town hall, and a hilltop castle, as well as being the starting point of the Harz narrow gauge steam railway. There are youth hostels at Leninstrasse 53 and Am Grossen Bleck 27. To reach either of these small towns take a train from Halberstadt. Services connect Halberstadt to Magdeburg and Halle. A few buses a day cross the old border to Bad Harzburg (6 DM), which has train connections to Hannover and Braunschweig. A short distance from Bad Harzburg is the old imperial town of GOSLAR, with numerous half-timbered buildings, the IMPERIAL PALACE and the frescoed 'Hall of Homage' in the town hall. Tourist information is at Marktplatz 7. The youth hostel is at Rammelsberger Strasse 25 (Tel. 05321 22240), just outside the old town, 13–21 DM.

The Rhine Valley

The section of the 820-mile-long Rhine that flows through Germany is considered the most scenic, and the popular image of sailing down the Rhine is a pleasure cruiser passing vineyards, castles and cliffs. This is founded on truth but is somewhat idealistic as the Rhine today is still Europe's main commercial waterway and as such takes its fair share of barges and freight loads. Köln-Düsseldorfer lines run boats from Frankfurt to Cologne which give a 50 per cent discount to Inter-Railers and is free to Eurail card holders. The most attractive segment of the journey is from Rüdesheim to Koblenz, or vice versa.

OBERWESEL is a lovely place, but almost closes down on Mondays. The youth hostel is fantastic, complete with swimming pool. It's at Auf dem Schönberg (Tel. 06744 7046) and costs 17 to 33 DM including breakfast. Phone to book in after 8 a.m. Stop off here on your way from Köln to Bingen – it's about three hours down the line – and finish your journey by boat.

Cologne (Köln)

The main reason for stopping off at Cologne is undoubtedly the cathedral (KÖLNER DOM) which took from 1248 to 1880 to complete; see the fourteenth-century stained-glass windows, altarpiece and the Shrine of the Magi. In the Second World War, 90 per cent of Cologne was razed to the ground, but amazingly the cathedral escaped almost intact. Open 10 a.m.–5 p.m. weekdays, 10 a.m.–1 p.m. Sat., 1 p.m.–5 p.m. Sun. For an impressive view of the city climb the 509 steps up the tower (2 DM, ISIC 1 DM), tower open 9 a.m.–5 p.m. daily.

From Cologne, you can take an hour-long round-trip on the Rhine for around 7DM. It makes two stops to allow break of journey, so if you wish to visit the ZOO, or take the cable-car across the river, this is a relatively cheap and pleasant way to do it. You also get a great view of the Dom from the river.

Other things of interest are the ROMAN-GERMANIC MUSEUM exhibiting Cologne's Roman remains and the WALLRAF-RICHARTZ-MUSEUM/MUSEUM LUDWIG with its impressive collection of German works. The MUSEUM OF ARTS AND CRAFTS at An der Rechtsschule includes vast collections of arts and crafts from the Middle Ages to the present day together with designs of the twentieth century. Open 10 a.m.–5 p.m. (until 8 p.m. on Tuesdays). Admission 3 DM. Even if you can only afford a few hours you should have no problems, as everything is near the station. Museums are closed on Mondays.

• **Excursion:** If you are based in Cologne, Aachen is well worth a half-day visit, being 40 minutes away by train. The RATHAUS and CATHEDRAL are of great interest in this ex-capital of the Holy Roman Empire.

STATION FACILITIES

	HAUPTBAHNHOF
Train information	Mon.–Sun.: 6 a.m.–11 p.m. (Tel. 0221–19419)
Reservations	Mon.–Sun.: 6 a.m.–9 p.m.
Tourist information	Mon.–Sat.: 8 a.m.–10.30 p.m., Sun.: 9 a.m.–10.30 p.m.; Winter, Mon.–Sat.: 8 a.m.–9 p.m., Sun.: 9.30 a.m.–10.30 p.m. Located directly opposite cathedral Unter Fetterhennen, 19
Foreign exchange	7 a.m.–9 p.m.
Left-luggage lockers	Always accessible
Left-luggage store	Mon.–Sun.: 6 a.m.–10 p.m.
Waiting room	In restaurant (with ticket only) and passageways
Bar, Buffet	7 a.m.–9 p.m. 'Milchstube','Bierfass', all hours except 4 a.m.–5 a.m. 'Treffpub'
Restaurant	8 a.m.–10 p.m. – 'Terrassen' and 6 a.m.–10 p.m. – 'Gaststätte'
Shops	Regular hours in pedestrian mall
Post office	Mon.–Sat.: 7 a.m.–10 p.m. Nord Tunnel, Sun.: 10 a.m.–10 p.m.

Daily trains to: Düsseldorf (½ hour), Hamburg (4 hours), Copenhagen, Hannover (3 hours), Mainz (1¾ hours), Frankfurt (2¼ hours), Würzburg (4 hours), Nürnberg (5 hours), Stuttgart (4 hours), Vienna, Munich, Innsbruck, Zürich, Basel (5 hours), Paris, Brussels (3 hours), Rotterdam (3¼ hours), The Hague (3½ hours), Amsterdam (4 hours).

There are two hostels in Cologne which are very good but suffer from the same problem – they fill up fast. The nearest to the main station, and reputedly the best, is at Siegesstrasse 5a (Tel. 0221–814711). It's a 20-minute walk across the Rhine, but is only two minutes' walk from the Deutz station and is well signposted. If it is full up you will be directed to a nearby hotel where you can get bed and breakfast for 30 DM – about double the hostel cost but quite reasonable for an hotel. You can also try the Youth Guest House at An der Schanze 14 (Tel. 767081), which is more luxurious, but further out. You cannot book by phone, so get there as soon as possible after reception opens at 11 a.m. Take U-Bahn lines 5, 15, 16 or 18 to Boltensternstrasse and then a five-minute walk. Price is 17–33 DM and includes breakfast, shower and linen. There are two camping sites at the end of the Rodenkirchen Bridge. Campingplatz der Stadt Köln is at Weidenweg (Tel: 831966). Although facilities are limited, there is a good bar across the road. Cost is 4.5 DM per person and 3 DM per tent. Tourist information will also find rooms from about 35 DM upwards. Salzgasse in the Old Town is where to go for eats, and there are all the usual excellent department stores with food halls for buying groceries.

The square immediately in front of the Dom is lively and interesting, often with street musicians performing, and a 'peace wall' to which you can contribute messages.

Telephone Code: 0221.

The Moselle Valley

Less commercial, and some say less scenic, is the Moselle region where wine making is the main regional industry, apart from tourism. Boats run between Cochem and Koblenz (KD lines with the same reductions as on the Rhine). The hostel at Koblenz is very good and overlooks the confluence of the Rhine and Moselle. It's at

Koblenz-Ehrenbreitstein on the right bank, bus 7, 8, 9, 10 from the station (Tel. 0261–73737). The towns to get off at are: BERNKASTEL-KUES, TRABEN-TRARBACH and COCHEM. You can hire bikes at Cochem. This is the region for wine tasting – ask at the tourist information offices for tours of the local cellars.

Frankfurt am Main

Frankfurt is Germany's most important finance and trading centre; a city of large skyscrapers with an important international airport and a much cleaned up red-light area right across from what is claimed to be Europe's largest railway station. If you head for McDonald's or Burger King across from the station you may be hassled. The Tourist Information Centre, opposite platform 23, is open Mon.–Sat. 8 a.m.–10 p.m. (9 p.m. off-season); Sun. 9.30 a.m.–8 p.m. An area worth visiting is around THE RÖMERBERG, with the rebuilt fifteenth-century RÖMER, or city hall, and ST NIKOLAIKIRCHE. Nearby is the DOM, built between the thirteenth and fifteenth centuries. The coronation of German Emperors took place here between 1562 and 1792. Amongst the museums that are worth a visit are the HISTORICAL MUSEUM, collections from the middle ages to the present day, and the GERMAN FILM MUSEUM, about the history and origins of the film industry. Museums generally open Tues.–Sun.: 10 a.m.–5 p.m., Wed.: 10 a.m.–8 p.m.

The youth hostel is pleasantly situated across the River Main and on the edge of the city's liveliest area for entertainment and reasonable eating places (with their copious cheap 'Apfelwein') – Sachsenhausen. The hostel is at Deutschherrnufer 12 (Tel. 619058). Take bus 46 from the Hauptbahnhof right to the hostel. The fruit stalls and shops in the underground mall in front of the station are quite good for stocking up on picnic items.

Telephone Code: 069

Trier

Germany's oldest city and one-time capital of the Western Roman Empire (with Roman baths, arches and amphitheatre remains to prove it), Trier has many interesting churches and museums, as well as the house where Karl Marx was born. Tourist information is next to the Porta Nigra, the (IYHF) youth hostel is at Am Moselufer 4, bus 2 or 8 from the station (Tel. 0651–29292) and the campsites are at Monaiserstrasse (Tel. 0651–86210) and Luxemburgerstrasse 81 (Tel. 0651–86921). For cheap eats try either of the two university Mensas at Universität Schneidershof or at the Tarforst campus. The Greek restaurant next to the youth hostel serves good, filling and reasonably-priced meals. For cheap beer and good food, head for the Loewenbrau Brewerie, near the amphitheatre. It is off the Gartenfeld Strasse, 100 yards after the railway bridge. The tree-shaded patio, where food and drink are served, is across the road from the main entrance. There is also a good market next to the cathedral and while you are there take a look at the impressive interior decor. For a good view of the city itself, follow the Romerstrasse up from the north bank of the Mosel to the Madonna statue.

Munich (München)

Munich is the capital of Bavaria and is regarded by some as the ultimate German city. It is beautifully landscaped, tastefully decorated, carefully laid out and has a glut of things to do and see.

Ruled for over 650 years by the Wittelsbach family who brought the world-famous art collections and rich architectural heritage to the city, Munich seems to have continual festivals all the year round: Fasching with its masked carnivals from February, ending on Shrove Tuesday; the beer inaugurations in March; the summer season of concerts and operas from May to August; the famous Oktoberfest beer festival lasting from end September to early October, followed not long after by the Christmas markets. And this doesn't even take into account the countless student-based activities going on round SCHWABING, Munich's lively Latin quarter.

STATION FACILITIES

MÜNCHEN HAUPTBAHNHOF

Train information	6 a.m.–11 p.m. (Tel. 19419)
Train price information	(Tel. 554141)
Reservations	9 a.m.–6 p.m., midnight in 'ABR Reisebüro'
Tourist information	Mon.–Sat.: 8 a.m.–10 p.m., Sun.: 1 p.m.–9 p.m.
Foreign exchange	6 a.m.–11 p.m.
Bar, Buffet	6 a.m.–9 p.m.
Cafeteria	6 a.m.–9 p.m.
Restaurant	6 a.m.–9 p.m.
Left-luggage lockers	5 a.m.–12 midnight
Left-luggage store	6 a.m.–11 p.m.
Shops	5 a.m.–12 midnight
Waiting room	All hours
Post office	Mon.–Fri.: 7 a.m.–9 p.m., Sat.: 8 a.m.–9 p.m.
Station shuts	11.30 p.m.–6 a.m.

Daily trains to: Paris, Brussels, Zürich, Milan, Vienna.

TOURIST INFORMATION

The Fremdenverkehrsamt (tourist office) (Tel. 239 1256/57) is at the front of the Hauptbahnhof, opposite platform 11, and is open daily 8 a.m.–10 p.m. The staff are helpful, fluent in English and will supply you with maps, details of walking tours and pamphlets and find you a room for 5 DM. Get the monthly programme of events and the 'Young People's Guide to Munich', which is excellent.

Munich's city transport system is one of the best in Europe, and also one of the most complicated. There are buses, trams, the U-Bahn and the S-Bahn. Note: Rail pass holders get free travel on the S-Bahn only. You need only one ticket even if your journey takes in the tram, bus and underground systems. For further information, pick up leaflets at the underground at Hauptbahnhof, or S-Bahn stations. Day tickets cost 9 DM for the inner zone and 15 DM for all zones.

Whilst it is tempting and apparently easy to travel free on public transport, you take the risk of an on-the-spot fine of 60 DM if a squad of police operates a random check (which are frequent). Ignorance is no excuse, the police reason that anyone who can work out how to get to their destination can operate the idiot-proof ticket dispensers or obtain a pass! Offenders or those unable to pay are taken to the police station for a statement. It obviously makes sense to have a valid ticket.

● **Addresses:**

POST OFFICE: Bahnhofplatz 1 (opposite station). Open 24 hours. Also poste restante here.

UK CONSULATE: Amalienstrasse 62 (Tel. 3816280).

US CONSULATE: Königinstrasse 5. (Tel. 28881).

CANADIAN CONSULATE: Tal 29 (Tel. 222661).

AMEX: Promenadeplatz 6, Mon.–Fri.: 9 a.m.–5.30 p.m., Sat.: 9 a.m.–12 noon (Tel. 21990).

MEDICAL HELP: Try university clinic at Ismaningerstrasse (Tel. 41401).

STUDIOSUS-REISEN (Student Travel): Amalienstrasse 73 (Tel. 500 60540).

TELEPHONE CODE: 089.

SEEING

MARIENPLATZ – the attractive pedestrian zone – is at the centre of Munich. The neo-Gothic TOWN HALL is located here (look out for the glockenspiel show at 11 a.m., noon, 5 p.m. and 9 p.m. May–Oct., 11 a.m. Nov.–Apr.), as is the old town hall (ALTES RATHAUS). On Sunday mornings in summer, a brass band in full Bavarian uniform plays in front of the town hall. Just off Marien-platz is the twelfth-century church of ST PETER. If a white disc is out on the platform, climb its tower (2 DM, 1 DM for students) for a view extending to the Alps (a red disc means you'll just see over Munich). Also near here is the FRAUENKIRCHE, with its green onion-topped twin towers, is the symbol of the city and houses various works of art, tombs and relics as well as the mausoleum of Emperor Ludwig IV (presently closed). ST MICHAEL'S CHURCH and the baroque THEATINER CHURCH are also worth a look. Eight blocks west of Marienplatz is KARLSPLATZ, the main square of Munich. All the city transport starts from here and SONNENSTRASSE, the main shopping street, begins. The palace of the Bavarian rulers (the RESIDENZ) houses a spectacular array of riches. Open Tues.–Sat.: 10 a.m.–4.30 p.m., Sun. till 1 p.m. North of the Residenz is the university area (Schwabing) with Leopoldstrasse at its centre.

Nothing much goes on in daytime here, but it's a lively place at night. To the east of Schwabing lies the ENGLISH GARDEN, ideal for sunbathing (nude!) and picnicking.

The ALTE PINAKOTHEK is one of Europe's finest art galleries. It specializes in early German, Flemish and Italian works and it's free on Sundays (closed Mondays). The NEUE PINAKOTHEK concentrates on modern art.

The DEUTSCHES MUSEUM is located on an island in the Isar River; it is the largest technical museum in the world (with lots of buttons to push), and has exhibits such as U-boats, a Messerschmitt jet fighter, a planetarium and old locomotives. Most explanations are in German only. Entrance 8 DM (ISIC 2.50 DM). The BAVARIAN NATIONAL MUSEUM gives a good introduction to what makes Bavaria different from the rest of Germany and has the most extensive collection of arts and crafts in the world (closed Mondays but open till 5 p.m. even on Saturdays; if you turn up after 3.30 they sometimes let you off without paying the admission fee).

The BMW MUSEUM (part of the factory) is well worth a visit if you have had enough of trains for a while. You can't get guided tours of the factory itself, but the museum is superb and includes a spectacular audio-visual show. It's the last stop on U-Bahn 2 and 3. While there, visit the park itself, scene of the 1972 Olympic Games and marvel at the impressive architecture either from ground level or from the top of the Olympia Tower. Entrance to the park is free, 5 DM for the lift up the tower, which is well worth it for the stupendous view, unless the weather is lousy. Don't eat in the restaurant at the top as the prices are exorbitant. An equally good panorama can be obtained free by walking up one of the hills in the Olympic Park. A break from sightseeing is offered by the rowing boats on the lake (7 DM for ½ hour).

SLEEPING

Munich is busy all year, particularly during the Oktoberfest when beds are very scarce. Still, there are plenty of places if you know where to look. Expect to pay about 25–40 DM for student accommodation, 17–33 DM at youth hostels and up to 70 DM in pensions. Try to arrange hostel accommodation ahead of time or turn up early! Ask at Tourist Information for the Accommodation Guide to Munich.

The cheapest sleep to be had is at the Youth Camp (Jugendlager-am Kapuzinerhölzl, known as the 'Big Tent') at Frank-Schrank Strasse 8 (Tel. 1414300); open end June–early September, 5 p.m.–9 a.m. For 6 DM you get an air mattress, blankets and a place in the circus tent, not to mention tea (free) in the mornings and evenings. You won't get turned away, and there is a great 'International' atmosphere, maximum stay is three days only. Take U-Bahn line U1 to Rotkreuzplatz, then tram 12 to Botanischer Garten. Take your passport for ID to avoid paying a 50 DM deposit for blankets; ask for plenty of these if it is late in the season as it can get chilly.

• **Youth hostels:** You must be under 27 or accompanying a child to use Bavarian youth hostels. Wendl-Dietrich Strasse 20 (Tel. 131156) is fairly central but large, impersonal, fills up early and is usually full of noisy adolescent school groups. It could be cleaner, and the lockers are dodgy. Security is a bit suspect too. Costs from 14.80 DM including breakfast. Take U-Bahn 1 to Rotkreuzplatz. The one at Burgweg 4-6, Pullach (Tel. 7930643 and 7930644), is more fun, but this renovated castle is a half-hour journey and also fills up early. There are no lockers and it has an infuriating token system for showers. The staff, however, are very helpful and it costs from 14 DM including shower and breakfast in a small dormitory. Take S-Bahn 7 (free on Inter-Rail) to Pullach, signposted from station. Last train from Munich is 10.40 p.m. and curfew is at 11.30 p.m.

Haus International, Elizabethstrasse 87 (Tel. 120060) is good but more expensive with prices from 35 DM for a shared room, to 59 DM for a single, so share in a large room to cut down costs. No IYHF card required. There is a disco in the basement and no curfew. Also Jugendgastehaus Thalkirchen (IYHF) at Miesingstrasse 4 (Tel. 7236550), where couples need to produce a marriage certificate to share a room. Take U-Bahn 1 or 2 to Sendlinger-Tor-Platz, change to U-Bahn 3 to Thalkirchen (Tierpark). If you're stuck for a place to stay try the Augsburg Youth Hostel, at Beim Pfaffenkeller 3 (Tel. 0821–33909), about 40 minutes away by DB train.

Some of the cheapest pensions are located in Schillerstrasse and Landwehrstrasse. Try Pension Schiller (Tel. 592435) at Schiller-strasse 11; further down the street at No. 32 there's Lugano (Tel. 591005). Westfalia at Mozartstrasse 23 (Tel. 530377) is also worth a try. For a reasonable hotel try the Helvetia in Schillerstrasse (Tel. 554745). The campsite, which is well equipped, is at Zentralländstrasse 49 (Tel. 7231707), open mid-March–Oct. Take U-Bahn 3 to Thalkirchen (Tierpark), then bus 57 to Camping platz (or a 20-minute walk). Although central and convenient, it can get very crowded and noisy, with cleanliness suffering as a result. 5 DM per person, up to 5 DM per tent.

You could try sleeping in the Hauptbahnhof although it is draughty, busy and you will get woken up and moved on by the police around 5 a.m.

EATING AND NIGHTLIFE

Bavarian cooking is tasty, filling and not for the weight-conscious. Munich's speciality is Weisswurst – a sausage made of veal and parsley. You can buy it at any number of stalls and eat it as a quick snack with a beer to keep you going. The VIKTUALIENMARKT is an attractive sight, but it's invariably cheaper to buy your supplies from one of the superb food halls of the department stores, Kaufhof, Hertie, Deutscher Supermarkt or the cheaper Pennymarkt and Aldi. The displays and high standards in these places really open your eyes if you've been weaned on dull supermarkets at home.

The student canteens (Mensas) have cheap lunches at Arcisstrasse 17 or Leopoldstrasse 15, open 11 a.m.–2 p.m., and all over Schwabing you'll find reasonably priced eating places. If you're desperate there's also a Wendy self-service outside the station. A quarter of the world's beer comes from Bavaria, and Munich is at the heart of this with its social life revolving round the beer halls and gardens. These are good places to eat, drink and make new friends. Avoid the touristy Hofbräuhaus as you're unlikely to meet the locals there; try instead the beer gardens in the English Garden. Augustinerkeller at Arnulfstrasse 52, Donisl at Marienplatz, and Hundskugel (Munich's oldest pub) at Hotterstrasse 18 are more representative. For cheap and delicious doughnuts and so on, try Strüdel Stube in Orlandostrasse (near the Hofbräuhaus).

For nightlife, Schwabing is the area to head for. Studiosus-Reisen, Amalienstrasse 73, have tickets for concerts, theatres, etc., with reductions. There's music and dancing at The Drugstore, Feilitzschstrasse 12, and the university has occasional 'events' such as open-air discos outside term-time which you can go along to if you can pass yourself off as a German student.

• **Excursions:** 22 km north-west of Munich is the concentration camp of DACHAU built in 1933. A visit here will put into perspective the atrocities that were committed and will leave an impression with you that all the opulence of Munich can't take away. The old administration block is now a museum, and a film in English is shown twice a day, check times at tourist information. Get there on the S-Bahn line 2, direction Peterhausen (free to Inter- Railers) to Dachau, then buses 720 or 722 to the camp (closed on Mondays). Buses are infrequent on Sundays and the alternative is a 45-minute walk.

NYMPHENBURG PALACE AND PARK is Munich's Versailles. Home of the Bavarian kings, situated in a 495-acre park, the palace makes a pleasant day trip. Closed Mondays. The surrounding park is free, but entry to the Palace is 6DM (4DM ISIC). Other ideas for trips are Europe's largest zoo, Hellabrunn, 6 km south of the city and the Benedictine monastery at ANDECHS (buses 951 or 956), whose beer hall serves some of the strongest home brew in Munich.

A good day trip from Munich is to the fairy-tale castle of NEUSCHWANSTEIN, which featured in the famous film *Chitty Chitty Bang Bang*, and was built by 'mad' King Ludwig II. Take the train to Fussen and bus Bf 971 (half-price on Inter-Rail) the 5 km to Hohenschwangau. It is then a steep 1 km walk up to the entrance. The bus fare is 1.80 DM and the entrance to the castle (open 8.30 a.m.–5.30 p.m. April–Sept., 10 a.m.–4 p.m. Oct.–Mar.) is 7 DM (4 DM on ISIC) including a rather hurried guided tour. While on the subject of films you may wish to spend some time at the Bavarian Film Studios which are near Pullach. Although quite expensive at 9.50 DM and the tour being only in German, you can walk through the U-boat used for the film *The Boat* and see other sights.

The Alps and the Romantic Road

The Romantische Strasse is the name for the undeniably scenic stretch from Füssen to the vineyards of Franconia. The towns en route are very picturesque, and this is the route to take for fairytale castles and medieval churches set among rolling green hills.

To get to those hidden little corners of Bavaria, the train is not the best way: use the Europabus 'Romantische Strasse'. They offer two alternative routes: Füssen to Würzburg, and Munich to Füssen (free to Eurail card holders). Make further enquiries at the Starnberger Bahnhof part of Munich station.

Places of note en route are: NÖRDLINGEN with its perfectly preserved circular medieval fortifications and fifteenth-century St George's Church; DINKELSBÜHL, also with a St George's Church which is a Gothic masterpiece, 'Deutsches Haus' and Old Town Hall; ROTHENBURG – visit the Rathaus, St Jakob's Church and the Folterkammer (torture chamber); and WÜRZBURG.

Würzburg

In the heart of wine country, Würzburg is *the* baroque city in western Germany. The Franconian RESIDENZ is the magnificent palace of the prince-bishops and is the main sight of Würzburg. Open Tues.–Sun.: 9 a.m.–5 p.m., 10 a.m.–4 p.m. Oct.–Mar. (4.50 DM, 3 DM on ISIC). The MARIENBERG FORTRESS, another of the princes' homes, is on the other side of the River Main, which intersects the town. Near the fortress is the KÄPPELE, an ornate baroque church which allows you an excellent view from the top. The MAINFRÄNKISCHES MUSEUM houses sculptures and carvings and is located in the Marienberg Fortress.

STATION FACILITIES

	HAUPTBAHNHOF
Train information	5.30 a.m.–10 p.m.
	(Tel. 0931–19419)
Reservations	5.30 a.m.–10 p.m.
Tourist information	Mon.–Sat.: 8 a.m.–8 p.m.
	Pavilion outside station
Foreign exchange	Mon.–Fri.: 6 a.m.–9 p.m., Sat.: 9 a.m.–1 p.m.
	(in next building along)
Café	Mon.–Fri.: 7 a.m.–8 p.m.
	Sat.: 7.30 a.m.–2.30 p.m.
	Sun.: 11 a.m.–6 p.m.
Restaurant	6.30 a.m.–12.30 a.m.
Bath, Shower	6 a.m.–10 p.m.
Left-luggage lockers	Always accessible
Left-luggage store	Mon.–Sat.: 7 a.m.–8 p.m.
Waiting room	In restaurants
Shops	Regular hours
Post office	Mon.–Fri.: 6 a.m.–9 p.m.
	Sat.: 6 a.m.–8 p.m., Sun.: 9 a.m.–8 p.m.
	(in next building along)

Daily trains to: Nürnberg (1 hour), Vienna, Munich (2½ hours), Stuttgart (2¼ hours), Mainz (2 hours), Paris, Cologne (3¾ hours), Frankfurt (1½ hours).

TOURIST INFORMATION

Located just in front of the station and in the centre at the Haus zum Falken, by the Marktplatz: Mon.–Fri.: 9 a.m.–6 p.m., Sat.: 9 a.m.–2 p.m. They'll find you a room for 3 DM (Tel. 0931–37398). STUDENT TRAVEL OFFICE: Jugendreisecentre, Blasiusgasse 11 (Tel. 0931–59150).

SLEEPING AND EATING

The IYHF youth hostel is at Burkarderstrasse 44 (Tel. 0931–42590), under 26 only, and costs 17–30 DM. The campsite is at Mergentheimerstrasse 13B (Tel. 0931–72536). Trams 3 and 5 get you there. The campsite is not signposted, but follow directions to the Würzburg Canoe Club and register in the club restaurant, whence you will be directed to your pitch. The cheapest hotels start from 60 DM, ask at the tourist office for suggestions.

Eat at the university Mensa in the Studentenhaus at the corner of Münzstrasse and Jahnstrasse. Open for lunch and dinner on weekdays, during term times only. There are several cheap fast food places around the centre, and if you have time try the local white wines.

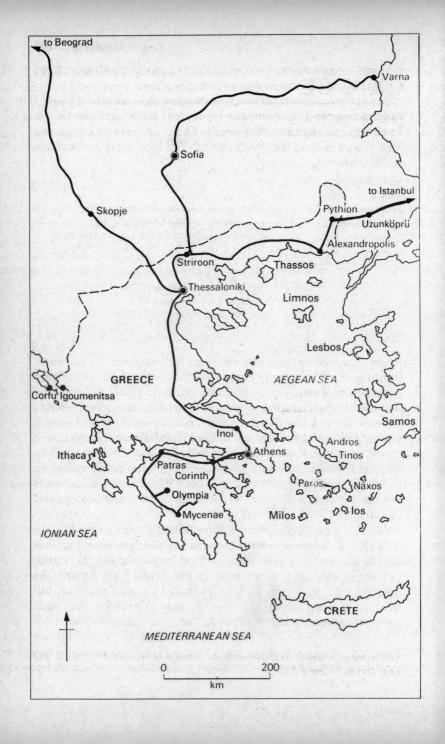

GREECE

Entry requirements	Passport
Population	9,900,000
Capital	Athens (pop.: 3,100,000)
Currency	Drachma
	£1 = approx. 324 dr.
Political system	Republic
Religion	Greek Orthodox
Language	Greek (some English and French spoken)
Public holidays	1, 6 Jan.; Shrove Monday; 25 March;
	Good Friday; Easter Sunday; Easter Monday;
	1 May; 3 June; 15 Aug.; 28 Oct.; 25, 26 Dec.
International dialling codes	From UK: 010 + 30 + number
	From USA: 011 + 30 + number
	To UK: 00 + 44 + number
	To USA: 00 + 1 + number
Railway office	1 Karolou St, Athens (Tel. 5224563)
	or 1f Filellinon St, Athens (Tel. 3236747)

Every year, Greece acts like a magnet to thousands of eurorailers from the north. So many come that the summertime population increases by about 50 per cent. The islands in particular offer the best under-30 social scene you're likely to find. Ironically, it's much easier to get to know Germans and Swedes here than Greeks, and you get to know them very well indeed if you share the same nudist beach, although it is, technically, only legal at three beaches in Greece. It's difficult to have a bad holiday in Greece, the birthplace of Western civilization, which provides a haven not only for lovers of nature, but also for those interested in history, archaeology and the arts.

Greek history begins about 2,500 BC with the Minoan civilization on Crete, a thousand years before the Mycenaeans got it together on the mainland. The classical period began during the eighth century BC and reached its peak in fifth-century BC Athens. As independent city-states the Greeks shared the same culture, but were always at each other's throats, until Alexander the Great sorted them out during the third century BC, uniting former rivals

Additional information on this country contained in *Greece* and *Europe – Grand Tour* factsheets (see p.13).

and himself conquering a world empire. By the fifth century AD, Greece had become part of the Byzantine Empire, and was eventually conquered by the Ottomans in the fifteenth century. The War of Independence in 1821 started the formation of the modern Greek state, a process which ended in 1947 with the return of the Dodecanese. They still play cricket on Corfu which, along with other Ionian islands, was under British rule till 1864. After the Germans pulled out in 1944, civil war broke out and continued for five years, seriously hindering Greece's postwar recovery. Away from the beaches, things are less serene. Relations with Turkey remain as strained as ever, particularly after the Turkish invasion of Cyprus in 1974. High inflation and low per capita income compared with other EC countries characterize the economy. Greece's recent history is almost as complex and unstable as her past. If stuck for conversation, it's safer not to discuss the monarchy (of her six kings since independence, four have been deposed and one assassinated).

• **Getting there:** Travelling there by train is still the cheapest way of getting to Greece, the islands and the sun. Charter flights offer little in the way of flexibility. No matter how bad things might sometimes seem by train, console yourself with the knowledge that they would have been a lot worse by bus. But there are problems in going by train, not least of which is deciding on your route. Note that it is now illegal to take into Greece *any* substance containing codeine – for example the common treatment for period pains, Feminax. You're OK if you have a doctor's note, however.

• **The Belgrade–Athens run:** Before the troubles in the former Yugoslavia, this notorious journey was a good alternative route into Greece. Of course, it is now more or less impossible to make this trip and the intrepid few who have overlanded on this route do not tell a pleasant tale. My advice is to stick to the Brindisi to Patras ferry. If you do decide to risk it, please heed this good advice:

1. If you can travel out of season, do so or at least try to avoid mid-July/August.

2. Go for the fastest train possible – it's well worth the supplement. Try and get on the through-train from Munich or

Vienna, or travel overnight in a couchette/sleeper. (It's advisable here to book as far in advance as possible.) You can book ahead to Munich before you go. A sleeper will cost about £18 but a couchette only around £7.

3. Reserve a seat well ahead of time or, if that's not possible, arrive early and look for German or Austrian coaches.

4. Take along plenty to eat and *drink*. Remember: the trains aren't air-conditioned and you don't know how long a train may stop en route.

5. Don't make arrangements to meet someone at the other end or keep your schedule too tight unless you can't avoid it.

6. Go on board determined to make friends, and try and look on the whole episode as an educational experience.

7. On the way back keep trying at the reservations office. You may be told at one window there are no seats for several days and get a reservation immediately at the next.

8. If you get on a train try to pay for a couchette or sleeper. Have plenty of 'hard' currency on you as dinars are usually refused. Always keep a receipt in case you are asked for extra payment.

9. Look out for Turkish or 'Yugoslav' guards trying to extract supplements on trains which are not exclusively reserved. Simply waving a Thomas Cook timetable can sometimes scare them off. Otherwise argue and kick up as much of a fuss as possible.

When you reach Thessaloniki, things pick up no end. When it comes to soft drinks and refreshments, it's a seller's market, a fact which the keen-eyed but smiling traders know all too well as they descend on those who had set off unprepared.

• **The Italian run:** The problems faced by travellers in Italy are normally a considerably watered-down version of those faced in 'Yugoslavia'. Trains are crowded and the toilets dirty. Your real problems start at Brindisi, beginning with the mile walk straight down to the docks. Avoid the rip-off Agenzie Pattimare reservation agency at all costs.

It can be windy on the Brindisi–Patras ferry, but don't let the cooling breeze kid you into not taking precautions against the sun. Putting a rucksack on sunburnt shoulders rather takes the edge off your holiday enjoyment. (See Eurail bonuses.) If you are going to Corfu, seriously consider flying from Athens, rather than taking the boat from Brindisi. It costs less (about £35) and only takes 50 minutes.

GREEK RAILWAYS
(Organismos Sidirodromoń Ellados, OSE)

A quick look at any rail map will show you that Greece's network is small. This is because Greece is a mountainous country and therefore many towns are not connected by rail, although OSE uses a large number of connecting buses, and the few trains there are will seem slow except by Eastern European standards. The international long-distance trains are somewhat optimistically called 'expresses', although some new trains on the Athens–Thessaloniki route have cut the travel time from seven hours to six and a half. Some of these require a small supplement of about 200 dr. Local trains are slow enough to enable you to strike up lasting friendships. (By the time you arrive you'll feel as if you were born with your fellow travellers.) There are some Inter-Rail bonuses in Greece, but always ask for student discounts.

The good news is that between now and 1997 a lot of money is being invested in OSE, particularly in northern Greece. Speeds, services and efficiency will improve things no end. The Patras–Athens run is earmarked for major investment, and that should come as a relief to many Inter-Railers!

● **Eurail bonuses:** Free:
—Eurail Pass and Eurail Youthpass travellers can use steamers (*Appia, Egnatia, Espresso Grecia, Castalia*) operated by the Hellenic Mediterranean and Adriatica di Navigazione between Patras and Brindisi and vice versa. However, between 10 June and 30 September, they must pay an £8 ($15) high-season surcharge. Travellers with Inter-Rail tickets will also have to purchase such a surcharge in advance, before embarkation. During July and August, advance reservation, which costs about £2 ($3.40), is recommended. Special accommodations (airline-type seats or cabins) and port taxes are extra – £5 each way and £2.50 extra for stopping off at Corfu. Before boarding, all passengers must check in at the Shipping Line Office at the pier.

Passengers who wish to break their voyage at Corfu must declare their intention of 'stop over' upon delivery of the ticket.

Reduced fares:
—30 per cent reduction on the published full fares of the Adriatica Line between Piraeus–Venice or Alexandria and vice versa, on the *Espresso Egitto*. Contact the local Adriatica offices. Check your dates carefully when taking this run as it can work out substantially cheaper to travel outside the high summer season which usually starts towards the end of July. If you do find yourself with time on your hands waiting for a ferry, the companies will usually let you leave your luggage in their offices while you head for the beach.

TRAIN INFORMATION

English is spoken by information officers at all major stations.

• **Reservations:** Wherever else in Europe you may decide against reserving, it's well worth thinking about it here. Go to an OSE office rather than the station – the staff are more helpful and it's generally less hassle. The rule is to book a seat as far in advance as possible for international trains. On some expresses (ask at station) reservations are obligatory. You can reserve up to a month in advance. It pays to be organized here; hundreds aren't. It's possible to reserve on internal routes in Greece, but you have to do it by post in advance and unless you have an extremely well-organized schedule (taking account of the Belgrade–Athens run) it's not worth the hassle. NB There are no tickets placed on reserved seats so chaos often ensues!

• **Night travel:** Couchettes and sleepers are both cheap by northern European standards. If you can get one, go for it.

• **Rover tickets:** The Greek Tourist Card is available only in second class for 10, 20 or 30 days unlimited travel for between one and five people. There are no child reductions. Prices for 10 days range from £29 for one person to £81 for five people. For 20 days the prices range from £43 to £129, and for 30 days from £57 to £177.

• **Ferries:** The only way to get to the islands. Tour agencies in Greece do not always advertise rival lines so it is worthwhile to tour all the agencies. In Piraeus, most of the agencies on the waterfront block offer a comprehensive chart of everything sailing that week, and some will also recommend cheap hotels in the area. On the islands, check and recheck: Greek ferry timetables change without notice from day to day, depending on the season and weather conditions.

TOURIST INFORMATION

For information about the country, accommodation and the main sights, see the National Tourist Organization of Greece (NTOG) known as EOT in Greece. For any other local information see the tourist police. Don't be put off by their name. Their role is to help you find accommodation and sort out your problems.

• **ISIC bonuses:** Up to 50 per cent off internal flights and ferries, up to 80 per cent reductions on theatres and museums. Olympic will grant reduction only if the internal flight is part of an international journey charged at a standard fare, and not Apex. The reduction only applies to jet aircraft and Boeing, not Domier or light aircraft. Consult the nearest Olympic offices or the Student Travel Service, 1 Fillellinon St, Athens (Tel. 01–3227993 or 3247433).

• **Money matters:** No more than 100,000 dr. may be imported, or 20,000 dr. exported.
Banking hours are Mon.–Thurs.: 8 a.m.–2 p.m., Fri. 7.45 a.m.–13.30 p.m. Also a word of warning: if you still have some dinar left over from Yugoslavia, you can only change them at the National Bank of Greece. It's best to change all your drachma before you leave Greece. All banks give the same rate and there are no commission charges. You can also change money at the Post Office (ELTA) and the Telecommunications Organization (OTE). Trying to change money at weekends other than in large resort hotels is a non-starter, so be prepared.

• **Post offices:** Stamps can also be bought from kiosks. The price is the same everywhere; in fact it is illegal for anyone to sell stamps for more than their face value.

• **Shops:** Hours can vary wildly. Generally open Mon., Wed., Sat.: 8 a.m.–2 p.m., Tues., Thurs., Fri.: 8 a.m.–1.30 p.m. and 5 p.m.–8.30 p.m. Supermarkets are open from Mon.–Fri.:

8 a.m.–8 p.m., and on Sat.: 8 a.m.–3.30 p.m. Non-food shops: Mon., Wed.: 9 a.m.–3 p.m., Tues., Thurs., Fri.: 9 a.m.–2 p.m., 5.30 p.m.–8.30 p.m., Sat.: 9 a.m.–3.30 p.m. Food shops: Mon.: 9 a.m.–3 p.m., Tues., Wed., Thurs., Fri.: 9 a.m.–2.30 p.m., 5 p.m.–8 p.m., Sat.: 9 a.m.–3.30 p.m.

● **Museums:** Usually open in winter 9 a.m.–3.30 p.m.; summer 8 a.m.–5 p.m. They tend to close on Mondays or Tuesdays. Students get a 50 per cent reduction.

SLEEPING

Greece presents the greatest variety of possibilities in all of Europe. Hotels are graded A, B, C, D and E. For a C-class hotel, expect to pay at least 2,000 dr. each. Student hostels are open to any paying customers. The youth hostels are nothing to get excited about. As usual, to stay you need an IYHF card. It's possible to get one in Athens if you haven't already got one. Some pensions and hotels charge 10 per cent extra for short stays during high summer and charge extra for showers. Off season, the boot's on the other foot and it's worth bargaining to get the price down. All hotel prices are fixed and should be posted at the reception. Expect to pay an extra 20 per cent in high season.

The National Tourist Board and the Tourist Guide of Greece, 137 Patissia St (Tel. 864 1688), issue a list with all the official campsites and facilities, giving an approximate price guide. Expect to pay at least 800 dr. It is illegal to camp outside the official campsites, since the country is increasingly concerned about such campers leaving litter, causing fires and destroying the environment. The National Tourist Office of Greece will provide you with a comprehensive list of campsites in the country.

On the islands, accommodation is hopelessly inadequate. Camping is illegal on many islands but nearly everyone is forced to do it at some stage as during July and August all the hotels and private rooms are full. There is some 'legal' camping on licensed campsites. The police are stepping up action (they can confiscate your passport) and the official policy of NTOG now is that you can't come to Greece by charter flight without having prebooked accommodation. Use your own discretion, but if you're camping illegally keep the place clean.

EATING AND NIGHTLIFE

Don't expect to eat as cheaply as you would have done a few years ago as high inflation continues to push up prices. Even old hands sometimes get a shock when they convert the bill into sterling or dollars. Always check the prices first in small shops and bakeries and make sure you know what you're paying for. If you're going to the islands it's easy to live off bread, cheese and water melon (karpouzi) during the day, and eat out at night. If you need that added luxury of a cup of coffee for breakfast to see you through the day, be sure to ask for Nescafé or you'll end up with sweet Greek coffee instead. An alternative is café frappé (iced coffee). This is much more refreshing.

When eating out, as often as not you'll be ushered into the kitchen. Take your time, as this is the local custom of choosing. Arni is lamb; moschari, veal; chirino, pork; kotópoulo, chicken. Avoid the fish unless you've got plenty of money or are on the islands where it's fresh. Moussaka is a combination of meat with potato or eggplant, in bechamel sauce. Dolmades are minced meat and rice wrapped in vine leaves and are delicious hot or cold. Eating out is a leisurely affair and gives one the opportunity in the islands of seeing what people look like with their clothes on. If you're down on your luck, there's always a souvlaki stand (meat kebab wrapped in bread) not far away. For drinks, don't overdo it with ouzo (the local aniseed spirit), or you'll know all about it the next morning. For the evening meal, try at least one bottle of the local retsina (with resin) before returning (as most do) to the aretsinato wine. During the summer months, the Athens Festival takes place. This includes open-air performances in the Herodes Atticus Odeon – an experience you're not likely to forget. For details on this and other events, contact the Athens Festival Box Office, 4 Stadiou St. There are numerous local festivals celebrating everything from Easter to wine. The Greeks use any excuse to have one, as they love to let their hair down and dance. Once a bouzouki gets going, anything can happen. Nightclubs are dull and expensive by comparison. Films are shown in their original language, and are always cheaper in the suburbs.

Northern Greece

If you're entering Greece from 'Yugoslavia' or Bulgaria, your first main centre will be THESSALONIKI. This is Greece's second city, founded in 315 BC. Although the station (like most in Greece) is unattractive, the people are very friendly and hospitable. Take a stroll through the OLD TURKISH QUARTER, visit the ARCHAEOLOGI-CAL MUSEUM and the third- and fifth-century churches of ST GEORGE and ST DEMETRIUS. Also see the Byzantine walls around the city – this can be an afternoon's walk. The castle at the top is closed for restoration. Tourist information can be obtained from the office at 8 Aristotelous Square (Tel. 031–263112 or 222935); or the tourist police at the New Railway Station (Tel. 031–517000), or at 10 Egnatia St (Tel. 541169), can help you.

As it is by the sea, Thessaloniki is relatively cool and the wide streets have many attractive shops not found in Athens. There is also an excellent copper market and several good beaches near the city with frequent buses and boats to them.

The youth hostel is at 44 Alex. Svolou Street (Tel. 031–225946). The YWCA at 11 Agias Sofias Street (Tel. 031–276144) and the YMCA at Hanth Square (Tel. 031–274000). Good 'C' grade hotels include the ABC, Continental, and Grande Bretagne. Camping grounds in and around the area are run by the Greek National Tourist Office, ask for a list from the local tourist police.

For an impressive day-trip from Thessaloniki, or even to stay for a few days, head east by bus (this is not a train route) along the coast to KAVALA. This prosperous market town has an amazing OLD QUARTER and a huge medieval AQUEDUCT leading from the hills. The Tourist Office is at the corner of Eleferion Sq. (Tel. 222425 or 228762). Open Mon.–Fri.: 7 a.m.–7 p.m., Sat.: 8 a.m.–2 p.m., and it helps accommodation seekers. Hourly ferry crossings are possible from here to the popular resort island of Thassos, an island composed of beach and greenery and small villages. Here you'll find many rooms for rent and a camp site on Pinos Beach (Tel. 71 170/3). There are many good beaches nearby, on the mainland, but the best are on SITHONIA, the westernmost prong of the HALKIDIKI peninsula. All are well connected to each other by bus.

Northern Greece is real 'spaghetti western' country. The mountains are rugged and the scenery wild and untamed. The two provinces of this area are Macedonia and Thrace.

South-east of Thessaloniki is the self-governing monastic commune of Mount Athos (no female has been allowed in for 900 years). If you want to visit, you'll have to go through your embassy and be able to give a sound reason for your visit, a letter of recommendation is usually required, and this should cite proven religious or scientific interests. To see some exceptionally early Christian art and visit nine Byzantine monasteries and nunneries at METEORA is much easier. The sight is breathtaking: 24 perpendicular rocks upon which, 600 years ago, the Byzantine monks chose to worship God and built their monasteries. Situated 21 km north of Kalambaka, it takes four hours to reach by train from Thessaloniki, change at Larissa. If you are planning to stay in the region, the tourist police station at 10 Watzipetrou Str, Kalambaka (Tel. 0432–22813) or 86 Papanastasiou Str, Larissa (Tel. 041–227900) can help you find private accommodation. Larissa itself is a picturesque town with a medieval fortress and an ancient theatre. The tourist office is at 18 Koumoundorou Str (Tel. 041–250919). If you are travelling to Athens from Larissa, stop via Thebes (Thiva), the legendary birthplace of Herakles, made famous by Oedipus. There are also many archaeological sites and museums which display the usual cultural heritage. North-east from Thessaloniki at Algia Eleni, near Seres, is LANGADA. The best thing to happen here is the ritual of the fire-walkers which takes place annually 20–23 May. The police station (Tel. 0321–63333) can give you more details and help find accommodation.

The Peloponnese

The most southerly part of Greece's mainland is separated from the central belt by the Isthmus of Corinth. The Peloponnese has remnants of every people who have occupied that land: Greeks, Turks, Franks and Venetians. It is a region that is becoming increasingly popular with tourists. On the main circular line from Patras to Athens lie Kalamata, Tripolis, Argos and Corinth. ARGOS is a busy city with little appeal, and few tourists. There are some interesting ruins and Roman Baths on the western side of town, but that's about it for sightseeing. Stay here overnight if you desire cheaper accommodation than elsewhere in the region. The cheapest hostel is Hotel Apollon, 15 Korai St (Tel. 280 12) which charges 1900 dr. for a single room. Near Argos lies the delightful, unspoilt town of NAFPILION (Nauplia) with a picturesque Venetian fortified islet in the middle of the neighbouring bay. Nafpilion is an ideal base by which to discover the surrounding areas since there are many frequent bus connections (the bus station is on Singrou St, near the base of the PALANIDI FORTRESS) to surrounding towns and cities. There is a good Youth Hostel, which does not require an IYHF card, at 15 Argonafton St (Neo Vyzantio St) (Tel. 0752–27754). A 15–20-minute walk from the bus stop, it charges 600 dr. per person, per night and charges a further 600 dr. for home-cooked dinner each night. You can rent bicycles from Riki and Pete, Navarino St (Tel. 24547) for 1,000 dr. per day, 5,000 dr. per week, and the Tourist Office can be found at Iatrou Sq (Tel. 0752–24444).

One of the major towns is CORINTH, though there are two Corinths: the new town, which has nothing much to recommend it, and the old town which has a lot hidden away in its quiet corners. The station will leave you in the new town, but buses leave every half-hour for 'Arhea Korinthos'. Here you can see columns from the sixth-century Temple of Apollo and the rostrum from which St Paul preached Christianity to the Corinthians. If you really want to catch these sights at their best, visit them around 8.30–9.30 a.m., as by lunchtime the coach tours from neighbouring areas arrive and the sites become besieged by tourists. For tourist information Tel. 0741–23282. If you are staying overnight in New Corinth, try Hotel Acti, 3 Ethnikis Anistasis St (Tel. 0741–23337) down by the sea, or camp at 'Beach Camping' (Tel. 25767 or 27967), which is 3 km west of town and charges 800 dr. per night. A regular train and bus service connects it to the city station.

Just down the line is MYCENAE which dates back to 3,000 BC and is one of Greece's high spots for archaeologists. Many of the treasures found here are now in Athens, but you can still see the 'Gate of the Lions', royal tombs and the 'Treasure of Atreus'. The small youth hostel is at Athens-Fihita, 20 Ifigenias St (Tel. 66285), which offers beds for 600 dr. Mycenae is also serviced by two campgrounds. Camping Mycenae (Tel. 66247) lies in the middle of the town, close to ruins and citrus fruit groves. It charges 340 dr. per person, 300 dr. per tent, and also offers a tent rental facility. Connections from and to Mycenae are easier by bus than by train, with Nafpilion and Argos being the most accessible.

Still going south, you'll come to EPIDAURUS whose main attraction is the well-preserved third-century BC amphitheatre, which seats 14,000, in which classical Greek dramas are staged during the summer months from June–September. Don't be put off by the plays being performed in Greek, they are well worth seeing for their authenticity, and by the end of the performance the language ceases to be a barrier. For information about the theatre and its performances contact the GNTO Festival Office, 2 Spyrou Miliou Arcade (Tel. 3223111–240 or 3221459) when you're in Athens. Most shows take place on Friday and Saturday evenings from late June until mid-August at 9 p.m. Tickets can also be purchased before the show at the theatre (Tel. 0753–22026) and cost around 1000–1700 dr. (500 dr. for students).

SPARTA is a town worth visiting just to see the evening *volta* in the mountain-surrounded town centre; but MYSTRA, 7 km away (about 200 dr. bus journey), has an impressive display of Byzantine churches, palaces and a castle.

PATRAS is the main town of the Peloponnese, the ferry landing from Brindisi, southern Italy. There's not much to see but if you're killing time look round the VENETIAN CASTLE, ARCHAEOLOGICAL MUSEUM, MUNICIPAL THEATRE and the churches of PANTAKRATOR and AGIOS ANDREAS. The busiest and most spectacular time to visit is in July and August, when many processions of the King Carnival take place, and the arts, theatre, dance and music are abundant. The police station (Tel. 061–220902/3) can help with enquiries, though a good camping site can be found from May to October at Agia Patron camping ground (Tel. 061–424133), 5 km outside Patras. Another campsite is Camping Golden Sunset Aliosos 25002. Take the bus to Achaion from the bus station. It's 19 km away from the centre of Patras, the conductors are willing to show you where to get off. For 300 dr. the ½-hour trip is well worth it. The youth hostel is at 68 Heroon Polytechniou St and costs 550 dr. (800 dr. during the summer), Tel. 061–427278.

About seven trains a day run the seven-hour trip to OLYMPIA, site of the first Olympic Games in Ancient Greece. There are many archaeological sites and museums in the city and its surrounding area, not surprisingly since the Temple of Zeus used to hold Phidias' gold and ivory statue of the God, one of the Seven Wonders of the Ancient World. The youth hostel is at 18 Prayitelous Kondyli Street

(Tel. 0624–22580), where there is often entertainment in the main street under the hostel (good fun but noisy). Camping Diana (Tel. 22314) is a shaded site 200 m uphill from Praxitelous Kondilia Ave where you'll find the Tourist Office (Tel. 0624–23125). Open: 9 a.m.–10 p.m. daily in the summer. The campsite charges 500 dr. per person, 400 dr. per tent and gives students a 10 per cent discount. For the tourist police telephone 22550.

Athens (Athinai)

Athens, 'the cradle of Western civilization', can offer you what is generally considered to be the high spot of a European tour: a visit to the 'high city' of the ancient Greeks, the Acropolis. It can also offer you dirty, squalid accommodation, unbearable heat, so-so food, and street after street of ugly concrete blocks. Modern Athens has nothing much to offer, but it's all worth while when you climb up to see the classical beauty of the white-stoned Parthenon, Temple of Athena and the beginnings of Western drama, the Theatre of Dionysus. If you're going island-hopping, Athens – or rather Piraeus, its port – is your starting point. Ferries leave from here for scores of islands (there are 1,500 to choose from in the Aegean and Ionian seas), and the average fare for a deck passenger on a five-hour sail is about 2,000–3,000 dr.

STATION FACILITIES
If you're travelling to the Peloponnese or Patras (for the ferry to Italy) use the Athinai-Peloponnese station, adjacent to the Larissa station (six Patras trains daily).

ATHINAI-LARISSA	
Train information	7 a.m.–midnight (Tel. 522 2491)
Reservations	At OSE office, Karolou 1–3
Tourist information	7 a.m.–12 midnight at tourist police station
Foreign exchange	7 a.m.–7 p.m.
Left-luggage office	6 a.m.–12 midnight
Restaurant	6 a.m.–12 midnight
Post Office	Mon.–Fri.: 7 a.m.–10 p.m. Closed at weekends.

Daily trains to: Thessaloniki, Belgrade–Trieste–Venice, or Belgrade–Munich–Dortmund.

TOURIST INFORMATION

The tourist police are at the station, and there's an information desk in the National Bank of Greece on Syntagma Square (Tel. 32 22545), open Mon.–Fri.: 8 a.m.–6.30 p.m., Sat.: 9 a.m.–2 p.m, Sun.: 9 a.m.–1 p.m. The main office of NTOG is at 2 Amerikis St (Tel. 3223111/9). Pick up the free map and leaflets on campsites, hostels, etc. and *This Week in Athens* which provides free information on clubs and sights. They don't operate an accommodation-finding service, but try the Hotel Chamber desk in the National Bank of Greece on Syntagma Square. The tourist police can be called by dialling 171. A good source for information on museums and shop hours is the *Athenian* which is published in English every month, although there are many others.

● **Addresses:**

POST OFFICE: 100 Eolou St, near Omonia Square. Open Mon.–Fri. 7.30 a.m.–8.30 p.m., Sat. 7.30 a.m.–2.30 p.m. Also Syntagma Square.

OTE OFFICE (main telephone office): 15 Stadiou Street. Open 7 a.m.–11.30 p.m. Reverse charge calls take two hours on a Sunday.

AMEX: 2 Ermou Street, Syntagma Square, weekdays: 8.30 a.m.–5.30 p.m., Sat.: 8.30 a.m.–1.30 p.m. (Tel. 324 4975).

UK EMBASSY: 1 Ploutarchou (Tel. 7236211/9). Open: Mon.–Fri. 8 a.m.–1.30 p.m.

US EMBASSY: 91 Vassilissis Sofias (Tel. 7212951/9). Open: Mon.–Fri. 8.30 a.m.–5 p.m.

CANADIAN EMBASSY: 4 Ioannou Genadiou St (Tel. 7239511/9).

AUSTRALIAN EMBASSY: 37 D. Soutsou St (Tel. 8211036). Open: Mon.–Fri. 9 a.m.–1 p.m.

FIRST AID: 21 Tritis Septemvriou (Tel. 150).

HOTEL CHAMBER OFFICE: 24 Stadiou Street (Tel. 3236641).

ISIC–USIT: 1 Filellinon Street, Athens (Tel. 324 1884).

EUROTRAIN: 11 Nikis Street (Tel. 3221267).

AMERICAN EXPRESS BANK: 31 Ponepistimiou Street (Tel. 3234–0781/4).

MIDLAND BANK: 19 Sekeri Street (Tel. 3647 410).

BARCLAYS BANK: 15 Vonkourestiou Street (Tel. 3644 311).

LATE-NIGHT CHEMIST: (Tel. 107).

RED CROSS FIRST AID CENTRE: #21, 3 Septemvrious St (Tel. 150 or 552 5555).

TOURIST POLICE: (Tel. 171). English spoken.
PHONE CODE: 01.

• **Getting about:** Looking at the taxis' tariffs, they seem a huge bargain, but by the time you've been ripped off – which seems to happen to most tourists – they don't work out as such a hot idea (each person pays what's on the clock so it doesn't help travelling in groups). Take the same precautions as you would in any other country. Remember the cab number, and if in doubt ask for a receipt. Do not only take an officially licensed cab because Greek taxis can be the bargain of Europe. The buses and trolley-buses are OK but usually packed (run 6 a.m.–midnight). You can take a bus out to the nearby beaches from the bus station in the centre of town. City buses are blue with three digit numbers, the standard fare is 50 dr. After midnight, there is only an hourly service.

SEEING

Athens reached its zenith around 400 BC when Plato, Socrates and Aristotle were strolling around the Acropolis which today is the heart of the city. What's worth seeing in Athens – the antiquities – are all clustered round the old town, or PLAKA district. The ACROPOLIS should be seen as soon as it opens at 8 a.m., before the hordes swarm up and destroy its atmosphere. The PARTHENON, the temple dedicated to the goddess Athena, is held up as the epitome of architectural perfection. See also the ERECHTHEION, TEMPLE OF ATHENA NIKE and the PROPYLAEA, the gates to the sacred site. The ACROPOLIS MUSEUM is a must. It contains some of the finds: statues, friezes, etc.

The Acropolis is open from Mon.–Fri. 8 a.m.–7 p.m., weekends 8.30 a.m.–3 p.m. and costs 1500 dr. (600 dr. on ISIC but free to EC students, and free to all on Sundays and public holidays). PNYX HILL offers a beautiful view of the Acropolis, and there's a *son et lumière* show here at 9 p.m. each night, which costs 400 dr. (150 dr. on ISIC).

The ancient AGORA, north of the Acropolis, was the marketplace and still has the remains of the old administrative centre. The TEMPLE OF HEPHAISTOS is considered the best preserved in Greece. This site is open from 8.30 a.m.–3 p.m. Tues.–Sun. It is well worth a visit (400 dr. admission, 200 dr. for students).

The NATIONAL ARCHAEOLOGICAL MUSEUM at 44 Patission St, has the best collection of ancient Greek artefacts in the world: gold death-masks, vessels, jewellery, statues, tombstones, frescoes, etc., dating from 1500 BC. Open Mon.: 11 a.m.–7 p.m., Tues.–Fri.: 8 a.m.–7 p.m., weekends: 8.30 a.m.–3 p.m. Admission 600 dr. (students 300 dr.).

SYNTAGMA (Constitution) Square, is the centre of modern Athens. This is where you'll find the hotels and cafés you can't afford. Constitution Square is flanked on one side by the Greek Parliament. From here take Amalias Avenue for the attractive NATIONAL GARDENS and HADRIAN'S ARCH. Also in this direction lie the PRESIDENTIAL PALACE and the OLYMPIC STADIUM.

The famous FLEA MARKET on Ifestou St, adjacent to Monastiraki Sq. makes a colourful walk and can produce some good bargains in equipment and leather goods. Beware of pickpockets. Closes 2 p.m. Sundays.

SLEEPING

There are literally hundreds of places to stay in Athens that fall into the economical category, and even though it's up to you to find your own room, unless you're arriving very late on an August night you should be OK. That's not to say that these places are clean, friendly or have even the bare essentials, but they are cheap. To be sure of somewhere with a roof over your head, always try to book in advance.

Head first for the Plaka as it's not only an attractive central place to stay (right underneath the Acropolis) but also one of the cheapest districts. Basically, the nearer to Syntagma Square you end up, the more you can expect to pay.

You may well find young blokes from various student hostels (unofficial ones, some of which are fairly grotty) joining the trains just before Athens extolling the virtues of their establishments and handing out leaflets. This is a good way of earning bed and board for those who plan on spending some time in Athens. Don't believe all they tell you about the price. Invariably, the accommodation looks nothing like it appears in the leaflet. The cheaper the hostel, the cheaper the security regarding belongings and valuables.

If you aren't completely numbed by the long, gruesome journey (particularly if you're hot off the notorious Belgrade–Athens run), try cutting right back on expenses and sleep on the roofs. Many hostels offer you a place for about 600 dr., and at least it's cool. For a single, on average, expect to pay 700–1,000 dr., doubles 2,000–3,000 dr. and dormitory beds 700 dr. In 1987 it was announced that sleeping on roofs was illegal, as tourists were being ripped off by hoteliers charging too much. It remains to be seen how strictly enforced this rule will be.

Try Student Hostel No 5, 75 Damareos St, Pangrati (Tel. 7519530). A bit out of town, but well worth the trouble of travelling to. Very clean, well organized and extremely friendly. Trolley-buses 2, 11 and 12. Single 1,200 dr. Also try Diethnes, 52 Peoniou St (Tel. 8832878) or Diana, 70 Patission St (Tel. 8223179). Directly opposite the station there's Olympos (Tel. 5223433). Highly recommended is Hostel Aphrodite, 12 Einardou St (Tel. 8810589). Cheap, friendly and three minutes from Larissis Station. The youth hostel at 57 Kypselis St (Tel. 8225860) is always pretty busy and not too central, but it's cheap (650 dr.). The YHA have accommodation at 1 Agiou Meletiou, and the YWCA at 11 Amerikis St (Tel. 3626180). For hotels, try round Apollonos St or Hotel Eva, 31 Victor Hugo St (Tel. 5223079) near the station. The Art Gallery, 5 Erechthiou Street (Tel. 9238376 or 9231933) is friendly, clean and within two minutes of the Acropolis. Not cheap at around 5,300 dr. for a triple, but worth it if you can afford it and desire a quiet area with large rooms. In the central area lies Festos, 18 Filellinon St (Tel. 323 2455) down from Syntagma Sq. It charges 900 dr. for a dorm bed, offers free luggage storage and has a curfew of 2 a.m. It also offers a bar with cut rate drinks in Happy Hour and inexpensive food. Hotel Acropole is two minutes' walk from the ferry port in Piraeas at 7 Gounari St (Tel. 417 3313). The nearest campsite is quite far out: 190 Athinon Avenue, Peristeri (Tel. 5814114); it is generally not worth the hassle of getting there, but if you must, take buses 822 or 823 from Eleftherias Square (Thission underground station). There is another campsite: Voula Camping, 3 Alkionidon (Tel. 895 2712). Take bus 118, 122 or 153 from Vass. Olgas Avenue.

If you're still stuck for a bed, drop into the ISYTS student centre at 11 Nikis St (Tel. 3233767 or 3221267), and they'll help you out.

EATING AND NIGHTLIFE

The advice is easy – head for the Plaka. There are lots of

restaurants, bars and discos there. The best club in town is Aigli at Hrodon Atlikou. The port of Piraeus is also lively at night, particularly Zea Marina, and in the National Park people gather on summer evenings to see performing artists.

For cheap eats, fill up on shish kebabs (souvlaki) and dolmades (vine leaves stuffed with meat). There are plenty of cheap supermarkets. Avoid fruit from stalls as it's overpriced and the quality suspect. Try Xynos or Aerides in the Plaka. Vegetarians are catered for at Eden, 3 Flessa St, Plaka, which is open every day, save Thursday, until midnight and is housed in a historic neo-classical building.

A general rule to remember, if you choose to eat out in Athens: if the signs are in English, then more often than not the food is more expensive and touristy.

• **Excursions from Athens:** 69 km away is the amazing TEMPLE OF POSEIDON on Cape Sourion. It dates back to 440 BC and is dedicated to the God of the Sea. Like the Acropolis, get there as early as possible; buses leave from Mavromateon St every half hour, until 9.30 p.m. Byron carved his name on to the temple, but although the Greek tourist brochures like to point this out to fame spotters, they do not recommend current visitors, famous or otherwise, to do the same. The site is open from Mon.–Sat.: 9 a.m.–sunset, Sun.: 10 a.m.–sunset, and admission is 300 dr. (students 150 dr.).

For DELPHI, 178 km from Athens, take the local train to Levadia and take the bus direct from there. Alternatively, take a KTEL bus from 260 Liossion Street (Tel. 8317096): approximately eight buses run a day. This is the site of the Delphic Oracle and was the holiest place in Ancient Greece. Little is left of the Temple of Apollo but there's still a fascinating museum (which houses the famous bronze charioteer), a 400 BC theatre and the stadium where the Pythian Games were held. Bus costs around 920 dr. The Tourist Office is at 44 Parlou St, close to the bus station (Tel. 82900). Open: Mon.–Sat. 8 a.m.–8.30 p.m.; Sun. 10 a.m.–3 p.m.; or at 45 Apollonos St, on the left and up the hill from the bus station lies the tourist police office (Tel. 82220), open 8 a.m.–2 p.m. At the top of the hill is the IYHF youth hostel (Tel. 82268). Open from March–November, it charges 680 dr. per bed. Other cheap hostels are near the former tourist office in Pavlou St. 3 km outside Delphi is the campground (Tel. 28944 or 82363) which charges 300 dr. per person, 500 dr. per tent. Buses for Volos, Evia, Sporades and Thessaloniki depart from Loission St, whilst taxis charge around 1,000 dr. from the port to Loission St Station. Buses for Patras depart from Kifissoo St.

The Islands

For a very large number of people, Greece is the islands. Each year quiet fishing villages are becoming both touristy and cosmopolitan, and while some remote islands probably still have a decade or so to go before they're turned into mini Majorcas, many have only a year or two, and some are there already. For a remote haven, choose an island which has only a weekly sailing from Piraeus – the fewer the ferries, the less the crowds, although, the less reliable the service. Another way to find a 'goodie' is to ask backpackers. There are six things to bear in mind:

1. Buy your ticket from one of the agencies in Piraeus, not on the boat – they often charge 20 per cent surcharge. Some of the Athenian hostels offer what appear to be bargain tickets – beware of hidden port taxes and surcharges. There are ten different quays at Piraeus, so it is definitely best to book in advance to avoid confusion. Daily departures from here include: Chios, Aegina, Crete, Paros, Naxos, Ios, Samos, Kos, Lesbos, Milos, Andros and Tinos in the summer. All other islands are reachable via connections.

2. Unless you enjoy a good strong gust knocking your tent down or throwing sand up in your face, avoid the southern Aegean islands in August. They can receive the incredibly strong meltemi (northern wind) which can really muck up your sunbathing and sightseeing.

3. If you plan on going far afield, go for an overnight boat as it costs no extra to sleep on deck and saves you the price of a night's accommodation at the other end.

4. The port authorities at Piraeus are contactable on (Tel. 01–451 1311) if there are any problems, and the Directorate of Tourism of Mainland Greece and the Islands is situated in Marina Zeas (Tel. 413 5716, 413 5730 or 413 4709).

5. Whichever ferry you disembark from, you will find touts peddling their accommodation. Much of it is cheap, but ensure that you know exactly where it is before you agree to anything – it is not uncommon for a 'within five minutes' walking distance' site to be, in reality, a half-hour bus trip away.
6. Plan in advance. Always check departure times for your next visit as soon as you've arrived on your island. Ferries out here are notoriously unreliable, so work out alternatives and plan for the worst. Keep some spare cash for port taxes.

The Argo Saronics

These islands are within four hours of Athens, and consequently are among the most touristy and expensive. AEGINA is the closest to Athens and sailings are from the central harbour at Piraeus (Tel. 4523 612). (For the other islands sailings are from Zea Marina, close to Piraeus.) Take the hydrofoils which supplement the steamer services and take half the time. The tourist police are on Leonardov Lada St (Tel. 22100). Look for bed and food around the port in Aegina town and admire the view from the TEMPLE OF APOLLO. The bay of Agia Marina has the best beaches but is packed out with Athenians at weekends. Also remember, Aegina is very much a family tourist area, so accommodation is not cheap and fills up quickly.

POROS is packed out in summer, but for a reason. It has beautiful beaches and lush pinewoods. The tourist information in the town of Poros will help you find a bed – avoid hotels. See the MONASTERY OF KALAVRIA. The tourist police are situated on Paraliaki Street (Tel. 0298 22256) open: 8 a.m.–2.30 p.m. Try to get out to the village of Trizina, close to Poros on the mainland. It lies close to the ancient city of the same name and is the legendary birthplace of Theseus.

HYDRA, nicknamed in the nineteenth century 'Little England', is 3½ hours from Piraeus and is one of the beautiful people's islands, consequently the prices, especially along the harbour, are crippling. For a truly memorable view, climb up to the hilltop monastery of AGIA TRIADA. Hydra is all you expect a Greek island to be: narrow winding streets, donkeys (no cars allowed), beaches and blue sea and sky. The tourist police at Navarhou N. Votsi St (Tel.

0298–52205) will find you rooms, which are cheaper at the other side of the town.

SPETSES is a small wooded island of great charm with AGII ANAR-GIRI as its best beach. The harbour town of Spetses has two cheap hotels (the Acropole and the Saronicos) and the tourist police on Botsari St (Tel. 0298–73100) will fill you in with any other information and help you may need.

The Cyclades

These are the most visited of the Aegean islands and thus the hub of the Greek ferry system in, and out of, season. There are 211 of them in all, but it's still possible to find a few of the inhabited ones that will offer you relative 'splendid isolation'. Visit the 'dry islands': SIFINOS with an estimated 365 churches and chapels on its land, and a gastronomic delicacy of roast kid and olives; SIKINOS which has a very good beach; SERIFOS with iron ore mines and annual August fiesta; and MILOS. All are relatively quiet, but their landscape is rather arid. Milos (Plaka) the capital is the discovery site of the Venus de Milo, and houses an archaeological folklore museum. ANDROS and TINOS are very attractive and large enough to allow the tourists to spread themselves out. TINOS becomes a sacred island on 15 August, and many pilgrims appear to attend celebrations in honour of the Virgin Mary. Her icon at the Church of Evangelistria is said to have miraculous properties. The tourist office, by the harbour, is open Mon.–Fri.: 7.30 a.m.–3.10 p.m.; Sat.–Sun.: 8 a.m.–1 p.m. and Tinos Camping (Tel. 22344 or 23548) is a ten-minute walk from the town, charging 400 dr. per person, 200 dr. per tent.

NAXOS: in Greek mythology this is the place where Dionysus sprang from the thigh of Zeus. It is the largest and most fertile of the island group. The tourist office can be found across the boat dock on the waterfront (Tel. 24525/24358), open daily 8 a.m.–9.30 p.m..; July–August: 8 a.m.–12.30 a.m. There are many pensions on the small hill behind the office. (Double rooms between 2,500–2,800 dr.). Much cheaper is Naxos Camping (Tel. 235 00/1) off Agios Giorgios Beach which charges 400 dr. per person and 200 dr. per tent. You can rent mopeds from 'Theoharis' (Tel. 23900), left of the tourist office and open daily from 8 a.m.–2 p.m., 5 p.m.–9 p.m. Expect to pay about 1,400 dr. including third party insurance and a helmet. The police (Tel. 22100/23280) are again left of the tourist office, take another right and a left to get there. The bus service for the islands is very good, and cheap. Try and get to the town of Aperanthos: the folk art and Michael Bardini (Cycladic Art) museums are open in the mornings for free. Apollon and Agia Anna have the best beaches.

If you do not want to leave the Greek mainland for too long take a boat or ferry from the mainland port of Lavrio to KEA (Tzia) to experience island life: a journey of only 90 minutes. It is a quiet picturesque island, and its most famous asset is a colossal archaic lion carved into the solid rock during the sixth century BC at the port of Karissa.

MYKONOS is *the* Greek island to experience tourism, not Greece. It's very beautiful, very very touristy, very expensive and very gay. There are nude beaches (the Paradise beach and Super Paradise – mostly gay) and countless discos, clubs and restaurants. There's also what was there before the thousands of tourists: whitewashed houses and windmills. There are a few reasonably priced hotels: the Phillippi (Tel. 22294) and the Apollon (Tel. 23271). Tourist information is available from both the tourist office (Tel. 23990) open 9 a.m.–9 p.m., and the tourist police (Tel. 22482), on the waterfront. Paradise Beach Camping is the only officially listed site on the island, and a van arrives to meet all boats as they arrive. Open from April–October it costs 400 dr. per person, 200 dr. per tent. Mykonos is very well connected by ferry – there is at least one ferry a day travelling to Tinos, Paros, Santorini, Ios, Naxos, Andros and to Piraeus. Although if you're travelling to the latter, less than half the time (though twice the price) are the Supercats Marine Co's hovercraft ferries (Tel. 01–3609911) which travel from Wednesday–Monday 9 a.m.–4 p.m. and cost 6142 dr.

There are also boat trips from Mykonos to DELOS, the ancient religious centre of the Greek world, where you can see the ruins of the Sanctuary of Apollo, the Terrace of Lions and the archaeological museum.

PAROS is a beautiful and very clean island, but very touristy, and all that makes it worth the trip is its beautiful old church, Panagia Ekatontapiliani. Boats depart, several times a day, to all the major nearby islands. A complete schedule is posted at the tourist office in the windmill by the dock (Tel. 22079), open daily, 8a.m.–10 p.m. Note that this office does not help with accommodation, but you'll find most of the hotels and rooms just off the waterfront and into the old town. Camping Karla (Tel. 22082) is 400m north of the town and charges about 700dr. per person and tent. ANTIPAROS, the virtually undeveloped, smaller island opposite Paros has a very frequent ferry service, so visit it as a day trip, or else find more secluded accommodation here. Camping Antiparos (Tel. 61221) lies 800m north-west of the town on AGIOS YIANNIS THEOLOGOS BEACH and charges 600dr. per person and tent. The island features some stalactite caves on its south side. Buses go directly to the caves every hour from 10.30 a.m.–2.30 p.m. A return trip costs about 600dr.

IOS used to be the place where students headed for – free and easy living with lots to do at night – but has now turned into a den of iniquity and is best avoided.

Santorini

4,000 years ago, a massive explosion left the outer rim of a volcano which became Santorini. From the harbour, get to the town of THIRA (ferries dock at Athinio now) where you can find rooms at reasonable prices. Beware of the hotel touts at Athinios: they will hustle you into a mini van and take you somewhere miles out of the town. The best beaches are Kamari, Monolithos and Perissa with its black sand. There are ruins from the Minoans, Romans and Venetians. The boat trip out to the little island of Mikra Kameni, where the volcano started and smoulders still, is worth it.

The monastery of Profitis Illias on the island's summit houses a great religious celebration each year on 20 July. All visitors are invited to join the islanders in a meal of traditional dry pea soup followed by an energetic course of folk dancing. Guest houses are operated by the GNTO at the small village of OIA on the north-west coast of the island, site of a spectacular sunset. Alternatively the Kontohori youth hostel, 25th Martiou St (Tel. 0286–22722/26577) offers a very good deal. If in doubt contact the tourist police further along the same road (0286–22649) for help. Perissa Camping is situated near the beach of the same name and charges 600dr. per person, 300–400 dr. per tent. The many travel agents in Thira's town square which book rooms, excursions, store baggage and exchange currency will ease any accommodation problems.

The Sporades

Some of the quietest islands in Greece are the Sporades, as they're further off the beaten track than the others. You approach them by boat from Kymi (port authority: Tel. 0222–22606), Agios Konstandinos (port authority: Tel. 0235–31759), or Volos (port authority: Tel. 0421–20115) which you reach by bus from Athens.

Alykon Travel, 98 Akadimias St, Athens (Tel. 362 2093) can help you with the best way to reach the islands. You can book accommodation before leaving the islands from the mainland at the Hotel Chamber of Greece, 2 Karageogi Servias St, Athens (Tel. 323 7193). Alternatively contact the islands' tourist police for information about villas, rooms to rent and camping grounds on the islands.

SKIATHOS is the most touristy, but that's because it's very beautiful. It's also lively, and one of the best Greek islands for nightlife. For a night's rest try one of the pensions on Evangelistras St in Skiathos town. KOUKOUNARIES is a superb beach surrounded by pine groves. Many homes advertise rooms to let ('dhomatia') on this island in the summer months and their prices are reasonable at about 2,200 dr. for a double room. Try Hadula Tsourou, 17 Mitrop. Ananiou St (Tel. 0427–22364) and Maria Papagiorgiou just off Grigoriou before Christina's Bar (Tel. 0427–21574), or if you have no joy, the tourist police (Tel. 0427–21111), who are situated on the left side of Papadiamandi St, along with most public facilities and moped rentals.

ALONISSOS is the smallest island. From the port of Patitiri, head for Marpounda or Kokinokastro where there's a good beach and some archaeological remains such as the sunken Byzantine ship at Agios Petras. The sea around this island has been declared a 'Marine Conservation Park', so remember to help the authorities and not to leave rubbish lying around. Ikos Travel in the island's main town PATITIRI will help you with rooms and accommodation, if you have no luck with the tourist police (Tel. 0424–91274). The official campsite is on Ikaros Camping (Tel. 65258) on Steni Vala Beach. It charges around 800 dr. per person and tent.

SKOPELOS has cheap rooms in its town and good beaches at STAFILOS and AGNONDAS. Inland lie the ruins of the medieval bishops' palace, and many churches and monasteries with icons. If you intend to stay in SKOPELOS try and get a room *up* the hill, even though it means further to walk, as the town sewage discharges into the harbour and can smell awful on a hot day. The tourist police (Tel. 0424–22235), and several other tourist information offices are situated on the waterfront.

SKYROS is the most beautiful and unspoilt island of the Sporades. Flat-topped white houses stand on the cliffs and folk crafts still flourish. The long dark sand beach is wonderful, and there are countless little coves for swimming and sub-aqua jaunts. Try the campsite (take bus from ferry to Magaria), or use one of the restaurants for a room. The police station is contactable by telephoning 0222–91274. The tourist office, Skyros Travel, operates all the information services you'll need, including help with accommodation, boat trips and buses.

North-east Aegean

If you don't mind going a bit further out of your way, the islands off the north-eastern Aegean have their rewards: Samos, Lesbos and Chios are the three most popular, and all are linked by boat services to the islands of the Dodecanese, Cyclades and Crete.

Samos, the birthplace of the goddess Hera (Juno) and Pythagoras, is heavily wooded with a rocky coastline and a good beach resort, Kokari. The capital SAMOS has a very good archaeological museum and Byzantine art museum. When you arrive go to Samos Tours at the end of the ferry dock (Tel. 0273–27715) or the tourist office further down the waterfront, by Pythagoras Sq. (less reliable for being open) (Tel. 0273–28530) for all the information you want. The tourist police are contactable, next door, on 0273–27404/27980. Accommodation is scarce in the summer months, but try the Pension Ionia (Tel. 0273–28782) or the Pension Avli (Tel. 0273–22939). The central island area around PYROS, and MYTILINIOS to the south-west are rich in archaeological sites and classical museums.

LESBOS, also known as Mytilene after its principal city, homeland to the prophetess Sappho, is a mass of olive trees and has some incredible, traditionally designed buildings in its port of Mithymna. The coast of Patraon in the northwest is abundant in archaeological finds, monasteries and there is a petrified forest at Sigri. To get to Samos from Piraeus, there is one service a day, and from Salonica, one service a week. The tourist police (Tel. 0251–22776) can help you with further travel and accommodation details, possessing a list for lower priced hotels and rooms to let in private houses. Try also the Association of Rented Rooms (Tel. 29081) on Mitropoleos Kamninaki. Expect to pay about 2000 dr. per double room.

CHIOS, home of Homer, has an interesting Byzantine monastery, the Nea Moni, plus all the usual Greek island charms. Because of its literary connections, the village of Vrontadg, 5 km from Chios, holds a 'Homeria' (events of art and literature) every summer. The tourist police, 37 Neorian St, on the north side of the harbour (Tel. 0271–26555), can help you find accommodation and fill you in on the details. A boat/ferry connects the island to Salonica once a week, to Piraeus once a day, and to the other North-east Aegean islands every hour. Contact the port authority (Tel. 22837) for more information.

The Dodecanese (South-east Aegean)

These are the most easterly islands of Greece, a few miles away from Turkey. The boat trip from Piraeus can take up to 20 hours, so unless you've a bit of time to spend – think again. Two of the largest ferries travelling this route are the Kamiros and Ialysos, which alternately have scheduled departures at 1 p.m. every day. These boats stop at Kos en route. You're rewarded for your efforts by superb beaches, mountains, medieval buildings and an air of historical importance which you don't find in any other group of islands.

The two main islands are RHODES and KOS, the latter of which is regarded as the birthplace of modern medicine as it was a healing centre of wide acclaim. The Knights of St John captured the islands in the fourteenth century, and they went on to be occupied by the

Italians during the Second World War. They were reunited with Greece in 1947. If you are travelling by ferry around these islands, expect cancellations due to rough seas, especially out of the summer season. Kos, Rhodes and Leros all have airports, and with a student discount of 25 per cent on Olympic Airways flights, air travel can become as competitive as unreliable services by sea.

RHODES: if you avoid the main town of Rhodes to escape from the package tourists, you're OK. In Rhodes town, see the old city, the Suleyman Mosque, and the Grand Masters' Palace. The tourist police and tourist information (Tel. 0241–27423) or at Rimini Square near Mandraki (the port area) (Tel. 35945) or the GNTO at 5 Archbishop Mekarios and Papagou Streets (Tel. 0241–23655/ 23255) will help you out with accommodation, bus and boat schedules. The old town has the best cheap places to sleep, such as Steve Kefalas's pension at 60 Omirou St (Tel. 24357), Pension Apollon further down at no. 28c (Tel. 32003), or Pension Massari, 42 Irodotou St (Tel. 22469) which charges 2700 dr. for a double room, 4000 dr. for quads with private baths included. If you're wanting to find the best hydrofoil, ferry and excursion boat information, look no further than Triton Tours, 25 Plastira St (Tel. 30657), open Mon.–Fri. 8 a.m.–2 p.m., 4 p.m.–9 p.m., Sat. 9 a.m.–1.30 p.m., 4 p.m.–8 p.m. The ferries to Israel stop at Rhodes, but only for a couple of hours; you can wait for the next boat provided you say so when you book. The west coast of Rhodes is incredibly windy, especially in comparison with the east coast where the best beaches are. Of these, Faliraki Beach is undoubtedly the best, even though it's packed for most of the season, and a campsite is situated near here, and 40 miles down the east coast at Lardos. If you want nightlife, you'll find it here. Discos are as plentiful as the bars. Some charge 1400 dr. entrance fee with plenty of free drink thereafter. Most shops stay open until well past 9 p.m., so stroll out in the evening to do your souvenir hunting.

LINDOS, along with Kameiros and Ialissos, has archaeological remains and is a particularly picturesque town, but the package-deal customers are here in swarms in summer, and as a result, prices become astronomical.

KOS comes very high in the list of archaeological sites and is a fascinating island: great beaches, ancient Roman and Medieval monuments, mosques, a Crusader fortress, mansions and a wonderful atmosphere. In the town, try the tourist police for a room, but camping, though not legal, is idyllic. There is an official campsite: Kos Camping (Tel. 23910 or 23275) in Psaldi, an inconvenient two kilometres out of town, though the rate of 750 dr. per person and tent is reasonable. The tourist police or tourist information office (Tel. 28724 or 24460) on the waterfront will be able to tell you the best way of getting there. Opening hours are: April to Oct.: 7.30 a.m.–9.30 p.m.; off season, Mon.–Fri.: 7.30 a.m.–3 p.m. On the outskirts are the ruins of Hippocrates' medical school and sanctuary, south-east of the city at the Aesculapium. Further west, on the coast road, lies the Petaloudes valley, where millions of butterflies gather each summer. For accommodation try Pension Alexis, at 9 Irodotou and Omirou St (Tel. 28798) in Kos Town. If it is boisterous nightlife you are after go to Tingaki, 10 km west; or visit Paradise Beach 50 km south of the capital, where you will find unspoilt sand, peace and quiet. Again, Kos has good ferry and boat links with the other islands and the mainland, but check with boat operators beforehand, since times are, as always, prone to change.

Crete

This is the most varied of all the islands, from the barren mountains to the beautiful old cities. Crete is the legendary birthplace of Zeus and home of the minotaur, and is divided into four regions with Agios Nikolaos, Rethymnon, Hania and Heraklion as their capitals. HERAKLION (Iraklion) is the main port of Crete with connecting ferries to Piraeus. Apart from the amazing ARCHAEOLOGICAL MUSEUM off Eleftherios Square, where you'll find the Hall of the Minoan frescoes, the city has little to recommend it. If staying, try the youth hostel at 3 Viranos St, just off 25th Augustou Ave (Tel. 286281) or one of the places in Handakos St. From Heraklion, you can visit the Minoan ruins at KNOSSOS, legendary home of the minotaur. The ruins open from Mon.–Fri., 8 a.m.–7 p.m. Sat.–Sun., 8.30 a.m.–3 p.m. Admission is 500 dr. (250 dr. for students). To get there take bus 2 which stops along 25th Augustou Ave. There are also ruins to visit at PHAESTOS, or the beach at PLAKIAS. The tourist office in Heraklion is opposite the Archaeological Museum at 1 Xanthoudidou St (Tel. 228203) or 228225), open: Mon.–Fri., 7.30 a.m.–2.30 p.m.

In western Crete look out for RETHYMNON with its Venetian and Turkish buildings. There is a youth hostel at 41 Tombasi St (Tel. 0831–22848), and the tourist office is on E.L. Venizelou Avenue (Tel. 0831–29148), whilst the tourist police are contactable on 28156. In HANIA (Chania), the elegant ex-capital of Crete, the Venetian architecture makes you feel you're more in Italy than in Greece. The tourist office at 40 Kriari St in the 'Pantheo' building (Tel. 0821 26426/42624) and the information bureau in the converted Turkish mosque, at 6 Akti Tobazi (Tel. 0821–43 3000), have, like the tourist police (Tel. 0821–24477) a printed list of all hotels on the island. Try the harbour area for rooms, or the youth hostel at 33 Drakonianou St (Tel. 0821–53565. Open from March–Nov.). For the high spot of your Cretan trip, walk along the 18-km SAMARIA GORGE, the largest one in Europe, a nature lover's dream, but in the summer a tourist haven. Take the bus to Xyloska, through the Omalos mountains, for this six-hour walk. The walk will end in the small town of Agia Roumelion, on the southern coast. From here you can get a bus to Loutro or Chora Sfakion where you can catch a boat back to Hania. Remember, before you set out for this trip, to bring your own refreshments and sensible footwear with you. You'll need them.

In eastern Crete AGIOS NIKOLAOS, like Malia, is the tourist trap. It's very picturesque but often short of rooms. Try the youth hostel at 3 Stratigou Koraka St (Tel. 0841–22823) for rooms, or enquire at the tourist information office at 20 Akti Koundourou (Tel. 0841–22357) for help. The harbour nightlife is the best thing about this town, and a nightclub 'Scorpios' plays dance music until the early hours. 52km west, at the village of PSIHROS, is the path that ascends to the Diktaian Cave (Dikteon Andron), the legendary birthplace of Zeus, and venue of cult worship. At the village you can hire a donkey from the locals if you do not wish to ascend to the cave by foot. Admission is 100 dr. for students. There are many other caves of archaeological, palaentological and historical interest, ask at the tourist information offices for more details. SITIA, east of the city, is near the fantastic palm beach of VAÏ, as seen in the Bounty Bar adverts, and the youth hostel at 4 Therissou St (Tel. 0843–22693) can usually squeeze you in. The tourist office for more information is at Iroon Politehniou Suq (Tel. 0843–25955).

If you're camping, there are a number of good sites on the island's coast. Camping Iraklion is only 6 km from Heraklion and has excellent facilities including supermarket and swimming pool. Camping Arkadia and Camping Elisabeth are beside excellent beaches and are just a few km from Rethymnon. Expect to pay about £3 per night.

There are daily sailings from Piraeus to the ports of both Hania (Tel. 0821–89240) and Iraklio (Tel. 081–226073), both of which take approximately 12 hours.

The Ionian Islands

These are the islands off the north-west coast, lusher than most, with Corfu as its main tourist trap, and Italian widely spoken.

Corfu

If you're taking the ferry from or to Italy, chances are you'll stop off here. Take the opportunity if you've a day or two to spare, particularly if you can avoid the terrible crush months of July and August. Corfu doesn't look terribly Greek; in some ways it's more like the French Riviera. The Venetians, French and British have all occupied the island and left their colonial marks in the buildings, food and people. If you are travelling from Patras, possession of an Inter-Rail + Boat does not make you second class (or even third class) but deck class, so the trick is to get on early and find a sheltered place to lay out your sleeping bag.

When you disembark, turn left to the Old Port; the road to the right of the Hotel Constantinopolis is where to start your search for a cheap bed. Try the Hotel Europa (Tel. 0661–39304), a short distance from the port, which charges about 4,000 dr. for a double room, and rents out mopeds for 3,000 dr. You are likely to be met at the port by a rep from this hotel – as well as reps from just about every other hotel with spare beds that day. Another recommendation is Hotel Elpis at 4 5H Parados N. Theotoki St (Tel. 30289) in an alleyway opposite 128 N. Theotoki St in the Old Port.

Basic double rooms cost about 2,000 dr., or 2,500 dr. for triples. Hot showers are an extra 100 dr. The tourist police, 31 Arseniou St (Tel. 0661–39503/39509), will fix you up in a private home if they like the look of you. Tourist information is in the Governor's House (Tel. 0661 30298 or 30360) between Mantzaran and Dessila streets. The youth hostels are far out and invariably full. The IYHF hostel is 4.5 km north on the main road from the port (Tel. 0661–91202), take the bus number 7 from Platia San Rocco to Kontokali for the 20-minute journey. The reception is open from 8 a.m.–12 noon, 5 p.m.–8 p.m. Camping Vatos, on the opposite side of the island to Corfu Town is cheap, friendly and has full facilities including bar, disco and a cheap restaurant. You can get free minibuses to and from the nearest beach as well as a free minibus service to the early-morning ferries. Pelekas Beach, on the west coast, is a favourite of eurorailers. The bus costs 140 dr. We don't recommend you to hire a moped, but if you must, make sure you get a helmet and haggle for the petrol, which is always an add-on at rip-off prices. Moped hire usually costs around 3,000–5,000 dr. The lively Pink Palace Hotel (Tel. 53103/4) at Agios Gordios is right on the beach and can be reached by bus from the Old Port. This place is a backpacker's heaven, so don't expect to relax here, because there are many activities designed for even the quietest person to join in the fun, such as the infamous ouzo circle. It charges from 2,100 dr. per person, with breakfast, dinner, showers and disco included. Laundry costs an extra 1,000 dr.

See Mon Repos where the Duke of Edinburgh was born. For your evening meal, the Old Port area is good. Try Pizza Pete at 19 Arseniou St, which serves brilliant vegetarian and pizza specials for 600–1,100 dr. (Open April–Oct. daily 9 a.m.–12 midnight.) Café Corner at 10 Agais Sofias is a licensed café in the old part of the town. English speaking service provides organic vegan dishes, and special dietary requirements can be catered for in advance (Tel. 26457).

Beware of some of the cheap food stalls as food poisoning seems to be a recurring hazard on the island.

There is much to offer in the way of culture on this island especially in the summer months. The festival of Corfu takes place in September, and features ballet, concerts, operatic and theatrical offerings. From June until then the GNTO put on a season of folkloric dances and 'Sound and Light' performances in English,

French and Italian at the old fortress to the north-east of the town. Out of season there are still the museums of Byzantine and Asiatic art and archaeology, plus the inevitable churches and museums to look round.

PAXI and its little neighbour ANDIPAXI, 30 minutes away, are becoming more touristy than is desirable due to their proximity to Corfu, but these small islands still have a lot of charm. Every day a car ferry leaves Corfu for Paxi, which takes about three hours' sailing. The island itself is covered with grape vines and olive trees, and on 15 August there is a festival gathering at the monastery of PANAYIA, and festivities carry on into the evening with dancing taking place in the main square in GAIOS. The tourist police (Tel. 0662–31222) should be able to help you find rooms to stay in. If you decide to risk the law and camp illegally on the sandy beaches, remember to be tidy and careful; fire can start particularly easily on undesignated sites.

ITHACA, the home of Odysseus, is a small mountainous island with many historical caves, particularly associated with the hero, and monasteries. Linked daily by boat from Paxi and Corfu, it has a cultural resurgence every July and August in the form of a music and theatre festival. The main town of VATHI has many shops and houses in the middle of a horseshoe-shaped harbour. Avoid the hotels for they are very expensive; try to find rooms to let by walking up Odysseus St, or enquiring at Polyctor Tours in the main square, or the tourist police (Tel. 0674–32205).

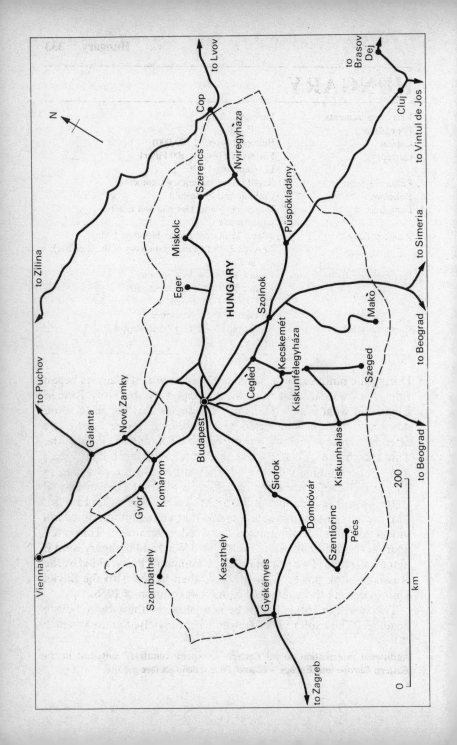

HUNGARY

Entry requirements	Passport
Population	10,585,000
Capital	Budapest (pop.: 2,200,000)
Currency	Forints (1 Forint = 100 Filler)
	£1 = approx. 136ft.
Political system	Republic/Parliamentary Democracy
Religions	Catholic and Protestant
Language	Hungarian (some German and English understood)
Public holidays	1 Jan.; 15 March; Easter Monday; 1 May; 20 Aug.; 23 Oct. (Proclamation day of the Republic); 25, 26 Dec.
International dialling codes	From UK: 010 + 36 + number
	From USA: 011 + 36 + number
	To UK: 00 + 44 + number
	To USA: 00 + 1 + number
Eurotrain office	Szabadsàg tèr 16, H–1395 Budapest 5 (Tel. 01–119 898)

During the ninth century, seven tribes of mounted Magyars began riding westwards, until they were stopped by the Holy Roman Empire in what is now Hungary. Gradually they began to settle down and became converted to Catholicism. Then during the fifteenth century, just when things were beginning to take off, the Turks turned up. A century and a half later, with most of the area's medieval monuments destroyed, the Austrians took over and in 1867 after several uprisings they agreed to grant Hungary equal status under the joint monarchy of the Austro-Hungarian Empire. This made Hungary unique as a region that successfully attained full independence after obtaining a devolved government. Things fell apart at the outbreak of the First World War, and Hungary went it alone until 1945. Two years later the Communist Party, aided by the Russians, took power. Hungary was then linked with the Soviet Union, despite the attempted counter-revolution of 1956.

Travel within Hungary can be very slow, so think twice before heading off to explore every corner. Fortunately, the areas which

Additional information on all Eastern European countries contained in the *Eastern Europe* and *Europe – Grand Tour* factsheets (see p.13).

have most to offer are the most accessible. If you only have time to visit one country in Eastern Europe, you can't go far wrong with Hungary. Budapest is, and always will be, one of the most beautiful of the world's cities. Its cuisine is unusual and well worth sampling. The people are friendly, but prices have increased dramatically since 1989–90. Tourism is the growth industry now. One of the areas that this new boom has focused on is Open-air Ethnographic Exhibitions, or 'Museum Villages'. These 'skanzens' (the name is from the first folk-culture museum, near Stockholm) appear all over Hungary – in the Danube Bend to the north of Budapest, the north-east and south of the Hungarian Plains to the east of the city, and in both west and south Transdanubia, to the west of the capital. Ask at tourist information for a special leaflet on them. Similarly, there is a specialist leaflet on the various sites of architectural interest throughout the country, which is worth acquiring from them. Hungary has been a pioneer regarding *Perestroika* and *Glasnost* and the number of western influences and the emerging capitalist economy are witness to this. Hungary has led the way in Eastern Europe these past two years, preferring to liberalize peacefully, with democratic elections ending the power of the Communist Party.

HUNGARIAN STATE RAILWAYS
(Magyar Államvasutak, MÁV)

Trains are considerably slower and dingier than they are in the West, as well as being crowded in the summer. There are often long gaps between services, too, but with patience it's possible to explore nearly all the larger towns and tourist centres on an Inter-Rail or BIJ ticket. Trains marked 'Sebesvonat' make only a few stops at major centres; other fast trains are marked 'Gyorsvonat'. The ultra-slow local ones ('Személyvonat') are noisy and take an age to get anywhere. Bear in mind when making your plans that the railway network is very centralized and that it's always easier to enter or leave Hungary via Budapest. As in other countries, BIJ ticket holders can break their journeys at any point without having to get their ticket stamped. As with the rest of Eastern Europe, queueing is a way of life, and unavoidable during the summer. Whenever possible, make your seat reservations in advance, at the MÁV booking office at Andràssy ùt 35, Budapest (Mon.–Wed.,

Fri.: 9 a.m.–6 p.m., Thurs.: 9 a.m.–7 p.m., Sat.: 9 a.m.–1 p.m.). It's worth keeping an eye out for any trains with new carriages, as they are a vast improvement on the old rolling stock.

• **Inter-Rail bonuses:** Free entry to Metró Museum, Metró Station Deák Ferenc tér, Budapest V; Transport Museum, Városligeti-Körut 11, Budapest XIV; and Horse Carriage Museum, Paràd-fürdö.

• **Rover tickets:** Unless you intend to do a great deal of travelling they do not offer particularly good value. Available for 10, 20 or 30 days in first and second class they cost from around £35 in second class for 10 days to £107 in first class for 30 days. You can buy two types of rover tickets in Hungary from any MÁV office. One covers the whole country and costs 800 ft. for 7 days and 1,200 ft. for 10 days, second class only. The second ticket is for the Lake Balaton area only and costs 200 ft. 7 days and 300 ft. for 10 days. If you are buying tickets as you go along there is, in theory, a 50 per cent reduction if you pay in a convertible currency. In practice, you will find that you are allowed to buy your ticket to the border in forints, but have to pay for the rest of the journey in a convertible currency.

Eurotrain offer Explorer passes in Hungary in first and second class (see p.33 for details).

TRAIN INFORMATION

Really, only German is understood. If you're getting nowhere, try and get your tongue round: 'Melyik vágányról indul a . . . vonat?' (From which platform does the train to . . . leave?)

• **Reservations:** (Helyjegy) To be sure of a seat, it's best to reserve at least two or three days in advance. This is obligatory on some international (Nemzetközi gyorsvonat) and other express trains.

• **Night travel:** Where necessary, Hungary borrows sleepers and couchettes from other East European countries. If you can't get a seat or lose yours to someone with a reservation (very common at Belgrade), try sleeping in the luggage car – this is more comfortable than being cramped in a single seat, but get there early. This appears to be tolerated by at least some guards in Turkey, Bulgaria,

Yugoslavia and Hungary. It is, of course, against all regulations, and this is information, not a recommendation.

● **Eating on trains:** All long-distance trains have either a buffet car or mini-bar which can be unbelievably bureaucratic and grubby. Station buffets are particularly good value, however, and quieter.

TOURIST INFORMATION

All towns have their own local tourist information offices (Idegen-forgalmi Hivatal) in addition to the newly privatized IBUSZ offices which deal with all aspects of travel and accommodation.

● **IUS/ISIC bonuses:** 25–30 per cent off other East European train fares. For further information, contact Express, Semmelweiss 4, Budapest (Tel. 01 178600).

● **Money matters:** 1 forint (ft.) = 100 fillérs.
Banking hours are generally 9 a.m.–5 p.m. (2 p.m. on Fri.), though the Hungarian National Bank closes at lunchtime. There's no minimum daily exchange amount, so only change money as you need it. You can do this on the train at the border, if you are lucky, but don't count on it. You are not allowed to take Hungarian currency out of the country, but you can change back up to half the amount you brought in, although this is limited to £50 or US $100. You may be directed to the restaurant car instead to spend your excess forints. Not all currency exchanges will change money back into hard currency – you have to look around. You are allowed to take out 500 ft. (really just a souvenir for all its value) and while you will be asked on the train about this they are unlikely to check. You will also be hassled quite openly in the station foyer at Keleti about changing money. Commission charges are very low (usually 1 per cent) and it's definitely not worth the risk of exchanging on the black market.

● **Goods:** Similar restrictions to the monetary ones exist for tobacco (250 cigarettes or 250 grammes), alcohol (one litre of spirits or two litres of wine), foodstuffs (and other goods that do not qualify as 'personal' – a limit of 5000 ft. worth on your first journey, and 500 ft. on subsequent journeys) being brought into the country. It is also illegal to sell/give away personal goods while in Hungary. On leaving, you cannot take objects (whether purchased or received as gifts) exceeding a value of 3000 ft. in total value out of the country. Within this, only 500 ft. worth of foodstuffs can be taken out of the country, and even then the list of prohibited foodstuffs (no quantity of which can be taken out of the country) is fairly all encompassing (e.g. fruit, chocolate, dairy products, vegetable oil, meat, spices, pharmaceuticals, imported drinks etc. etc. – ask for a full list from a tourist office). Tobacco has an exit limit of 400 cigarettes or 200 grammes, and alcohol has a restriction of one litre of spirits and *un*limited (!) quantities of wine.

• **Post offices:** Open Mon.–Fri.: 8 a.m.–7 p.m.; Sat.: 8 a.m.–1 p.m. The quickest service for phone calls, faxes, telexes and telegrams abroad is the Hungarian Post Services Centre (Budapest V, Petofi S. u. 17–19, Mon.–Fri.: 7 a.m.–8 p.m.; Sat.: 7 a.m.–8 p.m.; Sun.: 8 a.m.–1 p.m.). Stamps can also be bought from tobacconists. The rates for postcards abroad is 7–20 ft., for letters 12–30 ft.

• **Shops:** Most shops are open Mon.–Fri.: 10 a.m.–6 p.m. and Sat.: 9 a.m.–1 p.m., with food shops opening Mon.–Fri.: 7 a.m.–7 p.m. and Sat.: 7 a.m.–2 p.m. Late night opening on Thursday is usually till 8 p.m., with many tobacconists, pastry shops, foodstores and large shopping centres in general also opening on Sundays. As ever, phone TOURINFORM for further information on who opens when and for how long, on 117–9800. Growing numbers of round-the-clock foodshops are appearing in Budapest.

• **Cinemas, Theatres, Concerts:** An equivalent UK value for theatre tickets is approx. £4–5, and for that you will get a wide variety of shows. Cinema tickets go for about £1, and concert tickets for about £7.

• **Museums:** Open Tues.–Sun.: 10 a.m.–6 p.m. Closed on Mondays, admission is generally between 10 and 80 ft. (i.e. 70p max), and is usually free on either Saturday or Wednesday.

• **Bicycles:** Certain stations rent out bicycles throughout the year. By arrangement, these can be returned to any station. In Budapest, hire from Southern and Western railway stations (for further information Tel. MÁV 1228–049). Help with routes, maps, and other matters can be obtained from the Hungarian Cycling Federation, 1146 Budapest, Millenáris Sporttelep, Szabó János u3 (Tel. 1836–965).

• **Medical Care:** First aid is free, but a fee is charged for proper medical treatment, the rate of which depends on the institution concerned. Sickness Insurance is advised by IBUSZ.

SLEEPING

IBUSZ and the local tourist offices will fix you up in a private house for about £11.50 ($18) for two people per night (plus 30 per cent for the first night). These are your best bet, so ask for the IBUSZ leaflet on accommodation in private homes. They are graded into A, B and C, depending on the tourist potential of the area. In small towns, look for the sign Szoba Kiadó (or Zimmer Frei or Zimmer) and don't be afraid to accept offers of a room if you're approached on the street or at a railway station. If you're out of luck, the student travel service Express have several hostels and cheap student hotels. Beds in a hostel/student hotel start at about 250 ft. Doubles start from 500 ft. per room. Express also book rooms in private homes. There's no need to be a member of the IYHF, and it's possible for couples to get a room to themselves. Most hotels, especially the budget ones, are booked out months in advance and are expensive for what you get, but if you are desperate, one-star hotels both in and out of Budapest can be had for £8–15 for a double room with bathroom.

Camping is a realistic possibility though prices have recently risen; still, it is only about £1–2 for a tent site, and a charge of less than £1 per person. Ask for a camping map from IBUSZ. Also, ask them about obtaining a FICC-AIT-IA Camping Carnet, which entitles you to a 20 per cent reduction in fees. There are about 280 authorized sites, officially graded from 1 to 4, depending on the facilities offered. For more detailed information, contact the Hungarian Camping and Caravanning Club at Ulloi ut 6, Budapest (Tel. 01–336536), where you can get copies of their Hungarian camping guides, containing full details of the services offered and concessions that apply to each establishment.

During the summer, Hungary's population almost doubles and queues for accommodation can be frustrating. You can reserve hotel accommodation in Hungary through the IBUSZ office in Vienna, at Kärntnerstrasse 26, where it's possible to reserve accommodation ahead of time. They only deal with hotels, and will not help with other types of accommodation such as hostels or campsites. Also if you plan on staying at any of the Express hotels or hostels in Budapest and will be arriving before 6 p.m., you're given priority if you have an Express Student voucher, available from Ökista in Vienna but you have to do it at least 10 days in advance. Don't be surprised if you are asked to pay for accommodation in hard currency – another reason for not changing too much.

Registration with the relevant police station has been relaxed, so that visitors need only register when staying in private accommodation for more than 30 days, as registration for hotels, hostels, camping grounds, paying guest rooms etc. is arranged by the accommodation site itself.

EATING AND NIGHTLIFE

Hungarian food is excellent by any standards, and furthermore it's cheap. Try pörkölt (a pork stew with paprika), paprikás csirke galuskával (chicken with a sour cream paprika sauce) or goulash. Vegetarians should try Gombafejek rantuv (mushroom coated with breadcrumbs), and somlói galuska (sweet dumplings in rum and chocolate sauce) or rétes (strudel) to follow. The cheapest places are the self-service restaurants. Choose and collect your food, then pay the cashier. Look out for the tourist menus as they're normally exceptionally good value; if you're really broke and don't mind standing up, try any bisztró. Also try the Hungarian spirit, pálinka, a clear brandy made from apricots, cherries and other fruits. Unlike the rest of Eastern Europe, Hungary has quite a bit of nightlife, particularly in Budapest. There are student discos and open-air concerts, as well as nightclubs.

If you're travelling on to Romania, Poland or Bulgaria, stock up on food in Hungary before you leave. All the Eastern European countries have menus which are heavily reliant on meat, which causes headaches for vegetarian visitors.

Budapest

The heart of the capital is the Danube, looking far more impressive than it does in Vienna, and spanned by a nice collection of bridges. Buda, west of the river and set among gentle hills, is a mixture of winding medieval streets, viewpoints over the city and neat suburbs; Pest is the centre of commerce and government. The two were united, along with Óbuda, in 1873, to become Budapest. There's plenty to see and do and because food and transport are still relatively cheap by Western standards it allows your lifestyle, for once, to rise above its usual humble level (though prices have increased sharply since 1990). All in all, Budapest is more lively, cosmopolitan and Westernized than any other East European (and some western cities)!

STATION FACILITIES

There are three main stations: Déli (south, Tel. 1159096) which serves the south-west, Keleti (east, Tel. 1136835) and Nyugati (west, Tel. 1490115). For rail information within Hungary telephone MÁV Central Information (1227860) and for abroad 1224052. Operates between 6 a.m. and 8 p.m. Call the stations direct between 8 p.m. and 6 a.m. They are well equipped by Eastern European standards, and you shouldn't find anything too out of the ordinary here. If you are stuck, remember 'pályaudvar' means 'station'. Expect delays – especially left-luggage. Give yourself plenty of time, especially in the evenings.

TOURIST INFORMATION

There are IBUSZ offices in all the stations (daily 8 a.m.–1 p.m.; 2 p.m.–7 p.m. Weekends till 5 p.m.). In addition there are offices at V, Roosevelt tér 5 (Tel. 117 3555) and Petőfi tér 3 (Tel. 118 3925). The latter is open 24 hours and also operates an accommodation service. If you are booking accommodation through this office, always do it before changing your money as they sometimes insist on payment in Western currencies, preferably DM or US $. Budapest Tourist, which arranges private accommodation, is at V, Roosevelt tér (open Mon.–Sat.: 8 a.m.–9 p.m., Sun.: 2 p.m.–8 p.m.). They also have offices near the two main stations: Baross tér near Keleti, and Bajcsy Zsilinszky u 55, near Nyugati. If you're sick of queues and know exactly what you want to ask, you can phone for foreign language tourist information TOURINFORM (Tel. 1179800), or go direct to their offices at 1052 Budpest V, Suto ut. 2, 50 metres from the Dèak Tèr Metro Station, open every day of the year from

8 a.m.–8 p.m. They can also reserve accommodation and sell concert tickets. IBUSZ in Budapest are not all that helpful on general tourist information.

• **Addresses:**
MAIN POST OFFICE and International Telephone Exchange is on the corner of Petöfi Sándor u and Martinelli tér (also poste restante), open Mon.–Fri.: 8 a.m.–6 p.m.; 8 a.m.–6 p.m. Saturday and in the morning only on Sundays and public holidays. Twenty-four-hour post offices are sited at Keleti and Nyugati stations.
UK EMBASSY: Harmincad u 6 (Tel. 1182888).
US EMBASSY: Szabadság tér 12 (Tel. 1126450), after hours (Tel. 1530566).
CANADIAN EMBASSY: Budakeszi u, 32 (Tel. 1387712).
EXPRESS: Student Travel Centre, Semmelweiss 4 (Tel. 1176634 or 1178600). They sell IUS/ISIC cards, book student hostels, tours etc.
EUROTRAIN: Szabadsàg tèr 16 (Tel. 1119898).

• **Getting about:** Public transport is efficient and cheap. Buy tickets in advance for buses (blue, 15 ft.), metro, trolley buses and trams (yellow, 12 ft.) from Trafik shops. Validate the tickets on entering the vehicles/metro. Tram, bus and metro services run from 4.30 a.m.–11 p.m., with night services on the busiest routes. The metro has three lines, transfer at Dèak Tèr. There is also a one-day travel pass valid for all public transport in Budapest, for 120 ft. Given the low cost of transport, however, it is probably easier to pay for individual journeys. Do not be tempted to dodge paying because of the ease with which you can avoid paying; fines are 200 ft., and inspectors make a beeline for dishonest tourists. Taxis are relatively cheap if there's a crowd of you, and cost about 80 ft. per mile. It is advisable, though, to use taxis with visible meters, and if you do, do not hand large currency notes over to the driver. Some drivers overcharge those who cannot speak Hungarian. If you are on the receiving end of a driver who insists on trying to overcharge you, then dig your heels in, and call for the police. State taxis are the safest bet, and are identified by a black number plate.

SEEING

The old town of Buda has at its centre VÁRHEGY, Castle Hill, with its painted baroque houses and students' and artists' quarter. It also has the FISHERMEN'S BASTION (Halaszbastya), built between 1899 and 1905, which is noteworthy for its view of the Pest panorama, Buda hills, Margaret Island, and the bridges over the Danube. Crowning the hill is the thirteenth-century MATTHIAS CHURCH where the Hungarian kings were crowned. The ROYAL PALACE, virtually destroyed in 1944, is now rebuilt and houses two important museums: the HISTORICAL MUSEUM OF BUDAPEST and the NATIONAL GALLERY with its impressive collection of Hungarian art. The latter is particularly recommended for its world-class collection of modern works. The Margaret Bridge takes you to MARGARET ISLAND, lying in the middle of the Danube. The island is a recreation park and often has outdoor concerts and plays on summer evenings. For the best views over the city, cross the Elizabeth Bridge and climb Gellért Hill to the Liberation Monument. There is also a cable car from the Chain Bridge at Clark Adam Tér. up the hill to the former Royal Palace. You can get a bus back if you're shattered. The floodlighting on summer evenings makes a walk by the riverside well worthwhile. You can also get excellent views by taking a trip on the cog railway which runs into the Buda hills. Take the Metro to Moszkva Tér and then tram 56 for two stops to the start of the Pioneer railway, a narrow-gauge system operated almost entirely by children who do everything but drive the trains on the seven-mile route through the Buda Forest.

ST STEPHEN'S BASILICA is the impressive church on Pest beside the PARLIAMENT. A walk through the twenty-seven courtyards of this complex when the sun is setting over the Buda hills can be truly memorable. For bibliophiles, the PARLIAMENT LIBRARY is the fifth largest book collection in Europe, with 400,000 volumes. Visitors should register in advance for a guided 40-minute PARLIAMENT TOUR (Tel. 36–1–112–0600) around the CUPOLA HALL, MAIN CHAMBER (unless the National Assembly is in session) and ORNAMENTAL STAIRCASE of this neo-Gothic building. Two other museums of exceptional quality are the FINE ARTS and the HUNGARIAN NATIONAL. The Fine Arts is in Városliget (the City Park) which has rowing boats for hire on the lake, and amusement parks. In the centre of the lake is an island upon which is situated VAJDAHUNYAD CASTLE, built in all the major architectural styles from the eleventh to eighteenth centuries. If you want to cleanse your pores from the grime of train travel, try an authentic Turkish bath. It only costs

around 80 ft., and the price includes a massage. Try the old
Ottoman baths of Kiràly Fürdö on Föutca 84. Men's sessions
take place on Mondays, Wednesdays and Fridays, and women's on
Tuesdays, Thursdays and Saturdays, all from 6.30 a.m.–6 p.m.
Beware, though, of masseuses who will bribe you for more money
even though you have paid at the entrance. They understand
English when they want to. If you can, make your visit to Budapest
coincide with St Stephan's Day (20 August), when there is an
impressive firework display and holiday atmosphere. Or, alternatively, you could try to catch Budapest's SPRING FESTIVAL which
takes place over two weeks every March. Featuring both Hungarian
and foreign artists performing symphonic, chamber, sacred and
modern music programmes, along with ballet, folk, dance, theatre,
film, rock, jazz, fine art and gastronomy. An example of the
outstanding foreign talent attracted to this festival last year is José
Carreras.

The IBUSZ-organized excursions are expensive. Both boat and
coach tours around Budapest cost about £8.40 for three hours. Pick
up a copy of the 'Budapest Experience' which is issued monthly by
the tourist office and gives details of all special exhibitions,
sightseeing and a city map.

SLEEPING

Budapest gets busy in summer, so don't hang about getting
organized on the bed front. The IBUSZ or Budapest Tourist Offices
mentioned under the tourist information above will be able to help
you in this respect. Alternatively head for the student accommodation office at Hotel Universitas (open during June, July and
August) at Irinyi József u. 9. They charge 1200 ft. per night for a
double room, and provide a buffet. The hostel also holds its own
disco every week from Thursday through to Sunday at 9 p.m., and it
is very popular and very cheap. You can avoid long queues at the
agency desks at the stations by heading straight into the city centre,
depending on your arrival time, to a tourist agency who will also
make bookings. Private accommodation is your best bet, although
you can't get in until after 5 p.m. Expect to pay anything up to
800 ft. each. Head straight for the IBUSZ office at the station to fix
up your accommodation, or try the Express Desk at Semmelweiss
utca 4 (Tel. 178–100) or any tourist agency as there's little to choose

between them. You pay them in full when you make the booking. They will accept traveller's cheques and give you change in forints. If Hotel Universitas is full they'll give you alternatives in the same area. You can also try the Econotour Hostel at Kinizsi u. 2–6, which is the student quarter near the university, Hotel Lidó, Nánási ut 67 (Tel. 1886865), Hotel Express, Beethoven u. 7–9 (Tel. 1753082) or Elle Hostel, Kollégium, Budaörsi ut 101, open only in the summer months (Tel. 667–788).

Camping out is illegal but easy to get away with (and even if you are caught you won't be sent off to Siberia, so don't worry). There are about ten campsites in the surrounding areas of the city. Rosengarten Camping at Pilisis út 7 is open from 15 May–15 September and Camping Niche open from 15 March–15 October costs 570 ft. a night with free showers. Take a bus or tram to Moszkva Tér then bus 158 to the campsite. (Chairlift out here affords wonderful views over Budapest and Buda forest.)

If you are broke or really need a cheap place to stay, then try the three sites claiming to be the cheapest youth hostels in Budapest centre: the Hostel 'Landler', Budapest XI, Bartok Bela ut 17 (Tel. 1851444/1667305), 369 ft. per person in 2/3/4-person rooms; Hostel 'Vasarhelyi', Budapest XI, Krusper u. 2–4 (Tel. 1853794), 468 ft. per person in 2/4-person rooms with showers; Hostel 'Rozsa', Budapest XI, Bercsenyi u. 28–30 (Tel. 1666677), 439 ft. per person, in 2/3-person rooms. These three hostels are student accommodation belonging to Budapest's Technical University throughout the year, but are used as youth hostels in July and August. They all also offer free kitchen and washing facilities, and a free safe luggage room. The receptions of all three offer currency exchange facilities and tourist information, as they are registered as a travel agency. All three are centred around Gellert ter: from Deli station, take the No. 18 tram; from Nyugati station, by metro to Kalvin ter, changing to a No. 1 bus; from Keleti station, take the No. 7 bus.

The two official campsites are a good last resort as they're rarely full to capacity. Hárshegy is at Hárshegyi u. 5 (Tel. 1151482) and Római camping, Szentendrei u. 189 (Tel. 1887167). Both cost around 300 ft. per person if you've a tent. Hárshegy also have four-bed bungalows for around 1150 ft. Bus 22 from Moszkva terminal (metro line 2) will get you there. Check their availability through Budapest Tourist Office. To get to Római take the metro to Batthyány Tér, where you change to the suburban railway,

HÉV. Get off at Rómaifürdö, where it is within sight of the station. If you pay in a convertible currency there is a 10 per cent reduction. If you stay here you can also get free access to the outdoor pool next door.

EATING AND NIGHTLIFE

Hungarian cuisine is one of the best in Europe and in Budapest you can eat well in any price range. Fixed menus for lunch are common and rarely cost more than 300 ft. but you have to ask for them as they are not always displayed. Look out for places called bisztrós, büfés, self-services and grills for even lower prices. One night at least, though, have a real blow-out. Even in a tourist trap, with gypsy music, wine and all the trimmings, there should be change from 1000 ft. per person.

Try: New York Restaurant, Erzsèbet Krt. 9–11. Amazing fin-de-siècle decor, gypsy music and dancing. The carp from Lake Balaton are a speciality here.

Further along Erzsèbet Krt. 47 is the Royal Hotel, where you can enjoy classical music from a five-piece band along with an excellent meal with wine for less than 800 ft. (closes 9.30 p.m.). Another place worth trying is the Apostolok Restaurant, Kigyó u. 4–6 (Tel. 1183704) which should provide you with a good four-course meal for around 500 ft. or Kis Kakukk, Pozsonyi út 12, which is also very reasonable. An Italian restaurant on Museum Kit opposite the National Museum is also very good value.

The meals on the Danube are good, too. Boats leave from below the Duna Hotel at 5.30 p.m. and 8 p.m. and the cruise lasts two or three hours – plenty of time to enjoy the meal knowing it won't break the bank. Wine cellars (borok) often serve good meals and the Hungarian wines, particularly Tokaji and Egri Bikavér (Bull's Blood), are quite something. With food being so cheap you can also consider coffee and cakes or ice-cream on the terrace by the river at the Atrium or Forum Hotels for around 300 ft, although these luxury Western hotels, such as the Duna and Hyatt, impose fairly rigid dress standards and may refuse to serve you if you are casually dressed.

The other 'must' is a visit to a sixteenth-century pastry shop, known worldwide. Ruszwurm (Szentháromság 7, opposite the Matthias Church, closed Wednesdays) has its own varieties of cakes and strudels plus original furnishings and intricate bread sculptures.

If you are really broke, you can lunch at the Fortuna Café for only 50 ft. Although this place is really a workers' canteen (which converts to a disco at night) you can fill up for next to nothing. It is in Old Buda near the Matthias Church. Walk past the Hilton and it is on the left up a small alley.

The Planetarium (near Népliget Station on Metro line 3) puts on a different show each night of the week with lasers and special lighting effects set to Western music by performers like Deep Purple, The Who and Mike Oldfield in the Lazer Theatre. Admission is around 100 ft.

Check out the *Express Cocktail Ship*, one of the Danube cruisers which take you round Margaret Island. There's rock, dancing and boozing, all for around 150 ft., but times vary depending on the time of year, so make sure you get on the right boat, in front of the Duna Hotel. There's traditional folk dancing in Buda Park, and a list of events is published in 'Coming Events in Budapest'. There are also open-air concerts (rock and classical) on Margaret Island. For up-to-the-minute information, buy a copy of the 'Daily News', a newspaper published in English and German every day except on Sunday and Monday. Apart from reporting national and international news, it carries regular listings of English language films in Budapest and other cultural events, and is available from news-stands and hotels.

The Danube Bend

This has Hungary's most spectacular scenery and it's possible to see some of it on a day trip from Budapest. The Danube makes a dramatic sweep south, about fifteen miles from Budapest, and the mountain scenery and villages up here are the best you'll find in the country. Boats leave the capital from Vigadó tér dock at 7 a.m. and 7.30 a.m., 10 a.m. and 2 p.m. every day – later boats make it possible for you to stop off and sightsee before continuing your journey. (Further information on boats is available from Dunatours (Tel. 1314533), Bajcsy Zsilinszky u. 17, and also from Mahart, Belgrád RKP [Tel. 1181704].) The journey to Esztergom, the heart of medieval Hungary, takes five hours so it's best to take a single and return to Budapest by bus (to Szentendre) and then suburban train.

SZENTENDRE, the 'Town of the Arts', is an old Serbian market town and artists' hangout. Lots of small museums (Margit Kovács ceramics collection is superb), churches and baroque houses. The main square (Fö tér) is the venue for a summer festival and one of the many OPEN-AIR ETHNOGRAPHIC MUSEUMS ('SKANZENS') in Hungary (near Angyal St, about three miles' walk from the station) has examples of traditional buildings from all over the country. Try the Inns and Coffee Shops, for a taste of the culinary overlap of the many cultures in this town. There is an infrequent bus service. The tourist office is by the Danube at Somogyi Bacsó part. 6. The campsite is on Pap Island (Tel. 26–10697), and open from May until September.

A few miles up river, VISEGRÁD is right on a bend among the mountains. This was a Middle Ages stronghold and has a FORTRESS and ROYAL PALACE. Its rich past makes it popular with tourists but you won't find any cheap commercialism, so eat in the restaurants without any fear of being ripped off. Tourist information is at Föutca 3/a (Tel. 26 28330), and a camping site can be found at Széchenyi u. 7 (Tel. 26–28330), open from May until September.

ESZTERGOM has some of the oldest and best-preserved remains in Hungary – including the first cathedral of the Christian religion. This was the residence of the Magyar kings from the tenth to the thirteenth centuries, and has the honour of being the oldest Royal town in Hungary. Take in the CHRISTIAN MUSEUM and ROYAL PALACE remains, but most of all visit the BASILICA, the largest cathedral in the country. For around 10 ft. you can climb to the dome and walk around outside it to enjoy superb views over the surrounding country and into Czechoslovakia. Tourist information (Komturist) and Express is at Széchenyi tér (Tel. 484). Camping is provided at Vadvirág Camping, Bańomi–dülö (Tel. 174), open from 15 May–15 October.

The Hungarian Plain

East of the Danube lies the dusty central plain which is real Hungarian peasant land. An in-depth exploration of this region will

still produce pockets of rural life virtually unchanged for generations. Trains run through the Plain and the Budapest–Kelebia line
stops off at the main settlements like Kecskemét and Szeged.

KECSKEMÉT, home town of Kodály, has only a small area of old
town left, but what there is is good. Walk along BÁNK BÁN and
János Hoffman streets. The TOWN HALL on Kossuth tér is another
typical building. Express is at Rákóczi út 32. The campsite is 5 km
from the station at Sport u. 5 (Tel. 76–28700) for further details.

SZEGED, near the frontier with Serbia and Romania, was
completely destroyed by flood in 1879, but the town today still has
something to say of its rich past when it was under Turkish and,
later, Austrian rule. See the DÓM TÉR where the VOTIVE CHURCH is,
and Hungary's best Greek Orthodox Serbian church on the north
side of the square. Also worth seeing are the ruins of the former
CASTLE and a performance of the SZEGED OPEN-AIR THEATRE Festival. The local tourist information office is at Victor Hugo u. 1, but
you're best to try Express at Kigyo 3, which specifically deals with
accommodation in the summer months. Opening hours are Mon.–
Fri.: 8 a.m.–4 p.m. There are two good student hostels in this town.
'Apáthy', Szeged-Centre, Eotvos u. 4. (Tel. 23–155), and
'Semmelweiss' can be found on the street of the same name (Tel.
11–644), and charges only $3 a night. Camping is provided at Port
Fürdö, Középkiköto sor (Tel. 62–53795) which is open from
May until September.

The historic, Baroque city of EGER, in the north-east, is
Hungary's Bordeaux. This is where the good red wine (Bull's
Blood) you've been knocking back in Budapest originates. It is not
too surprising, therefore, that an interesting organized local tour
exists (at the unusually low price of £5), involving the 'Election of
the Wine-General of the Valley of the Beautiful Lady'. It should be
pointed out that the worthiness of any particular candidate for this
post is apparently directly linked to the candidate's ability to drink
as much wine as possible! For more information, contact Irene
Smuczer, Budapest Tourist, Eger 3300, Dobo I ut. 5 (Tel.
36–10019). Tourist information at Bajcsy Zsilinszky u. 9 (Tel. 36
11724, open 8 a.m.–6 p.m.) will give you a map and information,
and should you decide to stay they'll help out on accommodation,
and Express at u Szechenyi 1st ván 28 (Tel. 36–10727 or 11865,
open 8 a.m.–4 p.m.) will arrange a place in the Student Hostel.
DOBÓ ISTVÁN SQUARE is the town centre; just north of this is the

CASTLE. The Kazamata Restaurant in the centre, by the neo-classical CATHEDRAL, is exceptionally good value and the wine is a knock-out. Eger is a good place to base yourself if you fancy delving into the forests and villages of inner Hungary for a while, and there are various cheap hotels and campsites, such as Autós Camping at Rákóczi út 79 (Tel. 36–10558).

The bus ride to attractive SZILVASVARAD makes a pleasant day-trip. East of Eger is MISKOLC, east of which in turn lies the world-famous wine-producing town of TOKAJ. Further south and east of there is the NATIONAL PARK OF HUNGARY – 62,000 hectares of HORTOBAGY was declared a nature conservation area in 1973, and now visitors to the National Park can see the protected animals and beautiful plants, many of which can only be found in this region. Examples of this are the bird reservations, which contain one of the largest water-bird feeding and breeding sites in Central Europe, with over 160 species passing through here between early spring and late autumn.

Lake Balaton

Lake Balaton is Central Europe's largest lake, measuring 600 square kilometres and also known as the 'Hungarian Sea', with rolling hills and vineyards interspersed with picturesque old towns making up the surrounding countryside. This is the region you'll pass through if you're coming in from Austria, and if you've hit a good spell of weather this is where to break your journey, as there are good beaches and everything you need for a few days' beach-bumming, Hungarian-style.

SIÓFOK, on the southern shores of the lake, with warm shallow waters and an abundance of Hungarian beach bums in the summer, is a bit like Torremolinos for us; but if it's company you're after, head there. There are seven campsites around this area, the nearest, Aranypart Nyaralótelep (Tel. 84–11801) being 200 m from the train station. The equally cheap Mini Camping can be found at Szent Lászlo út. 74, two kilometres away. IBUSZ operates from Kele u. 1–3 (Tel. 84–11481), and bicycles can be hired from the train station if you can produce your ticket proving

that you have travelled by train. KESZTHELY has more to offer.
Apart from its beaches, there are various things to see: the first
European agricultural college, GEORGICON; the HELICON LIBRARY,
with many rare books and antiquities; and the BALATON MUSEUM.
BALATONFÖLDVÁR is probably the most scenic of the Balaton
resorts, with trees coming down close to the lakeside. It's a good
centre for watersports and has quite a bit of nightlife. Express office
at Jozsef A. u. 9 will fix you up with a room at the Express
International Youth Centre or Hotel Juventus for $3–$6 a night, as
will a number of other tourist agencies in town. A camping site is
located at Zalatour Camping, Balatonpart (Tel. 12–782).

TIHANY and BALATONFÜRED are on the northern shore and are
quieter and prettier. Tihany has Celtic and Roman ruins and a
beautiful yellow ABBEY looking down on the peninsula, where you
can hear a high standard of organ recitals given all year round. The
OPEN-AIR MUSEUM gives a good idea of the Balaton folk traditions,
and the thatched-roof houses set among the hills add to the charm.
The tourist office and exchange is at Balatontourist, 8200 Vesz-
prem, Kossuth L. u. 21 (Tel. 80–26277).

Balatonfüred is a health spa which tends to attract wealthy
Hungarians and Germans. See the MEDICINAL SPRINGS, busy
HARBOUR and ROUND CHURCH. The tourist office is Balatontourist,
8230 Balatonfürd, Blaha Lug u. 5 (Tel. 86–42822) and camping can
be found 600 km from the train station at XXVIIFICC Rally
Camping, Balaton földvár (Tel. 86–43823) by the water's edge, at
the biggest site in the country.

Day-trips to try in this area are the Lóczy Cave, the Gáspar and
Jókai look-out points and wine-tasting at Badacsony.

Western Hungary

Between Budapest and Austria lies TRANSDANUBIA, which now can
be overflowing with bargain hunting Austrians over for the day.
GYÖR is a large industrial city two hours from Budapest by train.
The OLD TOWN has been lovingly preserved. See the CARMELITE
CHURCH and Baroque CATHEDRAL. For entertainment sample the
gypsy atmosphere of Vaskakas Tavern beneath the Castle or the
magnificent Kisfaludy Theatre at Czuczor Gergely utca. Tourist

Information is at Aradi Vértanúk u. 22 (Tel. 961–1557. Open Mon.–Thurs.: 8 a.m.–4 p.m. Fri.: 8 a.m.–3 p.m. Sat.: 8 a.m.–11 a.m.), across from the Town Hall. Express at Bajcsy-Zsilinsky ut 41 (Tel. 28–833. Open Mon.–Fri.: 7.30 a.m.–12 noon, 12.40 a.m.–3.30 p.m.) can arrange accommodation during the summer in the KTMF Student Hotel. There is a camping ground at Kiskút-liget (open mid-April to mid-October), take bus 8 from the station.

Almost at the Austrian border (only 60km from Vienna) is SOPRON – over 700 years old, it is Hungary's 'Town of Museums', with over 400 protected buildings. This staggering statistic is in part due to the sheer diversity of sites on offer in Sopron – it was the location of the largest (18,000 square metres) Iron Age settlement in Europe, and a part of the amber road from the Roman period ran through here. A veritable ensemble of late Renaissance and Baroque structures are found in the inner city, with SZECHENYI PALACE, the DOMINICAN CHURCH, FABRICIUS HOUSE, the twelfth-century SYNAGOGUE, and the FRANZ LISZT MUSEUM. The SOPRON FESTIVAL WEEKS take place each year at the end of June and the start of July. Also worth visiting is a performance in the CAVE THEATRE in FERTO RAKOS (between Sopron and the protected environment area of Lake Ferto). Worthy of a day-trip is the ESTERHAZY PALACE (FERTOD CASTLE) the 'Hungarian Versailles' (modelled on the Habsburgs' palace at Schönbrunn) where Joseph Haydn spent some years as court musician. One of his compositions, the 'Farewell Symphony' received its first performance at the palace. The eighteenth century was when the MUSIC HOUSE was built as a home for him by the Esterhazys, and today it serves as the HAYDN MEMORIAL MUSEUM.

KŐSZEG is a quiet town on the Austrian frontier (except when the shoppers hit town!). It is famous for holding off the huge Turkish siege of 1532. On JURISICH TÉR, the cobbled main square, is the Gothic ST JAMES CHURCH with its wonderful frescoes. JÚRISICH CASTLE, where the Turks were beaten back, is now a historical museum (closed Mondays) and also has cheap accommodation from April to mid-October. The tourist bureau at Vàrkör Square and Express next door will help you out with a place to stay.

Express at Bajcsy-Zsilinsky ut. 41 (Tel. 28–833) can arrange accommodation during the summer in the KTMF Student Hotel, Ságván E. u. 3. The Hotel Aranypart, which also provides camping facilities is situated at Aldozat u. 12 (Tel. 26–442 or

033–242). There is another camping ground at Ciklámen Camping Kiskút-liget (Tel. 96–18–986, open mid-April to mid-October), take bus 8 from the station to travel the 3 km distance. There is a good hostel at Express Hotel Pk, Koseg Centre, Felszabadulás Park 2 (Tel. 322), and a campsite situated 1 km from the train station at Strand Camping, Strand-Sétany (Tel. 94–60155). The post office is open weekdays from 8 a.m.–8 p.m., and can be found at Jókai u. 10.

The South-west

Southern Transdanubia has a pleasant mild climate and has lovely green hills. NAGYKANIZSA is the major town of the Zala Hills which lie on the westernmost perimeter of the region; it is also home to many horse shows. Much of the architecture is eighteenth-century baroque and the town is surrounded by forest parkland and a rowing lake. The area is poorly connected by train so the bus service is the major form of transport to and around the neighbouring villages. ZALAKAROS is the major touristy centre of the district due to its famous medicinal baths at the Zalakaros Spa Centre. Information for accommodation can be obtained from Zala Country tourist office (Zalatour) in Lenin u. 13 (Tel. 93–11185), or at the IBUSZ office in Szabadság tér 21 (Tel. 93–11126). The nearest camping site is at Auto's Camping, Vár u. 1 (Tel. 93–19119) and is open from May until September. SZIGETVÁR which lies further to the west is yet another place famous for being besieged by the Turks in the sixteenth century. This story is told in the museum (open 10 a.m.–3 p.m., closed Mondays), in the fifteenth-century FORTRESS. Also visit the ALI PASHA MOSQUE which is now a church. The tourist bureau is located inside the Oroszlán Hotel on Zrinyí tér (Tel. 284) and will set up accommodation. From April to mid-November you can stay in dormitories in the Fortress itself.

MOHÁCS, which lies to the south-east of the region, is situated on the banks of the Danube and plays host to the BUSO PARADE of monstrous figures wearing traditional carved masks, held at the end of the carnival season year at the end of February on the last Sunday of Shrovetide. The great Battle of the Mohács of 1526 made the town well known, and a memorial site is open on the very fighting ground. The tourist office is at Tolbuhin u. 2 (Tel. 10–961).

Pécs

Pécs, the main city, situated five hours away from Budapest, and 30 km from Mohács, is home to many fantastic churches, such as the Romanesque CATHEDRAL, the former sixteenth-century Turkish MOSQUE OF PASHA GHAZI KASIM, and the enormous SYNAGOGUE which is open daily from 12.30 p.m. One of the city's most famous treasures is the painted burial chamber and MAUSO-LEUM unearthed in I. Istuán tér. A later, fourth-century ROMAN CRYPT and graves can be found in Geisler Cta utca, open from May through to October, closed Mondays and between 1–3 p.m. A walk down Káptalan u. brings you to Pécs' many museums, including the Vasarely Museum named after the initiator of 'op art' and Zsolany Porcelain Museum. There is a MINING MUSEUM on Déryné u. 9 which is open all day except Mondays, and has a superb working-class movement exhibition.

The tourist office at Széchenyi tér 9 (Tel. 13300), open in the summer months from 9.30 a.m.–8.30 p.m., will arrange accommodation for you, and can also exchange money, as can the IBUSZ office next door (closed Sunday). To get there take bus 3 from the railway station. The Barany and County office of the Express Youth and Students Travel Bureau is situated at Bajcsy-Zsilinszky u. (Tel. 12–793) and can organize accommodation in student hostels. To get there, turn right when leaving the train station. A good camping site is Familia Camping on Gyöngyösi 1 u. 6 (Tel. 72–29938) which is 2 km from the train station and provides catering facilities and tennis courts. For roofed accommodation, try the Hotel Balokány in Universitás ut 2 (Tel. 11966) which charges $4 per night, or the inexpensive Minaret Hotel at Sallai utca 35 which is an old monastery.

The environs of Pécs have much to offer for nice days out: take bus 35 into the scenic MECSEK HILLS and climb the 194 m TV TOWER, on the Misina Peak, for a stunning view, or try ABALIGET 15 km away which houses a stalactite cave and two artificial lakes for

rowing and swimming. Also, less than two hours away is the
GEMENC NATIONAL PARK, which has a reputation for being the
largest and most beautiful wildlife preserve in the country. A flood
plain forest, it contains stags, deer, wild boar, white-tailed eagles,
black storks and many rare European birds. For those wishing to
stay in this peaceful area, a camping site is located nearby with tents
for rent available. Contact tourist information (Tel. 72–78054) for
more details.

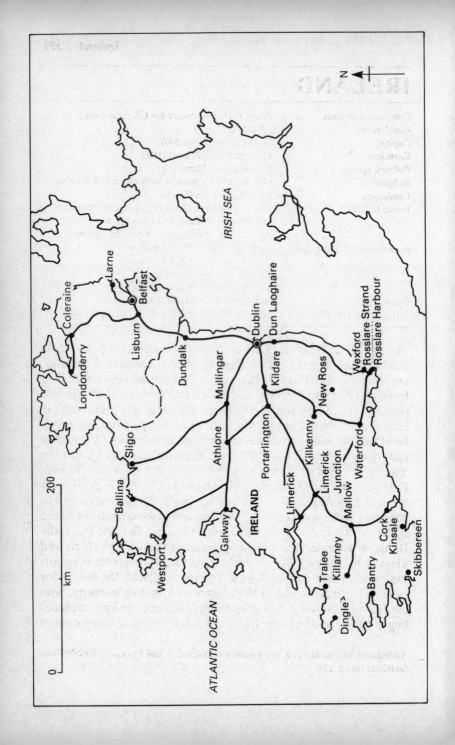

IRELAND

Entry requirements	Passport (not necessary for UK nationals)
Population	3,550,000
Capital	Dublin (pop.: 1,100,000)
Currency	£1 = approx. 0.97 punt (IR£)
Political system	Parliamentary Democracy
Religion	94% Roman Catholic, 4% Protestant, 2% Other
Languages	English and Irish (Gaelic)
Public holidays	1 Jan.; 17 March; Good Friday; Easter Monday; first Monday in June; first Monday in August; last Monday in October; 25, 26 Dec.
International dialling codes	From UK: 010 + 353 + number
	From USA: 011 + 353 + number
	To UK: 00 + 44 + number
	To USA: 00 + 1 + number
Eurotrain office (Compass Travel)	34 Lower Abbey Street, Dublin 1 (Tel. 01–741777 or 787028)

The history of Ireland is both turbulent and fascinating, as are its folklore and legends. The Romans never conquered Ireland, enabling the Celts to develop a pre-Christian native culture free from outside interference, and many examples of their art and civilization still exist today. The dawn of Christianity came with the arrival of St Patrick in the fifth century, when he is credited with banishing all snakes from Ireland. Ireland then became a centre of culture and learning, while the rest of Europe languished under the 'barbarian' invasion that followed the collapse of the Roman Empire. Their peaceful role as the scholars of Europe was however brought to an end when the Vikings began their attacks on the coastline in the ninth century. The Norsemen were finally defeated in the tenth century by the High King of Ireland, Brian Boru, at the Battle of Kinsale. The infighting amongst the various chiefs and kings that followed Boru's death gave the Normans their opportunity to extend their influence beyond England. By the Tudor period, parliament was in the control of a British minority, who gradually (following Cromwell's seventeenth-century crusade) began taking land from the Irish Catholics to give to loyal Protestant

Additional information on this country contained in the *Europe – Grand Tour* factsheet (see p.13).

settlers from Scotland and England, thus ensuring their allegiance to the English Crown. After the 1801 Act of Union, Ireland became a part of the United Kingdom, but the Great Famine (1845–1848, 1 million people died) that followed the repeated failure of the potato harvests gave rise to both an increase in Irish nationalism and the mass emigration of a further million people. A number of unsuccessful rebellions occurred before home rule was passed in 1914, but it was not until the Easter Rising of 1916, when a group of rebels took over most of Dublin and declared an Irish Republic, that the final impetus for independence arrived. In the seven days that followed the declaration, fierce fighting gutted the city, until Crown troops regained control. The brutal execution of the ringleaders sparked the War of Independence that led to the 1921 treaty removing British forces from all of Ireland, with the exception of the six counties that today constitute Northern Ireland to the north-east of the landmass. A further, civil, war was embarked upon, between the anti-treaty (republican) and the pro-treaty (free-state) forces. Finally, in 1937, the twenty-six counties became fully recognized and independent (Eire).

Outside the modern cities of Ireland are the villages and towns in the country, which give you a real understanding of Irish hospitality. Although trains will get you to all the main centres, the best way to get to grips with Ireland and her past is to hire a bike and cycle – even if you don't really know where you are going, it should be worth your while when you get there. The Irish are justifiably proud of their hospitality, and although not every Irishman is a William Butler Yeats, most have the 'gift of the gab' and will be only too happy to pass the time of day with you. Head to the local pub, enjoy the stout, and ask around for Bed and Breakfast. Unfortunately, Ireland is one of the most expensive countries in Europe (and this is most noticeable in the cost of eating and sleeping), so it is wise to budget carefully before coming.

• **Getting there:** The shipping lines which operate regular sailings from Britain to Ireland are Sealink, Stena Line and B&I. B&I offer students and IYHF card holders special discounts. Inter-railers get a 50 per cent discount, while students get 25 per cent off (50 per cent if you have a 'travel-save' stamp). See USIT, 52 Grosvenor Gardens, London SW1 (Tel. 071–730 8111), for details. If you're not a student, check all the other prices. Eurotrain offer a train/ferry ticket from London to Dublin for about £55 return on an

ISIC which is the best value of all. Irish Ferries operate Le Havre–Rosslare and Cherbourg–Rosslare, while Brittany Ferries operate Roscoff–Cork. Eurail Pass holders get to travel free on both services to Rosslare which is a considerable saving as the normal fare is around IR£63 ($100) adult single, IR£99 ($160) adult return. Inter-railers, again, get 50 per cent off these services.

IRISH RAILWAYS
(Iarnrod Eireann, IE)

Eurail Passes are valid in the Republic, as is Inter-Rail. Travelling on trains is extremely expensive in Ireland, but ISIC card-holders with a valid 'travelsave' stamp can receive up to 50 per cent off. A 'travelsave' stamp costs IR£7, available from USIT in either London or Dublin, and it entitles you to half price on all IE train and BE bus single adult fares over IR£2 on trains and provincial buses, half price on all single or return fares on Northern Ireland Railways and similar discounts on B&I car ferries and ships to the Aran Islands. The Irish Railways' Rambler tickets are a more expensive alternative, available from any station. The tickets can be for 4 of 8 days (IR£45), 8 of 15 days (IR£60), or 15 of 30 days (IR£90). Irish Bus (Bus Eireann) offer a similar deal: 3 of 8 days (IR£26), 8 of 15 days (IR£60), 15 of 30 days (IR£90). Combined rail and bus tickets are definitely the best value, with an 8-day ticket (IR£78) and a 15-day ticket (IR£115) being available. The relatively new Irish Emerald Card entitles you to free second-class travel on rail and bus both north (Northern Ireland) and south (the Republic) of the border: 8 of 15 days (IR£105), or 15 of 30 days (IR£180). Trains are reasonably fast around the Dublin area and to major towns, but don't expect speeds similar to those on the continent. In many areas (especially in the west) buses are the main form of transport.

- **Inter-Rail bonuses:**

Irish Ferries		Reduction %
Rosslare/Cork	Le Havre	50
Sealink Stena Line UK Ltd.		
Rosslare	Fishguard	30
Dun Laoghaire	Holyhead	50
B&I Line		
Dublin	Holyhead	50
Brittany Ferries		
Cork	Roscoff	50

- **Eurail bonuses:** Free:
—Ferry crossings on Irish Ferries between Rosslare (Ireland) and Le Havre (France) 21 hours or Cherbourg (France) 17 hours, and between Cork (Ireland) and Le Havre (France) 21½ hours. If cabin accommodation is requested an extra charge will be made. Port taxes are extra and payable in Irish pounds. During July and August advance reservation is recommended. It is compulsory if cabin accommodation is requested. Check the sailing schedule always.
—Free service on Expressway buses of Bus Eireann.

TRAIN INFORMATION

- **Reservations:** Are not necessary. If you want to make one, you must do so by 5 p.m. on the preceding day.

- **Night travel and eating on trains:** There are no night services in Ireland. Most long-distance trains have catering facilities ranging from bar service to set meals, but these are quite expensive.

- **Bikes:** Are often the only way to get to the local hostel and see the neighbourhood. They cost about IR£5 a day from most towns.

TOURIST INFORMATION

There are eighty-six offices scattered throughout Ireland, twenty-eight of which are open all year round, with others open Mon.–Fri.: 9 a.m.–5 p.m., Sat.: 9 a.m.–1 p.m. in summer. Each office gives information on its own region as well as for all of Ireland. They have a good selection of maps and literature; although these will cost you, the staff are always friendly.

Not all of Ireland is run as efficiently as the tourist board, so use their offices fully while you have the chance.

- **ISIC bonuses:** With the ISIC you can get a Travel-Save Stamp ticket. This entitles you to up to 50 per cent off all one-way journeys, on buses and trains, as well as reductions to some cinemas, theatres, and museums.

- **Money matters:** 1 Irish pound (£1), or punt, = 100 pence (p.). Banking hours are Mon.–Fri.: 10 a.m.–12.30 p.m., 1.30 p.m.–3 p.m. with an extension to 5 p.m. on Thurs. in Dublin. Some Trustee

Savings Banks stay open till 5 p.m., depending upon the day. For the rest of the country late-opening days vary. The British pound is now nearly equal to the Irish pound and is not interchangeable.

• **Post offices, shops and museums:** Tend to work around a 9 a.m.–5.30 p.m. routine. Some local shops stay open late, some to midnight. Museums vary the most, so always check with the nearest tourist information office.

SLEEPING

Hotels are very expensive so your best plan is to stick to approved Irish Tourist Board bed and breakfast (B&B, IR£10–15) and hostels (IR£4–8). Most approved premises display the triangular shamrock sign. For advance information on youth hostels contact An Oige, 39 Mountjoy Square, Dublin (Tel. 01–363111). There are approximately 40 registered holiday hostels, most of them marketed under the banner of Irish Budget Hostels, Co. Clare. There are also around 50 independent hostels of all sizes and with ranges of activities, who market themselves under the co-operative Independent Owners' Association. While some of the Association's listed hostels are of good standard, others are not. The Irish Tourist Board do not approve them, so be warned. Their information office is at Dooey Hostel, Glencolumcille, Co. Donegal (Tel. 073–30130). Get a copy of their directory, cost IR£1, from this address. The overall recommended guide is the Ireland '93 Accommodation (IR£4), which gives a complete list of all approved Bed and Breakfast, youth hostel, holiday hostel and caravan and camping accommodation. It is available in all Tourist Information Offices, as are the Irish Farm Holidays Guide and their guide on Town & Country Homes (IR£2). This lists all the approved B&Bs. If you require it, they'll book you a bed by phone for a small charge. Youth hostels tend to be situated in the most scenic parts of the country but are not always near a station. Beds cost between IR£4 and IR£8, depending on the hostel. Camping costs IR£3–IR£6 a tent on official sites, and is only for those who don't mind getting wet. (Tourist information provide a booklet priced at IR£1.)

EATING AND NIGHTLIFE

Food is also quite expensive in Ireland, particularly in tourist traps, and the only way to survive on a tight budget is to rely on the very good bakeries and 'pub grub' offers in most bars. Some restaurants outside Dublin shut by about 9 p.m., so eat early. Junk food addicts are more than adequately catered for, as in all cities. Ask at tourist information for their useful booklet 'Special Value Tourist Menu', which lists many restaurants throughout Ireland that provide enjoyable three-course meals at fixed prices. For bargains, you could turn to Chinese and Indian foods, or live off fish'n'chips, but bar food will keep you well fed for a reasonable price. Some guidebooks politely call Irish food wholesome, rather than basic, which is perhaps a more apt description. Pubs and cafés have a reputation for offering a wide variety of traditional dishes (tripe and drisin) at the aforementioned 'reasonable prices', but other than them, the only time you are likely to get the chance of traditional Irish cooking is in a guesthouse or B&B, if you are lucky, with Irish stew or boiled bacon and cabbage appearing on the menu. As eating out is so incredibly expensive, the pub will have to be the mainstay of the budget traveller. Pubs are referred to a lot in this section of the book: this is because they are the focal point of Irish life. Here you will find great foods, good beer and a real chance to meet the Irish who are a lovely, warm lot. Ask about to discover which pubs have folk/rebel music and dancing (ceilidh), and where the best draught Guinness is. If you need to relax, then do so over a pint of stout, while listening to the local characters swapping stories. With a little coaxing, these lads will be only too happy to let you know about the legends and folklore of the area, whether it be fairies, witches, leprechauns, or old-fashioned wars. And if sport is what grabs you, make tracks for the local Gaelic football pitch, and catch a game of the ancient Irish sport of hurling. Played with wooden bats (cumanns) and a leather ball (slitter), it is fast and furious, and one of the most exciting games in the world.

Dublin

There's no denying Dublin has character. The contrast of the elegant eighteenth-century quarter with the damp dingy slums only a mile or two away is as much a comment on the Irish mentality as anything. In Gaelic, the city's name means Blackpool – but this city is the very antithesis of that resort. This is the setting James Joyce used for *Ulysses* – his own home town. It's a rich experience, so don't try and hurry it.

STATION FACILITIES

Dublin has two main stations: Connolly, with northbound trains, and Heuston Station for trains to the south and west.

	CONNOLLY STATION
Train information	Mon.–Sat.: 9 a.m.–6 p.m. Use Booking Office on Sundays (Tel. 366222)
Booking office	Mon.–Sat.: 9 a.m.–7 p.m. Sun.: 10 a.m.–6 p.m.
Left-luggage store	Mon.–Sat.: 7.40 a.m.–9.30 p.m. Sun.: 9.15 a.m.–1 p.m., 5 p.m.–10 p.m.
Restaurant, Buffet	Mon.–Sat.: 7.30 a.m.–7.30 p.m.
Shops	Mon.–Sat.: 7.50 a.m.–6.30 p.m.

	HEUSTON
Train information	Mon.–Sat.: 7.20 a.m.–10 p.m. (Tel. 365421)
Reservations	Mon.–Sat.: 7 a.m.–9 p.m. Sun.: 8 a.m.–9/10 p.m. (Tel. 363333)
Left-luggage store	Mon.–Sat.: 7.20 a.m.–9 p.m. Sun.: 8 a.m.–3 p.m., 5 p.m.–9 p.m.
Restaurant	Mon.–Sat.: 7.45 a.m.–7 p.m. Sun.: 8.30 a.m.–10.30 a.m., 5 p.m.–7 p.m.

Daily trains to: Belfast, Sligo, Rosslare (Connolly); Cork, Galway, Limerick (Heuston).

TOURIST INFORMATION

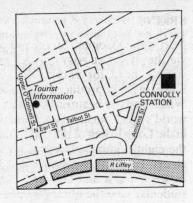

Main office: 14 Upper O'Connell St (Tel. 747733), open Mon.– Sat.: 9 a.m.–5 p.m. June: 8.30 a.m.–6 p.m., July and August: Mon.–Sat.: 8.30 a.m.–8 p.m., Sun.: 10.30 a.m.–2 p.m. Money exchange facilities provided Mon.–Sat.: 9 a.m.–5 p.m.; there is also a branch at the ferry pier at Dun Laoghaire, and at Dublin Airport.

● **Addresses:**

GENERAL POST OFFICE: O'Connell St, open daily from 8 a.m. to 8 p.m., Sundays 10.30 a.m.–6.30 p.m.

AMEX: 116 Grafton St (Tel. 772874), open Mon.–Fri.: 9 a.m.–5 p.m., Sat.: 9 a.m.–5 p.m.

ISIC–USIT (IRISH STUDENT TRAVEL AGENCY): Aston Quay, O'Connell Bridge, open Mon.–Fri.: 9 a.m.–6 p.m., Sat.: 11 a.m.–4 p.m. (Tel. 778117). Also a Eurotrain office.

UK EMBASSY: 33 Merrion Rd (Tel. 695211).

US EMBASSY: 42 Elgin Rd, Ballsbridge (Tel. 688777).

CANADIAN EMBASSY: 65–68 St Stephen's Green (Tel. 781988).

YOUTH INFORMATION CENTRE: Sackville Place (off O'Connell St) (Tel. 786844), open Mon.–Wed.: 9.30 a.m.–6 p.m., Thurs.–Sat.: 9.30 a.m.–5 p.m. Information on organizations, travel and accommodation.

EUROTRAIN/COMPASS TRAVEL: 34 Lower Abbey St (Tel. 741777).

PHONE CODE: 01.

● **Getting about:**

City buses operate from 7.30 a.m. to 11.30 p.m. Many of them start from O'Connell Street in the centre. You won't need them for sightseeing as it's all easily negotiated by foot ('shanks's mare' as they call it). Tel. 734222 for information on all public transport. Buy a weekly bus pass (IR£10.50) or bus and train pass (IR£14 plus ID photo for ticket) from Dublin Bus in Upper O'Connell Street.

SEEING

Start with O'Connell Street and your visit to the tourist office, then via the GENERAL POST OFFICE, where the Easter uprising of 1916 started, head for TRINITY COLLEGE. The oldest in Ireland, this university has produced such men as Thomas Moore and Oscar Wilde. See the beautiful LIBRARY which is the home of some of the world's most outstanding illuminated manuscripts. Pride of place, in the Long Room of the Old Library, is reserved for two volumes of the eighth-century 'Book of Kells' which you can look at free of charge between November and March or pay if you are visiting between April and October. Admission is IR£1.75 (IR£1.50 for students), and the library is open Mon.–Fri.: 9.30 a.m.–4.45 p.m.; Sun.: 9.30 a.m.–12.45 p.m. A recent addition to Dublin's list of tourist attractions is the College's 'The Dublin Experience'. Open seven days a week (10 a.m.–5 p.m.), this sophisticated multimedia interpretation of the city, and the country's history, costs IR£2.50 (IR£1.50 for students). At the back of the university, through the grounds, sit the Dail and Seanad, the seats of the Irish Parliament, at Leinster House on Kildare Street. You can visit only when Parliament is not in session. In the same street is the NATIONAL MUSEUM (closed Mondays), which is good for early historians and has a comprehensive exhibition on the 1916 uprising. Around the corner, on Merrion Street, is the NATIONAL GALLERY which has an excellent collection of Rembrandts along with a good modern section and several rooms devoted to portraits of modern Irish literary men such as George Bernard Shaw and Brendan Behan.

At Castle Street is, predictably, DUBLIN CASTLE – the historic heart of the city. Preceded by a Gaelic Ring Fort and a Viking Fortress, there are still significant portions of the original thirteenth-century Norman Castle remaining. The recently restored Gothic CHAPEL ROYAL features a particularly high standard of plaster and carved-oak decorations. Another component of the post-Medieval castle is the STATE APARTMENTS, which were built as the residential quarters of the Viceregal Court. These, along with the VIKING ('UNDERCROFT') FORTRESS and the Chapel Royal, are all open to visitors during the week from 10 a.m.–12.15 p.m. and 2 p.m.–5 p.m. and at weekends, and bank holidays, from 2 p.m.–5 p.m. As far as churches go, CHRIST CHURCH (started in 1038), and the twelfth-century ST PATRICK'S CATHEDRAL are the names to look for.

The most elegant buildings of Dublin are said to be the CUSTOM HOUSE, on the north bank of the River Liffey, and the Bank of Ireland in College Green (formerly Parliament House).

The JOYCE MUSEUM at Martello Tower (a little way out at Sandycove) looks at the life and works of the Irish author, James Joyce. Pick up the 'Ulysses' map from tourist information. For a breath of fresh air, head for ST STEPHEN'S GREEN, an oasis in the middle of the city and a popular place for office workers to enjoy packed lunches if the weather is fine. Just off the park, at Earsfort Street, is the new National Concert Hall, which features music to suit all tastes. Alternatively, you might like to visit the famous PHOENIX PARK, the largest enclosed park in Europe, which has featured everything from horse racing through rock concerts to a huge papal mass. Phoenix Park has the second highest obelisk in the world and one of the world's oldest zoos, famous for breeding lions. Don't be tempted to pitch your tent here, as the official residence of the President of Ireland is in the park and the police take a dim view of campers in the vicinity. Across the river from Phoenix Park is KILMAINHAM GAOL, a central character of Ireland's passionate history, as the leaders of the rebellions of 1799, 1803, 1848, 1867 and 1916 were detained here. A visit to the gaol includes a guided tour, an audio-visual presentation and an exhibition. Opening hours are June–Sept. 11 a.m.–6 p.m. daily. Off season: Sun. and Wed. only 2–6 p.m. Admission: adults IR£1.50, students 60p. For a few free pints of Guinness, go to their brewery at JAMES' GATE, watch the film about its production, then sup up.

SLEEPING

You can expect to pay IR£18 upwards in a hotel, so head for the student and youth hostels. Go round to the USIT office, Aston Quay (Tel. 6798833).

International Student Accommodation and Activity Centre (ISAAC), 2–5 Frenchman's Lane (Tel. 363877), is a very central old warehouse and the best deal in Dublin at around IR£5 a night. Also try The Young Traveller at St Mary's Place (Tel. 305000). It's a lot cleaner, but expect to pay IR£8.50 for B&B.

• **Youth hostels:** Mountjoy St (Tel. 301766) is very good and costs between IR£7.50–IR£9. The YWCA at Radcliffe Hall, St John's Rd

(Tel. 2694521) and Lower Baggot St are also worth checking out, as are the two independent hostels that charge between IR£5 and IR£7 a night: Cardijin House at 15 Talbot Street (Tel. 788484) and Kinlay House at 2–12 Lord Edward Street (Tel. 6796644).

• **Bed and breakfasts:** Try any along the Clontarf road, with views out to Dublin Bay. Particularly good is Mrs McKenna at 110 Sandford Rd, Ranelagh (Tel. 971375), as she always makes you feel very welcome. Or the Drumcondra area: Mrs Mooney, 20 St Lawrence Road, Clontarf (Tel. 339097) gives you a warm welcome, pleasant rooms and a wonderful full Irish breakfast to start off your day. Also check out Mrs Ryan, 10 Distillery Road (Tel. 374147). Expect to pay around IR£12 upwards for shared rooms. As these places are all in the suburbs, it's a good idea to make a reservation through the Tourist Office, approximate cost IR£1 + deposit, before heading out of the city.

EATING AND NIGHTLIFE

There are the usual fast-food chains in the centre, and also quite a few pubs now offering excellent-value lunches. If you're in town for a while, it's worth buying the tourist board's booklet 'Special Value Tourist Menu' which has a good choice of eating places in Dublin, offering three-course meals at fixed prices.

Anywhere around the university is your best bet, with restaurants catering for the student market. Try the students' restaurant in Earl's Port Terrace. Bewleys have cafés in Grafton St, South George St, and Westmoreland St, all doing good meals at reasonable prices. Cheaper places to eat include Flanagans in O'Connell St (across from the Tourist Information Centre), and Pat Grace's Fried Chicken Store in Merrion Row – good value fish and chicken dishes. Shop for food in Moore Street.

This is the home of the pub. It's at the centre of Ireland's social life, and the atmosphere in a good Dublin pub takes some beating. The following pubs all have something unique, whether it be folk music, good beer or a great atmosphere. Most have all three, and are the sort of places you'll be looking for to eat, drink and make merry: O'Donoghue's, Merrion Row, is always lively as is the Baggot Inn, Baggot Street. Mulligan's Pub, Poolbeg Street; Scruffy Murphy's, off Mount Street; An Beal Boacht, Ranelagh Bridge and The Four Seasons, Capel Street.

The South-east

Counties Wexford, Carlow, Kilkenny, Tipperary and Waterford are the home of Cistercian abbeys, Anglo-Norman castles, race-courses, crystal factories, early Christian relics, and tributes to the occasional US president who claimed Irish roots.

The Wicklow Mountains lie only ten miles from Dublin, and a day or two exploring this mountainous area from the base towns of Glendalough (with its eighth-century monastery) or Wicklow can be rewarding, before crossing the county border south into Wexford. ENNISCORTHY is a small town in the Slaney valley and on the main line south from Dublin. It was a storm centre during the 1798 rebellion against the British. The sixteenth-century castle is now a folk museum, and if you hit it in the first week of July, expect an even-better-than-usual atmosphere, as the Strawberry Festival livens things up considerably. The town also offers excellent angling. Further south and west, the port of New Ross contains St Maty's Abbey, with the largest collection of sepulchral monuments in Ireland. It also has the 600-acre forest of the John F. Kennedy Arboretum Park, nature-trails, gardens and panoramic views (May to August: 10 a.m.–8 p.m.; April and September: 10 a.m.–6.30 p.m.; October to March, 10 a.m.–5 p.m.). IR£1 admission for pedestrians. In WEXFORD, see the BULL RING and ruins of the twelfth-century SELSKAR ABBEY, and ask for information on the free guided walking tours at tourist information on Crescent Quay.

On the road into Carlow County from Bunclody, you might care to turn off the road to Tullow, to see the herbaceous ALTAMONT GARDENS (open every Sunday, 2 p.m.–6 p.m., till the end of October, admission £1, Tel. 0503–57128) with its homemade teas. The site dates from 1850. Nearby, CLONMORE CASTLE was completed in 1180 from the stones of a ruined abbey begun in the sixth century, but it is perhaps more for its Megalithic field monuments (Dolmen), that Carlow County is more widely known. Particularly noteworthy are the Haroldstown Portal Tomb (northeast of Tullow) and the Brownshill Dolmen (reputedly the largest in Europe, and dating from 2000 BC). TULLOW possesses a museum housed in a former church (open every Sunday afternoon of the year, and also open Wednesday afternoons in the summer), by the Slaney River Bridge. Nearby CARLOW TOWN, the capital, has a county museum (May to September: 11 a.m.–5.30 p.m., adults IR£1) in the Town Hall, and a castle dating from 1207 (access permission obtainable from the mineral water company who own the site it stands on). Boats are available for hire on the single waterway system of the Barrow Navigation. LEIGHLINBRIDGE has the oldest bridge on the system, guarded by the ruins of a twelfth-century Anglo-Norman castle. BAGENALSTOWN is a bit of a curiosity, its original plan being modelled on Athens. Also on the site is fourteenth-century BALLYMOON CASTLE. For walkers, the South Leinster Way is a pleasant component of the proposed round-Ireland walking route, from Wicklow in the northeast, via towpaths along the River Barrow, to GRAIGNAMANAGH in the south.

This ancient town, at the south-eastern point of Kilkenny County, contains the massive thirteenth-century Norman DUISKE ABBEY, fully restored, with a larger-than-life effigy of a Norman Knight inside. Guided tours of both the Abbey and the town can be arranged via the Kilkenny Tourist Office. Up the road at THOMAS-TOWN, lies the twelfth-century Cistercian JERPOINT ABBEY, well preserved and restored, with a guide service from mid-June to September (10 a.m.–6 p.m., adults 80p). The small town of KELLS, just west of Thomastown, is noteworthy as the only completely medieval walled town remaining in Ireland, with seven towers and some of its once-extensive monastic buildings still preserved today. KILKENNY CITY itself grew from a sixth-century monastic settlement established by St Canice (Cill Chainigh, Church of Canice). Under the Normans, it grew in importance; its peak of some 1500 years as a centre of civilization and culture came in 1642, when it became a major political capital during the Confederation of Kilkenny. ST CANICE'S CATHEDRAL was completed in 1285 (although its Round Tower is some 300 years older, and offers a staggering panorama to those who ascend its 167 steps), and as well as its own elaborate ornamentation, this impressive Gothic building has a large collection of sculpted monuments. The acoustics of this structure can be heard to best effect when the city's annual Arts Week takes place in August. Walking tours of the city as a whole depart from the tourist office at Shee Alms House, Rose Inn St (Tel. 21755) four times a day from March to October, and by arrangement in the off-season. They can also fix any accommodation problems for you. The city's CASTLE was completed in the fourteenth century, and acted as the home of one of the most powerful of the Anglo-Norman families in

Ireland. Still undergoing restoration, the LONG GALLERY of the building has an interesting collection of family portraits, but the building is perhaps most remarkable for its modern art gallery. (Castle opens from 10 a.m.–7 p.m. every day, adults IR£1 admission.) Also worth visiting in Kilkenny City is the ST FRANCIS ABBEY BREWERY, the ruined abbey being located in the yard of Smithwick's Brewery. Guided tours are available each day at 3 p.m. for the brewery (from June to 1 September). For sporting enthusiasts, a hurling match takes place most summer Sundays, in the city's NOWLAN PARK.

Crossing the border from Kilkenny into Tipperary County, seven ornate early Christian HIGH CROSSES can be found at Ahenny, Killamery, Kilree and Kilkieran. CARRICK-ON-SUIR contains a fine Elizabethan MANOR HOUSE residence of 1568, next to the remains of the c. 1450 CARRICK CASTLE (open mid-June to early September, adults 80p). On the way west to the racecourse at CLONMEL (one of many, in this, the horse county of Eire), is the TIPPERARY CRYSTAL WORKS, a recently established industry that carries on the region's world heritage of hand-cut crystal from glass blown on site. Guided tours give visitors the opportunity to view all stages of crystal production. The NORTH MUNSTER WAY can be picked up near here on the banks of the Suir, and followed on via Clonmel to the borders of County Cork. A medieval ecclesiastical centre, CASHEL is the location of the ROCK OF CASHEL, with the remains of its magnificent cathedral and Round Tower dominating the countryside. CORMAC'S CHAPEL is the finest remaining example from this period of architecture. In addition, a subterranean museum displays items of historical interest, and a full guide service is provided (June to mid-September, 9 a.m.–7.30 p.m., off-season 9.30 a.m.–4.30 p.m., admission IR£1.50). The nearby BRU BORU was recently developed as a major cultural centre for Irish music, drama and tradition, in the shadow of Cashel's ancient rock. North-east of Cashel, on the border with Kilkenny, are the SLIEVEARDAGH HILLS, an area strongly connected with many Irish groups, including the revolutionary nineteenth-century 'Young Irelanders' movement, and the local development of a coal-mining industry. The social history and geography of the area are the focus of a study weekend held in July. Passing through the capital TIPPERARY TOWN and its racecourse will bring you to the town of CAHIR and its CASTLE, built in the middle of the River Suir, and containing an audio-visual unit for the whole south-eastern area, and a full guide service; this facility is open from June to September 10 a.m.–7.30 p.m., and for the rest of the year 10 a.m.–6 p.m. each day except Sundays, 2 p.m.–6 p.m. (Adults IR£1, Tel. 052–41011). South and west towards the KNOCKMEALDOWN MOUNTAINS at the border with Waterford County, the limestone cave of MITCHELSTOWN should be visited (open all year, with guide service, 10 a.m.–6 p.m., admission IR£2, Tel. 052–67246), before passing on to the PRESIDENT REAGAN CENTRE at BALLYPOREEN, commemorating the birthplace of the former US President's ancestors, and his visit there in 1984. (Opened by appointment.)

County Waterford is best entered via THE VEE, a switchback route through the KNOCKMEALDOWN MOUNTAINS, which allows the visitor the best views of the beautiful border area. Nestling in the southern foothills is MOUNT MELLERAY, a Cistercian Foundation with over 60 monks. Proceeding south from here to the cathedral town of LISMORE, one can visit the majestic CASTLE perched above the River Blackwater, which is also the home of some magnificent gardens (open 1.45 p.m.–4.45 p.m. from 7 May to 7 September, except Saturdays, admission IR£1.50, Tel. 058–54424). Directly east of Lismore is DUNGARVAN, the historical and medieval significance of which is under-scored by the substantial Anglo-Norman CASTLE, which was sacked during the Cromwellian Wars. Portions of this castle still overlook the town's harbour. ST AUGUSTINE'S CHURCH in nearby ABBEYSIDE incorporates sections of an abbey of 1290 from the same site. And if, at the end of a hard day, you are seeking a change from the medieval castles and the early Christian monasteries so liberally distributed around southeast Ireland, then you could do worse than follow the N25 north from the coast, until you get to BALLINAVOUGH (near LEMYBRIEN), where the singular collection of antique dolls and toys (dating from 1820) of Mrs Helen Collendar can be viewed between 6 p.m.–9 p.m. every evening from 1 June to 1 September, at her home (admission IR£2).

Finally, head east to WATERFORD CITY, only an hour away from Rosslare, which has the ferry-link with Fishguard. A port founded by the Danes, it grew to be Ireland's fifth largest city, and walking tours of the city leave the Tourist Office (41, The Quay) and end at Reginald's Tower, visiting 10 historic locations en route, at 11 a.m. and 3 p.m., Monday to Saturday (IR£2 per person, information from the Tourist Office, or Tel. 051–94577 outside normal hours). REGINALD'S TOWER is a Viking fortification built about 1000 AD, which now contains the WATERFORD CIVIC AND MARITIME MUSEUM (10 a.m.–7 p.m. Monday to Friday, 10 a.m.–3 p.m. on Saturday). The FRENCH CHURCH was given to Huguenot refugees for worship in the seventeenth century, and is free to visit. The WATERFORD HERITAGE CENTRE is a well presented interpretative centre for the Viking and early Norman settlement of Waterford (Monday to Friday, 10 a.m.–1 p.m. and 2 p.m.–5 p.m., admission IR£1). Famous for its crystal, the WATERFORD CRYSTAL CENTRE is a logical place to visit at Kilbarry, with regular factory tours and a video presentation (tours at 10.15 a.m., 11 a.m., 11.45 a.m., 1.45 a.m. and 2.30 p.m. Monday to Friday; Video Presentation Area open Monday to Friday 9 a.m.–5 p.m.; Gallery Area open Monday to Friday 9 a.m.–5 p.m. and 10 a.m.–1 p.m. on Saturdays, until 11 September.)

Cork (Corcaigh)

3½ hours away from Dublin on the main line, Cork is a convenient stopover on the way to the south-west of Eire. Ireland's second largest city, it is bursting with history and charm. Its reputation as the 'Venice of Ireland' comes from its construction on a marsh ('corcaigh'), which has led to a large network of bridges being built to span the River Lee and her tributaries.

Starting in Washington Street, you can see the neo-classical construction of the COURTHOUSE, and further along on the Western Road is University College Cork, as well as the old COUNTY GAOL, where many republican prisoners were held and executed during the War of Independence. The gates of the Gaol are a replica of those at the Temple of Bacchus, in Athens. Off the Western Road is Fitzgerald's Park, which houses Cork's MUSEUM (10 a.m.–4 p.m.). If you are in the mood for a peaceful stroll or a picnic, then the Lee fields provide a perfect setting with beautiful scenery on the banks of the Lee. ST ANNE'S CHURCH ('Shandon') is known locally as the 'four-faced liar', and offers the opportunity of a go at ringing the bells, for visitors so inclined.

In Bishop Street, the large Gothic ST FINBARR'S CATHEDRAL stands on the site of the Saint's original monastic settlement of 620 AD, and boasts a golden angel who, legend has it, will blow its horn to signal the end of the world. Near St Finbarr's, on Barrack Street, is the ELIZABETH FORT: a star-shaped building which dates back to the sixteenth century. A walk down towards the docks area of the city will bring you to the City Hall. Enter to see the busts of the two Lord Mayors (Tomas McCurtain and Traolach McSuibhne) who died during the War of Independence.

Cork also boasts two breweries, 'Beamish and Crawford' in South Main Street and 'Murphy's' in Lady's Well: it's worth enquiring about brewery tours, as they do happen occasionally.

A good day-trip is to Dundanion Castle in BLACKROCK (take the No.2 bus) where in 1669, William Penn set sail for America. Just up the road, Blackrock Castle is a fine setting for a pint and a sandwich. Also worth a visit is BLARNEY CASTLE, just six miles down the road from Cork, the site of the famous Blarney Stone, where legend says you can gain the 'gift of the gab', once you have paid the IR£2.50 (students IR£1.50) for the honour of kissing it. A short (15 km) but sweet rail-journey away is COBH for a day out. Information on additional guided walking tours (two evenings a week in July and August, from outside the tourist office) can be obtained from the tourist office (Tel. 273251) on Grand Parade Street (open 9 a.m.—7 p.m. in the summer, Sundays 11 a.m.–1 p.m.).

SLEEPING

Avoid hotels as they are unbelievably expensive. Instead, head for the Western Road where you will find plenty of Bed and Breakfasts (B&B) and the Redclyffe 'An Oige' youth hostel (Tel. 432891). Independent hostels can be found at Sheila's Cork Tourist Hostel in Wellington Road (Tel. 021–505562, IR£5.50 per night) and Campus House at 3 Woodlands View, Western Road (Tel. 021–343531, same charge). Also, you could try Isaac's Hostel on McCurtain Street (only five minutes from the train station) and Kinley House on Infirmary Road (near the old North Infirmary, take the No.3 bus northwards). For all hostels, you should expect to pay between IR£4–8, and IR£10–12 for Bed and Breakfasts, many of which can be found in the university area. If you prefer the attractions of the open air, then the campsite on the Doughcloyne Road (take the No.14 bus) charges IR£3 per tent.

EATING AND NIGHTLIFE

Eating out in Cork can be an expensive business, so examine any menu carefully before ordering. The Lon Wah Chinese in Oliver Plunket Street does a good value high tea. There are plenty of fast-food joints in the city centre for burger addicts, and Garaboldies Pizzas are worth trying (off Paul Street). Best advice is to head for the pubs, where everything is happening, and fill up on pub grub over a good Cork pint of stout. For a possible added attraction, the Western Road also boasts the 'Western Star', frequently a watering hole of Cork's many international rugby stalwarts. For those who require more after all this, the De Lacy House (Oliver Plunket Street) offers the best in bands and a disco. Likewise, the Grand Parade Hotel (Grand Parade) gives a great choice with its two stages and three discos. But without a doubt, the most unusual venue in Cork is Nancy Speirs Backstage in Barrack Street, with its excellent architecture. To sample a local ceilidh (traditional dance) inquire at the Aras, Conradh na Gaeilge at Dyke Parade.

The South-west: West Cork and Kerry

Known as the 'Garden of Ireland', with its rugged unspoilt landscapes, commanding mountain ranges (Ireland's highest), breathtakingly beautiful lakes and islands, this region has people who will be more than happy to pass the time with you. It is practically impossible to travel through towns and villages here, without encountering the myths and legends which haunt the area. Old Celtic crosses, ruined abbeys, forts and castles, ringforts (mystical places where the Celts believed the fairy gods lived) are not in short supply here. Take care, however: this is the land of the 'banshee' (a mythical ghost who forewarns a death in your family if you are unfortunate enough to hear her scream), leprechauns (spirits who jealously guard the pot of gold that resides at the end of each rainbow), and tree gods (who will 'vix' or curse you, should you bring harm to the tree that they are assigned to guard).

Seventeen miles from Cork is Kinsale (Cionn-tsaile), an area steeped in history, for it was here that King Brian Boru defeated the Vikings at the 'old head of Kinsale' on the coast, where the ruins of a number of battlements and castles still remain. In 1601, the Spanish landed here to help O'Neill from the North against the English, only to suffer defeat a year later. A small, attractive fishing village, Kinsale is known as Ireland's culinary capital, and there is no shortage of Bed and Breakfasts here. Along with its twelfth-century church, 2 km up the road lies the Summer Cove Youth Hostel (Tel. 021–772309, IR£4 per night, March to December). Also at the same price is Dempsey's Hostel (Tel. 021–772124) on Eastern Road. For a great night out with traditional music (and the possibility of a ceilidh) head to 'The Spaniard' on the hill.

The town of Bantry (Beanntrai) is a peaceful place famous for its summer regatta and beautiful views of Bantry Bay. For B&B head to Atlanta House on Main Street (027–50237) where Pat will make you feel very welcome indeed. For a good meal, reasonably priced, try Pete's Grill, washed down with a pint and some atmosphere in the Anchor Bar near the bus stop. For a day-trip from Bantry, go to Glengariff (Gleann Garbh), for a walk up to Lady Bantry's View will provide you with an excellent all-round view of the countryside and bay for miles around. Alternatively, head to the parks and mountains of Goughan Burra (source of the River Lee) for a perfect picnic site. A third option for a day-trip is to the Island of Cape Clear (Oilean Cleire). Take the bus to Skibbereen (An Sciobarin), famous for its international busking festival, and from there travel on to Baltimore (Dun na Sead), where a ferry (IR£5 return) will take you out (remember to check the times of the boat back!) to an island so peaceful and trouble-free that there is no need for a Garda (police) station there. An Gaeilge (Irish Gaelic) is still the main language of the island, but everyone can also speak English. See the Ring of St Ciaran's Church and the Holy Well there, then head to the pub and chat to the locals. For your sleeping needs, there is a hostel at the South Harbour (028–39144, IR£4.50 per night).

Limerick

Ireland's third largest city is on the River Shannon, the longest navigable river in the British Isles. It is a port town with Georgian houses and elegant buildings which has had its ups and downs over the centuries. In recent years it has greatly benefited from the tax-free area round about nearby Shannon Airport which has brought much employment and economic regeneration. Buildings to see in the city include THE GRANARY, a former grain store later adapated to a bonded warehouse and now tastefully adapted for modern use, housing a pub and the local library. The tourist office is on Arthurs Quay (Tel. 061–317522). Also worth checking out are the CUSTOM HOUSE, TOWN HALL, KING JOHN'S CASTLE (built in 1210), and the nearby twelfth-century ST MARY'S CATHEDRAL. The town is famous for its beautiful handmade lace, and the Limerick Lace Collection can be seen in the CONVENT OF THE GOOD SHEPHERD in Clare St. (Open business hours on weekdays only).

The youth hostel is at 1 Pery Square (Tel. 061–314672). Ennis Road seems to be the place for B&B, but always check the prices, for while some are cheap, there are several which are very expensive indeed. The Limerick Hostel at Georges Quay (Tel. 061–45222) falls into the cheaper category, and charges IR£3.90 a night, with meals extra.

Eight miles from Limerick City on the main Shannon Airport/ Ennis/Galway road stands the fully restored fifteenth-century BUNRATTY CASTLE which houses a superb collection of fourteenth- to seventeenth-century furniture and furnishings. It is open to visitors daily, and medieval banquets and entertainments are held twice nightly. The FOLK PARK in the grounds of the castle contains farmhouses and cottages, a forge and other typical features of the traditional way of life. Just around the coast from Galway in the North Shannon region is Ballyvaughan which houses the spectacular Aillwee Cave, a 2-million-year-old cave complete with stalagmites and an underground waterfall, and once a prehistoric refuge for bears. It is open daily in the summer from 10 a.m.–7 p.m.

Galway

Galway is a seaport and university town which was ruled in the sixteenth century by Anglo-Norman tribes. It had extensive trade with Spain, particularly in the wine business, and it retains some Spanish architectural remains such as the Spanish Arch, one of the gateways to the old town.

TOURIST INFORMATION AND ADDRESSES

TOURIST OFFICE (Tel. 63081): One block east of the station, Victoria Place off Eyre Sq. Open Mon.–Fri.: 9 a.m.–6.45 p.m. Sat.: 9 a.m.–12.45 p.m. Also on the Promenade. Open June–August, Mon.–Sun.: 9 a.m.–6 p.m.
POST OFFICE: Eglinton St. Open Mon.–Sat.: 9 a.m.–5.30 p.m.
USIT (STUDENT TRAVEL): University College, New Science Building, Galway (Tel. 24601). Open Mon.–Fri. 10 a.m.–1 p.m., 2 p.m.–5 p.m.

SEEING

Eyre Square, where the station is, is the city centre. It is also the main bus station. Note the SPANISH ARCH, which is a half-mile walk from Eyre Square down Shop St, which becomes High St and finally Quay St. LYNCH'S CASTLE, down Shop St, is fourteenth-century, as is the CHURCH OF ST NICHOLAS, where is it said that Columbus prayed before setting out on one of his voyages of discovery. Walk round by the banks of the River Corrib and see the salmon jump at SALMON WEIR BRIDGE in the spawning season, and in the summer evenings check out the *Simsa*, a traditional music presentation in the Irish-speaking theatre (Taibhdhearc Na Gaillimhe) on Middle St (Tel. 095–62024).

SLEEPING, EATING AND NIGHTLIFE

In the centre of town you have no alternative but to use B&Bs or independent hostels. Try Mrs Barrett (Tel. 23249). A number of hostels offer accommodation for IR£5 a night: these are Woodquay Hostel (Tel. 62618), The Grand Holiday Hostel in Salthill (Tel. 091–21150), and The Arch View Hostel in Dominic Street (Tel. 091–66661). Try also Stella Maris in Salthill (Tel. 21950). If these are full up, look around the seaside suburb of Salthill area for B&Bs.

There is a selection of eating places in the 'Special Value Tourist Menu' booklet, and there's plenty of fish'n'chip shops to keep you going. 'Pucain' in Forster St, and Crane Bar, William St and Naughtons Bar, Quay St, are lively at night and have traditional music. Also worth a try is the King's Head on the High Street, which serves what must be the smoothest Guinness in Ireland. Pick up from the tourist office a copy of 'Passport to Galway' which is an excellent guide to the city events and the surrounding countryside. There are also books available for the energetic which describe the various footpaths in the vicinity.

• **Excursions from Galway:** 90 minutes on the motorship from Galway Pier in the summer months takes you out to the remote and fascinating ARAN ISLANDS: Inishmore, Inishmaan and Inisheer. Inishmore may be visited from Rossaveal Pier all year round. Do go into the pubs here to hear the Gaelic-speaking jaunting car drivers and have a chat with them (they are bilingual). Life out here is traditional; a hard life based on fishing. This is where the famous Aran sweaters come from and where tweed trousers and skirts are made to keep out the Atlantic winds. If you are looking for peace and solitude among spectacular granite mountains, this is where you'll find it. Visit the prehistoric forts and remains during your hike round these fascinating islands. Inisheer has a particularly nice sandy beach. There are plenty of B&Bs and camping is IR£2 on official sites with water and toilets. The Aran tourist office can help you find accommodation (Tel. 099–61263) though there are a couple of good hostels: one at Kilronan (Tel. 091–68905 or 099–61255), the other at Mainstir House Hostel on Inis Mor (Tel. 099–61169) which charges IR£6.50 a night and includes breakfast.

Neighbouring villages to Galway all have their beauty spots and interesting features. DUNMORE north-north-east from Galway, has its own well preserved abbey and castle, whilst TUAM, the major neighbouring town, has many remains that show it to be the twelfth-century seat of the kings of Ireland. For the tourist office telephone 093–24465. In the summer a steam railway (as used by John Wayne in his 1951 film *The Quiet Man*) runs the 20-minute route from the town to Atheny, and connects up with the main Dublin to Galway Intercity line. One kilometre off the main Galway to Limerick Road (N18) is Thor Ballylee, the tower home of the poet W. B. Yeats. Visits are available by coach from Easter to October, and the entrance is IR£2. For further information Tel. 091–31436.

The best way of exploring the area is by bicycle. These can be hired from 'Round the Corner' bicycle hire, Queen Street, Victoria Place, or at 'Europa Bicycles', Hunters Building, Earlsland (Tel. 63355 or 23307).

Connemara

Starting about twenty miles north of Galway is the famous rugged mountainous region of Connemara. The shoreline is unspoilt but jagged with several interesting traditional villages where English is rarely spoken, in favour of Gaelic. Connemara needs to be explored by bus or bike as there are no trains. If you are coming from Galway, the youth hostel at Indreabhán (also known as Inverin) is probably your best starting-off point. It is about 20 miles north of Galway (Tel. 091–93154). The nearby village of CARRAROE holds summer festivals and is worth a visit. Connemara ponies are wild, rugged creatures which can be seen in all their glory during August at the Connemara Pony Show in Clifden. Other accommodation can be found at Spiddal Village Hostel (Tel. 091–83555) where beds are IR£4.50 a night, and Lough Corrib Hostel in Camp Street, Oughterard (Tel. 091–82634) which charges IR£5, and is open from March onwards.

The North-west

Counties Mayo, Sligo and Donegal lack the charm, and warmer climate, of the south. They are serious counties, full of prehistoric remains and reminders of a turbulent past with the British. As the most inaccessible, they have also seen a lot of improvements in recent years and have much to recommend them. WESTPORT, in Clew Bay, is worth stopping at to see the beautiful estate of the Marquess of Sligo, two miles from the town. WESTPORT HOUSE is his Georgian mansion, open to the public April–Sept., full of beautiful things. You'll find Westport a busy place on the last Sunday in July, but all those people climbing CROAGH PATRICK aren't tourists, they're pilgrims as this is where St Patrick is said to have fasted and prayed. The tourist office (Tel. 098–25711) and the post office are in the Mall. Also try the Summerville Hostel (Tel. 098–25948) two miles west of town, the hostel on Altamount Street (Tel. 098–26644), and the Granary Hostel on The Quay (Tel. 098–25903) which charges IR£4 a night.

SLIGO, the county of W. B. Yeats, is incredibly rich in archaeological sites and atmosphere. This is the main town of north-west Ireland, with its population of only 25,000. The main sights are mountains – principally Knocknarea and Ben Bulben. Knocknarea is easy to climb and well worth the effort for the view you get from the summit, as well as the view on the summit itself: an 80 foot cairn, rumoured to be that of Maeve of Connacht, an amazon queen. The tourist office at Temple St (Tel. 071–61201) will give you help and information on sights and accommodation, and have guided walks at 11 a.m. every day during the summer. The main sight in the town of Sligo is the ruined thirteenth-century Dominican friary, SLIGO ABBEY, with its well preserved cloister and pillars. Also worth a visit is the COUNTY MUSEUM which has an extensive collection of first editions of Yeats, and concluding the poetic theme is the Yeats Memorial Building on Hyde Bridge, open in the summer on weekdays 10.30 a.m.–1 p.m. and 3 p.m.–5 p.m. Just outside the town is Carrowmore megalithic cemetery which contains an array of tombs dating back to 4,000 BC (Tel. 071–61534), open in the summer from 9.30 a.m. to 6.30 p.m., and admission is only 80p. If it is sea and sand that you desire, travel a little further out of the main town to Rosses Point, seaside village and holiday resort, 8 km from Sligo.

For accommodation try the youth hostel Eden Hill on Pearse Road (Tel. 071–43704).

East of Sligo and in the province of Connacht is LEITRIM, a village situated in a coarse fishing region and mountainous farmland. The tourist office operates from the county's capital of Carrick-on-Shannon during June to August, but it is best to telephone the Sligo office for any information. The nearest budget hostel is at Bundoran on the coast road by Donegal Bay, in the neighbouring county of Donegal (Tel. 072–41288) which charges IR£5 a night.

COUNTY DONEGAL is not served by rail, but if you want to do a bit of hitching, this region will provide you with an unspoilt, wild and beautiful terrain. The Glenveagh National Park 14 miles north-west of Letterkenny covers an area of 10,000 hectares and has various nature paths and a castle in its grounds. LETTERKENNY itself holds an International Folk Festival in August: information is obtainable from the tourist office in Derry Road (Tel. 074–21160). DONEGAL TOWN has its own fifteenth-century castle which is open in the summer months from 9.30 a.m. until 6.30 p.m. On the outskirts of the town on the road to Ballyshannon and Sligo is a craft village, open from Monday to Saturday. The tourist office (Tel. 073–21148) can help with accommodation, though there is a good hostel in the town at Ball Hill (Tel. 073–22174). Alternatively you can use coastal hostels after hiring a bicycle from C. J. Doherty (Tel. 073–21119), and explore the sublime landscape, but don't forget to take warm clothes! There is much here for the visitor to admire: Slieve League, for instance, near Carrick, has the highest sea cliffs in Europe, where a 600 m mountain seemingly falls into the Atlantic.

The tweed industry is alive and well here and is a thriving part of Ireland. Magees of Donegal is the main town exponent, though for the major centre of the handknits and weaving industry go to ARDARA near the west coast, west of Donegal itself. The most breathtaking route to get there is to travel via the Bluestack Mountains; once in the village itself you can hire a bicycle from Donal Byrme (Tel. 075–41156) and explore the coastal scenery. The nearest budget hostel can be found at Derrylahan Hostel in Kilcar on the northern coast (Tel. 073–38079) which charges IR£3.50 a night, or IR£2 a night for tents. Showers cost an extra 50p.

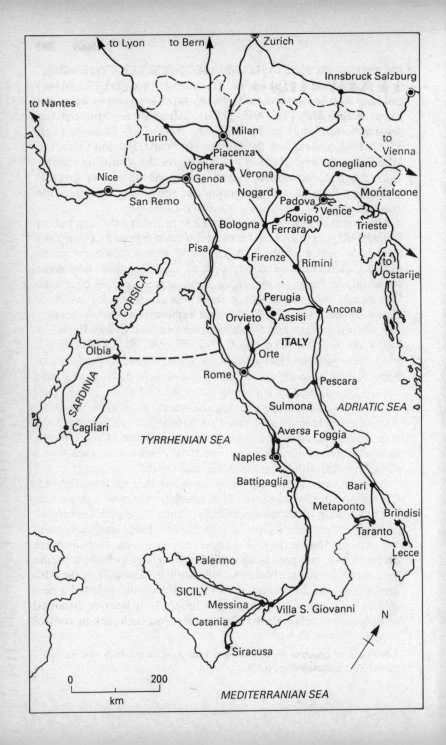

ITALY (Italia)

Entry requirements	Passport
Population	57,300,000
Capital	Rome (pop.: 3,800,000 +)
Currency	Lira
	£1 = approx. 2145 L
Political system	Republic
Religion	Roman Catholic
Language	Italian (English spoken in some major cities)
Public holidays	1, 6 Jan.; Easter Sunday; Easter Monday; 25 Apr.; 1 May; 1 June; 15 Aug.; 1, 7 Nov.; 8, 25, 26 Dec.
International dialling codes	From UK: 010 + 39 + number
	From USA: 011 + 36 + number
	To UK: 00 + 44 + number
	To USA: 00 + 1 + number
Eurotrain office	Via Nazionale 66, I–00184 Rome (Tel. 06–46791)

Italy is like a spoilt child. You'll be annoyed, frustrated and overwhelmed, and yet your greatest Inter-Railing stories will probably originate in this exciting and beautiful country. Whatever your personal feelings on Italians are, you've got to admit they have style. Who else could make a full-scale drama out of a potentially normal situation like seeing a relative off in a train; or challenge a restaurant bill with the gusto of life and death?

Italy's history is dominated by three familiar themes: Empire, Church and the Renaissance, all of which have played a major role in the forming of European culture. From the eighth century BC onwards, there were Greeks in southern Italy and Sicily, and Etruscans in the north. By the third century BC, the Romans were on the move, conquering an empire which was to reign supreme over much of the barbarian world, until its downfall in the fifth century AD. As the civil power of Rome declined, it found a new role as the centre of the Christian Church. Italy became disunited and power was left in the hands of local lords, each seeking control

Additional information on this country contained in the *Italy* and *Europe – Grand Tour* factsheets (see p.13).

of provincial kingdoms. Even the Pope and the Holy Roman Emperor could not agree as to who ruled what. Eventually the Pope, fed up with the whole affair after the city-states refused to submit to his authority, moved base to Avignon (1303–77). After this period of internal strife, the Kingdom of Naples and powerful city-states such as Venice and Florence, provided patronage for the arts. Among other factors which gave rise to this fifteenth-century Renaissance was the new humanism which produced men like Leonardo da Vinci and Michelangelo. Disunity and continued rivalry led to outside intervention by Spain and Austria and finally by Napoleonic France. This foreign domination created the desire for unity, initially under Garibaldi, leading to the ultimate unification of all Italy in 1870. After the First World War, Mussolini and the Fascists rose to power, which eventually brought about an alliance with Hitler during the Second World War. Since then, industrialization and emigration have characterized the economy, particularly in the south where poverty continues to be a problem. The wealthy north is a world away.

ITALIAN STATE RAILWAYS
(Ferrovie dello Stato, FS)

On paper, the Italian rail network should be one of the best in Europe. In reality, the railways can be quite inefficient but have improved greatly in the past few years. Most Italians accept that trains often run late and they manage to live with the bureaucracy and confusion of the whole system.

If you set out prepared for anything, you won't be surprised when a grandmother tries to board a busy train through your window, and ousts you into the corridor while she grabs your seat. Social friction within Italian society can only be worsened by the railways which ensure that those with money are provided with everything imaginable, while second-class passengers are treated as a subspecies. In peak season second class gets incredibly busy on the main lines, so either move early for a seat or, if it is a long trip, reserve. If there's a group of you, and things look busy, set one the task of getting in pronto without a rucksack to get some seats; then the rest can follow at leisure.

The late '80s have seen dramatic improvements on the Italian network – hourly services between Milan and Rome, with the first-class MiRo train taking only four hours to do the journey, and new sleepers and couchettes have improved overnight travel. The new rolling stock, though less quaint, is much more comfortable, and FS are spending some of the country's new-found wealth on improving the service, even for second-class travel.

The best of the non-supplement trains are the long-distance Espressos (if it's more than ½ hour late you can get a credit towards another ticket). They run frequently between Rome, Florence, Venice, Milan and Naples. Away from the main centres, things are not so rosy as you'll have to depend on the Direttos which stop at most stations or, even worse, the Locales which stop at every station. The Rapido is the top of the ladder for second-class travel, but for this privilege you'll have to pay a special supplement of about 30 per cent of the normal fare plus 2,500 L for a seat reservation. (Some Rapidos are first class only, so always check before boarding the train.) If you've always wanted to travel on a EuroCity, wait until you're out of Italy as you can pay up to 80 per cent of the ticket (usually 30 per cent). The station manager's office is always interesting as there's a 50/50 chance there'll be either a crucifix or a picture of Karl Marx over his desk.

The Italian Kilometric Ticket (no age restrictions) is valid for up to 20 trips, totalling up to 3,000 km, and can be used by as many as five different people. If this is the case, each trip is calculated by multiplying the distance travelled by the number of adults. This pass can be bought from every large station in Italy as well as from any Compagnia Italiana Turismo (CIT) office, and costs £152 first-class and £90 second-class if bought in London or around 310,000 L and 180,000 L when bought in Italy.

Note: When paying a supplement in Italy always check it covers the whole journey as often they're only sold in sections.

If you are intending to do a lot of travelling, it may be worth considering the 'Travel-at-Will' or BTLC ticket (Biglietto turistico libera circolazione) which is valid for 8, 15, 21 or 30 days in first and second class. This ticket frees you from paying supplements, even on Rapido trains, and is available only to tourists residing outside Italy. You can buy it in major Italian stations or from CIT or Wasteels in London before you go. It is possible to extend the validity of all but the 8-day ticket. Prices in second class are £88 for 8 days, £110 for 15, £126 for 21 and £152 for 30. Children under 12 get half price. Flexi Tickets are also available, second class costing £66 for 4 days travel out of 9, £94 for 8 of 21 days, and £120 for 12 of 30 days. Tourists can also buy circular tickets for journeys of over 1,000 km which start and finish in the same town, or start and finish at any frontier. These work out slightly cheaper than the normal fare but are likely to be of limited appeal as you are not allowed to go through the same town twice and every break of journey has to be endorsed. Day return tickets for journeys over 50 km have a 15 per cent discount, as do 3-day return tickets for journeys over 250 km. Families of at least four people travelling together qualify for a 30 per cent reduction on the full fare for adults and 65 per cent for children under 12, although the Kilometric ticket may work out better value. Fares are worked out on the actual distance travelled and cost approximately 5,800 L for 100 km, 11,600 L for 200 km, 29,000 L for 500 km and 52,200 L for 1,000 km in second class and roughly 40 per cent for first class.

- **Eurail bonuses:** Free:
—Eurail Pass and Eurail Youthpass travellers can use steamers (*Appia, Egnatia, Espresso Grecia, Castalia*) operated by the Adriatica di Navigazione and Hellenic Mediterranean Lines between Brindisi and Patras and vice versa. However, between 1 June and 30 September, they must pay a 14,000 L high-season surcharge. During July and August, advance reservation, which costs about 2,500 L, is recommended. Special accommodations (airline-type seats or cabins) and port taxes are extra. Before boarding, all passengers must check in at the Shipping Line Office at the pier. Passengers who wish to break their voyage at Corfu must declare their intention of 'stop over' upon delivery of the ticket. Holders of tickets for Corfu (as final port of destination) can in no case continue their voyage to Patras. In Brindisi, beware signs announcing 'Inter-Railers sailing to Greece this Way' – these will take you to the Agenzia Pattimare which has recently been ripping off innocent Inter-Railers to the tune of a £25 'reservation' fee. This is quite unnecessary. Instead, go straight to the shipping offices (Adriatica or HML) in the harbour, where you will be charged a port tax of around £5 (with an extra £2.50 if you stop off at Corfu). If you have a choice, Adriatica are less strict about deck passengers staying on deck than Hellenic. You will need to get your boarding card stamped by the police before embarking.

Reduced fares:

—About 20 per cent reduction on first-class fares for holders of Eurail Pass and on second-class fares for holders of Eurail Youthpass on the Steamship Company Tirrenia between Naples and Palermo, Naples and Malta, Syracuse and Malta and for crossings to Sardinia.

—20 per cent reduction on the normal fares of the Steamship Company DFDS between Genoa and Tunis, Genoa–Alicante and Málaga.

—30 per cent reduction on the published full fares of the Adriatica di Navigazione between Venezia–Piraeus–Alexandria, on the *Espresso Egitto* and/or its return. Contact the local Adriatica offices.

The following half-price reductions are granted by Europabus on transportation costs only and by local offices in Europe.

266 Venice–Florence
267 Florence–Rome
268 Rome–Naples–Pompeii–Sorrento–Amalfi
269 Palermo–Agrigento–Syracuse–Taormina–Palermo

TRAIN INFORMATION

The FS information officers generally speak English, but are sometimes less helpful than they might be, as they understandably get fed up with the long queues in the summer; so try and use your timetable whenever possible. Many stations now have Digiplan machines which issue free computerized print-outs of train times, and possible routes to your chosen destination.

• **Reservations:** Are optional on all non-supplement trains and can be made up to six hours before departure. It's a good idea to do this on runs between major cities, as the trains are always mobbed. It's also possible to reserve a seat for the entire journey from London to Italy or vice versa.

• **Left luggage:** Many Italian stations now seem to count a rucksack with bedroll and sleeping bag attached as three items, and charge accordingly. One notable exception is Venice.

• **Night travel:** This is a good move in Italy where prices are low and distances often long. You can get a couchette from Paris to Rome or vice versa for about 16,800 L. Within Italy, they are either first-class four-berth or second-class six-berth. Don't expect too much for your money – couchettes can be old and dirty. Avoid bottom bunks as headrests take up space, and it's even stuffier down there since the air conditioning often doesn't work. If you prefer to go up-market, there are also sleepers run by Wagons-Lits. If you're asked to give up your passport for the night, don't worry as this is standard practice. Many Italian trains also have pull-down seats. Make sure that your luggage will be secure while you are asleep.

• **Eating on trains:** There are mini-bars on all major trains, but if you're on a tight budget it would be quite a bit cheaper to take a picnic, as prices can be very high.

• **Scenic tips:** Without doubt, the finest way of arriving in north Italy is from Switzerland. The Bern–Brig–Milan and the Zürich–Lugano–Milan runs offer some of Europe's most spectacular Alpine scenery. If you plan on arriving from Austria, you won't be disappointed either, as the runs from Innsbruck–Bolzano to Verona and Vienna to Venice also offer some fine mountain views. One of the most popular routes is from Nice in France down to Pisa – which is no wonder, as there's a lot more than just the Mediterranean coast to feast your eyes on (the train makes its way past most of the Riviera beaches). Further down the same line, anywhere around the Bay of Naples has excellent coastal views, particularly along the narrow-gauge line to Sorrento, though this is a private railway. If you're arriving at Brindisi from Greece, there are three very different but equally scenic routes to choose from: along the southern coast to Catania in Sicily; up the Adriatic coast to Rimini; or over the mountains to Naples via Taranto. Remember to have both drachma and lire on you before attempting to use the ferry crossing. Some ships do not accept both currencies. Another beautiful run, brought to our attention by an Italian reader, is Sulmona to Isernia, part of the excellent electrified line from Rome to Pescara.

• **Bikes** and scooters can sometimes be hired from local tourist offices.

TOURIST INFORMATION

Italy is divided into twenty regions. Each region's capital city has its own tourist board called Assessorato Regionale Turismo (ART). Each of these regions is divided into provinces which, in turn, have their own tourist offices, Ente Provinciale Turismo (EPT) or Azienda Promozione Turistica (APT). Apart from promoting general tourism in their areas, the EPTs also publish free maps, brochures, etc., as well as helping with accommodation problems. For everyday purposes, look for the local tourist offices, Azienda Autonoma di Soggiorno e di Turismo (AAST). They have exactly the same function as the EPTs except they're limited to a particular town or resort. Before you set off to Italy, it's well worth writing in advance to their State Tourist Office (ENIT) at 1 Princes Street, London W1R 8AY, or Italian Government Travel Office, 630 Fifth Ave., New York, NY 10020, asking them to send you their excellent free 'Travellers' Handbook' which is updated annually and contains the latest information on everything you will need to know.

• **ISIC bonuses:** Between 20 and 50 per cent discounts on sea travel. For further information, contact STC Viaggi per la Gioventù, Via Nazionale 172, Rome.

• **Money matters:** The only unit of currency is the lira, for which there are notes for everything between 1,000 and 100,000 lire. Banking hours are Mon.–Fri.: 8.30 a.m.–1.20 p.m. and 3 p.m.–4 p.m.

Some exchange agencies (*cambio*) give a better rate: you will have to shop around. In general, a bank like Credito Italiano is better. The gettone (Italian phone token used as currency) is used as the equivalent of 200 L.

• **Post offices:** Open 8.30 a.m.–2 p.m. Mon.–Fri., till noon Sat. Letters can be sent to poste restante by adding 'Fermo Posta' to the name of the locality. On delivery at the central post office, you'll have to pay a small charge. Stamps are also sold at tobacconists'.

• **Shops:** Open from 8.30/9 a.m.–1 p.m. and from 3.30/4 p.m.–7.30/ 8 p.m., except in northern Italy where the lunch break is shorter and shops close earlier. Most stores take a half day on Monday, generally opening at about 3.30 p.m. Supermarkets can be difficult to find in town centres, so if you see one, use it.

For opening times of museums, check at the local AAST office. Many are shut on Sunday afternoons, Mondays and public holidays. Also, many churches shut between 12 noon and 3 p.m. NB. Most churches, especially the major cathedrals, will not admit people wearing shorts or with uncovered shoulders (or girls with short skirts), so dress sensibly and with respect, before venturing out.

SLEEPING

There is a vast array of hostels, hotels and pensions in Italy to choose from; each one has its own fixed charges, mostly 15,000–40,000 L, as worked out by the provincial tourist boards. These charges vary according to the grade and the season (hotels 1–5). Always check behind the door to see if it includes IVA (Italian VAT), breakfast, and a shower, as these are often extra. There are fifty-two youth hostels scattered throughout Italy (open for IYHA members only), as well as numerous student hostels in all the main towns (open to everyone). Many Italian hostels do not accept phone reservations. For further information on youth hostels in Italy contact Associazione Italiana Alberghi per la Gioventù (AIG), Via Cavour 44, 00184 Roma (Tel. 06–4882342). Hostels are not automatically your best bet as many operate an evening curfew (usually about 11.30) and shut during the siesta period. We've found inexpensive hotels are more reliable in their cleanliness and flexibility. Look for the signs Pensione, Albergo, Locanda and Soggiorno. Girls have another option by staying at the local Casa Famiglia which are run by nuns and offer a bed for about 10,000–20,000 L. Wherever you stay, don't be afraid to give up your passport when you check in as this is standard practice. If you're determined to save as much as you can, camping represents another alternative. The local AAST office has information on the prices of the nearest sites but, for the amount you save, it's often a lot more convenient to stay at a cheap pension in the centre.

EATING AND NIGHTLIFE

Finding a supermarket in the town centre, or a public toilet can be a problem in Italy. You may be forced into a café with high prices and an old crone posted outside the toilet demanding 200 L. To avoid this it's best to be organized. In general, the breakfast at a hotel or pension isn't worth it, as all you're likely to get is a cup of coffee and a roll (it's normally cheaper at the local bar). If you can do without breakfast, go straightaway to the nearest supermarket or local market. In the evening rosticcerie, trattorie, tavole calde and osterie represent the best value. Cheap restaurants can be found quite easily and the standard of the cooking is incredibly high, even on a fixed-price 16,000 L menu. In fact, Italy represents one of the best deals in Europe for good cheap meals. The pizza stalls give you a cheap and tasty lunch, and in the evening, especially in Rome, you're spoilt for choice. Some places bump up the bill if you've chosen to sit outside to eat your meal, so check first. When your bill comes, check it. Watch the *pane e coperto* – the bread and cover charge. It ranges from 1,000 L to 2,500 L but the average is 1,500 L. Also check whether the bill includes service (*servizio compreso*). All restaurants are now required by law to give you an official receipt. The reason so many Italians stage melodramas with the waiter is that the arithmetic can sometimes be dodgy, and never in your favour. Snacks and afternoon coffees can be a bad idea: they inevitably end up costing as much as a meal, so bear this in mind when you're at the supermarket. Expect to pay 17,000–25,000 L for a full meal with wine in a trattoria, and 15,000–20,000 L for the menu turistico.

Once the evening meal is over most Italians wander round to a few cafés and bars, soaking up the local colour. As Luigi Barzini comments in *The Italians:*

> *The show can be so engrossing that many people spend most of their lives just looking at it. There are usually café tables strategically placed in such a way that nothing of importance will escape the leisurely drinker of espresso or aperitivo.*

The disco and nightclub scene is not startling, but there are a few flash – and expensive – places in the main cities. Musical and cultural events are thick on the ground in places like Rome, Florence and Milan. Pick up the 'What's On' from the local tourist office of whichever centre you're in, and make use of your ISIC whenever you can.

Northern Italy

The north is where the money's made, and to a large extent stays. Parts of it are therefore industrial, and prices tend to be higher, but there are too many interesting towns in this area simply to head south regardless. Its regions include PIEDMONT where Turin is; the DOLOMITE RANGE (part of the eastern Alps); LOMBARDY, dominated by Milan; EMILIA-ROMAGNA where Ferrara, Parma and Bologna are located; the ITALIAN RIVIERA where Genoa and the resort towns lie; and VENETO, the region of beautiful Renaissance towns such as Verona, Padua, and its crowning glory – VENICE.

Piedmont and Trentino – Alto Adige

TURIN (Torino) is more of a stopping-off place than a tourist centre. It's on the main line to Rome, Florence, Naples and Paris and is one of Italy's main industrial centres, though there are seemingly hundreds of museums to choose from. The old SIXTEENTH-CENTURY QUARTER, however, is attractive enough to merit a visit, as is the former ROYAL PALACE (entrance 6,000 L), the PALAZZO MADAMA and the very good EGYPTIAN MUSEUM and ANCIENT ART MUSEUM in the baroque Palace of the Academy of Sciences, Piazza Castello (open from 9 a.m.–2 p.m. daily except Mondays, entrance 10,000 L). Another must to visit is the famous fake in the CHAPEL OF THE HOLY SHROUD, housed in a casket behind the apse of the DUOMO. Admission is free, though the cathedral is closed on Mondays and Sunday afternoons. If it's a view that you're after, climb up the emblem of the city, the MOLE ANTONELLIANA, and look over the city from its 548-foot height. The tourist office is at Via Roma 226 (Tel. 011–535181/535901) and there is an information office at Portanuova Station in the heart of the city and open Mon.–Sat.: 9 a.m.–7.30 p.m. Another unusual attraction is the free MEDIEVAL VILLAGE in the Parco del Valentino, situated next to the river. If you are choosing to stay, try the IYHF Ostello Torino, Via Alby 1 (Tel. 6602939) which is situated across the river from the park and charges 16,000 L for bed and breakfast. The camping site is further out at Campeggio Villa Rey, Strand Val. S. Martino 27 (Tel. 8190117) which is a good few kilometres from Station Portanuova and it charges 4,000 L per person and 3,500 L per tent.

The DOLOMITE REGION towns are a mixture of Roman ruins, medieval castles and baroque churches. The backdrop of the pink-coloured Dolomites and the proximity to Austria and Switzerland make this region feel like a totally different country. BOLZANO is on the main line from Munich, and is more Austrian than Italian in its language and character, but it is no less attractive. This is the capital of the Südtirol/Alto Adige area and was part of Austria till 1918. Tourist information is on Piazza Walther 8, where the GOTHIC CATHEDRAL stands (Tel. 975656). This tourist office gives excellent lists of accommodation information and can also direct you upon the best walks and hikes in the area. It is open from Mon.–Fri.: 8.30 a.m.–12.30 p.m., 2 p.m.–6 p.m.; Sat.: 9 a.m.–12.30 p.m. There is another tourist office on Piazza Parrocchia 11–12 (Tel. 993809), which is open Mon.–Fri.: 8.30 a.m.–12.30 p.m., 3 p.m.–5.30 p.m. The MUSEO DELL'ALTO ADIGE has a rare collection of local wooden sculptures and paintings and the village of GRIES, across the River Talvera, makes a lovely walk. There is a campsite at 'Moosbauer', Via San Maurizio 83 (Tel. 918492). Take bus No.8 from the station. BRUNICO, half an hour from the Austrian frontier, still feels like a part of Austria. The dominating Tyrolean CASTLE OF BISHOP BRUNO was built in 1251. Walk for half an hour to the PLAN DI CORONES for an incredible Alpine view. The tourist office is in Via Europa 22 (Tel. 857–22) just up from the bus station. TRENTO, half an hour from Bolzano on the line to Verona, is another Roman town on the Brenner route. Unlike Brunico, this town feels very Italian and, even though the inhabitants were Austrians till 1918, they now consider themselves true Italians. Walk down VIA BELENZANI and look at the Renaissance and Venetian palaces, the baroque church of SAN FRANCESCO SAVERIO, and the thirteenth-century bishop's house, IL CASTELLO DI BUON CONSIGLIO (the Castle of Good Counsel). Trento's tourist office, Azienda Autoviana, is in Via Alfieri 4 (Tel. 983880) and is open Mon.–Fri.: 9 a.m.–12 noon, 3 p.m.–6 p.m.; Sat.: 9 a.m.–12 noon. The hostel is the best place to stay while you're here. It charges 13,500 L per person, including breakfast, and is situated on Via Manzoni 17 (Tel. 234567). The mountain regions near Trento are good for day-trips. The tourist office in VANEZE, half-way up MONTE BONDONE (Tel. 47128) can help you with accommodation, if you decide to stay here, and can also help you with information on ski-lifts and maps. The Ski School, Monte Bondone (Tel. 47211) gives lessons and rents equipment.

Lombardy

This region stretches from the Italian-Swiss border and Lombardy lakes to the plains of the Po River valley, taking in places such as Como, on Lake Como, Bergamo, Mantua (Mantova) and its main city, Milan.

COMO is an ancient silk-producing city on the southern tip of Lake Como, half an hour away from Milan by train. Its architecture is very rich and you should head for the PIAZZA DEL DUOMO to see the old PRETORIAN PALACE called Il Broletto (1215). Next to this is the PALAZZO DEL COMUNE, and the Renaissance Gothic DUOMO from 1396. The Romanesque church of SAN FIDELE is reached by taking Via Vittorio Emanuele. Tourist information is on Piazza Cavour, and at the station. Highly recommended is taking a water bus up the lake which stops at all the small villages en route – it makes a lovely excursion from Milan. (Avoid the set tours as they are expensive and not good value.) The IYHF hostel is the 'Villa Olmo', on Via Bellinzona 2. Open from March–November, it is situated 1 km from the station and charges 13,000L for bed and breakfast (Tel. 031–573800). Try and stay at the village MENAGGIO on the lake side. The hostel there, Ostello della Gioventu, Via Quattro Novembre 38 (Tel. 0344–32356) is open from March to November, overlooks the lake and offers a superb three-course evening meal with wine for 9,500 L, and bed and breakfast for 10,000 L with no curfew or restriction on drink. An overnight train departs from here to Brindisi, so if you choose to travel, try to coordinate your arrival there with the September festival.

BERGAMO is divided into two: the lower city, built under the Fascists in the 1920s; and the upper city, a medieval settlement reached by funicular. Apart from the PALAZZO DELL'ACCADEMIA CARRARA with its collection of sixteenth-century art and furniture, forget the lower city. Once you've taken the funicular up head for the Piazza Vecchia where the PALAZZO DELLA RAGIONE stands. Opposite this is the PALAZZO NUOVO. The cathedral has a fifteenth-century interior and nineteenth-century exterior. VIA ROCCA takes you to a park which has a medieval lookout post from where the view over the Bergamasque valleys is particularly good. Tourist information is at 20 Viale V. Emanuele II, and the IYHF hostel 'Bergano' is at 1 Via Galileo Ferraris (Tel. 035–342349), 4 km from the railway station, open from Feb.–Nov. and charges 16,000L for bed and breakfast.

MANTUA was one of *the* Renaissance courts, ruled as it was for 400 years by the Gonzaga family. Their sumptuous palace (PALAZZO DUCALE) is on Piazza Sordello. There are over 500 rooms, including the miniature suite specially constructed to house the court dwarfs. It's free on ISIC, closed Mondays and open weekday mornings and Saturday afternoons. Opposite the palace is the medieval CATHEDRAL which is impressive enough, but pales into insignificance beside the beautiful Renaissance CHURCH OF SANT'ANDREA. The PALAZZO DEL TÈ was the Gonzagas' summer home, built in the early sixteenth century (closed Mon. and Sun. p.m.). The artist who painted the frescoes decorating the rooms here was Giulio Romano, and you can visit his sun house on VIA C. POMA, which is still well preserved. Tourist information is at Piazza Mantegna 6 (Tel. 0376–350681) and Piazza Sordello 23; watch out for their 1 p.m.–3.30 p.m. siestas. For cheap beds, try La Rinascita, Via Concezione 4 (Tel. 0376–320607), or the youth hostel Ostello Sparafucile (Tel. 0376–372465), a renovated medieval castle, open Apr.–Oct., on the outskirts. Take bus 2, 6 or 9 from p. Cavallolti to get there, and expect to pay 9,500 L for bed and breakfast. Camping is allowed here in July and August.

Milan (Milano)

Most eurorailers don't get off at Milan, or if they do they stay in the station till their connection comes. While Milan is not exactly Venice in the sightseeing stakes, it's got a lot more than most people realize, and as the rich man of Italy (every third building seems to be another bank), it has the perks of a high living standard (and higher standards of cleanliness) and more things going on in the evenings than elsewhere.

STATION FACILITIES

There are three stations in Milan (Centrale, Lambrate and Garibaldi). The last two are mostly used for local traffic and are less important. Some consider the Centrale station to be one of the most impressive in Europe, if only for its sheer size alone, which reflects past Italian confidence in their railway system. Since the fire in November 1983, the whole station has had a facelift making it even more spectacular. There are no shops nearby for picnic purchases, so buy in advance.

	MILANO CENTRALE
Train information	7 a.m.–11 p.m. (Tel. 222 441)
Reservations	7 a.m.–10 p.m. (6.30 p.m.–10 p.m. for couchettes and sleepers)
Tourist information	9 a.m.–12.30 p.m., 2.15 p.m.–6 p.m.
Foreign exchange	8 a.m.–7.30 p.m., Sundays 9 a.m.–2.30 p.m.
Left-luggage store	7 a.m.–10.30 p.m. (1,500 L)
Bar, Buffet	7 a.m.–12 midnight
Restaurant	11.30 a.m.–11.30 p.m.
Bath, Shower	7 a.m.–10.30 p.m.
Post office	Mon.–Fri.: 8 a.m.–2 p.m. Sat.: 8 a.m.–4 p.m.

Daily trains to: Amsterdam, Bern (4½ hours), Basel (5½ hours), Paris, Luxembourg, Vienna, Venice (3 hours), Frankfurt, Florence (3¼ hours), Rome (6½ hours), Bologna (2 hours), Brindisi, Naples, Nice (4¾ hours), Genoa.

TOURIST INFORMATION AND ADDRESSES

The Provincial Tourist Board is at Palazzo del Turismo, Via Marconi 1 (Tel. 809662), open Mon.–Sat.: 8 a.m.–8 p.m., Sun.: 9 a.m.–12.30 p.m., 1.30 p.m.–5 p.m. For information on Milan, go to the Duomo then walk to the left side of the square under the arches (opposite the Galleria Vittorio Emanuele). They will supply you with a free map of the city which marks the metro and main train/bus lines. Another useful free map gives locations of all the hotels and pensions within the commune. Get the free guide 'Tutta Milano' in English. They are sometimes not very helpful and not too keen to phone hotels for you.

POST OFFICE: Stazione Centrale or Piazza Cordusio 4 (near the Duomo); also poste restante. Open Mon.–Fri. 8.15 a.m.–7.40 p.m., Sat. 8.15 a.m.–5.40 p.m.

AMEX: Via Brera 3, beyond the p. Scala (Tel. 85571). Mon.–Fri.: 9 a.m.–5.30 p.m., Sat.: 9 a.m.–12.30 p.m.

UK CONSULATE: Via San Paolo 7 (Tel. 8693442; after hours Tel. 862490).

US CONSULATE: Piazza Carlo Donegari 1 (Tel. 652841; after hours Tel. 653131).

CANADIAN CONSULATE: Via Vittore Pisani 19 (Tel. 6697451; after hours Tel. 66980600).

AUSTRALIAN CONSULATE: Via Turati 40 (Tel. 4565078; after hours Tel. 6682481).

24-HOUR CHEMIST: Tel. 871442 or 192, or at the Central Station (Tel. 6690735).

'SOS FOR TOURISTS': Tel. 5456551. For legal complaints.

PHONE CODE: 02.

SEEING

The CATHEDRAL (Duomo), the white marble monument of Milanese wealth with 135 spires and over 2,000 sculptures inside and out, is the finest piece of Gothic architecture in northern Italy. It was started in 1386 and not completed till 1813. Ascend to the roof for the view. The building's situated at Piazza del Duomo, though you'd have a job missing it. The famous opera house, LA SCALA, with perfect acoustics, has been the scene of many a Verdi or Rossini première, and there's a museum there showing costumes, manuscripts and other operatic memorabilia. It's north of the Duomo, through the gallery, on Piazza della Scala (open 9 a.m.–12 noon, 2 p.m.–6 p.m., entrance 5,000L). The BRERA PALACE AND ART GALLERY, a few blocks north of La Scala on Via Brera, is Milan's finest gallery. Housed in a seventeenth-century palace is a varied collection of Italian art and a library of books and manuscripts (open 9 a.m.–2 p.m., closed Mondays, entrance costs 8,000 L, or is free to EC residents under the age of 18). The POLDI-PEZZOLI MUSEUM is a private collection with some rare sculptures, paintings and tapestries (closed Mondays, open weekdays until 6 p.m., Saturdays until 7.30 p.m., entrance 5,000 L), Via Manzoni 12.

The MUSEUM OF ANTIQUE ART is housed in the fifteenth-century SFORZA CASTLE (closed Mondays and at lunchtime, entrance is free). Among its collection is Michelangelo's 'Rondanini Pietà' –

his last, unfinished work. Enter from Corte Ducale, Piazza Castello. Behind the castle is the SEMPIONE PARK. SANT'AMBROGIO BASILICA, dating back to the fourth century, houses religious treasures and a few dead saints as well as a jewel-studded ninth-century altar. If you'd like to see the rapidly decaying masterpiece, Leonardo's 'Last Supper', go to the convent next to SANTA MARIA DELLE GRAZIE, though as the city's tourist trap they charge 10,000 L to see it; the EC regulations for under 18s still stand. The MUSEUM OF SCIENCE AND TECHNOLOGY, Via S. Vittore 21, is well worth visiting to see the complete aircraft and ships as well as working models of Leonardo's inventions. Open all day except Mondays, entrance costs 6,000 L.

For those of you sightseeing in a day, invest in a one-day tourist ticket costing 3,200 L for unlimited travel on buses, trams and the underground. Tickets are available from the Duomo (Cathedral) underground station and the Central FS and Cordorna underground stations. Otherwise, single fare tickets cost 1,000 L and must be purchased in advance from the aforementioned venues.

SLEEPING

You shouldn't encounter many hassles in finding a reasonably priced room in Milan, even in summer – and you won't have to walk far either as there are plenty of suitable places just north or west of the station except during an international trade fair. The tourist office will help you out if you've hit a fluke blackspot. The 'Piero Rotta' Youth Hostel, Via Martino Bassi 2 (Tel. 02–39267095), open from 7 a.m.–9 a.m., 5 p.m.–11.30 p.m., is half an hour away by metro, and allows only three days' stay at the maximum. Bed and breakfast costs around 20,000 L, but it is only available to IYHF card-holders.

For pensions in the 55,000–65,000 L range, try: Pensione Paganini, Via Paganini 6 (Tel. 273890); Pensione Trentina, Via Lippi 50 (Tel. 2361208), and Hotel Valley, Via Soperga 19 (Tel. 278228) are also close to the station and cheap. More centrally, there are a few pensions in Via Dante at 35,000 L per double, such as the Pensione Dante (Tel. 866471). They charge 60,000 L for a double with free showers. Also try Hotel Rivoli at Via Giovanni Lulli 11 (Tel. 2046815). Two more cheap hotels are Hotel Ballarin, Via Soncino 3 (Tel. 86451756) which offers single rooms for

17,000 L and doubles for 24,500 L, and the Hotel Commercio, Via Mercato 1 (Tel. 8058003) which has single beds with private showers for 20,500 L and doubles for 30,000 L. Milan's campsite (San do Nato) is not to be recommended – it is dirty and unsafe.

In recent years Milan has been taking over from Paris as Europe's foremost city for fashion and design. Consequently, many English-speaking models have been lured by the prospect of fame and fortune. If you've been travelling on your own and miss English-speaking company, try the American Hotel, Via Finocchiaro Aprile 2 (Tel. 666441) or Hotel Brussels, Piazza Castello 13 (Tel. 809361).

EATING AND NIGHTLIFE

There are trattorie and rosticcerie all over the city. The speciality of Milanese cooking is that they use butter, not olive oil as they do elsewhere in Italy. With the amount of money knocking about Milan, the Milanese tend to eat out a lot, so restaurants are more expensive here than elsewhere. For a cheap meal near the centre try Burghy, just out from San Babila underground station. There are plenty of cheap places in the Via Marghera area. If you want to go up-market without paying up-market prices, try Pane e Farina at Via Pantano 6 (Tel. 803274). Flash in Via Bergamini (near the Duomo) serves good value sandwiches and pizzas. The soup and panini bar is open all day except Sundays, where you can expect to pay around 2,000–4,000 L, and the restaurant is open at lunchtime and from 7 p.m.–midnight. Ice-cream lovers must head for Milan's most famous *gelateria:* 'Viel Gelati' on Via Lucia Beltrami, open from Thursday to Tuesday until 2 a.m. For an interesting evening and a closer look at some of Milan's large transvestite community try Scimmie at Via Ascanio Sforza 49. For pubs go to the Brera area; and try Giamaica at Via Brera 32.

Emilia-Romagna

This is the region from the southern Po Valley to the Apennine Mountains north of Tuscany. Its towns are medieval and Renaissance: Parma, Ferrara, Ravenna and Bologna. It has the richest cuisine in Italy, where tortellini, tagliatelle and Bolognese sauce originated, and from Parma has come Parma ham and Parmesan cheese.

PARMA, in the centre of the huge plain south of the River Po, is known for its architectural and gastronomic delights. PIAZZA GARIBALDI is the old town centre with the TOWN HALL, CLOCK TOWER and GOVERNOR'S PALACE. The DUOMO (Cathedral) is Romanesque and on its cupola is Correggio's 'Assumption of the Virgin Mary'. Also noteworthy in Piazza Duomo is the striking octagonal red marble BAPTISTRY. The HISTORICAL PHARMACY OF ST JOHN (in Piazza de San Giovanni) features some early decorative work of the definitive Parma Mannerist, Parmigianino. In contrast, the sixteenth-century MADONNA DELLA STECCATA (Steccata's Church, just off Piazza Garibaldi) marks the painter's last work for his home town, as he was imprisoned twice for failing to meet the deadline for completion of the frescoes, and left Parma soon after his release. The PALAZZO DELLA PILOTTA has been restored since its Second World War bombing to become the city's museum, and the NATIONAL GALLERY reviews the school established by Correggio in Parma, as well as the medieval-Renaissance Italian works. Tourist information (Azienda Promozione Turistica) is available at Piazza Duomo 5 (Tel. 0521-234735), and a youth hostel at 5, Parco Cittadella (Tel. 581546) provides rooms for 15,000 L without breakfast. This hostel is also the only site for a campground near Parma. Like the hostel, it allows only three days maximum stay and is open from April–October. Campsite charges are 5,000 L per person, 6,000 L per tent.

FERRARA today is an agricultural and industrial centre, lying on the rail line between Bologna and Venice, but hopefully you'll visit it to see what's left of one of the Renaissance's cultural centres. It was an independent duchy ruled by the dukes of Este, and in their courts flowered some of the most gifted philosophers, artists and writers of the Renaissance movement. The CASTELLO ESTENSE (the Duke's Castle) dates back to the fourteenth century. This fortress, surrounded by a moat and complete with dungeons and a beautiful chapel, is open to the public. The town's CATHEDRAL is of the twelfth century and stands opposite the thirteenth-century PALAZZO COMUNALE. The PALAZZO SCHIFANOIA, down Via Scandiana, is where the dukes went for amusement; it's now a museum; the archaeological museum is in the Renaissance

PALAZZO DI LUDOVICO IL MORO. Ferrara has a youth hostel, Via Benvenuto Tisi da Garofalo 5 (Tel. 0532–21098) and tourist information is at Piazzetta Municipio 19 (Tel. 0532–209370), which is open from Mon.–Sat.: 9 a.m.–1 p.m., 2.30 p.m.–7 p.m.; Sun.: 9 a.m.–1 p.m.

RAVENNA was the sixth-century western capital of the Byzantine Empire, and the birthplace of Christian Iconography; the early Christian mosaics are outstanding. Ravenna is an hour down the line from Ferrara, and two hours from Bologna. The tourist office at Via Salara 8 (Tel. 0544–35404) will supply maps, information and accommodation help. There is also an APT office on Via S. Vitale 2 (Tel. 35755–56). SAN VITALE, the octagonal church, contains some mosaics, but across the cloister is the TOMB OF GALLA PLACIDIA with the best mosaics in Ravenna. Dante is buried in the grounds of the CHURCH OF SAN FRANCESCO. The high spot of Ravenna is a visit to the seventh-century church of SANT' APOLLINARE IN CLASSE (bus 4 from the station). The beaches are good, but often mobbed in summer. There's a youth hostel, 'Dante', on Via Aurelio Nicolodi 12 (Tel. 0544–420405). It's good, quite cheap at 16,000 L for bed and breakfast, and reached by bus 1. For camping, head to Marina di Ravenna, or further along the coast to Camping Classe out at the Lido di Classe, which is extremely friendly and serves cheap food. Be warned, the camping sites are not cheap (though most include tennis courts and swimming facilities) and access to and from the town is difficult because bus services are poor. Also beware of mosquitoes; they thrive by the sea at night, and are only too glad to feast on foreign blood. Pack the repellant now! For a hostel try Albergo Minerva, Via Maroncelli 1 (Tel. 0544–34543), just to the right of the station, Albergo Ravenna (directly opposite Minerva) or Albergo Eva at Via Rocco Brancaleone 42 (Tel. 0544–39403). There's a student refectory at 8 Via Oberdan.

Bologna

The oldest university town in Europe (1076), one of the gastronomic centres of Europe, a Renaissance city of culture and learning, and today as red and communist as Moscow was. This is where some eurorailers met a tragic death in August 1980 when the station was bombed. Things are back to normal now, and what's left of the station still stands on the northern edge of Bologna and carries trains running to Florence, Venice, Rome, Vienna, Sicily and other destinations.

STATION FACILITIES

	BOLOGNA CENTRALE
Train information	8 a.m.–8 p.m.
Reservations	7 a.m.–9.45 p.m.
Tourist information	Mon.–Sat.: 9 a.m.–7 p.m., Sun. 9 a.m.–1 p.m. (Tel. 246541)
Foreign exchange	8 a.m.–10 p.m.
Left-luggage store	All hours
Cafeteria	Thurs.–Mon.: 11 a.m.–3 p.m., 7 p.m.–10 p.m.
Restaurant	11 a.m.–12 midnight (upstairs) 7 a.m.–12 midnight (downstairs)

TOURIST INFORMATION AND ADDRESSES

Apart from the one at the station (Tel. 246541), there are offices at Via Leopardi 1, Via Marconi 45, and Piazza XX Settembre. The main tourist office is at Palazzo Comunale (Tel. 239660). General siesta-time is 12.30 p.m.–3.30 p.m. They'll help out on accommodation (they book rooms for free) as well as providing the usual services.

POST OFFICE: Piazza Minghetti, Mon.–Fri.: 8.15 a.m.–6.40 p.m., Sat.: 8.15 a.m.–12.20 p.m.

STUDENT TRAVEL OFFICE: CTS, Via delle Belle Arti 20 (Tel. 264862).

24-HOUR CHEMIST: Tel. 192. Also late night chemists are at the train station (Tel. 246603) and at P. Maggiore 6 (Tel. 238509).

UFFICIO STRANIERI (FOREIGNERS' OFFICE): Tel. 337473/337475. Open Mon.–Sat.: 7.30 a.m.–11 p.m., Sun.: 8 a.m.–10 p.m.

PHONE CODE: 051.

SEEING

The main street is the VIA UGO BASSI with at one end the

pedestrianized PIAZZA RAVESNANA where two Gothic structures over 100 metres tall, the Garisenda and Asinelli towers, supply shade to sit under. Just off from here is the PIAZZA MAGGIORE, which on Sundays becomes the site of puppet theatre shows. The PIAZZA COMUNALE is a complex of palaces which contains the municipal art gallery (open 9 a.m.–2 p.m., closed Mondays). Seven churches joined into another conglomeration is what you'll find at the BASILICA SANTO STEFANO; the octagonal church of the Holy Sepulchre, the eleventh-century Church of the Crucifix and the Church of St Peter and St Paul all merit a look. The courtyard behind the Holy Sepulchre has the BASIN OF PILATE where Pontius Pilate is said to have washed his hands when symbolically absolving himself of responsibility for Christ's death.

SLEEPING, EATING AND NIGHTLIFE

The scope isn't huge in Bologna for budget beds, especially since the youth hostel is about three miles from the city at San Sisto, Via Viadagola 14 (Tel. 051–519202). To get there take bus 93 from Via de Mille or Via Irnerio (the main road running parallel to the train station on the right, off Via Independenza), or take bus 30 from the coach station on the corner. This hostel charges 16,000L for bed and breakfast, as does the second IYHF hostel further up the road; 'Le Torri San Sisto 2' at number 5 (Tel. 051–501810). The cheapest place in town is the Dormitorio Comunale. It has replaced the old hostel, but we can't vouch for it. Try Albergo 11 Guercino behind the station on Via Serra 7, Pensione Fiorita (Tel. 369893), or Locanda Testoni, Via Testoni 3 (Tel. 23968), or Hotel Touring, Via Mattuiani (Tel. 584305) where single rooms range from 17,000–34,000 L and doubles cost between 29,000 and 58,000 L. If you are arriving late, check outside the station's tourist office, for they post up-to-the-minute accommodation vacancies here after hours.

Eating's a totally different proposition: the only headache here is deciding where to go, as there are simply so many likely places. The cooking is terrific, and it's almost unheard of to have a bad meal. Vegetarians can find heaven at the Centro Naturista Bolognese in Via degli Alban 6, and though there is a university refectory, this is one place it'd be a shame to use as there are so many family-run trattorie. Try Osteria d'Orso on Via Montana, or the Trattoria at Via Broccaindosso 21A. If you're there in term-time, ask students in the university refectory (on Piazza Puntoni 1) for an idea of what's on, and while you're there get a good meal for 2,500L. Show the guard any student ID, and you'll be able to buy your meal ticket. Pick up the rest of the events from tourist information. In the evening the young crowd hang out around Piazza Maggiore.

The Italian Riviera – Liguria

From the French Côte d'Azur to Tuscany lies the Italian Riviera. It's not quite as flash as its French counterpart, but it's cheaper, which results in some of the bigger resorts being packed out in summer. Genoa is the main town of this region, though it's hardly a resort. There's a very comprehensive and picturesque rail line serving the Riviera which starts at Marseille in France, passes through the border at Ventimiglia and serves places like Bordighera, San Remo, Alassio, Albenga and Genoa. Rather than staying on the Côte d'Azur, you may wish to stop off on the border here at VENTIMIGLIA. Worth checking out for accommodation are the Hotel XX Settembre, Via Roma 16 or the Hotel Regina, Corso Genova 39. There are at least twenty-four trains a day, so hopping from one place to the next till you find the one you like best is easy. Each town has a tourist information office and they'll help out on accommodation.

BORDIGHERA was a favourite among European royals and the English aristocracy in the nineteenth century. The oldest part of the town is on the hill, and along the shore is the new town. Bordighera is an attractive garden-filled resort which prides itself on its abundant palm trees (they supply the Vatican with palms on Palm Sunday). Prices tend to be high here, so try sleeping on the beach (in an unobtrusive place as the police aren't at all keen on this practice) and avoid the restaurants without fixed menus. The tourist office, Ufficio Informazioni del Turismo, is at Palazzo del Parco (Tel. 0184–262322/3). In late July and August, the town presents the Salone Internazionale Umarismo, a humour festival, with performances taking place in the same building as the tourist office.

SAN REMO is the Riviera's largest resort, but unless you've money to waste in the Casino, stick tight to the beach. There are plenty of

pizzerias and cafés, but this resort is one of the most commercialized and we're not recommending it too highly. If you do decide
to stay, the tourist office at Palazzo Riviera (Tel. 0184–571571) can
help you find accommodation.

ALASSIO has a good mile-and-a-half beach. The new town's pretty
grim, but the old town down by the beach is lovely. This used to be
another haunt of the wealthy British, and there's tennis, golf and
skiing on offer. Off this stretch of the coast you'll find the island of
Gallinara, which historically belongs to Albenga, and was a haven
to fifteenth-century monks. For further information, the tourist
office is on Viale Gibbi 26 (Tel. 0182–40346).

ALBENGA was a strategic Roman port and you can visit the ROMAN
NAVAL MUSEUM here and see the remains of a Roman ship sunk in
the first century BC, which carried a cargo of 10,000 amphoras (wine
vessels). Today Albenga is a market town – though it is still the
historical centre of the western Riviera – and is more down to earth,
and Italian, than many of the surrounding resorts. As can be
expected in this country, this city has a wealth of cathedrals and
churches which outline its artistic, architectural and historical
development over the centuries.

Genoa (Genova)

The largest port of northern Italy with a medieval harbour-quarter,
Renaissance upper town of merchants' palaces and, above all this,
modern Genoa. Crowning this is the CIRCONVALLAZIONE A MONTE,
a boulevard which winds its way in and out of the hills, giving a
superb panorama over the city. Genoa became an important
cartographical school in the twelfth century, an artistic centre in the
sixteenth and seventeenth centuries when Flemish masters, including Rubens and Van Dyck, came over to paint the wealthy
merchants' portraits. This is also the birthplace of Christopher
Columbus, and the city where Marco Polo was kept as a prisoner of
war in 1298 after the sea battle of Ciurzola.

STATION FACILITIES

Genoa has two stations: the Porta Principe (main station) and

Brignole. Trains bound for the north use Principe, trains heading south use Brignole. Through-trains stop at both, except for those going north-west (Milano–Nice). They use only Principe. There are inter-station connecting trains regularly (at intervals of less than 30 minutes).

	PRINCIPE	BRIGNOLE
Train information	7 a.m.–11 p.m. (Tel. 284081)	7 a.m.–11 p.m. (Tel. 284081)
Reservations	7 a.m.–10 p.m.	7 a.m.–10 p.m.
Tourist information	Mon.–Sat.: 8 a.m.–7 p.m.	Mon.–Sat.: 8 a.m.–7 p.m.
Foreign exchange	Mon.–Fri.: 8.20 a.m.–1.20 p.m.	See train information
Left-luggage store	All hours	All hours
Cafeteria	11.30 a.m.–3.30 p.m. 7 p.m.–11 p.m.	6 a.m.–9.30 p.m.
Restaurant		11 a.m.–5 p.m.
Bar, Buffet	7 a.m.–11.30 p.m. (summer) 7 a.m.–11 p.m. (winter)	6 a.m.–9.30 p.m.
Post office	Mon.–Sat.: 8 a.m.–10 p.m. Sun.: 8 a.m.–12 noon	Mon.–Fri.: 8.15 a.m.–10 p.m. Sat.: 8.15 a.m.–2 p.m.

Daily trains to: Luxembourg, Frankfurt, Milan (1½ hours), Venice (4½ hours), Bologna (3 hours), Florence (4½ hours), Rome (5½ hours), Naples, Nice (3 hours).

TOURIST INFORMATION AND ADDRESSES

At the railway stations (Tel. 262633) and the main office at Via Roma 11 (Tel. 581407). Open Mon.–Thurs.: 8 a.m.–2 p.m., Sat.: 8 a.m.–1 p.m.
POST OFFICE: Palazzo Poste, Via G. Boccardo 2.
UK CONSULATE: Via XII Ottobre 2, 13th floor (Tel. 564833).
US CONSULATE: Piazza Portello (Tel. 282741).
24-HOUR CHEMIST: Piazza Acquaverde (Principe Station).
PHONE CODE: 010.

SEEING

Get hold of a map as it's a confusing city. Walk down VIA GARIBALDI and see the elegant sixteenth-century palaces. There are seventeen museums and galleries in this city, but we believe the following to be the cream of the crop. The PALAZZO BIANCO and PALAZZO ROSSO are now art galleries. The former contains a Flemish collection and the latter, which is the larger of the two, displays works by many famous masters such as Tintoretto, Caravaggio, Van Dyck etc. Other cultural sites worth a visit are the gallery and fine frescoes of PALAZZO CATALDI and the antiquities in PALAZZO DORIA TURSI. Moving on to a different heritage, the CHRISSONE MUSEUM houses a wonderful collection of Japanese and Chinese paintings and artefacts, including 1,000 engraved Japanese sabres. Via Balbi, running east from the main station, is a fine example of Old Genoa (as is Via Cairoli), and is also the site of the PALAZZO REALE FINE ART (and antique furniture) GALLERY. In the historical centre of the city, visit the DUOMO SAN LORENZO, off Piazza Matteoto, a cathedral that was constantly renovated from the ninth to sixteenth centuries. Nearby, the Via San Luca houses many interesting churches and monuments, but also look at the streets you're walking through, since the buildings here are as decorative as any museum's exhibits. Around the east of the harbour, the Via San Lorenzo leads past the twelfth-century cathedral of the same name, into Piazza de Ferrari. Beyond this square, Via Dante leads past the main post office to Piazza Dante, and the site of Christopher Columbus's childhood home.

SLEEPING, EATING AND NIGHTLIFE

Tourist information usually come up with plenty of pension suggestions. If you want a room with its own bathroom, then La Capannina, Via Tito Speri 7 (Tel. 317131) charges 25,000–45,000 L for its singles, and 40,000–71,000 L for its doubles. The International Youth Hostel 'Genova' in Via Costanzi (Tel. 010–586407) charges 18,000 L per night for bed and breakfast and is situated 3 km from the station, women can use the Casa della Giovane, P. Santa Sabina 4, near Via Fontane (Tel. 206632) for around 12,000 L.

There are scores of pizzerias and restaurants, and the prices all seem very much on a level in all quarters of the town, so go for one that's handy and displays its menu with prices quoted. Try the regional specialities of cima Genovese (stuffed cold veal) and pandolce (orange-flavoured cake).

Veneto

Veneto encompasses the north-eastern section of the Po Valley to the Dolomites and coastal resorts. This is the region around what many consider to be the most beautiful city in the world, Venice. Apart from this, there are the art towns of Padua and Verona, Belluno and Treviso close by.

Venice (Venezia)

Venice is absolutely unmatched by anything else in Europe; there really is nowhere else like it. It's a 'must' on any European tour, and it's worth all the crowds and hugely inflated prices, because you'll never forget it. The town consists of 117 islets connected by 400 bridges with 150 canals winding their way through the maze. There are no cars, only boats.

The history of Venice is long and colourful. Her buildings reflect her glorious past when she, as an independent city-state, ruled over most of the Mediterranean. During the Renaissance, Venice was *the* trading port with the Middle East, and she became the centre of European commerce. The doges (the city dukes or rulers) had enough money not only to build sumptuous palaces and churches, but also to commission large-scale works of art from the Venetian school (Titian, Tintoretto, etc.) and patronize science and the arts. Their 1,000-year independence came to an end in 1797 when Napoleon gave Venice to the Austrians. When Italy was united, Venice joined on, and its popularity as a tourist trap of the twentieth century has brought it new wealth, much of which is used to prevent the entire city sinking and being lost for ever.

STATION FACILITIES

The station is situated at the west end of the town right on the Grand Canal. It's easily possible to go everywhere by foot, but it's more fun to take the vaporetti (waterbuses) from outside the station. Nos. 1 and 34 take you down the Grand Canal to San Marco Square.

No. 2, which is the faster, limited-stop service, takes you to San Marco and Lido following the Giudecca Canal route.

SANTA LUCIA, VENEZIA	

Train information	7 a.m.–9 p.m.
	(Tel. 715555)
Reservations	7 a.m.–10 p.m.
Tourist information	8 a.m.–8 p.m.
Foreign exchange	Mon.–Sat.: 8 a.m.–7 p.m.
	Sun.: 8 a.m.–1 p.m.
Left-luggage store	Times vary according to season
Bar, Buffet	6 a.m.–9 p.m.
Waiting room	All hours
Post office	Mon.–Sat.: 8.30 a.m.–1.30 p.m.

Some trains stop only at Venezia–Mestre on the mainland, so check. To reach Venezia–Santa Lucia from Mestre, there are both trains and buses. Bus 2 from outside the station takes you into Venice proper.

TOURIST INFORMATION

The tourist office in the station (Tel. 719078) handles accommodation and little else except handing out maps. In summer, an office at the bus station in Pizzale Roma does the same. (Tel. 5287886). For information your best bet is to head for the central tourist office near San Marco Square at Ascensione 71F (Tel. 5226356), but this office will not help you with accommodation. The student tourist office (CTS) is at Dorsoduro 3252 (Tel. 705660); they'll help you out with accommodation and student travel. Tourist offices are always busy, so try and fix up accommodation beforehand. Also, all APT offices are outlets for the useful Youth Discount Passes (Carta Giovanni).

• **Addresses:**
POST OFFICE: Fondaco dei Tedeschi, near the eastern side of the Rialto Bridge. Telephone office here also.
AMEX: San Marco, 1471 San Marco. Mon.–Sat.: 8 a.m.–8 p.m.
UK CONSULATE: Dorsoduro 1051 (Tel. 5227207).
FIRST AID: (Tel. 113).
PHONE CODE: 041.

• **Getting about:** The waterbuses (vaporetti) cover all Venice. A trip on Line 34 is good, as it takes in quite a few sights. They run every 10 minutes from 5 a.m. to 12 midnight. Fares are around the 2,000 L mark. A 24-hour pass costs 12,000L. A 3-day pass is also available at 17,000L. There are also a few buses, but their routes are restricted. The gondolas look beautiful, but at 60,000 L an hour it's not surprising we haven't seen too many eurorailers on them.

SEEING

Venice is a place to wander in. There are so many little winding back-streets and alleys, unexpected quiet squares and little hump-back bridges that this is the easiest place in Europe to get lost in (no wonder Venice's famous son Marco Polo was so good at exploring). Many factors contribute to strangers losing their way in Venice, so a few cautionary words are in order before you attempt gleefully to pounce upon this city, armed only with your trusty tome of *Europe by Train*. First of all, Venice is divided into six main districts, and each district (or sestiere) can have duplicate street names, so be sure to *which* district your required street belongs. Next, streets do not possess individual numbers, but a sestiere number, which can go up to 6,000, but not in any obvious logical pattern. Thirdly, the most highly recommended tool for getting about in Venice is the red 'Edizioni Foligrat Mestre-Venezia' map. Use it as you seek out the following unmissable sights:

1. ST MARK'S SQUARE: The city revolves round this incredible piazza. ST MARK'S BASILICA and the DOGES' PALACE are here, as are the LAW COURTS, the beautiful CLOCK TOWER and the OLD LIBRARY – now an archaeological museum. The PIAZZETTA leads off from the square to the GRAND CANAL.

2. ST MARK'S BASILICA: This amazing Byzantine church, built in the eleventh century, is a riot of gold, marble and mosaic. It was originally the chapel for the Doges, and became the city cathedral in 1807. The four massive bronze horses over the doorway were brought over from Constantinople after it was raided in 1207. (Women: bring a shawl to cover your shoulders and arms; men: wear long trousers to be let in.) Climb up the Basilica for 2,000 L and a grand view.

3. DOGES' PALACE (Palazzo Ducale): This pink-and-white fairytale palace was the home of the Venetian government and the rulers of the republic. (Note the Tintoretto in the Grand Council Chamber.) The connecting bridge between the palace and the prison is known as the BRIDGE OF SIGHS. 4,000 L on ISIC, 8,000 L without reduction.

4. THE ACADEMY OF FINE ART (Galleria dell'Accademia) has the best of the Venetian school's work: Canaletto, Tintoretto, Bellini, Veronese, etc. Closed Mondays. Entrance costs 8,000 L and there are no ISIC reductions. Check opening times before you go with the tourist office near San Marco Square.

5. CHIESA DEI FRARI: After St Mark's, this is Venice's most prized church. It houses two Titians and a Bellini. Next to it is the SCUOLA DI SAN ROCCO with a collection of fifty-six Tintorettos on biblical themes. Entrance costs 6,000 L (4,000 L for reductions).

6. SCHOOL OF ST GEORGE: Beyond St Mark's Square at Calle dei Furlani. A frieze of paintings by Carpaccio – beautiful, and usually much quieter than the other museums. Entrance costs 4,000 L (3,000 L for reductions).

A few streets away from the 'sights' is the quieter, less touristy western side of Venice; a great place to go to escape the hordes.

• **Festivals:** The following is a selection of the many events that occur throughout the Venetian year. If possible, tailor your travelling plans to take in one. The 'Masked Carnival' takes place in the first two weeks of February, and the 'Festa del Redentore' (including an hour-long firework show) on the third Saturday of July. If you are in Venice in the last week of August and the first week of September, partake of the International Film Festival, and stay around for the 'Regata Storica' – a pageant of beautiful boats down the Grand Canal on the first Sunday in September.

• **Excursions:** Just east of Venice lies the LIDO, the beach resort of the rich and famous. Wander past the villas, casino and hotels, and imagine it as it was when Thomas Mann used it to inspire his novel, *Death in Venice*. Also worth a trip is the island of MURANO where Venetian glass is blown (but buy it in Venice itself as prices in Murano are inflated); BURANO, a colourful little fishing village; and TORCELLO with its Byzantine cathedral.

SLEEPING

Accommodation in Venice is not as troublesome as it used to be. Recently prices have levelled out, and it's no more expensive here now than in Rome or Paris. Watch out for hotel guides offering 'cheap' rooms at the station: some are not as good a bargain as they seem. The area near the station is as good as anywhere to look; just keep going from one pension to another. If all else fails, take the train (there is a flat fare of 1,000 L) to Mestre, eight minutes away, and base yourself there where beds and food are cheaper. It is now illegal to sleep in railway stations in Italy and if you risk it you are likely to have a hose trained on you and end up with a soaking. You should also seriously consider travelling to Padua for accommodation in high summer. It's only 30 minutes by train from Santa Lucia station and there is a regular service. Accommodation is much cheaper, even in the incredibly busy summer season, but you are strongly advised to book (and arrive) *well* in advance, as there can be an unwillingness to hold cheap rooms until your time of arrival, if demand is high.

• **Hostels:** The youth hostel is on the island of Giudecca at Fondamenta Zitelle 86C (Tel. 52 38211); take the waterbuses (costing 1,800 L) 5 and 8 from the landing stage along from the Piazza San Marco. Reception is open all day (11 p.m. curfew). Expect to pay 17,000 L for bed and breakfast. Also out here are a few pensions and a religious hostel (women only), Istituto Canossiane, Ponte Piccolo 428 (Tel. 52 21157). To get there take waterbus 5 to Sant' Eufernia, and walk to your left when you get off. Reception opens at 4 p.m., and it's 14,000 L each. More expensive is the Istituto Ciliota at San Marco 2976 (Tel. 5204888) which caters for women and married couples only. To get there take vaporetto 2 to San Samuele. A double room costs in the region of 65,000 L. Finally there's Domus Covanis, Dorsoduro 899, on Rio Foscarini (Tel. 52 87374). It's clean and convenient.

For camping, head to the beach on Litorale del Cavallino. Take vaporetto 4 from near San Marco to Punta Sabbioni. You'll find an endless stretch of camp-grounds in this area so you won't be short of choice. There is also a site at Fusina in Via Moranzani (Tel. 5470055), which you can get to by waterbus or road bus no. 13 from the railway bridge near Mestre station, though reports differ as to cleanliness. It costs 7,000 L per person and mosquito repellent is an essential addition to your camping gear. There are a number of sites on the mainland. Best bet is to take bus 5 or 19 from the bus station and get off at whichever one takes your fancy. Expect to pay about 4,000 L per night. Further out, on the island of Lido, the very basic campsite San Nicolò, Ballarin Giancarlo (Tel. 5267415), charges 4,000 L per person and 3,500 L per tent plus an extra 2,000 L if you have no camping carnet. Bus A from Lido ferry will get you there.

• **Hotels and pensions:** Don't attempt to stay in a single room – it'll cripple you financially. If you are travelling alone, find a partner quick, or head for a hostel. I suggest the Lista di Spagna near the station as there are many cheap pensions in this area. Locanda Stefania, Fondamenta Tolentini 181A (Tel. 5203757), is across the bridge at the station. Doubles cost around 42,000 L. The Hotel Villa Rosa at Calle della Misericordia 389 (off the Lista di Spagna) (Tel. 5216569), costs 45,000 L for a double with shower and balcony. Only two minutes' walk from St Mark's square is the 'Piccola Fenice' at the corner of Campo S. Angelo and Calle della Madonna (Tel. 5204909). It has only 15 rooms and charges about 30,000 L per person in a double or triple room. Breakfast is 7,200 L. Archie's House, Cannaregio 1814/B, San Leonardo (Tel. 720884) is only 10 minutes from the station. Locanda Ca' Foscari, Dorsoduro 3888 (Tel. 5225817) is clean and reasonably priced. Near the Mestre station, at Via Parini 4, you should be able to get a double for under 36,000 L. A friendly welcome and attractive rooms (double around 40,000 L) are offered at Col di Lana (signposted from just outside Mestre Station).

EATING AND NIGHTLIFE

Do not buy food and drink from stalls outside the station – items are half the price two minutes further on. There are quite a few fixed-price menus floating about and the food markets provide all you need for picnics. The main market is at the foot of the Rialto Bridge. There is also a cheap self-service restaurant here (expect to pay about 10,000 L). For trattorie the best area is Dorsoduro; there's a particularly good one at Dorsoduro 3922. If you're hard up and can't afford to eat at a trattoria, try the railworkers' café to the right of the station (Mensa Dopolavoro Ferroviario), or the students' Mensa at the end of Calle della Frescada. Warning: meals in restaurants are outrageously expensive.

Verona

It's not surprising Shakespeare chose Verona as his setting for *Romeo and Juliet* as it is a romantic city of palaces, churches, gardens and vineyards. It's about midway on the line from Milan to Venice and a popular destination with eurorailers who make their base here and travel to Padua and Venice for day-trips. From the station, it's a 15-minute walk to the centre of Verona, or take bus 1 to the PIAZZA BRÅ where the incredibly preserved ROMAN ARENA is. Tourist information offices are at Palazzo Barbieri, Cato Via Leoncimo 61 (Open Mon.–Sat.: 8 a.m.–8 p.m., Sun.: 9 a.m.–2 p.m., Tel. 592828) and Piazza Erbe 42 (Tel. 8030086). The Veronese merchants' palaces are located in the same square, and the adjoining PIAZZA SIGNORI contains the tombs of the Scaligeri, Verona's medieval enemies. Their house was the CASTELVECCHIO, which is now the showpiece painting and sculpture museum of Verona, open Tues.–Sun.: 8 a.m.–6.45 p.m. Admission is 5,000 L. The Romanesque church of SAN ZENO MAGGIORE is worth seeing for its bronze door-panels and the altar-piece by Mantegna.

For a bed, try the Casa della Giovane (for women), Via Pigna 7 (Tel. 596880), who charge about 17,000–25,000 L. Advance bookings taken. Open 8 a.m.–10.30 p.m. There is also the 'Ostello Verona' hostel at Salita Fontana del Ferro 15, 3 km from the station (Tel. 590360), just across the Ponte Pietra, and with bed and breakfast at 14,000 L a night it's good value. You can camp in the hostel grounds for 7,000 L. The hostel provides evening meals for 10,000 L extra. The chef will cater for vegetarians if notified in advance. The Elna Hotel, Via Mastino della Scala 9 (Tel. 500911) offers single rooms, with bathroom, from 45,000–61,700 L, and double rooms for 55,000–77,000 L. Alternatively, the Al Castello, Corso Cavour 43 (Tel. 8004403) offers singles for 30,000 L and doubles for 48,000–60,000 L, with bathrooms. Camping is available at Campeggio Castel San Pietro, Via Castel San Pietro 1 (Tel. 592037). Take bus 3 to Via Marsala. They charge 5,500 L per person and 4,000 L per tent and are only open in the summer months. Camping Romeo e Giulietta (Tel. 8510243) on the Via Bresciana 54 is open all year round. It is situated 5 km from the centre of Verona so take the APT bus to Peschiera from the train station.

Try Trattoria alla Canna at Via Scrimiari 5, Osteria al Cristo at Piazzetta Pescheria 6 or Trattoria da Mario, at Stradone Porta Palio for cheap set menus. Wash it down with the local Soave or Valpolicella wine. During the summer there are performances of opera in the 22,000-capacity Roman Arena. Seats start at about 22,000 L, but it's an experience you won't easily forget (check with tourist information).

Padua (Padova)

About 30 minutes from Venice lies Padua, the famous thirteenth-century university town. Today, it's not as attractive as it once was, due to heavy industry, so a one-day visit should suffice. Tourist information is at the station. Pick up maps here, and make use of the accommodation service which is free (open Mon.–Sat.: 9 a.m.–6 p.m., Sun.: 9 a.m.–12 noon). There is also a facility here where you can exchange money – cash and traveller's cheques. They take a 3,000 L commission (Tel. 049–793384.) There is normally only one person working here, so don't be surprised if it suddenly shuts at odd times, while they nip off for a break. There is also a downtown office at Riviera Mungai 22, which shuts at 6 p.m. and another at the entrance of the MUSEO CIVICO EREMITANI (same entrance for the Scrovegni Chapel) where you can get maps, hotels and change (open Tues.–Sun.: 9.30 a.m.–12.30 p.m., 2.30 p.m.–4.30 p.m.). If you're having real problems, the Foreigners' Office (Ufficio Stranieri) is based at Riviera Ruzzante and English interpreters are available from Mon.–Fri.: 10 a.m.–12.30 p.m.

The CAPPELLA SCROVEGNI is *the* sight of Padua: Giotto's masterpiece of medieval art that shook the theories of the time. Open from 9 a.m.–7 p.m. in the summer (until 6 p.m. in the winter) there is a 8,000 L entrance fee. Next door is the thirteenth-century CHIESA DEGLI EREMITANI where frescoes by the young Mantegna hang. Entrance is free, and the building is open from 8.15 a.m.–12 noon, daily. Further up Corso Garibaldi, on the Via Roma, and in the centre of the city, is the University. If you visit nothing else in the building of BOPALACE, visit the anatomy theatre; this breathtaking construction is the oldest in the world. The PALAZZO DELLO

RAGIONE, next door, keeps a magnificent thirteenth-century wooden horse and some beautiful frescoes. Entrance is 4,000 L and it is open Tues.–Sun.: 10 a.m.–6 p.m. If from here you walk up Piazza Antenore and turn right walking up Via del Santo, you'll come to IL SANTO on the Piazza. This is the church dedicated to St Anthony, which holds his remains and has thus become a site of pilgrimage. Note also that the building itself is constructed in six differing architectural styles. The SCUOLA SANT' ANTONIO contains four Titians also dedicated to this saint, the patron of Padua. Keep your eyes peeled, because all around Padua you'll find walls and gates, the majority of which date back to the sixteenth century. A useful item to invest in if you're on a cultural mission in the city is a 'Collective ticket' for Padua's museums and monuments. They cost in the region of 10,000 L (students 7,000 L) and are valid for a whole year. Buy them from the entrance of individual monuments and museums, or at the IAT offices in the city.

Accommodation shouldn't be a problem. The youth hostel here is a renovated medieval castle. It's at Porta Legnano in Montagnana (Tel. 0429/81076), an hour's bus ride from the bus station at Via Trieste, just in front of the station. You can also take a local train to Monselice, and change there for Montagnana. Buy your tickets from the booth here, or at any tobacconists instead of on the bus. In town, try the Ostello Città di Padova at Via Aleardi 30 (Tel. 049–875 2219). Also worth checking out is the Albergo Pavia, Via Papafava 11 (Tel. 049–875 1566). Expect to pay about 38,000 L for a double, 30,000 L for a single. The Casa Famiglia at Via Bixio 4, which only takes girls (Tel. 049–875 1554) is also worth trying. It is across from the station and to the left. It's run by nuns and costs 15,000 L per night. For food, go to the excellent food market, the Salone, near the university, or try one of the three Mensas: at Via San Francesco 122 (closed August), Via Padovanino, or Via Leopardi. In some people's opinion, the best place to head for is the Mensa in Via Piovego.

San Marino

On the slopes of Monte Titano, 23 km south-west of Rimini, you enter foreign territory. At just 61 square km San Marino is the world's smallest republic. It's also the oldest and has preserved its independence since the fourth century despite scheming princes and popes. It has a democratic constitution which so impressed Napoleon that he offered to enlarge the Republic. The offer was turned down – San Marino has never sought to expand but has been regarded as a place of sanctuary ever since it was founded (according to legend) by St Marinus, a Dalmatian stone cutter fleeing religious persecution. Garibaldi took up sanctuary there when fleeing from Venice in 1849.

Despite all this, there's rather a Toy Town feel to present-day San Marino. It is heavily reliant on tourism and milks its unique position for all it's worth. You no longer have to wave your passport on the border but you'll probably send postcards with the specially issued San Marino postage stamps (valued by collectors), and beware of getting too much San Marinese currency in your change – it has only souvenir value in the rest of Italy, and the Italian lira is valid here anyway.

Places of most interest are in the medieval capital, also called San Marino (see below) but a fairly shameless policy of reconstruction means that not everything is as steeped in ancient tradition as the San Marinese would have you believe. Amongst the more authentic pleasures of San Marino are the magnificent views of the Adriatic, and the duty-free drink.

GETTING THERE

There are no direct trains, so take the train to Rimini and bus the remaining 24km from there. Take the cable car from Borgo Maggiore at the foot of Monte Titano to San Marino (the capital).

TOURIST INFORMATION

There is a tourist office in the city of San Marino on the Contrada Omagnano 20 (Tel. 882410. Local telephone code 549).

SLEEPING AND EATING

San Marino has yet to respond to the needs of budget travellers and it's probably better to do a day-trip rather than an overnight stay. The cheapest hotels are in the region of 44,000–55,000 L. There are lots of good restaurants, although, again, you may find yourself paying over the odds. Duty-free drink makes this a good place to stock up on your favourite tipple.

SIGHTS

The Palazzo del Governo in San Marino city is a splendid neo-gothic affair (reconstructed in 1894). In front of the Palace is the Freedom Statue of San Marino. The palace is on the old town's main square – Piazza della Liberta. Just off the square is the neo-classical Basilica San Marino (1836). From the Basilica take the road south-east to the three peaks of Monte Titano with their three (rebuilt) medieval tower fortresses. For museums try the Garibaldi museum, the stamp and coin museum, the Museum of Weaponry, and the intriguingly named Museum of the Incredible but True. For cultural events, time your visit to coincide with 3 September, when the National Day of the Republic is celebrated with a Crossbow Competition.

Outside the city of San Marino, on the border, the medieval village of Verucchio has a tenth-century fortress (once the stronghold of Rimini tyrants), the Rocca Malatesta and a small Archaeology Museum with ceramics from 1400 BC Villanova culture. San Leo, also a border town, has a particularly fine Renaissance castle built by the Montefeltro Dukes of Urbino in the fifteenth century and containing a small picture gallery.

Tuscany

Italy's wealthiest region in every way. This was the birthplace of the Renaissance and, apart from the mountains and coastal beaches, it offers some of the finest old art cities in the world: Siena, Pisa and the Renaissance town itself, Florence. The countryside is beautiful – without the south's poverty or the north's heavy industry, and the trains serve even the smallest towns.

Florence (Firenze)

The Medici family made Florence the central point of the Renaissance, and her citizens included names like da Vinci, Botticelli, Michelangelo, Galileo and Machiavelli. The legacy lives on in today's Florence, and even the pot-smoking, guitar-strumming crowd that camp outside the Uffizi in summer can't take away from the centuries of elegance and careful detail that make this a pilgrimage centre for artists the world over. There are enough churches, galleries, palaces and museums to interest everyone, but there aren't enough beds, so come early to Florence, and avoid joining the throngs of August station-sleepers who wake up to find they've lost more than a good night's sleep, if they haven't been arrested first, as it is illegal to sleep on public ground such as stations.

STATION FACILITIES

FIRENZE SANTA MARIA NOVELLA

Train information	8 a.m.–9 p.m. (Tel. 288785)
Reservations	7 a.m.–9 p.m.
Tourist information	8.30 a.m.–9 p.m.
Foreign exchange	7.20 a.m.–1 p.m. Sat. and hols., otherwise
	7.20 a.m.–1 p.m., 2.35 p.m.–8 p.m. (poor rates)
Left-luggage store	All hours
Bar, Buffet; Restaurant	5.30 a.m.–11.20 p.m.; 11.30 a.m.–9 p.m.
Shops	8 a.m.–12 noon, 5 p.m.–7.30 p.m. exc. Wed. and Sun.

Daily trains to: Bologna, Venice, Munich, Vienna, Frankfurt, Pisa, Rome, Naples, Sicily, Paris, Milan.

TOURIST INFORMATION

The tourist office at the station branch (Tel. 283500) also deals with accommodation (commission 2,000–4,000L). Expect long queues. The city tourist office is at Via Manzoni 16 (Tel. 2346284 or 247814). They give out good maps of the city and a useful 1/3/5-day guide to the city which can help you plan the best sites to as many days. Open Mon.–Sat.: 8.30 a.m.–1.30 p.m. They do not book rooms.

• **Addresses:**

POST OFFICE: Via Pellicceria. Also poste restante and telephones. Open Mon.–Fri.: 8 a.m.–7 p.m.; Sat.: 8.15 a.m.–12 p.m.

AMEX: Via Guicciardini 49 (Tel. 288751), Mon.–Fri.: 9 a.m.–5.30 p.m., Sat.: 9 a.m.–12.30 p.m.

UK CONSULATE: Palazzo Castelbarco, Lungarno Corsini 2 (Tel. 284133/212594).

US CONSULATE: Lungarno Vespucci 38 (Tel. 217605).

STUDENT TRAVEL: Via dei Ginori 11 (Tel. 292150/289570).

24-HOUR CHEMIST: At the station by track 16, Comunale No.13 (Tel. 289435).

MOPED RENTAL: Excelsior, Via della Scala 48 (Tel. 298639) or outside the train station at Via Alamanni (Tel. 213307), charge is 30,000 L per day.

TOURIST MEDICAL OFFICE: 24-hour home visits (Tel. 475411).

POLICE: Via Zara 2 (Tel. 49771), English-speaking personnel available from 9 a.m.–2 p.m.

PHONE CODE: 055.

SEEING

First soak up the atmosphere in Florence: it is as important in this city as rushing around the never-ending historic sites; cars are banned from the city centre in the day, so it is easy to relax.

The DUOMO is the amazing multicolour cathedral with the huge dome which takes up a good chunk of the centre. It was started in 1296 and finished in 1434 – the dome was hailed as the wonder of the fifteenth century, but the façade of the cathedral today is only nineteenth-century. Climb the 464 steps (5,000 L) for an unrivalled view over Florence. The CAMPANILE was Giotto's idea and the BAPTISTRY is Romanesque and noted for its bronze doors by Ghiberti (open 9 a.m.–7.30 p.m.). The next sight of Florence has got to be the UFFIZI (30,000 L plus guidebook), one of the world's greatest art galleries housed in a Renaissance palace. There's such a glut of sheer genius here, you really can't cope; visit it more than once and try to avoid the crowds. It isn't quite the same trying to study the finer points of a Leonardo with school parties whizzing past and real art enthusiasts elbowing you out of the way to get a closer look. It's open Tues.–Sat.: 9 a.m.–7 p.m., Sun.: 9 a.m.–1 p.m. Closed Monday, as are most of Florence's sights. Still, we must be grateful we still have the Uffizi to visit, as Hitler ordered the collections to be destroyed in 1945, and the terrible flood of 1966 badly damaged many of its treasures.

Across from the Uffizi is the PALAZZO PITTI, a fifteenth-century palace which the Medicis used during the sixteenth century. You can wander round it today and see the Raphaels, Rubens, Titians, and on its ground floor the ROYAL APARTMENTS and MUSEUM OF GEMS. All the palaces and museums are open from 9 a.m.–2 p.m. and are closed on Mondays. The medieval BARGELLO PALACE holds the NATIONAL MUSEUM, which is an important sculpture collection. If you, like thousands of others, came to Florence to see Michelangelo's 'David' you'll find him in the GALLERIA DELL'ACCADEMIA on Via Ricasoli. The massive PALAZZO VECCHIO was the Medici residence from the fourteenth to the sixteenth century. Inside it's sumptuous – not surprisingly, they got the cream of Renaissance artists to decorate it. It's at Piazza della Signoria (closed Saturdays). The other palace you ought to see is the MEDICI on Via Cavour (open 9 a.m.–12.30 p.m., 3 p.m.–5 p.m., closed Wednesdays). They lived here from 1460 to 1540. There's a tiny chapel on the first floor, and a Medici Museum downstairs which is free on Sundays.

As far as churches go, take in the Medicis' Renaissance parish church, ST LAURENCE'S. Most of them are buried here in the MEDICI CHAPELS (closed Mondays), and there's a LIBRARY considered to be Michelangelo's architectural masterpiece. SAN MARCO is worth seeing for the monks' cells which Fra Angelico painted his unique shade of blue, and the BRANCACCI CHAPEL of Santa Maria della Carmine has some beautiful Masaccio frescoes. Giotto has some work in SANTA CROCE and next to this is the interesting PAZZI CHAPEL.

The PONTE VECCHIO was the only bridge to survive the war intact, when the Germans blew-up all the others but were rushed by New Zealanders of the 8th Army before they could destroy it. It dates back to 1345 and is famous for the gold- and silversmith shops that line it. The STRAW MARKET (Mercato Nuovo) makes a good shopping trip, and the BOBOLI GARDENS, behind the Pitti Palace, are good for a picnic and sunbathe; they close at night, however, and charge 5,000 L entry.

SLEEPING

Use the station tourist office and stress your price range. Florence is more expensive than average (now higher than Venetian levels), so be prepared to spend about 15,000 L in a hostel, 25,000 L in a pension and about 35,000 in a hotel for a single. Showers are invariably an extra 3,000 L and breakfast is rarely included.

● **Hostels:** The youth hostel is at 2/4 Viale Augusto Righi (Tel. 601451) with around 400 beds, but it's for IYHF members only and costs 18,000 L a night. Reception opens at 2 p.m.; take bus 17B from the station. Pio X-Artigianelli is another hostel at Via dei Serragli 106 (Tel. 225044). It's near the Pitti Palace, but it's small so try to get there early. Ostello S. Monaca, Via Santa Monaca 6 (Tel. 2396704), 17,000 L, is a private hostel near the centre, bus 11 or a fifteen-minute walk from the station. It is shut between 1 p.m. and 3 p.m., but you can reserve a place and leave your luggage at other times and register properly between 4 p.m. and 11.30 p.m.

● **Pensions:** There is a glut of suitable places within five minutes of the station. The only problem is that this is common knowledge, so get there early. If you come up with nothing in this area, drop off your pack if it's heavy as the other pensions are a good walk away. From the station, turn left then try places along Via Nazionale, Via Fiume, Via Fuenza, Via 28 Aprile, Via Guelfa and Via Cavour. We've tried the following and found them OK: Hotel Ester, Via Nazionale (Tel. 212741); Hotel Mia Cara at Via Fuenza 58 (Tel. 216053); Hotel Sofia, Via Cavour (Tel. 283930); Hotel Fiume (Tel. 211045). Also try Hotel Sampaoli at Via S. Gallo 39 (Tel. 284834) and Hotel Giovanna, Via Firenze 69 (Tel. 2381353).

Outside this section try Hotel Aldini, Via Calzaioli 13 (Tel. 214752), near the Duomo, or Hotel Davanzati at Via Porta Rossa 15 (Tel. 283414). If you fancy splashing out on luxury with your travelling companion try the Pensione Maria Luisa de'Medici, Via del Corso 1 (Tel. 280048) with its elaborate atmosphere. Double rooms with a bath and shower cost 63,000 L a night, 94,000 L for triples, and breakfast is served in the room. You must ring in advance to reserve, though.

● **Camping:** Viale Michelangelo 80 (Tel. 6811977) is a site open (6 a.m.–12 midnight) from April–Oct. but often full. It has good views of Florence and charges 5,000 L per person and 6,000 L per tent.

Take bus 13 from the cathedral. For all-year camping try Camping Camerata next to the youth hostel (Tel. 610300) on the 17b bus route. Neither will take bookings by phone although you can check how full they are first, before travelling. There is a municipal site at Villa Farvard, 6 km out of town, which provides **free shelter and showers**. Take buses 14a, b or c from the station and stop at Rocco Teddabla. Open from 7 p.m. to 10 a.m. Seven nights' stay allowed only in summer time. Security here is very good, and often people leave their belongings here while they excursion out to Pisa for the day, since it balances out the cost of sightseeing. Try the Norcenni Girasole Club campsite (Tel. 959666) 27 km south of Florence.

Travel at night from Florence to Venice and save yourself the cost of a bed: many night trains leave from the Campo di Marte station, and you arrive in Venice around daybreak.

EATING AND NIGHTLIFE

The Santo Spirito–San Frediano quarter has more economy restaurants than elsewhere, but really Florence isn't geared up for subsistence-level living. Cheapest of all is the station buffet – spaghetti for 3100 L.

The self-service restaurant at Piazza della Stazione 25 does a really cheap meal; a favourite (for a splurge) is Trattoria ZaZa at P. Mercato Centrale 26. A busy but good and cheap place is Trattoria il Constadino, Via Palazzuolo 69. If you've really reached rock bottom, Casa San Francesco on Piazza Sant' Annunziata (diagonally opposite Chiesa di Sant Annunziata), run by Franciscans, will do you a full lunch for about 9,000 L. They're only open for lunch, so you'll have to eat other meals elsewhere, and only use this if you are really broke. The university Mensas are on Via San Gallo 25 and Via dei Servi 66–68. For picnic food, the Mercato Centrale, near San Lorenzo, is your best bet. There are also a number of fast-food chains and, of course, ice-cream parlours. Florence is reputed to have the best *gelati* in Italy. Vivoli, on Via dell' Isola delle Stinche, is still held by many to produce the world's best. Use the take-away pizza places for economy shopping.

During July and August there are bi-weekly classical concerts held in the Pitti Palace courtyard, and there's a music festival in May. On 24 June there are fireworks on Piazzale Michelangelo after

the parade in sixteenth-century costume, and the soccer match of
the afternoon. On most summer nights, groups of students and
travellers congregate on the Ponte Vecchio, and at the Duomo and
Piazzale Michelangelo.

Nightclubs are expensive, charging between 12,000 and 15,000 L
for admission. The most international of those available is Space
Electronic, on Via Palazzuolo 37, open from 9.30 p.m.–1.30 a.m.,
complete with a pirhana-filled fish tank as decor.

Siena

Siena is Tuscany's second art city, but while Florence is Renaissance, Siena is medieval. It's 1½ hours from Florence, and there are
trains daily passing through Empoli and Poggibonsi. (Trains from
Rome go via Chiusi, and you have to change at these stops unless
you're taking a direct train.) The heart of the city is the PIAZZA DEL
CAMPO, where the Palio (an inter-district horse-race) is held as part
of the 2 July and 16 August celebrations, with fifteenth-century
costume parades and all-night dances following on. The closest
you'll get to the centre by bus from the station is Piazza Matteoti;
walk the rest. The Gothic TOWN HALL (Palazzo Communale) and
the bell tower in the piazza are well worth a visit. Entrance is only
2,500 L on ISIC. In the PIAZZA DEL DUOMO (bus 1: tickets at station)
is ST CATHERINE'S CATHEDRAL with its museum of art and sculpture
opposite. The CHIGI SARACINI PALACE is today a music academy, but
on request they'll show you round the Renaissance apartments and
gallery of Tuscan paintings. Further along you'll come to PIAZZA
SALIMBENI with its four palaces dating from the thirteenth to the
sixteenth centuries. The MUSEO CIVICO in the Palazzo Publico
houses an exceptional exhibition of Sienese art, including the
magnificent frescoes by Pietro and Ambrogio Lorenzetti: 'Alleg-
ories of Good and Bad Government and their Effect on Town and
Country'. These two paintings are responsible for many art
historical waxings upon space and perspective in Sienese art.
Admission to the museum is 5,500 L (students 3,000 L) and it is open
from Mon.–Sat.: 9.30 a.m.–6.45 p.m., Sun.: 9.30 a.m.–12.45 p.m.

The busiest and most colourful time to visit the city is on 2 July or

16 August when the 'Il Palio' takes place, a night-long celebration and torch-lit procession in fifteenth-century costume. The central event is a traditional horse-race around Piazza del Campo at 7 p.m. Standing room for the race is free, but arrive early, and remember to book accommodation in advance for this period.

Cheap rooms are a bit of a problem here, but you can try Locanda Garibaldi, Via G. Dupré 18 (Tel. 0577–284204). It's central and one of the cheapest in Siena. Or ask tourist information: they're at Piazza del Campo 5 (Tel. 0577–280551), open Mon.–Fri.: 9 a.m.–12.30 p.m., 3.30 p.m.–7 p.m.; Saturdays: mornings only. There's no shortage of good trattorie, and the Mensa Universitaria is on Via Sant' Agata. The IYHF hostel is at Via Fiorentina 89 (Tel. 0577–52212) about 1 mile from the centre. Beds from about 15,000 L, including breakfast. To get there take bus 4 or 15 from the station. The nearest camping ground is at Siena Colleverde, Strada di Scacciapensieri 47 (Tel. 280044). To get there take bus 8 from Piazza Gramsci. The site is open from March until November and costs 8,600 L per person, including tent.

Pisa

Head straight for the PIAZZA DEL DUOMO with its famous Leaning Tower which Galileo used in his experiments (bus 1 from the station), or a 1½ km walk. There is a tourist office also situated in this square, though the main office is at Lugarno Mediceo 42 (Tel. 050–203512). Beside the tower is the CATHEDRAL (open from 7.45 a.m.–12.45 p.m., 3 p.m.–6.45 p.m. daily) and the BAPTISTRY, the pulpit of which, by Nicola Giovanni, is the first Gothic sculpture in Italy, dating from 1206. Nearby is CAMPO SANTO, a twelfth-century cemetery built by the Crusaders. The MUSEO NAZIONALE DI SAN MATTEO, on the Arno near Piazza Mazzini, houses important works by many important fifteenth-century artists. Admission is 6,000 L and the museum is open from Tues.–Sat.: 9 a.m.–7.30 p.m., Sun.: 9 a.m.–1.30 p.m.

Lodgings are difficult if you arrive late. Try Locanda Galileo, Via Santa Maria 12 (Tel. 050–40621), down Via San Lorenzo, or Casa della Giovanni, Via F. Corridoni (Tel. 22732). The latter is a ten-minute walk, turn right from the station, and offers women bed and breakfast for 15,000 L. The campsite is at Viale delle Caseine 86 (Tel. 050–560665). It is about 700 m from Rossore station (the opposite side of town from the main station), bus 5 will see you there. Prices are about 6,000 L per person and 3,000 L per tent. Next to the site is a huge supermarket where you can stock up on food and drink at reasonable prices. The Mensa Universitaria on Via Martiri offers good food at cheap prices and is open from mid-September to mid-July from 12 noon–2.30 p.m. daily, and on weekdays for evening meals from 7–9 p.m. There are also other cheap places around the University.

Florence–Rome (Umbria)

It's a two-hour journey from Florence to Rome by the InterCity direct line, but why not take a detour to visit the attractive towns of Perugia and Assisi? If you choose the latter route and decide to stop off for a few hours at each place, here is some basic information on these two places:

PERUGIA is the capital of Umbria, and a beautiful medieval hill town about one and a half hours from Florence. Although the centre and university are quite modern, a walk up the side streets will take you back to the days of Perugino – Raphael's teacher. Sights to see are the CATHEDRAL, NATIONAL GALLERY OF UMBRIA, NATIONAL ARCHAEOLOGICAL MUSEUM and the ARCH OF AUGUSTUS. The GALLERIA NAZIONALE DELL'UMBRIA at the Palazzo dei Priori has a rich collection of paintings by Fra Angelico and Piero della Francesca. It is open from 9 a.m.–2 p.m., 3 p.m.–7 p.m., and entrance is 8,000 L. Next door is the COLLEGIO DEL CAMBIO where there are frescoes painted by Perugino in collaboration with Raphael. The opening hours are the same, but the price for entry is cheaper, at 3,000 L. If jazz is your scene then try to coincide your visit with the annual jazz festival which takes place from late June to early July. The youth hostel is 2 minutes from the cathedral on Via Bontempi 13 (Tel. 22880) and the price per person is about 12,000 L. There are many cheap pensions and guest houses in the city which charge between 25,000 and 45,000 L for a single room and between 50,000 and 60,000 L for a double. Try the Casa del Sacro Cuore, Via del Brozzo 12 (Tel. 33141) which has a restaurant, bar and disabled access. Tourist offices can be found at Via Mazzini 21 (Tel. 075–25341) or down the road, next to the town hall at the Piazza IV Novembre (Tel. 23327). They are open from 8.30 a.m.–1.30 p.m. and 4 p.m.–7 p.m. The camping site is at It Rocolo, Colle della Trinità and is open in the summer months only. Expect to pay about 6,000 L per person, plus 4,500 L per tent. If it's sun and swimming that you're after, Perugia is well linked by rail and bus to Lake Trasimeno – the largest stretch of water on the Italian peninsula.

ASSISI, famed for its saint, is also very near. In fact the city and its environs are encrusted with pious history and active monasteries. The thirteenth-century BASILICA OF ST FRANCIS AND SACRO CONVENTO is the first place to head for. There are two churches built one above the other, with a crypt that houses St Francis's tomb. The upper basilica is adorned by Giotto's frescoes illustrating the life of the saint, and there is also much work by Cimabue. Open daily, except for Sunday mornings when Mass is delivered in English at 8.30 a.m. Other religious structures to visit are the Romanesque CATHEDRAL OF ST RUFIUS and the BASILICA OF ST CHIARA where the body of St Claire is preserved in the crypt. Directly behind, outside the city walls, is a Franciscan shrine in SAN D'AMIANO built on the spot where St Francis heard the voice of Christ and wrote his Canticle of the Creatures.

In the centre of the city is the first-century BC TEMPLE OF MINERVA (now a church) behind which is located the Roman Forum. The tourist office is opposite these Roman columns on the Piazza del Comune (Tel. 075–812534) which is open 8 a.m.–2 p.m., 3.30 p.m.–6.30 p.m. Ask here for addresses of private homes and religious institutions that offer accommodation. A cheap hotel is situated nearby in Corso Mazzini 20 (Tel. 812922) and charges 60,000 L for a single room and between 70,000–85,000 L for a double. A hostel and campground is situated 1 km from Assisi at Fontemaggio. It charges 15,000 L for a bed and is only a short bus journey from the station to P. Matteotti. The IYHF 'Ostello della Pace' in Via Valecchi is 3 km away from the train station. Open all year round it charges 16,000 L for bed and breakfast (Tel. 075–816767). Also on the outskirts is the ROCCA MAGGIORE where for 3,000 L you can climb up for a stupendous view over the town and valley. Further over on the opposite side of the town is the CHURCH OF SANTA MARIA DEGLI ANGELI, in a suburb 5 km away, which contains the Porziuncula: the nucleus of the first Franciscan Monastery and the Cappella del Transito where St Francis died in 1226.

Rome (Roma)

Rome, the 'eternal city', is so called because it is a place of great beauty, contrast and life. There are really three Romes: the religious world centre of the Catholic Church, the incredible ruins of the centre of the Roman Empire, and modern, dirty, bustling Rome. All three seem incongruous, yet they live inside and beside each other with great ease. You'll soon realize Rome was built to rule and dominate the world. Everything is on a massive scale, solid and 'eternal'. You'll find the Romans proud, arrogant and conceited, but you'll look back on the overwhelming beauty and dimensions of St Peter's, the atmosphere in the Colosseum at dusk, and the Trevi Fountain when it's floodlit at night and buzzing with young people, and remember it affectionately.

STATION FACILITIES

	ROMA TERMINI
Train information	7 a.m.–11 p.m. (Tel. 4775)
Reservations	7 a.m.–10 p.m.
Tourist information	8.15 a.m.–7 p.m.
Foreign exchange (near platform 12)	Mon.–Fri.: 8.30 a.m.–1.30 p.m. in bank. Other times, window 28
Left-luggage store	All hours (Pay double for tents attached to outside of rucksack)
Bar, Buffet	6 a.m.–11.25 p.m. and 7.20 a.m.–8.40 p.m.
Cafeteria	10.30 a.m.–11 p.m.
Bath, Shower	7.20 a.m.–8.40 p.m.
Waiting room	Closed 4 a.m.–6 a.m.
Shops	7 a.m.–9 p.m.
Post office	Mon.–Fri.: 8.15 a.m.–8 p.m., Sat.: 8 a.m.–12 noon
Station shuts	1.30 a.m.–4.30 a.m.

It also has a morgue for 'departed' passengers.
Daily trains to: Pisa, Genoa, Nice, Milan, Innsbruck, Venice, Florence, Bologna, Ancona, Naples, Brindisi, Sicily.

Trains running from the north of Italy to the south and vice versa stop at Tirbutina station so you don't have to come into the centre.

TOURIST INFORMATION

Before leaving the station, go along to the EPT tourist office on platform 3 and pick up a map of the city, plus two booklets, 'Qui Roma' ('Here's Rome', current events, etc.) and 'Roma Giovane' ('Young Rome') as these are a great help in getting to know your way around.

Apart from the office at the station which does not provide camping information (Tel. 4871270/4824078), there's one at Via Parigi 5 (Tel. 4883748) (open Mon.–Sat.: 8.15 a.m.–7.15 p.m.) which is very near the station, and queues are shorter. To get there, leave the station by the main doors and head towards the large fountain. Once past this, take the small road which is the first turning on the right. Pick up 'Qui Roma' here and, rather than leave yourself open to their accommodation suggestions (all over 25,000 L), hand them some of our telephone numbers and ask them to phone for a reservation for you.

Generally, shops and churches are open 9 a.m.–1 p.m., 4 p.m.–8 p.m. Museums generally close about 1 p.m. or 2 p.m. and all day Monday, though the Campidoglio museums open late on Tuesdays and Saturdays. In August, Romans take their holidays and you'll find many restaurants shut.

● **Addresses:**

POST OFFICE: Piazza San Silvestro 19, open Mon.–Fri.: 8.30 a.m.–9.40 p.m. for poste restante, Sat.: 8.30 a.m.–11.30 a.m., telephones 8 a.m.–12 midnight.

AMEX: Piazza di Spagna 38, open Mon.–Fri.: 9 a.m.–5.30 p.m., Sat.: 9 a.m.–12.30 p.m. (Tel. 67641).

UK EMBASSY: Via XX Settembre 80a (Tel. 48 25551).

US EMBASSY: Via Vittorio Veneto 119a (Tel. 46741).

CANADIAN EMBASSY: Via Zara 30 (Tel. 440 3063).

CTS (YOUTH TRAVEL SERVICE): Via Genova 16 (Tel. 46791). They help out on accommodation, issue ISICs, etc. Also a Eurotrain office (Tel. 46791).

LATE CHEMIST: In station.

INTERNATIONAL MEDICAL CENTRE (English spoken): (Tel. 4882371 or 4881129).

CITY POLICE: (Tel. 67691).

PHONE CODE: 06.

• **Getting about:** The buses are cheap, costing 1,000 L and the underground continues to expand yearly (costs 700 L and 6,000 L for 10), but it's difficult as they keep finding new archaeological sites where they want to lay tracks. Bus tickets are valid for an hour and a half, and you may change the bus or tramway with the same ticket provided you do not exceed the time limit. On boarding the bus, you should cancel the ticket, in order that the time is readable. Buy tickets from Tabac shops or the stations. Buses run from 5.45 a.m.–12 midnight. You can buy a cheap route map from the bus kiosk at the station. (Few people buy metro tickets!)

Special weekly bus tickets for tourists are sold for 10,000 L at the Ufficio Abbonamenti (season-ticket office) of the ATAC on Largo Giovanni Montemartini and at the Ufficio Informazioni (enquiry office) on Piazza dei Cinquento. They are valid for the entire day and night network, with the exception of sightseeing tours, for eight days.

Avoid the taxis which are expensive, costing around 3,000 L for the first minute, with a surcharge of 3,000 L for night service, and extra for each suitcase.

There are many stands in the summer, throughout the city at various piazzas, which rent out bicycles, especially along the Via del Corso. The rates are generally 15,000 L a day. Near the Vatican is St Peter Rent, via Porta Castello 43 (Tel. 6875714) which also hires out mopeds and scooters and is open from 9 a.m.–7 p.m.

SEEING

Though the three sides of Rome (ancient, religious and modern) are virtually inseparable, we've tried to separate the sights into the three categories. If you give yourself a day for each you'll make it, but by the end you'll need to head for a beach to soothe your blisters in the sea. Ideally, give yourself 4–5 days here, and unless you're really flattened, use the afternoon siestas to get round the sights which are otherwise mobbed. A final word: be on your guard constantly for pickpockets, including young children begging to distract your attention and particularly the motorized ones who cruise about on mopeds and whip handbags off shoulders and wallets from pockets, then make off at great speed.

• **Ancient Rome:** The sites of ancient Rome are clustered round the

Piazza Venezia, the modern city centre, and lie on the PALATINE, CAPITOLINE and AVENTINE hills.

The COLOSSEUM is the biggest site of ancient Rome (free for lower levels, 6,000 L for upper). Open from 9 a.m.–7 p.m. in the summer months and 9 a.m.–3 p.m. in the winter, closed Sunday and Wednesday afternoons. This huge arena sat 55,000 Romans who passed many an afternoon watching the local Christians being eaten for dinner by lions, etc., or gladiators fighting it out to the bitter end. The Palatine Hill is where Nero, Mark Antony, Cicero and co. were based. The VILLA FARNESE incorporated many ancient structures into it when it was built in the sixteenth century, and the BOTANICAL GARDENS here were the world's first. See the frescoes on the HOUSE OF AUGUSTUS and the remains of the PALACE OF THE FLAVIANS and the PALACE OF SEPTIMIUS SEVERUS.

The ROMAN FORUM, adjoining the Palatine Hill, was the commercial, religious and civic centre of ancient Rome. Look out for the three TRIUMPHAL ARCHES, HOUSE OF THE VESTAL VIRGINS and the half-dozen temples. Enter by Via dei Fori Imperiali (closed Sundays and Tuesday afternoons, costs 10,000 L). Opposite is the IMPERIAL FORUM; Caesar started this annexe of the Roman Forum when the expanding empire's paperwork was getting too much for the one place. See TRAJAN'S FORUM with its famous column, and the BASILICA OF ST MAXENTIUS, the ancient law court and exchange (closed Mondays). The MAMERTINE PRISON, just off Via dei Fori Imperiali, is where Nero kept St Peter, and many others were tortured here.

The PANTHEON is the best preserved of all the sites of ancient Rome. It was started in 27 BC, rebuilt in AD 125 and, having been a temple to the gods for over 700 years, became a Christian church in the seventh century. The kings of Italy and the artist Raphael are buried here. It's at Piazza della Rotonda, near the Tiber. Entrance is free, and opening times are 9 a.m.–2 p.m. daily.

On the APPIAN WAY, the 2,300-year-old Roman road stretching as far south as Brindisi, you'll find the third-century BATHS OF CARACALLA (near Piazzale Numa Pompilio), and the CATACOMBS OF ST CALIXTUS. There are five tiers of burial chambers, and many Christian saints and martyrs here, at 110 Via Appia Antica (closed Wednesdays). The NATIONAL MUSEUM OF ROME has the world's best collection of artefacts from the Roman Empire (Via delle Terme di Diocleziano, closed Mondays). CASTEL SANT' ANGELO, built by

Hadrian in AD 139, was the Pope's fortress to flee to in times of danger. Now it's a museum of weapons, art and relics (Lungotevere Castello, closed Mondays). That leaves only the THEATRE OF MAR-CELLUS (13 BC), the PYRAMID OF CAIUS CESTIUS on Piazza San Paolo, and the remains of four ancient ROMAN TEMPLES in Largo Argentina. All the Roman remains that don't close on Mondays tend to close on Tuesdays.

• **Papal Rome:** The independent state of the VATICAN CITY is the spiritual centre for 627 million Roman Catholics. The Vatican has its own post office with stamps, printing press, currency, radio station, newspaper and railway, all within one square mile. The Pope's in charge here and the Swiss Guards keep order. ST PETER'S SQUARE is a seventeenth-century baroque masterpiece, designed by Bernini, which leads up to ST PETER'S BASILICA, the church whose incredible dome can be seen all over Rome. Inside the huge interior are works by Raphael, Michelangelo (his famous Pietà), Bernini and Bramante. (Don't wear shorts, or have bare shoulders, if you want to get in.) For the full emotion of this church to hit you – even if you're an atheist – come at 8 a.m. and climb the stairs to the top of the dome for a breathtaking view. The basilica itself is open from 7 a.m.–7 p.m. The VATICAN MUSEUMS which include such treasures as Michelangelo's SISTINE CHAPEL, the RAPHAEL ROOMS, the GRAECO-ROMAN MUSEUMS, and the VATICAN LIBRARY are located north of St Peter's on Viale Vaticano. It costs about 7,000 L on ISIC, 10,000 L without, but it's well worth it. There are four alternative routes to follow through the museums; we suggest you take C or D, and skip through the bits you're not interested in. They are open Mon.–Sat. and the last Sunday of every month, when admission is free for everyone. Museums close at 5 p.m. in summer, and last entry is at 4 p.m. The two churches that must be included here, though they're not located in or near the Vatican, are ST JOHN LATERAN with the HOLY STAIRS and SANTA MARIA MAGGIORE. The former is the church of the popes, founded in the fourth century. The stairs are believed to be those from the palace of Pontius Pilate which Christ ascended during his Passion. You can only climb them, however, if you're officially worshipping, and then you have to do it on your knees. The church is south-east of the Colosseum at Piazza San Giovanni in Laterno. The latter is another fourth-century church, though rebuilt in the thirteenth and with an eighteenth-century façade.

The campanile is the tallest in Rome and there are some interesting fifth-century mosaics (Via Liberiana 27). Mass is at 10 a.m. on Sundays, but come earlier to allow for queueing.

• **Modern Rome:** The squares of Rome are worth seeing as sights in themselves. The PIAZZA DEL CAMPIDOGLIO, designed by Michelangelo, is flanked by palaces and is considered to be the political city centre. Of the three palaces one is the senatorial office, one is the CAPITOLINE MUSEUM of antique sculptures, and the other is the CONSERVATORIO which has large chunks of hands, toes and heads from Roman statues. The Capitoline Museum, like the Vatican, offers free access on the last Sunday of each month, otherwise it charges 8,000 L entrance. Like all the other museums it closes at 2 p.m., and is shut on Mondays, so try and organize your sightseeing around its later opening times on Tuesdays and Saturdays from 5 p.m.–8 p.m., and 8.30 p.m.–11 p.m. on Saturdays.

The PIAZZA NAVONA is another Bernini work, as is PIAZZA BARBERINI. The SPANISH STEPS (Piazza di Spagna) are eighteenth-century and the Barcaccia fountain at the bottom attracts a young crowd of manwatchers, but *the* fountain of Rome has got to be the TREVI at Piazza di Trevi. This baroque work was finished in 1762. If you're looking for your Latin lover, come here after dark. The fountain's floodlit and the atmosphere typically Roman. Next to it is the BASILICA S. MARIA (opposite McDonald's) which is as beautiful as the more renowned tourist attractions, and far less crowded.

The MONUMENT TO VICTOR EMMANUEL II, in the Piazza Venezia, is the huge white marble 'wedding cake' at the end of Via del Corso. It was built in 1911 to celebrate Italy's unification. The VILLA BORGHESE, in the north of Rome, is the most splendid of Rome's parks. The zoo (open from 8 a.m.–6 p.m., admission 5,000 L) and two art galleries are out here, and though this seems like the best place to sleep out in Rome, it is very dangerous.

If you're in search of artistic modernism amongst the historical weight of Rome, visit the National Gallery of Modern Art on the Viale delle Belle Arti, which houses the biggest collection of Italian art from the nineteenth century to the present day. Entrance is 8,000 L and opening times are 9 a.m.–2 p.m. daily. There are many street markets in the city for those who wish to browse for material items and escape from the spiritual heritage. Via Sannio plays host to a new and secondhand clothing market, whilst that of the Porta

Portese is a curio heaven every Sunday morning. Arrive about 8.30 a.m. for the best viewing – it gets crowded quickly – and remember to watch your wallet.

SLEEPING

Though Rome gets packed in July and August, beds are never really a problem as there are literally hundreds of pensions, locande and alloggi. There are plenty of cheap places beside the station and, though this isn't right in the centre, it's not so far out you can't walk to the sights, and the prices are the cheapest in town. To help you find a place, use either CTS (see addresses), the Student Help Office or the tourist offices; but remember to get them to phone only your own suggested places, as theirs are all over the top.

There are three university halls of residence, which are opened from the end of July to the end of September by the IYHF. They are at Via Cesare de Lollis, 24/B (Tel. 063242571), (take bus 492 from the Termini station), 'CIVIS', 7 km from the station at Viale del Ministero degli Affari Esteri 6 (take Subway A to Ottaviano, then bus 32) and at Via D. De Dominicis (Subway A to Colli Albani, then bus 409). All charge around 18,000–20,000 L for bed and breakfast. Bookings for these hostels are handled by the one office (Tel. 3242571 or 3242573).

• **Student hostels:** The other youth hostel is at Viale delle Olimpiadi 61 (Tel. 3236279); it is 6 km out and reports on it vary dramatically (costs 18,000 L per night). To get there take the subway to Ottaviano and then bus 32. There's the Centro dei Giovane at Via degli Apuli 40 (Tel. 4953151); it's cheap and convenient but tends to fill up quickly, so get there early. Next door is the Hotel del Popolo (no. 4), (Tel. 490558), beds cost around 20,000 L per single. Cheaper at 18,000 L a night but far more crowded are the dorms at the English-speaking Pensione Ottaviano 4 (Tel. 383956) near Piazza de Resergimento. Another cheaper and recommended place is Pensione Lachea, Via San Martino della Battaglia 11 (Tel. 4957256). Here singles cost 25,000 L, doubles 38,000 L and triples 55,000 L a night. Advance reservations and deposits, though, are necessary.

• **Pensions near the station:** As you leave the station you can turn either right or left to begin your search. On the right is Via Palestro. At No. 9 of this street is Pensione Lella which charges around

60,000 L per double and at No. 35 is Pensione Michele (Tel. 4873359), with Pensione Katty (Tel. 4441216) on the third floor at the same address. At No. 15 is Pensione Bolognese, which has clean rooms and showers and costs about 50,000 L for a double, 65,000 L if you want a shower room (Tel. 490045). The Pensione at Piemonte at Via Vicenza 34 (Tel. 4452240) costs about 60,000 L for a double with showers.

On the left of the station you'll find another spate of pensions, and also several cheap eating-places. This is a very Roman working-class neighbourhood, full of colour and life. Via Principe Amedeo has a collection of very good bed bargains; all ask about 36,000 L a person. The pensions include Cotorillo, Contilia, Govoni and di Rienzo, which are all very acceptable. Next door at No. 79 is Hotel Pezzotti (Tel. 4466875) with free showers and adequate double rooms for 50,000 L; and at 79d on the sixth floor is Pensione Tony (Tel. 4466889). His rooms are clean and have their own shower. Another recommended place is the Pensione Germano, 14a Via Calatafimi (Tel. 486919), which is clean, friendly and inexpensive.

If things are desperate and you're sleeping out, no matter how desperate you are avoid flaking out in the park outside the station. Each summer the muggings seem to get more numerous and vicious, and the gypsies that hang out there should be watched like hawks. The park at Calle Oppio, near the Colosseum, is your best bet, but even that is to be avoided. One final piece of advice. Roman pensione owners are notorious for attempting the great tourist rip-off. Always check the prices with those posted in the room, and argue for the difference.

• **Camping:** There are several sites around Rome, but none are near the centre. One of the nearest, five miles out, is Flaminio, at Via Flaminia (Tel. 3332604). It is quite good and open all year but relatively expensive. To get there take the underground from Piazza Flaminio and request the stop for the camping site called Due Ponti, or take the tramline 225 (from Station Termini take bus 910) to the endstation Piazza Mancini, followed by bus 202, 203, 204 or 205 to the site. The prices here are cheap: cost is around £10 for two people and one tent, with free pool and video facilities. Single and double tents are also available for hire from the campsite. Try also Camping Roma on Via Aurelia. Take bus 38 from the train station to Piazza Fiume, then bus 490 to the terminus where you change to bus 246. For Camping Nomentano, Via Nomentana, take bus 36 from outside Termini Station to Piazza Sempione, then bus 336 to Via Nomentana. Salaria Camping, Via Salaria 2141 is still the cheapest in town.

EATING AND NIGHTLIFE

For about 15,000 L you can eat a good, filling meal in Rome. Almost every neighbourhood has its own collection of cheap trattorie and rosticcerie, as the Romans eat out a lot themselves. Go for the menu turistico and spoil yourself on the delicious pasta and pizza dishes which fill you up for very little money. There's little point buying food for picnics (though if you do, bar owners will let you eat it inside if you buy a drink from them) as good supermarkets are few and far between. Don't trail across town to follow our few suggestions; just eat at the nearest likely spot wherever you happen to find yourself, though remember that it is the smaller street establishments that offer the best prices. The Mensa Universitaria on Via Cesare de Lollis 20 is closed all August. Palmerie, Via Cimarra 415, is where some of the trendy Roman crowd hang out. The fixed-price menus are reasonable. The area on the right-hand side of the station as you leave is good for tourist menus. Especially good value is Osteria da Salvatore at Via Castelfidardo 39c. Expect to pay around 15,000 L, including drinks. For a good self-service restaurant, try the one at Piazza Cinquecento 47 near the station. For the vegetarian or the health conscious, try splashing out at L'Albero Del Pane, Dei Bianchi Vecchi 39, a health food store selling natural organic foods. Open from 9 a.m.–1.30 p.m., 5 p.m.–8 p.m. Giolitti's are reputed to have the best ice-cream in Rome. They're near the Pantheon at Via Ufficio del Vicario 40.

The Romans are big manwatchers, so when in Rome . . . sit out and scrutinize the passers-by in Piazza Navona or Piazza del Popolo, or go and revisit some of the sights when they're floodlit: the Trevi, the Colosseum, St Peter's, etc. You're likely to encounter young Romans in a trattoria, disco or bar. If opera is your cup of tea, try and make it along to the outdoor performances in the Roman Baths of Caracalla. Buy tickets from the Teatro dell'Opera. Avoid the discos: they are extravagantly expensive and not very exciting, ranging between 10,000 L and 25,000 L for entrance. If you have to get some music, venture to L'Esperimento in Via Rasella 5, the city's 'alternative' rock club with live bands nightly.

• **Excursions:** Nineteen miles east of Rome is the sixteenth-century Renaissance cardinals' palace, VILLA D'ESTE at Tivoli. The gardens with their 500 fountains are the main attraction here, and your ISIC will get you in free in daytime. Take a train from Rome station, or bus RT from Rebibbia (Underground B-line) if you don't have a rail pass. If you bus it, you could also take in HADRIAN'S VILLA (closed Mondays).

Mussolini's 1940s quarter of Rome – the EUR – has an amusement park (LUNA PARK) and the MUSEUM OF ROMAN CIVIL-IZATION which reconstructs ancient Rome as it was under Constantine in the early fourth century. Should you have hit a heatwave, the nearest beach is OSTIA-LIDO. It's not one of Italy's best but it's only eighteen miles away (metro Line B to Magliana then train to Ostia).

The fourth-century BC ruined city and monumental area of OSTIA ANTICA is only a further 5 km away, and can be reached by the same train or by coach (bus no. 04) which leaves Ostia–Lido every 15 minutes. The excavated ruins are accessible from 9 a.m.–6 p.m., and during the summer classic plays are staged on the Roman theatre. A good camping site is situated 3 km from the ruins at Capitol Campground, Via dei Castelfusono (Tel. 5662720). Its cost may not be the cheapest at 5,300 L per person with an extra 2,700 L per tent, but there is a free swimming pool and tennis court facilities. To get there take bus 5 from Ostia–Lido central.

More ancient ruins can be found at CERVETIERI, 44 km away from Rome, and built on a hill where the Etruscan town of Caere once stood. Its main attraction is the Etruscan necropolis about 2 km out of town (open from 9 a.m.–6 p.m., closed Mondays, and entry costs 8,000 L). The many tombs here are amazing for their interior decorations, from mythological wall paintings to 'The Tomb of the Reliefs', which is an immaculate replica of an Etruscan home carved entirely out of stone. To get to Cerveteri take a train from the Termini station to the seaside town of Ladispolista, and catch a bus from the corner of Via Cagliari for Cervetieri itself, or get a bus direct from Rome, on Via Lepanto. Buses run every half hour, and the whole journey takes approximately one hour.

Southern Italy

Using the old geographical 'boot' analogy of Italy, CAMPANIA is the ankle, BASILICATA the arch, PUGLIA the heel (the departure point for the Brindisi ferry to Greece), and CALABRIA the toe.

There's a lot to take in in Campania. Apart from the colourful chaos of Naples, there's the smouldering volcano of Vesuvius, the archaeological remains of Pompeii, Herculaneum and Paestum, the romantic towns of Sorrento, Amalfi and Positano and the islands off the coast of Naples: Capri, Ischia and Procida. The Italians head for Agropoli, Catellabate and Santa Marco, all south of Naples, for their holidays so these are places to avoid in August when all the natives are there but worth the trip at other times of the year.

Naples (Napoli)

Naples is a crazy city: overcrowded, dirty, smelly, and alive. It has possibly the worst traffic conditions you can imagine, with pollution to match, but no tour of Italy is complete without a stop here. If you've come down from Florence or Venice, you'll feel you're in a different country. The main streets are bustling with car horns and lunatic Vespa drivers, while the backstreets are right out of the Middle Ages – tiny, cobbled alleys (*viccoli*) where children kick footballs. Watch your belongings in this city; it has more crime than any other city in Italy. Naples has its own way of getting things done (much of it involving corruption, for the powers of the rival Camorra and Ndrangheta crime syndicates are legendary) which the visitor will find unfathomable. Unfortunately, you will also find that many of the sights are wholly or partly under restoration, or have strange opening times. Change your money *prior* to arrival in Naples. The banks here have a very high commission. Also: do not expect northern standards of hygiene; until 1973 (when a cholera epidemic broke out), Naples had no sewers; but things are much better now. Despite all this it is a vibrant and exciting city.

There is, though, more than one face to Naples. Once away from the choking Medieval centre, around what the locals call Spacca-

Napoli (literally, 'divides Naples', the string of narrow streets beginning with Via Tribunali which divides the old city from the new and runs along the route of the Old Roman Decumanus Maximus), you have a chance to explore both the countryside and seaside delights of the area.

STATION FACILITIES

Trains from Rome, and those going on to Sicily, invariably use the central station. The Rome–Bari trains stop at both stations, Piazza Garibaldi or Centrale. There's a connecting elevator between the two. Trains to Sorrento on the Circumvesuviana railway leave from Napoli PG. Space permits details of Napoli Centrale only as the most used by eurorailers.

	NAPOLI CENTRALE
Train information	7 a.m.–11 p.m.
Reservations	7 a.m.–10 p.m.
Tourist information	Mon.–Sat.: 8 a.m.–8 p.m.
	Sun.: 8 a.m.–1 p.m.
Foreign exchange	7 a.m.–9 p.m.
Left-luggage store	All hours
Bar, Buffet and Restaurant	6 a.m.–12 midnight
	(meals 11 a.m.–4 p.m.)
Bath, Shower	Tues.–Sat.: 8 a.m.–8 p.m.
	Sun.–Mon.: 8 a.m.–2 p.m.
Waiting room	All hours
Shops	6 a.m.–12 midnight
Post office	Mon.–Fri.: 8.15 a.m.–7.30 p.m.
	Sat.: 8.15 a.m.–1 p.m.

Daily trains to: Rome, Florence, Bologna, Genoa, Milan, Sicily,Venice, Brindisi.

TOURIST INFORMATION AND ADDRESSES

Apart from the one at the station (Tel. 268779), there's an office of Ente Provinciale per il Turismo at Piazza Gesù Nuovo (Tel. 5523328) and the main office at Via Partenope 10A (Tel. 7644871). The information outlet with the highest reputation is the Azienda di Turismo, P. Reale (Tel. 418744) open Mon.–Sat., 8.30 a.m.–2.30 p.m.

POST OFFICE: Piazza Matteotti, open Mon.–Fri.: 8.30 a.m.–7.30 p.m., Sat.: 8.30 a.m.–12 noon (Tel. 5511456).

AMEX: c/o Ashiba Travel, Piazza Municipio 1 (Tel. 5515303).

UK CONSULATE: Via Francesco Crispi 122 (Tel. 663 511), open Mon.–Fri.: 8.30 a.m.–1 p.m.

US CONSULATE: Piazza della Repubblica (Tel. 761 4303, 24-hour phone line).

24-HOUR CHEMIST: Mattera, Via Carbonara 43, also at the Station Centrale (Tel. 268881).

PHONE CODE: 081.

SEEING

Naples has none of the famous sights of Rome, Florence or Venice, but it still has much to offer. If you visited Pompeii or Herculaneum and were disappointed to find none of the artefacts – or bodies – there, then visit the NATIONAL ARCHAEOLOGICAL MUSEUM on Piazza del Museo (just outside the Piazza Cavour metro station). In this sixteenth-century palace you'll find one of the best Graeco-Roman collections in the world, as well as the frescoes and jewellery from Herculaneum, and the Borgia Collection of Etruscan art. It also houses the famous Farnese Bull. It is open from Tues.–Sat.: 9 a.m.–7 p.m., Sun.: 9 a.m.–1 p.m., and entry is 8,000L. Just around the corner of Via Duomo you'll find the SAN GENNARO CATHEDRAL where every year St Gennaro's blood apparently turns to liquid. You can tour the crypt and catacombs every day from 9.30 a.m.–noon. If you like churches, then Naples is for you, as it has some really fine examples. The church of GESU NUOVO on Piazza Gesu Nuovo (opposite the tourist office) may look like a prison on the outside, but inside it feasts on the Baroque style. Down the road lies the medieval church of SANTA CHIARA and nearby is SAN DOMENICO MAGGIORE, on the Piazza of the same name. The latter is a curious mix of Gothic and Baroque, complete with a thirteenth-century painting that spoke to St Thomas Aquinas. Off a small sidestreet to the north is the Chapel of SAN SEVERO which charges a small admission fee. Once inside though, it is worth it. There are some brilliant sculptures, including a Veiled Christ hewn out of one single block of marble; so realistic, you really feel that you are looking at the body through a veil.

The museums are no less breathtaking in content. The CAPO-
DIMONTE MUSEUM overlooks the city from its highest hill at VOMERO
and has collections of Fine Art from the fourteenth century
onwards, including the GALLERIA NAZIONALE. It was the view from
the belvedere of room 25 that inspired the saying 'See Naples and
die'. The Royal Apartments on the first floor of this former royal
estate include a parlour completely built from Capodimonte
ceramics. Bus 24 or the funicular take you there. Opening hours are
Tues.–Sat.: 9 a.m.–7 p.m., Sun.: 9 a.m.–1 p.m., and entry is
4,000 L. The CARTHUSIAN MONASTERY is also found here. The opera
house, TEATRO SAN CARLO (a source of much Neapolitan Pride, like
the football team), and the GALLERIA UMBERTO I, a nineteenth-
century shopping arcade, are near the CASTEL NUOVO on Piazza
Municipio. The castle was built in the late thirteenth century for
Charles I of Anjou, then rebuilt for the fifteenth-century Aragons
and is open daily.

The city's transport system has some useful offers for the tourist.
You can buy half-day passes for 1,200 L, they operate within the
timescales of 6 a.m.–2 p.m., or 2 p.m.–11 p.m. and are valid on all
buses, trams and funiculars, but not on the subway. A whole day
pass costs 2,000 L. The flat fare is 800 L for each single journey and
all tickets are available from convenience stores throughout the
city.

SLEEPING

Hotels have a reputation for unreliability as regards changing their
rates once you are in. Get a clear agreement before you move into
your room, but if there are still problems, phone EPT (Tel. 419888).
Try Hotel de la Ville, Vieo 5 Allessio al Lavinaio No. 16, which
costs around 12,000 L per night with a 2,000 L charge for showers.
Try also Hotel Casanova, Corso Garibaldi 333 (Tel. 268 287), which
charges 18,000 L for a single room and 38,500 L for a double, or
68,000 L for four. Breakfast is 4,500 L extra. To get there walk from
the station up Piazza Garibaldi and turn down the fifth road on your
right.

The youth hostel 'Mergellina' is excellent and is at Salita della
Grotta à Piedigrotta 23 (Tel. 7612346); 16,000 L covers bed and
breakfast, with a 9,000 L extra charge for other meals. Go to the
Margellirra stop on the underground. You can camp on the edge of

the volcano crater at Camping Solfatara (Tel. 8673413). You can either take bus 152 direct, or a local train from Piazza Garibaldi (directly underneath the central station) to Pozzuoli (the end of the line) and then a walk of 850 m, mostly uphill. The train is free on Inter-Rail.

EATING AND NIGHTLIFE

Pizza was born in Naples, so this is the place to find out just how far from the original the Pizzaland restaurant-chain really is. There are hundreds of cheap pizza places, and none charge more than 7,000 L for a plateful big enough for two. Look out for the sign 'vera pizza' (true pizza), as it's usually a mark of quality. If you're flush, try one of the seafood restaurants down by the port in the Santa Lucia district. Renzo e Lucia on Via Tito Angelini 31/33 do good baked fish, and Caffe Osteria at Via Miroballo 14 gives good value for money. The university Mensa is on Via Mezzocanone. Try the vegetarian-Indian Restaurant Campania, Gapala-Corso Vittoria, Emanuele, open 8 p.m.–12 midnight daily except Mondays. Cantina Triunfo is recommended, though it is pricey by some standards. It is at 64 Riviera di Chiala, not far from the hostel, and starts serving at 8.30 p.m. with meals costing about 30,000 L including wine. On the snack side, try the Neapolitan coffee (café lungo) with plenty of sugar and a cake. Sfogliatella is the speciality cake of the region, but there are many others to try. The more familiar chips and sandwiches are readily available, and the best place to find them is around the Piazza Garibaldi.

There are plenty of shady bars and rip-off joints down by the port. You'll find your evening strolls being interrupted by people trying to sell you anything from cabbage-leaf Marlboros (which pass off as the real thing till you light them) to watches made from bottle lids – some of these are worth buying for the craftsmanship involved. Also the 'genuine Scotch' is sometimes only cold tea. Be warned! Nightlife doesn't take off until around midnight, after the public transport systems shut, although taxis are affordable. The popular area seems to be around Piazza Amedo, where there are plenty of bars, piano bars and restaurants. Nightclubs are expensive, and cost around 15,000–20,000 L with a smart dress code and a free drink thrown in.

• **Excursions:** There are many places of interest within a day-trip visit from Naples. The PHLEGRIAN FIELDS (Campi Flegri), on the pensinsula north of Naples, still have some active volcanoes you can visit. MOUNT VESUVIUS hasn't erupted since 1944, but it could have another go at any time, as Etna's proved, so take the chair lift to the crater at your peril! If you do go, make sure it's a clear day, and go early. The private Circumvesuviana Line, from Stazione Vesuviana near Central Station – it is one floor underground at the station – serves this area, including Herculaneum and Pompeii, and it runs on to Sorrento, though it does not take the Inter-Rail ticket as pre-paid payment. It takes approximately 15 minutes to go from Naples to Herculaneum (descend at the Ercolano stop), and 45 minutes to Pompeii (make sure you get off the train at the Pompeii Scavi stop since the modern city is very dull). You can also get to Pompeii on the main Naples–Salerno train line from Napoli PG (free with an Inter-Rail ticket). Both HERCULANEUM and POMPEII have entrance charges of 10,000L from 9 a.m.–1 hour before sunset. These two towns fell foul of a Vesuvian outburst in AD 79. The latter was covered with ashes, the former with mud. Both offer a unique insight into first-century Roman Imperial life since you can see houses and baths preserved from that age. If you wish to stay in Pompeii, there is a good campsite by the Villa dei Misteri station, and camping Zeus is very convenient, cheap and friendly – no tent is necessary. From Naples, it is also possible to take a ferry over to the islands in the Gulf. Take the ferry from the port, or the hydrofoil from Megellina. CAPRI is the most touristy of the islands, and very expensive (but the beach at Marina Piccola is the best in the area, and the blue grotto is unmissable), while the Italians favour ISCHIA which is more 'authentic' and cheaper.

If you like Baroque architecture, then visit the town of CASERTA, 45 minutes by train from Naples, for its Bourbon Palace, PALAZZO REALE, also known as 'petit Versailles'. South of Naples lies the beautiful AMALFI COAST. It is a natural area of mountains, limestone rock and beaches; a great place to unwind after the chaos of the city. There are many small towns dotted along the coast, so the best way to take it all in is by hiring a scooter. AMALFI itself is a pleasant seaside town with a magnificent moorish style cathedral. The tourist office is at Corso delle Reppubliche Marinare 19/21. Since Amalfi can become quite touristy, it's better to stay at other small towns, like ATRANI, about a ten-minute walk away. Here we recommend staying by the beach at A Scalinatella, Piazza Umberto 1 (Tel. 089–871 492) for 10,000–15,000L per night. Make sure, while you're here, to visit the spectacular cliffside town of RAVELLO and the EMERALD GROTTO, about 4 km from Amalfi, in the bay of Corica dei Marini. The cave is full of stalagmites and caryatids, and is visited by boat tours.

If you're heading south for Sicily, you can stop off at Salerno and catch a bus (it takes about an hour) to PAESTUM, where you'll find three Greek temples, dating from 2400 BC, better than many in Greece, and some exceptionally impressive tomb paintings which also figure in the National Museum there.

Bari and Brindisi

Bari and Brindisi are places you'll find yourself at if you are travelling, by boat or ferry, to Greece or Yugoslavia. Neither offers much in the way of a pleasant cultural retreat, but nevertheless, you'll need to use the facilities there before you depart to nicer scenery. BARI, possibly as a way to attract the young tourist, has introduced a *Stopover in Bari* scheme whereby people under the age of 30 can enjoy free camping, buses throughout the town, free information centres, free museums, cheap meals, free luggage storage, free bikes, skateboards . . . in fact, most things for absolutely nothing. To get to the campsite, take buses 3 or 5 (free to the *Stopover* traveller) to Pineta San Francesco. The offer takes place in the summer months only, between mid-June and 8 September, although do be careful while you're here. Reports have come back to us that this area of town has become a haven for criminals and junkies, so make sure that you keep your belongings safe; if you're female, don't go out at night on your own; and don't tread on any needles. All the information you'll need about the *Stopover* is available from the booth at the station. Another part of the scheme that this place can help you with is the 'package' that puts you up in a private home for two nights for 25,000L. For more information, contact the main office at Via Dante Alighieri III (Tel. 5214538. Open: 8.30 a.m.–8.30 p.m. daily). There is also a 24-hour telephone hotline (Tel. 441186). If you're staying in this town out of season, then try the International Youth Hostel, 'Ostello del Levante' in Via Nicola Massaro 33, 8 km from the rail station (Tel. 080–320282) which gives bed and breakfast for 12,000 L. From Bari's port, ferries depart for Corfu, Dubrovnik and Patras, but don't just find out a time and turn up. It's best to book your voyage in advance, and even then, you need to get to the station at least two hours early so that you can pay your tax.

BRINDISI, as a place, is no better than Bari, so arrive here in the afternoon in time for the regular evening ferry service to Corfu and Patras. Most of the ferry lines offer discounts to the under 27s and ISIC card holders. Eurail and Inter-Rail pass holders are given free deck passage on Adriatica Lines and Hellenic Mediterranean Lines, but in the summer months from June–September, you must pay an extra tax of 18,000 L. The Brindisi boat offices are as follows: Adriatica Lines, Via Marlines le Regina Margherita 13 (Tel. 523825); Hellenic Mediterranean Lines, Corso Garibaldi 88 (Tel. 368232). The tourist office is EPT, lungomare Regina Margherita 5, at the dock to the left of the Station Marittima (Tel. 21944). Opening hours are Mon.–Sat.: 8.30 a.m.–12.30 p.m., 4.30 p.m.–7.30 p.m.

Sicily

The journey from Naples to Sicily takes about ten hours. Sicily is an interesting place to visit, and comes as a complete contrast to Italy, which is not surprising really as parts of it are nearer North Africa than mainland Italy. It's the largest island in the Mediterranean and because of its strategic position has been in the hands of just about every empire there ever was.

• **Getting there:** The standard ferry crossing is from VILLA SAN GIOVANNI to MESSINA on the train-ferry. In summer, the Rome–Sicily run gets crowded, so reserve ahead if you can. Once you're there you'll have to use the railway as your main sightseeing medium. The services are slow and typical of the rest of the Italian rail network. They are not, however, overwhelmingly crowded. The buses are reasonably punctual and usually air-conditioned.

Ignore the ferries from Naples to Catania, Syracuse and Palermo. They're expensive and if you're on Inter-Rail you'd have to pay to get over.

Sicily: the east coast

The port town of MESSINA, founded by the Greeks in the eighth century BC, has been rebuilt twice this century: once after the 1908 earthquake, and again after the bombing of the Second World War; consequently, there's not *that* much to see, but if you've time to kill waiting on a ferry, take in the following sights: the largest ASTRONOMICAL MECHANICAL CLOCK in the world in the thirteenth-century Norman cathedral, the church of ANNUNZIATA DEI CATA-LANI, and the NATIONAL MUSEUM. The tourist office is on Via Calabria Isolato 301 (Tel. 774236), and there's another at the station (Tel. 672944. Open Mon.–Sat.: 9 a.m.–7.30 p.m.). Half an hour from Messina is TAORMINA, a historical resort popular with middle-aged Italians. The GREEK THEATRE looks out over the smoking live volcano of MOUNT ETNA which makes this setting for Greek drama suitably dramatic. The PALAZZO CORVAIA, the Sicilian parliament house dating from the fourteenth century, is in Piazza Vittorio Emanuele, and the beach of MAZZARO can be reached by funicular.

CATANIA hasn't been swamped by Mount Etna since 1693, so the old town dates from the seventeenth century, but in 1992 the mountain steadily engulfed nearby villages and the countryside with an eruption. SIRACUSA is a strange mixture of ancient Greece and Rome. This was once as important a centre as Rome or Athens and there are plenty of archaeological sites to back this up. The ARCHAEOLOGICAL MUSEUM is at Piazza del Duomo and the remains are behind the present city. The GREEK THEATRE here is considered the best of its kind in the world. Opposite the theatre is the altar used for public sacrifices; a short walk takes you to the ROMAN AMPHITHEATRE from the fourth century BC. Tourist information is at Via San Sebastiano 43, and the youth hostel's at 45 Via Epipoli (Tel. 0931–711118). For pensions, try Centrale (Tel. 0931–60258) at the station, or Gran Bretagna, Via Savoia 21 (Tel. 0931–68765).

There is a camping site, Agriturist, at Loc Rinaura 115 (Tel. 721224).

Agrigento has frequent train services to other parts of Sicily. The main town is 8 km from the sea, where there is a resort called San Leone if you want to do the tourist bit. This hillside town is the site of the VALLEY OF TEMPLES, a collection of columns and temples dating from the sixth and fifth centuries BC. The tourist office is at Viale della Vittoria 255 (Tel. 0922–26926). There are two good campsites on the coast and the Nettuno has good showers and facilities and charges 3,500 L per night without tent. Take bus 10 from the station.

Palermo

The capital of Sicily has a modern north side and historic south side. The mixture of Arabic and Western is noticeable here, as can be seen in the PALACE OF THE NORMANS (see especially the PALATINE CHAPEL mosaics in the palace). Open Monday and Friday–Saturday from 9 a.m.–12 noon – unless the Sicilian Parliament is in session. Five miles away in Monreale is the NORMAN CATHEDRAL (open from 8 a.m.–12.30 p.m. and 3.30 p.m.–6.30 p.m.) with its unique biblical mosaics, and just next door the BENEDICTINE CLOISTER hides a garden with exquisite medieval columns. APT tourist information is available at Piazza Castelnuova 34/35 (Tel. 091–586122/583847) open Monday–Saturday from 8 a.m.–8 p.m.) and the train station (open 8 a.m.–2 p.m.). A late-night pharmacy, Lo Casco, can be found in Via Roma 1 (Tel. 6162117) near the train station. Try round the harbour for cheap rooms, or near the station on Via Roma and Via Maqueda. Pensione Sud, Via Maqueda 8 (Tel. 091–6175700) singles for 16,000 L, doubles for 26,000 L; Albergo Pretoria, Via Maqueda 124 (Tel. 091–331068) singles for around 18,000 L, doubles for around 28,000 L; and Albergo Rosalia Conca d'Oro, Via Santa Rosalia 7 (Tel. 091–6164543), singles for 20,000 L, doubles for 29,000 L, plus free beach tickets if you come in summer) are just a few suggestions. Palermo's nightlife is outside the city at Mondello, but for good eating the Da Pino, Via dello Spezio 6 on P. Sturzo, open Mon.–Sat., 12 noon–3 p.m., is highly recommended for its value and authentic Sicilian cuisine.

Sardinia (Sardegna)

The mountainous and untamed island of Sardinia is about halfway between Italy and Africa's northern coast. The 1.6 million Sardinians have a strong independent streak; the region has been granted its own autonomous status. The west of the island is hilly but mainly cultivated; the east is wild and almost completely untouched. There are about half a dozen towns in all, and only a few real roads, so be prepared to rough it a bit if you're camping – but camp all the same, as this is by far the best means of accommodation on the island, and the scenery and climate are beautiful.

● **Getting there:** From Italy there are ferries to Cagliari (the capital), Olbia (on the east coast), Porto Torres (the northern tip) and Golfo Aranci (on the Costa Smeralda). The best overnight crossing is with the Tirrenia Line from Civitavecchia (one hour north of Rome) to Olbia. It costs about 21,000 L for deck class and reservations in summer are advisable. The Tirrenia office in Rome is at Via Bissolati 41.

For a daytime crossing, the state railways one from Civitavecchia to Golfo Aranci is the cheapest. A second-class reclining seat will cost 15,000 L plus. The crossing takes about nine hours, and there are five crossings a day. At the other end, there's a train waiting to take you on to Olbia or Sassari.

● **General information:** Once you're there, the rail network connects up the northern and western coasts, but that's about it. Services are slow and a bit unpredictable, but it's a lot better than hitching it round.

As far as accommodation goes, the tourist office will help you out. Good cheap pensions are thin on the ground and hotels, where they exist, expensive. In the north, youth hostels are your best bet. They're cheap (around 9,000 L) and usually on the beach. Generally, though, you can't beat camping. There are several official sites, but the true joy comes only with setting up on your own.

Avoid the restaurants – they're aimed at the wealthy tourists. Go for pizzerie, tavole calde or rosticcerie. Fish and seafood are cheap on the coast (cook them yourself), and the markets provide ample picnic food. The local wine is Vernaccia.

Sardinia: the east coast

South from Olbia, which houses the island's ports, is the most unspoiled region of Sardinia. There are miles of beautiful quiet beaches, and in these parts the women still wear the national costume. NUORO and ARBATAX are particularly beautiful and are the sites of archaeological remains. To get to this area, you'll need to take the train from Macomer or Cagliari. The coast around SANTA MARIA NAVARRESE is good for beaches.

Going north from Olbia you enter COSTA SMERALDA, the 'millionaires' playground'. This is the most commercialized part, though it's not yet spoilt. If you have enough time, take a trip to Porto Cervo and see some of the most expensive real estate in Italy. Don't attempt to stay the night, however, unless you don't mind paying Aga Khan prices. Golfo Aranci is in this region, and from here you really have to bus it. ARZACHENA is worth heading for, and has some very good beaches. The tourist office is at Via Risorgimento (Tel. 82624). Again not on the rail line but worth seeing is SANTA TERESA DI GALLURA on the northernmost tip of Sardinia with a view of Corsica. This little fishing village is currently becoming 'touristy', so get there before it finally succumbs. The tourist office can be found at Azienda, Piazza Vittorio Emanuele 24 (Tel. 0789–754127), and can help you find accommodation.

Sardinia: the west coast

SASSARI, Sardinia's second city, has an interesting old medieval town which centres on the CATHEDRAL. There are a couple of churches and the SARDINIAN NATIONAL MUSEUM to see here, and tourist information is at Via Brigata Sassari 19 (Tel. 233534). This is your best base for exploring north-west Sardinia and you'll find cheap rooms and meals along Corso Vittorio Emanuele. An hour from here is one of the prettiest towns on the island, ALGHERO. It's more Spanish than Italian as for many years this was a Catalan colony. The churches are the main sites of the town, and from here you can take a boat out to CAPO CACCIA and the Neptune Grotto: a series of underground caves, some of which are still unexplored. The tourist office can be found at Piazza Porta Terra 9 (Tel. 919054).

Cagliari

The capital city of Sardinia. Ignore the new town and concentrate on the medieval centre, the CASTELLO, behind the harbour. The thirteenth-century CATHEDRAL is here and not far away is the second-century ROMAN AMPHITHEATRE. The NATIONAL ARCHAEOLOGICAL MUSEUM (closed Mondays, open 9 a.m.–2 p.m. and 3.30 p.m.–6.30 p.m. Fri. and Sat., Sun.: 9 a.m.–1 p.m. Admission 3,000 L) is famous for its collection of 'Nuraghic bronzes', and its Punic-Roman section. Tourist information is at Piazza Matteoti (Tel. 669255 or 664923. Open Mon.–Sat.: 8 a.m.–8 p.m., Oct.–April: 8 a.m.–2 p.m.), and for cheap beds and meals try the streets between Corso Vittorio Emanuele and Via Roma. While you're here, visit the flea market at Bastione di San Remy on Sunday mornings, and try to coincide your visit with the July–September arts festival. This is when plays are put on in the amphitheatre, so it is worth the trip.

Malta

If you're near to Naples, Calabria or Catania and fancy an island break which will steep you in history, a wonderful climate and won't break the bank, take a ferry over to the small country of Malta. Ferries are operated by the Tirrenia Navigation Co. and the Gozo Channel Co. and operate from Syracuse to Malta three times a week at a cost of around 17 Maltese pounds one way. (£1 is around LM 0.57.) Crossing time is three hours. There is also a daily catamaran service from Syracuse, Catania and Taormina/Naxos, crossing time is approximately eight hours.

The island's main centres are Valletta, Sliema, Mdina and Rabat, while the little neighbouring island of Gozo also begs a visit as a day's excursion since there is a 20-minute crossing every two hours, by the Gozo Chanel ferry service which operates from Cirkewwa in Malta to Ugarr Harbour in Gozo (Tel. 556114), costing about LM 1.50. To get to Cirkewwa, take buses 45 or 48 from Valetta, and bus no.25 to get from Mgarr to Victoria. The Youth Hostel Association on Malta ensures accommodation is no problem with cheap beds in all the main centres (average LM 1–2, which is around half-price; but you *must* show your 'Europe by Train' to qualify). Food too is good and cheap, and though the nightlife is tame by northern European standards the island has more than enough charm and colour to compensate for this.

The capital, VALLETTA, has as its not-to-be-missed-sights: the natural GRAND HARBOUR, used emphatically when Malta was the HQ for the Knights of St John in the sixteenth century; the GRAND MASTERS' PALACE; ST JOHN'S CO-CATHEDRAL; the PALAZZO PARISIO, home to Napoleon in 1798; the UPPER BARRACCA, from where the view over the Grand Harbour and the FORTRESS OF ST ANGELO is breathtaking, and the five Hostels of the Knights of St John – the AUBERGES. Tourist info is at 1 City Gate Arcade, Valletta (Tel. 227747). Open Mon.–Fri.: 9.30 a.m.–1 p.m., 3 p.m.–6 p.m., Sat.: 9.30 a.m.–12 noon. Gozo has two tourist offices, one at Palm St, Victoria (Tel. 556454), open Mon.–Sat.: 7.15 a.m.–7 p.m., Sun.: 8 a.m.–7 p.m., one other at Mgarr Harbour (Tel. 553343).

Seven miles from Valletta is the beautiful ancient capital of MDINA. See the MDINA GATE, the VILHENA PALACE, CASA INGUANEZ, the incredible baroque CATHEDRAL, the NORMAN HOUSE and the CHURCH OF THE ANNUNCIATION.

Try and visit TARXIEN (buses 8, 11 or 26 from Valetta), where there are remains of temples, stone tablets, stone idols and altars dating back to the third and fourth centuries BC and the GHAR DALAM CAVE and museum at BIRZEBBUGA (bus no.11 from Valetta), where there are semi-fossilized remains of extinct species from when the island was still attached to Africa. Pop over to Gozo to visit the fifteenth-century CITADEL, built by the knights, for a breathtaking view of the surrounding environs. If you are after sun and sand, the best beaches are to the north of the island at Mellieha Bay, Golden Sands (of course) and ARMIER (buses No. 50, 51 from Valetta), or to the south at Birzebuga. Ramala Bay on Gozo is exceptional for its beautiful red sand. While you're on Gozo you must visit DWEYRA BAY, near the town of St Lawrenz (take bus 5 from Victoria), there you'll find an inland sea, Fungus Rock and a sea-carved arch.

Youth hostels to base yourself at are in PACEVILLE at 30b Wilga Street (bus 67); in PAWLA: 17 Tal-Borg Street (buses 1, 2, 3, 4, 5) (Tel. 29361); in GHAJNSIELEM: 21a Cordina Street on Gozo (book through the Pawla hostel). The hostels are clean, comfortable and undoubtedly the best places to stay in Malta. There are no opening and closing times (you are given a key) but there is a night-time curfew. This applies to all hostels. Family rooms are available and though preference is given to the under-30s, others can still get in. Expect to pay between LM 1.75–2.75. The Youth Accommodation Centre International is based at 188 St Lucia St in Valletta, and offers cheap accommodation as do the guest houses whose prices vary between LM 3.50–5.50. Remember there are no organized or official camping sites on Malta. Gozo has four guest houses which charge around LM 3.50 for bed and breakfast. They are the Three Hills Guest House, Europe St, Victoria (Tel. 551895); The Grand Guest House, 56 St Anthony St, Mgarr (Tel. 556183); Lantern Guest House, Qbajja Road, Marsalforn (Tel. 556285); and St Joseph Guest House, 131 Conception St, Qala (Tel. 556573).

Valletta abounds in cheap eating places. In SLIEMA, try the Magic Kiosk, St Anne's Square. To sample some freshly caught fish take the bus to the south-east coast village of MARSAXLOKK and eat in any restaurant along the harbour. Nightclubs and discos are to be found in the St Julians Bugibba areas and are surrounded by bars and takeaways. On Gozo, in the winter, two clubs to visit are the Astra and Auroa in Victoria.

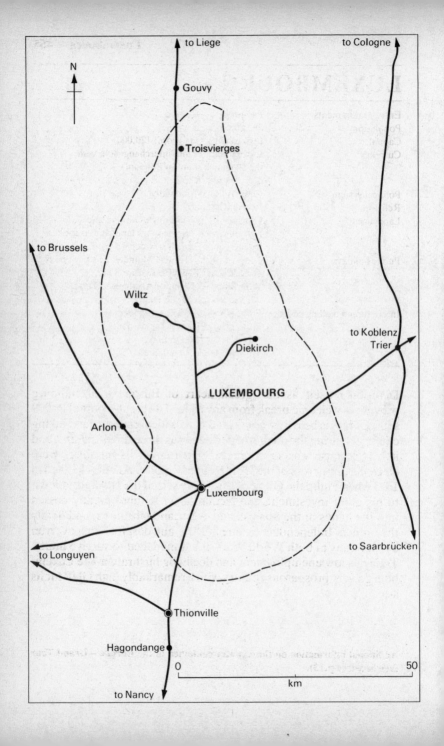

LUXEMBOURG

Entry requirements	Passport
Population	380,000
Capital	Luxembourg City (pop.: 120,000)
Currency	Luxembourg Franc (interchangeable with the Belgian but not in Belgium) £1 = approx. 52.5 fr.
Political system	Constitutional Monarchy
Religion	Roman Catholic
Languages	Officially French although German and Letzeburgesch (the people's language) is spoken by everyone. English is widely spoken.
Public holidays	1 Jan.; 11 Feb. Carnival Monday; Easter Sunday and Monday; 1 May; Ascension Day; Whit Monday; 23 June; Assumption Day; All Saints Day; 25, 26 Dec.
International dialling codes	From UK: 010 + 352 + number From USA: 011 + 352 + number To UK: 00 + 44 + number To USA: 00 + 1 + number

Describing itself as the 'green heart of Europe', Luxembourg provides a welcome break from any train. The greater part of its 999 square miles is heavily wooded and makes ideal camping and hiking country. During the medieval period it was three times the size, and its royal house was so important that four of its members were elected as emperors of the Holy Roman Empire. All this changed in 1443 when Philip the Good of Burgundy seized the city and added it to his other investment, the Netherlands. It subsequently passed into the hands of the Spanish and Austrian Habsburgs, and finally the French. Independence came in 1815, and despite being overrun by Germany in both World Wars, it has managed to survive intact. Today its low unemployment and declining birthrate make Luxembourg a very prosperous country with a remarkably high GNP for its size.

Additional information on this country contained in the *Europe – Grand Tour* factsheet (see p.13).

LUXEMBOURG NATIONAL RAILWAYS
(Société Nationale des Chemins de Fer Luxembourgeois, CFL)

With only 210 miles of track, this is the smallest national rail network in the world – it takes only two hours to cross the whole country. There are, however, sixty-four stations, so the train really can take you to even the most obscure corners, and there are no supplements to worry about. CFL also run many bus services on which Inter-Rail passes are valid. Network tickets are available for one day, five days or one month for second-class travel on all lines of the Luxembourg railway and bus system. Prices are 239 fr., 724 fr., and 1,923 fr. respectively. If you are taking a bicycle on your journey, a flat rate of 30 fr. has to be paid for its railcar transport.

All train and bus stations sell Billets Reseaux. These tickets are good for unlimited second-class train and bus travel. They are not valid on buses running within the capital. A one-day ticket costs 120 fr. Another type of ticket which is inexpensive for the non-Inter-Rail traveller is the Benlux Pass. This ticket entitles the holder to 5 days unlimited travel in any 17-day period in Belgium, the Netherlands and Luxembourg. It costs only 1,990 fr. (2,770 fr. for over 26s). This is not as expensive as a one-way ticket from Luxembourg to Amsterdam.

TRAIN INFORMATION

For information on international trains, go to the Rail Tour Office where English is spoken. If there's a queue, or it's a simple question, look for the information officers wearing yellow capbands.

• **Reservations:** It's not possible to reserve on internal trains, and on internationals it's optional, but must be done twenty-four hours in advance. Luxembourg is connected to the German and French railways' computer, so it's possible to reserve sleepers and couchettes in these countries.

TOURIST INFORMATION

Apart from the National Tourist Office to the right of the main station in Luxembourg there are local offices (Syndicats d'Initiative) scattered throughout the country. Most open at 8 a.m. and shut at 6 p.m. with a two-hour lunch break.

• **ISIC bonuses:** Some museums and galleries half price.

• **Money matters:** 1 Luxembourg franc (fr.) = 100 centimes. Banking hours are Mon.–Fri.: 9 a.m.–12 noon and 1.30 p.m.–4.30 p.m., though some banks are open earlier, longer or do not close for lunch; some are open on Saturday mornings. The Luxembourg franc is interchangeable with the Belgian franc, but you're best to change them before leaving the country.

• **Post offices:** Open Mon.–Fri.: 9 a.m.–5 p.m. Station branch open 6 a.m.–8 p.m.

• **Shops and museums:** Vary in their times of opening. Tues.–Fri.: 9 a.m.–12 noon and 2 p.m.–6 p.m. seems to be the general rule. All shops are closed on Monday mornings, and some museums are shut all day.

SLEEPING

Pick up the tourist board's excellent free guide on accommodation at the main office next to the station. This lists prices and facilities for all Luxembourg's hotels and pensions. If you're thinking about camping, ask for the free folder giving all the campsites and prices. There are twelve youth hostels for which you need IYHF membership, charging 290 fr. (250 fr. for under 26s) per night with breakfast included. The Luxembourg City youth hostel costs an additional 40 fr. per night. In addition, there are a large number of campsites throughout the country, a free list of which is available from the national tourist office. Expect to pay from 100 fr. per tent plus a further 80/90 fr. per person.

EATING AND NIGHTLIFE

Dishes have a strong French flavour and specialities include Ardennes ham which you can pick up at supermarkets and butchers' in town. Check up with the tourist offices for what's happening in the week ahead.

Luxembourg City

The old part of this 1,000-year-old city is on a high plateau overlooking cliffs, and the valleys of the Alzette River. Around the edge of the plateau is the PROMENADE DE LA CORNICHE which offers spectacular views over the city. Just below the promenade are the CASEMATES, thirteen miles of connecting underground passages, hewn from solid rock, from the times when this area was a fortress. You can explore these tunnels: enter from Place de la Constitution or from 'Bock' – fortress reconstruction. Also in the old town is the seventeenth-century CATHEDRAL OF NOTRE DAME and the NATIONAL MUSEUM on Fish Market Place (closed Mondays) which is free, and offers a selection of historical, natural, and artistic artefacts. Situated next door is the Folklore Museum, which is open from 2 p.m.–6 p.m. Two major sights are currently closed to the visitor; the Renaissance GRAND DUCAL PALACE is undergoing restoration, re-opening at the end of 1993. The Grand Duke's office is therefore replacing the Galerie d'Art Municipale for the duration of the year in VILLA VAUBON located in Avenue Eile Reuben. The main annual event in the city is the 'Schobermesse', an amusement fair and market which arrives on the last but one Sunday in August. A fleamarket takes place every second and fourth Saturday of the month. For those with a little bit of cash to spare and a head for heights, the Compagnie Aeronautique in Junglinster offer an original way to see the city by hot air balloon. Tel. 78 90 75 for further details. See also the EUROPEAN CENTRE, located in the western suburbs and the home of a number of European agencies including the Supreme Court of the EC, the General Secretariat of the European Parliament and others. After Brussels, Luxembourg can be regarded as the most 'European' of European cities. While you are in the vicinity, all Luxembourg's radio stations, including Radio Luxembourg itself, are close neighbours of the European centre at Kirchberg. Radio Luxembourg is contactable by telephoning 071–436 4012, in London.

STATION FACILITIES

	GARE DE LUXEMBOURG
Train information	7 a.m.–8 p.m.
	(Tel. 492424)
Reservations	7 a.m.–7.30 p.m. (Tel. 4990573)
Tourist information	Mon.–Fri.: 9 a.m.–7.30 p.m. summer,
	9 a.m.–12 noon, 2 p.m.–6.30 p.m. winter
	Sat.: 9 a.m.–12 noon (in Luxair building)
Foreign exchange	Mon.–Sat.: 8.30 a.m.–9 p.m.
	Sun.: 9 a.m.–9 p.m.
Left-luggage lockers	No access 1.30 a.m.–4 a.m. (60 fr.)
Left-luggage store	No access 1.30 a.m.–4 a.m.
Bar, Buffet	8 a.m.–7 p.m.
Restaurant	Mon.–Fri.: 12 noon–3 p.m.
	5 a.m.–12 midnight
Baker	open daily
Shops	6.30 a.m.–8 p.m.
Bath, Shower	6 a.m.–9.30 p.m.
Waiting room	All hours (ticket required)
Post office	Across from station
Station shuts	1.30 a.m.–4 a.m.

Daily trains to: Brussels, Strasbourg, Basel, Zürich, Milan, Koblenz, Paris.

TOURIST INFORMATION AND ADDRESSES

Next to the station is the Luxair Terminal building. In summer it opens 9 a.m.–7.30 p.m., 9 a.m.–12 noon and 2 p.m.–6.30 p.m. the rest of the year, and hands out free information on all Luxembourg, as well as handling accommodation enquiries. The Tourist Information Centre is at Place d'Armes (Tel. 222809), open 9 a.m.–7 p.m. summer, 9 a.m.–1 p.m. and 2 p.m.–6 p.m. winter (closed on Sundays).

POST OFFICE: 38 Place de la Gare. Mon.–Sat.: 6 a.m.–10 p.m. Post restante till 8 p.m.

LUXEMBOURG STUDENT TRAVEL (TEJ): Voyage SOTOUR, 17 Place du Théâtre (Tel. 222673 or 46514), open Mon.–Fri.: 8 a.m.–6 p.m., Sat.: 10 a.m.–4 p.m.

24-HOUR CHEMIST: Tel. 012.

UK EMBASSY: 14 Boulevard Roosevelt (Tel. 229864).

US EMBASSY: 22 Bd E. Servais (Tel. 460123).

AMEX: 6–8 rue Origer (Tel. 496041).
BUS INFORMATION: A one trip ticket costs 25 fr., all day tickets cost
120 fr., and are available from the driver, as are the better value
ten-trip tickets which several people can use.

SLEEPING

Stay close to the station for cheap hotels. If you have a car, go into
the suburbs, 5–10 km from the city centre for accommodation. Rue
Joseph Junck is a safe bet, as is rue de la Liberté. Doubles average
about 1,800 fr., but Axe, 34 rue J. Junck (Tel. 490953), has rooms
for less. Hotel Delta, 74–78 rue A. Fischer (Tel. 493096), have
cheapish doubles and triples. The youth hostel is good but is a bit
out of the 'shopping area', though right in the historical part of the
city. The scenery on the bus ride is worth the 10-minute trip. It can
sometimes be full of adolescent groups and there is a 9 a.m.
eviction, but apart from that it is comfortable and beautifully
located. Take bus 9 from the station. The fare is about 30 fr. and it
will cost you the same for your rucksack. If you don't fancy paying
the extra you can walk through the town to it in half an hour and
check out the places you want to come back to at night. The address
is 2 rue du Fort Olisy (Tel. 226889), and single beds cost 320 fr. per
night including breakfast.

Kockelscheuer Camping, 22 route de Bettembourg (Tel. 471815)
is a difficult 25–30-minute walk from the station so it is better to take
bus 2. Prices from 100 fr. per tent and 90 fr. per person.

EATING AND NIGHTLIFE

Food isn't terribly cheap, so use the supermarkets and bakeries
(pâtisseries) near the station. The latter offer good sandwiches, but
also try the delicious 'pâte au Riesling'. You'll find the usual
McDonald's-type fast-food places in this area as well. Try the
tourist menu at Le Papillon, 9 rue Origer. Always look out for the
restaurants which offer a 'Menu du Jour'. These meals are the best
buy of the day and are much appreciated by the locals who go
regularly to these restaurants. Prices range between 250–400 fr. For
such a lunch try the 'As Arcadas' in Rue J. Junck. Serving
Portuguese food, the 'menu du jour' is from 12 noon–2 p.m. and
costs 250–280 fr. with soup and dessert included. Place d'Armes is

where to head to in the evenings. People generally congregate here and often there are free concerts in the square. There are also fast-food restaurants in this part of town and McDonald's opened a new branch recently right beside the bandstand. The familiar sounding Pizza Hut has two outlets at Place d'Armes and at rue Origer, and both are open until midnight. The cheaper restaurants are on the outer roads of the city. The Taverne du Carvery on Avenue Marie-Therese is open until 11 p.m., and it serves vegetarian dishes and special diet cooking on request, prices start at around 220 fr. At a similar price is the Giardino on the Rte d'Esch. It also caters for vegetarians and is open until 11.30 p.m. Generally, the Italian and Chinese restaurants are the cheapest in town, with meals costing in the region of 100 fr.

'La Semaine a Luxembourg' is the 'what's on' and is available from tourist information as is 'Vade-Mecum', the cultural diary. Published every three months, it lists all theatres, concerts, films, galleries and museums. Winter is the Luxembourgian theatrical season, and for theatregoers the Theatre des Capucins in Rue des Capucins (Tel. 206 45) provides a varied and impressive programme all year round.

The most British of the city's 'eateries' is Scotts Pub and Restaurant, 4 Bisserreg (across the bridge from Rue St-Unic). It serves beer and snacks and many expatriots are found here.

The Countryside/Provincial Luxembourg

On the banks of the River Sauer lies the medieval village of ECHTERNACH. Though badly damaged in the Second World War (that's Germany just across the river) it has been well restored now, and the 1328 TOWN HALL is as good as ever. Echternach has a big International Music Festival each June (student tickets cost 150 fr. and are available from the tourist office) and a centuries-old dancing procession takes place on Whit Tuesday. The tourist office is contactable by telephoning 72230, and is open from 9 a.m.–12 noon and 2 p.m.–5 p.m. The BENEDICTINE ABBEY has some impressive frescoes and stained-glass windows and the buried remains of St Willibrord. There's a youth hostel at 9 rue André

Duchscher (Tel. 72158) or try Hotel Le Petit Poète, 13 Place du Marché (Tel. 72072). Doubles from about 1,200 fr. It's right in the centre of town.

The cheapest of the town's campsites, Camp Officiel, is near the bus station in rue de Drekirch (Tel. 72272). It charges 90 fr. per person, 100 fr. per site and is open from March until October. Buses are the easiest method of getting from Luxembourg City to Echternach. There are twelve buses daily, each taking just over an hour to travel the distance. Just a few minutes north of Echternach is a small wedge of a hiker's paradise: LITTLE SWITZERLAND. This is the Moellerdall section of the Ardennes, and a walk through the steep gorges and forest makes an exhilarating hour or so. Luxembourg has the densest network of marked walking paths in the world. National routes are marked by yellow signs. The YHA maintains the walking routes marked by white triangles, and maps are available from the YHA at 18 Place d'Armes (Tel. 225588) and cost 130 fr. In the northernmost part of the Ardennes is TROISVIERGES, the heart of hiking country.

The Clerve Valley leads to CLERVAUX, about an hour on the line from Luxembourg City. The castles of BOURSCHEID and CLERVAUX, both eleventh-century and in good repair, are here in fairytale settings. There are permanent exhibitions in Clervaux Castle, including Steichen's 'Family of Man' collection. Admission 40 fr. The tourist office at Clervaux (open from 2 p.m.–6 p.m., and in mornings of summer months) is next to the Castle (Tel. 92072). They'll help you find a bed. VIANDEN is definitely worth a visit. It is not directly linked to Luxembourg City by rail or bus; so travel via Echternach. Here you'll find cobbled streets and a magnificent castle which is the biggest one west of the Rhine. Admission is 110 fr. This was the cradle of the Grand-Ducal dynasty and dates back to the ninth century. Try the chairlift (télésiège) which operates from rue de Sanatorium and costs 140 fr., and also the open-air swimming pool with impressive views over the castle. Less scenic, but no less historic is the DOLL MUSEUM (Tel. 84591) which is open from Easter to October and features a display of over 200 dolls dating from 1860–1960. Admission is 70 fr. The Youth Hostel is situated over the bridge (and at the end of the Grande Rue) from the train station at 3 Montée du Chateau (Tel. 84177). You'll also be able to find numerous other cheap hotels along this road. The tourist office is in the Victor Hugo House close by the bridge (Tel.

84257, closed 12 noon–2 p.m.). Three camping sites are situated on the edge of the River Our; each costs about 100 fr. per person and per site.

The route from Luxembourg City to Clervaux has many interesting smaller towns which have a lot to offer in terms of countryside and history. MERSCH, just at the entrance to the valley of the Seven Castles, has prehistoric caves and the remains of a Roman villa and early feudal castle. It is also the site of many wooded walks. Maps and information are available from the tourist office at the town hall (Tel. 32523) and at St Michael's Tower in July and August (Tel. 329618), closed from 12 noon to 2 p.m. Further up the route lies DIEKIRCH, home of a beer festival on the third Sunday of July, and three camping grounds. Bicycles can be rented at Camping de la Sure (Tel. 809425) where maps and information are also available. The tourist office is contactable on 803023. WILTZ, like Clervaux, borders on a valley, and is divided into two parts as a result, with a castle situated on the higher plateau. An international open-air theatre festival in July takes place in the amphitheatre in the castle yard, and a folklore museum is housed in the former castle stables. A walk through the town leads along a path of stone crosses which remember the plague. For tourist information tel. 957444 (office closed between 12 noon and 1.30 p.m.). The youth hostel is situated on rue de la Montagne (Tel. 95062) and has kitchen facilities.

Travelling back along the opposite end of the country is the village of BASCHARAGE, located on the main road from Luxembourg to Paris. Here you can get guided visits to the brewery, Brasserie Nationale, with a free drink of beer (Tel. 50 901 121), or to gem-cutting workshops (Tel. 50 90 32). You must telephone in advance to book.

If your destination is France, stop off at ESCH-SUR-ALZETTE, Luxembourg's second city, located south, on the French border and only 20 km away from Luxembourg City with a direct rail link. It is a good place for shopping at reasonable prices and houses the National Museum of the Resistance. The tourist office can be found at the Town Hall, office 8 (Tel. 547383, open Mon.–Fri.: 7.30 a.m.–12 noon, 1.30 p.m.–5 p.m.).

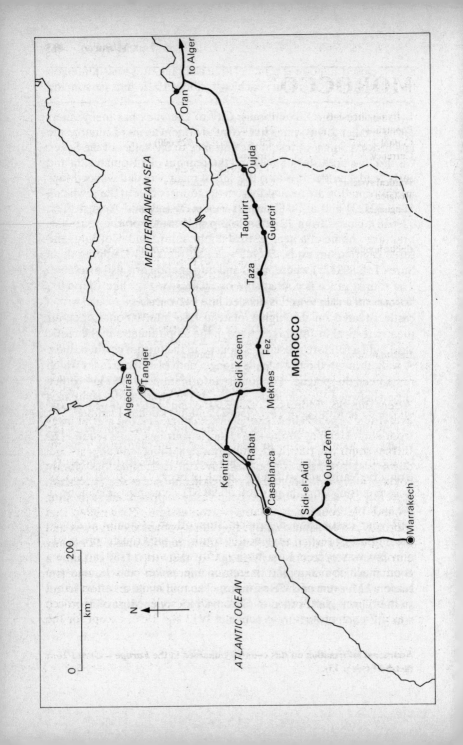

MEDITERRANEAN SEA

MOROCCO

ATLANTIC OCEAN

to Alger

Oran

Oujda

Taourirt

Guercif

Taza

Fez

Sidi Kacem

Meknes

Tangier

Algeciras

Kenitra

Rabat

Casablanca

Sidi-el-Aidi

Oued Zem

Marrakech

N

0 200 km

MOROCCO

Entry requirements	Passport
Population	22,100,000
Capital	Rabat-Salé (pop.: 925,000)
Currency	Dirham
	£1 = approx. 13.58 dh.
Political system	Constitutional Monarchy
Religion	Muslim
Languages	Arabic (French and Spanish also official languages) (English spoken in tourist towns)
Public holidays	1, 11 Jan.; 1st of Moharram (moveable); 3 March; Moulid El Nabi (moveable); 1 May; Aid Es Seghir; 6 Nov.; 18 Nov.; Aid El Kebir (moveable).
International dialling codes	From UK: 010 + 212 + number
	From USA: 011 + 212 + number
	To UK: 00 + 44 + number
	To USA: 00 + 1 + number
Eurotrain office	112 avenue d'Espagne, Tangier (Tel. 09–35540)

After Europe, Morocco comes as a bit of a culture shock: everything appears alien, exotic and exciting, and if it's a 'far away from home' feeling you're after, this is your best destination. The further south you travel, the more 'foreign' things will appear – get down to Marrakesh if you possibly can to sample the vibrant colours, new smells and tastes, and baking hot sun of this Arab land. Recently the rail network has been vastly improved and travelling around the country is relatively trouble-free. Remember that Morocco is a Muslim country, therefore women should dress and act accordingly when travelling in more remote areas. For many eurorailers Morocco is the highlight of their trip. It is certainly a country which makes a tremendous impression on you, and is a place which everyone 'doing Europe' should make an effort to get to in order to glimpse a non-European lifestyle. Most of Morocco was a French protectorate between 1912 and 1956, except for the

Additional information on this country contained in the *Europe – Grand Tour* factsheet (see p.13).

north which was Spanish. The lowland areas, where the trains run, are the richest and most populous parts of Morocco.

• **Getting there:** There are various ferries from Spain to Tangier and Ceuta in Morocco, with the Algeciras–Ceuta being the shortest and cheapest crossing, but as it's not on the railway it might be easier to use the Algeciras–Tangier crossing. It costs about 2,100 pesetas with 30 per cent Inter-Rail/Eurail reductions. Don't rely on the information posted in Algeciras Ferry Terminal; ask. Avoid any dealings in drugs *completely*. The border guards do not look kindly on anyone caught in possession.

To get from Ceuta to Tetouan, walk from Ceuta port to town centre, then catch bus (48 ptas) to border. Then take another bus (or share a petit-taxi) to Tetouan. The bus option in Morocco can be worth pursuing – they're very cheap and quite comfortable. Tetouan–Sidi Lyamani by bus is a beautiful run and you can connect from there to trains in Casablanca.

MOROCCAN RAILWAYS
(Office National des Chemins de Fer, ONCF)

Recently there has been a big improvement in Moroccan trains, although they still do not run as frequently as you might wish. The Inter-Rail card is valid here (Eurail is not) and the railway runs to the main tourist towns and regions. There are three classes on the trains: first, second and 'Economique'. Your Inter-Rail or BIJ ticket entitles you to use the second-class facilities. It is well worth paying the supplement of around £2 to travel in an air-conditioned carriage. The rail network runs south from Marrakesh to Casablanca and Rabat, then splits at Sidi Kacem, one line going north to Tangier, the other to Oujda and over the border to Algeria. You can even charter a train!

The Trans-Maghreb Express which travels from Casablanca through Mekenes, Fes and the fringes of the Atlas mountains to terminate in Algeria is a laid-back, but beautiful route to travel upon, if you are intending to pass through, rather than stay in, Morocco.

• **Inter-Rail bonuses:** The Algeciras–Tangier crossing has 30 per cent discount for Inter-Rail, 20 per cent discount for Eurail.

- **Rover tickets:** The Carte d'Abonnement is valid for unlimited travel for one month on all trains but the fast TNR services. It costs 1,146 dh. for first-class and 767 dh. for second.

TRAIN INFORMATION

You'll find the odd official who speaks pidgin English, but generally you'll have to resort to French, which is the official second language.

- **Reservations:** Not compulsory, but not a bad idea if you're on a long haul in peak season.

- **Night travel:** Sleeping cars are first class only and come in singles or doubles. They're fairly expensive so unless you're feeling particularly delicate, try and schedule your travelling for daytime. Second-class cars are often very full at night.

TOURIST INFORMATION

Most towns have both a tourist office and a Syndicat d'Initiative. The tourist office should be your first port of call as they have information on all of Morocco, and will also help find a bed if necessary. When you're organized, make your way back to the Syndicat d'Initiative which has leaflets on local sights, etc. Most offices have leaflets on all the places you are likely to visit in Morocco, so stock up at the first one you come to.

A word of warning: unofficial guides (mostly young boys) will pester you with their dubious services. A good impersonation of Finnish usually puts them off your track. Hustlers are another problem: they'll approach you in the medina and kasbah (old fortress), be incredibly friendly, and be conversant in a dozen languages. Ignore and avoid them. Finally, when you're at the sights don't feel obliged to accept the custodian's offer of a guided tour or feel it necessary to give him a tip, as he is already paid by the government and does very well from other tourists. If you do want an official guide – head for the nearest tourist office ('syndicat d'initiative') where you can expect to pay about 30 dh. for half a day of the guide's time. If you wear contact lenses, bear in mind that it can be very dusty, and you may be more comfortable wearing glasses if you have them.

• **Money matters:** 1 dirham (dh.) = 100 francs.
Banking hours are Mon.–Fri.: 8.15 a.m.–11.30 a.m., 2.15
p.m.–4.30 p.m. (during Ramadan 9.30 a.m.–2 p.m.). Banks charge
no commission and have the same rate of exchange everywhere.
Buy dirhams in advance if arriving outside banking hours. Keep
your receipts as you will probably be asked to produce them when
changing dirhams back, and remember to use banks – the rate on
the boat back to Spain is a rip-off.

• **Post offices:** Open Mon.–Sat.: 8.30 a.m.–12 noon, 2.30 p.m.–6
p.m. (Closed Sat. p.m.)

• **Shops:** Open Mon.–Sat.: 8.30 a.m.–12 noon, 2 p.m.–6.30 p.m.
Bargain like mad wherever you go in the markets (souks), even
when you see the 'prix fixe' sign. Haggling is a way of life here and,
unless you manage to get the price down by at least 50 per cent,
consider yourself a failure. Remember: you can never start low
enough. Check with the Syndicats for opening times of museums
and other sights.

• **Buses:** More frequent and cheaper than trains, though they are
less comfortable. If you are trying to board a bus at an intermediate
stop between its point of departure and its destination – be warned!
You will find it difficult to get a space, and this means you could be
waiting at your stop for longer than you bargained for.

SLEEPING

Morocco is a country where it pays dividends to be tough. You can
live off next to nothing if you don't mind roughing it a bit. Camping
and youth hostelling ('Auberges de Jeunesse') are very cheap, as
little as 15 dh. a night under canvas or 20 dh. in a hostel dormitory,
but you're not guaranteed central locations or Swiss conditions. The
medina hotels/pensions offer the most central and colourful locations and are usually cheaper than the places in the new areas of
town. Hotels are graded from one to five stars and there are fixed
maximum prices for each category. You usually pay by the room, so
doubling up with friends can bring the unit cost of a room down. The
cheapest hotel rooms of class 1/2 cost somewhere between 60 and
110 dh. (£4–£7) for a double room, with an extra £1 for shower and

breakfast. You will find the *Non-Classé* hotels are cheaper than those listed (*Classé*), by the tourist offices. If you find the water is hot at any time of day, seize the chance for a shower while you can (these usually cost 5–8 dh.) as the plumbing here is decidedly erratic. As far as public toilets go, always carry your own loo paper.

EATING AND NIGHTLIFE

If you've an iron stomach, take full advantage of it in Morocco by eating in the kasbahs and from shishkebab stands. Most decent restaurants offer a good selection of Moroccan dishes. Try harira, a rich soup of chicken, peppers and spices, followed by touajen (lamb or chicken stew) or couscous, Morocco's most famous dish (made from semolina, with lamb, fish or chicken). Alternatively, try the Djaja Maamra – steamed and stuffed chicken with couscous, almonds and raisins. If you like something sweet to finish the meal, ask for kab el ghzal (almond pastries) and some mint tea. Don't take chances with tap water; drink only mineral water, which you have to ask for by brand name. You can usually trust Sidi Ali or Sidi Harazem brands. One important point to remember: there is little, or no, alcohol in this country. Often it is difficult in the more remote places to find meals during the day, so eat well at night. The local Syndicat will let you know where the nearest belly-dancer performs and what's happening on the disco scene.

Tangier

This isn't the best Morocco has to offer, but if you're on a day trip from Spain, it'll show you some of the exotic and colourful differences between Europe and North Africa. As Tangier receives more than its fair share of tourists, be particularly on your guard for hustlers. Many readers feel the best advice on Tangier is to head straight for the rail station and take the first train out. This is primarily because of the excessive amount of hassle one experiences here, so be warned.

The main market place, GRAND SOCCO, connects the medina and

the new town. Tourist information (Tel. 9382 39/40) is at 29 Boulevard Pasteur (open Mon.–Fri.: 9 a.m.–3 p.m. in summer, otherwise 8.30 a.m.–12 noon and 2.30 p.m.–6.30 p.m.), as is the post office. In the medina, the rue Mokhtar Ahardan is where to look for cheap hotels and restaurants. The Pensione Palace (Tel. 09–39248) is at No. 2 and costs about 30 dh. per person. If you really want to spoil yourself, head for the Grand Hotel Villa de France, 143 Hollande St (Tel. 31475), which overlooks the town. In addition to the four-star view (Noel Coward used to stay here), you can expect an equally superb double room and service for about 180 dh. The beaches and nightlife are both good, though single girls on the beach are in for a hard time. If you decide to stay, visit the SULTAN'S PALACE, which is now a museum containing a fine collection of Moroccan art, carpets, jewellery and weapons. Six miles out of town and in sight of the Rock of Gibraltar lies the camping site Tinjis. It is situated east of the city on the Malabata Rd near Camping la Miramonte Mar-Bel. To get there walk along the Doubonah Rd and turn right, or along the rue de la Vieille Montagne (the prolongation of the avenue Allal Ben Abdellah).

If you are leaving the country from here, remember to turn up early for the boat as you will end up having to queue for several things like passport control, forms for passport control, customs and – finally – the boat itself. To buy a discounted ferry ticket back to Algeciras you must produce a photocopy of your Inter-Rail/ Eurail Pass (the Cafe Terminal across from the main station will do one cheaply). The Eurotrain office is at 112 avenue d'Espagne (Tel. 09–35540). Try the campsite Tinjis. To get there walk along the Doubonah Road and turn right, or along the rue de la Vieille Montagne.

A useful point of information that will save you unnecessary trekking: the train station (GARE DU PORT) is right below the ferry terminal in the city. Most trains leave from this stop, as well as from the GARE DE VILLE, which is 300 m beyond the port gate.

Rabat

From Tangier to the capital of Morocco – Rabat – is about five hours on the main line. This is a clean, organized and structured city. It has numerous parks and gardens, and most of the town is new and affluent by Moroccan standards. There is a kasbah in the old town but the medina lacks atmosphere, and you feel you're back in Europe a lot of the time.

TOURIST INFORMATION AND ADDRESSES

TOURIST INFORMATION: Angle Avenue Al Abtal, Rue Oued Fes (Tel. 07–751 71/79) or Syndicat d'Initiative at rue Patrice Lumumba (Tel. 723272), which is nearer the station and is open from 8.30 a.m.–6.30 p.m. every day in season.

POST OFFICE: Avenue Mohammed V. Open Mon.–Fri.: 8 a.m.–12 noon; 2 p.m.–6.45 p.m., Sat.: 8.30 a.m.–12 noon.

AMEX: In Rabat Hilton (Tel. 772151). Take bus for Agdal.

UK EMBASSY: 17 Boulevard Tour Hassan (Tel. 720905).

US EMBASSY: 2 Avenue de Marrakesh (Tel. 766265).

CANADIAN EMBASSY: 13 Zankat Joafar Essodik, Agdal (Tel. 771376).

MEDICAL ASSISTANCE: (Tel. 74411).

PHONE CODE: 07.

POLICE: Rue Scekamo (Tel. 19).

SEEING

The TOUR HASSAN minaret in the twelfth-century mosque and the MAUSOLEUM OF MOHAMMED V are close to each other, and about a mile's walk away is the CHELLAH, an Arab necropolis built in the old Roman section of Rabat called SALA COLONIA. There are gardens here that are ideal for a picnic. The OUDAIAS KASBAH fortress has another beautiful garden, a Moorish café, and the MUSEUM OF MOROCCAN HANDICRAFTS: carpets, musical instruments, furniture, etc. (open 8 a.m.–12 noon, 2 p.m.–6 p.m., closed Tuesday and Saturday p.m.). The ROYAL PALACE is also located here in the capital, though it dates only from the 1950s.

SLEEPING, EATING AND NIGHTLIFE

Try to book your rooms in advance, especially if you are planning to visit Rabat in July, since it can become vastly overcrowded in this month. The Youth Hostel on 43 Rue Marassa (Tel. 725769) is cheap, but not great. Instead stick to the new town area around the train station: here you will find many hotels situated in the surrounding roads. For camping, take bus 6 or 24 to Salé terminal and follow the signs for Camping Municipal. For cheap hotels, try the Hotel France which is on the edge of the medina and costs around 50 dh. for a clean double with washing facilities (cold water, as in most cheap Moroccan hotels!). Alternatively, in the medina, try Hotel Marrakesh, rue Sebbahi (Tel. 727703). Enter the medina on Avenue Mohammed V and turn right three blocks later: singles around 30 dh. – good value. The medina is also the place for cheap eats. There are plenty of stalls and restaurants, with the Restaurant El Bahia on Avenue Hassan II offering good food at budget prices. It's located to your right as you approach the medina from Avenue Mohammed V. For an evening stroll, walk round the Oudaias Kasbah as the sun is sinking. If you want to brave a nightclub investigate around Sahat Melilya and Témara Beach areas.

Casablanca

This is the largest, and in many ways the least attractive, of Morocco's towns. With over two million inhabitants and a busy port, Casablanca is a crowded, modern and somewhat squalid city, and the only thing romantic about it is its name and Play-it-again-Sam image. Take the train to the Port Station for the medina, beaches etc, but be careful taking photographs as some of this is a sensitive military area. Casablanca has got some character and among its sights are the neo-Moorish public buildings round the PLACE DES NATIONS UNIES and the MAHKAMA (regional courts). A *must* to visit is the world's largest mosque: HASSAN II MOSQUE, which has room for 80,000 worshippers and a 172-metre minaret. If you decide to stay, try the youth hostel at 6 pl. Amiral Philbert (Tel. 22 05 51) which charges 22.50 dh. per person including breakfast. To get there turn and keep walking right from the station, turning up the first small flight of steps on the left. The tourist office at ONCF, 98 Boulevard Mohammed V (Tel. 20577/220706), and at SS Rue Omar Slaovi (Tel. 271177), can provide good maps and disco listings for the party animals. The journey south to Casablanca from Tangier is no problem as it involves the best trains in Morocco;

however, if you're going further south make sure you have supplies with you as the buffets are awful. Also, if you can afford it, pay the supplement from second to first class (if you're travelling in peak season). Still, you shouldn't judge Morocco by Casablanca. Travel through to Fez or Marrakesh for a more representative image.

Marrakesh

This red-ochre city on the edge of the Sahara desert is what you expect Morocco to be like: vibrant markets with snake-charmers, fortune-tellers and acrobats; palm trees; remains from ancient dynasties, and incredible midday temperatures of around 105°F (August maximum).

On arrival get hold of a 'petit-taxi' (regular ones cost double) and haggle to fix a price for a ride to the Djemma el Ina. Or you can save 10 dh. and take a 3 or 6 bus from outside the station. You'll be dropped off in the city's main square, and from there it's no problem finding a cheap hotel bed. To walk takes about 30 minutes.

TOURIST INFORMATION AND ADDRESSES

TOURIST OFFICE: Place Abdelmoumen ben Ali on Avenue Mohammed V (Tel. 431088/438889). English spoken. Ask for a map and a list of accommodation (though it doesn't list the real cheapies). Open Mon.–Fri.: 8.30 a.m.–12 noon, 2.30 p.m.–6.30 p.m. Sat.: 8.30 a.m.–12.30 p.m. If you have already picked up leaflets on the city elsewhere, don't bother making the one-mile trek here unless you're desperate for them to book an hotel for you. Also, there is a Tourist Centre at 179 Bd Mohamed V (Tel. 432097/434797).
POST OFFICE: Place du 16 Novembre, off Avenue Mohammed V. Open Mon.–Fri.: 8.30 a.m.–12.15 p.m. and 2.30 p.m.–6.45 p.m.
AMEX: c/o Voyages Schwartz, rue Mauritania, 2nd floor (Tel. 436603/433321). Open Mon.–Fri.: 8.30 a.m.–12.30 p.m., 3 p.m.–6.30 p.m.
CHEMIST: Near Hotel Marrakesh, Place de la Liberté. Open till 10 p.m.
ALL-NIGHT CHEMIST: Rue Khalid Ben Ovalid (Tel. 430415).

EMERGENCY PHONE NO: 19.
PHONE CODE: 04.

SEEING

The DJEMMA EL FNA (Assembly of the Dead) is the showpiece of Marrakesh. This square is the hub of life of the city. In daytime it's a busy colourful market, and at night the street artists arrive. (Be particularly careful of your valuables here.) The medina is particularly lively and there are various photogenic markets like the ones for musical instruments or wool dyers. The old theological school, BEN YOUSSEF MEDERSA, has some fine marbles, mosaics and wood-carvings, and the pale green twelfth-century minaret of the KOUTOUBIA MOSQUE is Morocco's best example. The BAHIA PALACE is nineteenth-century and the PALACE EL BEDI is sixteenth-century. The SAADI MAUSOLEUM contains the remains of various sultans and is free, though the guide expects a tip. The bus station is at Bab Doukkala. Buses to the beach leave from here, but they travel at a relaxed pace. If it is spectacle that you are after, coincide your visit with the annual two-week Folklore Festival held in the BEDI PALACE at the end of May/beginning of June. Evening shows (tickets cost about 50 dh.) of authentic, visual performance span the whole spectrum of Moroccan music. Failing that, go and see the souk of camels (traditional trading station) which takes place every Thursday.

SLEEPING, EATING AND NIGHTLIFE

Head for the Djemma el Fna area for cheap hotels and restaurants. Hôtel de France, 197 rue Zitoun el Kedim (Tel. 443067), and further down on the right; Hôtel de Medina have doubles for about 50 dh., the latter with hot showers included. The youth hostel's good by Moroccan standards. It's near the station on Route Al Jahidh, Quartier Industriel (Tel. 432831); it closes 9 a.m.–2 p.m. and after 10 p.m. It is this same area, around the station, that is the best place to find the cheapest, classified, hotels; so look around. The same area is abundant in French-style restaurants and also contains the majority of the city's bars. Café-Restaurant Oriental at 33 rue Bab Abnaou (off the Djemma el Fna) do good menus at reasonable prices. Other reasonable hotels are situated near the

Djemma el Fna. The Hotel da la Jeunesse at 56 Derb Sidi Banloukate (Tel. 43631) is one of the best budget hostels on this street, charging 40dh. for a double room and 50dh. for a triple, including cold showers. Try the Café Restaurant Marocain at pl. Djemma el Fna nearby, open from 8 a.m.–11 p.m. The Rue Bani Marin just off from here houses other good food venues like Mik Mak on Placc Foucald which has an excellent patisserie.

Meknes

On the eastern line to Fez and the Algerian border, and 4½ hours from Tangier, lies the imperial city of Meknes. From the station, turn left for the medina, hotels and the old town. Tourist information is at Place Administrative (Tel. 05–21286/524426) and is open Mon.–Fri.: 8 a.m.–2 p.m.; Sat.: 8.30 a.m.–12 noon, 3 p.m.–6 p.m. English is spoken, and some literature is available. Another Tourist Centre can be found at Esplanade de la Foire (Tel. 520191). MANSOUR, the pavilion where the seventeenth-century Sultan Moulay Ismail received ambassadors, is up here. There are UNDERGROUND CAVES where the Sultan's slaves were kept which can be viewed if you ask the guards nicely. The elaborate TOMB OF MOULAY ISMAIL is further up on the right. The mosque in which the tomb is located is the only one in the country to admit non-Muslims. Dress appropriately so as not to cause offence. There are two outstanding palaces in this city. The DARJAMI PALACE, at the back of place el Hedir, now a museum, was formerly a nineteenth-century Moroccan Palace. The DAR EL-KEBIRA (Great Palace) was once the largest in the world. The theological school BOU INANIA is the elaborate fourteenth-century building in the medina.

SLEEPING, EATING AND NIGHTLIFE

Around Place el Hédime there are quite a few cheap hotels, but if you don't fancy these the best alternative is camping. The best site is Camping Esplanade near the Heri, on the other side of the medina from the tomb of Moulay Ismail. The youth hostel's a dead loss, but if you're desperate it's at Boulevard Okba Ben Nafii (Tel. 05–

24698) (near Hôtel Transatlantique). Far better is the friendly and safe Hotel Maroc, 103 av Benbrahim (Tel. 03–30703) just off the av Romazine. Doubles cost about 50 dh. The Hotel Excelsior, 57 av des F.AR. (Tel. 21900) just around the corner from the bus station has good rooms, with doubles costing 61 dh., 85 dh. with shower and 87 dh. with a bath. For food, rue Dar Smen and Avenue de Romazine are the best ideas. Moroccan-style nightlife is not hard to find in Meknes.

Fez (Fes)

The oldest imperial city in Morocco is today considered her cultural and intellectual centre. The huge medina here is unmatched elsewhere in North Africa. You could easily spend days in it; the colours, smells, filth and constant arguments are as endless as the memories you will keep of Fez.

TOURIST INFORMATION AND ADDRESSES

TOURIST INFORMATION: La Délégation Régionale du Tourisme, Place de la Résistance, Immeuble Bennani (situated at the end of Avenue Hassan II) (Tel. 623460/626297). Open Mon.–Thurs.: 8.30 a.m.–12 noon, 2.30 p.m.–6.30 p.m.; Fri.: 8.30 a.m.–11.30 a.m., 3 p.m.–6.30 p.m.
Le Syndicat d'Initiative et du Tourisme, Place Mohammed V (main square of the city) (Tel. 624769). Open Mon.–Fri.: 9 a.m.–12 noon, 3 p.m.–6 p.m.; Sat.: 9 a.m.–12 noon.
POST OFFICE: Avenue Mohammed V (corner of Avenue Hassan). Open Mon.–Thurs.: 8.30 a.m.–12 noon, 2.30 p.m.–6.30 p.m.; Fri.: 8.30 a.m.–11.30 a.m.; 3 p.m.–6.30 p.m.
BUS STATION: CTM, Boulevard Mohammed V (Tel. 22041) with buses to Rabat, Casablanca, Marrakesh, Meknes, and Tangier. Private buses from Gare Routière in Bab Boujeloud.
ALL-NIGHT CHEMIST: Av Abdelkrim El Khattobi (Tel. 623380).
PHONE CODE: 05.

SEEING

Expect to get lost in Fez: the MEDINA is so sprawling and

unstructured it's inevitable. There is a map to help you out, but it is
not well detailed. You will inevitably be pestered by unofficial
guides, so be careful. The majority of them will hang out in Bab
Boujeloud, so watch out in this area (also for pick-pockets), and if
you do accept an offer, barter him down to about 15 dh. and
emphasize that you wish to go sightseeing, not shopping (he will
receive a commission on any goods you buy, and you will end up
paying more as a result). Official guides are available at the hotels or
tourist offices for 30 dh. for a half day. There are countless souks in
the medina to look at, but only ferret out the tannery one if you've
got an iron stomach: the sight of vast vats of coloured dyes is
intriguing, but the smell is not.

Before entering into the medina, check out the DAR BATHA
PALACE, which now houses the MUSEUM OF MOROCCAN ARTS AND
CRAFTS (open 9–11.30 a.m., 3–6 p.m, closed Tuesdays) and features
all local artisan traditions. The medina is the location of the
tenth-century minaret of the KAROUYINE MOSQUE, built in the
fourteenth century and the Karonic University, MEDERSA, which
claims to be the oldest in the world along with the theological
schools of ATTARINE and BOU INANIA.

SLEEPING, EATING AND NIGHTLIFE

Round Bab Boujeloud you'll find a few cheap (and fairly nasty)
hotels with doubles for 50–60 dh. Other cheap non-classified hotels
are found in the new city, around the area of Avenue Mohammed
V. The youth hostel on 18 rue Abdeslam Serghini (Tel. 624085) is
good value and, by Fez standards, very clean and comfortable.
Reach it by walking six blocks down from the tourist office along
Boulevard Chefchaouni, turn left to street below and look for sign.
Follow the arrows from Place Mohammed V, it is about 5 km from
the station. For hotels try the Excelsior at 107 rue Larbi el Kaghat
(Tel. 25602), or the Hotel Renaissance at 47 rue Abdekrim
el-Khattabi (Tel. 22193) near the Avenue Mohammed V, which
charges 40 dh. for a double room, but has no showers. The Hotel du
Commerce in Pl. des Alaouites in Fes el-Jdid is very clean and
charges 60 dh. for a double room and an extra 4 dh. for showers.

Bab Boujeloud and the medina are the cheap eating districts. The
place Mohammed V also boasts plentiful eating places, but is more
expensive. The youth hostel has a kitchen, so you could buy food

and cook it yourself (watch the meat). Avoid the local delicacy, bisteela (which is pigeon, vegetables and nuts, covered in sweet pastry!). An evening stroll in the old Jewish quarter is more rewarding than the formal entertainments you'll find.

Off-the-track places

Many of Morocco's best places are not on the railway, so buses are the only answer. TETUAN, 1½ hours away from Tangier (cost about 30 dh.), is a relatively unspoilt town with a fascinating medina – eat there and try round Place Hassan II and Avenue Mohammed V for rooms. The tourist office is situated on the latter (Tel. 7009). ASNI is thirty miles from Marrakesh and buses leave hourly from the station. It's more fun to share a taxi with several others and a full load should mean your share of the fare comes to between 10–15 dh. This is in the HIGH ATLAS mountain region in the Sahara. IMLIL, accessible by 'taxi' (communal truck), is even more spectacular. This is surrounded by the mountains and you can start a climb of MOUNT TOUBKAL (13,671 feet) from here. The town's refuge is your best bet for a bed, and it has cooking facilities. Don't attempt the mountain unless you're experienced and well equipped.

ESSAOUIRA is a Berber town on the south coast. If you're tired out with travelling and need a break before the long haul back home, sleep here free on the beaches and take advantage of this opportunity to share in a very un-European culture and lifestyle. Take a leisurely walk up to the eighteenth-century Moorish fortress (the SKALA) at sunset. The tourist office is on Porte Portugaise.

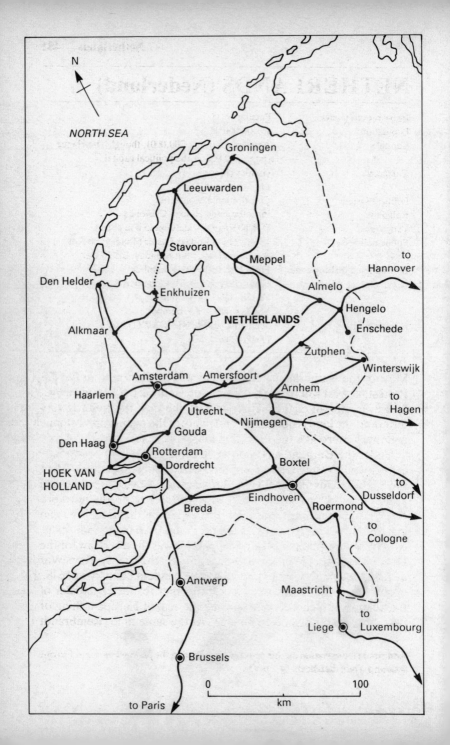

NETHERLANDS (Nederland)

Entry requirements	Passport
Population	15,500,000 +
Capital	Amsterdam (pop.: 700,000), though The Hague (pop.: 500,000) is the political capital
Currency	Guilder (Florin)
	£1 = approx. f.2.85
Political system	Constitutional Monarchy
Religions	Protestant and Roman Catholic
Language	Dutch (English widely spoken in cities)
Public holidays	1 Jan.; Good Friday; Easter Monday; 30 Apr.; Ascension Day; Whit Monday; 25, 26 Dec.
International dialling codes	From UK: 010 + 31 + number
	From USA: 011 + 31 + number
	To UK: 09 + 44 + number
	To USA: 09 + 1 + number
Eurotrain office	Schipholweg 101, NL–2316XC Leiden (Tel. 071–253 333)

Most of the Netherlands' major cities are concentrated in the flat Protestant west where one has visions of windmills, tulips and clogs. However, not all of the Netherlands is like this; the south is very different: the land is not all flat, and many of the people are Catholic and much more like the French in many respects.

Under the Burgundians and the Habsburgs, Holland was politically linked to Belgium to form the Netherlands (lowlands). Then the Spanish King Philip II started to levy heavy taxes to pay for his army, fighting for the Catholic cause in Europe. As the northern Netherlands had mostly become Protestant by this time, you can imagine this didn't go down too well. Philip tried to smooth things over by sending in Spanish governors. This was the last straw for the Dutch who, under William of Orange, fought the Eighty Years War against the Spanish, emerging as an independent country in 1648.

After this, the Dutch really got it together for the remainder of the seventeenth century and showed the rest of Europe a thing or two about seafaring and commerce. At the same time, Rembrandt

Additional information on this country contained in the *Netherlands* and *Europe – Grand Tour* factsheets (see p.13).

et al. were hard at work creating the Dutch golden age of arts and science. Symbolically, the Netherlands' eclipse by Britain in the eighteenth century was begun by William III moving across to England to share the throne with Mary. After the Napoleonic Wars and French domination, life for the Dutch gradually developed into parliamentary democracy.

NETHERLANDS RAILWAYS
(Nederlandse Spoorwegen, NS)

Dutch Railways are as trouble-free and efficient as you're likely to find anywhere in Europe. There are frequent intercity services between all parts of the Netherlands, at least once an hour. The short distances involved mean you can see most of the Netherlands while based at one city. Be careful not to end up on the 'stop-trains' which do just that, before connecting up to the main intercity network. Supplements are only necessary on EuroCity trains. Electric trains often consist of portions for two different destinations.

• **Eurail bonuses:** Free passage on ships of BV Rederji NACO between Enkhuisen and Staveren or vice versa between 15 May and the first week in September.

TRAIN INFORMATION

There should be no problem with language as nearly everyone speaks English. Ask at the information desk for the booklet called 'Travelling By Rail in Holland' which has a useful map with frequency times.

• **Reservations:** It's not possible to reserve seats on inland trains or the Amsterdam–Brussels run. Also it's not compulsory to reserve seats on the international trains, despite what they might tell you at Amsterdam Train Information Office. Trains are often very full, so if the queues are small, go ahead and reserve one. If they are not, you could literally be waiting for hours in the summer to make your reservation.

• **Night travel:** There are couchettes and sleepers on international routes only. There is an all-night service between Utrecht, Amsterdam, The Hague and Rotterdam running every hour.

• **Eating on trains:** All intercities have the usual mini-bars while only international trains have diners.

• **Scenic tips:** If you're fortunate enough to be travelling at any time from March to May through the bulb fields (Bollenvelden) region (on any runs between Amsterdam, Haarlem and Leiden) you will be amply rewarded.

• **Bikes:** The Netherlands are ideal for cycling – it's flat and there are cycle tracks everywhere. Most stations hire out bikes and give reduced rates if you show your ticket. It usually costs only about £2 per day, but often you must leave a large deposit.

• **Rover tickets:** The Rail Rover ticket is available for one or seven days. The prices are £17 and £39.50 for second class. In addition you can buy a Public Transport Link Rover which extends the Rail Rover ticket for use on all public transport, including Amsterdam and Rotterdam Metros, but excluding KLM Airport buses. The prices are an additional £2 and £7.50. The new Holland Rail Pass is valid for unlimited travel for any 3 days in a 10–15 day period and costs £25. Supplements still need to be paid for EuroCity trains but it is valid on ordinary Netherlands Railways intercity services. The frequency of service in the Netherlands is such that you should never need to use an international express train for a domestic journey. You can buy it before you go from Netherlands Railways, 25/28 Buckingham Gate, London SW1E 6LD (Tel. 071–630 1735). If you buy it in the Netherlands you need to show your passport and provide a passport-size photograph.

   If you are travelling as a group, consider the Multi Rover Ticket which gives two to six passengers unlimited rail travel for one day (off peak only). It costs £25.50 for two passengers to £42.50 for six. The Teenage Rover is a similar ticket for those aged 10–18, and allows travel for any four days in a ten-day period and is only available in June, July and August. Finally, there is the Benelux Tourrail which gives free rail travel in Belgium, the Netherlands and Luxembourg (including Luxembourg country buses) on 5 out of 17 days. It cannot be used with the Public Transport Link Rover and is only valid when accompanied by a passport. The ticket costs £51 for adults, £38 for ages 4–25 and 50 per cent extra for first-class use.

TOURIST INFORMATION (VVV)

The local offices are run by individual towns and can be found in every town and village in the Netherlands. They find you accommodation if required and supply you with all the information about the area. If you plan to cycle, ask for a cycle map. Unfortunately it's not always free, so inquire first. Free maps are available from the Netherlands Board of Tourism in London.

• **ISIC bonuses:** Up to 50 per cent reduction on museums. You can get into all state museums free once you've bought your museum card (f. 15 for those under 26, f. 40 for those over) from any state museum. For further information, contact NBBS, Dam 17, Amsterdam. In the States you can buy a Holland Leisure Card from the Netherlands National Tourist Office which for around $8 gives you free museum entrances and many other bonuses.

• **Money matters:** 1 guilder (florin) (f.) = 100 cents (c.).
Banking hours are Mon.–Fri.: 9 a.m.–4 or 5 p.m.; there are also exchange offices in twenty-seven railway stations, some of which are open in the evenings and at weekends. Some VVV tourist offices also exchange money. 'Store front' style exchange shops can charge as much as 9 per cent commission, so steer clear!

• **Post offices:** Open Mon.–Fri.: 9 a.m.–5 p.m. and, in major towns, 9 a.m.–4 p.m. on Sat.

• **Shops:** In general, Mon.–Fri.: 8.30/9 a.m.–5.30/6 p.m. and on Sat.: 8.30/9 a.m.–4 p.m.

• **Museums:** Most state museums are free on Mondays. Anyone can buy a museum card which is essential for anyone taking sightseeing at all seriously. Most museums charge about f. 5 for admission.

SLEEPING

If you're spending a lot of time in the Netherlands, it's a good idea to ask for the tourist board's publications on camping and hotels; the purpose-made 'Youngster' brochure lists all youth hostels and sleep-ins. No special documents are necessary on any of Holland's 2,000 or so campsites. Expect to pay about f. 15 per night. For the fifty-two youth hostels, you have to be an IYHF member; charges vary from f. 20 to f. 30, depending on whether breakfast and an evening meal are included. Student hostels are open in summer and are fairly lax as long as you look like a student. Hotels are graded on a star basis with breakfast usually included in the price. Expect to pay f. 50 minimum for a one-star single room. Fortunately, the Netherlands has plenty of boarding houses and private houses, most of which are very relaxed; these are your best bet. The local tourist offices keep a list and will find you a place for a small commission. Things get busy in July and August in Amsterdam and other tourist centres, so try and get along early.

EATING AND NIGHTLIFE

Most of the Dutch go in for a koffietafel (sandwich lunch and coffee) which is just as well, as evening meals have a tendency to be very high in carbohydrates. The best advice is to follow their example at lunchtime. There are over twenty-six types of cheese, so there's no excuse for sticking to just Edam and Gouda. There are numerous regional specialities to sample; one of the best is nieuwe haring (new herring) – this is salted herring roe and is surprisingly tender and savoury. Follow the example of the Dutch and eat it from the street stalls. It's at its best during the first few weeks in May and makes a welcome change from hamburgers. For your main meal in the evening, keep your eyes skinned for one of the 600 restaurants which serve the tourist menu. This is filling and cheap and is the same price everywhere, so if you like what's on it, don't waste your time looking elsewhere. If you prefer something a little more exotic, try 'rijsttafel' from one of the numerous Indonesian restaurants in most cities. The VVV offices will keep you informed as to what's going on locally. In the larger cities there are plenty of nightclubs and discos, but expect to pay out quite a bit. Cinemas always show films in the original language with Dutch subtitles. Prices usually start at about f. 15 and performances begin at about 7 p.m. and 9.30 p.m.

The Northern Netherlands

Much of this area has been reclaimed from the sea and so is characteristically flat. FRIESLAND is a wildlife and bird sanctuary, and this province is more like a separate country (with its own language and separate history) than a part of Holland. The best places to make for are ZAANDAM, the 'living museum': a reconstructed village of mills and old houses; ALKMAAR (fifty minutes from Amsterdam) with its cheese market on Fridays at 10 a.m. until 12 noon from mid-April to mid-September; HOORN, which puts on a crafts and folklore market; and the capital of Friesland, LEEUWARDEN. Apart from being the birthplace of Mata Hari (her house is now the Museum of Frisian Literature), the town is also a birdwatchers' paradise; you can wade out to the islands on organized treks. See the FRIES MUSEUM, OLDEHOVE TOWER and PRINCESSEHOF MUSEUM of unique ceramics.

Amsterdam

There are two distinct faces to Amsterdam: one, the quiet graceful old town of endless canals, narrow houses and tiny winding streets; the other, the harsh reality of twentieth-century capitalist consumerism: fast food, fast sex, loud music and drug pushing. The two sides live incongruously together and have made Amsterdammers famed for their tolerance of different standards and others' opinions. There are so many things to experience in this city that it is pretty well essential to see it during any comprehensive European tour. You can also buy bulbs and herrings.

STATION FACILITIES

	AMSTERDAM CENTRAAL STATION
Train information	Mon.–Fri.: 8 a.m.–10 p.m., Sat. and Sun.: 9 a.m.–10 p.m. (Tel. 1202 266 or 106–8991121)
Reservations	Mon.–Fri.: 8 a.m.–8 p.m., Sat. and Sun.: 9 a.m.–5 p.m.
Tourist information	April–Sept.: daily, 9 a.m.–12 midnight Oct.–Mar.: Mon.–Fri.: 1 p.m.–6 p.m. (in VVV office outside station)
Foreign exchange	24 hours a day
Left-luggage lockers	No access Mon.–Sun.: 1 a.m.–5 a.m.

AMSTERDAM CENTRAAL STATION	
Left-luggage store	5 a.m.–1 a.m.
Bar, Buffet	7 a.m.–7 p.m.
	6 a.m.–11 p.m. on platform 10a
Waiting room	All hours on platforms 7a, 10a, 13a
Shopping	6 a.m.–11 p.m. in central tunnel
Station shuts	Open 24 hours

Daily trains to: Hamburg (6 hours), Düsseldorf (2½ hours), The Hague (¾ hour), Brussels (2¾ hours), Paris (6 hours), Internal trains run approximately every 15 minutes.

TOURIST INFORMATION

The VVV Amsterdam tourist office is just opposite the station at Stationsplein 10. From Easter–June and September Mon.–Sat.: 9 a.m.–12 midnight, Sun.: 9 a.m.–9 p.m., July and August Mon.–Sun.: 9 a.m.–12 midnight, October–Easter Mon.–Fri.: 9 a.m.–6 p.m., Sat.: 9 a.m.–5 p.m., Sun.: 10 a.m.–1 p.m. and 2 p.m.–5 p.m. (Tel. 6266444). Another is at Leidsestraat 106, open daily in the summer months 9 a.m.–11 p.m.; out of season: 10.30 a.m.–5.30 p.m., closed Sundays. Ask for the publication 'Use It', a student-orientated magazine on what's where and how much. 'What's on in Amsterdam' lists current events. Tickets for public transport, city walks, excursions and low-priced maps and guides are also available here.

• Addresses:

POST OFFICE: Singel 250–256, Mon.–Sat.: 8 a.m.–3 p.m.
AMEX: Damrak 66 (Tel. 262042), Mon.–Fri.: 9 a.m.–5 p.m., Sat.: 9 a.m.–12 noon, 1 p.m.–4 p.m., Sun.: 11 a.m.–4 p.m.
UK CONSULATE: Koningslaan 44 (Tel. 6764343).
US CONSULATE: Museumplein 19 (Tel. 6790321), open Mon.–Fri.: 9 a.m.–3.30 p.m.
MEDICAL HELP: Tel. 6642111 for doctor or dentist.
24-HOUR PHARMACY: Tel. 6948709.
CRISIS CENTRE: JAC, Amstel 30 (Tel. 6242949).
NBBS: Rokin 38, near Dan Square. Sells Eurotrain tickets.
PHONE CODE: 020.

• **Getting about:** Information and a map of the city's buses, trams and underground are available from the GVB pavilion in front of the station. If you're going to make more than three journeys, invest in a twenty-four-hour pass which costs f. 9, or if you are staying longer, the two-day or three-day passes are considerably good value costing f. 12.10 and f. 14.80 respectively. Multi-ride tickets are also good value, sold in strips of fifteen or ten and usable throughout the Netherlands. The fifteen-strip ticket is sold in post offices and tobacconists and costs f. 9.05, the ten-strip ticket is sold on buses and costs almost the same: f. 9. If you need to buy tickets on the bus, board the bus from the front, and stamp the ticket on your first journey, since unstamped ones are invalid. Be warned: bus inspectors are extremely vigilant, especially in Amsterdam in the summer months, and it is not uncommon for up to six inspectors to board one vehicle at each exit, thus ensuring fare dodgers are quickly found!

• **Drugs scene:** There are nearly as many pushers as eurorailers in Amsterdam station. It's up to you whether you get involved with them, but the best advice is not to. Contrary to what you might believe, possession of *any* amount of drugs is a criminal offence, although you are likely to be fined only for possession of less than 30 grams of hashish. Any more, and you are in serious trouble, with legal consequences to match.

SEEING

The four main canals (the Singel, Herengracht, Keizergracht and Prinsengracht) wind their way past the main sights, so in many ways the canal boats give you the best introduction to the city. They may really make you feel like a tourist but they're cheap during the day. Watch out at night – they can cost up to four times as much for the same trip. HERENGRACHT passes the rich seventeenth-century merchants' houses; at MUNT on the SINGEL is a colourful flower market.

DAM SQUARE is the heart of the city. It lies at the end of the main shopping thoroughfare, the DAMRAK, but its attraction is often clouded by the litter and the numbers of undesirables who hang around there. Still, it's always lively, and you can often find buskers and street artists performing. To the east of the Dam lies the old city centre, beautifully preserved in its seventeenth-century splendour. This area is known as WALLETJES, and you'll do best exploring it in daytime as parts of it (Oudezijds, Achterburgwal, Oude Zijds Voorburgwal and their surroundings) have a totally different character at night when they turn into the sex streets of Europe. JORDAAN is another district worth a wander. This is the Bohemian and working-class quarter bordered by Prinsengracht, Brouwersgracht, Marnixstraat and Elandsgracht. There's a good Saturday market on Lindemarkt, open on Fridays and Saturdays from 9 a.m. to 5 p.m.

Just west of the Dam is the WESTERKERK which has a good view from its tower. Round the back is ANNE FRANK'S HOUSE where she wrote her famous diary while in hiding with her family from the Nazis for two years. See the Anti-Semitic Exhibition downstairs. It's at Prinsengracht 263, open Monday to Saturday: 9 a.m.–5 p.m. and Sunday: 10 a.m.–5 p.m. Entrance f. 6.

The RIJKSMUSEUM at Stadhouderskade 42 is one of the world's great art museums and comes top of the list of Amsterdam's forty museums. It's really big on Rembrandts (his 'Night Watch' is there) and the Dutch masters. Open Tues.–Sat.: 10 a.m.–5 p.m., Sun.: 1 p.m.–5 p.m. Entrance f. 6.50 for adults. The ROYAL PALACE on Dam Square is held up by 13,659 bits of wood; this led it to be known as the 'Eighth Wonder of the World'. Also there is the NIEUWE KERK, though there's nothing new about this late Gothic church which dates from around 1500. Entrance costs f. 6. Just behind it is a 'tasting house', THE THREE BOTTLES (De Drie Fleschjes), which dates from 1650. Try the Bols and Hoppe liqueurs.

If you are planning on visiting a lot of museums it is advisable to invest in a museum card which gives you unrestricted entry to most collections in the country. After visiting five or six museums it has paid for itself, and can be purchased at any museum ticket office. As far as the museums are concerned, the favourites are the AMSTELKRING (Our Lord in the Attic) at Oude Zijds Voorburgwal 40, a preserved seventeenth-century house where repressed Catholics used to hide; REMBRANDT'S HOUSE at Jodenbreestraat 4–6, which contains virtually a complete collection of the artist's etchings and some drawings; the STEDELIJK MUSEUM at Paulus Potterstraat 13, which has a diverse modern art collection (including a lot of paintings by the Russian artist Malevich); and the VAN GOGH MUSEUM, just along the street at No. 7 (closed Mondays).

The Fleamarket at Waterlooplein is also worth a visit. Haggle and barter to get the best deal. Amsterdam is also the diamond centre of the world. Information about tours of cutting rooms is available from VVV, Amsterdam Tourist Office.

Being so flat, the Dutch go in for cycling in a big way. It's a cheap and fun way to get about and in fact can also be the quickest. You can rent a bike at several places in the city, although the most convenient is next to the station at Stationsplein 6: Rent-a-bike. You can extend this to the canals as well, by hiring a canal bike from four moorings in the city centre. The cost is f. 16.50 for two and f. 24.50 for four, per hour, with a returnable deposit of f. 50 when you 'park' the bike at any of the mooring points. Open from 9 a.m. to 11 p.m. in summer and 7.00 p.m. in autumn. You can pick up bikes at the Leidseplein (between the Marriot and American Hotels); between the Rijksmuseum and the Heineken Brewery; Prinsengracht at the Westerkerk, near the Anne Frank House and on the Keizersgracht, near the Leidsestraat. A company called 'Yellow Bikes' organizes bike tours throughout Amsterdam from 30 March until 31 October. For further details tel. 6206940. Do watch out for bike-thieves in the city, and people who throw bikes into the canals!

SLEEPING

As Amsterdam is the fourth most popular European city (after London, Paris and Rome), it's busy in summer, and often all the hotels are full. Still, you'll always find a bed in one of the hostels or the Sleep-In: check 'Use It' for current location. Be prepared for problems from hoteliers, as well as drug pushers at Amsterdam Centraal, trying to fill up their rooms out of season. It is possible to book accommodation via the Netherlands Reservation Centre in the Hague (Tel. 070–320 2500).

• **Hotels:** One hotel which is good value is the Hotel Schröder, at Haarlemmerdijk 48b (Tel. 26 62 72), ten minutes west of the Central Station. Singles are around f. 35, doubles f. 60. This includes breakfast. Showers are f. 2. There is a minimum two-night stay in the busy season.

Also recommended is the Frisco Inn at Beursstraat 5 (Tel. 6201610). Five minutes' stroll from Central Station. Centrally located with good security. Singles, doubles and dormitory accommodation, dorms from around f. 25, many with private showers. Very helpful and friendly staff with a lively bar. Even if you're not staying there it's worth checking out for its daily happy hour, weekly half price night, regular live music and for Rover, possibly Amsterdam's largest cat.

Other recommendations are:

Van Onna, Bloemgracht 102 (Tel. 626 58 01).

Pax, Raadhuisstraat 37 (Tel. 624 97 35).

Hotel De Beurs, Beursstraat 7 (Tel. 622 23 08/622 07 41).

Hotel Fantasia, 16 Nieuwe Keizergracht (Tel. 624 88 58).

Hotel Acro, Jan Luykenstraat 42–44 (Tel. 662 05 26). Clean, comfortable and quiet.

Young Budget Hotel Kabul, Warmoesstraat 38–42 (Tel. 623 71 58). Lively and good value. Near the station, but also the red-light area. A walk down Raadhuisstraat, Beursstraat, Bloemgracht or Stadhouderskade will produce something, unless the city's bursting at the seams.

• **Private accommodation:** The average is f. 45 per person; VVV will fix you up for a f. 4 fee.

• **Hostels:** Vondelpark IYHF hostel, Zandpad 5 (Tel. 683 17 44). You'll need membership. Around f. 23 in dorms. Tram 1, 2 or 5 from station to Leidseplein, then a five-minute walk. They don't take telephone reservations – go early.

Stadsdoelen IYHF hostel, Kloveniersburgwal 97 (Tel. 624 68 32). f. 21. This is more central. Take tram 4, 9, 16, 24 or 25 to Muntplein.

Hotel Kabul (Student Hostel), Warmoesstraat 42 (Tel. 623 71 58). Dormitory, single or double accommodation. Near station (and red-light district). Very noisy – the bar closes at 4 a.m. Dorm accommodation for f. 19.

The Sleep-In is open late June–early September and at Easter. Tends to be a bit sleazy and promiscuous. Check address as it changes location annually, currently at 's Gravesandestraat 51–53 (Tel. 694 74 44) at the metro stop Weesperplein, or a 10-minute walk from Central Station. Cheapest in town are two Christian hostels at f. 15 for bed and breakfast. The Shelter is the more central at Barndesteeg 21 (Tel. 6253230) but is in the red-light area. Approach the hostel from the Damrak side rather than from Nieuwmarkt. The Eben Haezer is at Bloemstraat 179 (Tel.

6244717) and is reached by taking tram 13 or 17 to Marnixstraat. Give the 'Boatels', behind the station, a miss, as they are illegal, dirty, smelly and dodgy for leaving luggage in. Hans Brinker Statel, Kerkstraat 136–138 (Tel. 622 06 87) is excellent and cheap.

For camping try Vliegenbos at Meewenlaan 138 (Tel. 636 88 55). To get there take bus 32, 36, 38 or 39 from Central Station, or try the brilliantly cheap Zeeburg at IJdijk 44 (Tel. 694 44 30) which costs about £1.50 a night, is aimed at young travellers and has regular live music. Take bus 22 or 37 from the Central Station.

Sleeping out is risky and best avoided. If you must, try Juliana-park, Beatrixpark or Vondelpark. Do not even think about the Central Station; it is both noisy and dangerous.

EATING AND NIGHTLIFE

There's a glut of cafés and restaurants near Dam Square, round the red-light district and Leidsplein: Dutch, Chinese, Italian and Indonesian. Go for the dag's menu and fill the gap with deep-fried poffertjes (mini-doughnuts) from street stalls. For Indonesian rijsttafel avoid the more expensive restaurants around Damrak and head for Binnen Bantammerstraat to the south-east of Central Station. Ask a local for precise directions. The many restaurants are authentic and great value. Although we have no particular preference, try the Azie or the Ling Nam.

A lively Irish pub is Mulligans on the Amstel, about 200 yards from Mint Square on the right. It opens at 2 p.m. and serves Guinness, live music and Irish stew. Vegetarian restaurants are plentiful; try Bolhoed in Prinsengracht 60–62 near Anne Frank's House, Harvest in Govert Flinkstraat 251 (which is open 5.30 p.m.–9.30 p.m. Tuesdays to Saturdays and offers special dietary requirements upon advanced request, as well as an art gallery), and Bent Hamazan Kosher restaurant at Anteliersstraat 57/2 (open daily from 5 p.m. until 10 p.m.). The further out of the town centre you go the cheaper the beer gets; Heineken costs around f.7 around Rembrandtsplein, f.5 in and around the red light district and in Happy Hours only f.3. There are several good street markets to buy picnic supplies from, and if you want to go out for a drink, head for the Leidseplein, Rembrandtsplein or Thorbecke-plein.

If you want to see 'sin city' and wander through the notorious red-light district of Zeedijk, go east of the Damrak to the area bordered by Warmoesstraat, Zeedijk and Damstraat. Go carefully here as the crime rate is high. In particular, don't take photographs as some of the locals don't like it and your camera may end up in a canal.

Recommendations for restaurants are: H88 at Herengracht 88 (also a student hostel); and Egg Cream at Sint Jacobsstraat 19, open 11 a.m.–7.30 p.m. Also worth checking out is the Great Rijsttaffel at Mandarin Rokin 26, as are the Prins van Oranje behind Central Station and the Sonja in front of the station. For dancing, etc., try Melkweg at Lijnbaansgracht 243a or Cool Down at Korte, Leidse-warsstraat 26. The nicest old cafés are off Jordaan. Good for a gas (and it can literally be a 'gas' if you're on the wrong end of it) is the café Chris at Bloemstraat 42, whose toilet can be flushed only from the bar!

Carillon concerts are organized at the Old Church – check the noticeboard on the door for details. For free pop concerts head for the Vondelpark (Tuesdays).

There is a host of nightclubs in the city. Limelight at Spuistraat 6 and Korskoff at Lijnbaansgracht 161 are both free, whilst Paradiso at Weteringschans 6 and Roxy at Singel 465 are two of the trendiest clubs and cost f. 10 entrance. Check the magazine 'Wild' for more details. Most cinemas are located around the Leidsplein and Rembrandtsplein areas, the programmes change on Fridays, so check the 'what's on' in the newspapers that day for listings.

Outside Amsterdam

LEIDEN is half an hour south-west of Amsterdam and makes a pleasant day trip. This is where Descartes first published his *Discourse on Method*, and the University is still considered the Netherlands' finest. Tourist information is at Stationsplein 210. See the OLD TOWN, BOTANICAL MUSEUM, the RIJKSMUSEUM VAN OUD-HEDEN (National Antiquities). Both these are on Rapenburg. To clamber in a windmill and nose about, go to the MOLEN MUSEUM DE VALK, Tweede Binnenvestgracht 1. Try sleeping at Witte, Wittes-ingel 80, and eating at Repelsteetje on Breestraat 19 (closed Mon.

and weekends). The Eurotrain office is at Schipholweg 101 (Tel. 071–253 333).

WASSENAAR lies on the coast ten kilometres from Leiden. It houses a campsite and amusement park, whilst a nudist beach lies further down at Scheveningen. A good B&B is pension 'Koning' at Kleverlaan 179 (Tel. 023–261456) which charges £24 each per night for double or family rooms including breakfast, colour TV and bathroom facilities.

The Hague (Den Haag)

As a major world political centre, The Hague has more than its fair share of smart elegant buildings and beautiful people. There are two royal palaces, over twenty excellent museums and two government bodies based in Den Haag: the Dutch government located in the attractive BINNENHOF, and the International Court of Justice housed in the PEACE PALACE.

STATION FACILITIES

There are two stations in The Hague: Holland Spoor handles all international trains and Amsterdam trains, while Centraal Station handles trains to the east (Utrecht), south (Rotterdam) and short intercity and suburban lines.

	HOLLAND SPOOR	CENTRAAL STATION
Train information	7 a.m.–11 p.m. (Tel. 899 1121)	7 a.m.–11 p.m. (Tel. 899 1121)
Reservations	–	Mon.–Fri.: 8 a.m.–8 p.m. Sat.: 9 a.m.–5 p.m. Sun.: 10 a.m.–5 p.m.
Tourist information	–	*Summer*: Mon.–Sat.: 9 a.m.–9 p.m. Sun.: 10 a.m.–7 p.m. *Winter*: Mon.–Sat.: 9 a.m.–8 p.m. Sun.: 10 a.m.–5 p.m.
Foreign exchange	Mon.–Sat.: 8 a.m.–8 p.m. Sun.: 9 a.m.–5 p.m.	Mon.–Fri.: 7.30 a.m.–9 p.m. Sat.: 8 a.m.–9 p.m. Sun.: 9 a.m.–9 p.m.

	HOLLAND SPOOR	CENTRAAL STATION
Left-luggage lockers	All hours	All hours
Cafeteria	Mon.–Fri.: 7 a.m.–7 p.m.	Mon.–Sat.: 6.30 a.m.–10 p.m.
	Sat.: 8 a.m.–7 p.m.	Sun.: 7.30 p.m.–10 p.m.
	Sun.: 9 a.m.–5 p.m.	
Restaurant	–	Mon.–Sun.: 6.30 a.m.–10.30 p.m.
Waiting room	All hours	All hours

Tram 12 connects the two stations, or take a through-going train (free).

Daily trains to: Amsterdam (¾ hour), Rotterdam (20 minutes), Antwerp (1½ hours), Brussels (2 hours), Paris (5½ hours) and Cologne (4 hours).

TOURIST INFORMATION

Is outside Central Station at Koningin Julianaplein 30. Open April–Sept., Mon.–Sat.: 9 a.m.–8 p.m., Sun.: 9 a.m.–5 p.m. There is another office situated at Gevers Deynootweg 126, Scheveningen, which is open out of season Mon.–Sat.: 9 a.m.–6 p.m., and from April to Sept., Mon.–Sat.: 9 a.m.–9 p.m., Sun.: 9 a.m.–5 p.m. Pick up the walking tour leaflet (f. 1.50).

• Addresses:
POST OFFICE: Nobelstraat, open Mon.–Fri.: 8.30 a.m.–6.30 p.m., Thurs.: till 8.30 p.m., Sat.: 9 a.m.–6 p.m.
UK EMBASSY: Lange Voorhout 10 (Tel. 3645800).
US EMBASSY: Lange Voorhout 102 (Tel. 3624911).
CANADIAN EMBASSY: Sophialaan 7 (Tel. 3614111).
AUSTRALIAN EMBASSY: Koninginnegracht 23–24 (Tel. 3630983).
MEDICAL HELP: Tel. 3455300.
NBBS (EUROTRAIN): Schoolstraat 24, Den Haag (Tel. 3465819).
POLICE: 070–31049 11.
PHONE CODE: 070.

SEEING

The BINNENHOF – the Dutch Westminster – is a complex of buildings with the thirteenth-century KNIGHT'S HALL at its centre. This is open to the public and is worth a look. There are carillon concerts at noon in summer and on Thursdays the imposing Lange Voorhout (where the UK and US Embassies are) turns into an open-air antique market. There is an abundance of museums in the city. The main attractions are the MAURITSHUIS MUSEUM, Plein 29, with its superb collection of Dutch art, including 16 Rembrandts, open Tues.–Sat.: 10 a.m.–5 p.m., Sun.: 11 a.m.–5 p.m., admission f. 6.50; the GEMEENTE MUSEUM (Hague Municipal Museum), Stadhouderslaan 41, the city museum with a collection of musical instruments and Mondrian's major works, open daily from 11 a.m.–5 p.m., admission f. 7; and the GEVANGENPOORT (Prison Gate) MUSEUM, Buiten-hof 33, a morbid torture chamber stuffed with medieval instruments to set your nerves on edge, open Mon.–Fri.: 10 a.m.–4 p.m., admission f. 5. Another interesting find is the PUPPET MUSEUM at Nassau Dillenburgstraat 8, which houses puppets collected from all corners of the world from the last 200 years. Admission is only f. 1 on Sundays between 12 noon and 2 p.m. A performance is given for adults on Friday evenings. The MESDAG PANORAMA is a popular place to visit, with the world's largest circular painting, at a mile long. Open Mon.–Sat.: 10 a.m.–5 p.m. Sun.: 12 noon–5 p.m. At Zeestraat 65, entrance f. 4.

Don't bother with the miniature city, MADURODAM, open April–December until 9.30 p.m. Trams 9 or 1 or bus 22 will take you out to Holland's Disneyland. It's aimed at kids and expensive. This city, built to a 1/25th scale, has everything from trains to houses and street lamps – and everything works.

As this is Holland's 'greenest city', there are plenty of picnic and unofficial camping places to be had. Try the Haagse Bos, Westbroekpark or Clingendael Park. The latter plays host to a Japanese Garden, entrance is by Wassenaarseweg and is open from mid-May to mid-June. A number 18 bus will take you there from the station. If you fancy beach-bumming it, SCHEVENINGEN is your nearest place (it's also good to sleep out on). Ten minutes from The Hague is the town of DELFT, famous for its pottery. You can see it being made at the Porceleyne Fles, Rotterdamseweg 196.

Bicycles can be rented at various venues in the city, though most outlets will want f. 100 deposit. The Garage du Nord at Keijerstraat 27, Schevenigen (Tel. 3554060) charges f. 9 a day and wants an identity card as deposit.

SLEEPING

Hotels aren't cheap, so try the alternatives. The VVV have a list with private accommodation. For camping try Ockenburg at Wijndaelerweg 25 (Tel. 3252364) near the beach (tram 3 from the station) and Duinrell, Wassenaar (Tel. 301751/19314). The youth hostel at Monsterseweg 4 (Tel. 397 00 11) is very good. Take buses 122, 123 or 124 for the five-mile journey from the station. Two hostels that charge between £6 and £10 a night are Marion at Havenkade 3/3a (Tel. 3543501) and Herberg Vlietzigt, Jaagpad 7, Rijswick (Tel. 015 131004).

EATING AND NIGHTLIFE

Scheveningen is lively at night and your best bet for cheap eats and bars, though some can be fairly rough, so shop around. For groceries, try the market at Markthof, near Binnenhof, or on Grote Markt Straat. The city has plenty of the usual fast-food outlets like McDonald's and Burger King, but far more filling is the inexpensive Italian fare served at Broodjeszaak Panini at Gortstraat 16. For the vegetarian diet De Puinruimer, in Columbusstraat 46, offers a good menu, though it is closed on Sundays and Mondays. 'T Goude Hooft at Groenmarkt 13 has an old Dutch interior and does three-course meals for around f. 18. All through the summer, on a Friday night at 11 p.m. there is a free firework display from the pier in Scheveningen.

Rotterdam

The largest port in Europe and second largest in the world, Rotterdam is Holland's second city after Amsterdam and, were it not for a Nazi air raid in 1940, would still be her rival in architectural terms. The rebuilt Rotterdam is an attractive, very modern city, best seen from the 600-foot-high Euromast.

	ROTTERDAM CENTRAAL STATION
Train information	Mon.–Fri.: 8 a.m.–10 p.m., Sat.: 9 a.m.–6 p.m., Sun.: 10 a.m.–9.30 p.m. (Tel. 4 117 100 – Abroad) (Tel. 8991121 – Netherlands)
Reservations	Mon.–Fri.: 8 a.m.–10 p.m., Sat.: 9 a.m.–6 p.m., Sun.: 10 a.m.–5 p.m.
Tourist information	9 a.m.–10 p.m. (Tel. 06–3403 4065)
Foreign exchange	8 a.m.–9 p.m.
Left-luggage lockers	No access 1 a.m.–5 a.m.
Left-luggage store	6 a.m.–10 p.m.
Restaurant	6 a.m.–11 p.m.
Waiting room	All hours
Station shuts	1 a.m.–5 a.m.

TOURIST INFORMATION

MAIN OFFICE: VVV, Coolsingel 67, on the corner of Stadhuisplein (Tel. 34034065). Open April–Sept.: Mon.–Thurs.: 9 a.m.–5.30 p.m., Fri.: 9 a.m.–9 p.m., Sat.: 9 a.m.–5 p.m., Sun.: 10 a.m.–4 p.m., October–March: closed Sunday.

DOCTOR AND 24-HOUR CHEMIST: Tel. 4362244.

NBBS: Reiswinkel–Meent 126 (Tel. 4149485) sell Eurotrain tickets.

PHONE CODE: 010.

SEEING

You can tour round the massive port by boat if you've spare cash, or else wander round some of its thirty miles yourself. The BOYMANS-VAN-BEUNINGEN MUSEUM on Mathenesserlaan is a superb modern-art museum, and the ETHNOLOGICAL MUSEUM at Willemskade 25 has a superb collection of world culture consisting of over 100,000 items. Close to the station is the GROOTHANDELSGEBOUW, a huge complex of offices, restaurants, entertainments, etc. One part of Rotterdam which wasn't wiped out was DELFSHAVEN from where the Pilgrim Fathers left in 1620 en route for America. In Delfshaven they are restoring the 110 buildings left and turning the area into a craft centre.

Not far from Rotterdam is the only remaining area with lots of windmills: Kinderdijk. Go on Saturday afternoons in summer and see all nineteen at work. The cheese town of GOUDA is 25 minutes by train from Rotterdam. See its colourful cheese market in the central market on Thursday mornings (9 a.m.–10 a.m.) from 5 July–30 August.

Rotterdam's youth hostel is at Rochussenstraat 107 (Tel. 4365763), take tram 4 to Dijkzigt, B&B f. 24. The Sleep-Inn (Tel. 121420) is open summers at Mauritsweg 29, B&B f. 12; under 27s only. For camping, try Kanaalweg 84 (Tel. 4159772), bus 33.

The Southern and Eastern Netherlands

The southern part of the Netherlands, bordered by Belgium, has as its main stopping-off places the beautifully situated, historic town of BREDA, and the reconstructed medieval town of MIDDELBURG, with its miniature town on a 1/20th scale, 'Walcheren'.

When in LIMBURG, the south-eastern province between Germany and Belgium, look in on MAASTRICHT with its nine castles and 120-mile network of man-made tunnels. UTRECHT is the main town of the east. It has a medieval city centre and a thirteenth-century cathedral. For real train buffs, there's a railway museum in the old station here, housing old steam locomotives. See also the CENTRAAL MUSEUM with its Viking ship, the MUSIC BOX MUSEUM and the RELIGIOUS HISTORY MUSEUM in Het Catherine Convent.

ARNHEM suffered great damage in 1944 (as seen in 'A Bridge Too Far'), but the twelfth-century DOORWERTH CASTLE outside the town has survived. The main reason to stay in Arnhem is for its proximity to the fascinating OPEN-AIR MUSEUM just north of the city. There are working farms, mills and houses here to give you a fully rounded picture of traditional Dutch rural life. There's also a zoo and safari park with a mini-train running through it, and a costume museum.

Haarlem

Fifteen minutes from Amsterdam is Haarlem, one of Holland's most historic and well-preserved towns. While you are at the tourist office pick up a copy of 'Zandvoort Haarlem', a multi-lingual guide to the city.

TOURIST INFORMATION

MAIN OFFICE: Stationsplein 1 (Tel. 023–319059). Schoolplein 1 (Tel. 023–317947).
POST OFFICE: Gedempte Oude Gracht 2 (Tel. 319066). Open Mon.–Thurs.: 8.30 a.m.–6 p.m., Fri.: 8.30 a.m.–8.30 p.m., Sat.: 9 a.m.–12 noon.
POLICE: Tel. 06–11 (emergency number).

SEEING

The GROTE MARKET is the historical centre where the RENAISSANCE MEAT MARKET, ST BRAVO'S CATHEDRAL, which houses the grave of Frans Hals, and the fourteenth-century TOWN HALL are located. See also the FRANS HALS MUSEUM at Groot Heligland 62, which displays not only a fine collection of the painter's own work, but also that of other seventeenth-century Netherlandish masters, and a comprehensive modern art collection. Concerts are held in the museum every third Sunday of the month from September until May. The museum is open daily from 11 a.m.–5 p.m., and entry is f. 2/f. 4. Other museums of interest are the TEYLERS MUSEUM at 16 Spaarne, the oldest museum in the country, which exhibits scientific antiquities, fossils and minerals, open Tues.–Sat.: 10 a.m.–5 p.m., Sun.: 1 p.m.–5 p.m., admission f. 4, and the FAMILIE TEN BOOM MUSEUM, at 19 Barteljorisstraat, which is devoted to the life and works of a family who in the Second World War saved the lives of many people in hiding from the Nazis. It is open Mon.–Sat.: 10 a.m.–6.30 p.m.

Day excursions can be taken from the town to smaller places of interest. ZANDVOORT is the nearby coastal resort, with miles of sandy beaches and dunes, which was awarded a prize by the European Environmental Organization for its safe and hygienic beaches and clean water. For tourist information tel. 250–17947, and for accommodation try De Brandig at Boulevard Barnaart (Tel. 0257–13035). SPAARNDAM is an old village built further inland along a Dutch dike, and is legendary because of Hans Brinker, the boy who put his thumb into a hole in the dike and saved the village from flood.

SLEEPING AND EATING

The youth hostel Jeugdherberg is at Jan Gilzenpad 3 (Tel. 023–373993). To get there take bus 6 from the station; beds cost around f. 18.50. The nearest camping site is de Liede at Liewegje (Tel. 023–332360). It is open all year round and provides excellent facilities: a canteen, showers and laundry facilities. The VVV can put you up in a private home if you do not have any success here.

The fast-food freak can find haven at McDonald's in Grote Houtstraat 75, whilst the vegetarian is well catered for at the Eko Eet Cafe in Zyl Straat 39 which is open until 9.30 p.m. For cheap meals try the Italian 'Mario' Restaurant at Rijksstraatweg 29 and the Chinese 'New China' at Pr Beatrixplein 5, both open until 10 p.m.

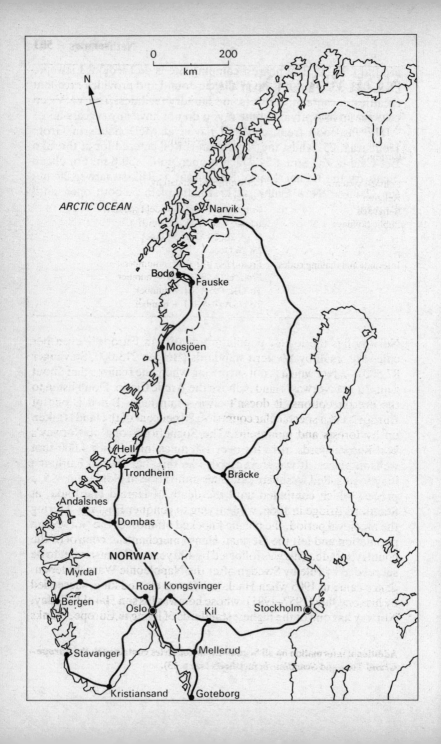

N

0 ——— 200
km

ARCTIC OCEAN

Narvik

Bodø
Fauske

Mosjöen

Hell
Trondheim   Bräcke

Andalsnes
Dombas

NORWAY

Myrdal
                Roa   Kongsvinger
Bergen
        Oslo   Kil   Stockholm

Stavanger   Mellerud

        Kristiansand   Goteborg

NORWAY (Norge)

Entry requirements	Passport
Population	4,200,000
Capital	Oslo (pop.: 465,000)
Currency	Kroner
	£1 = approx. 10.29 kr.
Political system	Constitutional Monarchy
Religion	Lutheran
Language	Norwegian (English widely spoken)
Public holidays	1 Jan.; 4, 8, 9, 11, 12 April;
	1, 17, 20, 30 May; 30 June;
	25, 26 Dec.
International dialling codes	From UK: 010 + 47 + number
	From USA: 011 + 47 + number
	To UK: 095 + 44 + number
	To USA: 095 + 1 + number

Norway has the lowest population density in Europe – even her cities are small by Western standards (Bergen 213,000, Stavanger 87,500) – a fact which is not surprising when one realizes that about a quarter of Norway's land is above the Arctic Circle. Don't listen to the preconceptions, it doesn't always rain here. But it is one of Europe's most spectacular countries: 80 per cent of the land is taken up by forests and mountains. The Sognefjord, one of Norway's best-known fjords, runs for over 100 miles inland with 4,000-foot walls in places. It was from fjords like this that Harald Fairhair's longboats sailed westward, after his unification of Norway in 885, a process which continued until the death of Harald Hardrada, at Stamford Bridge in 1066, while trying to conquer England. During the medieval period, the plague knocked off most of the Norwegian population and left the German Hansa merchants in control of the country's trade. This was followed by 400 years of Danish rule, to be succeeded by rule by Sweden after the Napoleonic Wars. Independence came in 1905 when Haakon VII was elected king, succeeded by his son Olav (1957–1991), whose heir was his son Harold. Today, Norway has one of the highest standards of living in Europe, thanks

Additional information on all Scandinavian countries contained in the *Europe – Grand Tour* and *Scandinavia* factsheets (see p.13).

to cheap hydro-electric power and the discovery of oil. Norway's well worth the inconvenience of getting there – even if you can only afford a quick train through.

NORWEGIAN STATE RAILWAYS
(Norges Statsbaner, NSB)

The Norwegians have one of the cleanest and most efficient railway systems in Europe and even though a majority of the trains are pretty slow, pass through some of the most spectacular scenery. There are no supplements in Norway so Inter-Rails are valid on all trains. The fastest and most comfortable trains are the Ekspresstog (Et, expresses). They run between all the major cities and stop only at main stations. The regular day-trains are the Hurtigtog (Ht, fast) but they're only slightly better than the locals (Persontog, Pt), which stop at every station. NSR have an office in London at 21–24 Cockspur Street SW1 (Tel. 071–930 6666). They are also agents for Swedish railways.

● **Inter-Rail bonuses:**

Hirtshals–Kristiansand	50%
Larvik–Frederikshavn	50%
Flåm–Bergen and other services by Express Steamers and	
Fjord Steamers run by 'Fylkesbaatane i Sogn og Fjordane'	50%
Buses in North Norway (Nordland, Troms and Finnmark)	50%

● **Eurail bonuses:**

Hirtshals–Kristiansand	30%
Flåm–Bergen and other services by Express Steamers and	
Fjord Steamers run by 'Fylkesbaatane i Sogn og Fjordane'	50%

● **ScanRail bonuses:**

Flåm–Bergen and other services by Express Steamers and	
Fjord Steamers run by 'Fylkesbaatane i Sogn og Fjordane'	50%
Larvik–Frederikshavn	50%

● **Nordturist bonuses:**

Flåm–Bergen and other services by Express Steamers and	
Fjord Steamers run by 'Fylkesbaatane i Sogn og Fjordane'	50%
Larvik–Frederikshavn	50%
Fauske–Narvik–Kirkenes (bus)	50%

TRAIN INFORMATION

No problems here as everyone speaks good English. NSB also publish an excellent free series of leaflets giving maps and descriptions of their main tourist routes.

• **Reservations:** Domestic reservations (20 kr.) are compulsory on all major routes, so check first. They should be made in advance, but if you don't have the time you can still do this on the train, though this won't guarantee you a seat, and you'll still have to pay. You may get a discount for more than one domestic reservation at a time. If you're travelling to Copenhagen you're advised to reserve thirty-six hours in advance and forty-eight hours at weekends. International seat reservations cost 15 kr. Reserved seats are not always marked, so don't be surprised if you get moved on, just when you thought it was safe to get comfortable. On the other hand, don't be too surprised to find someone already sitting in a seat you have reserved in advance. Be polite, and remember: if you reserved the seat, you have the right to it.

• **Night travel:** Second-class sleepers with three berths cost about 100 kr.; with two berths 200 kr. Standards are high – video and snacks are available. 50 kr. buys you an excellent hearty breakfast.

• **Eating on trains:** Expresses have dining cars, and if you have a bit of money to blow the food is excellent, as is the scenery. All other trains have buffets which serve hot meals as well as snacks.

• **Scenic tips:** There are more scenic routes in Norway than anywhere else in Scandinavia, and possibly even Europe. The jewel of them all is the Bergen–Oslo run. Be sure to get hold of the free NSB leaflets which give good descriptions of the various lines.

• **Rover tickets:** *Nordturist* (Nordic Tourist Ticket): available in the Nordic countries and in most European countries. Valid for unlimited railtravel in Norway, Sweden, Denmark and Finland for 21 days. Also valid for some ferries.

Class:	1st	1st	2nd	2nd
Prices in Kroner (1991):	adults	youth 12–25	adults	youth 12–25
	2365	1775	1775	1320

ScanRailpass: ScanRail is quite similar to Nordturist, but is only valid for certain days within a period of time. Available in North America (French Rail Inc.), Australia (Bentours), Singapore, New Zealand, Hong Kong and UK (NSR Travel). Valid for travel by train (and a few ferries) in Norway, Sweden, Denmark and Finland.

Class:	1st	2nd
4 days out of 15 days	USD 179	USD 145
9 days out of 21 days	USD 299	USD 239
14 days in 1 month	USD 459	USD 349

Midtukebillett and mini-group do not exist any more. *Minipris* has been introduced instead. Valid for direct travel on 'low-trafic' departures (most trains Monday–Thursday and Saturday). Price one-way, unlimited distance (1992): 490 kr. With *'Customers Card'* you can obtain 30–50 per cent reduction on normal 2nd class fare. Price 1992: 370 kr., valid one year.

TOURIST INFORMATION

There's a tourist office (turistinformasjan) at every major town, and in most villages, in Norway. They help to find accommodation if necessary and have a good supply of local information leaflets. Extended hours always operate from the beginning of June–end of August. Norway's one of the most health-conscious of all European countries, and at weekends you'll find, depending on the season, the ski slopes, forest tracks and waterways well used by the 'great outdoors' fanatics. For detailed information on hiking and mountaineering, contact DNT, Stortingsgata 28, PO Box 1963 Vika, 0125 Oslo.

• **ISIC bonuses:** 50 per cent discounts on museums, theatres and some coastal steamers. Also 30 per cent reductions on some bus services. For further information, contact UR Universiterssentret, Blindern, Oslo (Tel. 02–466880).

• **Money matters:** 1 Norwegian kroner (kr.) = 100 øre.
Banking hours are Mon.–Fri.: 8.30 a.m.–3 p.m. (3.30 p.m. in winter). Some stay open till 5 p.m. on Thursdays.

• **Post offices and shops:** Mon.–Fri.: 8/9 a.m.–4/5 p.m., late-night opening Thursdays till 7 p.m.; closed Saturday p.m.

• **Museums:** Vary throughout Norway, but the general pattern is 10 a.m. opening and early closing at 3 p.m. or 4 p.m.

EATING AND NIGHTLIFE

Norway is one country you're bound to lose weight in; it's not that the food is bad, or that you'll be press-ganged into spending all day out hiking in the fjords – it's just that food is so expensive here that you'll rarely be able to afford the luxury of a full stomach. This is *the* problem in Norway: it's quite easy to spend 100 kr. a day just feeding yourself with average-quality meals. (That said, it is now much on a par with places like Venice or Florence, and at least the quality is excellent here.) Avoid expensive meat dishes and turn instead to fish, and try and copy the locals: eat a full breakfast of smørbrødbord, have a snack at lunch (bought from a market/shop) and aim for a koldtbord (cold table) meal in the evening where you can eat as much as you like, or a fixed-price menu. If you're planning on self-catering a lot in Norway (and you should), bring some basic supplies with you from home.

The Norwegians have a reputation for being quite a serious lot, and to an extent that's fair comment – though catch them after a few drinks at night and you'd never believe it. They're very culture-conscious, and much effort is made to preserve the folk songs and dances of their forebears – the displays of these you may encounter are not put on purely as commercial stunts for the tourists.

SLEEPING

Norwegian law allows you to camp for free anywhere you want for two nights, provided you keep 150 m from all buildings and fences, and do not litter or vandalize the area. If you are camping while you are in this country remember to bring your own supply of camping gas since it is not freely available in Norway.

Check out Den Norske Turistforening (DNT, the Norwegian Mountain Touring Association) for unusual accommodation. They sell maps and keep many attractive mountain huts (hytter) all over the country. Expect to pay about 40–125 kr. per night, with a 45 kr. surcharge to non-members. Huts are open from the end of June to the beginning of September. The best place to contact them is at Roald Amundsengate 28 in Oslo.

There are 78 Youth Hostels in the country and standards vary, as do prices (between 60–100 kr.). Only a few are open all of the year round. Alternatively, try booking a private room through the tourist office; it is reasonable to pay from 150 kr. for a single to 200 kr. for a double room.

The Southern Coast

If you've arrived in Norway at Stavanger, it'll take you about eight hours to get to Oslo. There's not that much to keep you here but if you've time to spare, the OLD TOWN gives you an idea what Norway was once like. The medieval CATHEDRAL is a good example, and is located in the colourful MARKETPLACE. If you've three or four hours to kill, the Stavanger–Sand ferry takes you through some fjords which will whet your appetite for what's to come. The 'Stavanger Guide' from the tourist pavilion has a map and all the information you'll need if you decide to stay longer.

Between Stavanger and Oslo is Kristiansand, which has ferry connections to Hirsthals in Denmark (50 per cent reduction with Inter-Rail and Eurail). There is some good scenery here and some good beaches on the nearby islands.

Oslo

On Norway's south-eastern coast at the head of a 60-mile fjord lies Oslo, the oldest of the Scandinavian capitals. Outside the city limits are acres of forests, hills and unspoilt countryside which the Oslo-ites use at every opportunity to pursue their many outdoor activities. The town itself has no distinctive style, and you have to look below the surface for its real attractions: the museums and parks.

STATION FACILITIES

Smoking is banned in the Central Station as in all public buildings in Norway. There is an Inter-Rail Centre, open 7 a.m.–11 p.m. mid-June–end September, offering showers (10 kr.), phones, food and information. All eurorailers welcome.

OSLO (CENTRAL)	
Train information	6.30 a.m.–11 p.m. (Tel. 171400)
Reservations	8 a.m.–9 p.m. (Tel. 171401)
Tourist information	8 a.m.–11 p.m. daily (Closed winter 3 p.m.–4.30 p.m.)
Foreign exchange + post office	7.00 a.m.–11 p.m. summer, 8 a.m.–7.30 p.m. winter
Left-luggage lockers	No access when station is closed (1 a.m.–5 a.m.)
Bar/Café	7 a.m.–11 p.m.
Restaurant	7 a.m.–11 p.m.
Waiting room	All hours, except 1 a.m.–5 a.m.

Daily trains to: Gothenburg, Stockholm, Stavanger, Trondheim, Bergen, Copenhagen, Hamburg.

TOURIST INFORMATION

Pick up maps, guides and 'what's on' information from the tourist office in the Central Station. The Norway Information Centre is in the Old West Station (Tel. 830050). They are extremely helpful and will give you maps, the 'Oslo Guide', 'Oslo This Week' and ferry and bus timetables. Mon.–Fri. (May–Sept.): 8.30 a.m.–7 p.m., Sat.–Sun.: 9 a.m.–5 p.m.

● **Addresses:**
POST OFFICE: Dronningensgate 15, open Mon.–Fri.: 8 a.m.–8 p.m., Sat.: 8 a.m.–3 p.m. Kongensgate 21 for telephones (telegrafen). Open Mon.–Fri.: 8 a.m.–9 p.m. Sat./Sun.: 10 a.m.–5 p.m. (Tel. 405420).
AMEX: c/o Winge Travel, Karl Johansgate 33 (Tel. 429150), open Mon.–Fri.: 8.30 a.m.–5 p.m., Sat.: 8.30 a.m.–1 p.m. No traveller's cheques exchange, but there is an Amex money dispenser outside.
STUDENT TRAVEL AND NORWEGIAN YOUTH HOSTEL ASSOCIATION: Terra Nova Travel, Dronningensgate 26 (Tel. 421410), open Mon.–Fri.: 8.15 a.m.–3.15 p.m.

NUH (Norwegian Youth Hostel headquarters): Dronningensgate 26. Pick up list of hostels here, although it is similar to that given at Terra Nova.

DEN NORSKE TURISTFORENING (Norwegian Mountain Touring Association): Stortingsgaten 28 (Tel. 832550). If you've come to Norway to climb or camp, call in for leaflets on mountain huts, etc. Open weekdays: 8.30 a.m.–4 p.m., Thursday till 6 p.m.

UK EMBASSY: Thomas Heftyesgate 8 (Tel. 552400).

US EMBASSY: Drammensveien 18 (Tel. 448550).

CANADIAN EMBASSY: Oscargate 20 (Tel. 466955).

AUSTRALIAN GOVERNMENT INFORMATION OFFICE: Jernbanstorget 2 (Tel. 414433).

24-HOUR CHEMIST: Jernbanstorget Apotek. Opposite Central Station.

PHONE CODE: 02.

• **Getting about:** City transport is good and you can use your ticket to transfer to any form of transport within an hour. These include buses, trams, undergrounds, ferries and local trains (free on Inter-Rail). Pick up the transit map at the station or tourist information. The Oslo Card (95 kr. for one day, 140 kr. for two and 170 kr. for three) is good value and gives free transport and entry to most of the sights; a student card gets reductions on most things too. A single ticket costs 15 kr., but try the 24-hour pass on all means of transport which costs only 30 kr.!

SEEING

The Rådhus (Town Hall) is down by the harbour. This avant-garde 1950s structure was decorated by contemporary Norwegian artists and can be visited free. From the Rådhus Gate you can enter AKERSHUS CASTLE, built by King Haakon V around 1300, then rebuilt in Renaissance style by Christian IV. It's open weekdays 10 a.m.–4 p.m. (May to September); and in the grounds of the castle is the NORWEGIAN RESISTANCE MUSEUM describing the Nazi occupation of Norway. The ferry from the Rådhus over to the peninsula of BYGDØY takes you to five very interesting places:

1. The incredible NORSK FOLKEMUSEUM with 150 wooden buildings filled with material artefacts recreating Norway's past. These include Ibsen's study, houses from Lapland and museums of domestic furniture, clothes and implements.

2. THE VIKING SHIP HOUSE: Three preserved Viking longboats from AD 800–900.

3. KON-TIKI MUSEUM: The rafts used by the explorer Thor Heyerdahl on his voyages.

4. The NORWEGIAN MARITIME MUSEUM.

5. The FRAM MUSEUM: The ship used in the Polar expeditions of the nineteenth and early twentieth centuries.

All these museums are within walking distance of one another and are open 10 a.m.–6 p.m.

The VIGELAND SCULPTURE PARK and VIGELAND MUSEUM (admission 10 kr.) show the work and the background of the Norwegian artist Gustav Vigeland. This park is one of Norway's finest and 1,750 sculptures dotted round it have been termed everything from 'obscene' to 'serene'. To get there take the 2 or 20 bus from National Theatret. The other famous Norwegian artist, EDVARD MUNCH, has his MUSEUM in the east of the city at Tøyengata 53 (admission 20 kr. – 10 kr. students). It's a particularly fine gallery, housing literally thousands of his Expressionist works. Both these museums tend to close on Mondays, except in high season but for more time-efficient sightseeing, note that these museums both stay open until 7 p.m. for the rest of the week. Check first with tourist information. The NATIONAL GALLERY is at Universitetsgata 13, and has Norway's principal art collection.

SLEEPING

Oslo's not easy on eurorailers. Forget hotels completely and concentrate on the few hostels and campsites, or settle for private accommodation. You can get a room in a private house for 150 kr. single, 250 kr. double, and you must stay at least two nights. Both youth hostels are very good, clean, efficient, and with plenty of facilities, but they could hardly be called central.

Haraldsheim is at Haraldsheimveien 4 (Tel. 222965). It charges average prices. Reservations cost 13 kr. and are recommended. It's open all year and is at the bottom of the hill from Sinsen tram terminus (trams 1 or 7). Price is 136 kr., including breakfast, per night. The other Oslo Youth Hostel is at Sognsvn 218 (Tel. 237640) and costs 145 kr. including breakfast for members. It is open from the beginning of June to late August. Take the underground to

Kringsja Station. The Seamen's Hostel, Oslo Sjømannshjemmet, Fred Olsengate 2 (Tel. 412005), has fair rooms. Reception is open twenty-four hours. The cheapest place in town is to be found at KFUM in Mollergata (Tel. 02–421066). For 70 kr. a night, in July and August, it provides sleeping accommodation and kitchen facilities. Reception is open 7.30 a.m.–11 a.m. and 5 p.m.–12 midnight, though it is advisable to book in advance.

If you don't mind an institutional atmosphere, Holtekilen Summer Hotel at Micheletsvei 55 (Tel. 533853) is good value. You can choose between the ten-bed classroom accommodation (it's a school except in summer) or if you're keen to escape the classroom, the hotel side does doubles for a bit more.

The campsites are Bogstad Camping at Ankerveien 117 (Tel. 507680) (bus 41) and the Ekeberg site at Ekebergveien 65 (Tel. 198568) which is more central but only open late June to late August (bus 24 from in front of Central Station. Showers are hot and free, but shared with the adjacent football pitches). The cheapest camping you will find in Oslo is around 60 kr. per tent although you are allowed to camp free in any of the wooded areas north of the city provided it is away from public areas. Head 50 minutes up the line to Moss for a YH Sleep-in for 75 kr.

EATING AND NIGHTLIFE

Here more than anywhere else in Europe, you'll find prices sky-high. Don't attempt restaurants or stopping off for a coffee and cake (25 kr.). Eat like the Norwegians: a hearty breakfast and big dinner and expect to average 100 kr. for a full meal. There are fast-food chains – Wimpy and Kaffistovas – which can help eke out the finances, and Kveldsmat on Universitetgata, off Karl Johansgate, is cheap. Vegetarians should venture to Vegeta Vertshus at Munkedamsveien 3b which is the largest vegetarian restaurant in the city. Small main meals cost about 48 kr. but go for the 98 kr. meals which include dessert, a drink and coffee.

• **Excursions:** Skiers should find the world's oldest SKI MUSEUM interesting. It's located inside the take-off point of the huge Holmenkollen ski jump. Exhibits here trace the history of the sport and produce evidence that it dates as far back as about 500 BC. Take the Holmenkollen railway from its underground station and walk about ten minutes from the station. EKEBERG PARK gives a great view over Oslo from its hills where Stone Age carvings from 1,000 BC have been found. If you're a group of four and have cash to spare, why not take a torch-lit sleigh ride through the woods here? (Contact Ekeberg Rideskole through tourist information.)

Oslo–Bergen: the Sognefjord

The rail run from Oslo to Bergen is one you should go out of your way to take. The scenery is incredible and during the course of this six-hour journey, you'll pass through fjords, glaciers, tundra, mountains, lakes, plateaux and gorges. Should you choose to break this journey and savour its delights slowly, stop off at MYRDAL and take the other line for the twelve-mile and 3,000-foot journey down to FLÅM. Should you decide to stay at Flåm, the Solhammer Pension, across the river from the station, is reasonable, and there's camping next door (Tel. 056 32121) (though if you don't camp freelance here you never will). The campsite has good facilities, but showers are extra. Expect to pay around 40 kr. per tent. The tourist office in FLÅM is right next to the train station (Tel. 32106) and is open from June–mid-August 8.15 a.m.–8.30 p.m. From Flåm you can tackle the fjords. A favourite trip of mine (and it won't take you out of your way from Bergen) is to take the ferry to GUDVANGEN from Flåm. This two-hour trip takes you past the spectacular scenery of the Nerøfjord, and calls at some isolated settlements en route whose sole means of communication is the ferry. From Gudvangen take the bus to Voss where you're back on the Bergen line again.

Another trip worth taking is from Flåm to Voss, which is 70 minutes east of Bergen on the Oslo rail line. It costs around 76 kr. with Inter-Rail and includes bus and ferry connections. There is a commentary in English on both the train section (from Flåm to Myrdal) and the ferry. The bus ride is particularly spectacular as you cross the roof of Norway via the steep road and many hairpin bends. If you stop off in Voss there is a very good folk museum including a restored farm which dates back to the seventeenth century.

The tourist office can be found in Tinghose (Tel. 511716), about five minutes from the station. For the Youth Hostel, turn right at the station and walk along the lake side (Tel. 512205).

Bergen

During the thirteenth century Bergen was the first capital of Norway. Now, the colourful harbour, red-roofed houses and spruce trees nestling under imposing Mount Fløyen give Bergen the reputation of being Norway's most attractive city. This was the northernmost city in the Hanseatic League and the HANSEATIC MUSEUM – a reconstruction of a sixteenth-century merchant's house – makes an interesting visit. This is in the quarter called BRYGGEN, and in the old timber houses today weavers and craftsmen carry on their trade. Take a guided tour when visiting ROSENKRANTZ TOWER and KING HAAKON'S HALL; it makes the visit all the more interesting. Also take the funicular up Mount Fløyen and see the view. If you enjoy walking, buy a one-way ticket for 13 kr. (persons under 18 years qualify as children and pay only 6 kr.) and walk back down through the lakes and mountains. The cable car operates every half hour from the early morning to 11 p.m. The RASMUS MEYER collection is an art gallery on the edge of the LILLE LUNGENGARDSVATNET park with many works by native artist Edvard Munch, and the GAMLE BERGEN (old town) with its traditional timbered buildings makes a pleasant walk. The Romanesque church of ST MARY'S is considered Norway's most beautiful church. Tourist information have details on the May–June INTERNATIONAL FESTIVAL held here, and also about the trips to the fjords that start from Bergen.

TOURIST INFORMATION AND ADDRESSES

Tourist information pavilion at Torgalmenning (Tel. 321480): walk for ten minutes up Kaigaten from the station. Open 2 May–30 Sept.: 8.30 a.m.–9 p.m., Sundays 10 a.m.–7 p.m. Off season: 1 Oct.–1 May: open 10 a.m.–3 p.m., closed Sundays. They change money, book you into private houses and supply maps and 'The Bergen Guide'.

POST OFFICE: Smästrandgate. Open 8 a.m.–5 p.m., Thurs.: till 7 p.m., Sat.: 9 a.m.–1 p.m.

24-HOUR CHEMIST: Accident Clinic, Lars Hillesgate, No.30 (Tel. 321120. (A chemist at the bus station stays open until midnight.)

STUDENT TRAVEL: Universreiser a/s Parkveien 1 (Tel. 326400). 25 per cent reductions on steamer fare to Newcastle.

PHONE CODE: 05.

BUSES: For those of you who want to see the sights quickly, special tourist tickets are available on the buses. Unlimited travel within the city for 48 hours costs 45 kr., or 48-hour tickets for Bergen and its surrounding areas cost 60 kr. Be warned, time starts ticking away from the moment you start using it.

A quick journey, which combines historical interest with beautiful countryside, is to Troldhaugen, Nordas Lake, the home and burial place of composer Edvard Grieg. Get there by taking any bus from the 18–19–20 platform to Hop – they depart about every fifteen minutes. It is open in the summer 9.30 a.m.–1.30 p.m. and 2.30 p.m.–5.30 p.m. During the Festival period recitals take place on Wednesday and Sunday evenings, tickets can be obtained from the tourist office.

SLEEPING, EATING AND NIGHTLIFE

If you are dumping rucksacks, note that left luggage is much cheaper than the lockers. For accommodation the tourist pavilion charges 15–20 kr. commission per person. Private homes are expensive and charge around 145–170 kr. for single rooms and 235–295 kr. for doubles. A deposit is also required.

The youth hostel is nearly always full (Bergen is very touristy), so call first. It's in a good position, halfway up Mount Ulriken. It costs 136kr., including breakfast. Open May–Oct. On bus route 4 at Ravneberget (Tel. 292900), but apply at IYHA office at Strandgaten 4. There's a YMCA Interpoint hostel at Kalfarv 77, open from 1 July–15 August, costing 75kr., 10 minutes' walk from the station.

Bergen's main camping site, Bergenshallens Camping (Tel. 270180) is a ten-minute journey from the city centre at 24 Vilh, Bjerknesver, take bus 3. It is only open in the summer and is very busy, so if you want the fresh outdoors check with the information centre first to find out if room is available. A new campsite to try is

Bergen Camping Park at Haukås i Åsane on Road no.1 (Tel. 248008). You can either bring a tent or use one of the camping huts.

The Polar Bear Bar in Ole Bulls Plass 9–11, just around the corner from the taxi central, offers the cheapest menu outside the fast-food chains. Ham or vegetarian salads can cost around 25 kr., soup 15 kr. and a good old English fried breakfast clocks in at only 29 kr. At night it becomes a Maxime nightclub, where you can bop away to your heart's content from 9 p.m.–3 a.m. Cafe Opera, at 24 Engen, is a little more expensive for food, but its atmosphere is more conducive, with live bands and art exhibitions making up the surroundings. Foreign newspapers and board games are available on request from the counter. Open 11 a.m.–1 a.m., Fridays and Saturdays until 3 a.m. Vegetarians are catered for at the Spisestedet Kornelia, at Fosswinklegate 18. Open from 11 a.m.–8 p.m., it serves organic vegetarian and Italian lunches, herbal teas and home-made ice-creams. On the whole though, the food and nightlife news is not too good. All you'll be able to afford are picnics and some of the fairly boring café-type places. Try Peppe's Pizza in Bryggen's, Finnegården 2A – all-you-can-eat pizza and salad for 65 kr. on Mondays (no wine though!). The restaurant in the Fantoft Sommerhotel is decent and offers a 20 per cent students' discount (bus 14 or 15) and Hulen is a club run by the town's university students in an old air-raid shelter beneath Nygaardsparken. If you're over 20 (and can prove it) you can go to the disco and drink there. Location is at 47 Olav Ryesvei, and opening times are Wednesday/Thursday 8 p.m.–1 a.m., Friday/Saturday 9 p.m.–3 a.m.

If all this travelling is making you want to crash out at the movies, there is no problem with language, as all films are shown in their original language with Norwegian subtitles.

Trondheim to the North Cape

The rail line runs to Bodø, capital of the Nordland province and land of the midnight sun. This is the northernmost region of Europe and its beauty is beyond the scope of any guidebook's description, so we won't start coming out with the standard string of superlatives, as you'd probably find it corny. Just take it from us you won't regret your trip up there but expect it to be slower than travel in the more built-up areas of Norway; just sit back, relax and enjoy this area's ambience. FAUSKE is the northernmost point of the Norwegian rail network. The easiest and quickest way to travel north and on to FINNMARK and LAPLAND (unfortunately there are no trains here) is to take the train to Fauske, from here take the bus to NARVIK and onwards. This bus journey takes five hours and costs 309 kr. or 155 kr. with a 50 per cent discount for Inter-Rail or Nordtourist pass holders.

Narvik – North Cape – Narvik

A worthwhile detour off the rail system is the superbly scenic bus journey from Narvik to North Cape – the land of the midnight sun and the most northerly point of Europe.

This trip necessitates at least two overnight stops, but the reward is breathtaking scenery over all of its 739 km length.

The most popular expedition starts with the midday bus from Narvik arriving at Alta 11¼ hours later.

There is a convenient Youth Hostel in Alta, but in common with most hostels this far north it does not open until mid-June. There are also two campsites with cabins to rent, one being on the E6 road into Alta (ask the bus driver for the rock paintings).

· The North Cape bus continues on its way next morning at 7.35 a.m., arriving at Europe's northernmost point at 1 p.m. The North Cape Hall is worth a visit, even if just to sip a coffee overlooking the Arctic Ocean.

For those wanting to stay longer, there is a Youth Hostel at Honningsvag and cabins to rent (expensive). The adventurous might consider joining up with the coastal voyage or continuing to Kirkenes on the Russian border. Otherwise, the return bus to Alta departs at 2.55 p.m., arriving back in Alta at 7.55 p.m., for an overnight stop. The journey continues to Narvik at 9 a.m. the following morning. NB: There is a 50 per cent reduction over this route with Inter-Rail or Nordturist. This does not apply to the Honningsvag to North Cape section or to the ferry crossings.

ACCOMMODATION

Alta

Youth Hostel at Alta Vandrerhjem, Midtbakken 52 (Tel. 084–34409). Close to the centre of Alta.

Camping/cabins   (a) Alta River Camping Øvre Alta (Tel. 084–34353). 4½ km from Alta centre.
                                   (b) Bossenkop Camping on E6 (Tel. 084–35226), near to rock paintings.

North Cape

Youth Hostel and cabins at Nordkaap Vandrerhjem, Skipsfjorden (Tel. 084–75113).

If you are wanting to visit the LOFOTEN ISLANDS travel from Bodø by Nordland Express and change at Narvik. The journey costs 439 kr., but does not include an overnight stay in Svolvaer. Narvik also has a separate rail link – the Ofoten Line – which runs the 27 miles to the border and on to Sweden. It is a particularly scenic journey and for many years it was the world's most northerly railway. Today, it is still the most northerly electrified line and carries about half the total goods transported by Norwegian Railways, mainly about 20 million tons of Swedish iron ore.

When in Narvik, tourist information can be found in the main street in Kongensgate 66 (Tel. 082–43309, Mon.–Sat.: 9 a.m.–9 p.m. Sun.: 12 noon–9 p.m.). Note that the exchange rate offered here is not that good, but you can book private rooms from here at a fee of 20–25 kr. with single rooms for about 110 kr. and doubles for 210 kr. The Youth Hostel (Tel. 425 98 55 234) is situated beside the harbour at Havnegate 3 (turn left from the tourist office and walk down Kongensgate for 10 minutes); expect to pay about 120 kr. per night, 150 kr. for non-members. Reservations are recommended.

The campsite is crowded and uneven and doesn't have showers, but you can get cheap showers and sauna in town at the Seaman's Mission, near the harbour. It is open from 4 p.m. to 10 p.m. and has a pool table, as well as cheap coffee and snacks. From June to August you can take a 15-minute cable car ride in the 'Gondolbaner' for magnificent views of the area and, at night, the midnight sun. The service runs from 10 a.m. to midnight or later depending on weather conditions and costs 50 kr. If you are intending to take the early morning train out of Narvik bear in mind that the station

closes from 10.30 p.m. to 5 a.m. As things go the station buffet is
reasonably priced, with coffee at around 8 kr.

Trondheim

Trondheim is the historical capital of Norway, founded in 997 by the
Viking king, and now saint, Olav Tryggvason. Now, in the 1990s, it
boasts the second largest university in the country and has become a
centre for technology, research and business enterprises. Pick up a
map and the 'Trondheim Guide' at the station. The tourist office is
over the bridge along Søndregate, then turn right into Kongensgate
and walk along to the market place. The office is on the corner (open 1
June–18 June: Mon.–Fri.: 8.30 a.m.–8 p.m.; Sat.: 8.30 a.m.–6 p.m.;
Sun.: 10 a.m.–6 p.m., 19 June–31 May: Mon.–Fri.: 9 a.m.–4 p.m.;
Sat.: 9 a.m.–1 p.m.). A godsend to broke tourists is the Youth
Information Centre at Munkelgate 15. Open weekdays from 8 a.m.
to 7 p.m., in midsummer it has a list of all host families in the area who
will put you up for free. It also provides pool, darts and English
newspapers, for a little recreational break. The sights of the city are
the medieval NIDAROS CATHEDRAL, erected over the grave of St
Olav, and host to the Norwegian Crown Jewels now on public
display, the twelfth-century ARCHBISHOP'S PALACE and the interesting RINGVE MUSEUM OF MUSIC HISTORY, the KRISTIANSTEN FOR-
TRESS and the old town bridge, from where the view of the wharf row
is excellent. The recently opened TYHOLT TOWER is worth visiting.
From this rotating 80-metre tower you can view all Trondheim and
the Trondheimsfjord. The youth hostel is at Weidemannsvei 41 (Tel.
530490). If you are wanting to camp, the nearest campsite is 10 km
out at Sandmoen Camping (Tel. 886135). A 44 bus will take you there
from the bus station and tents are charged at 90 kr. each. With a
Eurail ticket you can travel for free on the NSB buses in the direction
of Stjordal or Storlien. This is excellent if you want to stay at the
Vikhammer Camping, 15 km north of Trondheim (Tel. 976164) or
Storsand Camping, 17 km north of Trondheim (Tel. 976360). The
majority of restaurants in Trondheim are situated around the area of
Kjopmannsgt, and fast-food venues gather around Olav Tryggva-
sons gt. Pizzakjelleren at Fjordgt 7 challenges the famished traveller

to eat as much as he or she can for 49 kr., and is open until 4 a.m.

In July and August there is an Inter-Rail Centre at Trondheim Rail Station which offers cooking facilities, seat reservations and all the usual Inter-Rail facilities, with a frequent day and night service to Bodø, Oslo, and Stockholm.

POST OFFICE: Dronningens gt 10. Open Mon.–Fri.: 8 a.m.–5 p.m., Sat.: 9.30 a.m.–1 p.m.

CHEMIST: St Olav Vaktapotek, Kjopmannsgt 65 (Tel. 523122). Open 8.30 a.m.–12 midnight all week.

FEMALE CRISIS CENTRE: Tel. 523420.

UK CONSULATE: Sluppenveien 10 (Tel. 968211).

PHONE CODE: 07.

Bodø – Mo-i-Rana

It's 11½ hours from Trondheim to Bodø, but the scenery and the comfortable trains make it feel a lot less. The bus ride from Bodø to Narvik joins up the northern part of the Norwegian railway system and is a fabulous experience. 50 per cent discount on fare with Inter-Rail and Nordturist card. From 2 June–10 July, the sun never sets here. 3½ hours before Bodø is MO-I-RANA, located on a magnificent fjord. The Youth Hostel (Tel. 087–50963) is open from May to September and costs 110 kr. If you hit a particularly good spell of weather, walk up Mount Ronvik, taking your camera with you. This is the coastal area that you should be in if you want to see the Northern Lights (Aurora Borealis) between November and February – although this does depend upon meteorological conditions. The 1956 CATHEDRAL is about the only noteworthy building in the town, but you don't come here for the towns. Head instead for SALSTRAUMEN where every six hours millions of gallons of water squeeze through a tiny passage between two fjords, making a spectacular sight. Buses sometimes run to coincide with the tides – ask for the timetable at tourist information, 32 kr. with Inter-Rail.

TOURIST INFORMATION AND ADDRESSES

Bodø's Tourist office is at Sjøgata 21, open Mon.–Fri.: 9 a.m.–

5 p.m.; Sat.: 10 a.m. to 2 p.m. in season. Books private accommodation for you. Flatvold Youth Hostel is at Nordstrandvn 1 (Tel.
081–25666). A new, very good hostel with all facilities, ¾ mile from
station. Open 20 June–16 Aug. The station buffet is OK for good
and filling food. If you stay at the campsite you may get the
occasional free fish from fishermen nearby. The site, 3 km from
town at Bodøsjøen, has free cooking facilities and superb views of
the fjord. It is on bus route 12 (Tel. 081–22902), and costs 40 kr. per
tent.

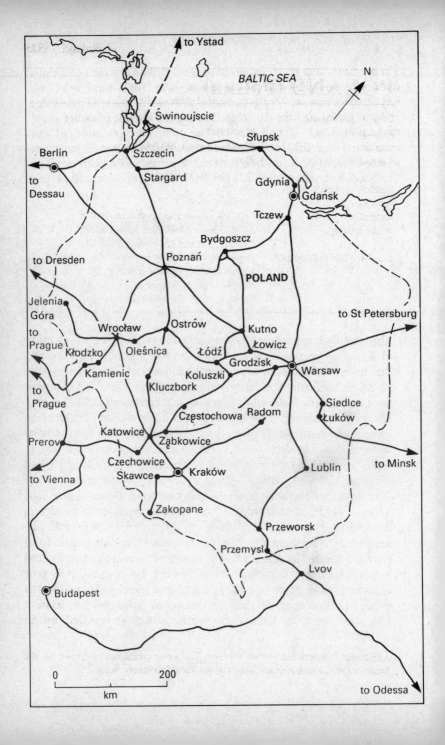

POLAND (Polska)

Entry requirements	Passport and visa (not available at border)
Population	37,500,000
Capital	Warsaw (pop.: 1,700,000)
Currency	Zloty
	£1 = approx. 24,778zl.
Political system	Republic
Religion	Roman Catholic
Language	Polish (German and English spoken)
Public holidays	1 Jan.; Easter Monday; 1 May; 3 May;
	18 July; 15 Aug.; 1, 11 Nov.; 25, 26 Dec.
International dialling codes	From UK: 010 + 48 + number
	From USA: 011 + 48 + number
	To UK: 00 + 44 + number
	To USA: 00 + 1 + number

The seemingly impossible has happened in Poland with the election of a Solidarity prime minister, but the harsh economic measures that have been adopted to pay for the failures of Communism have made life difficult. Solidarity's long struggle reflects the independent spirit of the Poles who resent outside pressure from the Soviet Union or wherever. This fact becomes understandable when one looks at the history of Poland, a country which has had more than its fair share of invasion and occupation. This process began in the tenth century with the eastward expansion of Germanic tribes, and continued long after the area came under the protection of the Holy Roman Empire. As an independent kingdom, Poland came into being in 1025; since then the country has been conquered and boundaries changed many times. In 1795 and 1939 Poland disappeared off the map altogether as it looked like doing again for a time in 1982, under martial law. It was eleven years ago that Poland began a democratic movement in Eastern Europe and it is now launching changes in internal political and social systems towards greater democratization and liberalization. Solidarity has come a long way since its humble beginnings when it was led by an

Additional information on all Eastern European countries contained in the *Eastern Europe* and *Europe – the Grand Tour* factsheets (see p.13).

electrician. Since 1991 Poland is in the Inter-Rail scheme and more worth visiting than ever.

POLISH STATE RAILWAYS
(Polskie Koleje Państwowe, PKP)

Polish trains are slow and busy, but cheap. Tickets are sold according to the type of train you want to travel on. Avoid the Osobowe and Pośpieszne categories and go for the Ekspresowe expresses whenever possible. It is probably worth paying the small additional fare for an upgrade to first class to ensure a seat. All the large cities have their own commuter trains called pociągi ēlektryczne which are even more crowded than normal. Don't be talked into buying a Polrailpass from any Orbis office unless you plan on spending a lot of time going around in circles as fares are so cheap. The pass costs around £25 for 8 days to £35 for one month second class. It is also available from Wasteels in London. Poland is in Inter-Rail. Watch out for the change to a winter schedule on 1 September; if you are in Poland then – your Thomas Cook timetable will not correspond.

Watch out for organized gangs of thieves on trains, especially at Warsaw station. The tactic seems to be that one group distracts the tourist whilst another member cuts off any accessible luggage.

TRAIN INFORMATION

Few officials speak English, so if you want to make a reservation write down the name of your destination and the time your train leaves. Most people speak some English, but if stuck try German in the south or French in the north and if really stuck, try: 'Z którego peronu odjezdza pociąg do . . . ?' (From which platform does the train to . . . leave?)

• **Reservations:** If you want a seat, you'll have to make a reservation as trains are always crowded to capacity. Go to the station at least one day in advance (several days for the Warsaw–Kraków–Zakopane run). For international trains you'll have to use Orbis or the international windows and face the queues. Look out for windows marked 'Polres': they deal with seat reservations (miejscówka) which are compulsory on express and international trains.

• **Night travel:** Don't expect high standards unless you're willing to travel first class. Reserve well ahead of time at Orbis, Polres and travel agents, particularly for couchettes, which are always cheaper than paying for a night's accommodation. You may have no alternative but to reserve a couchette if you are going to Czechoslovakia, as you will probably be told they are the only seats available. International journeys are still cheaper to Russia, Czechoslovakia and Romania. Some couchettes can only be booked shortly before departure.

• **Eating on trains:** There's either a WARS restaurant or buffet car on all long hauls in Poland, but some international trains have few facilities.

TOURIST INFORMATION

There are local Informacja Turystyczna (IT) offices in every major town. If you plan to stay for a while, it's worth buying 'A Guide for Young Tourists' from any Ruch kiosks in Poland.

• **ISIC bonuses:** For an IUS card you have to go to Almatur in Warsaw; this gives you 25 per cent reductions on international trains within the former Eastern Bloc. New ISIC cards are combined with the IUS card.

• **Money matters:** 1 zloty (zl.) = 100 groszy (g.) (never used). Banking hours are Mon.–Fri.: 8 a.m.–1 p.m. Some banks Sat.: 8 a.m.–10.45 a.m. It's also possible to exchange money at Orbis, at travel agents and post offices, hotels, and hundreds of Kantor kiosks (bureaux de change), which may give slightly better rates.

Currency exchange has been opened to the free market, thus eliminating the need for a black market at a stroke. You now get the same rate everywhere and so living here for foreigners can be very cheap. You should still keep your exchange receipts as they may be checked when you leave. You aren't allowed to take zlotys out of the country, and as they are worthless anywhere else anyway you might as well spend them all.

• **Post offices:** Open Mon.–Fri.: 8 a.m.–8 p.m. Getting mail sent on is more trouble than it's worth (allow at least three weeks). Most embassies will keep your letters for at least two weeks.

• **Shops:** For food, 8 a.m.–7 p.m., others 11 a.m.–6 p.m. For opening times of museums, etc., check with the local IT office.

• **Visa:** Obtain your visa in advance from any Polish consulate in Europe, cost £20. Visas are not available at the border.

SLEEPING

It can be difficult to find a room in Poland without having fixed it up beforehand. To do this contact Polorbis (see p. 60 for address). They will issue you with student accommodation vouchers ($7 for students). These vouchers allow you to stay at any of the ISHs (international student hostels) (open July, Aug. and Sept.) in Poland if you're a student or under 25. If you haven't already done this, then your best plan is to arrive as early as possible in the day – and even this does not ensure you a bed at an ISH. Vouchers are a prerequisite in Warsaw, so don't waste time going along unless you have them. If you've no luck with the ISHs, try the Polish Youth Hostel Federation (PTSM). Most require an IYHF card, but it's not always essential. The good news is that they're very cheap, the bad news is that they're like overcrowded prisons. There are a huge number of hostels ('schroniska mlodzieżowe') in Poland all of which are spartan even by Western YH standards.

The more money you have, the fewer your problems are likely to be. PTTK is an organization which runs cheap hotels called 'Domy Turysty'; you can find out about these from the local IT office, but don't build your hopes up as they are nearly always full. Standard Polish hotels are not too expensive. Another organization called 'Biuro Zakwaterowania' arranges for you to stay with private families. Be careful about accepting offers of private rooms on the street as the room in question might well be a long way out of town. Finally, if you're really desperate, try the long queue at the Orbis office; they might have a spare bed in one of their hotels, if you're prepared to pay the high prices asked.

With almost seventy well-equipped sites, camping is another budget option in Poland. Prices are likely to be around 20,000 zl. per person but are rising fast. Some sites have bungalows available for hire, a bed here will be around 60,000 zl. Ask for details and location at the local tourist information.

EATING AND NIGHTLIFE

The austere economic measures have affected tourists as well as the Poles, but things are improving and new restaurants appear almost daily. Things are not as bad as the media make out, for it's still possible to eat very well if you know where to look. Pork, fish or poultry will normally be the best bet. You can get a good meal (but not a gastronomical delight) at the top hotels and restaurants. Expect to pay around 60,000 zl. for a three-course meal. Avoid station restaurants completely, except in Warsaw, and only go there if you are stuck.

Nightlife is slowly resurfacing with the freeing up of society. It revolves around kawiarnie (cafés) and winiarnie (wine bars), and in some places student clubs. Polish vodka is, of course, internationally well known.

Warsaw (Warszawa)

The beautiful city of Warsaw could have looked very different today had the patriotic Poles decided to replace the bombed buildings of 1944 with concrete blocks, instead of rebuilding replicas of the original nineteenth-century structures. Ignore the few Stalinesque buildings that have crept in, and judge the city instead on her elegant palaces and parks. Her past is bloody and tragic, and you only have to look back to 1943 when Hitler ordered that no stone of Warsaw should be left standing, for evidence of this. The HISTORICAL MUSEUM OF THE CITY, on the Old Town Market Square, has film captured from the Nazis which shows the systematic destruction of this city, and there are reminders of the holocaust dotted all round the centre.

TOURIST INFORMATION

The Warsaw information office is located at pl Zamkowy 1/13 (Tel. 6351881). The main Orbis office is at ul Bracka 16 (Tel. 260271), open Mon.–Fri.: 8 a.m.–7 p.m., Sat.: 8 a.m.–5 p.m. The Orbis branch at Marszakowska 142 sells international train tickets and changes traveller's cheques.

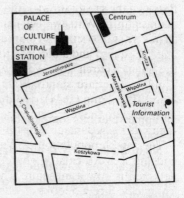

- **Addresses:**

MAIN POST OFFICE: Świętokrzyska.

AMEX: Orbis, Marszałkowska 142.

ALMATUR (Polish Student Travel): At the university on ul Kopernika 23 (Tel. 263512). Open Mon.–Fri.: 8.30 a.m.–8 p.m. (4.30 p.m. Sept.–June), Sat.: 10 a.m.–6 p.m., Sun.: 10 a.m.–4 p.m. in season.

OUR ROOTS (Jewish Information and Tourist Bureau): Grzybowski Sq 12/16 (Tel. 200556). Open 9 a.m.–5 p.m. Sells publications, in English, describing walks of particular historical interest.

UK EMBASSY: Aleja Róż 1 (Tel. 281001).

US EMBASSY: Al Ujazdowskie 29/31 (Tel. 283041).

CANADIAN EMBASSY: ul Matejki 1/5 (Tel. 298051).

AUSTRALIAN EMBASSY: ul Estońska 3–5 (Tel. 176081).

FIRST AID: Hoza 56 (Tel. 999).

STATIONS: There are three stations in Warsaw, but the only one you're likely to use consistently is the new Centralna. Train information: Tel. 200361. Wasteels office is also at Centralna Station.

PHONE CODE: 022.

- **Getting about:** Buy your tram and bus tickets at the kiosks marked Ruch (bilety tramwajowe and bilety autobusowe). Buy as many as you think you'll use in one go (at the station) to avoid queues. Buses marked with letters are expresses and cost twice as much as normal buses. After 11 p.m. all fares are doubled. Don't forget to get your ticket punched by the machine at both ends of the bus or tram, or you risk a 200,000 zl. fine if you're caught; as the standard fare is only 480 zl. it is hardly worth the risk.

SEEING

Between the STARE MIÁSTO (old town) and the AZIENKI PARK lie the main sights of Warsaw. The centre of the old town is the beautiful RYNEK STAREGO MIASTA (market square). Rebuilt baroque houses line the square and a block to the south lies ST JOHN'S CATHEDRAL, the main church for Warsaw's deeply religious Catholics. In Zamkowy Square stands Warsaw's oldest monument, the Sigismund III column (1644), and this adjoins the ROYAL CASTLE which dates back to the fourteenth century and is still being worked on to repair its 1940s damage. The tin-roofed baroque PALACE is close by.

The Jewish population of Warsaw was wiped out under Nazism and the PAWIAK PRISON where 35,000 were executed and 65,000 detained is now a museum. The JEWISH HISTORICAL INSTITUTE at Tiomackie Street 5 looks at what happened in the famous Warsaw Ghetto, and the MAUSOLEUM TO STRUGGLE AND MARTYRDOM, across the river in Praga, is housed in the former Gestapo HQ and prison.

AZIENKI PALACE AND PARK were built for the last Polish king in the eighteenth century. The palace has been restored and there are many other buildings and monuments in this graceful park. On the southern edge of the park is the monument to Chopin, and on Sunday afternoons there are often Chopin recitals. The WILANÓW PALACE AND PARK was one of the seventeenth-century kings' summer houses. The restored palace can be visited, and while you're out here you can visit the MUSEUM OF THE POLISH POSTER in the palace grounds. The palace is closed Tuesdays, the museum shuts Mondays and you reach them by bus B from ul Marszał-kowska.

Markets remain a good way to see ordinary life and the daily market on ul Targowa, Bazar Różyckiego (take tram 7) and the Sunday flea market in Skra Stadium off Wawelska are worth a look. The Saturday bazaar in the Praga district (Stadion ló-lecia) is also interesting.

SLEEPING

Finding a bed in Warsaw can be a depressing and soul-destroying experience. Your best course of action is to go to the Almatur office (see above) and ask them for the addresses of their current ISHs (they change locations annually). These are open July–August and are cheaper if you are a student. Almatur also have lists of the campsites. If you're an IYHF member, go along to PTSM at ul Chocimska 28 for a list of Polish hostels. The two in Warsaw are cheap, rule-ridden and fairly depressing. They're at Karolkowa 53a (Tel. 328829), tram 24, and Smolna 30 (Tel. 278952), tram 8, but you must arrive before 9 a.m. to be in with a chance, though the latter is becoming more relaxed about rules. PTTK at ul Marszał-kowska 124 will give you a list of their Domy Turysty. The best campsite is Gromada on ul Żwirki i Wigury (Tel. 254391). There are bungalows here as well as tent sites, and they offer one of the best deals going: about 60,000 zl. per person in a four-person bungalow (bus 128, 136 or 175 from Centralna, direction airport). Hotels are likely to be too expensive to be a serious option, but Hotel Druh at ul Niemcewicza 17 (Tel. 6590011) from 380,000 zl. for doubles is not too bad. Take tram 25 towards pl. Narutowicza.

EATING AND NIGHTLIFE

Make up for all the hardships you've had to endure by eating out in style. Food here is cheap enough to let you eat in all the best restaurants and still think you got a bargain. If you're cutting back on food too, eat in the milk bars (bar mleczny), but only if you're prepared to risk salmonella, or at the university cafeteria on campus at ul Krakowskie Przedmieście. For food try the Krokodyl, Rynek Starego Miasta 21, on the old town market square, Rycerska, ul Szeroki Dunaj 9–11, Mekong (for oriental food) Wspólna 35, or Pizzeria Bambola at ul Putawska and ul Wspólna.

The kawiarnie and winiarnie are the hub of social life in Warsaw, as elsewhere in Poland. It's not difficult to find good ones, but the Fukierowska wine-cellar at Rynek Starego Miasta 27 (Old Town Market Square) is Poland's best and dates back to 1590. Also look up Pod Herbami on ul Piwna. For dancing, Hybrydy, ul Kniewskiego 7/9, is a lively student disco. The cinema is cheap, and Bajka, ul Marszałkowska 136/138, shows Polish films with English or French subtitles. For opera, concert or theatre tickets, go to the Orbis office. If you need to get rid of some zlotys try the Centrum shopping centre on ul Marszałkowska near Central Station.

Cracow (Kraków)

A visit to Cracow in the south is a must as it is the ancient city of Polish kings and culture. Gothic, Renaissance and Baroque architecture reflect this long history. It is the only city in Poland to survive the war and has retained its medieval air.

TOURIST INFORMATION

Wawel Tourist is near Gówny station at ul Pawia 6/8 (inside the Hotel Warszawski) (Tel. 229730). Pick up 'What, Where, When in Cracow', open Mon.–Fri.: 8 a.m.–7 p.m. Orbis is in the main square at Rynek Główny 41 (Tel. 224035).

Addresses:
POST OFFICE: corner of Westerplatte and Wielopole.
AMEX: at Orbis in the Hotel Cracovia, ul Marszałka Focha (Tel. 222885).
ALMATUR: Rynek Główny 7/8 (Tel. 226123).
US CONSULATE: ul Stolarska 9 (Tel. 221400).
PHARMACY: Komorowskiego 11 (Tel. 223027). Open 24 hours.
TRAINS: Make sure you get off at Kraków Główny, a 10-minute walk from the centre, and not one of the suburban stations. Train information: Tel. 222248.
PHONE CODE: 012.

SEEING

To see the sights, wander around the old town (STARE MIASTO) which is surrounded by a park where the old walls once stood. At the centre is the huge central market square, RYNEK GLÓWNY, with its Renaissance mercantile CLOTH HALL (museum upstairs) and CATHEDRAL from which spire the bugler plays an unfinished warning daily, reminiscent of when the Mongol hordes surrounded the city. WAWEL CASTLE dominates the River Vistula and encloses a CATHEDRAL, overseen for many years by Karol Wojtyla (now Pope John Paul II). The fifteenth-century COLLEGIUM MAIUS on sw Anny is the oldest building of the famous JAGIELLONIAN UNIVERSITY and is well worth a visit. The old Jewish quarter of KAZIMIERZ has Poland's oldest synagogue, the STARA SYNAGOGA at Szeroka 40. Also try listening to the first independent commercial radio station in Eastern Europe on Radio Marpolska, a far cry from the seven minutes of illegal radio from Solidarity during the 1980s.

SLEEPING

The Biuro Zakwaterowan, ul Pawia 8 (Tel. 221921) will arrange accommodation. There are three hostels – ul Oleandry 4 (Tel. 338822), tram 15, ul Kościuszki 88 (Tel. 221951) and ul Złotej Kielni 1 (Tel. 372441). You could also try the Dom Turysty at Westerplatte 15–16 (Tel. 229566) which is on the edge of the old town. For camping try Camping Krak on ul Radzikowskiego 99 (Tel. 372122), bus 208, open mid-May to mid-September. Hotel Pollera is only five minutes from the station and old city at ul Szpitalna 30 and costs 168,000 zl. (Tel. 221044). It is highly recommended.

EATING AND NIGHTLIFE

Street stalls are often the best place to eat, but few restaurants will stretch your budget either. Try Staropolska, ul Sienna 4; Balaton, ul Grodszka for Hungarian food or Jadlodajnia Stanislaw at ul Mikolajska 16 for a haunt popular with the locals.

Cracow has better nightlife than much of Poland because of the university. Try the student club Pod Jaszczurami at Rynek Główny 8 or the disco Rotunda, ul Oleandry 1.

• **Excursions:** Less than two hours away is the town of OSWIECIM, better known as AUSCHWITZ, site of the largest concentration camp in Hitler's 'Final Solution'. There are actually two camps, Auschwitz itself and the huge BIRKENAU about 2 km away. The Auschwitz camp, now a museum providing a harrowing impression of life and death in the camps, is a 3 km walk from the station but is poorly signposted. You may prefer to take a bus or taxi; neither will stretch your budget. Watch the spine-chilling film showing the camp just after liberation. An all-inclusive coach trip from Cracow costs around £6.

The salt mine at WIELICZKA is an amazing complex of under-ground chambers, including the CHAPEL OF THE BLESSED KINGS, intricately carved from salt. The guided tour lasts 3–4 hours. Try and go early to be finished by lunchtime. Open 8 a.m.–9 p.m. in season.

Częstochowa

Częstochowa is the most important religious site in deeply Catholic Poland. Pilgrims come from around the world to the JASNA GORA MONASTERY to see the BLACK MADONNA, an icon which is said to have cried during a seventeenth-century Swedish siege. The tourist office is at Aleje NMP 63 (Tel. 41360). The youth hostel, at ul Waclawy Marek 12 (Tel. 0331–31296), is on the other side of town. The campsite is basic, but cheap, and is at ul. Oleńki 3 (Tel. 47495).

Tatras Mountains

Sixty miles south of Cracow is the beautiful TATRA NATIONAL PARK with lofty 6,000-foot mountains of granite and limestone. ZAKO-PANE is the largest town in the area and is a good place to base yourself to explore the surrounding area. You may choose to take the bus from Cracow to Zakopane: it is quicker, more scenic and costs about £1 one-way. A funicular railway runs to the top of MT GUBALOWKA (3,720 feet) and a cable car up MT KASPROWY WIERCH (6,510 feet). There is a great hike to the top of MT GIEWONT (6,260 feet) which takes about six hours. You will have a magnificent view from each peak. MORSKIE OKO is a beautiful mountain lake about 40 mins from Zakopane by bus, and well worth the trip. The tourist office is at ul Kosciuszki 7 and the PTTK at ul Krupówki 37 will give you information on mountain shelters. The youth hostel is at ul Nowotarska 45 (Tel. 0165–4203). For camping, try Pod Kro-kiwa, ul Żeromskiego (Tel. 2256) opposite the foot of the ski jump.

Malbork

The castle by the River Vistula (Wisła) in Malbork is one of the most awesome military fortifications in Europe. The sheer scale of the project is best appreciated from the opposite bank of the Wisła (best photographs as well). The construction of the Marienburg was begun by the Teutonic Knights in 1274 after they were driven out of Palestine. In 1309, the Marienburg became their European headquarters and powerbase, and remained so until 1457 when the Grand Master was forced to flee to Königsberg (though the power of the Teutonic Knights had been on the wane since their defeat at the battle of Grünwald in 1410). From May–Sept. the castle is open Tues.–Sun.: 9 a.m.–4.30 p.m.; at other times of year, Tues.–Sun.: 9 a.m.–3 p.m. Admission costs just over £1 (£3 if you want a tour in English). Malbork is on the main train line between Warsaw and Gdańsk.

Gdańsk

The port of Gdańsk in north-eastern Poland is famous as the birthplace of Solidarity and has a lot to offer the eurorailer with its historic old town dating from the time of the medieval Hanseatic League, when the city was known as Danzig.

TOURIST INFORMATION AND ADDRESSES

TOURIST OFFICE: ul Heweliusza 27 (Tel. 314355), open Mon.–Fri.: 9 a.m.–3 p.m., Sat.: 8 a.m.–4 p.m., Sun.: 8 a.m.–3 p.m.
ORBIS: in Hotel Hevelius, ul Heweliusza 22 (Tel. 314777), open Mon.–Fri.: 10 a.m.–5 p.m.
POST OFFICE: ul Pocztowa and ul Dluga.
AMEX: at Orbis in Monopol Orbis, pl Gorkiego (Tel. 311466).
ALMATUR: Dlugi Targ 11 (Tel. 317801), open Mon.–Tues. and Thurs.–Fri.: 9 a.m.–3 p.m.
TRAINS: Gdańsk Glówny is 10 minutes from the centre. Train information: Tel. 310051.
PHONE CODE: 058.

SEEING

Around the market square, DLUGI TARG, is the headquarters of the old Hanseatic League and the imposing TOWN HALL which contains a very interesting HISTORICAL MUSEUM (closed Mondays). There is a great view from the tower. Walk along ul Mariacka to see the grand façades of seventeenth-century burghers' houses. North of the old town is the home of Solidarity, the former LENIN SHIPYARDS, now Gdańsk Shipyards (STOCZNIA GDAŃSKA) and a monument to workers killed during the rising of 1970. During the summer Gdańsk is packed with beachgoers, try STOGI BEACH (tram 9); although heavily polluted, windsurfing is popular. East of Gdańsk is the beautiful Mazurian lakeland. Take the train via Olsztyn.

SLEEPING

There are many hostels in the area, but the most central is at ul Walowa 21 (Tel. 312313), five minutes from the station, closed 10 a.m.–5 p.m. Be aware of the fact that dormitories are mixed. Use the Biuro Zakwaterowan at ul Elźbietańska 10–11 (Tel. 312634) to help you find a room. For camping try Gdańsk-Jelitkowo, ul Jelitkowska (Tel. 532731). Tram 5 or 8 from the Oliwa train station to the last stop, then a short walk. For a hotel try Hotel Jantar on Dlugi Targ 19 (Tel. 316241) for a good location from around 80,000 zl. A short train ride away at the seaside town of Gdynia is a YMCA, 10 minutes' walk from the station at ul Zeromskiego 26 (Tel. 48/58 203115), open 15 June–31 August.

EATING AND NIGHTLIFE

Milk bars are probably your best bet. If you want to splash out try Pod Łososiem, ul Szeroka 54, which serves excellent fresh fish. Flisak, ul Chlebnicka and Kameralna, ul Dluga 57 are popular student clubs.

Toruń

Toruń is best known nowadays as the birthplace of Nicolaus Copernicus, but in its heyday during the late Medieval period

Toruń was one of the most important of the Hanseatic trading cities, evidence of which remains today in its host of Gothic ecclesiastical and secular buildings. The town's economy went into a sharp decline after the Polish Partitions. Toruń (or Thorn as it was then called) remained under Prussian and German control until 1919 when the Treaty of Versailles handed it over to the recently formed Polish state as part of the 'Polish corridor'.

TOURIST INFORMATION

The best source of information on the town is the PTTK office at pl Rapackiego 2 (Tel. 24926/28228). Open Mon.–Fri.: 8 a.m.–4.30 p.m., weekends: 10 a.m.–1 p.m. ORBIS is just off Rynek Staromiejski at ul Zeglarska 31 (Tel. 22553). Open Mon.–Fri.: 9 a.m.–5 p.m., Sat.: 9 a.m.–2 p.m.

● **Addresses:**

ALMATUR: ul Gagarina 21 (Tel. 20470). Near the university. In summer, student residences are converted into temporary hostels.
STATIONS: Most trains stop at Toruń Główny (main station), about two miles from the centre, across the River Vistula (Wisła). Buses 12 and 22 maintain a frequent service between the station and pl Rapackiego. Toruń Miasto is much closer to the centre.

SEEING

As well as the TOWN HALL, which ranks amongst the best of Europe's secular Gothic buildings, there are several fine red-brick churches and the remains of the town's fortifications. The streets of the old Hanseatic town are charming, if slightly run-down. The house in which Copernicus was born now contains a MUSEUM dedicated to the astronomer and his work.

SLEEPING

There are several decent, affordable hotels in the town centre. The Pod Orłem at ul Mostowa 15 (Tel. 25024) and the Polonia at pl Teatralny 5 (Tel. 23028) are both within five minutes' walk of Rynek Staromiejski. Private rooms can be arranged through the office at Rynek Staromiejski 20. The PTTK Dom Turysty at ul

Legionów 24 is quite far out from the centre, as are the IYHF hostel at ul Rudacka 15 (Tel. 27242) and Camping Tramp at ul Kujawska 14 (open May–Sept.), both of which are in the area around Toruń Główny.

EATING

The local speciality is gingerbread, which is widely available in the Old Town. There is a good selection of cafés with seats outside, especially along ul Szeroka. The restaurants of the Polonia hotel (see above) and the Kosmos on Ks J. Popiełuszki provide reasonably priced meals, but better quality food at much the same price is available at the restaurant of the Zajazd Staropolski hotel on ul Zeglarska.

Poznań

Due to its position at the crossroads of several important trade routes, Poznań flourished in the fifteenth and sixteenth centuries, though the following two hundred years saw a marked decline in the city's fortunes. The Industrial Revolution saw the city's revival, but by then Poznań was the Prussian city of Posen. Following German unification in 1871 an attempt was made to Germanize the city. Resistance to this policy established Poznań as a centre of Polish nationalism. A successful uprising by the local Polish population in late 1918 ensured the city's incorporation in the reconstituted Polish state.

TOURIST INFORMATION

Stary Rynek 77 (Tel. 526156). Open Mon.–Sat.: 8 a.m.–4 p.m. Good range of material on the city and surrounding area. Helpful, well informed staff. ORBIS have offices at pl Wolności 3 (Tel. 524011) (sells international train tickets), al Karola Marcinkowskiego 21 and ul Święty Wojciech 33.

● **Addresses:**
POST OFFICE: The main office is on al Marcinkowskiego.

ALMATUR: al Aleksandra Fredry 7 (Tel. 523645).
STATIONS: Poznań Główny is about 15–20 minutes' walk from the
Stary Rynek at the heart of the old town. Trams 5 and 21 connect
the station to the city centre.
PHONE CODE: 061.

SEEING

The impressive MAIN SQUARE (Stary Rynek) is lined by gabled
houses. The most important public buildings are located in the
centre of the square. Pride of place goes to the TOWN HALL (now
containing the MUSEUM OF THE HISTORY OF POZNAŃ). At noon the
figure-play on the Town Hall clock re-enacts the local legend of the
two rams which saved the city from burning down. To the rear of the
Town Hall is the WEIGHING HOUSE. The red-brick buildings of the
old ecclesiastical quarter are a 15-minute walk away across the
River Warta. The imposing castles of ROGALIN and KÓRNIK (seven
and fourteen miles from Poznań respectively) are easily reached by
bus.

SLEEPING

Hotels are expensive by Polish standards, but private rooms are
available from the Biuro Zakwaterowania at ul Głogowska 16 (Tel.
60313) across from Poznań Główny, or from the ORBIS office in
the Hotel Poznań on pl Henryka Dabrowskiego (Tel. 331811) near
the bus station. As regards location, you cannot better the PTTK
Dom Turysty at Stary Rynek 91 (Tel. 528893). Of the five IYHF
hostels, the two most convenient are at ul Berwińskiego 2/3 (Tel.
663680) and al Niepodległości 32/40 (Tel. 56706). Both the
campsites are far from the centre; the Streszynek at ul Koszalińska
15 (Tel. 47224) is easier to reach (bus 95), as well as having a
pleasant lakeside setting.

EATING AND NIGHTLIFE

The Pod Koziołkami, Stary Rynek 64 serves good, cheap meals and
Polish beers and spirits. The food at the U Dylla, Stary Rynek 37 is
similar in quality and only slightly more expensive, but only
expensive imported beers and spirits are sold. The Pod Korona, off

the Stary Rynek at ul Zamkowa 7 offers good-value meals (wide variety of traditional Polish dishes), while the Przyneta at ul Święty Wojciech is noted for its fish specialities. One of the better milk bars is the Mewa on pl Wolności. Poznań produces two good-quality beers, Lech and Ratusz, which make a pleasant change from the ubiquitous Tatra Pils. If the tourist office cannot help you find the type of pub or club you are looking for, the most obvious place to ask around is the Odnowa, the largest of the student clubs, at ul Święty Wojciech 80/82.

Wrocław (Breslau)

After Prussia seized Breslau from Austria in 1763, Breslau developed into Prussia's second most important city (after Berlin). By the early twentieth century, Breslau was one of the leading cities of the new German state. At that time, Poles constituted only around 3 per cent of the population. So important was the city to Germany, that Polish leaders never envisaged Breslau would become part of Poland in the aftermath of the Second World War, but that was indeed what occurred. The German population fled, or were forced out, leaving the depopulated city to be filled with Poles from the city of Lwów (Lvov), which Poland had lost to the USSR. Breslau was then re-named Wrocław, though many Silesians still use the Germanic name (as they do for other towns in Silesia). Today, Wrocław is a university town and cultural centre, famous for its 100 bridges spanning the river Oder (Odra), its canals, parks and gardens.

TOURIST INFORMATION

Tourist Information is at Rynek 38 (Tel. 443111). Open Mon.–Sat.: 10 a.m.–4 p.m. ORBIS is close by at Rynek 45 (Tel. 447946/447679/ 444109). Open Apr.–Sept., Mon.–Sat.: 8 a.m.–5 p.m.; Oct.–Mar., Mon.–Fri.: 8 a.m.–5 p.m.

• **Addresses:**
POST OFFICE: The main office is at ul Zygmunta Krasińskiego 1. Smaller offices operate in front of Wrocław Główny and at Rynek 28.

ALMATUR: ul Tadeusza Kościuszki 34 (Tel. 443003). On a street between the main train station and the Rynek.

STATIONS: Your most likely point of arrival is the main station Wrocław Główny, about 10–15 minutes' walk from the Rynek. Trains from Jelenia Góra arrive at Wrocław Świebodzki, on the fringe of the old town. Wrocław Nadodrze receives trains from Łodz. Tram 0 or 1 to the centre.

PHONE CODE: 071.

SEEING

The MARKET SQUARE (Rynek) is dominated by the fourteenth-century TOWN HALL with its astronomical clock, one of the most impressive public buildings in Poland. The building now houses the TOWN MUSEUM, which is worth visiting if only to see the interior of the Town Hall. Around here are many medieval houses which have benefited from the town's conservation programme. The university area is a short walk from the Rynek, with the ecclesiastical quarter further on, across the River Oder on Ostrów Tumski. Walking along the Oder affords particularly fine views of the ecclesiastical district. By the river is the NATIONAL MUSEUM, best known for its collection of medieval stone sculptures and Silesian wood carvings. Close by is Breslau's major tourist attraction, the PANORAMA RACŁAWICKA (open daily 8 a.m.–5 p.m., £1.50). The panoramic painting (120 m long and 15 m high) depicts the defeat of the Russians in 1794 by the people's militia led by the national hero Tadeusz Kościuszko. The Prussian King Frederick the Great had a residence at the Spaetgens Palace down near the river, which is worth a look. The Sudeten Mountains can be reached from Wrocław by heading south towards the Czech border.

SLEEPING

There are several affordable hotels along ul Piłsudskiego, right opposite Wrocław Główny: at no. 98 the Piast (Tel. 30033); at no. 66 the Polonia (Tel. 31021); at no. 100 the Grand (Tel. 36071); and at no. 88 the Europejski (Tel. 31071). Private rooms can be booked at the Biuro Uslug Turystycznych at ul Pilsudskiego 98. The PTTK Dom Turysty is well located, close to the Rynek at ul Karola Szajnochy 11 (Tel. 443073). Of the two IYHF hostels, one is in the area behind Wrocław Główny at ul Kołłataja 20 (Tel. 38856). The other, at ul Na Grobli 30 (Tel. 37402), is not easy to reach by public transport (nor is the campsite nearby). The campsite near the Olympic Stadium at al Ignacego Paderewskiego 35 (Tel. 484651) is better in any case. Trams 16 and 17 run along ul Adama Mickiewicza: the stadium is off to the left.

EATING AND NIGHTLIFE

Two particularly good milk bars are the Ratuszowy at Rynek 27a, and the Miś, close to the university at Kuźnicza 48. For cheap but substantial meals try the KDM restaurant at Tadeusza Kościuszki square 5/6, or the Ratuszowa, beneath the New Town Hall at Rynek 9. The Pod Chmielem beer hall at ul Odrzańska 17 (between the Rynek and the Oder) offers surprisingly good-quality meals in lively surroundings. The main student club, the Pałaczyk, is at ul Tadeusza Kościuszki 34, in the same building as the ALMATUR office. The Rura at ul Łazienna 4 offers live music nightly (blues and, especially, jazz).

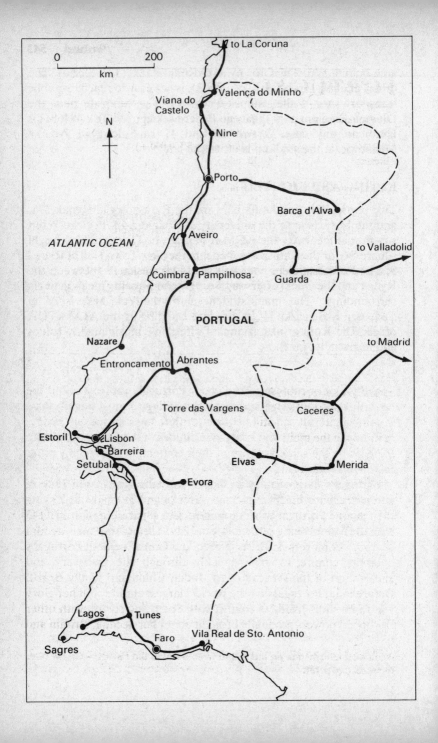

PORTUGAL

Entry requirements	Passport
Population	10,100,000
Capital	Lisbon (pop.: 1,500,000 +)
Currency	Escudo
	£1 = approx. 219$
Political system	Republic
Religion	Roman Catholic
Language	Portuguese (some English spoken in cities)
Public holidays	1 Jan.; 3 March; 17, 24, 25 April;
	1 May; 10, 18 June; 15 Aug.; 5 Oct.;
	1 Nov.; 1, 8, 25, 26 Dec.
International dialling codes	From UK: 010 + 351 + number
	From USA: 011 + 351 + number
	To UK: 07 + 44 + number
	To USA: 07 + 1 + number
Eurotrain office	Rua C.C. Branco 20, P–1100 Lisboa
	(Tel. 01–525709)

There's a lot of rubbish talked about Portugal, not least about the beautiful unspoilt Algarve where, according to most guidebooks, inviting a girl out can still be misinterpreted as a proposal. Today, certainly in the main tourist areas, attitudes of the young people are likely to be the same as those of their contemporaries in any other European country.

Portugal's early history is shared with the rest of the Iberian peninsula, with the Phoenicians, Greeks and Romans all leaving their mark. Portugal was recognized as a separate nation in 1143 with the Moors being pushed out in 1249. Throughout the fifteenth century, explorers such as Vasco da Gama helped Portugal's overseas empire to grow quickly through the discovery and exploration of the African coast, India, China and finally Brazil. Before long, Portugal had the world's largest empire, but her glory was to be short-lived, as conflict with Spain and rivalry with other European powers gradually brought about her decline. Britain and

Additional information on this country contained in the *Europe – Grand Tour* factsheet (see p.13).

Portugal share a 'special relationship' with an alliance going back more than 600 years. Eventually, even the royal family packed their bags and set off to Brazil during the Napoleonic Wars. Recently, the 1974 revolution has brought about a more liberal constitution and since 1986 Portugal has been a member of the EC. Portugal remains one of Europe's most affordable countries, where it's possible to cultivate a good tan and eat well while doing it.

PORTUGUESE RAILWAYS
(Caminhos de Ferro Portugueses, CP)

The British originally built the Portuguese network with a wide gauge for extra comfort. Much of the 3,600-km network is electrified, but you will also find some of the more remote inland lines are narrow-gauge and steam-hauled. The fastest of the non-supplement trains are the expresses (directo). Next down the list are the semi directos, which stop nearly as often as the slow regionals. Away from the Lisbon area, services can be very slow, so you might feel justified in paying the extra supplements for the intercity rápidos; this works out at about 25 per cent above the normal tariff. The standard has improved in recent years, though.

TRAIN INFORMATION

English is spoken by most information staff.

● **Reservations:** Are optional on inland trains and are quite cheap. For international and express trains, reservations are free of charge providing they are made the day before departure. In general, trains are crowded so it's best to reserve seats in advance.

● **Supplements:** Eurail Pass holders need to pay a supplement to travel on express trains. Some rápido trains carry a saloon observation car which requires a supplement to travel in it. Don't buy tickets on the train as you face a whopping surcharge. It's far better to queue at the station if you possibly can. Ask first about the train you are taking. It is worth paying the small supplement on the Lisbon–Porto line.

● **Night travel:** There are no couchettes, but the sleepers are cheap.

• **Eating on trains:** All trains except the regionals have mini-bars, but only the rápidos can be relied upon to have dining cars.

• **Scenic tips:** As with Spain, there are enough problems getting where you want to go without worrying about scenic routes; however, the run from Valença in the north down to Lisbon is one of the best Portugal has to offer. Also try the line from Porto along the Douro valley and its branch lines, such as the one to Braganza. Always check the timetabling of trains with the posters on station walls, as printed timetables cannot always be relied upon to be accurate.

• **Rover tickets:** Available for 7, 14 or 21 days in first and second class. The 'Tourist Ticket' is valid for all trains on the network and costs 15,200 $, 24,050 $ and 34,060 $ respectively for second-class travel.

• **Time difference:** Portugal is in the same time-band as the UK, so remember to put your watches back an hour when travelling from Spain and take account of the difference when planning journeys from timetables.

TOURIST INFORMATION

Is provided by the government-run Postos do Turismo. They have offices all over the country and stalls at major stations.

• **ISIC bonuses:** The main perk here is admission to the cheap student restaurants on your ISIC. In addition about 1,200 places – discos, theatres and so on – also offer discounts. For further information contact Turismo Social e Juvenil, Turicoop (1st floor), Rua Pascual do Melo, Lisbon.

• **Money matters:** 1 escudo ($) = 100 centavos. 1,000 Escudos is known as a 'conto'.
Banking hours are Mon.–Fri.: 8.30 a.m.–2.45 p.m. There are late-night exchange facilities at major tourist resorts.

• **Post offices and shops:** Open Mon.–Sat.: 9 a.m.–1 p.m., 3 p.m.–7 p.m. (closed Saturday p.m.).

• **Museums:** Open 10 a.m.–5 p.m., although some close for lunch and most are closed all day Monday.

SLEEPING

The government-run tourist board controls all the accommodation within Portugal and will book you a room if required. Hotels are graded from one star to five, boarding houses (estalagem, albergaria, pensão), one to four. By law, prices should be shown at reception and behind the door of each room. A double room in a three-star hotel costs about 4,000 $ a night. A student hostel tends to be more expensive than a cheap pensão. There are seventeen youth hostels (Pousadas de Juventude) in Portugal, all requiring IYHF cards, and most with an 11 p.m. curfew, prices 600 $–1,100 $. Camping is another possibility: sites are generally close to towns, cheap, but may be quite basic except in the Algarve, where you have to have a Camping Carnet and things are quite plush. I recommend cheap hotels and boarding houses. They're normally near the stations, and as prices are unaffected by location it's not really worth shopping around.

EATING AND NIGHTLIFE

Food is cheap in Portugal and eating out is a relatively inexpensive affair (900 $ to 1,400 $), except in the Algarve where prices are marked up for the tourists.

Go for fish dishes, especially chowders if you get the chance: they're invariably cheaper and tastier than meat dishes. National specialities include 'linguado delícia' (sole cooked with banana). If you don't like fish, pork represents the best value among the meat dishes. Vegetarians will have to cope largely with omelettes and salads. A bottle of wine is often thrown in for the price of the meal; if not ask for the local plonk (vinho da casa). The port is excellent but, rather surprisingly, it's not drunk a lot in Portugal. The other wines are excellent too.

If you're living on the beaches and need a meat 'booster', keep your eyes skinned for the mobile shops which serve cheap steak sandwiches (pregos).

Taverns tend to be very basic, but go down well with the local lads.

Bullfighting in Portugal is not as gory as it is in Spain – they're not allowed to kill the bull – but it's still a national obsession. Of the two types of Portuguese bullfights, the 'tourada à antiga' is perhaps the more spectacular. Here the bullfighter is dressed in eighteenth-century costume and fights from a horse.

Discos and bars are at their best in Lisbon, though by northern European standards many of the discos are pretty tame, and you'll do better heading for a bar which has 'fados' (melancholy Portuguese ballads) on the bill. There are no licensing hours in Portugal, so things can often drag right through the night till dawn.

Lisbon (Lisboa)

This westernmost capital of Europe escaped many of the influences that shaped the rest of the continent: among them the Reformation, the Industrial Revolution and the Second World War. It has developed out on a limb at a different pace and in a different way, and if any one force can be said to have affected its development, it was – and is – the sea. Lisbon was rebuilt after the 1755 earthquake; only the old Moorish quarter of Alfama escaped destruction. Essentially, it's a pleasant city to visit: beds and meals are cheap and plentiful, the nightlife's lively and there are several places of great interest to visit.

STATION FACILITIES

International trains and northern and eastern trains use Santa Apolónia Station. Trains to the south and south-east leave from Barreiro Station (linked to Santa Apolónia by a ferry across the Tagus – free on Inter-Rail); trains to Sintra and the west use Rossio (on bus routes 9, 39–59 from Santa Apolónia), and trains for Estoril and Cascais use Cais do Sodré Station (bus 35).

SANTA APOLÓNIA	
Train information	8 a.m.–10 p.m. (Tel. 326226)
Reservations	9 a.m.–8 p.m. Window 11
Tourist information	9 a.m.–2 p.m., 4 p.m.–7 p.m.
Foreign exchange	9 a.m.–8 p.m.
Left-luggage lockers	No access 2 a.m.–5 a.m.
Left-luggage store	7 a.m.–1 a.m.
Bar, Buffet	7 a.m.–11 p.m.
Shops	Mon.–Sat.: 7 a.m.–12 midnight
Waiting room	All hours
Post office	Mon.–Fri.: 9 a.m.–7 p.m.
Station shuts	2 a.m.–5 a.m.

Daily trains to: Porto, Madrid, Irún, Paris.

TOURIST INFORMATION

The Portuguese National Tourist Office (Tel. 3463643) is in Palácio Foz on Praça dos Restauradores, open Mon.–Sat.: 9 a.m.–8 p.m., Sun.: 10 a.m.–6 p.m. The Municipal Tourist Office is at Rua Jardim do Regedor; and the national tourist office headquarters is at Avenida Augusto de Aguiar 86 (Tel. 575015), open Mon.–Fri.: 9.30 a.m.–5.30 p.m.

• **Addresses:**
POST OFFICE ('Correio'): Praça do Comércio, open Mon.–Fri.: 9 a.m.–7 p.m.
AMEX: Star Travel Service, Avenida Sidónio Pais 4A, open Mon.–Fri.: 9.15 a.m.–12.30 p.m., 2 p.m.–6 p.m. (Tel. 539871).
UK EMBASSY: Rua S. Domingos à Lapa 35–39 (Tel. 661191).
US EMBASSY: Avenida Dôs Forças Armadas (Tel. 725600).
CANADIAN EMBASSY: Rua Rosa Aravjo 2, 6th floor (Tel. 562547).
AUSTRALIAN EMBASSY: Avenida da Liberdade 244 (Tel. 539108).
BRITISH HOSPITAL: 49 Rua Saraiva de Carvalho (Tel. 602020).
EUROTRAIN: Rua C.C. Branco 20 (Tel. 525709).
24-HOUR CHEMIST: British Hospital, Rua Saraiva de Carvalho 49 (Tel. 602020).
PHONE CODE: 01.

• **Getting about:** It's best to get your tram or bus ticket from a Carris kiosk rather than on the vehicle, where it costs about 110 $. A four-day pass costs 980 $ and is valid on buses, trolleys and subways. Buy it from Carris booths in the main stations, open 8 a.m.–8 p.m. The metro system is limited, but a fast way of getting around and only costs around 50 $. If you're travelling in a group, taxis work out cheap at 75 $ per kilometre.

SEEING

It's pointless our suggesting a route round the ALFAMA district as it's so sprawling you're bound to get lost, so just wander through at your own pace, and if you happen to pass the church of SÃO MIGUEL or LARGO DO SALVADOR 22 (sixteenth-century mansion house), look in. This is one of Europe's most colourful districts, especially in the morning when the fish market's on, or on Fridays (washday) when the narrow streets are hung with locals' shirts and undies. The area is enclosed roughly by the banks of the Tagus, the castle, the church of St Vincent-outside-the-walls, and the cathedral. ST GEORGE'S CASTLE, the fortress on the hill, has dominated Lisbon in one form or another for 1,500 years. Its gardens of peacocks and flamingos make a good vantage point to look over the city. Near the centre is the SÉ (cathedral), worth a look for its ambulatory and burial chapel. A good view of Lisbon is obtained by taking the ASCENSOR DE SANTA JUSTA for 25 $ up the ornate tower created by Eiffel.

On the outskirts of the city are quite a few sights worth visiting. Go to the BELÉM quarter (tram 15, 16 or 17 from Praça do Comércio), get off at the Museu Nacional dos Coches, and head for the HIERONYMITE MONASTERY (Mosteiro dos Jerónimos, closed Mondays). Here Vasco da Gama is buried, as are various Portuguese kings. The affluent merchants in the spice trade put up most of the money for this beautiful place which was built in the early sixteenth century. Opposite is the MONUMENT TO THE DISCOVERIES (180 $, free with ISIC). Take the lift (free) for a view of the city. Also in this district is the TOWER OF BELÉM (400 $, free with ISIC), one of Lisbon's landmarks, an elegant mixture of Gothic and Renaissance architecture.

As far as museums go, the GULBENKIAN arts and culture centre, Av. de Berna 45 (closed Mondays), the MUSEU NACIONAL DE ARTE ANTIGA, Rua das Janelas Verdes 95, and the FOLK ART MUSEUM, Av. Marginal, Belém, are the best.

• **Excursions:** SINTRA, twenty-five miles north-west of Lisbon, is one of Portugal's oldest towns and was part of the famed Grand Tour in the nineteenth century; it was favoured by Byron. The summer residence of the royal family was here and the PENA PALACE and PARK are well worth the day trip (closed Wednesdays and public holidays). The MOORISH CASTLE is a must with its fantastic views. The park has more than 400 kinds of trees and many rare plants. Also out here is the sixteenth-century monastery of SANTA CRUZ DE CAPUCHOS and MONSERRATE PARK. From June to September the Sintra Festival attracts large numbers of music, opera and ballet enthusiasts and the piano concerts are incredibly popular. Tourist information is at Praça da República (Tel. 9235079).

If you want a day on the beach, head for ESTORIL, a jet-set resort sixteen miles west of the city, or CASCAIS, two miles further on. If you want to stop off here but can't afford the hotel prices, head a few miles back towards Lisbon and get off the train at Oeiras. Here you can enjoy a fine beach and an excellent modern, cheap and friendly hostel just a stone's throw away. It is at Catalazete, Estrada Marginal (Tel. 4430638). It's quite small and fills up quickly so don't waste time in booking your place.

From Cascais you can catch a bus to CABO DA ROCA, the most westerly point in Europe, with a memorable view from the lighthouse. No. 45 departs from Cascais at 11 a.m., 3 p.m. and 6.45 p.m. and returns at 11.50 a.m., 4 p.m. and 7.30 p.m. A more frequent bus (no. 403) runs from Sintra. Get off at the Azoia turn-off and walk the last couple of miles. Another idea is to visit QUELUZ, the town eight miles north-west of Lisbon, where the rococo palace used to entertain VIPs of the Portuguese government. It's stuffed full of antiques and can be reached by train from Rossio Station (closed Tuesdays).

SLEEPING

An average double in a pension is about 2–3,000 $, a single 3–4,000 $. There are plenty of cheap places in Lisbon – not everywhere is clean and quiet, but the ones listed are about as close as you'll get. If these don't come up lucky, try yourself round Rua da Alegria, Rua dos Correiros, Rua Augusta and Praça da Figueira. The youth hostel, at Rua Andrade Corvo 46 (Tel. 532696), is cheap and a 20-minute walk from the centre, but next to Picoas Metro. As far as camping goes, there are plenty of sites – and free beach camping close by – but the best site is the Parque Nacional de Turismo e Campismo (Tel. 704413) (bus to Parque Florestal, Monsanto). As regards cheap hotels, Residencial Mansarde, Avenida da Liberdade 141, 5th floor (Tel. 372963), charges about 3,000 $ for doubles. At No. 53 of this street, Pensão do Sul (Tel. 365647) has cheap rooms, as does Pensão Pembo at No. 11 (Tel. 325010). Pensão Ninho de Águias, Costa do Castelo 74 (Tel. 860391), is of very high quality. Doubles start at 3,200 $ including breakfast. Pensão São João da Praça on São João da Praça 97 (Tel. 862591) is near the Alfama district and asks from 2,500 $ per double.

EATING AND NIGHTLIFE

Between the port and the Praça da Figueira is the best district.

Lisbon is no longer as cheap as in the eighties, so choose your district carefully. Try Rua dos Correeiros (near Terreiro do Paco). Use the Mercado da Ribeira outside the Cais do Sodré for picnic food, and watch out you don't get stuck on Sundays, especially in July, when many places close. Fish is generally good value, but don't eat the bread and savouries put out on the tables unless you're prepared to pay the extortionate prices that are often asked for them. Restaurante Trevo da Madalena and Restaurante Central on Rua da Madalena both do meals around 900 $, or try Gloria on Rua da Gloria 39A. The area near the youth hostel is quite good for eating places.

Nightlife starts late and can get pretty lively. The authentic Portuguese folk music, the fado, is performed in several restaurants and cafés. Don't go till around midnight, unless you're happy to share your evenings with coach parties from package tours. Sr Vinho, Rua Praças 18, and the Patio das Cantigas, Rua São Caetano 27, offer authentic fados, but not for under 1,000 $. Taxi drivers can be a good source of information on the location of an authentic fado. Lively nightlife can be found in the Barrio Alto, especially around Rua Díario das Notícias. Port, the national drink, can be sampled at the Port Wine Institute, Rua S. Pedro de Alcantara 45, from 10 a.m.–12 midnight. From May–Sept. the Lisbon Amusement Park gives you somewhere to spend time before heading for the bars or cafés later on. The fair goes on till 1 a.m. and can be reached by the underground (station Entre-Campos). The best club in town is Trump's on Rua da Imprensa Nacional.

Northern Portugal

If you're approaching Portugal from the north, the places worth stopping for are Viana do Castelo, Óbidos on the Costa de Prata, and Coimbra. PORTO is an industrial town, very much a mixture of old and new. Tourist information at Rua Clube dos Fenianos (Tel. 02–312740). Climb the Igrejados Clerigos church tower, then visit one of the 20 or so Porthouses for a free tour and tasting, though avoid buying any in the Porthouses' own shops as you will probably find it cheaper in town. Much of this region is unspoilt, as most eurorailers head for either Lisbon or the overrated Algarve. The youth hostel is at Rua Rodrigues Lobo 98 (Tel. 65535). Take bus 19 or 20 from Praça da Liberdade, but arrive early as it is often full. The campsite is at Rua Monte dos Burgos (Tel. 812616). Bus 6 from Praça do Liberdade. A day trip to REGUA in the Douro Valley is possible from Porto. This is one of Europe's most scenic routes.

VIANA DO CASTELO: this pretty little fishing resort, 1½ hours from Porto, has a vantage point for views over the whole region: the BASÍLICA OF SANTA LUZIA. You can take the funicular up or, better still, walk up the twisting road past the pine and eucalyptus trees till you reach the top. Back down in the town, look out for the reminders of the Renaissance in the buildings of the PRAÇA DA REPÚBLICA and the church of SÃO DOMINGOS. If you're here in the third week of August, you'll catch the festival: bullfights, processions, fireworks, dancing, etc. The MUNICIPAL MUSEUM has a collection of the ceramics Portugal is famous for. Rooms aren't a problem: try the streets off Avenida dos Combatentes, or camp at CABEDELO BEACH.

ÓBIDOS is a little medieval village, seven miles from the sea, and is worth seeing for its preserved CASTLE, old TOWN WALLS and the two churches of SANTA MARIA and the MISERICÓRDIA. Tourist information is on Rua Direita.

Coimbra

This university town is second only to Lisbon in terms of historical and cultural importance. It is set among the beautiful forests and woods of the Beira Litoral region, and is about 2½ hours from the capital. Get off at Coimbra 'A' station, walk two blocks east for the turismo in Largo da Portagem. It's open Mon.–Sat.: 9 a.m.–8 p.m., Sun.: 10 a.m.–5 p.m., and operates a currency exchange desk (Tel. 39–23886).

The UNIVERSITY is the best sight of the town. The OLD LIBRARY (Biblioteca), the CHAPEL and the MUSEUM are all impressive (knock on the door to be let in) and the CEREMONIAL HALL is decorated with some fine 'azulejos' (ceramic tiles). The MACHADO MUSEUM nearby is a former episcopal palace, and today houses many of Portugal's artistic treasures. The town's CATHEDRAL is twelfth-century, as is the Cistercian convent, MOSTEIRO DE CELAS. Not far out is a reconstructed village of all the famous buildings in Portugal, miniature-size: PORTUGAL DOS PEQUENINOS.

For cheap beds, look out for 'dormidas' round the station: Rua da Sota and the streets around should produce something. The youth hostel is at Rua Henriques Sêco 12 (Tel. 39–22955). Take bus 7 from Coimbra A to Liceu José Falcão. Recommended. The campsite at Praça 25 de Abril (Tel. 712997) costs around 400 $. For eats, try 'Zé Manel', Beco do Forno 12, just off Rua da Sota. Apart from good cheap food, this place has character. Open 12 noon–3 p.m., 5 p.m.–10 p.m. and closed Mondays. Much cheaper food than in Lisbon. Fado can be found, along with several bars, on Travessa da Rua Nova.

An unspoilt resort where traditional Portugal survives alongside tourism is Nazare, 5 km (bus) from Valado on the Lisbon–Coimbra line. There is a nice beach and a funicular (20 $) to the old town.

The Alentejo

This huge region is the hinterland of Portugal between Spain and the Tagus. It is off the beaten track – a good place for avoiding your fellow tourists. The main town is EVORA, three hours from Lisbon. See the fourth-century ROMAN TEMPLE OF DIANA, the chapel (CAPELA DE OSSOS) containing the bones of 5,000 monks, the SÉ (cathedral) and the MUSEU D'EVORA (free on ISIC).

The youth hostel is at Rua da Corredoura 32 (Tel. 66–25043). Camping is on the Alcáçovas Road (320 $ per person), outside town. Food is cheaper than in Lisbon. Good regional specialities can be found at Restaurante Faísca on Rua da Raimundo.

The Algarve

Portugal's famous southern region used to be one of the best-kept secrets in continental Europe; mile after mile of white sand interspersed with picturesque fishing villages. Sadly that is no longer the case as the package holiday industry has really taken off in a big way in the Algarve since the early 1970s. Many of the small villages have been turned into overgrown building sites, crowded with British package holidaymakers and overpriced accordingly.

The Algarve has practically no evidence left of its historical past. Most of the small villages were flattened by a major earthquake in 1755, and only FARO, LAGOS and SAGRES (home of Prince Henry the Navigator) have any traces worth visiting. The region as a whole retains some appeal, if you can manage to avoid all the busy package resorts, including QUARTEIRA, VILAMOURA, MONTE GORDO and (especially) ALBUFEIRA. These over-commercialized villages really have nothing to offer other than superb beaches. If you're lucky, you might find a few empty feet of sand all to yourself among the package tourists. One good place to base yourself is the small town of Lagoa, between Albufeira and Lagos. There is a complex specially designed for young travellers, which offers the major service of sending transport to meet all local trains in the small towns. It is open from the end of May to the beginning of October. It is a self-contained unit with a choice of three restaurants/snack bars, and a disco with parties most nights. Accommodation is in dormitories or tents. Also there is a shuttle bus all day to its own beach which gives access to other, more secluded beaches. It is very popular among eurorailers because of the cosmopolitan atmosphere. For further information contact Astor Hostels, Thurloe St, London SW7.

One advantage of the huge package trade is that English is practically the second language of the region. The local cuisine is worth investigating – plenty of fish and seafood delicacies – and regional wines are really cheap. House wines are normally less than a pound (about 240 $) even in some of the better cafés and restaurants. The region is a paradise for those interested in sport, assuming they're not short of a few quid, and there are many exclusive golf and sports clubs tagged on to the bigger hotels.

Finding an inexpensive base in the Algarve is next to impossible during the peak summer months from June to August. Look out for 'casas particulares' (private accommodation) or else consider sleeping on the beach. If you've really set your heart on spending a few days in the Algarve then you ought to consider arriving out of season. March and April are good months, when the weather is mild with temperatures occasionally straying into the low 70sF. Cheap accommodation is also relatively plentiful in towns like Faro and Lagos. The weather can become quite windy after September so bear this in mind before packing too much suntan lotion later on in the year.

The Algarve is well connected by rail from Lisbon and the north, and the region's main line runs across from Lagos, through Faro, to Vila Real de Santo António in the east.

LAGOS is the region's westernmost town of any size and has a colourful past dating back to the time of the Celts. There's still quite a bit to see, including the scattered remains of the MEDIEVAL WALLS and the magnificent church of SANTO ANTONIO, on Rua Silva Lopes, which contains some of Portugal's finest gilt carvings. The REGIONAL MUSEUM next door has an interesting, if rather disjointed, collection of artifacts telling the town's history. The TOURIST OFFICE is on Largo Marquês de Pombal (Tel. 63031). Accommodation is more expensive than elsewhere but there is a wide choice, and many private rooms.

Faro

Faro, the Algarve's capital, is well worth at least a day trip. Its jumbled streets spread out from a small MARINA just along from the railway station. Faro has an empty old CATHEDRAL just opposite the BISHOP'S PALACE. Nearby is an ARCHAEOLOGICAL MUSEUM, the better of a couple of modest museums in town. Try and get to the CARMELITE CHURCH at Largo do Carmo, near the main post office as the church has a spectacular gilt interior, and a bizarre CHAPEL OF BONES behind it. The chapel was built by an over-zealous bishop in the last century using the skulls and bones of over 1,200 monks. Faro is your best bet for accommodation in the Algarve if you insist on arriving mid-summer. Room prices are over-inflated but you may find something away from the smart shopping centre part of town – aimed very much at the British tourist with lots of cash. Try PENSÃO RESIDENCIAL MARIM on Rua Gonçalo Barreto (Tel. 089–240–63). The TOURIST OFFICE, open daily 9 a.m.–8 p.m. in the summer, is on Rua da Misericórdia but don't expect much help in finding cheap accommodation.

When crossing from Portugal to Spain there is no rail connection between the border and Huelva. Take the train to the border, then the ferry at Villa Real de San Antonio, then walk into town (15 minutes) where a bus leaves for Huelva where you can again join the train, or stay on the bus to Seville (3 hours).

SAGRES has some excellent beaches, is off the package tour track and popular with backpackers. It is best reached by the frequent buses from Lagos. Private rooms are widely advertised; expect to pay 1200 $–1700 $. The youth hostel is in the FORTRESS (Tel. 82–64129). The main street, Praça da República, is the centre of nightlife and good cheap restaurants.

For a total contrast, head inland for a day. The contrast with the heaving coastal resorts in many of the isolated rural villages is amazing, although you'll need to take the bus or cycle since the railway sticks rigidly to the coast! If you're heading east into Spain, VILA REAL DE SANTO ANTÓNIO sits right on the border and is a pleasant little town for a few hours' stop. Even if you're not heading onward through Spain, day trips from Vila Real across to AYAMONTE take 15 minutes by ferry (every half-hour, costs 70 $) and customs formalities are minimal.

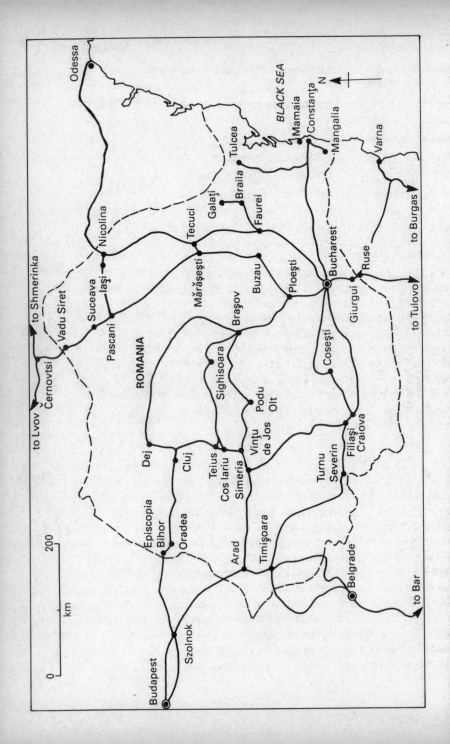

ROMANIA (România)

Entry requirements	Passport and visa (available at border, take dollars)
Population	22,800,000
Capital	Bucharest (pop.: 2,300,000)
Currency	Leu
	£1 = approx. 705 lei
Political system	Republic
Religion	Romanian Orthodox
Language	Romanian (a little French and German spoken)
Public holidays	1, 2 Jan.; 1, 2 May; 1, 25, 26 Dec.
International dialling codes	From UK: 010 + 40 + number
	From USA: 011 + 40 + number
	To UK: 00 + 44 + number
	To USA: 00 + 1 + number

Romania is keen on encouraging and developing tourism, especially after the extremely violent revolution which overthrew the Stalinist Ceauşescu regime in December 1989 and which affected all facets of Romanian life. Although the new Government under the National Salvation Front has yet fully to convince the populace of its democratic intentions, things have become more lax for the eurorailer.

Once a Roman province, the area was overrun by Asian, Slavonic and Turkish tribes giving a real mixture of peoples including many gypsies. Moldavia in the east and Wallachia in the south were united to form Romania in 1859. Transylvania, the area in the central part, is full of forests, its beauty and diversity overshadowed by the legend of Count Dracula. Initially allied to the Germans during the Second World War, the Romanian leadership was overthrown by anti-Fascists in 1944 and, following liberation by the USSR, became a Communist republic in 1946.

From 1965 to the December revolution of 1989 the country was led by Nicolae Ceauşescu and remained firmly Stalinist, and, as Ceauşescu established his cult of personality, became one of the most repressive countries in Eastern Europe. The secret police, the Securitate, vigorously and brutally enforced the Ceauşescu regime

Additional information on all Eastern European countries contained in the *Eastern Europe* and *Europe – the Grand Tour* factsheets (see p.13).

and were widely feared. There was widespread destruction of rural villages and of historic Bucharest at Ceauşescu's whim to enforce his own policies and ensure central control. Ironically, as Ceauşescu distanced himself from the USSR and embarked upon his own maverick foreign policy, the regime enjoyed some support from the west until glasnost established itself in the USSR.

Chronic economic mismanagement and privation under the Ceauşescu regime have made Romania one of the poorest countries in Europe. The new Government has taken steps to begin the mammoth task of reconstruction. However, food and general shortages may continue and the potential of the market economy has yet to be fully realized.

Although the democratic sentiments of the National Salvation Front have been questioned by many Romanians, the tourist infrastructure is rapidly being expanded and the warmth of the people is entirely genuine. Romania is on the threshold of a new era and remains one of the last European countries where you are less a tourist and more a genuine traveller.

ROMANIAN RAILWAYS
(Căile Ferate Române, CFR)

In recent years Romania has improved its services considerably in response to increased demand. Most trains are still dirty and overcrowded by Western standards, so imagine what they were like before. To travel at reasonable speed and comfort on any of the Rapide (fast) and Accelerate (semi-fast) trains you will have to pay a supplement. To avoid this, you have to travel on the local tren de persoane trains – a fate worse than death. In other words, pay the supplement. Never rely on split-second connections – there are often delays, sometimes running into hours, for example on the Budapest–Bucharest run.

• **Inter-Rail bonuses:** Free entry to the railway museum at Gara de Nord, Bucharest.

TRAIN INFORMATION

English is not widely spoken, so be prepared with a French back-up. If all else fails, try: 'De la ce peron pleacă trenul spre . . . ?' (From which platform does the train to . . . leave?)

• **Reservations:** Compulsory on all trains except the tren de persoane. The best strategy is to reserve your place out as soon as you arrive, especially on crowded routes, such as Bucharest–Constanţa. Reserve your exit seat before entering the country – queues are horrendous.

• **Night travel:** Couchettes and sleepers hardly come up to Western standards and need to be booked well in advance, particularly on the Bucharest–Budapest run. Kick up a fuss if officials demand additional 'reservations' once you're aboard. Rates vary according to distance.

• **Eating on trains:** There are restaurants on many long-distance fast trains, and buffets on shorter-distance fast trains.

TOURIST INFORMATION

ONT is the national tourist organization. They have offices in all large towns which give out information and help in finding a room.

• **ISIC bonuses:** Reductions for all international rail travel in Eastern Europe. Also museum entrances reduced with an IUS card. For further information, contact CATT, Str. Oneşti 4–6, Bucharest 1.

• **Money matters:** 1 leu (plural, lei) = 100 bani. (Not used.) Banking hours are Mon.–Sat.: 9 a.m.–12 noon, 1 p.m.–3 p.m. (closed Saturday p.m.).
   The leu has undergone high inflation recently and there is a black market paying over the official rate. Although the risks are also greater because of informers, there is now probably more chance of being duped by a fraudster than being jailed. Cigarettes, especially Kent or Marlboro, are an alternative informal means of exchange and are useful for tipping. There is also a good black market for coffee. Extra hard currency is useful.

• **Post offices, shops and museums:** All vary their times of opening, depending on the district. Most keep to the 9–5 routine six days a week. In Bucharest, some shops open on Sunday mornings.

SLEEPING

One's choices are limited in Romania by the absence of cheap class-three hotels but rooms in private homes may now fill this gap; expect to pay in hard currency. Hostels (căminul de studenți) are run by the student travel service, CATT, and give preference to large groups when they open during July and August. If you're lucky and make the effort to get to the hostel direct, you will find it inexpensive, although prices have recently shot up. Most euro-railers camp and accept the poor facilities, or pay for a class-two hotel which can be anything up to 1,600 lei for a double room. All hotel bills/campsites must be paid for in hard currency, and receipts must often be produced from where you changed your money: you may have great difficulty if you have changed unofficially.

EATING AND NIGHTLIFE

Eating is more expensive than elsewhere in Eastern Europe, and the food is generally of low quality, as is the beer. Don't expect to be able to put a picnic lunch together from a supermarket unless you happen to like jam, which is colossally oversupplied. Romania's nightlife is not up to Hungary's standards, but after a few glasses of țuică, the local plum spirit, you'll never know the difference.

Bucharest (București)

The journey here on the dismal trains is not one of Europe's best and you'll probably wish you hadn't bothered halfway through the night, but take heart: Bucharest is known as the 'Paris of Eastern Europe', though considering the lack of nightlife and scarcity of actual 'sights', this is a bit over the top, as much of historic Bucharest disappeared under Ceaușescu's bulldozers. The atmos-phere following the democratization of Romania is exciting, however, as the Romanians exercise their newly found freedoms.

STATION FACILITIES

There are four train stations, Gara de Nord, Băneasa, Obor and Basarab. Gara de Nord is the biggest station and is used most by eurorailers. Beware of beggars and conmen here.

GARA DE NORD

Train information	24 hours (Tel. 052)
Reservations	24 hours
Tourist information	See below
Foreign exchange	8 a.m.–6 p.m.
Left-luggage lockers/store	24 hours
Café, Restaurant	6 a.m.–12 midnight
Waiting room	24 hours
Post office	24 hours

Daily trains to: Athens, Cluj, Belgrade, Berlin, Basel, Budapest, Munich, Paris, London, Prague, Sofia, Warsaw, Vienna, Zürich.

TOURIST INFORMATION

The station office is open 7 a.m.–9 p.m. weekdays, 7 a.m.–3 p.m. weekends. The main tourist office is at Blvd Magheru 7 (take tram 87 from the station to Piaţa Romană), open Mon.–Sat.: 8 a.m.–8 p.m., Sun.: 8 a.m.–2 p.m., info only 8 a.m.–4.30 p.m. Mon.–Fri. Don't be surprised if there are no street maps available – if this is so, the main tourist office has one on its wall which you can consult, or take yourself off to Hotel Griviţei on Calea Griviţei 130 near the station for maps at 7 lei. You can change money at all offices. CATT, the youth tourist service that deals with groups (the whole of Romanian tourism centres on groups), is at Strada Oneşti 4–6. Left-luggage is only for Romanians – foreigners have to use the 'Hand Luggage' office near Platform 13. The CFR offices are at Brezoianu Street 10, in the Tarom Building, and on Calea Griviţei, open Mon.–Fri.: 7.30 a.m.–6 p.m., Sat.: 7.30 a.m.–12 noon.

• **Addresses:**
POST OFFICE: Str. Matei Millo 10, off Calea Victoriei, open 7 a.m.–midnight daily.
UK EMBASSY: Str. Jules Michelet 24 (Tel. 111634).
US EMBASSY: Tudor Arghezi 7–9 (Tel. 124040).
CANADIAN EMBASSY: Nicolae Iorga 36 (Tel. 506330).
24-HOUR CHEMIST: Blvd Magheru 18. Also at Gara de Nord.
PHONE CODE: 0.

• **Getting about:** Buses, trolley-buses and trams are cheap, and tickets can be bought from all kiosks. Taxis too are a bargain. A metro system is still being built in Bucharest, with three lines having been completed. This merely adds to the chaos as some roads have been closed and many tram routes have been cancelled. Beware of pickpockets, especially on buses which are chronically over-crowded.

SEEING

Modern Bucharest is hard on the eye, so ignore the new and concentrate on the old. The name Bucharest was given to this town in 1459 by none other than Dracula, a local lad, known here as Vlad the Impaler. By far the most pleasant day's sightseeing is spent out on the HERĂSTRĂU PARK where the VILLAGE MUSEUM is, along with many bars. This collection of peasant houses gathered from all over the country is open 9 a.m.–6 p.m. (5 p.m. Monday). Parks and museums are Bucharest's main assets. LIBERTY PARK, the STUDENT PARK on Lacul Tei, or the central CIŞMIGIU PARK are great meeting places and the places to head for to meet young Romanians. Go to Piaţa Unirii for the bustling market where Romania's gypsies sell their wares. As far as museums go, out of the forty or so to choose from, I'd recommend the HISTORY MUSEUM; the former royal palace, today the NATIONAL ART MUSEUM; and the GEORGE ENESCO MUSEUM. For an insight into turbulent recent history visit the TV station (bus 131 from Piaţa Aviatoriler) and observe the bullet-ridden buildings where the opposing factions of the 1989 revolution battled for control of the media. Also view the Victory of Socialism Boulevard to the monumental HOUSE OF THE REPUBLIC constructed by Ceauşescu for his own purposes, and bear in mind that over one-fifth of Bucharest was destroyed in their construction. Take the Metro to the Piatza Uniiri stop.

SLEEPING

The ONT office (see above) may arrange rooms in private homes or you may be approached directly at the station which will usually be cheaper. For a bed in a student hostel, go to ONT or CATT and ask them for addresses as these change yearly. Camping is out at Camping Băneasa (Tel. 794525) and not very appealing. It is reached by taking bus 205 from Gara de Nord to its terminus at Plata Presei Libere, then bus 148. The site is hidden in the trees, has poor facilities and is very expensive. Grade-two hotels are your best bet in Bucharest. Get a list from ONT and if you're told they're all full, ignore it and go along to the hotels regardless and ask at reception. There are quite a few near the Gara de Nord, charging about 880–1,020 lei single, and 1,400–1,760 lei for a double. Try Hotel Dunărea, Calea Griviţei 140 (Tel. 173220); Hotel Bucegi, Strada Witing 2 (Tel. 159350); Hotel Cişmigiu, Blvd M. Kogălniceanu 18 (Tel. 147410).

EATING AND NIGHTLIFE

The twenty-four-hour stand-up Buffet Expres are the cheapest form of eats, but a lot of the food is fairly revolting and high in stodge content. For quick self-service snacks you could also try the self-service restaurants at the Dorobanţi or Lido Hotels. For a pizza joint, Salon Spaniol at Calea Vitorei 116 is favoured by students but closes at 6 p.m. Traditional Romanian cuisine can be found at Hanul Manuc at Strada Iuliu Maniu 62, a bar/restaurant in an attractive setting. Good food and authentic gypsy music can be found at La Doi Coçosi at Şoseaua Străuleşti 6. Next to the History Museum at Strada Stavropoleos 5 is Caru cu Bere which does some fine meals and has a good selection of beers.

As far as nightlife goes, don't build your hopes up as it's a bit of a non-event and the streets are darker than you might be used to. ONT will tell you what's on in town, but usually the choice is between the Circus at Aleea Circului, the cinema or the theatre. The University Student Club is an alternative on Saturdays where you can meet young Romanians, a surprising number of whom speak English. It's on Calea Plevnei 61 (Metro–Eroiler) and you need your ISIC/IUS. If you are a student and have the advance approval of the Institute of Architecture you can gain entrance to the Architects Club on Strada Academiei 2–4 (near the Intercontinental Hotel). The Club is popular with the locals and the entertainment varies from disco and jazz to theatre and film. The Institute is near the Club.

• **Excursions:** SNAGOV, 25 miles to the north, is well worth a day trip. The lake here is a great place for swimming and boating during the summer. Take a boat to the island in the middle of the lake, to visit the sixteenth-century MONASTERY where the infamous Vlad the Impaler (Dracula to some) has his final resting place. No women are permitted to enter the monastery.

Transylvania

This picturesque region, home of the notorious Count Dracula, is Romania's most scenic. The Transylvanian Alps and the small peasant villages with their rich, active folklore make travelling here interesting and rewarding. The best towns to base yourself in are Braşov or Sighişoara.

BRAŞOV, about 2½ hours from Bucharest, is on the edge of the Carpathian Mountains and set among the Transylvanian Alps. In its old town are the BLACK CHURCH and the TOWN HALL – both fourteenth-century, but the main attractions are outside the town. The Disneyesque CASTLE OF BRAN, Dracula's summer house, is reached by bus 12 to the bus station, then bus 23 (runs Mon.–Sat. only) to the castle, and is open from 9 a.m.–6 p.m. (closed Monday). Postăvarul, 9 Eroilor Blvd (Tel. 42840), will give you details of the best excursions. It is about 2 km from the train station and reached on bus 4. CATT in Strasma Armata Roşie will hand you this year's list of student hostels (bus 4 from station). Just past the Hotel Carpati is the Braşov University Rector's Office, which will find you a cheap room on production of a student card (open Mon.–Fri.: 10 a.m.–5 p.m.). Camping Zimbrul is on the road to the mountain resort of Poiana–Braşov. Take bus 4 to Parc Central, then bus 20. Braşov saw heavy fighting in the revolution of December 1989 and many buildings, especially on Piaţa Teatrului, are pock-marked by bullets, save the Communist Party building which remained oddly unscathed.

SIGHISOARA, 2¼ hours away from Braşov, is a beautiful medieval town, as yet unspoilt by tourism. This is an ideal spot to break the long haul from Bucharest to Budapest (nearly 14 hours), and it offers more in the way of sights than Braşov. The OLD WALLED TOWN is well preserved and among its sights are the CLOCK TOWER, the TOWN MUSEUM (closed Monday), the GUILD TOWERS, and the BERGKIRCHE, a church with good views over the town. The CHURCH

OF THE MONASTERY off Clock Tower Square is the town's oldest building and not far from here is Dracula's father's house. ONT is across from the main thoroughfare of Str. Ch. Gheorghiu-Dej. It's open Mon.–Sat.: 8 a.m.–1 p.m., 2 p.m.–8 p.m., Sun.: 8 a.m.–11 a.m. Get your map here. You've a choice of camping at Campground Hula Danes (bus direction 'Medias') about 2½ miles from town, or paying up for Hotel Steaua, Strada Ch. Gheorghiu-Dej (Tel. 950–71930). To meet the locals and have a drink, try the beer hall at 34 Piata Lenin.

The FĂGĂRAS MOUNTAINS of the Carpathian Range make a great place to go hiking amongst the 6,000-foot peaks and 70 lakes. GARA SEBEŞ OLT on the main line from Braşov is a good place to start. There are mountain huts (Cabanas) spread throughout the region high up on the slopes. Get a map ahead of time in Braşov and reserve Cabana beds through the tourist office there. Make sure to bring a lot of food and a good pair of shoes.

Moldavia

This region of Europe is known for beautiful painted mountain monasteries of northern Bucovina, small rural villages and its completely unspoilt lifestyle, where locals still wear national costume and not a word of English seems to be spoken. The trains are pitifully slow and you can't afford to be in a rush. Ask at Bucharest for times and routes – mostly you have to change to the smaller lines at Cluj.

SUCEAVA is the capital of Moldavia and the best starting point for a tour of the monasteries. The FOLK ART MUSEUM is a worthwhile visit. It's in the sixteenth-century 'Princely Inn' at Strada Ciprian Porumbescu 5 and in only an hour or two fills you in on the culture of the people that surround you. The ONT office is at Nicolae Bălcescu 2 (open Mon.–Sat.: 8 a.m.–8 p.m., Sun.: 9 a.m.–12 noon), and they'll supply you with bus schedules and details on the monasteries.

THE MONASTERIES: VORONET is the most famous and ancient of the monasteries, dating back to 1488. It's known as the 'Sistine Chapel of the East', owing to its amazing frescoes and unique shade of blue. 'The Last Judgement' is the most amazing fresco in Moldavia, showing a whole panoply of figures and scenes from the Bible. HUMOR, a nearby village, has a monastery obviously built by misogynists (the devil is portrayed as a woman in the frescoes), and from here you can set off for SUCEVIŢA MONASTERY. This one is absolutely covered in fascinating frescoes inside and out, from portraits of Plato to the 'Arabian Nights'. There is also a small museum here. The actual village of Suceviţa has got to be the most charming in Romania. There is a wonderful view over the monastery from the hill opposite and you can camp at the bottom of the hill.

To experience religious life visit the PUTNA MONASTERY where you will rub shoulders with chanting monks. There is no shortage of accommodation here with a large hotel, campsite and bungalows.

The Black Sea Coast

Romania's coastline starts at the Danube delta on the Russian frontier and stretches south for about 150 miles to the Bulgarian border. The resorts are dominated by huge hotels, and the main town on the coast is the ancient port of CONSTANŢA. The city is a curious mixture of Roman, Greek and Eastern Byzantine (there's even a mosque and minaret here). See the remains of the ROMAN DOCKS with its huge piece of preserved mosaic, the ARCHAEOLOGI-CAL MUSEUM and the ROMANIAN NAVAL MUSEUM. Outside the Archaeological Museum is a statue of the city's most famous resident, the poet OVID. Part of the beach is sheltered by a tree-and-hedge wind-break; however, you may find that Constanţa gets busier than the other resorts in summer, so use your rail ticket to the full and head off for somewhere smaller down the line. Camping at Constanţa is at Mamaia. Take trolley-bus 150 from the station, and it is a two-minute walk to the site, situated by the sea and usually very crowded in summer. The resorts of Mamaia, Efone Nord, Efone Sud, Neptun, Saturn and Mangalia are all good places to soak up the sun in more isolated surroundings.

TULCEA is the gateway to the Danube delta. Nature lovers should take a boat trip to see the wildlife in this unique delta; over 300 species of birds, 60 species of fish and well over 1,000 species of plants are to be found in the shelter of this protected area. Excursions are organized by ONT in the Hotel Delta, ten minutes' walk down the quay from the station at Strada Isaccea 2 (Tel. 14720). Hotel Egreta is the cheaper hotel at Strada Păcii (Tel. 17103). The nearest camping site is at Maliuc (two hours by ferry) and is infested with mosquitoes.

Western Romania

All trains east to Romania from Hungary and Yugoslavia pass through this area, once known as THE BANAT when it formed part of the great Habsburg Empire. The land is mostly flat and is dominated by the three cities of Timişoara, Oradea and Arad.

Timişoara

TIMIŞOARA, which played such an important role in the revolution of 1989, is an interesting city whose architecture reflects its population of Hungarians and Serbs (now deported). The Hungarian people of western Romania led the fight against Ceauşescu and so it is no surprise that the December 1989 revolution started here and made the city world famous. The impressive DICASTERIAL PALACE on str. Ceahlău is an indication of the great opulence of the old Habsburg rulers. Around the picturesque square PIAŢA UNIRII is a baroque CATHOLIC CATHEDRAL and a SERBIAN CATHEDRAL, as well as the MUSEUM OF FINE ARTS. The ETHNOGRAPHIC MUSEUM at str. Popa Şapcă is in the remains of the old Magyar fort around which the city grew. Take a walk along the BEGA CANAL through a whole series of parks and visit the THERMAL BATHS on Bulevard Vasile Parvan. For a bit of fun go to the PUPPET THEATRE at Piata Furtuna. The tourist office and CFR international booking office are both at 6 B-dul Republicii. The cheapest place to stay is the campground in the Pădurea Forest (tram 1) where there are also bungalows. You could also try to get a place in the dormitories from CATT, but these are often full with groups.

Arad

ARAD is dominated by a huge star-shaped eighteenth-century CITADEL, around which the River Mureş flows through a park. The HISTORY MUSEUM (closed Mondays) is housed in the PALACE OF CULTURE on Piata George Tonescu and has displays on the complex history of the whole area. The Philharmonic Orchestra is also located here. Bulevard Republicii is the main street and here you will find the tourist office at number 72 just across from the neoclassical TOWN HALL. There is also a tourist office geared towards foreigners next door in the Hotel Astoria at number 89 (Tel. 16650). For accommodation the youth hostel organization CATT is at 16 Piata Avram Iancu. To get to the Subcetate campsite follow the river south of the Citadel, about a mile or so from the bridge near the Park Hotel.

There are a whole series of fairs and gatherings in the villages around Arad well worth day visits, especially the 'Kiss Fair' in HĂLMAGIU in March, as well as festivals in PÎNCOTA (February), BÎRSA (April), SÎNTANA (May) and AVRAM IANCU (June). Ask at the tourist office for exact dates.

Oradea

ORADEA is a common stopping-off point on journeys from Budapest to Bucharest although probably does not warrant any more than a day's visit. Oradea has its own CITADEL and the largest baroque CATHOLIC CATHEDRAL in Romania. Nearby is the grand BISHOP'S PALACE which was based on the Belvedere Palace in Vienna and is now a large MUSEUM (open Tues.–Sun.: 10 a.m.–6 p.m.) which has displays on the history and people of the Crişana region. Tourist information is on the main shopping street at 4 Piata Republicii and the CFR Railway office is at number 2. Cheap places to stay are hard to come by so you should try the campground five miles south east of Oradea at Băile Felix (tram 4 or 5), near the famous thermal baths, or else contact CATT at 9 str. Vulcan. There are many

fascinating caves in the area; try to visit the VADU CRIŞULUI CAVE
(take a slow train east from Oradea) which has tours 9 a.m.–6 p.m.
each day.

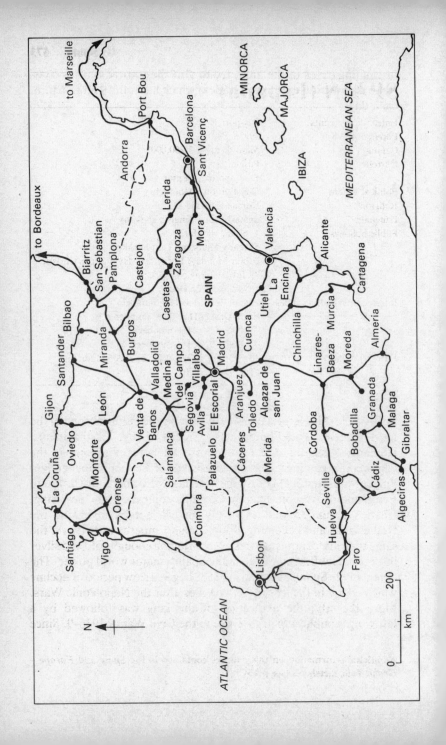

SPAIN (España)

Entry requirements	Passport
Population	39,000,000
Capital	Madrid (pop.: 3,250,000)
Currency	Peseta
	£1 = approx. 178ptas.
Political system	Constitutional Monarchy
Religion	Roman Catholic
Language	Spanish (some English spoken)
Public holidays	1, 6 Jan.; 19 Mar.;
	Maundy Thursday; Good Friday;
	Easter Monday; 1 May; 23 May; Corpus Christi;
	29 July; 15 Aug.; 12 Oct.;
	1 Nov.; 6, 8, 25 Dec.
International dialling codes	From UK: 010 + 34 + number
	From USA: 011 + 34 + number
	To UK: 07 + 44 + number
	To USA: 07 + 1 + number
Eurotrain office	Jose Ortega y Gasset 71, E–28006 Madrid
	(Tel. 91–4011300)

Spain is the third largest country in Europe and culturally one of the most diverse. The Phoenicians, Greeks, Celts, Carthaginians, Romans, Visigoths and Moors were all here. Throughout the Christian reconquest, Spain consisted of several independent kingdoms united in 1479 by the marriage of Isabella of Castile to Ferdinand of Aragon. Shortly after this unification, the new king, Charles I, landed well and truly on his feet by inheriting the Netherlands and becoming Holy Roman Emperor in 1519. At the same time his 'conquistadores' were bringing enough gold and silver back from South America to make Spain a major world power. The defeat of the Spanish Armada in 1588 began a slow period of decline which ended in the loss of her colonies after the Napoleonic Wars. More recently, the abdication of the king was followed by a left-wing republic which gave rise to the Civil War of 1936–9. Since

Additional information on this country contained in the *Spain* and *Europe – Grand Tour* factsheets (see p.13).

the death of the dictator Franco in 1975, King Juan Carlos has steered Spain towards democracy and since 1986 Spain has been a member of the EC.

SPANISH NATIONAL RAILWAYS
(Red Nacional de los Ferrocarriles Españoles, RENFE)

The last year or two has seen significant improvements on RENFE. Supplements required on all fast trains: from Talgos to the less steep Rápido supplement. RENFE are spending a lot of money ordering 155 m.p.h. trains to develop the Madrid–Seville line and cut the travel time from six hours to three. You often have to change trains at the Spanish border, so don't go for a sleeper from France unless you're travelling on a Talgo which adjusts its wheels to the broader gauge. Check carefully in the timetable to see if you will have to change. The 'Automotor' trains which cover the medium-haul routes at semi-fast speeds are both comfortable and air-conditioned, and are a better bet than non-air-conditioned expresses. It's safe to say that all non-supplement trains are pretty slow and crowded, but they'll get you there in the end. The Tranvias and Correos (locals) crawl along and are only for the stalwart. Some routes are now impossible without supplements being paid, Algeciras–Madrid being an example. The RENFE computer is linked to BR, so you can book ahead before you leave, either at Victoria Station or through appointed BR travel agents.

● **Non-RENFE lines:** A few lines in Spain are not run by RENFE and do not accept rail passes. They are the narrow-gauge lines Hendaye to Gijon, Gijon to Ferrol, Palma to Inca, Valencia to Gandia and Barcelona to Montserrat.

TRAIN INFORMATION

English is not always spoken, so it pays to have a Spanish back-up prepared. Expect long queues. At present, due to the ETA terrorist attacks, left-luggage facilities at Spanish stations are sometimes withdrawn, or subject to security checks such as X-ray examination. There are normally alternative non-official facilities though; usually in the form of some little fellow posted by the station door or in the nearest café who'll guard your luggage for the same hours at the same fee. If in doubt ask at the station.

• **Reservations:** If you can face the queues it's always advisable to reserve a seat in Spain. Unfortunately, if you decide not to reserve there's often no way of telling if someone else has, as reserved seats are not always indicated. On many occasions you settle down in an apparently empty compartment, only to be thrown out just when you thought you were safe. *Reservations are obligatory on all expresses.*

• **Night travel:** Spanish couchettes sleep six and are sometimes very old and dirty – more often than not you are better off on the floor. Sleepers are cheap, however, so all's not lost. For a journey under 550 km, a berth in a tourist-class sleeper will cost about 1,800 ptas.

• **Scenic tips:** In Spain, it's normally effort enough to get from A to B without thinking about scenic routes. Entering from France, the most scenic route is from Toulouse over the Pyrenees, arriving at Barcelona, although if you return to France by this route you can expect to be searched thoroughly, especially if travelling from Barcelona. The main line from here on to Madrid takes in much that is typically Spanish without you having to go out of your way. If it's mountains you're after, then it's best to head towards the north-west (León-Túy) or the south (Córdoba–Málaga, Granada–Almería).

• **Rover tickets:** In 1987, RENFE introduced their first rover ticket, the Tarjeta Turistica, which allows unrestricted travel within the country and covers all supplements except sleepers and seat reservations. Prices range from £60 for a second-class ticket valid for 8 days to £150 for first class valid for 22 days. Children between 4 and 12 pay half the appropriate adult fare. The ticket can be bought by anyone living outside Spain and can be used at any time of the year. A Flexi Card allows 4 days travel in 15 days and costs about £45 second class. Also, the Chequetren is available for individuals or families and gives a discount of 15 per cent when tickets or services to the value of either 25,000 ptas. or 35,000 ptas. are bought in advance for 21,000 and 30,000 ptas. respectively. There is a 50 per cent discount for families of at least three people travelling on journeys of more than 100 km. The first person pays the full fare while the rest pay only half fare. Children aged between 4 and 12 pay only 25 per cent of the full fare. This discount also applies to supplements. RENFE operates a discount for all standard fares on about 300 days per year called Blue Days (*dias azules*) when you can expect a further 25 per cent or so reduction (50 per cent with a RENFE Youth Pass). The number of Blue Days varies according to the time of year with all of February included but only 16 days in June. There is also a straight 20 per cent reduction for individuals taking return journeys of more than 100 km, which is applicable to all types of train and all classes. At the top end of the market there is the Al Andalus Express (a sort of Spanish Orient Express), which runs from Seville to Málaga. Prices are expensive, so it's beyond the means of most eurorailers. For further information contact Marsans Travel Ltd, 7A Henrietta Place, London W1M 9AG (Tel. 071–493 4934).

TOURIST INFORMATION

The government-run tourist office has branches in all major towns and at many stations. They have an excellent collection of free handouts on all the regions of Spain. In addition, there are local city tourist offices which supply maps and more detailed information.

• **ISIC bonuses:** Reduced entrance to the Prado and Bellas Artes museums. For further information, contact Viajes TIVE, Fernando el Católico 88, Madrid.

• **Money matters:** 1 peseta (pta.) = 100 centimos (c).
Banking hours are generally Mon.–Fri.: 8.30 a.m.–1.30/2 p.m., Sat.: 8.30 a.m.–1 p.m. From June–Sept. banks may be closed on Saturdays. Shop about, as there's no set rate of exchange, and commission rates are high. The 'La Caixa' bank rate is very poor.

• **Post offices:** Open Mon.–Sat.: 9 a.m.–2 p.m. and often later in larger cities. 'Lista de Correos' = poste restante.

• **Shops:** Open Mon.–Sat.: 9 a.m.–1.30 p.m., 5 p.m.–7.30/8 p.m. (closed Saturday p.m.), but the department stores in large provincial capitals may be open from 10 a.m.–8 p.m.

• **Museums:** Vary considerably; most open 10 a.m. and shut again for lunch 12.30/1 p.m., opening again at 4 p.m. till 7 p.m.

SLEEPING

Every large town in Spain has a Brujula office to help find rooms for a small fee. In addition the tourist information office issues lists to help freelancers. You shouldn't have any problems as there's always plenty of cheap accommodation around the stations, all of which is inspected and graded by the government. By law, prices should be shown behind the door of each room. During the summer it's legal for prices to be increased by about 15 per cent, so don't get too excited until you've worked it out. Hotels start at about 1,200 ptas. for a single and prices are nearly always charged by the room, not per person. Pensiones and Hostales are officially graded (Hs = hostal, HsR = hostal residencia, P = pensión, CH = casa de huéspedes and, cheapest of all, F = fonda). For the bare necessities, expect to pay about 900 ptas. per person. Always check to see if breakfast is included in the price; don't assume the management will tell you. Hot showers are another extra which can cost up to 250 ptas. If you think you're being done, the mere mention of 'libro de reclamaciones' (complaints book) should sort out your problems. To use any of Spain's seventy youth hostels, you'll need an IYHF card. At 500–650 ptas. a night, they are easily the cheapest accommodation you're likely to find. If you are thinking about camping, go to ANCE, Principe De Vergara 85, 2° Ocha, 28006 Madrid; they will give you a map and a rundown on official campsites. Prices start at about 275 ptas. per person per night. Sleeping on the beaches is another alternative, but don't make it too obvious or you'll attract trouble from the police or worse.

EATING AND NIGHTLIFE

Spain offers some of the most affordable restaurants in Europe. Give your stomach a chance to adapt to the excess of olive oil, and don't have too much seafood to start with. Once you've adapted to local conditions, there's an endless variety of regional specialities to sample, all at reasonable prices. Go for the tourist or house menu where possible, as it's usually a safe bet and works out a lot cheaper than ordering individual dishes. Expect to pay anything from 600 to 1,300 ptas. for your evening meal and remember that the Spaniards don't eat until at least 9 p.m.–10 p.m. If there's no fixed tourist menu, ask if they do combinados – an all-in feast on one plate which often includes something to drink as well. For those low in funds, try tapas – delicious and varied titbits that are sometimes free – available at most bars. Local wine is cheap at about 180 ptas. a bottle, and is a much better buy than beer, though it's often rough and tastes like weak sherry. Wine cellars and bars are cheaper and have more local colour than the discos which make their living by fleecing tourists at the resorts.

The bullfighting season runs from March to October and is recommended only for the bloodthirsty. Anyone who wants to see one, but is put off by the violence, should head for Portugal.

Madrid

Although Madrid was the 1992 Cultural Capital of Europe, it is not one of Europe's most attractive capitals and is certainly not to everyone's taste. The old town has charm, the nightlife is amongst the hottest in Europe and the Prado is definitely one of the world's great art galleries, but the sprawling concrete districts and lack of major sights entice one to leave Madrid in favour of Toledo or Seville. Still, sleeping and eating aren't a problem and many argue that Madrid is worth the trip for the tapas and nightlife alone.

STATION FACILITIES

Madrid has three stations: Chamartín, serving the north-east, France and eastern Spain; Atocha, serving Portugal and the south of Spain; and Norte (also called Principe Pio) handling what's left. Some trains, e.g. the Paris–Algeciras Express, pass through more than one of them. There are interconnecting trains every 20 minutes, and also an underground service. Because of bomb scares, the left-luggage lockers can only be used after your kit has been X-rayed. This is tough luck at Chamartín, but at Atocha head for some of the bars behind the station (round Calle de Rafael de Riego), and deposit your rucksack for 150 ptas. There is tourist information at Chamartín. (We give no information on the Norte Station as it is little used by eurorailers.) Trains may be diverted from Atocha to Chamartín due to building work – check locally and in Thomas Cook's timetable.

	CHAMARTÍN	ATOCHA
Train information	7 a.m.–10 p.m. (Tel. 530 0202)	7 a.m.–10 p.m.
Reservations	8 a.m.–9 p.m.	9 a.m.–9 p.m.
Hotel reservations	9 a.m.–11 p.m.	–
Foreign exchange	7 a.m.–10 p.m.	8.30 a.m.–9.30 p.m.
Restaurant, Cafeteria	12 noon–4 p.m. 7 p.m.–12 midnight	7 a.m.–12 midnight
Shops	7 a.m.–11 p.m.	–
Waiting room	All hours	All hours
Tourist information	Mon.–Fri.: 8 a.m.–8 p.m. Sat.: 9 a.m.–1 p.m.	–
Post office	Mon.–Fri.: 9 a.m.– 2 p.m., 5 p.m.–10 p.m. Sat.: 9 a.m.–2 p.m.	Mon.–Sat.: 9 a.m.–2 p.m. 7 p.m.–10.30 p.m.
Station shuts	12 midnight–5 a.m.	12 midnight–5 a.m.

Daily trains to: Bilbao, Paris, Zaragoza, Barcelona, Valencia, Alicante, Granada, Córdoba, Seville, Lisbon.

TOURIST INFORMATION

The main national office is at Maria de Molina 50, and there's another one at Plaza de España which is better. Both are open Mon.–Fri.: 9 a.m.–7 p.m., Sat.: 9.30 a.m.–1.30 p.m. The municipal office is at Plaza Mayor 3, open 10 a.m.–2 p.m., 4 p.m.–7 p.m., Saturday 10 a.m.–2 p.m.; closed Sunday; and the provincial office is at Duque de Medinaceli 2. Pick up a free map and information leaflets here including a very good list of pensions.

● **Addresses:**

POST OFFICE: Palácio de Comunicaciones, Plaza de Cibeles. Open Mon.–Fri.: 9 a.m.–10 p.m. and Sat.: 9 a.m.–8 p.m., Sun.: 10 a.m.–1 p.m. Poste restante and telegraphs here.

AMEX: Plaza de las Cortes 2 (Tel. 4295775). Open Mon.–Fri.: 9 a.m.–5.30 p.m., Sat.: 9 a.m.–12 noon.
UK EMBASSY: Fernando el Católico 16 (Tel. 3190200).
US EMBASSY: Serrano 75 (Tel. 5763400).
CANADIAN EMBASSY: Núñez de Balboa 35 (Tel. 4314300).
AUSTRALIAN EMBASSY: Paseo de la Castellana 143 (Tel. 2798501).
EUROTRAIN: José Ortega y Gasset 71 (Tel. 4011300).
PHONE CODE: 91.

• **Getting about:** For price and speed, the metro is the best means of getting about. It runs till 1.30 a.m. and has nine lines. Buy tickets from machines (125 ptas. per trip, 490 ptas. for ten) or kiosks and hang on to your ticket till you've finished the journey. Buses are pretty efficient, microbuses are the more luxurious versions of the same theme and both cost the same as the metro.

SEEING

The PRADO MUSEUM is the reason why thousands of art-lovers descend on this city each summer. There are over 3,000 master-pieces here, mainly collected by the Spanish royal family in the seventeenth and eighteenth centuries. The old Spanish masters (El Greco, Goya, etc.) are well represented, and there's a fair number of Flemish works collected by the Habsburg kings of the sixteenth century. There's such a glut of genius here, you'll need to pay two or three visits at least. The entrance is reasonable at 400 ptas., but ISIC holders are free. Near the exit is a shop selling very reasonably priced reproductions, postcards and books. The Prado is open daily, except Mondays, May–October, Tues.–Sat.: 9 a.m.–7 p.m., Sun.: 9 a.m.–2 p.m., November–April, Tues.–Sat.: 10 a.m.–5 p.m., Sun.: 10 a.m.–2 p.m. Your ticket to the Prado also admits you to the CASÓN DEL BUEN RETIRO, near Retiro Park, to see Picasso's famous painting 'Guernica'. Open Tues.–Sat.: 9 a.m.–6.45 p.m., Sun.: 9 a.m.–1.45 p.m. The ROYAL PALACE is the only other 'must' in Madrid. A 45-minute guided tour will take you through the various apartments and the Royal Armoury, which is considered one of the world's best collections of medieval weapons. The palace gardens, especially the CAMPO DEL MORO, are particularly fine and make good venues for regal picnic lunches. Entrance costs 500 ptas., 350 ptas. on ISIC. The BOTANIC GARDENS, near the Prado, is also a nice place to have a quiet picnic. Entrance costs 50 ptas.

Parks are, in fact, Madrid's speciality, very busy and colourful on Sundays. The RETIRO PARK in the city centre is huge and, apart from its rowing lake, theatre, fountains and statues, the CRYSTAL PALACE of the Bourbon kings is here. North-west of the palace is another park on ten times the scale of the Retiro, which the young Spaniards tend to patronize at weekends: the CASA DE CAMPO has among its attractions a zoo, amusement park, swimming pool and outdoor theatre.

OLD MADRID lies between PUERTA DEL SOL (known as the centre of Spain) and the Crystal Palace; notice the descriptive pictures above the street signs to help the illiterate seventeenth-century locals. These narrow winding streets are the most colourful and interesting in Madrid. If you're feeling particularly penitent you can even buy a hair shirt here. The taverns in the alleys off the PLAZA MAYOR are good starting places for your evening's pub crawl, Madrid-style. On Sunday mornings there's a flea market (the Rastro) off the southern corner of the square where gypsies often congregate and put on street shows.

SLEEPING

Cheap beds aren't a problem here, even in summer. The tourist offices will advise you on accommodation, but won't arrange it for you; Brujula, a private placing agency, will do this for a small fee. They have kiosks at the stations, but you shouldn't even need them as there are hundreds of suitable places, many near the centrally located Atocha Station, in streets like Calle Toledo. Try the Hotel Residencia Finistere at No. 113, where you can expect to pay around 2,500 ptas. for a double with a shower. If you're really cutting corners and don't mind other people's nocturnal 'goings-on', or the odd bed-bug, the area south of Puerta del Sol will produce some very cheap (750–1,500 ptas.) casas de huéspedes. The university let out rooms to those wanting to stay five or more days, and there are two youth hostels which aren't too far away from the centre. One's at Calle Santa Cruz de Marcenado 28 (Tel. 247 4532) and the other's at Casa de Campo (Tel. 463 5699) in the park there. You need IYHF membership, and a bed will cost about 500 ptas. Ask at Turismo for the camping leaflet, and don't risk the parks unless you're desperate.

The street with more cheap beds than anywhere else is Gran Vía in central Madrid. Hostal Alcázar-Regis, on the 5th floor of No. 61 (Tel. 247 3549), is good value for what you get; La Costa Verde (9th floor) is cheaper, and Buenos Aires (Tel. 247 8800) on the 2nd floor have singles for around 1,900 ptas. and doubles for 2,700 ptas. Hostal Amayo (Tel. 222 2151) on the 1st floor of No. 12 and at No. 38, Hostal California (Tel. 222 4703) and Don José (Tel. 232 1385) have good rooms, and Hostal Margarita at No. 50 (Tel. 247 3549) is reasonable with singles from 2,200 ptas. Camping Madrid (Tel. 2022835) is reasonable, but a long way out. Take the metro to Plaza de Castilla, then bus 129.

EATING AND NIGHTLIFE

Tapas (the tasty snacks served in infinite varieties to accompany your drink) are at their best in Madrid. Most Madrileños spend between 6 p.m. and 10 p.m. on the tapas circuit in either Pasage de Matheu or the area round Plaza Mayor. Mussels, mushrooms, omelettes and filled rolls are some of the savouries with which to bridge the gap till dinner, washed down with sangría or wine. The main meal of the day is eaten at lunchtime (2 p.m.–4 p.m.) and dinner, around 10 p.m., is quite a light affair. Argüelles, on the metro, is the city's main student quarter. Make for this area to eat cheaply and meet the university students. The bars along Calle de la Princesa are a safe bet to make friends, and back in the centre Calle Echegaray and Ventura de la Vega, off Calle San Jerónimo, also have cheap restaurants. Restaurant Copatisan, Calle del Barco 16–18, is very cheap and very good. Closed Aug. For a good paella try Restaurant El Parque, Fernando el Católico 78.

The nightlife starts with the pub crawl and continues in the salas de fiesta (nightclubs), winding up around 3 a.m.–4 a.m. At weekends, things are twice as lively and the discotecas (which are on the expensive side) hold afternoon as well as evening sessions to cope with the insatiable demand ('afternoon' in Spain seems to mean 7 p.m.–10 p.m.), try Archy's at Marquis de Riscal 11. The salas de fiesta shows range from awful cabarets to sex shows.

This list of current events in the 'Guía del Ocio' is all you need. Avoid the heavily advertised flamenco shows, as they're incredibly commercial and plastic, and ask about for the best discos, etc., in the bars along the Aurrera in the Argüelles quarter.

• **Excursions:** Thirty miles from the Norte Station is the huge granite palace of EL ESCORIAL. This was King Philip II's country house and though it took over twenty years to complete, it still looks more like a high-security prison than a palace. The guided tours take you round the museums, library, church, art gallery and royal apartments and cost 500 ptas. (open 10 a.m.–1 p.m., 3 p.m.–7 p.m.). A few miles further on is the VALLE DE LOS CAÍDOS – a memorial to those who died in the Civil War, and where Franco is buried. Or if you just want to cool off, stay in the train to Cercedilla and take the branch line up into the Sierra de Guadarrama Mountains.

ARANJUEZ, en route south to Córdoba or Seville, is worth a stop-off to see the ROYAL PALACE, the SAILOR'S HOUSE, the PRINCE'S GARDEN and the FARMER'S HOUSE. The campsite here, Soto del Castillo, will entice you to stay a night or two as it's about the best one in Spain.

Northern Spain and the Basque Country

This region runs from the foot of the Pyrenees to close to Portugal. It is one of Spain's least touristy areas, and the lush forests, good beaches and historic towns make it worth exploration. The Basques – possibly the oldest ethnic group in Europe – have their own very separate history, culture and language. Since Franco's death, the ETA (Basque Liberation Front) have been increasingly active in their terrorist acts of bombings and murder, and the issue is still anything but settled. There have yet to be any tourist casualties.

San Sebastián

This was, until recent terrorist attacks, one of Spain's major holiday resorts for the rich and famous. Now its position as one of the main Basque cities makes it a slightly less safe bet for a family holiday, but the choice is yours; the odds of anything nasty happening are weighted heavily in your favour and the political graffiti is interesting. It's an attractive place; the beaches are good and it will break up a run from Paris to Madrid nicely.

TOURIST INFORMATION AND ADDRESSES

TOURIST OFFICES: C. Fueros 1, and Reina Regente (ground floor, Victoria Eugenia Theatre), open Mon.–Fri.: 9 a.m.–1.30 p.m., 4 p.m.–7 p.m., Sat.: 9 a.m.–1 p.m.
POST OFFICE: Calle Urdaneta 9.
FIRST AID: Cruz Roja, Calle Matia 7 (Tel. 214600).
PHONE CODE: 943.

SEEING

The SAN TELMO MUSEUM, in a sixteenth-century Renaissance monastery on Calle Coro, will fill you in on the differences between the Basques and the Spanish or French; or visit the AQUARIUM down on the port to see the collection of sea creatures. The fish market is well worth a visit, as is Constitution Square, a former bullring. From the beach you can rent out a boat and go over to the island of SANTA CLARA, or else just laze about on the beaches of LA CONCHA and ONDARRETA. On the coast is the living sculpture 'Bones of the Wind' by Eduardo Chillida.

SLEEPING

During the summer, cheap beds are hard to find. Try the excellent campsite on the Carretera de Monte Igueldo (about five miles from the station – take the Barrio de Igueldo bus from Alameda de Boulevard) or the two youth hostels at Ciudad Deportiva Anoeta (Tel. 452970) and Parque Ulia (Tel. 293751). The best pension deals are at Pensión La Perla, Loyola 10 (Tel. 428123). The cheapest you'll find is Fonda Aruaga at Narrica 3 (Tel. 420681) with singles from 2,000 ptas. It's also possible to sleep on the beach, but more risky.

EATING AND NIGHTLIFE

It's not easy to cut corners in San Sebastián for two reasons: first, there are hardly any places with tourist menus in the eurorailer's budget range; and secondly, the food is so good you won't feel like living off bread, cheese and fruit. This is one Spanish town where the food is consistently good and, of course, the fish dishes are excellent. The city actually has a Gastronomic Academy, and the exclusive and chauvinistic male-only dining clubs frequently sponsor eating contests. There are several bars and restaurants in the central square, Plaza del 18 de Julio, but watch the prices here.

For pre-dinner 'tapas', or 'pinchos' as they're known locally, try the bars along Calle Fermin Calberton and, for dancing, La Piscina, Ondarreta, is meant to be pretty hot. There are festivals all summer, the most interesting being the Basque folklore one, the jazz festival (July) and the international film festival (September). Ask at tourist information for details.

Pamplona

The picturesque old town is well worth a visit at any time of the year but more so from 6–14 July for the Festival de San Fermín, better known as the Running of the Bulls. A favourite of Hemingway, the festival is a week-long spectacle of singing, dancing and most of all drink. It is arguably the best street party in Europe: the whole town is bedecked in red and white and in fiesta mood.

The actual bull run begins at 8 a.m. when a group of bulls pursues crowds of people to the bull-ring. Although it may be tempting to prove your machismo and run with the bulls, bear in mind that it is dangerous (because of the crowd of runners as much as the bulls) and, in the event of injury, your insurance cover will probably be invalid. Anyway, the best part of the fiesta is the exuberant nightlife around Plaza del Castillo and Calle Navarrería.

Tourist information is at C. Duque de Ahumada 3 (Tel. 948–220741), open Mon.–Fri.: 10 a.m.–2 p.m., 4 p.m.–7 p.m.; Sat.: 10 a.m.–2 p.m. They will help with accommodation, but you will have to be extremely fortunate or resourceful to find a bed during the fiesta. Try Fonda La Montañesa, C. San Gregorio (Tel. 948–224380) or Casa Huéspedes Santa Cecelia, C. Navarrería 17 (Tel. 948–222230). The nearest campsite is Camping Ezcaba (Tel.

948–330315) with excellent facilities and a free swimming pool, 7 km away but with bus connections. If you're out of luck do not be tempted to sleep rough in the unsafe Plaza del Castillo but head for the other side of the bull-ring to a park. Showers are available at Calle Eslava 9, open Tue.–Sun.: 7.30 a.m.–9.30 p.m. and are widely used by bedless travellers.

If you can tear yourself away from the festivities the MUSEO DE NAVARRE has some excellent murals. The CATHEDRAL with its beautiful Gothic cloisters, and the CITADEL are also worth a look.

Santander

The port town of Santander is wedged between the Basque and Galician regions in the province of Cantabria. This part of northern Spain is mountainous with a rugged coastline, and contains some of the world's best prehistoric cave art in the ALTAMIRA CAVES.

The beaches at Santander are the main reason to stop off, particularly the ones at EL SARDINERO, COMILLAS and LIENCRES. The area by the harbour is the 'new town' and this is where the restaurants and bars are located. Tourist information is at Jardina de Pereda, open Mon.–Fri.: 9 a.m.–1.30 p.m., 4.30 p.m.–7.30 p.m.; Sat.: 9 a.m.–12 noon (Tel. 42–216120). There are plenty of cheap hostales, or campsites outside the town.

An interesting excursion from Santander is inland to the picturesque village of MEDINA DE POMAR with its fascinating monastery (open 10 a.m.–1.30 p.m.) and collection of churches.

Santiago de Compostela

This is the main town in the beautiful province of Galicia, though if you really wanted to explore the dramatic Atlantic coastline you'd be better staying at La Coruña, on the main line to Madrid. Santiago was a popular place of pilgrimage in the Middle Ages for up to two million Christians a year who made the journey here to

see where the Apostle St James is buried. The CATHEDRAL dominates the town, but it's difficult to isolate other main sights as the
whole inner town is a national monument, and deserving of it. The
cathedral was started in the eleventh century but encompasses
many architectural styles. The student quarter lies between the
cathedral and the university and this is the best area to head for at
night. The tourist office is at Rúa del Villar 43, closed Saturday
p.m., all day Sunday and 2 p.m.–4 p.m. daily (Tel. 15 84081), and
they have a list of the pensions with their prices posted up, but once
you're at Turismo you're already in Santiago's main hostel street.
Try Hospedaje Santa Cruz at No. 42, or Pensión Lens at No. 73.
You may have trouble during the annual festival (15–31 July) or
around religious feast days when pilgrims still flock into the town.

Barcelona

Situated across the Pyrenees from France and on the Mediterranean south of the Costa Brava, Barcelona seems to have as many
links with France as with Spain. It's proud of its position as capital of
Cataluña, and the language you'll hear in the streets, Catalan, is
derived not from Spanish but from the French langue d'oc.

The old quarter of BARRIO GÓTICO with its medieval streets is
particularly lively, though the whole city is bustling and vivacious.
Regarded as the literary capital of Spain, and with an important
university, Barcelona has the added attraction of its proximity to
the Mediterranean and good beaches.

Last year was a particularly big year for Barcelona, as the host of
the summer Olympic Games. 150,000 jobs were created for the
construction of the Olympic Village on the coast in old Barcelona.
Literally thousands of millions of pounds have been spent on
ancillary projects to make Barcelona a great centre for urban
tourism. No doubt the eurorail market will also benefit.

STATION FACILITIES

Barcelona's main station, Sants, handles most major trains;
rápidos to Valencia stop at the smaller Paseo de Gracia (there are
connecting trains every twenty minutes).

	SANTS
Train information	6.30 a.m.–10.30 p.m.
	(Tel. 490 0202)
Reservations	7 a.m.–8 p.m.
Tourist information	7.30 a.m.–10.30 p.m.
	daily
Foreign exchange	Open weekends
Bar, Buffet	7 a.m.–11 p.m.
Restaurant	12 noon–3 p.m.
Shops	7 a.m.–10.30 p.m.
Post office	–
Station shuts	12 midnight–4 a.m.

Daily trains to: Paris, Geneva, Valencia, Zaragoza, Madrid, Irún.

TOURIST INFORMATION AND ADDRESSES

TOURIST OFFICE: Gran Vía de Les Corts Catalanes 658 (Tel. 3017443), open Mon.–Fri.: 9 a.m.–7 p.m., closed Saturday p.m. and Sundays. Ask them for their list of budget accommodation, along with your map and leaflets. Also in Término Station.
POST OFFICE: Plaza d'Antoni López, open Mon.–Sat.: 8.30 a.m.–9.55 p.m., Sun.: 10 a.m.–12 noon. Stamps from the basement.
AMEX: Paseo de Gracia 101, open Mon.–Fri.: 9.30 a.m.–6 p.m., Sat.: 10 a.m.–12 noon (Tel. 217 0070).
UK CONSULATE: Avenida Diagonal 477 (Tel. 322 2151).
US CONSULATE: Vía Laietana 33 (Tel. 319 9550).
CANADIAN CONSULATE: Vía Augusta 125 (Tel. 2090634).
PHONE CODE: 93.

• **Getting around:** Although walking is the best way to see Barcelona, there is good public transport by bus and metro. Plaça de Catalunya is the main terminus. Bus and metro rides are 90 ptas., but you can save money by buying a multi-ticket at metro entrances. A T–1 card for 500 ptas. allows 10 trips by bus and metro, whilst a T–2 card for 460 ptas. allows 10 trips on the metro only.

SEEING

Head for the BARRIO GÓTICO and look out for the GREAT ROYAL

PALACE in Plaza del Rey, the CATEDRAL DE SANTA EULALIA and the
DIPUTACIÓN PROVINCIAL (council buildings). The hub of the city,
however, is LAS RAMBLAS. This collection of streets starts at the port
and runs to the city centre at Plaça de Catalunya. For sheer
entertainment value you can't beat Las Ramblas. It's the Piccadilly
Circus of Barcelona, so popular that you pay for a folding chair to
spectate, come nightfall. The incredible and unmissable cathedral
of TEMPLO EXPIATORIO DE LA SAGRADA FAMILIA is the work of the
Catalan architect Gaudí; however, his death before construction
was completed put a spanner in the works as he didn't leave any
plans. Work is now proceeding, however. South of Barrio Gótico is
MONTJUICH PARK, the setting for the Olympics. The buildings
originally erected here for the 1929 International Exhibition were
refurbished specially for the Olympics. The model town in PUEBLO
ESPAÑOL is well worth seeing as it shows all the different regional
styles of architecture in Spain. Take the funicular up, and admire
the view over the port and city or for even more dramatic views,
take the tram and the funicular up to TIBIDABO. There are also good
views from Palan Nacional and Mirador de L'Alcade (near Parc
d'Attractions).

The PICASSO MUSEUM is at Calle de Montcada 15 (entrance 400
ptas.) and has lots of his works from the early sketches to his final
masterpieces.

SLEEPING

The youth hostel on Passeig Pujadas 29 (Tel. 300 3104) charges
750 ptas., breakfast extra. Reception closed 10 a.m.–5 p.m. but you
can leave luggage and reserve a bed after 3 p.m. It has only 68 beds,
so get there as soon after 8 a.m. as possible; its big drawback is the
midnight curfew. There are also youth hostels at Passeig de Nostra
Senyora del Coll. 41–51 (Tel. 213 8633), Numancia 149–151 (Tel.
230 1606) and Duquesa d'Orleans 58 (Tel. 205 0961). The latter is a
long way from the centre of town, however. For camping, there are
quite a few sites; the nearest one is four miles out on the Espluges
bus route: Camping Barcino (Tel. 3728501). The university at Calle
Mestre Nicolau 14 (Tel. 250 1419) offers both sexes bed and
breakfast for 800 ptas. Your best bet for cheap casas and hostels is in
Las Ramblas. Pensión Fernando, Calle Ferran 31 (Tel. 301 7993),
is cheap and friendly; Hostal Alicante, Ronda Universidad 4 (Tel.

318 3470), is a good splurge. Hostal Noya, Ramblas 133 (Tel. 301 4831), and Hostal Canaletas on the 3rd floor (Tel. 301 5660) start around 1,000 ptas. for singles and are situated right in the city centre. Although it can be quite rowdy, the Kabul Young Budget Hotel is cheap and central at Pl. Reial 17 (Tel. 318 5190). Mixed dormitories and free (but cold) showers. There is no curfew or lock-out and it costs only 1,000 ptas. or so. Although you get breakfast and can buy sandwiches at the bar, you are better eating around the Plaça de Sant Jaume. Some distance out is the Youth Hostel Ocata at El Masnou. To get there, take a suburban train from Barceloneta metro station to Ocata station (20 minutes). Turn right out of the station, left at the Banco de Bilbao and head up the hill. If all else fails, there's a Brujula (accommodation-finding kiosk) at Término Station, and if you arrive exhausted in mid-August this is your best move.

EATING AND NIGHTLIFE

The Catalans eat late. Dinner time averages 9 p.m.–11 p.m. There are plenty of places offering menu del día in Barrio Gótico, and if you get a chance to sample the regional speciality, Catalan stew, escudella i carn d'olla, do so. Casa José, Pl. San José Oriol 10, is the cheapest, though not friendliest, feed in Barcelona. Cosmos, at Ramblas 34, does a good meal with coffee for about 600 ptas. If you're feeling extravagant, go to Barceloneta, the area of colourful winding streets down by the port, and savour the fresh seafood concoctions in Casa Costa on Juicio. Vegetarians should head for Restaurante Biocenter on C. Pintor Fortung 24, open afternoons except Sundays.

If you've money to blow, go to the nightclubs and discos like Georgia, Pelayo 58, or El Cordobés on Ramblas Capuchinos, but for our money strolling through the Ramblas, stopping at a few cafés en route, is better value. It gets quite lively at the top of the Montjuich on summer evenings, but if that's too sedate for you, head down to El Barrio Chino (near the docks). By Spanish standards some of the shows down there are pretty hot stuff, but bear in mind that this is the red-light area and can be rather sleazy. Be wary of your valuables.

• **Excursions:** The town of MONTSERRAT is 38 miles from Barcelona, reached by Catalan Railways (from Plaza de España – about £5 with Inter-Rail discount). Set among the mountain peaks, there is a Benedictine monastery and a Gothic basilica. It's a nice day trip if you're sick of crowds.

If the oppressive heat of the city is getting you down, you've not far to go to get to the good but crowded beaches of the COSTA BRAVA and the COSTA DORADA. LLORET DE MAR is infested with package tourists but pretty, while S' AGARÓ is the St Trop of the Costa Brava. Stay at SAN FELÍU DE GUIXOLS and travel in the two miles to S' Agaró to save yourself a fortune. Buses run to these and other, closer resorts from Vergara 5, Barcelona.

About 60 miles south of Barcelona, on the Costa Dorada, lies TARRAGONA. Although touristy and surrounded by oil refineries, the culture vultures may wish to stop off here and visit the ruins of the provincial Roman capital of Hispania. If you are coming from Barcelona, sit on the right-hand side of the train for a visual extravaganza! Tourist information is at 4 Fortuny (Mon.–Fri.: 8.45 a.m.–2.35 p.m., Sat.: 9 a.m.–2 p.m.) where you can pick up leaflets with lots of useful information. Rambla Nova is the main street in Tarragona, and along this long, tree-lined avenue you will find an information kiosk and the post office, as well as countless places offering cheap food. The ARCHAEOLOGICAL MUSEUM has a fascinating collection of mosaics and is one of the most important in Spain. It is part of the CYCLOPEAN WALLS, which run for about 1 km along the highest part of town, starting at the end of Rambla Vella which runs parallel to Rambla Nova. The wall, which varies in height from 12–40 feet, was built around 600 BC. Also visit the ROMAN AMPHITHEATRE and the thirteenth-century CATHEDRAL in the old town. The youth hostel is at Avenida President Companys s/n (Tel. 977–210195). It normally has 90 beds, but in July and August the number jumps to 190. There are also a number of cheap hotels south of the Rambla Nova and the campsite is a couple of miles east of the town. Take bus 3 or 3A from the Rambla Nova.

Just over the border from France is PORT BOU. Situated in a natural amphitheatre and nestling beside the Mediterranean, Port Bou is a delightful spot for the travel-weary eurorailer to relax and toast for a day or two. The vast railway station is out of all proportion to its surroundings but it is only a short walk to hotels and the rather pebbly beach. Tourist information at the harbour is open throughout the day Mon.–Sat., but only on Sunday mornings.

Although there is no youth hostel and the locals don't like you sleeping on the beach, the Hotel Juventas is highly recommended at around 2,400 ptas. for a double with washbasin and shower next door. It is at Avenue de Barcelona 3. There isn't really much to do in Port Bou but lie on the beach and watch the skinny-dippers. There are plenty of good cafés, but although the seafood is good value the prices are not all that cheap.

Andorra

This small autonomous principality of 51,000 people lies within the Pyrenees mountains between France and Spain. Andorra was founded in 784 by Charlemagne and is under the joint suzerainty of the Bishop of Urgel (Spain) and the French President. The official language is Catalan and both French francs and Spanish pesetas are used.

Andorra can be reached by train from Toulouse, Barcelona or Perpignan to La Tour-de-Carol. From there it's a two-hour bus journey (60 F) round hairpin bends to the Andorran capital ANDORRA LA VELLA. The bus doesn't connect with all the trains, so check the timetable first. The scenery on the way to La Tour-de-Carol is fairly dramatic and, once inside Andorra, the mountains are equally spectacular, making for a few days' good hiking. The tourist information office in Andorra la Vella is at Carrer Dr Vilanova (Tel. 20214). They'll provide you with maps and accommodation lists. There are no youth hostels in Andorra, but finding a room in a Residència should be no problem. Prices start at around 65 F. The owner will take your passport for registration with the police.

Because of Andorra's duty-free status, Andorra la Vella is extremely commercialized, resembling a Spanish Costa resort. One consequence of this is that you can pick up extremely cheap duty-frees – for example, one litre of Polish vodka for £3.50! Goods tend to be priced in francs in the north of the country and in pesetas in the south. However, you can pay in either currency and when changing money you can get your cash in whichever currency you want. This can be handy if you are visiting only France, or only Spain.

The main sight in Andorra la Vella is the sixteenth-century CASA DE LA VALL, the seat of the Andorran government. It's open 10 a.m.–1 p.m., 3.30 p.m.–6.30 p.m., Mon.–Fri. and 10 a.m.–1 p.m. Sat. and is free with an official guide. Aside from Andorra la Vella there are a number of other small, less commercialized towns in Andorra which could be used as a base for exploring the countryside. The National Festival is on 8 September with a pilgrimage at the sanctuary of MERITXELL.

Valencia

If you're taking a detour off the railway to visit the Balearic islands of Majorca, Menorca or Ibiza, Valencia is logically en route, so you may feel like stopping off here. There's nothing very exciting here, but it is the point of departure for steamers to the islands, as are Alicante and Barcelona.

STATION FACILITIES

	VALENCIA TÉRMINO
Train information	24 hours (Tel. 3520202)
Reservations	8 a.m.–10 p.m.
Tourist information	At town hall
Foreign exchange	8 a.m.–9 p.m.
Left-luggage store	All hours
Bar, Buffet	6 a.m.–1.30 a.m.
Cafeteria	7.30 a.m.–11.30 p.m.
Waiting room	All hours
Station shuts	3 a.m.–5 a.m.

Daily trains to: Barcelona, Alicante, Córdoba, Madrid.

TOURIST INFORMATION AND ADDRESSES

TOURIST OFFICE: Calle de la Paz, open Mon.–Sat.: 10 a.m.–2 p.m., 4 p.m.–8 p.m., Sun.: 10 a.m.–2 p.m.
POST OFFICE: Plaza del Pais, Valenciano 24.

AMEX: c/o Viajes Melia, Calle de la Paz 41, open Mon.–Fri.: 9.30 a.m.–1.30 p.m., 4.30 p.m.–8 p.m., Sat.: 9.30 a.m.–1 p.m.

US CONSULATE: Calle de la Paz 6 (Tel. 3516973). Mon.–Fri.: 10 a.m.–1 p.m.

FERRIES TO THE ISLANDS: Transmediterránea, Avenida Manuel Soto Ingeniero 15 (Tel. 3676512).

PHONE CODE: 96.

SEEING

The PALACE OF THE MARQUÉS DE DOS AGUAS is about the most interesting building around. It's eighteenth-century rococo and contains about the best collection of Spanish pottery in Spain (2 p.m.–4 p.m., siesta, closed Sunday p.m. and all day Monday). The GOTHIC CATHEDRAL is also worth a look: climb its tower for a view over the city. Apart from these, the MUSEO PROVINCIAL DE BELLAS ARTES is the only other place really worth visiting, with works by Goya amongst others. Free entry, open Tues.–Sun.: 10 a.m.–2 p.m., closed Mondays. The best beaches are further south at BENIDORM and ALICANTE, but there are closer ones on the Costa del Azahar accessible by bus.

SLEEPING, EATING AND NIGHTLIFE

The youth hostel is at Avenida del Puerto 69 (Tel. 3690152) on bus route 19. Open July–September. Round the Plaza del Mercado are plenty of grotty casas and fondas with beds around 800 ptas. The cleanest and cheapest is Hostal del Rincón at C. Carda 11 (Tel. 3316083). The Barrio del Carmen is the area both for cheap eating and for nightlife. Rice dishes are the Valencian speciality, but you often have to watch the prices. There are lots of spit'n'sawdust bars in this area which vary from colourful and 'ethnic' to grimy and revolting.

Castile: Central Spain

About two hours from Madrid lie two towns which should ideally be included on any Spanish itinerary: ÁVILA and SEGOVIA. Ávila (famous because of Saint Teresa) has some of Europe's best-preserved medieval battlements, dating from the eleventh century, and there are other buildings in the town from this same period. Tourist information is at Pl. de la Catedral (Tel. 918–21 13 87), open Mon.–Fri.: 9 a.m.–8 p.m., Sat.: 9 a.m.–3 p.m., Sun.: 11 a.m.–3 p.m. There's no problem finding cheap rooms. Segovia has a ROMAN AQUEDUCT antedating Christ, a fourteenth-century ALCÁZAR (palace) (rebuilt in the nineteenth century), and dozens of churches in different architectural styles. The tourist office is at Plaza Mayor 10 (Tel. 911–430328), open Mon.–Fri.: 9 a.m.–2 p.m., 4.30 p.m.–7 p.m., Sat.: 9 a.m.–2 p.m., and there are plenty of cheap rooms nearby. Try Fonda Cubo, third floor at Plaza Mayor 4. Whilst both these towns are interesting enough to make the effort to get to them alone, you'd be absolutely crazy not to make it to the town of Toledo.

Toledo

This is the town which can show you the past four centuries of Spanish history and culture in one or two days. From the Moorish and Visigothic mosques and synagogues to the Renaissance buildings of the Spanish Inquisition, every architectural style is represented and wonderfully preserved. It's interesting to note that Toledo was one of the world's few centres of Arab, Jewish and Christian co-existence. It's possible to make Toledo a day trip from Madrid (it takes 1½ hours) but you'll kill yourself trying to see all the sights in just one afternoon. Perched up on the high town are buildings such as the MOSQUE OF THE CHRIST OF LIGHT (tenth century), the SYNAGOGUE OF SANTA MARÍA LA BLANCA, the incredible medieval CATHEDRAL; and dominating the violet-coloured sky is the ALCÁZAR which once housed El Cid. EL GRECO lived in Toledo, and his HOUSE AND MUSEUM can be seen (closed Sunday p.m. and Mondays, admission 200 ptas.). There are many more things to see: go along to Turismo, just outside the Puerta de Bisagra (closed Saturday p.m. and Sundays), and pick up your glossy leaflets and map. This office, like many of the sights, takes a long siesta and doesn't reopen till 4 p.m. From the station (at the foot of the hill) take the bus marked Santa Barbara to the centre.

For accommodation, there are two campsites: Camping El Greco (Tel. 925–213537) and Circo Ronano (Tel. 925–220442). The first is the better of the two, and charges 350 ptas. per person. A mile out of town on the N401 road. Tourist information will suggest pensions of which perhaps Pension Descalzos, C. de los Descalzos 32 (Tel. 925–222888), is the best. Fonda Lumbreras, Calle Juan Labrador 7 (Tel. 925–221571), or Fonda Escobar, Cuesta de Santa Leocadia 4 (Tel. 925–229465), are good bets. Shop around for your meals and eat at the fixed-price menu places near the central Plaza de Zocodover if possible. This is where it all happens in Toledo, especially at night. There is a RENFE office just off the main square too, where you can get info or book tickets.

The youth hostel is in a castle ten minutes' walk from the station and town centre. It's at Castillo de San Servando (Tel. 925–224554) and is beautiful inside with a super pool, though slightly more expensive than a normal Spanish hostel.

Salamanca

Further down the line from Ávila is Spain's oldest university town, Salamanca. The main reason for going there is to see Spain's most beautiful square, the PLAZA MAYOR, built by Philip V in the eighteenth century. From the station take bus 1 to the centre of the town where tourist information is at Gran Vía 41 (Tel. 923–268571), closed Saturday afternoon and all day Sunday. An afternoon should be long enough to take in the main sights: the square, university, OLD AND NEW CATHEDRALS, and HOUSE OF SHELLS, but if you come in term-time you might want to stay a night for the active student nightlife. Look for a room round the Plaza Mayor and Calle Meléndez, which are also the main areas for cheap food.

Burgos

Most Madrid–Paris runs go through this old tenth-century capital of Castile. Franco was declared military commander here in 1936 and none other than El Cid is buried in the CATHEDRAL that you should head for, as the rest of the town has nothing spectacular in it. Entrance 300 ptas. Tourist information is at 7 Pl. de Alonso Martínez (Tel. 947–20 31 25). Open Mon.–Fri.: 9 a.m.–2 p.m., 4.30 p.m.–6.30 p.m., Sat.: 10 a.m.–1.30 p.m. The youth hostel is at Avenida General Vigón (Tel. 947–22 03 62) or try Hostal Victoria, C. San Juan 3 (Tel. 947–20 15 42), near the tourist office. The nearest campsite is large and well equipped, but a 3.5 km bus ride from the centre. It's at Fuentes Blacas (Tel. 947–221016) and costs 325 ptas. per tent, 375 ptas. per person. A short walk away is the Carthusian monastery Cartiya de Miraflores, which is open Mon.– Fri.: 9.30 a.m.–1 p.m., 3.30 p.m.–6 p.m., Sat. and Sun. 12 noon–2 p.m., 3 p.m.–6 p.m., and has some ornate tombs.

Valladolid

Just over an hour from Burgos is the university city of Valladolid. If you take a break here, visit the sixteenth-century house of MIGUEL DE CERVANTES, who wrote *Don Quixote*, off the Calle Miguel Iscar, the CATHEDRAL, the cloisters of the sixteenth-century S. GREGORIO COLLEGE, and the UNIVERSITY. Tourist information is at 3 Pl. de Zorrilla.

Cuenca

If you're heading for Valencia and the Costa del Azahar, and fancy a short break in the five-hour journey from Madrid, take an hour or two off at Cuenca, about halfway up the line. Walk round the old town, starting at the PLAZA MAYOR, and take in the CITY HALL, the CATHEDRAL and the incredible fourteenth-century HANGING HOUSES on the banks of the Huécar River. Turismo is at Dalmacio Garcia Izcara 8 (Tel. 966–22 22 31). Open Mon.–Fri.: 9 a.m.–2 p.m., 4.30 p.m.–6.30 p.m., Sat.: 9.30 a.m.–1 p.m. Pension Centrale (Tel. 966–211511) at C. Alonso Chirino 9 is good for a cheap bed.

More expensive but with great views is Posada de San José (Tel. 966–211300) at C. Julian Romero 4 near the cathedral.

Costa del Sol

This exploited cement-heap of coastline, best reached via Málaga, is all that you'd expect. It's difficult to know you're in Spain, the food and nightlife are plastic and often vulgar, and you'll begin to understand the background to the jokes about package deals to Torremolinos. Don't come here to look for quiet fishing villages, deserted beaches or friendly locals. However, if you're low on cash, keen to rough it on the beach, meet Europeans and pick up a tan, then you'd be hard pressed to find a better deal in Europe. If you avoid July and August and the main package-holiday resorts, you'd be amazed how different a picture can emerge.

Málaga

Don't stay in Málaga too long: not just because you run a higher risk of getting mugged here than anywhere else in Spain, but because the resorts are often crowded, and it's advisable to make for one and get established first, then head back for a day trip to see this city's sights.

Tourist information in Málaga is at Calle de Larios 5 (Tel. 952–213445), open 9 a.m.–2 p.m. (1 p.m. on Sat., closed Sun.). If you feel you're being followed from the station, turn round and take a good look, then stick to major streets. The instances of eurorailers being followed from station to tourist information and being mugged en route are amazing. Whatever happens, don't even think about sleeping out at Málaga Station. We realize you'll probably know plenty of people who have and have come out unscathed, but we also know scores who've had their rucksacks actually cut off their backs and been threatened at knife-point to hand over their valuables. Honestly, it's not worth the risk. The British Consulate is at Edificio Duquesa, Duquesa de Parcent 8 (Tel. 952–217571), in case anything nasty happens. The US one is at Avenida Fuengirola (Tel. 952–461865). Tourist information will give you a leaflet on Málaga's sights. Take in the ALCAZABA Moorish palace and GIBRALFARO CASTLE if you can. 'El Corte Inglés', the big department store, is useful to stock up in. Usually its toiletries, etc., are cheaper than at the resorts, and its cafeterias are worth a visit too. If you must stay, try Hostal Residencia Chinitas Pasaje Chintas 2 (Tel. 952–214683).

The Resorts

The resorts to the east of Málaga are less exploited, but the beaches aren't so good. In places like CASTELL DE FERRO and TORRENUEVA you'll avoid the package tourists, but will find the facilities basic. It's easier coming down from Granada to get to the eastern resorts and using the bus for the last lap.

West of Málaga, the electric train runs as far as FUENGIROLA, stopping at Torremolinos, Benalmadena, and Los Boliches en route. This train is free on Inter-Rail, but to get on to Marbella or further west, you have to resort to buses.

TORREMOLINOS is the most commercialized centre. Look for rooms in hostels leading down to the beach and, as far as eating and nightlife goes, you'd have a job actually to miss the tourist menus, bars and discos, so there's no problem there. Tourist information is on Bajos de la Nogalera (1 p.m.–4.30 p.m. siesta). If this doesn't appeal, move on to other resorts till you find a suitable one. MARBELLA is slightly more 'up market', so prices can be higher here. There's a good youth hostel here on Trapiche (Tel. 952–771491) but it may be closed temporarily, and for pensions, try round Aduar or Germán Porras. FUENGIROLA'S a good compromise between the two and, with its four miles of beaches and many cheap beds and restaurants, an attractive proposition to the footsore eurorailer.

Andalusia (Andalucía)

This is stereotyped Spain: flamencos, bullfights, Moorish palaces and hilltop villages. This region is bordered by the Mediterranean, the Straits of Gibraltar and the Gulf of Cádiz, and the principal centres are Seville, Granada and Córdoba.

Seville (Sevilla)

If Madrid disappointed you, head for Seville. It's a great city to visit: typically Spanish and colourful, and as alive at night as in the day. There are plenty of sights and cheap beds and it seems impossible to hit a day in summer when the heat doesn't drive you into the nearest shady park for a siesta, no matter how dedicated a sun-worshipper you might be. The railway station is called Santa Justa.

TOURIST INFORMATION AND ADDRESSES

TOURIST OFFICE: Avenida de la Constitución 21B (Tel. 4221404), open 9.30 a.m.–7.30 p.m., Mon.–Fri. and 9.30 a.m.–2 p.m. Saturday.
POST OFFICE: Avenida de la Constitución 32, open Mon.–Fri.: 9 a.m.–9 p.m., Sat.: 9 a.m.–2 p.m.
AMEX: c/o Viajes Alhambra, Teniente Coronel Segui 3, open Mon.–Fri.: 9.30 a.m.–1 p.m. and 4.30 p.m.–7.30 p.m., Sat.: 9.30 a.m.–1.30 p.m.
UK CONSULATE: Plaza Neuva 8 (Tel. 4228875).
US CONSULATE: PEU Paseo de las Delicias 7 (Tel. 4231885), open 9 a.m.–1 p.m., 2 p.m.–4.30 p.m., closed Wednesday p.m., Saturdays and Sundays.
FIRST AID: Avenida Menendez Pelayo (Tel. 4411712).
PHONE CODE: 95.

SEEING

The CATHEDRAL and ALCÁZAR complex should be your first stops.

The cathedral, the third largest in the world, is built on the site of a former mosque (entrance 300 ptas.), and the Moorish tower, LA GIRALDA, is a leftover from this period. Leave the cathedral at Puerta de los Naranjos, cross the plaza to Puerta Oriente and you'll come to the fourteenth-century Alcázar palace with its combination of Moorish and Gothic architecture (600 ptas., free with ISIC).

PLAZA DE ESPAÑA and the nearby parks offer romantic settings for the evening stroll, and you can hire out boats at reasonable rates and row round the Spanish Square taking it all in.

Behind the cathedral is the picturesque old Jewish quarter of SANTA CRUZ. There are guided tours, but you're better off wandering round yourself.

SLEEPING

Concentrate your efforts on finding a cheap pension (there's no convenient campsite or central youth hostel). Down from the Plaza de Armas Station or in the Santa Cruz area are your best bets, especially around C. Mateos Gago. Rooms start about 3,000 ptas. single. Try to get fixed up early as Seville's popular with eurorailers and Spaniards alike. The hostels on Archeros are among the best in town. Try Pérez Montilla at No. 14 (Tel. 4361740) or Casa de Huéspedes Orellana (Tel. 4362259) at No. 19. Another good street to try is Calle San Eloy with the Hostal La Gloria at No. 58 (Tel. 4222673) among the best. Sleeping rough in the parks is a dicey proposition as you have not only the police to contend with, but also the local rats. The youth hostel is at Calle Issac Peral 2 (Tel. 4613150). Take bus 34 from opposite Hotel Alfonso XIII to the last but one stop.

EATING AND NIGHTLIFE

Prices in Seville tend to be over the top, but there are plenty of central places with fixed tourist menus, and there are even a few fast-food places creeping in now. Again, the area round the Plaza de Armas Station isn't bad, and you can eat for about 900 ptas., but some of these places aren't too fussy about hygiene.

The Barrio Triana is a good place to make for to try the local tapas, though some bars seem a bit hostile to women coming in on their own. Casa Manolo at San Jorge 16 in the Barrio Triana is cheap and lively. But best value is El Diamante, Constitución 10, where an all-you-can-eat buffet costs under 900 ptas. Speciality dishes can be found everywhere but are especially good at Mesón La Barca at C. Santander 6.

Going to a flamenco is *the* thing to do in Seville. There is no shortage of venues, and by and large they're good value. Avoid the heavily advertised ones and try and make your drinks last as long as possible, as they're (surprise, surprise) overpriced. Los Gallos at Plaza Santa Cruz 11 charge about 2,800 ptas. for entrance, including your first drink. This is about average, but the entertainment here is above average.

• **Excursions from Seville:** The sherry capital of JEREZ DE LA FRONTERA is about two hours from Seville. If you're in this region in the first week of May go down for the fiesta. There are free guided tours and liberal samplings at the bodegas of Sandeman, Gonzalez Byass, etc. CÁDIZ, another 50 minutes away, hasn't much to commend it unless you're after a heavy nightlife scene.

If you are going on to Portugal, take the train to Huelva, then a 15-minute walk to the bus station for the bus to the ferry at Ayamonte (about 500 ptas.).

Granada

Bus 4, 5, 9 or 11 will take you from the station to the centre of Granada, and once you've found your bed and left off your things, you should walk up to the incredible ALHAMBRA, *the* sight of the city.

TOURIST INFORMATION AND ADDRESSES

TOURIST OFFICE: Calle Libreros 2 (behind the cathedral) (Tel. 225990). Mon.–Fri.: 10 a.m.–1 p.m., 4 p.m.–7 p.m. Sat.: 10 a.m.–1 p.m. Also: Plaza Mariana Pineda 10 (Tel. 226688). Same opening hours.

TRAIN INFORMATION: Tel. 223497.

POST OFFICE: Puerta Real, open 9 a.m.–2 p.m., 4 p.m.–6 p.m., closed Saturday p.m. and Sunday (Tel. 224835).
AMEX: c/o Viajes Bonal, Avenida Calvo Sotelo 19, open Mon.–Fri.: 9.30 a.m.–1.30 p.m., 5 p.m.–8 p.m.
PHONE CODE: 958.

SEEING

The huge Arabic fortress on the hill dominating the city – the ALHAMBRA – is one of the world's best-preserved Moorish palaces. The ALCAZABA and WATCH TOWER go back to the ninth century, and you should visit GENERALIFE, the summer house of the sultans, the fourteenth-century palace, and see the incredible mosaics and examples of Muslim art. Go early in the day to get its full atmosphere. If you want to see the whole lot – castle, Generalife, royal palace, as well as the remaining grounds – the cost is 525 ptas. The Alhambra is open daily from 9 a.m.–6 p.m., but if you are here on a Saturday, do head up there in the evening when the whole inside is lit up from 8 p.m.–10 p.m.

Opposite the Alhambra is ALBAYZÍN, the hilltop Arab quarter with its crowded, winding streets; and on the other hilltop is the gypsy quarter of SACROMONTE. Down in the town take in the Renaissance CATHEDRAL (150 ptas.) and ROYAL CHAPEL, with its elaborate tombs.

SLEEPING

The youth hostel is the best deal in Granada. It's in the Colegio Emperador Carlos at Camino de Ronda 171 (Tel. 272638). It's not too far from the station and a 20-minute walk from the town centre. Other hostels near the station abound in Calle San Juan de Dios. For pensions, try round the station on Avenida Andaluces, or the road up to the Alhambra, Cuesta de Gomérez. Hostal Residencia San Joaquin, Mano de Hierro 14 (Tel. 282879), is excellent, and the Sierra Nevada campsite at Carretera Madrid (Tel. 232504) is OK. It is on bus line 3.

EATING AND NIGHTLIFE

Round Cetti Meriem is the place for cheap meals. La Riviera at No.

5 starts meals around 600 ptas. and has a good selection. Avoid the 'gypsy flamenco' at Sacromonte come what may, and instead head for the bars in the centre. As far as nightlife's concerned, save your pesetas and go for a nocturnal stroll up by the Alhambra instead. The old Arab quarter, Albayzín, has atmosphere and most bars serve cheap food but you should watch your valuables after dark.

Córdoba

The Roman and Moorish remains are the reasons to include Córdoba in an itinerary. This was the eighth-century capital of Moorish Spain, though in many ways today's Córdoba looks as if it's had its heyday.

TOURIST INFORMATION AND ADDRESSES

TOURIST OFFICE: C. Torrijos 10, open Mon.–Fri.: 9.30 a.m.–2.30 p.m. and 5 p.m.–7 p.m., Sat.: 9.30 a.m.–1.30 p.m. (Tel. 471235). The Municipal Tourist Office is at Plaza de Judas Levi 3 (off Manriques), open Mon.–Fri.: 8.30 a.m.–1.30 p.m. (Tel. 290740). POST OFFICE: Cruz Conde 21, open 9 a.m.–2 p.m., 4 p.m.–6 p.m., closed Saturday p.m. and Sunday. PHONE CODE: 957.

SEEING

The main area to concentrate on is the JUDERÍA (old Jewish quarter) with its maze of narrow, twisting streets. Here you will find the MEZQUITA, built in the eighth century; it was the largest mosque in the world before the Christians made it into a cathedral in the thirteenth century. The structure has an incredible array of decorated arches and pillars, and if you climb the tower you'll see how big the mosque must have been, as the cathedral fits into its original centre. During the summer it is open from 10.30 a.m.–1.30 p.m. and 4 p.m.–7 p.m. and at other times from 10.30 a.m.–1.30 p.m. and 3.30 p.m.–5.30 p.m. Entry is 400 ptas. The fourteenth-century SYNAGOGUE isn't exactly riveting, and the MUSEO MUNICI-PAL could be missed out too, unless you're keen on bullfighting. The ALCÁZAR, the palace of the Catholic monarchs, is at its best floodlit at night. It's on the banks of the Río Guadalquivir and the Moorish gardens, towers and fountains make it an interesting place to take in. If you do want to go in, last entry is at 7 p.m. Entrance is free on Tuesdays, otherwise 200 ptas.

SLEEPING, EATING AND NIGHTLIFE

Cheap pensions are on Calle Rey Heredia, at La Milagrosa, No. 12 (Tel. 473317); 1,100 ptas. per person. Check out the Hostel Mari, Calle Pimentero 6 for only 800 ptas. per person. The IYHF hostel is Residencia Juvenil Córdoba at Pl. de Judas Levi (Tel. 290166). It is a sparkling new building with marble floors in the heart of the Judería. Highly recommended. There's camping about a mile out at Carretera Córdoba–Villaviciosa (Tel. 275048). Buses run every 10 minutes from the campsite to town. Tourist menus are found most easily in the old quarter and, for tapas and bar crawls, try the Jewish quarter (round the Mezquita). Flamenco here is among the best in Spain, but avoid the expensive private shows: the bar on Calle La Luna is a good place to see students gathering to sing, play the guitar and dance flamenco.

Ronda

The main line from Córdoba to Algeciras passes through this delightful town impressively perched on a gorge. See the CASA DEL REY MORO and the RENAISSANCE PALACE. Also take a look at the eighteenth-century bridge spanning the deep gorge beneath the town, as well as the former Moorish fortress and baths, and the cathedral. For a room try around the tourist information office at Pl. de España. Open Mon.–Fri.: 9.30 a.m.–2 p.m., 5 p.m.–7 p.m., closed Saturday afternoon and Sunday (Tel. 871272). There is plenty of budget accommodation.

Algeciras

TOURIST OFFICE: Juan de la Cierva, open Mon.–Fri.: 9 a.m.–2 p.m., Sat.: 10 a.m.–1 p.m. Hostels are cheap and plentiful, so accommodation shouldn't be too much of a problem here and you may prefer to stay here than in more expensive Gibraltar. There is a campsite at Playa Rinconcillo (Tel. 661958), about 3 km from the town centre. Take the bus: Rinconcillo.

If you are using Algeciras as the departure point for a trip to Morocco, buy your ticket from the first office selling ferry tickets to Tangier or Ceuta. Although there are a number of operators on this route they all charge roughly the same and are quite expensive at around 2,700 ptas. single and 5,400 ptas. return. It's no cheaper to buy at the ferry terminal than at any of the offices in town. A cheaper crossing is to Ceuta for around 1,440 ptas. single which also avoids Tangier. If you are going on this trip remember to get your passport stamped during the voyage. The town itself is rather unremarkable and down at heel, but does have good views of Gibraltar, which you can reach from here by bus for around 200 ptas.

Avoid the overnight Paris–Irún–Algeciras train (particularly on Thursday and Friday nights) as it is very overcrowded and full of Arab immigrant workers returning to North Africa. Consequently the return route will be just as busy. The guard has a permanent escort of two armed security guards – which says it all!

Gibraltar

First settled by the Moors, then the Spanish took over, followed by the British in 1704. Despite strong Mediterranean influences, Gibraltar is distinctively British, with British police, troops, beer and currency. The reopening of the frontier with Spain in 1985 means that eurorailers can get here easily. The most convenient way is by bus from Algeciras to La Linea (140 ptas.), then walking across the border.

You can take a look at the MOORISH CASTLE, though it is no longer open to the public. Visit the GALLERIES in the Rock (70p). Another 'hole' in the Rock is the natural ST MICHAEL'S CAVE (£1.50). Concerts and *son et lumières* are often held here. The GIBRALTAR MUSEUM (£1) chronicles the Rock's history from Neanderthal times. All these sights are open 10 a.m.–5.30 p.m. Also, take the cable car to the top of the Rock. The famous apes are up here, cared for by the British Army. Feeding times are 8 a.m. and 4 p.m.

Tourist Information is in Cathedral Square (Tel. 76400), open Mon.–Fri.: 8 a.m.–5.30 p.m.; the London office is at 179 The Strand, WC2R 1EH (Tel. 071–836 0777). Accommodation in Gibraltar is difficult as there are no youth hostels or campsites. The cheapest hotel is Queen's on Boyd Street (Tel. 74000). Singles cost £22 and doubles £32. The cheapest beds are at Toc H Hostel (Tel. 73431) on Lime Wall Road, and although it is usually full, standards are not very high.

Ferries run from Gibraltar to Tangier, but, at about £28 return, it is cheaper to go from Algeciras. In general, though, Gibraltar represents good value as there is no VAT.

N.B. Gibraltar closes down on Sundays in a big way!

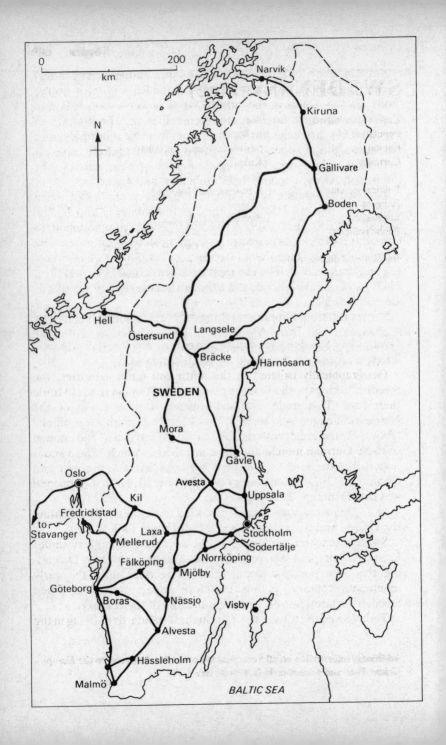

SWEDEN (Sverige)

Entry requirements	Passport
Population	8,644,000
Capital	Stockholm (pop.: 1,600,000)
Currency	Krona
	£1 = approx. 9.51 kr.
Political system	Constitutional Monarchy
Religion	Lutheran
Languages	Swedish, English
Public holidays	1, 6 Jan.; 17, 20 April; 1, 28 May;
	8, 20 June; 31 Oct.; 24, 25, 26 Dec.
International dialling codes	From UK: 010 + 46 + number
	From USA: 011 + 46 + number
	To UK: 009 + 44 + number
	To USA: 009 + 1 + number

Over half of Sweden's land surface is covered by forests and lakes, an area larger than the whole of the British Isles.

Geographically isolated in the ninth and tenth centuries, the Swedish Vikings pushed eastwards down the Russian rivers to trade their furs. This trade eventually caught the attention of the Hanseatic League who were always keen to capitalize on others' labour. By the fourteenth century, all Scandinavia had had enough of these German merchants who controlled so much. The Swedes hoped that the Union of Kalmar between Sweden, Norway and Denmark (1397) would change all this; instead, all that happened was that Denmark came out on top.

In 1523 Gustav Vasa was elected king for successfully defeating the Danes, and from then on the Swedes never looked back.

Sweden reached her zenith in the seventeenth century under Gustavus Adolphus who procured a Baltic empire for her. Defending this new position meant constant warfare until the early nineteenth century; it was therefore widely welcomed when Sweden declared herself neutral at the end of the century.

Today Sweden enjoys one of the highest standards of living in the

Additional information on all Scandinavian countries contained in the *Europe – Grand Tour* and *Scandinavia* factsheets (see p.13).

world and a quality of life to go with it, thanks to the highly developed social welfare system. Sweden applied for membership of the EC back in 1991 and may be entering soon.

• **Getting there:** The alternative routes are London–Dover–Ostend and up through Germany, or from Harwich to the Hook of Holland, then up. This takes about 22–25 hours to reach Stockholm. For full details ask British Rail or NSR Travel, 21–24 Cockspur Street, London SW1. By sea there are four sailings a week from Harwich to Gothenburg (50 per cent discount for ISIC card holders) and twice a week from Newcastle to Gothenburg in high season. Also there's another ferry to Esbjerg in Denmark which connects up to a through-train to Copenhagen, and a line operates from Newcastle to Esbjerg.

SWEDISH STATE RAILWAYS
(Statens Järnvägar, SJ)

Swedish trains are efficient, clean and comfortable. They are very rarely late and run frequent services (every hour or so) to most of the major cities. The journey from Stockholm to Malmö takes only six hours, and to Narvik in the far north of Norway twenty hours. New fast trains (the X–2000s) have started running between Stockholm and Gothenburg travelling at 130 m.p.h. The journey takes just under three hours and the trains have audio channels in seats and outlets for computers! The long-distance Inter City and Rapid trains are the fastest, followed by the expresses which are used on regular routes. The local trains are not as slow as in some countries, but still stop at every station. There are supplements only on City Express trains, but see Reservations. Ask at stations for a free copy of SJ Tågtider timetables.

• **Inter-Rail bonuses:**

	FROM	TO	REDUCTION %
Stena Line	Gothenburg	Frederikshavn	50
Silja Line	Stockholm (1)	Helsinki (1)	50
	Stockholm (1)	Turku (1)	50
T.T. Line	Trelleborg	Travemünde	50

(1) A ticket bought for Stockholm–Turku is not valid for Stockholm–Helsinki.

- **Eurail bonuses:** Free:
—Steamer service of the Silja Line between Stockholm and Aland Islands–Turku. (Full fare is charged for cabin space and reservation is compulsory between Sweden and Helsinki.)
—Ferry crossings operated by the Scand Lines between Helsingborg and Helsingør (Denmark).
—Ferry crossings operated by Stena Line between Gothenburg and Frederikshavn (Denmark).

Reduced fares:
—50 per cent reduction on the Danish Navigation Company, Øresund, on the hydrofoil between Malmö and Copenhagen (reservation compulsory).

TRAIN INFORMATION

No problems here, as everyone speaks perfect English and queues are never too long.

- **Reservations:** (20 kr.) Are compulsory on X-2000 trains. On all other trains you can board without tickets or reservations and buy them from the conductor. Reservations cost 20 kr. at the ticket desk and 25 kr. on the train.

- **Night travel:** Is relatively cheap in Sweden at about 80 kr. for a couchette and about 160 kr. for a tourist-class sleeper.

- **Eating on trains:** All long-distance expresses have a buffet or dining car, other trains have only snack bars.

- **Cinema couch:** A new service on the night train Luleå–Stockholm is the cinema couch, with a film saloon and bistro. Films change regularly and cost 40 kr. entry.

- **Scenic tips:** Any line north of Stockholm is of interest, particularly from Östersund onwards, either to Trondheim in Norway or to Kiruna in the far north.

- **Bikes:** Bikes go as luggage as Swedish trains have no guard's vans. This means that your bike may not travel on the same train, so to be sure it arrives with you, send it two days in advance. Cost per bike is 75 kr.

• **Rover tickets:** The Nordic Railpass ('Nordturist Medtåg') is valid for 21 days in Sweden, Denmark, Norway and Finland for unlimited rail travel. For details see p.37.

A popular card is the 'Inlandsbanan' which is valid for the Inland Railway travelling 800 miles down the backbone of Sweden from Gallivare in the north to Kristinehamn in the south, with one short stretch involving travel by bus. The card, which gives unlimited travel on the line, is valid for either 14 or 21 days. It costs around 650 kr. for 14 days and 700 kr. for 21 days.

TOURIST INFORMATION

Every Swedish county has a tourist board in addition to the local tourist information offices called 'Turistbyrå'. They are very helpful and always have a good selection of maps and brochures.

• **ISIC bonuses:** Few reductions here; the main one is 20 per cent off tours and day trips to historic places. For further information, contact SFS Resebyra, Kungsgatan 4, Box 7144, 10387, Stockholm (Tel. 08–234515).

• **Money matters:** 1 krona (kr.) = 100 öre.
Banking hours are Mon.–Fri.: 9.30 a.m.–3 p.m. Bank charges are high for traveller's cheques (approximately 35 kr.) so it makes sense to cash large denominations. 'Forex' offices, found in the major cities, will change traveller's cheques for 10 kr. commission, however, and are worth looking out for. Credit cards are widely accepted in Sweden.

• **Post offices and shops:** Post offices open Mon.–Fri.: 9 a.m.–6 p.m., and 9 a.m.–1 p.m. on Saturdays. Most shops are open 9.30 a.m.–6 p.m. on weekdays and until 1 p.m. and 4 p.m. on Saturdays. In some larger towns department stores stay open until 8 p.m. or 10 p.m. with some opening Sundays 12 noon until 4 p.m. The poste restante service is free in Sweden, and stamps are sold at newsagents as well as post offices.

• **Museums:** Normally open from about 10 a.m.–5 p.m.

SLEEPING

All regional and local tourist offices have free lists of hotels and campsites; many also have a room-finding service called Rumsför-medling. They charge a commission of about 40 kr., and can find you a room in a private house or in a hotel. In smaller towns and villages look for the sign Rum (the Swedish equivalent of B&B, except there's no breakfast). At about 200 kr. for a single, this represents as good value as you're likely to get. Youth hostels are great and cost about 76–80 kr. per night; add another 25 kr. to this if you're not a member. Camping's no problem thanks to the Allmansrätt law which allows anyone to camp on unfenced land for one night only – and please be careful about fire. Tourist informa-tion will direct you to suitable places. If you prefer your comforts, most towns have campsites with excellent facilities costing about 70–80 kr. per tent, but these require a camping pass (43 kr.) obtainable at the site.

EATING AND NIGHTLIFE

Eating out is incredibly expensive in Sweden even at fast-food joints: £1.30 for a small hamburger, £2.50 for a large one, £1.50 for a Coke. Always check to see if there's a tourist menu or a cheap set meal (dagens rätt) for between 45–55 kr. More often than not, you'll be forced to eat from supermarkets, which is no bad thing as the quality and choice are excellent. Most of the regional speciali-ties, such as smoked reindeer meat from Lapland, are expensive and confined to the best restaurants. Smörgåsbord is cheaper here than in Norway, so if you feel like a Scandinavian splash-out do it here.

Nightlife is what you make it in Sweden, and there's no shortage of options in the larger towns. Alcohol and tobacco are expensive and controlled by the government, but there's not much the government can do during the midsummer festival when everyone lets rip with non-stop dancing and drinking, particularly in the north.

Stockholm

All the qualities one associates with the Swedes are reflected in their capital. It's tidy and well laid-out, socially minded and efficiently run, and the high level of money floating around has permitted them to improve their environment with schemes like making the city's waterway safe for swimming and erecting new buildings with more of an eye towards appearance than to economy.

It's difficult to make out on a tight budget here, as even supermarket food is expensive, but you'll get by if you follow our suggestions and use your common sense.

STATION FACILITIES

	STOCKHOLM CENTRAL
Train information	24 hours (Tel. 020–757575)
Reservations	Domestic: 24 hours (Tel. 225060)
	International: 7 a.m.–10 p.m. (Tel. 227940)
Tourist information	Summer: 8 a.m.–9 p.m.
	Winter: 8.30 a.m.–5 p.m.
Foreign exchange	8 a.m.–9 p.m.
Left-luggage lockers	No access 1 a.m.–4.30 a.m.
Left-luggage store	6 a.m.–10 p.m.
Café, Bar	6.30 a.m.–10 p.m.
Restaurant	6.30 a.m.–12 midnight
Provisions	7 a.m.–10 p.m.
Post office	Mon.–Fri.: 7 a.m.–10 p.m., Sat.: 10 a.m.–7 p.m.
Station shuts	Mon.–Sat.: 1 a.m.–4.30 a.m., Sun.: 1 a.m.–5 a.m.

Frequent trains to: Malmö, Copenhagen, Gothenburg, Oslo, and all Sweden.

TOURIST INFORMATION

Apart from the station, there's an office in the centre at Sweden House (Sverigehuset), Kungstradgården, opposite the department store NK. Pick up maps and 'Stockholm This Week' and take a look at 'Stockholm on a Shoestring'. The Swedish Institute on the first floor gives out free factsheets on Sweden, and everyone involved seems incredibly helpful.

- **Addresses:**

POST OFFICE: Vasagatan 28–34, open 8 a.m.–8 p.m., Sat.: 9 a.m.–3 p.m., Sun.: 9 a.m.–11 a.m. Also Central Station (see opening hours above).

AMEX: Birger Jarlsgatan 1 (Tel. 6797880). Open Mon.–Fri.: 9 a.m.–5 p.m., Sat.: 10 a.m.–1 p.m.

UK EMBASSY: Skarpögatan 6 (Tel. 6670140).

US EMBASSY: Strandvägen 101 (Tel. 7855300).

CANADIAN EMBASSY: Tegelbacken 4, 7th floor (Tel. 237920).

AUSTRALIAN EMBASSY: Sergelstorg 12 (Tel. 6132900).

24-HOUR CHEMIST: Apoteke Scheele, Klarabergsgatan 64 (Tel. 248280 or 218934).

SVENSKA TURISTFÖRENINGEN: Drottninggatan 31–33 (Tel. 7903100). Call in for information if you're camping or hostelling in Sweden.

PHONE CODE: 08.

• **Getting about:** The underground and buses are good and charge by the zone. Three-day transit passes cost about 105 kr. (including free entry to some museums and ferries); twenty-four-hour passes cost about 30/55 kr., depending on the areas covered. Buy these at tourist information or stalls in the underground. The 'Stockholm Card' (Stockholmskortet), also known as the 'Key to Stockholm', is available for 135 kr. per day. One adult and two children to 18 can use the same card. It gives you free travel on buses and underground trains as well as suburban trains (also free on Inter-Rail), museum entrances and sightseeing trips by bus or boat. It also gives you a free excursion by boat to Drottningholm Palace. If you are only staying one day, you will need to cram in a lot to make it worthwhile, as many museums shut at 3 or 4 p.m. The banks also hand out free city maps, and if nature calls the best toilets are in the department stores such as NK. Look out for the underground station at Kungsträdgården – it is like a long art gallery of decorated walls.

SEEING

Close to the centre lie the islands of GAMLA STAN, SKEPPSHOLMEN and DJURGÅRDEN where the vast majority of sights are located. Gamla Stan, or the Old Town, dates back to the mid-thirteenth century. The narrow medieval streets are full of trendy shops and restaurants, nightclubs and studios. The eighteenth-century ROYAL PALACE is in Gamla Stan, and parts of it are open to the public till about 3 p.m. daily, except Mondays. The NATIONAL MUSEUM and

MODERN ART GALLERY are located east of the Old Town at Skeppsholmen, and east of this again is the Djurgården, an island almost entirely devoted to recreation. Take the ferry over from Slussen or Nybroplan, or walk from Strandvägen. This is where the seventeenth-century warship *Wasa* is on view. This flagship of the Swedish navy only lasted ten minutes on her maiden voyage before sinking into oblivion, till she was rediscovered in 1956 and brought up. She's in a remarkable state of preservation and is well worth the 30 kr. fee (students 20 kr.).

If you're heavily into ships and naval history, the MUSEUM SHIPS at Sjöhistoriska museet (Tel. 6664900) will be of interest. Here you can see an ice-breaker, lightship and medieval ship. Open daily 10 a.m. to 5 p.m. during the summer.

Sweden's open-air museum, SKANSEN, is definitely one of Europe's best. It's called 'Sweden in Miniature' with good reason, as an afternoon spent there will fill you in more on Swedish folklore, architecture and history than will a week touring the country. There are over 150 buildings of authentic Swedish design, demonstrations of folk dancing, craftsmen at work, a zoo, an aquarium and lots more. Open Apr.–Sept.: 8 a.m.–11.30 p.m.; Oct.–Mar.: 8 a.m.–9 p.m. (the buildings 11 a.m.–5 p.m.). Entrance costs 25 kr.

GRÖNA LUND, or Tivoli, is the amusement park on Djurgården. It is Stockholm's version of the famous Copenhagen Park and is a favourite family attraction.

The Swedish 'House of Culture' (KULTURHUSET) at Sergelstorg is a good example of the country's social-mindedness. Exhibitions of crafts and art are always on and there are free 'creative activities' for anyone who wants to participate so, if you're feeling inspired, jog along and model or paint your masterpiece. There's also a library and access to foreign newspapers and records. It's open in summer, Mon.–Fri.: 9 a.m.–6 p.m. and Sat.–Sun.: 11 a.m.–5 p.m. The only dance museum in the world is at FOLKETS HUS, Barnhusgatan 12/14.

SLEEPING

Hotellcentralen at Central Station will give you a map and list of hostels and hotels or find you a hostel space for a fee of 12 kr. per person, or a hotel bed for a fee of 24 kr. per room. The International Youth Centre will also help out if you're really stuck. You'd do well to make use of these services, especially in peak season, as beds (especially cheap ones) are thin on the ground. Hotelltjänst (Tel. 104467) can arrange, free of charge, private accommodation at the station if you're staying more than two days, but in general in summer there are never enough to go around. If it's at all feasible to call ahead and reserve, do so; and this goes for hostels, campsites or hotels. (English is widely spoken.)

The most memorable place to stay in Stockholm is definitely on board the af *Chapman*. This youth hostel is a nineteenth-century sailing ship, fully rigged and decked out, and harboured opposite the Gamla Stan; it costs 90 kr. for a 'berth' in a four–eight-bed cabin for IYHF members, non-members pay a supplement of 25 kr. You need to pre-book or turn up early – 9 a.m. at the latest – to stand a chance; to reserve, call 6795015. The other central youth hostel, open only in summer, is also popular and good: Frescati Hostel at Professorsslingan (Tel. 159434) is part of Hotel Frescati and offers great doubles for around 175 kr. per person. There's also a youth hostel on Skeppsholmen beside af *Chapman* (Tel. 6795017). Large and good value. There's a YMCA hostel (KFUM) at Garden Jyllandsgatan 16 (Tel. 7526456), which costs 70 kr. and is open from 20 July–16 Aug. Take underground 11 to Kista (Sorogatan exit).

For hotels try one of the following: Domus Hotel, Körsbärs-vägen 1 (Tel. 160195), singles 495–750 kr., doubles 590–850 kr., Pensionat Oden, Odengatan 38 (Tel. 6124349), or Gustavs-vikshemmet at Västmannagatan (Tel. 214450). Skeppsholmen Hotel is opposite af *Chapman*.

Out of the four city campsites, the nearest ones are Ängby Camping on Lake Mälaren (Tel. 370420) on underground 17 or 18, and Bredäng Camping (Tel. 977071) on subway 13 or 15 to Bredäng Station. For a list of Swedish youth hostels contact STF at Drottninggatan 31–33, and for student hostels contact SFS at Kungsgatan 4, Box 7144, Stockholm (Tel. 234515).

EATING AND NIGHTLIFE

Face the fact, you're going to have to spend twice as much as you would in southern Europe to eat out here. Picnics are the answer, in conjunction with bar meals ('Bars' are basic self-service restaurants here). In conventional restaurants look out for 'Dagens rätt' (today's special) for a slightly cheaper lunch or snack. Buy in supplies at Östermalms Saluhall or Hötorgshallen, the two big indoor markets. The central supermarkets also do a good line in groceries and the prices are cheaper than in the indoor markets. While smörgåsbord are filling and tasty, they also tend to be pricey; however, if you arrive in Stockholm Central after a long train journey, treat yourself to the excellent stora frukost (eat-as-much-as-you-like breakfast 6.30 a.m.–10 a.m., closed Sunday). It's about 55 kr. and will keep you going all day. At Norrlandsgatan 5, Pk-Building, there is a good vegetarian restaurant where you help yourself and pay according to weight. Hot vegetarian dishes are served all day. If you're cutting all corners and don't mind plastic atmospheres and fast food, there are a number of outlets to choose from. There are several McDonald's and a Wimpy beside the Kulturhuset. In the evening Gamla Stan tends to be the best area to head for. There are plenty of pubs and clubs with bands for around 50 kr. For cheaper entertainment, go over to Skansen or Gröna Lund where there's usually dancing, etc. Check with 'Stockholm This Week' for current events. The music pub 'Victoria' and Café Opera, both on Kungsträdegården, are good places to meet young Stockholmers. The latter resembles the bar in the TV series 'Cheers'. At midnight the chairs/tables are cleared for a disco to begin. Entry is free before 11 p.m.

• **Excursions:** The old university town of UPPSALA is 45 minutes away by train. On a day trip here you can see the medieval CATHEDRAL, sixteenth-century CASTLE, the oldest UNIVERSITY in Sweden, pre-VIKING BURIAL MOUNDS, and the UPPLANDS MUSEUM which details the city's history and customs. Turn right on leaving the station for tourist information at Sit Persgatan 4 (Gamla Torget) (Tel. 018 117500) or try the tourist information at Uppsala Castle – open May–Sept. (Tel. 018–153033). An alternative excursion is to DROTTNINGHOLM PALACE, the residence of the royal family, built in the seventeenth century, five miles west of the capital on the island of Lovön. It's all very pretty: Chinese pavilion, unusual 200-year-old theatre, etc. To get there, either head for Klara Mälarstrand (near City Hall) and take the steamer, or take the underground to Brommaplan and then change to Mälaröbuses. To see at least some of Stockholm's 24,000 islands in the archipelago take a bus out to the TV tower at KAKNÄSTORNET. This 508-foot tower is reputed to have the fastest lift in Europe, but the view is worth it once your stomach has settled down. There is also a cafeteria and restaurant with prices which are not as extortionate as you will find in similar towers in other countries. Open from 9 a.m.–10.30 p.m. mid-April–September, 9 a.m.–6 p.m. mid-September–mid-April (Tel. 086–678030).

Malmö

The southern Swedish area of Skåne with its endless fields and sandy beaches is home to Malmö, Sweden's third largest city and one of the venues for the 1992 European Football Championships. Malmö is a pleasant stop-off and is easily reached by hydrofoil from Copenhagen, or by train from Stockholm or Gothenburg. On arrival, a good place to head for is another of the excellent Inter-Rail centres, on Stortorget 24 (Tel. 118585). They'll help out with free showers, advice and rucksack storage. Your ticket gains you entry.

The train station is handily placed just north of the GAMLA STAN (Old Town), the area to concentrate upon. The STORTORG is a massive market square, built in the sixteenth century, and the centre of things. Look for the RÅDHUS (Town Hall) on one side of the square; it is worth the tour inside. Don't miss the LILLA TORG, an idyllic square of medieval houses and cobblestones off the Stortorg, and full of stalls and buskers in the summer months. Take a look at the ST PETRI KYRKA, a Gothic church behind the Rådhus. The MALMÖHUS is Malmö's castle, once a prison, with Lord Bothwell, Mary Queen of Scots' last husband, on its guest books. The museums here are excellent, and bear in mind that an entry-ticket bought here is then valid for the rest of the day at the other city museums. There is a good beach south of the Slottspark, further on from the castle.

Tourist information is at Skepsbron 1 (Tel. 341270), a short walk from the station. The staff are extremely helpful. Camping is your cheapest bet in Malmö, as in much of Sweden; bus 11A will take you to Sibbarp Camping at Strandgatan 101. Otherwise there are hostels at Dahlemsgatan 5, the Kirsebergs hostel (Tel. 342635), or further out at Backavagen 18, where you'll find the IYHF hostel (Tel. 82220). Pick up the 'Malmö This Month' guide, which is free and widely available, for details of events going on.

Gotland

Sweden's largest island of Gotland is known for its medieval remains and its connections with the Hanseatic League. To get here you need a ferry from Oskarshamn or Nynäshamn over to VISBY, the major town on Gotland. Ask tourist information for connection times and details, but fares are likely to be 150 kr. (one-way), less 25–35% for student discounts. In Visby, tourist information is at Strandgatan 9 at the harbour (Tel. 0498 10982). Before heading off to the unspoilt countryside of Gotland, preferably on a bike, which can readily be hired at a number of shops between the ferry terminal and the tourist information for around 40 kr. per day, wander through Visby and take a look at the OLD CITY WALLS, the Viking remains in the GOTLANDS FORNSAL MUSEUM and the ST MARIA CATHEDRAL.

Gothenburg (Göteborg)

Sweden's second city is about four hours from Stockholm, and the detour to the west coast provides an interesting alternative route to get down to Copenhagen, as the direct line running straight down to Malmö is not that interesting. But if you go down that way it is worthwhile stopping off at the pleasant university town of LUND, four hours from Gothenburg, which has a magnificent cathedral with moving clock and an interesting outdoor museum (Kulturen) with demonstration crafts and old houses. Gothenburg's big on parks, museums and canals – in fact there's a distinct British feel to it, and it is known as Little London. Its harbour is the largest in Scandinavia.

STATION FACILITIES

	GÖTEBORG CENTRAL
Train information and *reservations by phone*	Mon.–Fri.: 5.40 a.m.–9 p.m. Sat.: 5.40 a.m.–8.15 p.m., Sun.: 6.30 a.m.–10 p.m. (Tel. 031–805000)
Tourist information	At 'Östra Nordstan' (2 minutes away) in Nordstan Shopping Centre Mon.–Fri.: 9.30 a.m.–6 p.m., Sat.: 9.30 a.m.–3 p.m.
Foreign exchange	Mon.–Fri.: 8 a.m.–9 p.m.
Left-luggage lockers	24 hours
Left-luggage store	Mon.–Fri.: 8 a.m.–9 p.m. Sat.: 7 a.m.–8 p.m., Sun.: 8 a.m.–9 p.m.
Cafeteria	Mon.:–Sat.: 6 a.m.–8.30 p.m. Sun.: 6.30 a.m.–10 p.m.
Restaurant and bar	Mon.–Thurs.: 11 a.m.–1 a.m. Fri.: 11 a.m.–2 a.m., Sat.: 1 p.m.–2 a.m. Sun.: 1 p.m.–11.15 p.m. Pub open daily until 12 midnight
Shops	Supermarket at station Mon.–Fri.: 6 a.m.–11 p.m. Sat.–Sun.: 7 a.m.–11 p.m. Other shops at 'Östra Nordstan' (2 minutes away)
Post office	At 'Östra Nordstan' (2 minutes away) Mon.–Fri.: 10 a.m.–7 p.m., Sat.: 10 a.m.–3 p.m.
Ticket office	Mon.–Fri.: 8.30 a.m.–7 p.m. Sat.: 9 a.m.–4 p.m. Sun.: 11 a.m.–6 p.m.
Station shuts	12 midnight–5 a.m. Access to waiting room with ticket

Daily trains to: Oslo, Stockholm, Malmö, Copenhagen, northern Sweden. From Göteborg harbour, ferry services to: Denmark (daily), West Germany (daily), England (3 times/week) and Holland (2 times/week).

TOURIST INFORMATION AND SLEEPING

Apart from Östra Nordstan, the main tourist office is at Kungsportsplatsen 2, open daily during summer 9 a.m.–8 p.m., otherwise 9 a.m.–5 p.m. Both offer an accommodation service including private accommodation lodgings for singles 180 kr., doubles 130 kr. per person. Their hotels start from about 350 kr. single, 450 kr. double, and they take 50 kr. commission. The youth hostel is good and not too far out. Ostkupan (Tel. 031–401050) at Kallebäck is about two miles from the centre on tram 5 to St Sigfridsplan, then bus 62 or 64 to Gräddgatan, open summer only. There is a new private hostel (Tel. 031–136467) on board a boat, the M/S *Seaside*, about 300 m from the station, along Packhuskajen (Tel. 031–101035). There's also a YMCA hostel at Garverigatan 2 (Tel. 031–803962), open 12 July–16 Aug. and costing 70 kr. Take Tram 1, 3 or 6 to Svingeln.

Kärralund (Tel. 031–252761) is the most central campsite and is reached by tram 5 to Welandergatan. Rather pricey.

You can either buy a 24-hour pass for the excellent bus and tram system for around 30 kr., or invest in the 'Key to Gothenburg' (Goteborgskortet) which gives you free public transport, museum entrance, a sightseeing tour of the city centre, free on the famous 'Paddan' sightseeing boats, and many other things such as a free day trip to Denmark, free entrance to the Liseberg amusement park and much more. It costs around 100 kr. for 24 hours, 135 kr. for 48 hours and 225 kr. for 72 hours. Children pay approximately 50 per cent of the adult price. Always check prices and discounts on offer first.

SEEING

The centre of Gothenburg is very modern but if you head off to HAGA, the old district of wooden houses and coffee shops, you'll see a different side of the city. Of the many parks worth visiting try to take in the BOTANICAL GARDENS, SLOTTSKOGEN with its zoo, lakes and birds, and LISEBERG LEISURE PARK which has everything from discos to fun fairs. The ART CENTRE on Götaplatsen are interesting places, and for the nautically minded the MARITIME MUSEUM (Sjö-fartsmuseet) has ships from Viking times to the present day for groups only. The KRONHUSET is the oldest building in the city and its museum, telling Gothenburg's history, includes such exhibits as reconstructed shops of the last century. The neo-classical CATHEDRAL is also worth visiting. The FESKEKÖRKA, a nineteenth-century building filled with fish stalls and vendors is situated by the moat close to Huitfeldtsplatsen. The 7 a.m. auction is worth getting up for.

EATING AND NIGHTLIFE

Along Kungsportsavenyn (the main boulevard) are restaurants of all kinds and descriptions (from Chinese to Scottish), and alongside them are the increasingly popular fast-food chains. Fish and seafood are naturally in abundance in Gothenburg and often the dagens rätt will include a local fish dish. La Gondola at Kungsport-savenyn 4 does good large meals at moderate prices, and they have outside table service. For picnic food, the markets on Kungstorget are best.

At night, a lot of the young locals seem to gather round Kungsportsavenyn to cast an eye over the visiting talent; otherwise, you're most likely to meet the resident students in the bar at the Students' Union, Kårhuskällaren, which is near Götaplatsen. Behind the market on Kungstorget is Ölhallen, an authentic Swedish pub, and there are quite a few disco and jazz clubs, though their entrance fees put most of them safely out of the average eurorailer's reach.

Lapland

If you were put off going up to Lapland in Norway, let yourself be persuaded now you're in Sweden. It's easier here: the trains run right up to RIKSGRÄNSEN, just before the border and NARVIK in Norway. From Stockholm to the border is a straight 24 hours, though the conditions on the trains don't make this seem as much of an ordeal as it sounds, and the scenery once you're around GÄLLIVARE or KIRUNA is breathtaking. Once you're up there, there's an inland line from Gällivare down through JOKKMOKK and ARVIDSJAUR to ÖSTERSUND. It's legal to camp on unfenced land for one night so you can go it alone in a big way, especially out of season. Make sure you leave the place tidy afterwards though, and treat the plants with respect! Unless you've skin like leather, take with you mosquito repellent of some sort as they're out in force up there. The Svenska Turistföreningen, Box 25, Drottninggatan 31–33, Stockholm, are the people to write to for information on mountain tourist stations and huts, and suggested hiking routes. To get the most out of a trip to Lapland, plan and book ahead as much as possible. Don't just wander aimlessly on to the train in Stockholm with no food or proper walking boots and expect to pick up relevant supplies once you're there, and don't go with fantasies in your head of great wilderness adventures with Lapps, reindeer and huskies. It's a bit like that, but in reality the towns are a bit grey and morose, and the Lapps (they call themselves Sami) are pretty sick of wide-eyed tourists pointing and gawping at them from June to September. If you do go make sure you have the right equipment with you. Good preparation will ensure you get the most out of this breathtaking area.

Gällivare

This strategic mining town is at the junction of the main line to Narvik and inland line to Jokkmokk. If you've time to kill here waiting for connections, go to the nearby iron mines at MALMBER-GET and take the tour round (check times with tourist information), or go to the museum at VASARA where there are skis dating back before the time of Christ. Apart from the ETTORE CHURCH and the largest log cabin in the world, that's about it here. The tourist office is near the station at Storgatan 16, and is open Mon.–Sun.: 9 a.m.–9 p.m. in summer. They'll give you details on how to get up to the Stora Sjöfallet National Park and the surrounding mountains. If you're staying, ask about the private accommodation here. The youth hostel is at Andra Sidan (Tel. 0970–14380), five minutes from the station. Costs 90 kr. for a member, 120 kr. for a non-member.

If you're travelling up to Kiruna and beyond, consider returning via Narvik and Fauske in Norway. (A bus connects the two and Fauske is on the Bodø line.) If, on the other hand, you are heading down to LULEA, take some time out to visit the excellent Museum of Lapp Culture. In addition to being free of charge, you can also get cassettes to wander around with, explaining the exhibits as you go along. The youth hostel (Tel. 0920–52325) is open all year round, take bus 6 from Lulea.

Kiruna

As the city's fairly unattractive, use Kiruna as a base for the surrounding countryside. Tourist information is at Hjalmar Lund-

bohmsvägen 42, open 9 a.m.–9 p.m. weekdays, 1 p.m.–8 p.m. Sun.
in season. There's a youth hostel called STF Vandrarhem Kiruna,
housed in a big yellow building with an old people's home behind it,
at Sky Hegatan 16A. It is only open in mid-summer and charges
111 kr. (79 kr. with ISIC). There is a campsite about a mile from the
station, Radhusbyn Ripan (Tel. 13100). Costs around 60 kr. per
tent, cabins also available from 125 kr. per person, sharing. Or
tourist information will get you into private houses. There are mine
tours at Kiruna for 65 kr.

If you are going on from Kiruna to Narvik, the north side of the
train is the one to sit on to see the most spectacular scenery.

Jokkmokk

The SWEDISH MOUNTAIN AND LAPP MUSEUM has special displays on
Lapp history and culture and is well worth the 20 kr. entrance fee.
You'll find tourist information at Stortorget 4, open Mon.–Fri.: 9
a.m.–7 p.m.; Sat. and Sun.: 11 a.m.–7 p.m., during the summer,
mid-June–August. The tourist office give out 'Polar Certificates' to
prove you've made it to, and crossed, the Arctic Circle (well, your
Mum'll like it). The GAMLA KYRKA (Old Church) is the other main
sight. There's a youth hostel at Stockgatan 24 (Tel. 0971–11977),
open summer only, and an official campsite, Notuddens, about a
mile from the centre.

Arvidsjaur

The LAPP VILLAGE in the town of Arvidsjaur is still used today by
Lapps visiting the town for festivals and gatherings. Tourist
information is at Östra Skolgatan 18, open 9 a.m.–8 p.m. daily in
the summer, and they'll arrange private accommodation for you.
The campsite at Järnvägsgatan 111 (Tel. 0960–13420) does huts as
well as tent sites, and opposite the station is the Central Hotel at
Järnvägsgatan 63 (Tel. 0960–10098) with rooms at 300 kr. single,
350 kr. double. The youth hostel is at Östra Skolgatan 9 (Tel.
0960–12413), 300 m from the station.

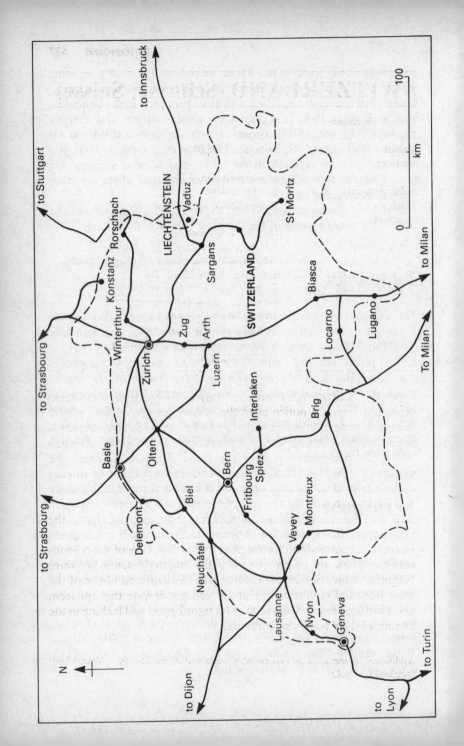

SWITZERLAND (Schweiz; Suisse)

Entry requirements	Passport
Population	6,850,000
Capital	Bern (pop.: 145,000)
Currency	Swiss franc
	£1 = approx. SFr. 2.22
Political system	Federal Republic
Religions	Roman Catholic and Protestant
Languages	German, French, Italian, Romansch
	(English widely spoken)
Public holidays	1, 2 Jan.; Good Friday; Easter Monday;
	Whit Monday; Ascension Day; Corpus Christi;
	1, 15 Aug.; 1 Nov.; 25, 26 Dec.
International dialling codes	From UK: 010 + 41 + number
	From USA: 011 + 41 + number
	To UK: 00 + 44 + number
	To USA: 00 + 1 + number
Eurotrain office	Bäckerstrasse 52, CH–8026 Zürich
	(Tel. 01–2423000)

Cross the border from France or Italy to Switzerland and almost immediately you'll notice even the wood-piles are neater. Where the Swiss obsession for punctuality and cleanliness comes from is open to debate, but we suspect it's an ongoing process started when the Romans cleaned up after the Celts. Then along came the Germanic tribes who brought with them the work ethic we still see in their Swiss descendants, only now it's in the form of high finance and flashy watches. By the end of the thirteenth century, William Tell and his friends were demanding independence from the Habsburgs. This sparked off a proud tradition of self-government among the cantons which continues to this day. One of the reasons why the Swiss are so prosperous is the country's neutrality since Napoleon's invasion of 1815. Physically, Switzerland is one of the most beautiful countries in Europe and yet despite this apparent good fortune, many Swiss seem a bit tight-lipped and lacking in the vitality of their Italian neighbours.

Additional information on this country contained in the *Europe – Grand Tour* factsheet (see p.13).

SWISS FEDERAL RAILWAYS
(Schweizerische Bundesbahnen, SBB)
(Chemins de fer fédéraux, CFF)
(Ferrovie federali svizzere, FFS)

Swiss federal railways and various private railway companies combine to give one of the most extensive and efficient services in Europe. There are even plans (called Rail 2000) to improve services with new lines and half-hourly service with fast new trains to rise to the challenge. The private outfits tend to serve the resort areas, except for the two largest. Most notable is the Bern–Lötschberg–Simplon line (BLS), Europe's largest private operation, which runs in friendly rivalry with the federal railway. International and intercity trains are federal-run, and intercity or express trains run hourly between all the main centres, while inland expresses run at least every other hour. There is a supplement on only two inland routes: the Bernina Express and the Glacier Express. From Chur to Tirano or v.v. it is about 20 SFr. each way and from Zermatt to St Moritz or v.v. it is about 8 SFr. each way including seat reservation. A useful spin-off are the free maps and leaflets given out to lure custom.

● **Inter-Rail bonuses:** Free entrance to Swiss Transport and Communications Museum, Lidostrasse, Lucerne.

On most private railways of Switzerland, Inter-Rail will bring you a 50 per cent reduction, so always ask first (see Appendix II). One that doesn't is Furka Oberalp.

● **Eurail bonuses:** Free:
—Regular steamer services on the lakes of Geneva, Lucerne, Thun, Brienz, Zürich, Neuchâtel, Biel, Murten, on the Rhine from Schaffhausen to Kreuzlingen and on the Aare from Biel/Bienne to Solothurn. Seasonal services – please consult timetables.

Reduced fares:
—50 per cent reduction on steamer services on Lake Constance between Romanshorn and Friedrichshafen and between Rorschach and Lindau.

● **Europabus:**
A 10 per cent reduction is granted by Europabus on transportation costs only and by local offices in Europe on:
200 St Moritz–Munich.

TRAIN INFORMATION

English is widely spoken throughout Switzerland and most Swiss timetables have an English section. If you have no luck finding anywhere to stay, look out for the travel-aid men with red, white and yellow armbands.

• **Reservations:** Must be made for the Glacier Express and the Bernina Express. It's probably only worthwhile reserving if you are going to Italy, where overcrowding can be a problem. Otherwise, don't bother unless you hit a particularly busy weekend. It's not possible to reserve on internal Swiss trains anyway. EuroCity trains have supplements, so ask first.

• **Night travel:** Wagons-Lits run sleepers on all international routes at their standard rates and couchettes are also available. SBB have no services on any inland runs.

• **Eating on trains:** Most stations are fairly well provided for, which is just as well as even the mini-bars are very expensive. If you've money to burn, the self-service buffet is much better value than the dining cars. Believe it or not McDonald's have coaches on certain trains between Basel and Geneva, so it's now possible to have a Big Mac should you feel the urge.

• **Scenic tips:** To get to grips with Switzerland's many scenic rail routes would take at least a month and involve paying out vast amounts for private lines. Swiss Pass or Swiss Card holders get round this problem, but most eurorailers have to be content with mainline runs. The possibilities are endless, without even leaving the main lines. All the main centres make excellent bases for touring the Alps. From Zürich take the main line to Chur, then the narrow-gauge Rhaetian Railway to Tirano – Europe's highest line at 7,400 feet as well as one of the most spectacular. At Chur an alternative is to head towards Zermatt. This line passes over the Oberalp (6,700 feet) and through the Furka tunnel but it gives no reduction to Inter-Railers.

Lucerne offers the greatest possibilities; foremost among them is the main line to Milan through the nine-mile-long Gotthard tunnel which took 2,500 men over seven years to construct in the 1880s. If this isn't spectacular enough, take the branch line to Locarno where you change trains for Domodossola in Italy. This line is a real favourite, passing through some incredible gorges. For the best view sit on the left-hand side. Also from Lucerne, the line to Interlaken is equally awe-inspiring. If you haven't already seen enough and don't mind paying out, take the private line up to Kleine Scheidegg where, after you change trains, the line goes under the Eiger and on to the Jungfraujoch, Europe's highest station at 11,300 feet. Private lines also take you up to Mounts Rigi, Pilatus and Titlis from Lucerne, so good luck if you've got the money. Bern makes an alternative base for any of these trips, but if, like most eurorailers, you're in a hurry the main line to Milan via Brig will not be a disappointment. At Brig, if you've spare cash why not head for Zermatt, and take the cogwheel train up to Gornergrat and see the Matterhorn from close up. Approaching from the west, the train follows Lake Geneva as far as Lausanne where the line splits to enter Bern or Brig – either route is beautiful. The Martigny to Le Châtelard (and on to Chamonix) route is another classic. Sit on the left-hand side for the best view.

● **Rover tickets:** There are a number of tickets available in Switzerland, but a lot of these are designed to get people from airports and border crossings to ski resorts. The most useful is the Swiss Pass. It is available for four days, eight days, fifteen days or one month (prices: £77, £97, £112, £154 in second class) and gives free travel on state railways, steamers, post buses, town buses and trams plus reductions on private lines. The new Flexipass is valid for three days within fifteen and costs £77 in second class. A number of Regional tickets are also available. They are valid for seven or fifteen days. With the latter the holder gets five days of free travel plus ten days of half-price travel. Prices range from £24 to £64 depending on the region and class and length of ticket.

If you intend to stay mainly in one place and/or use many private lines, consider the Swiss Card which gives free travel from the border to a destination and back plus reductions on other journeys. £44 for one month. In general, though, the Swiss Pass is the best bargain. If accompanied by a parent, children under 16 travel free on the Swiss Travel System, and unmarried 16–25-year-olds pay half price.

● **Bikes:** Can be hired at most SBB stations and some private ones; cost approximately SFr. 14 a day for a basic six-gear model. Racing and mountain bikes are also available.

TOURIST INFORMATION

Every town has its own well-organized tourist office usually situated near the station. They keep a good selection of maps and leaflets, as well as running a room-finding service. Ask for the Swiss Holiday Card map: this shows the rail network of the country.

• **ISIC bonuses:** There's a variety of reductions on internal fares and in some museums. For further information, contact SSR Leonhardstrasse 10, Zürich, or SSTE, 3 rue Vignier, Geneva.

• **Money matters:** 1 franc (SFr.) = 100 centimes (c.).
Banking hours are Mon.–Fri.: 8.30 a.m.–4.30 p.m. (often closed 12 noon–2 p.m.). Many stations have exchanges which stay open seven days a week. Switzerland is a good place to change money, as few banks charge a commission and rates are generally favourable. Post offices open Mon.–Fri.: 7.30 a.m.–6 p.m. (often closed 12 noon–1.45 p.m.), Sat.: 7.30 a.m.–11 a.m. Shops open Tues.–Fri.: 8.30 a.m.–6.30 p.m., and Saturdays until mid-afternoon. Many shops shut for lunch 12 noon–2 p.m., particularly in small towns.

SLEEPING

Availability and price are the two main problems you're likely to face in Switzerland. During the summer, the tourist resorts are packed and then there's always that unexpected conference in town. To avoid paying through the nose for somewhere to stay, arrive as early in the day as possible and start looking right away. Tourist offices keep lists of hotels and hostels in the area, and some will find you a room if required for a small charge. Hotels tend to be expensive with singles costing around SFr. 40, so think twice before committing yourself. Even a dormitory bed in a student hostel will set you back SFr. 28 or more. Youth hostels often provide the only answer; there are over 100 of them in Switzerland, most of which are very clean and have excellent facilities. IYHF cards are required and you can expect to pay SFr. 10–20 for a bed. Swiss campsites are among the best in Europe, and at only 7 or SFr. 8 per person you can't go wrong. If you're forced to the hills to sleep out, remember it can get bitterly cold in Switzerland at night even during the summer. Free accommodation is listed in a new brochure, 'Schlafplätze für Unkomplizierte', available for a small fee from the Vereinigung Ferien und Freizeit, Wasserwerkstrasse 17, CH–8035 Zürich.

EATING AND NIGHTLIFE

Although Switzerland used to be *very* expensive, prices have not risen so fast here, although budget travellers will still find it a bit of a struggle to eat out. Fortunately, a lot of the regional specialities can be bought from supermarkets (try Co-op or Migros) and prices are certainly not as bad as in Scandinavia. Alpine areas have a good selection of cheeses and cold meats ideal for picnics. The cheapest restaurants (Gemeindestube) don't serve alcohol, so if you want a glass of wine with your meal you'll have to check out the fixed-price menus. Look out for Rösti (a filling potato dish from the German area) or Berner Platte (a mixture of ham, bacon, and sausage with potatoes and green beans or pickled cabbage). If you can get a group together it's worth going for a fondue. The Swiss don't exactly specialize in budget entertainment; as a result, most young people take to the bars which serve excellent beer. During the summer, but also in spring and autumn there are plenty of local folk festivals going on in the mountains, and on 1 August the sky is set alight by fireworks commemorating the founding of the Swiss Confederation.

Zürich

The largest city of Switzerland and home of the 'gnomes' (as Harold Wilson so aptly put it) of the international money market. Walking on the average Zürich pavement, you're literally on top of gold: vaults containing much of the world's gold reserves lie buried beneath them. Zürich is one of Europe's most expensive cities, and in our estimation doesn't merit more than a couple of days of a tight timetable, though there's no denying the Old Town is picturesque. Situated in northern Switzerland, not far from the German border, Zürich handles trains to an impressive number of destinations in Switzerland, France, Germany, Belgium, the Netherlands, Hungary, Austria, Yugoslavia and Italy.

STATION FACILITIES

	ZÜRICH HAUPTBAHNHOF
Train information	Daily 6.30 a.m.–8.45 p.m.
	(Tel. 2115010)
Reservations	7 a.m.–7.30 p.m.
Tourist information	Mon.–Fri.: 8 a.m.–10 p.m.;
	Sat., Sun.: 8 a.m.–8.30 p.m.
	(no commission, including coins)
Foreign exchange	6.15 a.m.–10.45 p.m.
Left-luggage lockers	No access 12 midnight–4 a.m.
Left-luggage store	Closed late evening to early morning
Self-service buffet	6 a.m.–1 a.m.
Restaurant	6 a.m.–11.40 p.m.
Bath, Shower and Shops	In complex under Bahnhofplatz
Post office	Mon.–Fri.: 7.30 a.m.–6.30 p.m.
	Sat.: 7.30 a.m.–11 a.m.
Station shuts	12 midnight–4 a.m.

TOURIST INFORMATION

The main office is on Bahnhofplatz 15, just outside the station. It's open Mon.–Fri.: 8 a.m.–10 p.m., weekends: 8 a.m.–8.30 p.m. There are leaflets on everything here and an accommodation service for SFr. 3–5 (Tel. 2114000).

Though the Swiss Student Reception Service is mainly a travel agent, it does also have information on Switzerland. It's at Leonhardstrasse 5 (Tel. 2423000) and sells Eurotrain tickets.

• **Addresses:**

AMEX: Bahnhofstrasse 20, open Mon.–Fri.: 8.30 a.m.–5.30 p.m., Sat.: 8.30 a.m.–12 noon (Tel. 2118370).
UK CONSULATE: Dufourstrasse 56 (Tel. 2611520).
US CONSULATE: Zollikerstrasse 141 (Tel. 552566).
PHONE CODE: 01.

SEEING

Getting around Zurich is simple on the modern transport net of buses, trams and S-bahns. Multiple-strip tickets are sold from automated ticket machines, but the best bet is the day card for

SFr. 5.60 which allows unlimited travel on all forms of transport for 24 hours. To the right of the Limmat River is OLD ZÜRICH with its sixteenth- and seventeenth-century guild houses, now restaurants and trendy shops, and close by the town's two medieval churches: FRAUMÜNSTER on the left bank and GROSSMÜNSTER, the austere Protestant cathedral, on the right. For a view over the old town, climb to LINDENHOF just up from the Fraumünster. BAHNHOF-STRASSE is said to be 'the most beautiful shopping street in the world' – it may well be, but it's certainly one of the most expensive; it runs down from the station to the lake where you can indulge in a boat trip if the weather's up to it. The lake is also great for safe, clean swimming and sunbathing. The ZOO in the Zürichberg woods and BOTANICS at Zollikerstrasse are wonderful picnic spots on good days, and on bad the SWISS NATIONAL MUSEUM behind the station and the RIETBERG MUSEUM in the Wessendonck villa at Gabler-strasse are excellent. The latter has one of the best collections of non-European art in Europe. The Swiss National Museum opens Tues.–Sun.: 10 a.m.–5 p.m.; closed Mondays. Admission free. The Rietberg Museum opens daily (except Monday) 10 a.m.–5 p.m. (9 p.m. on Wednesdays). Admission SFr. 3 (SFr. 1 with ISIC). There are all sorts of boat trips on Lake Zürich lasting 1½–4 hours which Inter-Railers get concessions on, or there's the trip down the River Limmat which takes you through old Zürich. Enquire at the Hauptbahnhof about the private mountain trains (Inter-Railers: always check in case you don't get half price on the line you've chosen) and strongly consider the chance to get up to an Alpine village, away from the bourgeois bustle of Zürich. From the Hauptbahnhof, take the train for about an hour to SCHAFFHAUSEN, then a further 20 minutes to STEIN AM RHEIN. This beautiful little place with its half-timbered houses and wonderful location can also be reached by boat from Schaffhausen quay. Inter-Railers get concessions and you can take the boat as far as Konstanz.

SLEEPING

It's probably best to forget hotels and keep it as basic as you can. The campsite on the Zürichsee is very good (train to Wollishofen, then 10-minute walk) and works out as your cheapest option. It's at Seestrasse 559 (Tel. 4821612). Between 27 July and 30 Aug., there's a YMCA Interpoint hostel at Stockerstrasse 18 in Horgen, which is a short train ride out of Zurich; costs SFr. 20.

The youth hostel's big and not strictly run. It's at Mutschellen-strasse 114 (Tel. 4823544) and is reached by tram 7 to Morgental (1 a.m. curfew; reception closes 9 a.m.–2 p.m.). There is a handy supermarket opposite the hostel, which is cheaper than those in town. For cheap pensions and one-star hotels, try the following: Foyer Hottingen, Hottingerstrasse 31 (Tel. 2619315) run by nuns and only for women or married couples; St Josef, Hirschengraben 64 (Tel. 2512757); Justinusheim, Freudenberg Strasse 146 (Tel. 3613806); or Hinterer Sternen, Freieckgasse 7 (Tel. 2513268). These range from SFr. 30–65 singles, SFr. 40 upwards for doubles.

EATING AND NIGHTLIFE

Round the station's as good as anywhere for cheap places, or use one of the many central Migros cafeterias. Jelmoli, the department store on Bahnhofstrasse, does good meals – the best value is the all-you-can-eat breakfast for SFr. 13. There's enough there to keep you sustained till dinner. The Mensa at Rämistrasse 71 does cheap meals for students (shut during the summer), and there are a few beer halls where you can pick up Würst snacks for not too much. The bars, discos and clubs are all around Niederdorfstrasse. There are also a substantial number of gay bars in the city.

Lucerne (Luzern)

If you can only stop once in Switzerland, make it at Lucerne. It's Switzerland's prettiest, and most touristy, town, and in this country that's saying something on both scores. Set on Lake Lucerne with the Alps in the background, it's beautifully preserved and has everything you always associated with Switzerland. It's 1½ hours from Berne and only ¾ hour from Zürich.

TOURIST INFORMATION AND ADDRESSES

The tourist office is a block from the station at Frankenstrasse 1, open Mon.–Fri.: 8.30 a.m.–6 p.m., Sat.: 9 a.m.–5 p.m. Closed Sun. (Tel. 517171). When closed use room-finding service at the station.

If you're staying a while, consider the Lucerne season ticket, which admits you to monuments, the beach and trips on cable railways and steamers. Underneath the railway station is a set of shops, including a good but pricey supermarket – open at odd hours and on Sundays. POST OFFICE: Frohburgstrasse, open Mon.–Fri.: 7.30 a.m.–6.30 p.m., Sat.: 7.30 a.m.–11 a.m.
AMEX: Schweizerhofquai 4, open Mon.–Fri.: 8 a.m.–12 noon, 2 p.m.–6 p.m., Sat.: 8 a.m.–12 noon. Exchange till 5 p.m.
PHONE CODE: 041.

SEEING

The fourteenth-century covered wooden bridge, KAPELLBRÜCKE, spanning the River Reuss, is the symbol of the town. Walk over it to see the 120 paintings dating from the sixteenth to the eighteenth century which tell the town's history. The adjoining WATER TOWER served as a lookout tower, prison, and archive store. On Kornmarkt is the beautiful old TOWN HALL, and on WEINMARKT are old painted houses. The SPREUERBRÜCKE is another covered bridge, this time with paintings on the 'Dance of Death'. For a superb view of the town and its surroundings, climb the westernmost tower on the old city wall (closed in winter).

The SWISS TRANSPORT MUSEUM sounds boring as hell, but is actually quite interesting, and free to Inter-Railers. It's at the end of the park en route to the campsite (bus 2 from the station). On Furrengasse is the small but interesting PICASSO MUSEUM (Am Rhya-Haus). The WAGNER MUSEUM in the suburb of TRIBSCHEN shows the house where he worked and lived, and some of his possessions. You can get here by bus 6/7 or by the boat from in front of the station (Inter-Rail concession). The GLACIER GARDEN is a beautiful rocky area formed during the Ice Age. Entrance to it and the PANORAMA (a huge 360° painting) is SFr. 7.50. Even if you don't go into these two attractions, it is worth walking up the Löwen-strasse to them, to view the beautiful LÖWENDENKMAL – a superb rock carving of a dying lion, to commemorate the Swiss Guards who died protecting the French king and queen.

SLEEPING

If you're intent on a pension or hotel (you must be mad), use the station's accommodation service (open 2.30 p.m.–10 p.m.) and clearly state your price range. The campsite is excellent: its situation couldn't be improved – near the beach and the lake – and to get to it you can walk through the park. It's at Lidostrasse (Tel. 312146) on bus route 2 and costs SFr. 5 per person and SFr. 2.50 per tent. The youth hostel Am Rotsee on Sedelstrasse 12 (Tel. 368800) has over 200 beds and is very reasonable at about SFr. 20 (SFr. 27 non-members). It's not central and closes 9.00 a.m.–4 p.m. Bus 18 to the Gopplismoos stop in Friedental, then a two-minute walk or the more frequent bus 1 to Schlossberg, then a 10-minute walk will get you there. Try to arrive early, as we've had reports of 1½ hours queueing, even at 5 p.m.; the wise arrive early, leave their form and YHA card in the box provided and return before 10 p.m. Hotel Weisses Kreuz at Furrengasse 19 (Tel. 514040) is an old city hotel within the SFr. 60–75 bracket, and is as good as you can expect. You can also try the Touristenhotel, St. Karliquai 12 (Tel. 512474). Dorms SFr. 34, ISIC reduction SFr. 27, or Pension Proffilla (Tel. 224280) from SFr. 50. Also try Schlüssel Franziskanerplatz 12 (Tel. 231061), singles in the SFr. 35–45 bracket, and is well located for the Old Town.

EATING AND NIGHTLIFE

In general both tend to cater for monied European tourists, but if you walk the length of Hertensteinstrasse, you should come up with some suitable pub or restaurant, even if it's just Migros at No. 46, or a fast-food place.

Apart from the International Music Festival (mid-August–early September), Lucerne is exceptionally sedate. A pub with a collection of eurorailers determined to make merry will probably be your high spot, unless your budget is elastic.

• **Excursions:** The steamer cruises down the VIERWALDSTÄTTERSEE (Lake Lucerne to us) are well worth it. Inter-Railers go half price, and you leave from the quay near the station (ask tourist information for details of the alternatives).

The huge towering mountain dominating Lucerne is MOUNT PILATUS (7,000 feet). To get up there, you'd do best to take the boat from Lucerne to ALPNACHSTAD (half price Inter-Rail) and then travel up on the steepest cogwheel railway in the world. Return by cable car to KRIENS then bus 1 back to Lucerne. It's well worth the effort, and really is an experience you won't forget, assuming you manage to avoid the mid-afternoon crowds and can afford the fare of around SFr. 66.

Berne (Bern)

There's nothing to keep you in Berne for much more than a day if you're a restless type, even though it is the capital of Switzerland. It's pretty but not spectacular, and once you've seen the CLOCK TOWER, BEAR PIT (complete with bears), GOTHIC CATHEDRAL and BERNESE HISTORICAL MUSEUM you've more or less done the rounds unless you collect Swiss stamps and want to visit the POSTAL MUSEUM.

STATION FACILITIES

	BERN BAHNHOF
Train information	7.30 a.m.–8.30 p.m.
	(Tel. 211111)
Reservations	7.30 a.m.–8.30 p.m.
Tourist information	Mon.–Sat.: 9 a.m.–6.30 p.m.
	Sun.: 10 a.m.–5 p.m.
Foreign exchange	6.10 a.m.–9 p.m.
Left-luggage lockers	No access 12 midnight–4 a.m.
Left-luggage store	6 a.m.–11 p.m.
Bar, Buffet	4 a.m.–11.30 p.m.
Shops	Tue.–Fri.: 8 a.m.–6.30 p.m.
	Sat.: 8 a.m.–4 p.m.
	Mon.: 2 p.m.–6.30 p.m.
Bath, Shower	6.30 a.m.–8 p.m.
Station shuts	12 midnight–4 a.m.

Daily trains to: Brussels, Basel, Milan, Zürich, Lausanne, Geneva.

TOURIST INFORMATION AND ADDRESSES

The main tourist office is the one at the station. When they close,

they leave information on accommodation posted up outside, and
there's a free phone to make reservations. Open Mon.–Sat.:
9 a.m.–6.30 p.m., Sun.: 10 a.m.–5 p.m. (Tel. 227676).
POST OFFICE: Schanzenpost 1, open Mon.–Fri.: 7.30 a.m.–6.30
p.m., Sat.: 7.30 a.m.–11 a.m.
AMEX: Bubenbergplatz 11, open Mon.–Fri.: 8.15 a.m.–12.30 p.m.,
1.30 p.m.–6 p.m., Sat.: 8.15 a.m.–12 noon (Tel. 229401).
UK EMBASSY: Thunstrasse 50 (Tel. 445021).
US EMBASSY: Jubiläumstrasse 93 (Tel. 437011).
CANADIAN EMBASSY: Kirchenfeldstrasse 88 (Tel. 446381).
AUSTRALIAN EMBASSY: Alpenstrasse 29 (Tel. 430143).
PHONE CODE: 031.

SLEEPING

Definitely avoid hotels here and stick to the youth hostel or
campsite. The hostel is at Weihergasse 4 (Tel. 226316) near the
Houses of Parliament. It closes 10 a.m.–5 p.m. and is run quite
strictly and costs SFr. 17 including breakfast. Camping Eichholz is
down by the river (Tel. 542602), a bit out of the city. Tram 9 to
Eichholz. For a central pension, try Hotel Bahnhof-Süd, Bumpliz-
strasse 189 (Tel. 565111), or Hotel National, Hirschengraben 24
(Tel. 251988) next to the station.

EATING AND NIGHTLIFE

For picnic food there are shops in Marktgasse and Zeughausgasse
near the station, or there are always Migros for cheap meals. About
the only place you can afford, or would find remotely lively, is the
Kornhauskeller on Kornhausplatz. It may bust your budget to eat
there, but go for the local beer.

• **Excursions:** The best day trip you can take from Berne is to the
ancient town of FRIBOURG, only 20 minutes away. The river that
runs through it, the Sarine, is commonly regarded as the boundary
line between the French- and German-speaking sections of Switzerland. Visit the ÉGLISE DES CORDELIERS with its original St Anthony
altar-piece, and take in the view from the bridges that span the
river. Most of the sights are on rue de Morat: the church mentioned
above, the CATHEDRAL, the sixteenth-century TOWN HALL and the
MUSEUM OF ART AND HISTORY.

The Bernese Oberland

The region round INTERLAKEN is stunning in its beauty, but from a eurorailer's point of view, unless you're stopping off to ski or climb, there's not that much to see apart from the scenery. Balmers Gasthaus, Hauptstrasse 23/25 (Tel. 036–221961) is great value: for SFr. 16 in dormitory, SFr. 26 in doubles, and even provides space under shelters outside when overfull. Contrast the quieter Youth Hostel further out at Aareweg 21 (Tel. 036–224353), take Bus 1 from the station. Only an hour from Berne, Interlaken is a good base for heading off into the Bernese Oberland. Inter-Railers get a 50 per cent reduction on the private railways that take you there. If you've decided that, now you're this far, you want to spend a bit of time here, consider buying the rail pass from this area's private railways board. It costs SFr. 125 for five days' unlimited travel out of fifteen days on most trains, cable cars and 'gondolas' which hoist you up the thousands of feet in next to no time. It also gives you the remaining ten days' travel at half price; still it is a lot of money, and remember you can still travel half price on your Inter-Rail. Tourist information is at Höheweg 37 in the Metropole Hotel, as well as at Westbahnhof; and for rooms, look at the bulletin board at Westbahnhof listing the hotel rooms as well as the 'Zimmer frei' (private apartments) alternatives.

GRINDELWALD is *the* destination for serious climbers (though LAUTERBRUNNEN is equally beautiful if you're not a climber). What with the NORTH FACE OF THE EIGER, the JUNGFRAU and the MÖNCH, you won't know where to begin. There are hourly trains here from Interlaken, and Inter-Rail's only valid on the route to Jungfraujoch. If you get this far, don't leave till you've taken the cable car to MÄNNLICHEN, WENGEN and from Grindelwald up to PFINGSTEGG. From Pfingstegg, walk to STIEREGG. More than likely, this will be the high spot of your travels in this spectacular country. KLEINE SCHEIDEGG and JUNGFRAUJOCH are also in this area and accessible with the help of an extortionately priced mountain railway. If you're staying, try for the youth hostel Die Weid at Terrassenweg (Tel. 036–531009), or camp. If this has whetted your appetite, you might as well carry on to the MATTERHORN. Your best base for excursions here is ZERMATT which you reach by private railway from BRIG or VISP (Inter-Railers half price). Tourist information is to the right of the station. They'll fix you up with maps, hiking suggestions and a bed. Hotel Bahnhof (Tel. 028 672406) opposite the station is reasonable and has dormitories as well as rooms for around SFr. 19 The youth hostel costs about SFr. 13.50 per night (including breakfast). Curfew is at 10 p.m., but can be flexible – check first! (Tel. 028 672320.)

Lausanne

The French Alps are visible from Lausanne, home of the most spectacular Gothic building in Switzerland: its cathedral; the old medieval quarter is the most interesting (as the rest of the town is very modern) and here you'll find the HÔTEL DE VILLE, the EARLY GOTHIC CATHEDRAL and the CHÂTEAU SAINTE MAIRE, formerly the Bishop's Palace and now the seat of government for the canton. The funicular to OUCHY will take you down to the busy port which looks over to Lake Geneva and the Alps. Of the museums try to take in COLLECTION DE L'ART BRUT in the Château de Beaulieu where there are interesting exhibits by psychologically disturbed people, criminals and recluses.

TOURIST INFORMATION AND ADDRESSES

TOURIST OFFICE: 2 Avenue de Rhodanie, open Mon.–Sat.: 8 a.m.–7 p.m., Sun.: 9 a.m.–12 noon, 1 p.m.–6 p.m., and at the station. They'll kit you out with maps, etc., and arrange accommodation. Ask for the Lausanne Official Guide.
POST OFFICE: 43 bis Avenue de la Gare, open Mon.–Fri.: 7.30 a.m.–12 noon, 1.30 p.m.–6.30 p.m. (closed Saturday p.m.).
AMEX: 14 Avenue Mon Repos, open Mon.–Thurs.: 8 a.m.–12.15 p.m., 1.45 p.m.–5.30 p.m., Fri.: 8 a.m.–5.30 p.m.
PHONE CODE: 021.

SLEEPING

The youth hostel is down by the lake at 1 Chemin du Muguet (Tel. 265782), SFr. 15 includes breakfast. Bus 1 to Batelière (direction

La Maladière), then follow the signs. The campsite is also by the lake, Camping de Vidy-Lausanne (Tel. 242031) at 3 Chemin du Camping and has tents, caravans and bungalows for hire. It is highly recommended. For rooms or dormitories, try Foyer la Croisée, 15 Avenue Marc Dufour (Tel. 204231).

EATING AND NIGHTLIFE

Food shouldn't be a problem. There are plenty of grocers' and bakers' shops to buy from, and no shortage of affordable restaurants, but watch out down in Ouchy – many restaurants are overpriced, as are many of the small Swiss cafes. Restaurant Manora in Place St Francais is a good self-service restaurant worth a visit. There are a few good supermarkets, open seven days a week, at the bottom of Avenue d'Ouchy. There's no unique nightlife here, except in the Festival and Fête in late June, when the town offers plenty to do at night.

If you're staying at the youth hostel consider taking a wander into the park opposite and eating at the café bar next to the tennis courts. Although the menu is somewhat restricted, they do an excellent range of pizzas at reasonable prices and both the staff and the customers are young and friendly. If you've just come off a train after a long journey and can't wait for food, McDonald's is facing the main entrance to the station. But watch the traffic as the trolley-bus terminal is here and these vehicles are noise-free as well as pollution-free.

Basel (Basle)

Situated on the crossroads of France, Germany and Switzerland, Basel is the country's second city and is considered the cultural capital of Switzerland. From Basel you can take the train just about anywhere in Europe, from Warsaw to Stockholm.

STATION FACILITIES

As Basel is the border, the French effectively share the station with the Swiss. You'll find information for both SNCF and SBB at the station. French trains stop at the west end of the station.

BASLE BAHNHOF

Train information	SBB 6 a.m–9 p.m.
	(Tel. 2726767)
	SNCF 7.30 a.m.–7 p.m.
	(Tel. 2715033)
Reservations	8 a.m.–7.30 p.m.
Tourist information	Mon.–Fri.: 8.30 a.m.–7 p.m.
	Sat.: 8.30 a.m.–12.30 p.m., 1.30 p.m.–6 p.m.
Foreign exchange	Mon.–Sat.: 6 a.m.–11.15 p.m.
	Sun.: 6 a.m.–10.30 p.m.
Left-luggage lockers	No access 12.30 a.m.–4 a.m.
Left-luggage store	5.30 a.m.–12 midnight
Bar, Buffet	6 a.m.–11 p.m.
Shops	Mon.–Fri.: 7 a.m.–6.30 p.m.
	Sat.: 7.30 a.m.–4 p.m.
Bath, Shower	Mon.–Sat.: 7.30 a.m.–4 p.m.
Post office	Mon.–Fri.: 7.30 a.m.–12 noon,
	1.45 p.m.–6.30 p.m.
	Sat.: 7.30 a.m.–11 a.m.
Station shuts	12.30 a.m.–4 a.m.

TOURIST INFORMATION AND ADDRESSES

As well as the one at the station, there's a tourist office at
Blumenrain 2. Closed Sat. p.m. and Sun. (Tel. 2615050).
POST OFFICE: Nauenstrasse, next to station. Open Mon.–Fri.: till
6.30 p.m., Sat.: till 11 a.m.
AMEX: c/o Reisebüro Kundig, Aeschengraben 10, open Mon.–Fri.:
8.15 a.m.–6 p.m.
PHONE CODE: 061.

SEEING

It's the museums in Basel that hog the limelight. If you're tired of
trudging round museums and galleries, just take in the two bare
essentials: the FINE ARTS MUSEUM and the KIRSCHGARTEN MUSEUM,
housed in an old patrician mansion at Elisabethenstrasse 27. As for
the town itself, the twelfth-century MÜNSTER (cathedral) is surrounded by medieval houses and stands in an attractive square. The
TOWN HALL is on Market Square, and there are still markets held

here today; THREE COUNTRIES' CORNER is the spot where the Swiss, French and German borders all meet. Just east of the tourist office lies the Münsterplatz where walking tours start.

SLEEPING

The large youth hostel is at St Alban-Kirchrain 10 (Tel. 2720572). It's clean, friendly and has double rooms and dorms. A three-course supper costs 7 SFr. 1 a.m. curfew. Take tram 1 one stop, then tram 3 to second stop. As far as hotels go, try the following, but insist on their cheapest rooms: Hotel Stadthof, Gerbergasse 84 (Tel. 2618711); Hotel Klingental Garm, Klingental 20 (Tel. 6816248). These one-star hotels have single rooms (without bath) starting at about 40 SFr.

Cheaper hotels are a short journey over the French border in Mulhouse.

EATING AND NIGHTLIFE

You shouldn't have many problems finding shops and cafés to feed yourself from, there are plenty of alternatives. Zum Goldenen Sternen, the oldest pub in Switzerland, at St Albanrheinweg 70, is good for a drink, but watch the food prices. 'This Week in Basel' will fill you in on events, and if you're there around Ash Wednesday, you should catch some local festivities.

Geneva (Genève)

This is perhaps the most international of all European cities, home to dozens of multinational organizations and peace-negotiating bodies such as the Red Cross and United Nations. The town has a rich and well-cared-for air, and is a good place to break up a long haul like Paris–Rome.

STATION FACILITIES

	GENÈVE CORNAVIN
Train information and reservations	8 a.m.–7.15 p.m.; Sat.: 8 a.m.–6.15 p.m.; Sun.: 10 a.m.–6.15 p.m. (Tel. 7316450)
Day tickets	4.30 a.m.–11.10 p.m.
Tourist information	Mon.–Sun.: 8 a.m.–8 p.m.
Foreign exchange	Mon.–Sun.: 6 a.m.–9.45 p.m.
Left-luggage lockers	No access 1 a.m.–4 a.m.
Snack bar	5.45 a.m.–12 midnight
Post office	6 a.m.–10.45 p.m. (next building)
Station shuts	1 a.m.–4 a.m.

Daily trains to: Lausanne, Basel, Bern, Zürich, Milan, Rome, Nice, Barcelona, Lyon, Paris.

TOURIST INFORMATION

The station office operates all year round, and is better than the administrative office at Tour de l'Ile (Tel. 738 5200).

• **Addresses:**
POST OFFICE: Poste Montbrillant (next to the station).
AMEX: 7 rue du Mont Blanc, open Mon.–Fri.: 8.30 a.m.–5.30 p.m., Sat.: 9 a.m.–12 noon (Tel. 7317600).
UK CONSULATE: 37–39 rue Vermont (Tel. 7343800).
US CONSULATE: 1–3 Avenue de la Paix (Tel. 7387613).
MEDICAL HELP: PMC 'Permanence', rue Chantepoulet 21.
PHONE CODE: 022.

SEEING

Most of the things to see in Geneva can be taken in on the one main walk. Starting from the station, walk down RUE DU MONT BLANC till you're at the lake, then turn right on QUAI DES BERGUES, cross the river on the PONT DE L'ILE to the PLACE BEL-AIR, then head on to the PLACE NEUVE down RUE DE LA CORRATERIE. Once here, enter the park which contains the university and the famous statue to the Reformation. The VIEILLE VILLE is the old cobblestoned quarter round the CATHÉDRALE ST PIERRE, where Calvin preached. On RUE HÔTEL-DE-VILLE is the TOWN HALL where the Geneva Convention was signed, and some seventeenth-century houses built by Italian religious refugees. The best museums are the PETIT PALAIS (Impressionist paintings), INSTITUT ET MUSÉE VOLTAIRE, 25 rue des Délices (Voltaire's house), and the PALAIS DES NATIONS on Avenue de la Paix. Don't miss the INTERNATIONAL RED CROSS AND RED CRESCENT MUSEUM at 17 Avenue de la Paix. Closed Tuesdays. Open 10 a.m.–5 p.m. Geneva is the world's top watchmaking centre, so hide your Japanese digital and wander round the superb CLOCK MUSEUM, 15 rue de Malagnou (closed Mondays). Boat trips on Lake Geneva (Lac Léman) are pleasant, but compare prices first. Sunbathers should head for Nyon, on the way to Lausanne, which has a good lakeside beach.

SLEEPING

Summer in Geneva makes affordable beds scarce, so arrive early and immediately aim at getting fixed up. Ask tourist information for their list of foyers, dormitories, etc., and phone around. The youth hostel is at 30 rue Rothschild (Tel. 7326260, 10 minutes from Cornavin station via rue de Lausanne). Reception closes 10 a.m.– 5 p.m. and costs SFr. 16 including breakfast. The nearest campsite is Sylvabelle, 10 Chemin de Conches (Tel. 3470603); take bus 8 or 88 from the station. There's a YMCA hostel at 9 Avenue Ste-Clotilde (Tel. 3218313; bus 1, 4 or 44 to Place du Cirque; open 11 July–16 August) which costs SFr. 14. Home St Pierre, at Cour St Pierre by the cathedral, is a great place. It takes only women and is deservedly popular (Tel. 3103707). Contact the 'cooperative universitaire pour logement' for a room in one of the four university halls of residence (Tel. 7812598). They charge around SFr. 30 each. Alternatively, you could stay just over the border in France, at Bellegarde, which is much cheaper.

EATING AND NIGHTLIFE

Geneva definitely aims its tourism at the well-heeled, but there are some Migros and budget restaurants dotted around. A picnic down by the lake is your cheapest and most memorable option, but if it's wet, try the restaurant opposite the station on 17 Place Montbrillant, or Le Zofage, the university's place at rue des Voisins, with cheap filling plats du jour.

Tourist information will tell you what's on. Geneva actually has the most swinging nightlife in Switzerland, but then that's not hard. Before you get excited, I'm afraid there's probably nothing much you can afford, so content yourself manwatching in Place Molard or head for a lively bar like Mr Pickwick's Pub, 80 rue Lausanne.

The Grisons (Graubünden)

From the source of the Rhine east to the River Inn and on to Austria is the canton of Grisons. Here you'll still hear Romantsch spoken along with Swiss-German. CHUR is the cultural and administrative centre, and such flashy resorts as St Moritz are in this region. The trains are narrow-gauge, but Inter-Rails are valid. Take the CHUR–ST MORITZ line (two hours), even if you don't get off at the other end, as the scenery is quite beautiful.

Chur

Walk through the old-town streets with their medieval houses and pass through the old gate to the CATHEDRAL, with its pre-Christian sacrificial stone. The HOF (Bishop's Palace) next door is still in use, so don't nose about too much. The pub in there (the Hofkellerei) is a good watering-hole, but a bit touristy in summer. Tourist information is at Grabenstrasse 5 (Tel. 081–221818), and there's a good youth hostel at Berggasse 28 (Tel. 081–226563). Ask at the station for a map to get you there.

St Moritz

The actual town's nothing special, and apart from the ENGADINE MUSEUM en route to the famed healing waters of the MAURITIUS

SPRINGS which reconstructs life of days long ago, there's not much else to see. But people don't come here to sightsee, they come to ski or climb. The general information centre is Kur-und-Verkehrsverein on Via Maistra 12, open Mon.–Fri.: 9 a.m.–12 noon, 2 p.m.–6 p.m., Sat.: 9 a.m.–12 noon (Tel. 082–33147).

If your time's short, do just two things: take the cable car up the 8,000-foot MUOTTAS MURAGL and walk the path along the SILS LAKE. If you're staying, try your best to get into the youth hostel at Via Surpunt 60 (Tel. 082–33969). It's beautiful, and cheap by Swiss standards. There's camping at Olympiaschanze (Tel. 082–34090) about 30 minutes from the station. Forget hotels; you're outclassed here, I'm afraid.

If you're heading for Italy, take the train in the direction of TIRANO on the Italian border (1½ hours) as the scenery around here and on the Passo del Bernina is incredible. Get off at every station and make a day of it, if you've time, as this is the highest line in Europe without cogs or cables.

Ticino

This region, next to Italy and known as the 'Swiss Riviera', has the best of both countries: the scenery, tidiness and efficiency of Switzerland, and the sun, language and ambience of Italy. Lugano and Locarno are the main centres and the area round the lakes of Lugano and Maggiore makes wonderful camping, swimming and walking, away from the crowds. The climate is particularly mild throughout the year.

Lugano

This is a particularly pretty town of sunny piazzas, palm trees and the dominating Monte San Salvatore. It's on LAKE LUGANO, and lies on the Zürich–Milan main line. Stroll through the little winding streets on the hill at SAN LORENZO for a view over the town, stopping off at SANTA MARIA DEGLI ANGIOLI to admire the sixteenth-century frescoes. Walk down to the lake and Riva Albertolli 5 where the tourist office is. They're open Mon.–Fri.: 8 a.m.–12 noon, 2 p.m.–6 p.m., Sat.: 9 a.m.–12 noon, 2 p.m.–5 p.m. and they'll give you maps, lists of the local mountain huts, and arrange accommodation (Tel. 091–214664).

The VILLA FAVORITA CASTAGNOLA houses one of Europe's finest private art collections: Rembrandts, Dürers, Rubens, etc. It's open Fri. and Sat.: 10 a.m.–12 noon, 2 p.m.–5 p.m., Sun.: 2 p.m.–5 p.m., 7 SFr. From the Paradiso quarter, it's a 10-minute ride on the funicular up MONTE SAN SALVATORE, with a great view over the Alps and lakes. The funicular from Cassarate up to MONTE BRÉ on the other side of the town is another scenic excursion. The MUSEUM OF EXTRA-EUROPEAN CULTURES, on Via Cortivo 24 has displays from Oceania, Indonesia and Africa. Open Tues.–Sun.: 10 a.m.–5 p.m. Entrance SFr. 6.

There's a youth hostel in Lugano-Crocifisso at 6942 Savosa (at the terminus of bus 5) of an exceptionally high standard (Tel. 091–562728). Aris Pensione, Via Geretta 8 (Tel. 091–541478), in nearby Paradiso is a good place to stay or eat, with rooms averaging SFr. 50 per person and meals SFr. 15. For hotels, try the Montarina which has rooms from SFr. 35–50 and dormitory accommodation at SFr. 15. It's at Via Montarina 1 (Tel. 091–567272). There are plenty of markets and food shops offering Swiss-quality Italian food. Commercio on Via Ariosto do great pizzas. In the evening there are often concerts down by the lake, but nightlife here is fairly sedate in general.

Locarno

From Lugano it's about half an hour to Ticino's capital BELLIN-ZONA, and from there another half-hour will take you into Locarno, the best place to base yourself for trips round LAKE MAGGIORE. To explore this region you'll need to resort to buses. One of the buses from Locarno station goes through Ascona, Brissago and crosses the Italian border at Madonna di Ponte. Get off at Brissago and make for the island where there's a beautiful botanical garden.

Back in Locarno itself there's a MUSEUM OF MODERN ART in the Pinacoteca Casa Rusca, with the works of Jean Arp and Filippo

Franzoni on permanent display. Funiculars take you up to see the town's landmark, the MADONNA OF THE ROCK (Madonna del Sasso). Try the Gottardo (Tel. 093 334454) above the station for a bed. The private Centrovalli railway from Locarno to Domodossola on the Milan–Brig line is well worth re-routing for. The left-hand side offers the best views of the fantastic scenery.

Liechtenstein

Entry requirements	Passport
Population	29,000
Capital	Vaduz (pop.: 4,870)
Currency	Swiss franc
	£1 = approx. 2.22 SFr.
Political system	Constitutional Monarchy
Religion	Predominantly Roman Catholic
Language	German; English and French widely spoken
Public holidays	1, 6 Jan.; 23 Feb.;
	19 March; 9, 12 April; 1, 20, 31 May;
	10 June; 15 Aug.; 8 Sep.; 8, 25 Dec.
International dialling codes	From UK: 010 + 41 + number
	From USA: 011 + 41 + number
	To UK: 00 + 44 + number
	To USA: 00 + 1 + number

This small alpine principality nestles between Switzerland and Austria. It has enjoyed sovereign status as an independent country since the early 1800s, although the Swiss currency is used. There is a separate identity to this little country which makes it worth a stop.

TRANSPORT

The railway plays a subsidiary role in the country as it passes through only a part of the country and has only two stops. However, the Postbus network is well developed. The best way to enter the principality is by Postbus from either Buchs or Sargans in Switzerland. Services are frequent and the journey times are thirty minutes and fifteen minutes respectively. Bus prices are very reasonable: a monthly pass costs SFr. 15, whilst all journeys up to 13 km are SFr. 2 and those over 13 km SFr. 3. Cross-border routes e.g. Feldkirch–Vaduz or Sargans–Vaduz cost SFr. 3.

SEEING

The capital, VADUZ, is the seat of government and the home of the Prince of Liechtenstein and his family. The Tourist Information is centrally located at Städtle 37 (Tel. 075 21443) and they will provide information and maps on the whole principality and help you with accommodation. You can also get your passport stamped here for just SFr. 1, just to prove you've been.

Liechtenstein is a philatelist's dream and the POSTAGE STAMP MUSEUM in the centre of Vaduz has many rare stamps both of Liechtenstein and other countries. It has free admission and is open April–October daily from 10 a.m.–12 noon and 1.30 p.m.–5.30 p.m. The LIECHTENSTEIN STATE ART COLLECTION at Städtle 37 is worth a visit for its fine interchanging exhibitions from the collections of the Princes of Liechtenstein as well as from other private and public collections. Open April–October 10 a.m.–12 noon, 1.30 p.m.–5.30 p.m. daily, Nov.–March 10 a.m.–12 noon, 1.30 p.m.–5 p.m. daily. Admission SFr. 3, or SFr. 1.50 to students with identification.

Also worth seeing is the LIECHTENSTEIN NATIONAL MUSEUM at Städtle 43. Open May–Oct. 10 a.m.–12 noon, 1.30 p.m.–5.30 p.m. daily, Nov.–April 2 p.m.–5.30 p.m. (closed Mondays). Admission is SFr. 2, SFr. 1 to students. It exhibits good displays of archaeological finds, local folklore, history and a good collection of weapons.

There is good hiking throughout Liechtenstein; many of the better routes and organized tours start at MALBUN. Other towns worth visiting are TRIESENBERG: see the WALSER MUSEUM with its historical collection on the local Walser community. Admission SFr. 2, students SFr. 1. Open Tues.–Fri.: 1.30 p.m.–5.30 p.m., Sat.: 1.30 p.m.–5 p.m., Sundays (June–August only) 2 p.m.–5 p.m. BALZERS is also interesting, notably for Gutenberg Castle and its varied churches.

SLEEPING

The youth hostel here is one of the friendliest we have come across. Reopened last summer after renovation, it's at Rüttigasse 6 (Tel.

075 25022) and is modern and clean. Showers, sheets and breakfast are included in the SFr. 16.30 price. IYHF membership required. Take the Postbus to the stop 'Hotel Mühle'. Alternatively try the Rheinweise Youth Centre (Tel. 075 81514) between Schaan and Buchs, SFr. 9. Campsites are at Triesen (Tel. 075 82686) or Bendern (Tel. 075 31211). If all else fails, tourist information may find you a room in a private house and many inns have rooms, although both these options are more expensive.

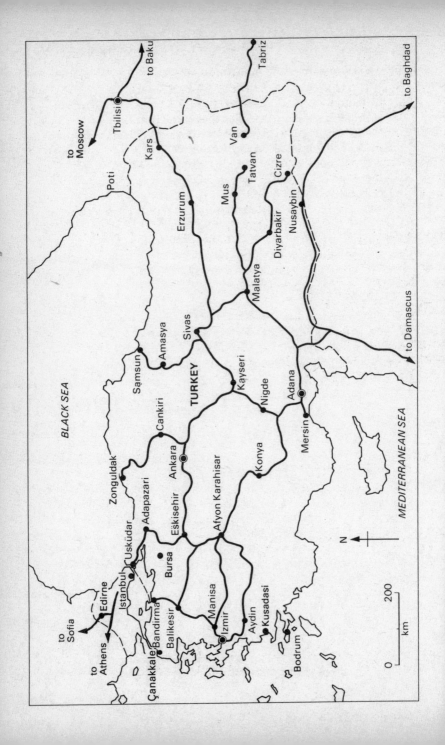

TURKEY (Türkíye)

Entry requirements	Passport and visa (£5 at border)
Population	57,000,000
Capital	Ankara (pop.: 3,460,000)
Currency	Lira
	£1 = approx. 13,120 TL
Political system	Republic
Religion	Muslim
Language	Turkish (some English, French and German spoken in cities)
Public holidays	1 Jan.; 23 April; 19 May;
	3½-day Muslim lunar holiday in spring; 30 Aug.;
	4½-day Muslim lunar holiday in summer;
	28, 29 Oct.
International dialling codes	From UK: 010 + 90 + number
	From USA: 011 + 90 + number
	To UK: 99 + 44 + number
	To USA: 99 + 1 + number

Only 3 per cent of Turkey is in Europe, the rest lies firmly in Asia. The Islamic and European blend of culture makes Turkey a fascinating experience and quite different from a jaunt through Europe. Of its previous civilizations, the best-preserved remains are to be found on the west and south coasts, the Aegean and Mediterranean. Until 1453 the European area of Turkey was under the umbrella of the Christian Byzantine Empire, but the Ottoman conquest put a stop to this. From then on there was no looking back, and under Süleyman the Magnificent (1520–63) the Ottoman Empire reached its zenith; it was largely thanks to him that the Christianity-versus-Islam wars of the sixteenth century were staged. It wasn't till the eighteenth and nineteenth centuries that this powerful empire went into decline; however, once it did the gradual process of westernization began. After the First World War Turkey was divided into British, French and Italian spheres of influence.

Additional information on this country contained in the *Europe – Grand Tour* factsheet (see p.13).

For those travelling Turkey in detail, a new guide, *The Good Tourist in Turkey* (Mandarin Paperbacks) may be useful. Aimed at the environmentally aware traveller, it explores in depth the entire country area by area.

The result was the War of Independence 1919–23. No one did more for the modernization of Turkey in the twentieth century than their national hero Atatürk, and tremendous progress has been made. Travelling in Turkey for women alone is no worse than anywhere else in southern Europe, so don't get the idea the Turks are a hostile and unfriendly lot as portrayed by the film *Midnight Express*. If you're befriended over there by a local, the hospitality they'll show you will leave any European pleasantries standing. Don't be surprised if Turks come up to you in the street and ask if they can talk to you to practise their English.

Nevertheless, steer very well clear of anything likely to be remotely connected with drugs. In particular, don't carry any loose tablets, even aspirin, and if you do have medicines with you carry a copy of the prescription if possible, or the original container. Since November 1989 British citizens (although not Americans, Canadians or Australians) require a £5 visa which you can get when you arrive. It must be paid for in hard currency – no coins are accepted.

TURKISH STATE RAILWAYS
(Turkiye Cumhuriyeti Devlet Demiryollari Isletmesi, TCDD)

In 1990 all of Turkey joined the Inter-Rail scheme ('European Turkey' joined in 1985). To coincide with this there has been a general improvement in services, although you can still expect the journey from northern Greece to Istanbul to take more than a day and the trip from Athens to take up to 40 hours. If you are coming direct from central Europe remember that you *must* have a transit visa for Bulgaria unless you travel through Yugoslavia and change at Thessaloniki in northern Greece. If you decide to travel through Bulgaria, get your transit visa before you leave home.

Railway services in Turkey are slow. Students can get a 10 per cent discount on train fares (20 per cent on return tickets). Apart from the lines in European Turkey and the Haydarpaşa–Ankara run, you are well advised to use the buses. These are fast, cheap and often modern Mercedes-Benz vehicles. Free drinks en route are often included. For a rough guide to the main services, consult Thomas Cook's Overseas Timetable.

For short journeys, use a Dolmuş – these are communal taxis which run on set routes. Stop them by waving. Outside the cities they are usually beat-up Ford Transit or VW vans. Very cheap.

TRAIN INFORMATION

English is spoken by the information staff in big cities, while German is more useful elsewhere throughout Turkey.

• **Reservations:** It's always advisable to reserve between Istanbul and Ankara, particularly if you want a couchette or to travel first class.

• **Night travel:** Generally, this is the best way of travelling in Turkey. There are first- and second-class couchettes to choose from.

• **Eating on trains:** Always be prepared with your own drinks. All expresses have a mini-bar or buffet.

TOURIST INFORMATION

There are tourist offices in all the major cities and tourist centres.

• **ISIC bonuses:** 50 per cent off museums, cinemas, concerts, and 10–20 per cent off rail tickets within Turkey. For further information, contact the nearest Turkish tourism and information office. Some places will not accept student cards as there are so many Turkish fakes.

• **Money matters:** 1 Turkish lira (TL).
Banking hours are Mon.–Fri.: 8.30 a.m.–12 noon, 1.30 p.m.–5 p.m. Twenty-four-hour exchange facilities are thin on the ground and there are none at the stations, although there is a small exchange office at Istanbul station, if you can find it at the opposite end of the platform from the station entrance. It is open at weekends and has an average exchange rate; also inflation is a way of life in Turkey. In 1980 the rate was 120 per cent, and although it dropped a couple of years later to only 30 per cent, it has been creeping up again. The rate last year was around 63 per cent, so bear this in mind when looking at prices. Remember to spend all of your lire before leaving the country as you will find it difficult, if not downright impossible, to exchange – particularly in Greece, although relations between these two countries have been improving in recent years. It is possible to convert lira back to a foreign currency before leaving Turkey if the original exchange slips are produced to prove it has been legally exchanged originally.

• **Post offices:** Open Mon.–Fri.: 8.30 a.m.–12 noon, 1 p.m.–5.30 p.m. Major post offices stay open till 12 midnight, Mon.–Sat. and 9 a.m.–7 p.m., Sun. Many post offices have exchange facilities; compare the rate to the banks'.

• **Shops:** Open Mon.–Sat.: 9 a.m.–1 p.m., 2 p.m.–7 p.m., Sun.: closed.

• **Museums:** All museums shut on Mondays, except for the Topkapi Palace which shuts on Tuesdays. Entry usually costs 5,000 to 10,000 TL.

• **Mosques:** A note to non-Moslems – when visiting a mosque footwear is removed and normally left on a rack or occasionally with an attendant outside, women especially should dress modestly. At the better known mosques overalls are provided for those deemed unsuitably dressed.

SLEEPING

There's no problem finding cheap accommodation in Turkey, but we can't guarantee you'll be happy with the standards of cleanliness. Tourist information help out here and will find you a room in your price bracket. Basically, the hotels registered with the tourist board are called 'touristic' and are graded de luxe, or 1–5 stars. Also there are plenty with no grades at all, many of which are dirty but safe enough. In general, though, discretion is the better part of valour when it comes to a shady set-up. Expect to pay from $10 upwards for a half-decent double (more in Istanbul). Always check the room first and be prepared to bargain if the price seems too high. This tends to be the norm along the Bosphorus, but you can get a reduction with an ISIC card in some places off season. There are a few 'pansiyons' in Turkey and they can be the best places to stay but there still aren't too many of them. Student dormitories are another option during July and August, as are youth hostels of which there are about 45 in Turkey; most of them allow you to stay if you have a student card, but it's best to have an IYHC to be on the safe side. Campsites are growing in number but are still a bit primitive in their facilities.

EATING AND NIGHTLIFE

Turkish cuisine is among the best in Europe for sheer good value. The variety of dishes is staggering and, as often as not, you're invited into the kitchen to choose your own. (If you don't like the look of things while you're in, now's your chance to skip out with a suitable excuse.) Turkish specialities include dolmas (just about anything stuffed with rice) and anything called 'şiş' (like şişke-bab) is done on a spit. Kadin budu is a concoction of fried rice and meatballs and, literally translated, means 'woman's thigh' (we don't quite see the analogy). Then how about kadin gobegi ('woman's navel') for dessert? The wine's not bad and the grape brandy, raki, is hot stuff. Expect to pay around 25–35,000 TL for a full meal including wine, though you *can* eat for a lot less. For a snack, try lahmacun, a type of pizza. Do not ever drink the tap water, especially in Istanbul and Izmir.

The Turks are big folk-dancers and you should be able to catch each region's favourite without too many problems. The Turkish coffee houses (Kahve) are great meeting places, although male only, and, of course, there's always the Turkish bath. Go and see a belly dancer if there's one advertised, even though they're terribly commercialized these days, but avoid the poor Western imitations of discos and clubs, although the major cities and resorts are improving.

Istanbul

Incredible mosques share the spotlight with bazaars and the largest Roman building in the world in this fascinating city, and the blend of Asia and Europe makes it quite unique. If you're thinking of a trip to Turkey, make this your destination. It's often dirty and is pretty rough in some parts (women alone should take extra care), and the intensive train travel will give you ulcers, but there's so much here to catch the eye and imagination that it's all worthwhile. The early morning call to prayer floating amongst the minarets is unforgettable.

STATION FACILITIES

Sirkeci (Tel. 5270050) is the main station of Istanbul; from here leave the trains bound for Sofia, Belgrade, Athens and the West. Haydarpaşa (Tel. 3360475) is the city's other station, on the opposite shore of the Bosphorus; services to Asia, Ankara, Anatolia, Iran, Syria and Baghdad leave from here.

Facilities at both stations tend to close down at night and there is no bath/shower at either station. Sirkeci Station has tourist information, exchange facilities and left-luggage. Although this is only a trolley on the platform it is fairly safe as there are many attendants about. Many nearby hotels offer left luggage facilities but satisfy yourself on their security before committing your luggage.

TOURIST INFORMATION AND ADDRESSES

TOURIST OFFICES: 57 Meşrutiyet Caddesi, Galatasaray (Tel. 1456875); Divan Yolu Caddesi, Sultanahmet (Tel. 5524903); entrance of Hilton Hotel; Karaköy Harbour Terminal; Yeşilköy Airport; Sirkeci Station; Yalova Harbour Terminal. Open Mon.–Fri.: 8.30 a.m.–6.30 p.m., Sat.–Sun.: 9 a.m.–5 p.m.

POST OFFICE: 25 Yeni Postane Sokak (two blocks from Sirkeci Station). 24-hour currency exchange.

AMEX: Hilton Hotel. Open daily 8.30 a.m.–8 p.m. (Tel. 1329558).

TOURIST POLICE: Across from St Sophia at beginning of Yerebatan Caddesi, open 9 a.m.–8 p.m. (Tel. 5274503).

UK CONSULATE: 34 North Meşrutiyet Caddesi, Tepebasi (Tel. 1447540).

US CONSULATE: 147 Meşrutiyet Caddesi, Tepebasi (Tel. 1436200).

STUDENT TRAVEL: YEDITUR, Inönü Caddesi 37/2, Gümüssuyu (Tel. 1499619/1525921). Student cards and travel.

MEDICAL HELP: For an ambulance call 100 Siracevizler Caddesi (Tel. 1444998).

PHONE CODE: 1 (Taksim, etc.), 3 (Asian side), 5 (Sultanahmet, etc.).

• **Getting about:** There are cheap buses which leave from Taksim Square. The communal taxis are also a good buy. They have routes between the main quarters, though if you specify you should get dropped off where you ask. Most taxis now have meters, but check,

and if there isn't one then agree a price before you start your
journey. Even if there is a meter check that the driver turns it on to
avoid later difficulties. Frequent suburban trains run along the main
line from Sirkeci. Inter Rail is valid.

SEEING

Basically, Istanbul divides into two main areas which are further
subdivided into several small districts. The European part of the
city is divided by the GOLDEN HORN, and the European and Asian
parts are separated by the BOSPHORUS STRAIT. The vast majority of
sights are on the southern bank of the Golden Horn.

OLD STAMBOUL is the old walled city across the Golden Horn and
it looks like something out of the 'Fry's Turkish Delight' advert. For
the best panoramic view of the old town, climb the Galata tower.
The mosques and palaces are wonderful examples, as good as you'll
find anywhere, especially ST SOPHIA, built in AD 347 by Constantine,
then rebuilt in the sixth century after a fire, and turned into a
mosque after the Turks captured the city in 1453. Today it's a
museum, though some of the original mosaics can still be seen. The
BLUE MOSQUE dating from the seventeenth century is an amazing
feat of engineering, built, as it was, to bend with the force in times of
earthquakes – a performance it has done twenty times already. You
can go into any mosque in Istanbul as long as you take off your shoes
and keep quiet. Not far from the Blue Mosque is the ornate
FOUNTAIN OF SULTAN AHMET. The Roman HIPPODROME was the
venue for chariot racing, and today there's a MOSAIC MUSEUM.
Nearby you can catch a glimpse of underground Istanbul at
YEREBATAN SARAYI (Sunken Palace), a vast man-made cavern built
in the sixth century for water storage should the city be besieged.

The GRAND BAZAAR (or Kapaliçarşi) is colourful and entertaining, but barter like mad before buying anything. The palace of
the Ottoman Sultans, TOPKAPI SARAY, is today a complex of
museums: have a look in the HAREM and TREASURY. There's enough
here to interest you for hours (open 9 a.m.–5 p.m., closed Tuesdays
and half price at weekends). The other notable museums are: the
ARCHAEOLOGICAL MUSEUM, the MUSEUM OF THE ANCIENT ORIENT,
and the MUSEUM OF TURKISH AND ISLAMIC ARTS, all of which are
self-explanatory. Another couple of mosques worth taking in on
your itinerary are the BEYAZIT, near the university, and the

sixteenth-century SULEYMANIYE. As a break from the hot dirty city, take a cruise down the Bosphorus. Boats leave Galata Bridge on three-hour round cruises between Europe and Asia. They are around £3 ($4.80), great fun and highly recommended. You can also get five-hour trips which stop off in Asia for four hours' sightseeing (fare about £5.50/$8.50). Boats leaving from the palace end of the quay allow you to visit four small islands, the Princes' Islands. There's a round trip every half-hour.

The 'modern' city is on the north side of the Galata Bridge and includes Istanbul's underground – the Tünel – with only two stations. Tickets are 400 TL. The Genoese Galata tower is now a nightclub. Also on this side of the Golden Horn is the nineteenth-century Dolhambaçe Palace.

SLEEPING

As long as you're not expecting Scandinavian-style cleanliness, you'll cope fine in Istanbul. Beds are cheap and plentiful, and as prices vary little between districts aim for the most central or convenient. Round the station is OK, but a bit on the noisy side. The central Sultanahmet quarter is near the sights and about the best place to head for. Although we concentrate on the Sultanahmet quarter, you may also find cheap places on the Haydarpaşa side of the Bosphorus.

Istanbul Youth Hostel, 63 Cerrahpaşa Cad, Aksaray (Tel. 212455), is OK, but hardly central, open only in summer. The only IYHF hostel in Turkey, the Yücelt Hostel, is in the Sultanahmet district at 6 Caferiye Sok (Tel. 5136150/1) and is clean, if crowded. The staff are helpful with onward travel arrangements. Beds from $5. There are several campsites, but Yeşilyurt (Tel. 5744230) or Ataköy (Tel. 5596000) are two of the nicest. The Sultan Tourist Hotel on Yerebatan Cad (Tel. 5207676) is good, with doubles around $12, or try the Gögür on Divan Yolu Cad (Tel. 5262319), or the Yöruk at 35 Inçiliçavuş Sok (Tel. 5276476).

Also worth checking out is 'Family Pansion' at Piyerloti Cad, Kadirga Harman, Sokah No. 4, Çemberlitas (Tel. 5283746). A safe bet is the Hotel Buyuk Sanid, at Hudavendigar Cad 35a (Tel. 5267229). You'll find the rooms as clean and secure as any you'll find in Turkey. Camping Florya is excellent, with its own stretch of beach and a cheap restaurant/bar. Take the local train to Florya, and prepare for a half-hour walk.

Don't try sleeping rough in Istanbul, it's not worth the risk; there are too many stories of muggings and rape. Don't bother with the black market here either, as police informers are out in abundance, especially in summer, and manage to make a good living out of turning in mugs who accept their offers. The same goes for drugs.

EATING AND NIGHTLIFE

You'll be pleasantly surprised on both scores here. It's possible to eat exceptionally well for next to nothing, whether you eat from the street stalls or at top restaurants. Fish and seafood are particularly good: go down to the Galata Bridge where there are dozens of seafood restaurants, or eat from the pavement fish-grilling stalls. If you've saved sufficient by getting into cheap accommodation, treat yourself to a proper Bosphorus meal (about 40,000 TL) of meze (mixed starters) and fresh fish. You'll have no trouble finding plenty of suitable places to patronize. The area behind the station (Eminonu) is a good one. Our only particular recommendation is the Murat Restaurant on Ordu Cad, Aksaray. Reasonable menus at good prices, next to the Hacibozan Ógullari Baklavaci.

Don't bother with the fabricated westernized nightlife of discos and nightclubs. To get a taste of real Istanbul, eat late and wander along Meşrutiyet Cad and sample the music in the little cafés. Sultanahmet Square will also be lively but can get pretty seedy late-on. There are a few pubs in the area, however, where you'll meet up with other eurorailers and hitchers. One in particular worth a visit is the Pudding Shop, on Divan Yolu Cad (off the Sultanah-met), which is one of Europe's classic meeting places, like Harry's Bar in Venice. The Istanbul Festival is on from mid-June to mid-July but it's fairly classically minded (opera, concerts, etc.). Ask at tourist information for details. If you're after belly dancing, head for the Galatasaray district and Istiklâl St; or if you've promised yourself an authentic Turkish bath, ask at tourist informa-tion for their recommendations. Cağaloglu Hamami at Yerebatan Cad in Cağaloglu is excellent – the full works for 50 or 60,000 TL.

North-west Turkey

BURSA was, for a short while, the capital of the Ottoman Empire. It is a popular resort area because it is only 20 minutes from the sea and is also close to the best-known Turkish ski resort ULUDAG. You can get to Bursa by taking a ferry from Istanbul to Yalova and then a bus. While in Bursa see the GREAT MOSQUE, GREEN MOSQUE and GREEN TOMB. Nearby are two interesting museums, the ETHNOGRAPHIC MUSEUM and the TURKISH AND ISLAMIC ART MUSEUM (entrance 60p/$1, closed Mondays). Tourist information is in the centre of town near the covered market. For accommodation try the Yeni Ankara at 48 Inebey Caddesi, along Tahtakale Caddesi, or camp on top of Uludag at Millipark Camping (take the cable car).

Çanakkale is a good case to visit the area of the First World War Dardanelles Campaign and the scene of a much earlier campaign, Troy. The bus from Bursa takes about five and a half hours (costs £3/$5). In Çanakkale itself there is a museum with archaeological artefacts from Troy and a CASTLE with its World War One artillery and damage. A minesweeper in the park around the castle is now a monument to Atatürk, who was the Turkish commander during the Dardanelles Campaign. The helpful tourist office is next to the harbour. The best place to look for hotels is around the town centre. Çanakkale comes to life every August with the Troy festival. Across the Dardanelles from Çanakkale lies the scene of the bloody campaign, and GALLIPOLI (Gelibolu) itself. You can take a ferry across to ECEABAT and then hire a taxi to look around the battlefield, where the ANZACS (Australia and New Zealand Army Corps) suffered horrendous losses at Anzac Cove in Churchill's ill-fated campaign. The whole peninsula is a vast war memorial and all cemeteries are well signposted and maintained. Full details from the tourist office. Twenty miles south is TRUVA (TROY). There are many buses from the bus station to Troy. The ruins of nine separate cities are not that interesting in themselves, but with a bit of background knowledge and some imagination they are evocative (entrance £1.50/$2.50), especially with the wooden horse replica.

Aegean Coast

KUŞADASI has not benefited from the growth of tourism, but it is a good base to explore the fascinating Greek and Roman site of Ephesus. To get to Kuşadasi either take a train to Izmir and then a two-hour bus ride or take the ferry straight from Istanbul. The small fortified PIGEON ISLAND is about the only thing worth a visit in Kuşadasi. The tourist office is in the port and is very helpful. There are many cheap sea-front hotels and pensions here, the best area being around Aslander Caddesi. The real reason for coming here is EPHESUS (EFES), a huge 2,000-acre site chock full of classical ruins, which can become incredibly hot during summer. To reach the site take a dolmuş to Selçuk and ask to get off at Ephesus. It is best to look around yourself as tours can be very pricey. See the GRAND THEATRE, the TEMPLE OF HADRIAN and the FOUNTAIN OF TRAJAN just to name a few. The site is open each day 8 a.m.–6.30 p.m. and admission is about £3/$5.

Three and a half hours east by bus are the amazing white cliffs and thermal pools of PAMUKKALE. There are also ruins of the ancient city of HIERAPOLIS at the top of the cliffs. Other classical ruins along the Aegean coast are BODRUM (HALICARNASSUS) and BERGAMA (PERGAMON) and are well worth a visit.

Ferries link a number of ports to the nearby Greek islands. Although fares are quite steep, this is a way of avoiding the sometimes nightmarish Athens–Istanbul run. Ferry services include Cesme–Chios (single £12.50/$20), Kuşadasi–Samos (£15.50/$25), Bodrum–Kos (£9.50/$15), Marmaris–Rhodes (£12.50/$20), Ayvalik–Lesbos (£18.75/$30).

Mediterranean Coast

This coastline has many beautiful beaches and resorts and is a good place to unwind and relax, but beware: there are often thousands of other people there with the same objective. The train runs down to MERSIN, in the eastern part of the coast, which is a bustling place and is best passed through. The tourist office is at the harbour, near where Turkish Maritime Lines run a service to the Turkish-controlled NORTHERN CYPRUS (ferry $16, students get a 10 per cent discount). If you go to Northern Cyprus, get the immigration authorities to stamp a separate sheet of paper rather than your passport because you may not be allowed entry back into Greece if they see you have been to the Turkish-controlled area of Cyprus.

Small beach towns run along the coast west of Mersin. KOCAHA-SANLI can be reached by bus and is a large campground right on the beach, a beautiful place. Also try the town of KORYKOS, with its two scenic castles, one on an island offshore, and beaches. There is no shortage of pensions or campsites here.

Central Anatolia

Central Anatolia is a desolate plateau region of extreme temperatures. It is also home to the capital of modern Turkey, Ankara, and the old capital of the Seljuk Turks, Konya.

Ankara

Ankara was once a small, unimportant town, but in the 1920s Atatürk made it the capital of the new Turkish Republic and it has boomed ever since to become a sprawling metropolis.

TOURIST INFORMATION

The main tourist office is at 121 Mustafa Kemal Bulvari (Tel. 188700). There is also an information office at 4 Istanbul Caddesi. Ask for a map and the useful 'Ankara Guide'. Both are open Mon.–Fri.: 8.30 a.m.–5.30 p.m., and in season 8.30 a.m.–6.30 p.m. and Sat. and Sun.: 8.30 a.m.–5 p.m.

● **Addresses:**
POST OFFICE: Atatürk Bulvari, open 24 hours with 24-hour currency exchange.

AMEX: 7 Cinnah Caddesi (Tel. 1677334), open Mon.–Fri.: 9 a.m.–6 p.m., Sat.: 9 a.m.–1 p.m.

STUDENT TRAVEL: Emek Işhani, Kat. 11 No. 1109, Kizilay (Tel. 1181326).

UK EMBASSY: 46A Şehit Ersan Caddesi (Tel. 1274310).

US EMBASSY: Atatürk Bulvari 110 (Tel. 1265470).

CANADIAN EMBASSY: 75 Nenehatun Caddesi (Tel. 1361290).

AUSTRALIAN EMBASSY: 83 Nenehatun Caddesi (Tel. 1361240).

MEDICAL HELP: Hacettepe University Hospital, Hasircilar Caddesi (Tel. 3103545).

TRAINS: Railway station on Hippodron Caddesi. Overnight services from Istanbul, also connections east.

PHONE CODE: 4.

SEEING

As the city is so sprawling a map is an excellent investment. ULUS is the old section of town where many of the sights are, including the Citadel and the Museum of Anatolian Civilizations. The CITADEL is itself a small walled city with winding lanes, a great place to wander. The BAZAAR and a MOSQUE are also within the Citadel's walls. The MUSEUM OF ANATOLIAN CIVILIZATIONS is a world class museum with exhibits from the huge number of cultures which grew up in this cradle of civilization (open Tues.–Sun.: 9 a.m.–5.20 p.m., admission £1.50/$2.50) and is situated in a restored covered bazaar.

The other main sight of Ankara is the huge MAUSOLEUM OF ATATÜRK, the national hero, in a large park. It is a monument to the man whose adopted name means literally 'Father of the Turks'. There is also a museum of his life and personal effects, open Tues.–Sun.: 9 a.m.–12 noon and 1 p.m.–5 p.m. Also check out the ETHNOGRAPHIC MUSEUM and the TEMPLE OF AUGUSTUS.

SLEEPING

Most of the cheap places to stay are in Ulus. You could try the Cumhuriyet Student Hostel in Cebeci (Tel. 3193634), open summers. Ask the tourist office for a list of hotels. Also try the Beyrut Palas Oteli at 11 Denizciler Caddesi (Tel. 3108407) or the Otel Bulduk, Sanayi Caddesi 26 (Tel. 3104915).

EATING AND NIGHTLIFE

Ulus does not have that great a selection of restaurants; try along the Çankiri Caddesi. The bazaar is always a good place to explore. To meet some Turkish students try the Café Melodi on Atatürk Bulvari.

Konya

KONYA is an important centre of Islam in Turkey and was once capital of the Seljuks. It is still a big pilgrimage centre. It was here that the famous Order of the Whirling Dervishes started. See the MONASTERY and TOMB OF MEVLANA, the founder of the Dervishes, the ARCHAEOLOGICAL MUSEUM and the MARKET. The tourist office is on Mevlana Caddesi (Tel. 33–111074). For accommodation try the Çatal Pansiyon (Tel. 33–114981) near the tourist office or Otel Konfor, 51 Eski Garaj Caddesi (Tel. 33–113103). The cheapest beds are likely to be on the rooftop at Otel Mevlana, 1 Cengaver Sok (Tel. 33–119824).

Eastern Turkey

The east of Turkey becomes wilder and harsher, that is until you get to LAKE VAN, where the land is green and the mountains beautiful. The city of VAN is three miles from the lake, the largest in Turkey. Outside the city is the imposing CITADEL and ANCIENT CITY on the ROCK OF VAN, once the capital of the Urartian Empire. There is also a small archaeological museum. The tourist office is at 127 Cumhuriyet Caddesi. Other places to visit around the lake are the ARMENIAN CHURCH on the island of AKDAMAR or the scenic mountains around the town of HAKKARI. The ferry across Lake Van takes about four hours.

KARS in the north-east is not too thrilling itself, but from here you can visit the incredible remains of the ancient Armenian city of ANI, 28 miles away. For accommodation try Hayat Oteli, 155 Faikbey

Caddesi. The tourist office on Lise Sokak (Tel. 021–123000) will get you the permit you will need to visit Ani as it is very close to the border with Armenia. To get to the ancient city either rent a minibus, get a taxi or catch the early bus (6 a.m.). The ruins are very impressive but unexcavated and well worth a visit to this spooky abandoned city.

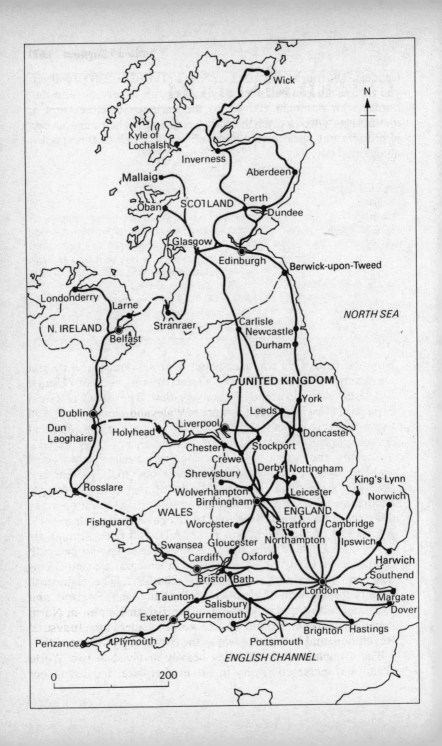

UNITED KINGDOM

Entry requirements	Passport
Population	57,100,000
Capital	London (pop.: 7,550,000)
Currency	Sterling
	$1 = approx. 58p
Political system	Constitutional Monarchy
Religion	Protestant
Language	English, also some Welsh and Gaelic in some areas
Public holidays	1, (2, 3 Scotland) Jan.; (17 March Northern Ireland); Good Friday; Easter Monday; 1st Monday in May; Spring Bank Holiday; (Early August Bank Holiday, Scotland), Late August Bank Holiday; 25, 26 Dec.
International dialling codes	To USA: 010 + 1 + number
	From USA: 011 + 44 + number
Eurotrain office	52 Grosvenor Gardens, London SW1 (Tel. 071–730 3402)

Even the British get confused about their nationhood, so it's not uncommon to hear 'England', 'Great Britain' and the 'United Kingdom' used incorrectly in conversation. The island of Great Britain isn't just England; it comprises Wales and Scotland too. Add to this Northern Ireland, and you have the United Kingdom of Great Britain and Northern Ireland, more commonly known as the UK.

England, the largest of the four countries, has always attracted the majority of immigrants from pre-Celtic times to the present day. With the Normans in 1066 came feudalism and a power struggle among the nobles. Pretty soon the barons were in a position to lay down the law and force King John to recognize their rights in 1215. By the end of the Tudor era, Henry VIII had been through six wives, and England was a prosperous nation. The seventeenth century saw a Civil War between the Parliamentarians and Cromwell, and the royalist supporters of Charles I. The eighteenth century began with the union of Scotland and England and continued with the development of the British Empire in North America and India. Britain was the world's leader in the Industrial Revolution, and became known as the 'workshop of the world'.

The economic strain of being heavily involved in two World Wars, and increased rivalry in the marketplace, has led to her decline as a world power. From a eurorailer's point of view, the United Kingdom offers a diversity of not just geography but of history and culture too – all you'd expect from a country made up of four separate nations.

BRITISH RAIL (BR)

In recent years, British Rail have streamlined their services and improved their corporate image: preparing for privatization perhaps? In terms of speed and comfort the InterCity 225 and other InterCity services rank almost on a par with France and are certainly as good as in Germany although, as in most other countries, the commuter services could be improved. There are five main categories of trains: (1) The new electric InterCity 225s which run from London to Leeds and Edinburgh. (2) InterCity 125s, named for the speed they travel at. These excellent trains, the fastest diesels in the world, are still used on most long hauls. (3) The other InterCity services are either diesel or electric and reach 110 m.p.h. on long runs. (4) Regional Railways run a network of cross-country trains supplementary to the main InterCity routes. These are particularly useful for avoiding transfers in London and other cities. (5) Local trains which run on more out-of-the-way routes or in the suburbs of the large towns. There are no supplements to worry about on any of these services.

New fast trains are planned for the Channel Tunnel when it opens next year, but the new high speed line from London to the Channel planned for 1997 remains a subject of heated debate and the Tory Government has not yet resolved matters.

● **Inter-Rail bonuses:** Up to half price to point of departure from the UK, plus reduction as follows:

Company	Route	Reduction
Sealink Stena Line	Dover–Calais	30%
	Folkestone–Boulogne	30%
	Fishguard–Rosslare	30%
	Holyhead–Dun Laoghaire	50%
	Stranraer–Larne	33%
Sealink Newhaven–Dieppe	Newhaven–Dieppe	30%
Sealink Stena Line	Harwich–Hoek van Holland	30%

Company	Route	Reduction
Hoverspeed (Hovercraft/Sea Cat)	Dover Hoverport–Calais/Boulogne	50%
P&O (European Ferries)	Dover–Calais/Boulogne	30%
P&O (European Ferries)/RMT	Dover–Oostende	30%
P&O (European Ferries)	Portsmouth–Le Havre	30%
Scandinavian Seaways (DFDS)	Harwich–Esbjerg	50%
	Newcastle–Esbjerg	50%
B&I Line	Holyhead–Dublin	50%

TRAIN INFORMATION

All main stations have their own information counters and there are free timetables for the main-line routes.

• **Reservations:** Only compulsory on certain services, as indicated by [R] in the BR timetable, otherwise advisable on main lines in summer, particularly around holiday weekends. Cost £1 for standard class for up to four people travelling together, £2 each for first class.

• **Night travel:** No couchettes, only sleepers at £20. Standard-class ticket holders share a two-berth compartment, £22 for first class. A bonus is free tea and biscuits in the morning. All sleepers are air-conditioned and modern.

• **Eating on trains:** Expensive restaurant cars run on all main lines, Mon.–Fri. Buffets with average-priced snacks run daily on the major routes and some local trains have trolley service.

• **Scenic tips:** There's nothing in Britain to compare with Switzerland or Norway, but the Lake District and parts of North Wales are interesting enough. The really scenic routes are up in the Scottish Highlands, particularly the Fort William–Mallaig and Glasgow–Oban runs. Ask for the 'Scenic Rail Journeys' leaflet at the British Tourist Authority.

• **Rover tickets:** There are several, depending on how much of the country you want to see. The All-Line Ticket is valid for either seven or fourteen days and costs around £265 and £400 respectively for first class. Standard-class tickets for the same periods are £160 and £225 respectively, with children aged between five and fifteen paying two-thirds of the appropriate adult fare. This ticket is valid for all stations and Sealink services to the Isle of Wight. In addition, a 20 per cent reduction on the Windermere Iron Steamboat Company's steamers in the Lake District. The BritRail Pass and Flexipass are available only outside the UK and are valid for 8, 15, 22 days or 1 month (or 4 days from 8, 8 from 15 and 15 from 1 month). For prices see the Introduction, p.32). If you just want to visit a certain part of England and Wales there are a total of 19 regional rover tickets available for seven consecutive days between Easter and October. There are also Flexi-Rovers for 4 days out of 8 in some areas. They cost from £27.50 to £48. All prices are standard class and some tickets are restricted to outside of weekday morning rush hours. If you are visiting or staying in Scotland, the Freedom of Scotland Ticket is a good buy and costs £56 for 7 days and £92 for 15 days. It is available only in standard class and also gives you free use of Caledonian MacBrayne sailings on the Firth of Clyde. If you are particularly attracted to the Highlands and Islands, an all-encompassing pass valid for all forms of land and sea transport called the 'Travelpass' is available for £35 for 7 days in March, April, May and October and £55 between June and September. For 13 days the price is £50 and £70 respectively. Note: British Rail calls itself ScotRail in Scotland and has recently embarked on an ambitious programme to modernize and improve stations and rolling stock. The Freedom of Wales pass is good for 7 days and costs £40 and the Northern Ireland Rail Runabout costs £27.50 and is valid for 7 days from April to October. Those resident outside Britain and France could consider the BritFrance Railpass (p.32).

• **Bikes:** There are no facilities for hiring out bikes at British Rail stations, so ask at the tourist office for local suggestions.

• **Coach travel:** If you have bought your Inter-Rail card in the UK or are travelling with a Eurail Pass, you can save money travelling to London and on to Dover with National Express (Caledonian Express in Scotland). They travel to 1,500 locations. A single from Edinburgh to London can be as low as £10. Those under 23 can get a 33 per cent Discount Card for £5.

TOURIST INFORMATION

Every major city or town has its own tourist information office, and they will fix you up with accommodation for around £1 and supply you with maps and leaflets. There are also regional and national tourist boards who supply information.

• **ISIC bonuses:** Up to 50 per cent reduction at some monuments where you have to pay, but (in the main) museums and galleries are free. For further information, contact ISIC, London Student Travel, 52 Grosvenor Gardens, London SW1W 0AG (Tel. 071–730 3402), or NUS Travel, 12 Dublin Street, Edinburgh (Tel. 031–556 6598).

• **Money matters:** 1 pound (£) = 100 pence (p).
Banking hours are generally Mon.–Fri.: 9.30 a.m.–3.30 p.m. but over the last year or so have started to vary, particularly in Scotland where the much greater use of cash dispensers and computers means many banks, particularly in cities, now open to 5 p.m. All Scottish banks used to close between 12.30 p.m.–1.30 p.m. but many are now open all day. You may still find some banks in Scotland opening late on a Thursday and in England some banks even open on a Saturday morning. Beware of unfamiliar Bureaux de Change which charge high commissions and have poor exchange rates. Scottish banks issue their own notes and you may get some funny looks if you use them in England. When leaving the UK take English notes, as Scottish ones might as well be from Paraguay, although a Scottish note has been gratefully accepted in Albania!

• **Post offices:** Open 9 a.m.–5.30 p.m., with sub-post offices generally closing for lunch; Sat.: 9 a.m.–1 p.m.

• **Shops:** 9 a.m.–5.30 p.m. is average. Large stores take no lunch breaks, and in London and major cities shops are open late on several days of the week. Many cities have shops that stay open very late and open all day Sunday – these are convenient, but watch the prices.

• **Museums:** 10 a.m.–5 p.m. is the norm, and in many cases entrance is free.

SLEEPING

The wonderful institution of Bed-and-Breakfast (B&B) is the cornerstone of accommodation in Britain, and between B&Bs and youth or student hostels you should easily get by. B&Bs average £10 (£18 in London) and this includes an English breakfast (bacon, eggs, etc.) which should keep you going all day. Always go for small B&Bs where you'll feel like one of the family and will get good value for money. Hotels in Britain are very expensive and are best avoided. Many universities let out their student flats and hostels in summer, and these average about £10 a night. Youth hostels charge according to your age, location and the facilities on offer. Expect to pay between £3 and £12. If you're thinking of doing much hostelling, pick up the 'YHA Guide to England and Wales' or 'Scotland YHA Guide' which will show you the locations, etc., of the hostels. It's possible to join the IYHF at most of the large hostels for around £8 (£4 for under 21s). As far as camping goes, the vagaries of British weather may make this a dicey proposition, but if you're keen count on £2–4 a night, and bring mosquito repellent and warm clothes.

The English, Scottish and Welsh Tourist Boards have guides called 'Where to Stay' costing £6.95, £3.25, and £2.25 respectively. These aren't bad, though they're a bit sparse on cheap suggestions. You'll do better getting the lists of local campsites and accommodation from tourist information, or using their bed-booking service for about £1.

EATING AND NIGHTLIFE

British food has a bit of a bad reputation, but during the past decade or so much has been done to overcome this, and eating out in Britain today is no longer an expensive and tasteless affair. If you've got the cash, go for the traditional dishes like roast beef and Yorkshire pudding, or Scotch salmon and beefsteak. Often you'll find these on the set-lunch menus offered by hotels, and this is your chance to cash in and sample them at a reasonable price (£5 upwards). Always check if VAT (a 17½ per cent tax) is included in the price, before deciding. For your picnics, look out for the impressive variety of British cheeses, Cheddar, Cheshire, Wensleydale, Double Gloucester, Stilton, etc., and shop at stores like Marks & Spencer, Waitrose, Safeway and Sainsbury's, where you can be sure the produce is fresh and reasonably priced. While in the UK, at least once try to partake in the age-old custom of afternoon tea. This filling snack of scones, jam, cream and tea is often served in even the most luxurious hotels for only a pound or two, and it really gives an insight into the civilized Britain of yesteryear.

It's possible to make out in Britain on very little indeed if you know where to look. All the major centres have fast-food chains of some description, and even the smallest village has its own local fish'n'chip shop where you can fill up for just about £2. Chinese and Indian meals are also good value, as (in general) are pub lunches.

The pub is the mainstay of British social life and this is where you should make for to meet the locals. Many pubs, however, are soulless places and don't merit five minutes of your time, so be selective and choose either one with a historical connection or those that go to the effort of putting on live music. Pubs open 11 a.m.–11 p.m. (10.30 p.m. in some areas), though some still close between 2 or 3 p.m. and 5.30 p.m. All pubs close for about three hours in the afternoon on Sundays. You must be over 18 to drink alcohol. The English and Welsh pride themselves on their 'real ale', the Scots on their whisky and the Irish on their Guinness.

London is the home of British theatre and cinema – but this doesn't mean other cities are dead ducks; Edinburgh's International Festival and Fringe in August–September puts London in the shade for the three or four weeks it's on. In general, the live music and dancing scene is better in Britain than in most other European countries. Liverpool and Manchester are frequently ahead of London for trend-setting. Pick up the tourist board's list of current happenings from whichever town you're in, and remember to try for student discounts on theatre tickets, etc.

London

London is a must in any European wanderings. There are three Londons to take into account: the CITY of London (the financial and administrative centre of Great Britain), WESTMINSTER (the political, royal and religious centre), and the WEST END (home of the British theatre and cinema, smart shops and clubs). Each area has a different feel to it, and the combination of all three with over a thousand years of history and traditions, plenty of open green spaces and the buzz of Europe's largest city, makes a visit here unforgettable.

STATION FACILITIES

There are eight major stations in London, all interconnected by the fast and efficient tube (underground railway). To ensure you're at the right station, here's a quick checklist of which station serves where:

• **Charing Cross:** Handles suburban lines and the London–Folkestone and London–Hastings trains.

• **Euston:** Central England and the north-west, Birmingham, Coventry, Liverpool, Manchester, Glasgow and on to Dublin.

• **King's Cross:** The north-east, Leeds, York, Hull, Newcastle and on to Edinburgh and Aberdeen. From Newcastle you can sail to Norway, Denmark and Sweden.

• **Liverpool Street:** The area north-east of London, Cambridge, Harwich, Norwich. From Harwich you can sail to the Netherlands, Germany, Sweden, Norway and Denmark.

• **Paddington:** The south-west of England, Exeter, Plymouth, Penzance, Bristol, Swansea, Oxford, Gloucester.

• **St Pancras:** Trains bound due north, Nottingham, Derby, Leicester, Sheffield.

• **Victoria:** South-east England, Newhaven, Brighton, Eastbourne, Hastings and Dover, the main gateway to France, Belgium, Spain, Italy, etc. The 30-minute train journey to Gatwick Airport leaves from here too. If you're travelling by hovercraft to France, this is also where you depart for Dover Priory. The Continental travel office is here.

• **Waterloo:** Trains to the south of England, Bournemouth, Portsmouth, Southampton and Weymouth.

We are reliably informed by British Rail that the stations detailed on page 679 are the ones you are most likely to use.

	KING'S CROSS	VICTORIA
Train information	24 hours (Tel. 071–278 2477)	7.30 a.m.–9.30 p.m. (Tel. 071–928 5100) (24 hours) Travel to Continent (Tel. 071–834 2345)
Reservations	Mon.–Sat.: 7.15 a.m.–10.30 p.m. Sun.: 8 a.m.–10.30 p.m.	8 a.m.–9.30 p.m.
Tourist information	–	9 a.m.–9 p.m.
Foreign exchange	Sun.–Thurs.: 8 a.m.–8 p.m. Fri. and Sat.: 8 a.m.–9.30 p.m.	T. Cook office 8.15 a.m.–9 p.m.
Left-luggage lockers	–	Always access
Left-luggage store	24 hours except Sat.: 11 p.m.– Sun. 7 a.m.	7 a.m.–10.30 p.m.
Bar, Buffet	Mon.–Sat.: 11 a.m.–11 p.m. Buffet 24 hours, Sun.: 12 noon– 2 p.m., 7 p.m.–10.35 p.m.	Buffet 24 hours
Restaurant	Mon.–Sat.: 7 a.m.–10 a.m. 11 a.m.–7 p.m.	7 a.m.–10 p.m.
Self-service	7 a.m.–9 p.m. daily	–
Showers	Open 24 hours	None
Post office	In road opposite station	In Buckingham Palace Road opposite station
Station shuts	Only Christmas Day	Always open

	EUSTON	LIVERPOOL STREET
Train information	Mon.–Sat.: 7.15 a.m.–10.30 p.m. Sun.: 8 a.m.–10.30 p.m. 24-hour telephone service (Tel. 071–387 7070)	7.15 a.m.–10.30 p.m. daily (Tel. 071–928 5100) (24 hours)
Reservations	7 a.m.–11 p.m.	Mon.–Sat.: 8 a.m.–6.45 p.m.
Tourist information	Mon.–Fri.: 8 a.m.–8 p.m. Sat.: 8 a.m.–6 p.m.	8 a.m.–6 p.m.
Foreign exchange	6.30 a.m.–11 p.m.	7.30 a.m.–8.30 p.m.
Left-luggage lockers	None	None
Left-luggage store	Open 24 hours	7 a.m.–10.30 p.m.
Bar, Buffet	7 a.m.–10 p.m.	7.30 a.m.–10.30 p.m.
Restaurant	7.30 a.m.–10 p.m.	Mon.–Fri.: 8 a.m.–9 p.m.
Bath, Shower	Mon.–Fri.: 7.30 a.m.–10 p.m. Sat.: 11 a.m.–10 p.m. Closed Sunday	None
Shops	8 a.m.–6 p.m.	Various times, Mon.–Sat.
Post office	None	None
Station shuts	Open 24 hours	Open 24 hours

CROSS-CHANNEL FERRIES

The ferries to Calais, Dieppe, Boulogne and Ostend are usually packed out in high season, so before embarking on the crossing take a look at the alternatives open to you. Sealink, Hoverspeed, P&O and Scandinavian Seaways ferries offer discounts to Inter-Rail holders. By far the most civilized form of Channel crossing is to use the Jetfoil from Dover to Ostend. For the £8 Jetfoil supplement you get a guaranteed seat, far shorter crossing, and a speedier city-to-city connection. Another good alternative is to route your journey via Holland. The Harwich–Hook of Holland ferries are very good and there's not much in it financially, although these cruise-liner ships offer either an overnight or full-day sailing.

TOURIST INFORMATION

England, Wales and Scotland have separate Tourist Boards, all of which have offices in London. The Tourist Information Centre run by the London Tourist Board at Victoria Station forecourt, carries information on London. Leaflets, maps, guidebooks, tourist tickets for buses and the underground, and sightseeing tour and theatre tickets are available. Same-day hotel accommodation can be booked. The Centre is open seven days a week, 9 a.m.–8.30 p.m. with longer hours in July and August. Liverpool Street station also has a Tourist Information Centre open Mon.–Fri.: 9.30 a.m.–6.30 p.m., Sat.: 8.30 a.m.–6.30 p.m., Sun.: 8.30 a.m.–3.30 p.m. and provides information on London and Britain generally. Theatre and tour tickets are also available.

The British Travel Centre provides information on all of the United Kingdom and is located at 12 Regent Street, Piccadilly Circus, London SW1, open Mon.–Fri.: 9 a.m.–6.30 p.m., Sat. and Sun.: 10 a.m.–4 p.m. (open later on Saturday May–September). Information on Northern Ireland is available from the Ireland desk of the British Travel Centre. The Scottish Tourist Board is at 19 Cockspur Street, London SW1, and is open Mon.–Fri.: 9 a.m.–5 p.m. The Welsh Tourist Board has an information desk in the British Travel Centre.

The City of London Information Centre, with detailed information on the City as well as more general information, is directly across the road from St Paul's Cathedral. It is open Mon.–Fri.:

9.30 a.m.–5 p.m., Sat.: 10 a.m.–4 p.m. during April–September and 9.30 a.m.–12 noon October–March.

There is also a telephone information service on 071–730 3488 from 9 a.m.–6 p.m. Monday to Friday.

• **Addresses:**

POST OFFICE: King Edward Building, King Edward Street (tube, St Paul's), open Mon.–Fri.: 8 a.m.–7 p.m., Sat.: 9 a.m.–12.30 p.m. This is where all poste restante mail will end up. The twenty-four-hour post office is at St Martin's Place, Trafalgar Square.

AMEX: 6 Haymarket (tube, Piccadilly). Exchange open Mon.–Fri.: 9 a.m.–5 p.m., Sat.: 9 a.m.–6 p.m. (8 p.m. in season), Sun.: 10 a.m.–6 p.m. (Tel. 930 4411).

US EMBASSY: 24 Grosvenor Square, W1 (Tel. 499 9000) (tube – Bond St).

CANADIAN HIGH COMMISSION: MacDonald House, 1 Grosvenor Square, W1 (Tel. 629 9492) (tube – Bond Street).

AUSTRALIAN HIGH COMMISSION: Australia House, The Strand (Tel. 379 4334) (tube – Aldwych).

NEW ZEALAND HIGH COMMISSION: New Zealand House, Haymarket (Tel. 930 8422) (tube – Charing Cross).

EUROTRAIN: Tel. 730 3402, or kiosk at Victoria Station (Tel. 630 8132).

WASTEELS: 121 Witton Road, SW1 (Tel. 834 7066).

PHONE CODE: 071 (inner London), 081 (outer).

• **Getting about:** The tube is efficient and fast, but expensive and often crowded. Pick up an underground map, free at any station, and hang on to your ticket till the journey's through because you cannot get back out without it. Tubes run 5 a.m.–12 midnight. Like the tube, the red double-decker buses operate on a zone system, and you pay the driver or conductor on the bus, while the single-decker Red Arrows are express buses with ticket machines on board. There is an excellent network of night buses which run 12 midnight–5 a.m. on certain routes; all leave from Trafalgar Square.

If you're in London for a while, pick up the leaflets on the London Explorer tickets and Travelcards, but these are expensive by other European standards. Travelcards are valid on tubes, buses and local BR services. A one-day card (all zones) costs £3.20 (not valid on night buses) and also covers BR services in and around London. Cards for longer periods require a photograph. The prices vary according to the number of zones. Most sights are in zone one. The

Visitor Travelcard is only available from travel agents outside south-east England – get it or a voucher for it before you leave home. It is available for one, three, four or seven days (costs about £2.60, £8.80, £12.40, £20.50) and comes with a wallet of discount vouchers. If you're taking a tube after 9.30 a.m. and returning to the same place the same day, buy a cheap day return which will save you up to a third. Unless you're in a desperate rush, don't bother with the expensive taxis and, though it's impossible to get round all the sights on foot, try to see as much as you can of London through walks. The 'London A–Z' (about £1.95) is the best long-term map investment you can make.

SEEING

London has swallowed many villages into its bulk in the course of its development, but even today each village (now district) has its own character and traditions. Soho, Hampstead and Chelsea are as different from each other as individual towns. It's easy to divide London into its three sections but this would neglect the areas that fall between, like trendy COVENT GARDEN, or the intellectual centre of BLOOMSBURY where the BRITISH MUSEUM and London University are located. Don't forget either the wonderful days out you can have at the maritime centre of GREENWICH, or at the Royal Botanical Gardens at KEW, or HAMPTON COURT PALACE, and many more. This rundown is just a small sample of what you can see, but once you've made your visit to tourist information, you should be in a position to work out your own best itinerary.

The City of London

The London of the eleventh century is that area known as 'the City'. In this 'square mile', the wheelings and dealings of the Stock Exchange and big business take place, and the Bank of England and Royal Exchange have their headquarters here. The sights include: the beautiful Renaissance cathedral of ST PAUL'S (the one Charles and Di chose for their wedding in 1981), where Nelson, Wellington and Wren are buried; FLEET STREET, the former home of the British press; the INNS OF COURT and the OLD BAILEY – the heart of the British legal system; and the TOWER OF LONDON which dates back to William the Conqueror and has served as prison, palace and mint. The Crown Jewels, the White Tower and Tower Green where Henry VIII had Anne Boleyn and Katherine Howard executed, are among some of the sights to see here. Near the Tower is the famous TOWER BRIDGE. The newly opened TOWER HILL PAGEANT, opposite the Tower, takes visitors in computer-controlled cars on a journey back to London in Roman times through to today. At the foot of Tower Bridge, on the southside of the Thames, is the newly developed BUTLER'S WHARF. This incorporates restored historic buildings and modern commercial units such as Sir Terence Conran's GASTRODROME. The BARBICAN is also in the City (tube Barbican or Moorgate). This arts centre has concerts, plays and exhibitions as well as the superb MUSEUM OF LONDON which is free and open Tues.–Sat.: 10 a.m.–6 p.m., Sun.: 2 p.m.–6 p.m.

Westminster and the West End

Roughly, this stretches from HYDE PARK (the famous expanse with Speakers' Corner – a national venue for impromptu free speech on Sundays) to WESTMINSTER ABBEY, the incredible Gothic church so central to the country's history. WHITEHALL and the HOUSES OF PARLIAMENT, the centres of British government and administration, are along here, and so is the timekeeping landmark of London, BIG BEN. To go in and listen to Parliament (a fascinating experience), line up at St Stephen's entrance opposite the Abbey. THE MALL is the boulevard leading from TRAFALGAR SQUARE, home of the NATIONAL GALLERY, to BUCKINGHAM PALACE, the home of the monarchy, which is not open to the public. The hub of the capital is PICCADILLY CIRCUS with its statue of Eros. Leicester Square, London's movie centre, is near here. Just to the north is SOHO; the recent cleaning up of this area means that it no longer lives up to its seamy reputation except as a rip-off for tourists. London's CHINA-TOWN is here, centred on Gerard Street. To the east is COVENT GARDEN, once a vegetable market, now a shopping arcade. You can normally catch some excellent street performances here, which are well worth waiting around for.

The BRITISH MUSEUM (tube Tottenham Court Road or Russell Square) is worth at least a day of anyone's time (everything, from the Elgin Marbles to Magna Carta is here). The other main museums are at South Kensington: the VICTORIA AND ALBERT, the NATURAL HISTORY, the GEOLOGICAL and SCIENCE MUSEUMS are next door to each other. Some of these have started to charge for entrance – check with tourist information. The ROYAL ALBERT HALL is close by. See the posters outside for what's on. The Proms are held here from July to September.

The famous department store HARRODS where you can buy 'absolutely anything', is in KNIGHTSBRIDGE. Wander round the food hall there – they sell every type and variety of eats you'd ever imagined. Other shops worth taking in for their sheer entertainment value are LIBERTY'S (the neo-Tudor building on Regent Street) and FORTNUM AND MASON, Piccadilly. Excellent shopping is also available right along OXFORD STREET.

MADAME TUSSAUD'S wax museum, where the famous are immortalized, is on the Marylebone Road (tube Baker Street). Shakespeare's GLOBE THEATRE Museum has been reconstructed on its original site on the banks of the Thames. 1 Bear Gardens, Bankside. If you are tired of the city's rush, head into one of the parks – tour LONDON ZOO (Regent's Park), try rowing on the Serpentine (Hyde Park) and look out for the Buddhist Pagoda (Battersea Park).

If you want to feel like a real tourist and can afford the £7 fare, consider a narrated bus tour run by London Transport which departs from Baker Street, Piccadilly Circus, Marble Arch and Victoria Station. Central London and its landmarks are included. However, you may feel that use of public transport, a travelcard and a guidebook of your own and at your own pace is better value.

SLEEPING

The possibilities are endless, but in the lower price bracket (£10–£15) you can't expect too much in the way of comfort. London is busy all year, but in the summer it's absolutely packed and advance booking is recommended. The London Tourist Board run an advance booking service from 26 Grosvenor Gardens. Booking can be made by credit card on 071–824 8844, and on-the-spot booking can be made at the Tourist Information Centres.

Student and Youth Hostels average £12, halls of residence about £15 and B&Bs £18. Staying with a local family is becoming increasingly popular and there are an increasing number of agencies which will organize this type of accommodation. A minimum stay of a few days may be a requirement together with a deposit in advance. Ask for leaflets at the London Tourist Board offices at Victoria station.

There are six youth hostels. The recently renovated City of London Youth Hostel, 36 Carter Lane (Tel. 071–236 4965 – tube, St Pauls); Holland House, Holland Walk, Kensington (Tel. 071–937 0748 – tube, Holland Park); 4 Wellgarth Road, Hampstead (Tel. 071–458 9054 – tube, Golders Green then bus 210 or 260); 38 Bolton Gardens (Tel. 071–373 7083 – tube, Earls Court); 84 Highgate West Hill (Tel. 071–340 1831 – tube, Archway then bus 148, 210 or 271); 14–18 Noel Street (Tel. 071–734 1613 – tube, Oxford Circus) which is perhaps the most central.

Other hostels: these range from a tent city to charity set-ups. A comprehensive list can be obtained from tourist informations. Try some of the following – Tent City, Old Oak Common Lane (Tel. 081–743 5708 – tube, East Acton); Fieldcourt House, 32 Courtfield Gardens (Tel. 071–373 0152 – tube, Gloucester Road); Astor Museum Hostel, 27 Montague Street (Tel. 071–580 5360 – tube, Tottenham Court Road); International Students House, 229 Great Portland Street (Tel. 071–631 3223 – tube, Great Portland Street); Centre Français, 61 Chepstow Place (Tel. 071–221 8184 – tube, Notting Hill Gate).

If you're staying a while, two good ideas are to contact either the London University Students' Union (Tel. 071–636 2818) or Universal Aunts (Tel. 071–351 5767). Although slightly more expensive than youth hostels, university residences generally have better facilities and are well located. They are obviously not available during term time. Either make advance arrangements with Mrs Fennell at Kings College (Tel. 071–351 6011), who can arrange accommodation at most of the university halls of residence, or contact the individual hall direct. Among the best are: Wellington Hall, 71 Vincent Square (Tel. 071–834 3980 – tube, Victoria); Ingram Court, 552 Kings Road (Tel. 071–351 2488 – tube, Fulham Broadway); Lightfoot Hall, Manresa Road (Tel. 071–351 2488 – tube, Sloane Square); Queen Elizabeth Hall, Campden Hill Road (Tel. 071–937 5411 – tube, High St Kensington). A good women-only hostel is Queen Alexandra's House at Brenner Road, Kensington Gore (Tel. Mrs Makey 071–589 3635 – tube, South Kensington).

Some of the cheaper B&Bs are soul-destroying places and you're invariably better off in a hostel, but anyway the areas to head for are Earls Court, Paddington and Bayswater.

Some of the better affordable hotels include Simone House Hotel, 49 Belgrave Road (Tel. 071–828 2474 – tube, Victoria); Luna House Hotel, 47 Belgrave Road (Tel. 071–834 5897 – tube, Victoria); Leinster Hotel, 7–11 Leinster Square (Tel. 071–229 9641 – tube, Bayswater); Vicarage Hotel, 10 Vicarage Gate (Tel. 071–229 4030 – tube, High St Kensington); Abbey House Hotel, 11 Vicarage Gate (Tel. 071–727 2594 – tube, High St Kensington). If you feel like treating yourself and are happy to stay a little way outside London, try the award-winning Chase Lodge, 10 Park Road, Hampton Wick, Kingston Upon Thames (Tel. 081–943 1862), which has ten attractive rooms in the friendly surroundings of a Victorian house and garden.

There are six readily accessible campsites to London. Ask at tourist information for details. Arguably the best is Picketts Lock, Picketts Lock Lane, Edmonton (Tel. 081–803 4756). Tube to Seven Sisters, rail to Lower Edmonton and then bus W8. Although ten miles from the centre it is remarkably well equipped.

Overall, Tent City is probably the most central and will certainly be the cheapest.

With violence on the increase, sleeping rough is not really an option and the police are clamping down on the more favourable areas along the embankment at Westminster Bridge and in Hyde Park.

EATING AND NIGHTLIFE

Eating for under £5 is no great problem with the spate of fast-food chains, Indian and Chinese restaurants and very good supermarkets increasing every year. Many pubs serve lunches and, of course, there's always the great British invention, fish'n'chips. Always check if VAT is included on a menu as this tax can fairly bump up the bill. You can't go too far wrong for fast food in McDonald's and Pizzaland, but branches of Wimpy vary dramatically. For the best non-European meals, head for Soho and the excellent Chinese restaurants. Marks & Spencer, Safeway and Sainsbury's are all reliable for high-quality groceries, and if it's a good day you can do no better than get a picnic together and head for one of the parks.

For a fairly cheap meal, try the Country Life vegetarian restaurant at 123 Regent Street, W1. Open Mon. 11.30 a.m.–6 p.m., Fri. 10.30 a.m.–3 p.m. In Soho, Poons, Leicester St, Lee Ho Fook, Macclesfield St, and Chan May Mai, Lisle St, are all good value. For Indian food try around Bayswater, or for unbeatable value the Oval Tandoori Restaurant at 64A Brixton Road SW9, which, although out of the centre, is worth the effort to get there. For good value Chinese food, try the Man Lee Hong restaurant on Lisle Street near Leicester Square or Wong Kei, 41–43 Wardour Street. For excellent crêpes try Le Shop (formerly the Asterix Créperie) at 329 King's Road, Chelsea SW3. Vegetarians can't do much better than try Rhavi Shankar, 133–35 Drummond Street.

Nightlife and London are inseparable from each other. London's no longer swinging the way it was in the 1960s, but there's still a lot happening. Your best source of information are the weekly magazines *Time Out* and *City Limits*. The theatre is firmly entrenched in London's nightlife, and you really ought to try and make it along to a show. Pick up the fortnightly London Theatre Guide at any theatre or information office. Take along your ISIC to any theatre displaying (S) in its write-up, and you will be able to get cheap standby tickets before the curtain rises. In summer there's open-air Shakespeare in Regent's Park. Expect an average theatre ticket to cost £9. There's a half-price theatre ticket booth in Leicester Square. There's music to suit all tastes on offer, from the 'Proms' classics in the Albert Hall to punk in The Marquee, 105 Charing Cross Road. Also try the Wag Club at 35 Wardour Street. Ronnie Scott's at 47 Frith Street is internationally known for jazz and expensive at £12 entrance (£6 students); rather cheaper is The Bass Clef at 35 Coronet Street.

There are endless lists of pubs, and these are as good a place as any to watch the locals in their habitat. Try the Sherlock Holmes, 10 Northumberland St, The Sun in Lamb's Conduit St WC1, or Ye Olde Cheshire Cheese, just off Fleet St. The Firkin chain of pubs are well worth visiting. There are three in the city centre and several more spread round the periphery. The Goose & Firkin in Borough Road (Tube: Elephant & Castle) has a piano player on Friday and

Saturday nights which livens up the friendly atmosphere. The Flounder & Firkin is in Holloway Road in the north, the Ferret & Firkin is in Lots Road, Chelsea, the Phoenix & Firkin at Denmark Hill Station (nine minutes from Victoria) and the Fox & Firkin is in Tavistock Crescent in Notting Hill. With over 4,000 pubs in London, you're bound to find one to your liking. If you're after some 'heavy nightlife', a wander through Soho should take good care of that, or if you want to be entertained while having a drink, try the Allsop Arms, 137 Gloucester Place. The Centre at 12 Adelaide St WC2 is a good meeting place for the under 25s. Leicester Square in particular is crawling with clubs, pubs and buskers.

South-east England

If you're arriving in Britain from France or Belgium, chances are your first impressions will be of DOVER or FOLKESTONE. Dover, with its famous chalky white cliffs, dates back to the Romans and there are still remains to be seen from their time. If you've a bit of time to spend before making the direct two-hour journey to London, take in the CASTLE, with its Roman PHAROS, the PAINTED HOUSE (a Roman townhouse off New St, closed Monday). Tourist information is near Dover Priory Station and at Townwall St. They'll give you help with accommodation if you're staying overnight. The youth hostel is at Charlton House, 306 London Road (Tel. 0304 205108), and there's a summer-only YMCA Interpoint hostel at 4 Leyburne Road (Tel. 0304 206138; costs £4.50).

Half an hour up one of the lines to London lies the ancient pilgrimage centre of CANTERBURY. The CATHEDRAL, where St Thomas à Becket was murdered in 1170, is well worth breaking your journey for, and not far from here you can see the remnants of the old city walls at DANE JOHN GARDENS. ST MARTIN'S CHURCH has evolved from fourth-century Roman villas and is one of the oldest churches in England. There are various remains of long-defunct religious orders: ST AUGUSTINE'S ABBEY outside the city's East Wall, and EASTBRIDGE HOSPITAL on St Peter's St, open Mon.–Sat.: 9.30 a.m.–5.30 p.m. Food and beds shouldn't cause you any problems, but Canterbury can easily be seen as a day trip from London. The tourist office is at 34 St Margaret's Street.

Southern England

The Southern counties of Surrey, Hampshire and Sussex have their fair share of beautiful countryside and wealthy, well-kept towns. Particular places of interest are Chichester and Winchester. Lying 1½ hours from the capital on the London–Portsmouth line, CHICHESTER is a charming market town and holds a summer theatre festival worth investigation. The ROMAN PALACE at nearby Fishbourne (open daily 10 a.m.–4 p.m.) has the best-preserved mosaic floors in the country. Tourist information is at St Peter's Market, West St, open Mon.–Sat.: 9.15 a.m.–5.30 p.m. WINCHESTER is a wonderful place, an archetypal English town. The CATHEDRAL is its pride, and rightly so. Walking down Cathedral Close, you'll come to WINCHESTER SCHOOL, England's first 'public' (private) school, which has nurtured the sons of the élite for six centuries. Winchester was the ancient capital of England under King Alfred the Great, and his statue stands at one end of the High Street. A good youth hostel is to be found in the City Mill, near the statue (Tel. 0962 53723). Not far from here (on bus route 214) is CHAWTON, home of the English novelist Jane Austen of *Pride and Prejudice* fame. Her house is open 11 a.m.–4.30 p.m. Winchester is on the London–Weymouth line, about 1½ hours down the line from London. Another ideal day trip from the capital is to BRIGHTON. Since the mid-eighteenth century, this has been a popular holiday resort, especially with the Victorians. In 1783 the ROYAL PAVILION was constructed when the Prince Regent came to settle here, and it's here and to the PALACE PIER you should head. Wander round the narrow streets from the Old Steine to West St. Tourist information is in the Guildhall on the Broadway, open Mon.–Sat.: 9.30 a.m.–6 p.m., Sun.: 2 p.m.–5 p.m. in season. Brighton has a reputation for hectic nightlife, no doubt influenced by the number of students in the town. Head for the Zap Club, Old Ship Beach, with live events every night. For a cheap bed, try the new private hostel at 75 Middle St (Tel. 0273–777717). It's £9 a night, good, central and fun.

PORTSMOUTH is less than two hours from London Waterloo. It is a centre of Britain's maritime heritage. The naval dockyard contains a museum and two historic ships: HMS *Victory* (Nelson's flagship at Trafalgar) and HMS *Warrior* (Britain's first ironclad). The Tudor warship MARY ROSE is preserved in Portsmouth after being salvaged from the seabed. See SOUTHSEA CASTLE where Henry VIII stood as he watched *Mary Rose* sink. Take the local train to Portchester and see the Roman and Norman castle with its huge keep and a church inside the walls.

A ferry leaves from Portsmouth to the ISLE OF WIGHT, which has a completely different feel from neighbouring Hampshire. Take a bus to Queen Victoria's favourite holiday retreat, OSBORNE HOUSE and enjoy the sandy beaches of VENTNOR and SHANKLIN.

South-west England

From the rail network point of view, we've divided the country so that we start the south-west at Salisbury and Bath, and extend down to Devon and Cornwall. This region is one of England's most picturesque and has some of the country's best weather.

Salisbury

Salisbury is dominated by its thirteenth-century CATHEDRAL, with the tallest spire in England. Take the tour round the cathedral and visit the cloisters and Chapter House. CATHEDRAL CLOSE was a religious city and you can still see some of its buildings, especially MOMPESSON HOUSE, now cared for by the National Trust.

Salisbury is on the London–Exeter and Bristol–Portsmouth lines, 1½ hours from London. This is the best place to stay if you want to visit the ancient religious site of STONEHENGE, ten miles north of Salisbury. If you know nothing of its history or aren't really interested don't bother making the trip as you won't understand what all the fuss is over. All that's there is a circle of stones they make you pay £1.30 (£1 for students) to see, but they probably date back as far as 2600 BC, and the huge bluestones were dragged around 300 miles from Wales, so that makes them rather special. It's thought they were an astronomical calendar, and later on, in 250 BC, the Druids used them for their sun-worshipping festivals. Another stone circle is at AVEBURY – the village is actually inside the circle, so it is free. Ask at tourist information about getting there. The CITY MUSEUM in Cathedral Street has a fascinating exhibition which tells you everything but 'why', about the site. The Salisbury tourist office is at Fish Row (Tel. 0722–334956), open Mon.–Sat.: 9 a.m.–7 p.m. in season, and they'll help with accommodation. There's a youth hostel at Milford Hill (Tel. 0722–327572) and several reasonable B&Bs.

Bath

Just 15 minutes from the city of BRISTOL, and in the south-west corner of the Cotswolds, lies the elegant Georgian spa town of Bath. This town was second only to London for style in the eighteenth century; successive generations of the aristocracy came to 'take the waters' and left behind an architectural legacy as rich as you'll find in England. Trains run hourly from London and the journey takes only 1¼ hours; if you're travelling on to Oxford you change at Didcot and Bath's proximity to Bristol means you could also use it as a jumping-off point for Devon and Cornwall.

SEEING

The heart of Georgian Bath is the CIRCUS, the circle of townhouses where the artist Gainsborough lived at No. 17, and William Pitt, the Prime Minister, at Nos. 7 and 8. Leaving the Circus at Brock St, you come to ROYAL CRESCENT, considered England's most attractive street. Visit No. 1 for an idea of elegant Georgian living. The MUSEUM OF COSTUME is particularly interesting, housed in the ASSEMBLY ROOMS on the Circus. From the Abbey Churchyard you enter the ROMAN BATHS AND MUSEUM. Take the tour, and visit the PUMP ROOM where the hot spring water is pumped. This complex is open 9 a.m.–7 p.m. daily. If you're there in the mornings and fancy treating yourself to a taste of elegant British life, sit down in the Pump Room for a coffee and enjoy the sounds of The Pump Room Trio (Mon.–Sat.: 10 a.m.–12 noon).

SLEEPING

Tourist information at The Collonades (Tel. 0225–462831) will find you a room for a commission, or pick up a list of places from them. Open Mon.–Sat.: 9.30 a.m.–5 p.m. There's a youth hostel at Bathwick Hill (Tel. 0225–465674), about a mile from the city (take minibus 18 from Orange Grove, by the Abbey), and a YMCA House at Broad Street Place (Tel. 0225–460471) accepts both sexes. For B&Bs, look around the Wells Road or, for one nearer the station, try Prior House, 3 Marlborough Lane (Tel. 0225–313587), around £10 each. There's a campsite three miles out, at Newton Mill. It is very good and is served by bus 5 from the bus station (Tel. 0225–333909).

EATING AND NIGHTLIFE

There are plenty of bakers, pubs and supermarkets, so meals shouldn't pose any problems. The City Market is good for fruit and vegetables, and Molehill Café, 14 George St, is about the best place in town. After 8 p.m., it becomes a club with live music. Take out a weekly membership for about a pound, if you're staying for a while. The Bath Festival is on in late May, and ask at tourist information for the monthly 'What's On'.

Devon and Cornwall

The main centres to base yourself to explore these regions are Exeter, Plymouth or Penzance.

EXETER is the county town of Devon and is dominated by its impressive medieval CATHEDRAL. From the station of St David's, take the bus into the centre. Tourist information in the Civic Centre on Paris St (Tel. 0392–265700) will give you all you need on the region, including the national parks of Dartmoor and Exmoor. While in Exeter, take in the fourteenth-century GUILDHALL and go for a drink in the SHIP INN where Sir Francis Drake went for a jar. The youth hostel at 47 Countess Wear Rd, Topsham (Tel. 039287–3329), is a short distance out, but good (bus 187 or 356 from Paris St bus station). Alternatively, try the Exeter Student Guest House, 16 New North Rd (Tel. 0392–52493).

PLYMOUTH has been a major port since the fourteenth century. It was here Drake spotted the Spanish Armada and the *Mayflower* set sail to discover the New World. Spend an afternoon wandering round the Elizabethan BARBICAN QUAY, NEW ST with its timber merchant houses and the ruins of the fourteenth-century castle.

PENZANCE, 2½ hours further down the line, has a history of pirates and invaders, and makes an interesting day trip. Take in the MARKET HOUSE and MORRAB GARDENS where subtropical plants flourish, thanks to the exceptionally mild climate. From Penzance you can sail out to the Scilly Isles, or visit ST MICHAEL'S MOUNT, three miles east of the town – a castle and mountain where St Michael is said to have appeared. LAND'S END is most definitely worth a visit now you are this far south in England. There are some really scenic walks to do along the rocky cliffs, and you can have your picture taken with a distance post showing how far it is to John O'Groats in northern Scotland, and to your home town.

The Midlands and East Anglia

The university towns of OXFORD and CAMBRIDGE, with their beautiful cloisters and unique building formations, are a must on a serious tour of Great Britain, and Shakespeare's home town STRATFORD-UPON-AVON, however commercialized it is becoming, is still well worth a visit. Most of the Midlands is industrial and not worth stopping off at, while East Anglia is the flat land, taking in places like Cambridge, NORWICH, KING'S LYNN and the NORFOLK BROADS.

Oxford

Home of Britain's oldest and highly prestigious university, which
has dominated the town for over 700 years, Oxford lies 45 minutes
from London's Paddington Station, and can easily be taken in on a
day trip from the capital.

STATION FACILITIES

Train information	Mon.–Sat.: 8.30 a.m.–7.30 p.m.,
	Sun.: 9.30 a.m.–7.30 p.m.
Reservations	Mon.–Fri.: 9 a.m.–5 p.m., Sat.: 9 a.m.–12 noon
Tourist information	8 a.m.–7 p.m.
Foreign exchange	8 a.m.–7 p.m.
Left-luggage lockers	All hours

Daily trains to: London, Reading, Birmingham, Manchester, Liverpool, Worcester.

TOURIST INFORMATION AND ADDRESSES

Tourist information is at St Aldate's (Tel. 726871), open Mon.–
Sat.: 9 a.m.–5.30 p.m., Sun.: 10 a.m.–4 p.m. Pick up their 40p
leaflet and their accommodation list.
STUDENT TRAVEL: 13 High Street. Open Mon.–Fri.: 9.30 a.m.–5.30
p.m., Sat.: 10 a.m.–3 p.m.
LATE MONEY EXCHANGE: Lewis's Bank, in Selfridge's department
store, Westgate. Open till 5 p.m. Mon.–Fri., Sat. till 12 noon.
PHONE CODE: 0865.

SEEING

Carfax Tower is at the centre, and from here most of the university
colleges are only a few minutes away. CHRIST CHURCH, the
sixteenth-century college with its beautiful library, housing the
spoils of Henry VIII's monastic plunderings, is down St Aldate's.
North of this is MERTON COLLEGE, dating from the thirteenth
century and with a notably attractive chapel; and next door is ORIEL.
Take Bear Lane now, then cross the High Street to reach
BRASENOSE COLLEGE and ALL SOULS (probably the most prestigious

collection of academics around – all specially appointed to the college). At the north end of the square is the BODLEIAN LIBRARY, built in 1602 and containing over three million books. The atmosphere in here must be sampled at first hand. MAGDALEN COLLEGE (pronounced 'maudlin') on the High Street makes a lovely walk through its fifteenth-century cloisters, and the ASHMOLEAN MUSEUM on Beaumont Street (Italian and English art) is worth seeing. Turn up Cornmarket Street at Carfax and, after the new shopping centre, you'll reach BALLIOL and ST JOHN'S colleges. Opposite Balliol, Latimer and Ridley were burned by Bloody Mary in 1555, with Bishop Cranmer following a year later.

If you want to be terribly traditional and you've managed to hit a sunny afternoon, hire out a punt at the CHERWELL BOATHOUSE for about £4 an hour. Worth a quick mention here is BLENHEIM PALACE, birthplace of Winston Churchill and ancestral home of the Dukes of Marlborough. You can visit the mansion for £4.50 in season (bus 420 or 423 from Cornmarket Street).

SLEEPING

An accommodation search agency called Citycomm Ltd has an extensive database of all types of available accommodation in Oxford and its surrounding area. They will arrange accommodation according to individual requirements for a booking fee of £2.50 per person. The cheapest are likely to be college rooms during the summer from around £7.50. Citycomm is centrally located at 2 Market Street (Tel. 794994). If you don't use the tourist office's or Citycomm's services, try calling in at the many B&Bs in Abingdon Road. The youth hostel is a little too like school to be comfortable; it's on bus routes 72 and Nipper 73 at Jack Straw's Lane (Tel. 62997). There's camping at Cassington Mill Caravan Park, five miles out (Tel. 881490) and at Oxford Camping International (Tel. 246551) on Abingdon Road. Mrs R. Old at 58 St John Street (Tel. 55454) is worth a try for B&B. Oxford does get busy in summer, but owing to its proximity to London, it's possible to take it in as a day trip.

EATING AND NIGHTLIFE

There are plenty of places ideal for eurorailers for, though an Oxford student may be a cut above the average, all students still look for the same type of things when it comes to eating and what to do at night. Brown's Restaurant and Wine Bar seems pretty popular from all appearances. It's at 7 Woodstock Road, and the food and atmosphere are very acceptable. Another place worth a mention is the local for Christ Church college, The Bear in Bear Lane. There are plenty of pubs; and if you want to meet the students, simply go to the pubs closest to the colleges; The Kings Arms in Holywell Street is particularly well attended. Oxford's July–August Festival is fairly classical; to find out the latest events, pick up the 'What's On' at the tourist office.

Stratford-upon-Avon

About 1½ hours from Oxford and 2½ from London (Paddington Station) lies the Elizabethan town of Stratford, birthplace of William Shakespeare. The house where he was born in HANLEY STREET in 1564 is charming, or would be if it weren't for the hundreds of tourists trying to get around it. He's buried in Holy Trinity Church. Shakespeare's wife's house ANNE HATHAWAY'S COTTAGE can be visited at Shottery. Americans might also like to visit the Elizabethan HARVARD HOUSE, where the parents of John Harvard (of University fame) lived. The Royal Shakespeare Theatre and the new Swan Theatre put on productions of outstanding quality, though the cheapest tickets are about £5–£8 (Tel. 0789–292271 for information on what's playing). While you're in the area, you can pop into Shakespeare's mother's house and complete the family socializing. The HOME OF MARY ARDEN in the village of Wilmcote can be reached by local train in a matter of minutes. The countryside around Stratford, the COTSWOLDS, possibly represents England at its best: rolling green hills and picturesque limestone cottages. Try to take in the beautiful towns of Broadway and Chipping Camden on a trip from Stratford.

TOURIST INFORMATION AND ADDRESSES

The tourist office is at 1 High St (Tel. 0789–293127), open Mon.–Sat.: 9 a.m.–5.30 p.m., Sun.: 2 p.m.–5 p.m. in season.

They'll give you a leaflet on accommodation, but the best bets are B&Bs on Evesham Place or Shipston Road.

• **Youth hostel:** Hemmingford House, Alveston (Tel. 0789–297093). Bus 518 from the bus station.

• **Camping:** The Elms, Tiddington (Tel. 0789–292312). Bus 518.

Cambridge

Oxford's great rival is the similarly ancient market town and prestigious university of Cambridge which dates back to the thirteenth century and has names like Darwin, Newton, Byron and Milton in its old registers. Cambridge is 60 minutes from London (Liverpool Street or King's Cross Station), and once you arrive at the station, the bus to Market Square will take you to the centre of things.

STATION FACILITIES

Train information	Mon.–Sat.: 5.35 a.m.–10.35 p.m.
	Sun.: 7 a.m.–10.45 p.m.
	(Tel. 311999)
Reservations	Mon.–Sat.: 8 a.m.–8.30 p.m., British
	Mon.–Sat.: 9 a.m.–5.30 p.m., Continental
Left-luggage lockers	All hours
Left-luggage store	Mon.–Fri.: 7 a.m.–7 p.m., weekend: 9 a.m.–1 p.m.
Bar, Buffet	Mon.–Sat.: 7.30 a.m.–9.45 p.m., Sun.: 9.30 a.m.–9.30 p.m.
Station shuts	1.20 a.m.

Daily trains to: London, Birmingham, Peterborough, Norwich.

TOURIST INFORMATION AND ADDRESSES

The tourist office is at Wheeler St (Tel. 322640), open Mon.–Fri.: 9 a.m.–6 p.m., Sat.: 9 a.m.–5 p.m., Sun.: 10.30 a.m.–3.30 p.m. in season. Pick up the 35p 'Brief Guide' leaflet and ask about their walking tours.

CYCLE HIRE: Cambridge Cycle Hire, 118 Milton Road. £3 a day.
PUNT HIRE: Scudamore's Boatyards, Silver Street, or Magdalene
Bridge. £4.80 per hour plus £30 deposit.
PHONE CODE: 0223.

SEEING

The area between Magdalene Bridge and Silver Street is the one to
concentrate on. The town itself is quite substantial, and the
university colleges are set apart, literally in a world of their own.
THE BACKS are the meadows and fields on the other side of the Cam,
and the best way to drink in this pastoral atmosphere is to hire a
punt and view the colleges from the river. An absolute must is a visit
inside KING'S COLLEGE CHAPEL, the largest chapel in Europe and
one of the most beautiful churches in Britain. Entry to all the
colleges is free, except QUEEN'S (50p). They are all closed, however,
from early May to mid-June, for exams. Take in ST JOHN'S, TRINITY
and especially CLARE COLLEGE gardens.

SLEEPING

Tourist information will find you a bed for a £1 fee or hand you a list
of local B&Bs. The best place to find a cheap B&B is near the
station at Tenison Road or Jesus Lane in the town. Try any of the
following in that lane: Mrs Spalding at No. 56 (Tel. 353858), Mrs
Day at No. 72 (Tel. 356961), or Mrs Owen at No. 65 (Tel. 60648).
The youth hostel is at 97 Tenison Road (Tel. 353858), conveniently
near the station and with cycle hire next door, and there's camping
at Cambspeed Caravan Site, Wimpole Road, Barton. Not that
good, 2½ miles west on bus routes 118, 120 or 175 from Drummer
Street.

EATING AND NIGHTLIFE

There are hundreds of pubs and shops, and the picnic bar in Marks
and Spencer, Market Square, is the best source for picnic food. The
Anchor, Silver Street, is next to the river, a good place to meet
students, and does good pub food. The Blue Boar, Trinity Street is
also recommended. The Maypole, in Portugal Place, does excellent
cocktails.

Ask tourist information for the 'What's On', as there's always a round of plays, films or debates. The best value is the Cambridge University Amateur Dramatic Club, Park Street. Their productions are good and their prices low, £1.50–£4 (Tel. 352000 to see what's playing). In mid-June, 'May Week' is on, when the students are enjoying their new-found freedom after the exams. Many good amateur plays and other events are on, and you may see one of the famous May Balls or a graduation ceremony on at Senate House.

Wales

Wales is a rugged land of 8,000 square miles and boasts that if it was flattened out, it would be bigger than England! Of its 2¾ million people, about a third speak Welsh, though you will notice bilingual signposts everywhere. It is wilder than England and less dramatic than Scotland. For a short while you'd never know you were over the English border, but travel to one of the national parks, or listen to the soft-spoken Welsh in the west and north, and you'll be glad you took in this extra country.

South Wales

South Wales was once internationally famous as a centre of coal mining and heavy industry, but the shift away from heavy industry in Britain today was reflected in the closing of the last colliery in the Rhondda Valley in 1990. Over the past decade, tremendous changes have taken place in the SOUTH WALES VALLEYS where vast land reclamation schemes have completely transformed areas of former industrial dereliction and have resulted in the re-greening of the valleys. Head for the BRYN BACH COUNTRY PARK or the CWM DARRAN PARK to see the beauty of the valleys, where you will find it hard to believe heavy industry once stood in these scenic spots. The RHONDDA HERITAGE PARK gives a fascinating insight into the regeneration projects and the important cultural and industrial heritage of the valleys. The valley railway lines from Cardiff, which run frequently, make the whole area easily accessible. (Take the line to Rhymney for the first two parks, and to Treherbert for the Rhondda park.) A Valley Lines Day Ranger offers unlimited travel for one day.

Cardiff

Cardiff, the Welsh capital city, is about two hours from London and an hour from Bristol. It is a reasonably attractive town, with an increasing amount to merit a stop. The CASTLE is an amazing blend of ruins and architectural styles. The CIVIC CENTRE, TECHNIQUEST and NATIONAL MUSEUM OF WALES are all worth a look, while the open-air WELSH FOLK MUSEUM at St Fagan's is fascinating. Take bus 32 out there, it's open Mon.–Sat.: 10 a.m.–5 p.m. (Tel. 0222–569441). Cardiff Tourist Information is at 8–14 Bridge St and is open daily 9 a.m.–7 p.m. Ask for the free entertainment and visitors' guides (Tel. 0222–222281). Try the youth hostel at Wedal Road on bus line 80 or 82 (Tel. 462303). There are plenty of pubs and clubs on and around St Mary Street, but perhaps the most notable are the Philharmonic and the Four Bars opposite the castle, which sometimes has jazz upstairs. The narrow Victorian shopping arcades, interspersed with newer centres, are good for a ramble.

South Wales National Park

The BRECON BEACONS NATIONAL PARK is a great place to stop off from a hectic European tour and get some good walking done in lovely countryside. BRECON is a charming unspoilt market town. It is a good base to explore the area, with a main tourist information centre (Tel. 0874–4437) able to give details on walks, mountain-bike hire etc. The Youth Hostel is a mile or so out, at Ty'n-y-Caeau (Tel. 0874–86270). Enjoy the mountain views, if you are fortunate enough to get good weather. Brecon is linked by bus 21 to Abergavenny, which is on the Crewe–Cardiff railway line.

The DAN-YR-OGOF caves complex, within the Brecon Beacon Park, is an excellent day-trip, well worth the visit. Open daily from 10 a.m. A guide will show you around the caves, including Britain's largest show-cave. The complex currently holds nine major tourism awards. Rail buffs will not want to miss out on the BRECON MOUNTAIN RAILWAY while in the park, one of a series of 'Great Little Trains of Wales'. The journey takes about an hour, with a working steam-engine and enclosed coaches which give all-round visibility for viewing the scenery. Rail passes are not accepted, but ticket prices are not excessive at £3.40 return (Tel. 0685 4854).

Further west and south in Wales, trains will take you from mainline Swansea to Tenby and Pembroke in the PEMBROKESHIRE COAST NATIONAL PARK. Tenby is an unspoilt seaside resort in lovely Carmarthen Bay with an attractive blend of architecture, while PEMBROKE is a fortified town with a magnificently preserved castle as its centrepiece (open daily 9.30 a.m.–6 p.m.). The Pembrokeshire Coast Park contains some of the best beaches anywhere in Britain and a series of dramatic coastlines. The islands just off the coast are homes and breeding grounds to seals and many types of birds. From Fishguard on the north Pembrokeshire coast, the ferry leaves to Rosslare in Ireland.

Mid-Wales

Mid-Wales is the least visited part of the country, an area of quiet towns, hidden valleys, and perhaps the place where you are most likely to discover traditional Wales. The area is best reached by train services from Shrewsbury, which will take you through to ABERYSTWYTH, the best known resort here. The town of Aberystwyth is a pleasant Victorian seaside resort, but there is also a sizeable student population as this is the seat of the University of Wales. Take the CLIFF RAILWAY up the 2-in-1 gradient to the top of Constitution Hill, where you can make the most of the view with the huge lens of the Victorian CAMERA OBSCURA. Early Welsh manuscripts are to be found in the NATIONAL LIBRARY, and the ABERYSTWYTH ARTS CENTRE is worth a look. Tourist information is at Lisburn House, Terrace Road, open daily 10 a.m.–6 p.m.

Another interesting rail outing is the VALE OF RHEIDOL STEAM RAILWAY to Devil's Bridge, a picturesque trip of about three hours, costing £8 return.

Right up the coast from Aberystwyth, just south of Porthmadog, PORTMEIRION is well worth a stop. In a beautiful coastal location, this amazing village is the fantasy creation of Sir Clough Williams-Ellis. Clusters of pastel-coloured houses surround a piazza with fountains, columns and statues, right in the middle of a subtropical woodland. You certainly won't forget this extraordinary place if you come here, one of the prime tourist attractions of Mid-Wales. It is best to stay in less attractive Porthmadog and to take bus 97 direct to the village.

North Wales

North Wales is an area of dramatic countryside, with a very different character from the south. Welsh is widely spoken in the towns and valleys up here. Fast trains can bring you to the main centres from London, and the coast is also served by direct services from Manchester and the West Midlands.

The SNOWDONIA NATIONAL PARK covers half of North Wales and is one of Europe's best regions for getting away from it all. The terrain is ideal for climbing, hiking, camping and hostelling. A good springboard for ventures into the Snowdonia Park is CARNARFON, reached by taking the train to Bangor, then the bus. Carnarfon is home to arguably the most splendid castle in Britain, the place where the investiture of Prince Charles as the Prince of Wales took place. LLANBERIS is a great place for a base, with plenty of hostels and guesthouses, near to the 3560-foot MOUNT SNOWDON itself. Take the privately run SNOWDON MOUNTAIN RAILWAY to the summit for an expensive £12 return, or alternatively go up with it and then walk back down yourself.

Other great castles in the area are Harlech, Conwy and Beaumaris on the island of Anglesey (Ynys Môn). Conwy also has Britain's smallest house; Ty Bach is on the quayside with a frontage of a mere six feet.

If you are interested in ecology, conservation and the environment a visit to the Centre for Alternative Technology is a must. Set in a slate quarry overlooking the Snowdon National Park, near Machynlleth, the centre is a maze of windmills, aerogenerators, solar heating panels and water turbines. It is three miles from Machynlleth Station, where you can get a bus to the adjacent village of Pantperthog. Open daily 10 a.m.–7 p.m. (Tel. 0654–2400). Entrance costs £2.75 (students £1.60).

Each July the small town of LLANGOLLEN hosts the INTERNATIONAL EISTEDDFOD, a music festival which attracts competitors from over 30 different countries. There's also a steam railway here. Buses run from Wrexham and Chirk railway stations to Llangollen.

Northern England

It is said (by Northerners) that you will know you've reached northern England when travelling from the south as soon as the beer is drinkable and strangers in pubs start a conversation with you.

Although northern England does have more than its fair share of industrialized cities with all the attendant problems, it does have areas of outstanding beauty, interest and character.

A 'lung' of green surrounded by the industrialized towns of the north Midlands and by Sheffield and Manchester is the PEAK DISTRICT NATIONAL PARK in Derbyshire. This was Britain's first national park and is the second most visited national park in the world, so it has to be worth a stop. A Derbyshire Wayfarer Pass for around £4.50 allows one day's unlimited bus and rail travel within Derbyshire. A good base is MATLOCK at the terminus of the railway from Derby. The Youth Hostel is at 40 Bank Road (Tel. 0629–582983), a few minutes from the station over the river and straight up the hill. Matlock itself is dominated by the ruined RIBER CASTLE, presently a fauna reserve which has great views. Take a walk along the river to MATLOCK BATH in a limestone gorge for a cable-car ride for £4 up to the Heights of Abraham for more splendid views. An excellent view of the cable-cars, gorge and Matlock Bath can be had from the White Lion Inn at Starkholmes, perched above Matlock and below Riber Castle. Not only does it have unrivalled views and the best beer in the area, it also serves reasonable food and one of our researchers drinks there! Further north, BUXTON, a former spa town, and CASTLETON, for its caverns, are well worth a look. The scenery throughout the Peak District is excellent and well suited to walking, but keep to defined footpaths to avoid further erosion of the most popular paths. Tourist Information at Matlock Bath (Tel. 0629–55082) and Buxton (Tel. 0298–5106) will provide information on the best walks, other sights and affordable accommodation.

Chester

Chester is a real gem of a town, easily reached by train from neighbouring Liverpool or Manchester. It is famed for its complete run of Roman walls which, unlike York's, can be walked right around. Inside the town, the medieval streets with their half-timbered houses can easily be explored on foot.

The CATHEDRAL on Northgate Street is well worth a look. See the ROWS, a unique set of two-tier medieval houses with shops built in, and the ruins of the half-excavated ROMAN AMPHITHEATRE, designed to seat over 7,000 spectators (open daily 10 a.m.–6 p.m.). If you have the time, bus 40 will take you to CHESTER ZOO, where you can catch good views of the animals, which are not kept behind bars. Open 10 a.m.–5 p.m. daily, admission £5.

Tourist information is at Northgate Street (Mon.–Sat.: 9 a.m.–5.30 p.m.) or at the Chester Visitor Centre (open daily 9 a.m.–7 p.m.). The Youth Hostel is pleasant and is at 40 Hough Green (0244–680056). Take bus 16 or 17 to save yourself the two-mile walk. Good B&Bs are to be found along Brook Street. Chester has a large number of pubs, some of which are located in wonderful historic buildings.

Liverpool

Liverpool is similar to Glasgow in that it has received a lot of bad press internationally and has a bad public image. In fact the crime rate is no higher than in any other major city and the people are renowned for their wit and friendliness. Tourism is a growth industry in Merseyside, and many people who come solely because of the Beatles are surprised to find much more.

STATION FACILITIES

	LIME STREET STATION (INTER CITY)
Ticket office	Mon.–Sun.: 5 a.m.–1 a.m.
Travel centre	Mon.–Sun.: 8 a.m.–8 p.m.
Left-luggage	Mon.–Sat.: 6.30 a.m.–10 a.m., 10.30 a.m.–6 p.m., 6.30 p.m.–9.30 p.m.
	Opens 7 a.m. Sun.
Telephone	051–709 9696
Restaurant	Mon.–Sun.: 7 a.m.–10 p.m.

Daily trains to: London, Manchester, Birmingham, South-West, Wales, Scotland, Lake District, Newcastle.

• **Merseyrail Underground:** Lime Street, James Street, Central and Moorfields stations in the city centre. Underground and bus information (Tel. 051–236 7676). Frequent trains to Southport, Chester, Ormskirk, Wirral, North Wales, Manchester.

TOURIST INFORMATION

There are information offices on Lime Street (Tel. 051–709 3631) and in Clayton Square shopping centre and the Albert Dock. Bus information from Merseytravel office, Williamson Square.

SEEING

ALBERT DOCK on the waterfront is the largest grade 1 listed building in the country. It has been restored and now hosts an array of small shops, cafés and exclusive apartments. The Albert Dock also hosts the northern branch of London's famous TATE GALLERY. Admission is free although there is often a small charge for admission to special exhibitions. Also at the Albert Dock is the MERSEYSIDE MARITIME MUSEUM – a museum which traces Liverpool's maritime history. Nearby is the PIER HEAD which holds the three buildings which dominate Liverpool's skyline. From here you can still get a Ferry 'Cross the Mersey. Other things to see in the city centre include the two modern cathedrals. LIVERPOOL CATHEDRAL is a huge gothic building completed in the 1980s. It is the second largest Anglican cathedral in the world after St Paul's and houses the largest pipe organ in Europe. There are often recitals on bank holidays. In complete contrast at the other end of Hope Street is the Catholic LIVERPOOL METROPOLITAN CATHEDRAL – a concrete and glass circular structure known locally as 'Paddy's Wigwam'. Inside the spray of light from the stained glass can be quite beautiful. If you've come to Liverpool in search of the Beatles, stop off at one of the information shops first. These will give you information about all the walking and coach tours available. The original Cavern club was demolished some years ago but a faithful replica has been constructed a little further down Matthew Street in the Cavern Walks Shopping Centre. If you want to see Penny Lane, Strawberry Fields etc., take a coach trip. Liverpool is famous for its footballing tradition. During the football season, matches can be seen on a Saturday at Liverpool or Everton FCs.

SLEEPING

The YMCA, YWCA and numerous small B&B hotels can be found on Mount Pleasant near the Catholic cathedral and 10 minutes' walk from the station.

EATING AND NIGHTLIFE

There are numerous fast-food and fish and chip shops dotted throughout the city centre. Alternatively, make a picnic with food from one of the city centre shops. Liverpool also has a great selection of ethnic restaurants and those in 'Chinatown' are excellent and great value, and especially popular for Dim Sum – the very tasty and varied snacks. There are some great venues for live music; a local will help out with inside knowledge. Also sample the varied pubs. One of our favourites is the Swan on Wood Street for its selection of good beers and interesting characters.

The industrial north has a few saving graces from its heavy-industry towns in the form of the YORKSHIRE MOORS in the east, and the LAKE

DISTRICT in the west. The moors are wild, untouched terrain, ideal for hiking and camping as long as you don't mind isolation. The NORTH YORK MOORS NATIONAL PARK has a tourist office at PICKERING STATION, which is as good a place as any to base yourself. The LAKE DISTRICT NATIONAL PARK is considered to be the country's best. The main centres, and also the most touristy in summer, are KESWICK, WINDERMERE and GRASMERE. There's a station at Windermere, and for Keswick use PENRITH. For tourist information, contact the office in Victoria Street, Penrith, open 10 a.m.–8.30 p.m. in season. There are thirty youth hostels (the world's highest density) and the Park Service run a series of free guided walks and courses in summer.

York

York dates back to Roman times and is considered Britain's best-preserved medieval city with the finest Gothic cathedral. It lies about halfway between London and Edinburgh on the east-coast line, and with the fast 125 intercity service, it takes only 2½ hours from the capital. A visit is most highly recommended.

STATION FACILITIES

Train information	8 a.m.–9 p.m.
	(Tel. 642155)
Reservations	8 a.m.–9 p.m.
Left-luggage store	Mon.–Sat.: 7.15 a.m.–9.15 p.m.;
	Sun.: 11.15 a.m.–6.45 p.m.
Bar, Buffet	7 a.m.–10 p.m.
Bookshop	6.30 a.m.–6.30 p.m.

Daily trains to: London, Edinburgh, Leeds, the Midlands, the West Country, South Wales, Liverpool, Manchester, Scarborough, Harrogate.

TOURIST INFORMATION AND ADDRESSES

The tourist information centre is in Exhibition Square and at the station, and is open Mon.–Sat.: 9 a.m.–8 p.m., Sun.: 2 p.m.–5 p.m. in season. They run a free two-hour walking tour from the Art Gallery at 10.15 a.m., 2.15 p.m. and 7.15 p.m.
PHONE CODE: 0904.

SEEING

There are four main entrances to the city: BOOTHAM GATE, MICKLE-GATE, MONKGATE and WALMGATE, and the city is surrounded by three miles of defensive walls which make an attractive walk. York MINSTER (the cathedral which had a tied school) is amazing: the Great East Window is as big as a tennis court, and all the stained glass is medieval. Once you've wandered around the cathedral, visit the CASTLE MUSEUM which is an exceptionally good folk museum with reconstructions of streets, people and implements of the last century. For evidence of the Romans, go to the MULTI-ANGULAR TOWER in the Yorkshire Museum Gardens. The JORVIK VIKING CENTRE in Coppergate is an essential stopping-off place if you are keen on history. York of 1,000 years ago comes to life in this fascinating museum, complete with authentic smells. Do get there very early as two-hour queues are not uncommon, such is its excellent reputation with visitors. Real train enthusiasts will like the NATIONAL RAILWAY MUSEUM down by the station – plenty of steam locos, etc. There are many other historic and interesting places, like the TREASURER'S HOUSE, CLIFFORD'S TOWER, and the wonderful old shopping streets of medieval York like the SHAMBLES, and the site of the old whipping post, WHIP-MA-WHOP-MA-GATE. Pick up detailed leaflets from tourist information. While you're in the area, you might want to visit CASTLE HOWARD, the beautiful eighteenth-century setting of the TV version of *Brideshead Revisited*. Ask tourist information for the best buses.

SLEEPING

Tourist information will give you lists of B&Bs and hostels, or find you a room for free (with a £1.75 deposit). York can get very busy in summer, so get fixed up as soon as you arrive. The area round Bootham is not bad for B&B, and there's a youth hostel at Water End, Clifton (Tel. 653147), though it's usually full. Without curfews are Bishophill House, a private hostel at 11–13 Bishophill Senior Road (Tel. 625904) and the International House, 33 Bootham (Tel. 622874) only 300 yards from York Minster. For B&B try Bishopthorpe Road in Bootham, or the Mount area down Blossom Street. The campsite, open May–Sept., is three miles out of town at Bishopthorpe (Tel. 704442).

EATING AND NIGHTLIFE

There are bakers' shops, markets and pubs a-plenty in York. York Wholefood, 98 Micklegate, do good meals upstairs, and Kooks at 108 Fishergate (closed Mon.) is also worth a try. With over 150 pubs, you shouldn't get stuck for a watering hole. The Black Swan in Peasholme Green is a suitably olde-worlde place, but there are many more dotted around.

York–Edinburgh

Fifty minutes further up the line from York is the cathedral town of DURHAM. You should take an hour or two of even the most hurried journey off, and catch the next 225, to see the magnificent CATHEDRAL and CASTLE there (not open to the public as it is part of the university). They face each other over Palace Green in a dramatic setting. The cathedral is eleventh-century and is considered one of Europe's finest Romanesque examples; and the castle dates from the same time with fourteenth-century additions. The fortified town of BERWICK-UPON-TWEED is the border between the ancient enemies, Scotland and England. Should you break your journey here, see the old city walls and elegant eighteenth-century TOWN HALL. From the border it's an hour to Edinburgh, Scotland's majestic capital.

Scotland

If you're visiting Scotland for the first time, the chances are you'll want to come again. The scenery in the Scottish Highlands is outstanding: the glens and mountains, lochs and islands are unique in their unspoilt beauty. Were the weather only a bit better, Scotland would be the answer to everyone's holiday problems; however, let's be honest – you don't come here for a tan, you come to hike on the hills or wander through the historic streets of Edinburgh. That said, the months between June and September can sometimes offer weeks on end without rain: it just depends on your luck. The rail network is a bit restricted up north, but if you travel up the east coast to Inverness, then west to Kyle of Lochalsh, taking the boat from Mallaig, then back down the west coast via Oban to Glasgow, Scotland's largest industrial city, you'll get a good idea of the geography. The Mallaig to Glasgow west coast line is one of Britain's most scenic rail journeys. Now, without going into a detailed account, until the eighteenth century, the English and the Scots had nothing in common and, as far as many Scots are concerned, they still don't. Remember this when you're making small talk with them, and do try not to refer to the whole of Great Britain as just 'England' – it doesn't go down well.

Edinburgh

The elegant city of Edinburgh can't fail to strike the visitor as dramatic: built on extinct volcanoes with a fairytale castle dominating the city, and hills and the sea all around. It's the artistic, commercial, academic and legal centre of Scotland and its history goes back to the seventh century. As soon as you walk up the hill from Waverley Station you're in the centre of things, with the castle and 'old town' behind and to your left, and the 'new town' from the Georgian era on your right, to the north of Princes Street, the main shopping thoroughfare.

STATION FACILITIES

	WAVERLEY STATION
Train information	Mon.–Sat.: 8 a.m.–11 p.m., Sun.: 9 a.m.–11 p.m. (Tel. 556 2451, 24 hours)
Reservations	Mon.–Sat.: 8 a.m.–8 p.m., Sun.: 9 a.m.–8 p.m.
Tourist information	100 yards from station (on top of Waverley Shopping Market)
Foreign exchange	3 a.m.–12 midnight
Left-luggage store	Mon.–Sat.: 6 a.m.–10.50 p.m. Sun.: 7 a.m.–10.50 p.m.
Bar	Mon.–Sat.: 7 a.m.–1 a.m. Sun.: 12.30 a.m.–2.30 p.m., 6.30 p.m.–11 p.m.
Restaurant	6.30 a.m.–10.30 p.m.
Bath, Shower	3 a.m.–12 midnight
Station shuts	12.30 a.m.–2.30 a.m.

Daily trains to: Aberdeen, Birmingham, Bristol, Glasgow, Inverness, Liverpool, London, Manchester, Perth, Stirling.

TOURIST INFORMATION AND ADDRESSES

The Edinburgh and Scotland Tourist Information Centre is on the top of Waverley Market, just up the ramp and to your right from the station, open weekdays 8.30 a.m.–9 p.m., Sun.: 11 a.m.–9 p.m. in season (Tel. 557 1700). Ask for 'What's On'. Good Bureau de Change (Tel. 557 2727). Packed with useful information, such as where to eat and what to see, the pocket-sized EDINBURGH CITY GUIDE is one of the best all-round city guidebooks. Good value at around £2.50 in bookshops. The Centre also serves as a ticket-booking agency.

POST OFFICE: 2–4 Waterloo Place (at east end of Princes Street), open Mon.–Fri.: 9 a.m.–5.30 p.m., Sat.: 9 a.m.–12.30 p.m. Currency exchange.

AMEX: 139 Princes Street, open Mon.–Fri.: 9 a.m.–5 p.m., Sat.: 9 a.m.–12 noon (Tel. 225 7881).

US CONSULATE: 3 Regent Terrace (Tel. 556 8315).

AUSTRALIAN CONSULATE: 80 Hanover Street (Tel. 226 6271).

MEDICAL HELP: University Health Service, Bristo Square (Tel. 667 1011).

CAMPUS TRAVEL EUROTRAIN: 5 Nicolson Square (Tel. 668 3303).

PHONE CODE: 031.

SEEING

The medieval ROYAL MILE was so called because it stretches from the CASTLE to the royal palace of HOLYROOD. You can't possibly miss the CASTLE which dates back to the seventh century. It stands on an extinct volcano and can be seen from virtually every corner of Edinburgh. Though entrance is £2.20 (there's no student discount), if you're keen on history it's worth it. The Scottish Crown Jewels are on display here and you can see the twelfth-century QUEEN MARGARET'S CHAPEL, the smallest in Scotland and the oldest building in the city. Walking down the Royal Mile, you'll find GLADSTONE'S LAND, a beautifully preserved seventeenth-century townhouse in the Lawnmarket, well worth a visit at £1.80, and behind this is LADY STAIR'S HOUSE with Burns, Stevenson and Scott mementoes. ST GILES' CATHEDRAL, the Gothic 1385 High Church of Scotland, is on the right, as are various buildings of the Scottish parliament. Halfway down in the Canongate is JOHN KNOX'S HOUSE and the

MUSEUM OF CHILDHOOD, an interesting collection of toys and games from bygone days. At the foot of the Royal Mile is the splendid PALACE OF HOLYROOD HOUSE. Open 9.30 a.m.–5.15 p.m. and Sun.: 10.30 a.m.–2.30 p.m. in season. Admission is £2, students £1. It is the official residence of H.M. Queen in Scotland and steeped in past tragedy and history with many good tapestries and paintings. After a tour of the sixteenth-century palace, clear your head with a good blast of Scottish air up another of Edinburgh's extinct volcanoes, ARTHUR'S SEAT, or walk to CALTON HILL at the east end of Princes Street to look at 'Edinburgh's Disgrace': the replica of the Athens Parthenon, built to commemorate Scottish dead in the Napoleonic Wars, that ran out of money and remains unfinished.

On one side of Princes Street are the city's main shops, while opposite are gardens and the two neo-classical art galleries: the NATIONAL GALLERY OF SCOTLAND and the ROYAL SCOTTISH ACADEMY, both particularly impressive. WALTER SCOTT'S MONUMENT, the huge Gothic tower in Princes Street Gardens, affords a good view from the top, and from here a walk up Hanover Street will take you down to Queen Street where, along on the right, you'll find THE ROYAL MUSEUM OF SCOTLAND. Bus 23 or 27 from Hanover Street will take you down to the BOTANICAL GARDENS which are a glorious picnic venue and you'll find the NATIONAL GALLERY OF MODERN ART near DEAN VILLAGE on Belford Road. If you've any time left, search out the GEORGIAN HOUSE in CHARLOTTE SQUARE, THE PEOPLE'S STORY MUSEUM in the Canongate Tollbooth, THE ZOO, one of the finest in Britain, and take bus 41 out to CRAMOND, down by the sea. During the International Festival and its Fringe in August literally thousands of events are staged: plays, concerts, exhibitions; and every church hall in the city has some group performing in it. Thousands of students descend on the city, as tickets start as low as £5. Running at the same time are the film and jazz festivals, and the bonanza of the MILITARY TATTOO with enough kilts and bagpipes to satisfy even the most ardent American. Tattoo office: Tel. 225 1188, Fringe office: Tel. 226 5257.

Go to INCHCOLM ISLAND in the Firth of Forth for a great day out. The 'Iona of the East' has a beautiful medieval abbey and hundreds of seabirds nest here. It is also home to grey seals. To get there take a train to DALMENY and walk 10 minutes to the pier at South Queensferry, and then a ferry which usually leaves across from the Hawes Inn, where Robert Louis Stevenson is known to have downed a few (cost £4.50 return, £3.50 for students). Runs May–Sept.

SLEEPING

Aside from late August–September (Festival time), a bed's not too much of a hassle, and the tourist information centre will help you out. They're open till 9 p.m. and have a free list of suggestions but advance booking is recommended. For B&Bs, take a bus out to Newington and look along Newington and Minto Streets, or try the Bruntsfield area.

• **Hostels:** The youth hostels are at 18 Eglinton Crescent (Tel. 337 1120) and 7–8 Bruntsfield Crescent (Tel. 447 2994).

The University Halls of Residence, Pollock Halls, 18 Holyrood Park Road (Tel. 667 1971), are very good and offer 1,500 single rooms at around £9.70 for students, £16.25 otherwise. Take buses 21 or 33 to the Commonwealth Pool.

The High Street Hostel (Tel. 557 3984) at 8 Blackfriars Street is situated halfway between the castle and the Palace of Holyrood House and only a few minutes' walk up the hill from Waverley Station. It costs £6.20 and you don't need an IYHF card. It is open 24 hours. There is a free left-luggage service and showers. Accommodation is in dormitories of about 12 beds. To camp, take bus 33 out to Little France, Old Dalkeith Road (Tel. 664 4742).

• **Hotels:** The Roxburghe Hotel, Charlotte Square (Tel. 225 3921) is a fine, recently refurbished central first-class hotel for the Adult Eurail market while Johnstonburn House Hotel at Humbie, half an hour east of Edinburgh, is a country house hotel of great character and quality, offering traditional comforts and excellent cuisine in an historic setting. The Adult Eurail market will also find the Greywalls Hotel in Gullane, near Edinburgh a delightful place to dine or spend a weekend. This luxury country house hotel is a fine example of a traditional British estate, and apart from its exceptional restaurant and good accommodation, it has the luck to be situated right next to one of Britain's finest golf courses – Muirfield, dramatically positioned right next to the sea but don't expect to be able to play as it's somewhat exclusive! Take the train to Drem and a cab from there. Booking ahead in summer is advisable. (Tel.

0620–842144). More accessible hotels by rail are in Linlithgow and North Berwick.

EATING AND NIGHTLIFE

Cheap eats are no problem in Edinburgh and it's possible to fill up for under £3 at either a fish'n'chip shop or a filled baked potato carry-out; Edinburgh specializes in these, and there are Spud-U-Like shops or similar around the centre. Try The Baked Potato Shop on Cockburn Street. Pick up the free leaflet from tourist information on restaurants. Pubs often offer cheap lunches, and this capital has over 500 to choose from. The University Students' Union at Teviot Row (up the Mound, and George IV Bridge) do meals for about £1.50, or try Henderson's Salad Table, 94 Hanover Street, for healthy meals around £7.50. Also good value is Bell's diner at 26 St Stephen Street in Stockbridge (Tel. 225 8116). It's a very popular eating place, selling home-made burgers, salads, delicious sweet courses and house wines. Also try the Buffalo Grill on Chapel Street for around £8 or the Cellar No. 1 on Chamber Street for a wine bar with good food for around £5. Book ahead. Edinburgh has restaurants representing a huge number of countries; try the Coconut Grove on Lochrun Terrace.

If you're here in Festival time, the nightlife position is unmatched anywhere else in Britain. Go along to the Fringe Club, in Teviot Row, off Bristo Square (Tel. 667 2091), where performers, the media and the public gather to socialize (£16 membership for the Festival's duration, bring a passport photo). Be sure to pick up the Fringe programme for the widest range of entertainment you're likely to find anywhere. If you're visiting at any other time, pick up 'What's On' from tourist information and combine some events with a visit to some of the city's pubs; a popular pub crawl is along the nineteen bars of Rose Street. Many students hang out in the George Square area pubs such as the Pear Tree, Maxie's Bistro, and the up-market, continental wine bar, Negociants, opposite the Teviot Row Students' Union. Café Royal, just behind the large Wimpy at the east end of Princes Street, is an outstanding example of a fine Victorian pub. Check out the ceiling in their upstairs bar. They do good bar lunches too, as does The Abbotsford on Rose Street.

If you are splashing out, try Jackson's Restaurant in Jackson's

Close, off the Royal Mile. They do an excellent menu including traditional Scottish food and wine.

Check out what's playing in the Film House (Lothian Road), the Tollcross Cinema, the Cameo (on Home Street, showing arty films), or the Grassmarket Theatre.

Glasgow

Just 45 minutes on one of the half-hourly expresses from Edinburgh is Glasgow, Scotland's largest city and business centre. While it does not have the immediate visual presence of Edinburgh, Glasgow is still a beautiful Victorian city and well worth a visit. Thanks to the 'Glasgow's Miles Better' campaign which started some years ago, it is gradually shaking off an unfair reputation for being violent and dirty. In recent years many buildings have been cleaned and the environment generally improved, although for many years it has had more parks per head of population (780,000) than any other city in Europe – a fact which has surprised many visitors. In Glasgow it's not so much the buildings you come to see (as with Edinburgh) but the people. They are regarded as the warmest, most outgoing lot in Britain, and a visit to a few pubs will confirm that. Previously it has hosted a Garden Festival and was the 1990 European City of Culture.

SEEING

When you get off the train at Queen Street Station go straight ahead into George Square and turn right into St Vincent Place. The tourist office is on the left-hand side (Tel. 041–204 4400), where you can pick up leaflets, get information about places to see and book accommodation. Without doubt the major attraction is the BURRELL COLLECTION, an 8,000-piece artistic treasure trove, gathered together over a lifetime of collecting on every continent by Glasgow shipping magnate Sir William Burrell. Entry is free to the collection, which was donated to the people of Glasgow in 1944 but opened only in 1983. The award-winning building housing the collection is situated in POLLOK COUNTRY PARK. Take a train from

Glasgow Central to Pollokshaws West and then the free bus from
the entrance next to the station. If you don't want to wait for the bus
(every 20 minutes) walk through the 361 acres of parkland and
gardens and see the herd of Highland cattle near to Pollok House.
In Pollok House is one of the finest collections of Spanish paintings
in Britain. Entry to both museums is free of charge and they have
the same opening hours: Mon.–Sat.: 10 a.m.–5 p.m., Sun.: 12
noon–6 p.m. The ART GALLERY AND MUSEUM, at Kelvingrove, is
also worth visiting as it houses Britain's finest civic collection of
British and European paintings including Salvador Dali's 'Crucifix-
ion'. Charles Rennie Macintosh came from Glasgow and many of
the buildings he designed can be seen in the city. The Headquarters
of the CHARLES RENNIE MACINTOSH SOCIETY (formerly Queen's
Cross Church) are at 866 Garscube Road, open Tues., Thurs., Fri.:
12 noon–5.30 p.m., Sun.: 2.30 p.m.–5.30 p.m. In the city centre you
can visit and have tea at the WILLOW TEA ROOM, a famous Macintosh
building recently restored, at 217 Sauchiehall Street (Tel. 041–332
0521) Mon.–Sat.: 9.30 a.m.–5 p.m. Well worth a look is the BARRAS
at weekends. On London Road and Gallowgate to the east of the
centre, this is possibly the world's largest open-air market with an
amazing variety of stalls and shops. An interesting look at Victorian
life in Glasgow can be had at THE TENEMENT HOUSE 145 Buccleuth
Street, a first-floor Victorian flat furnished with the trappings of a
Victorian family. Open Mon.–Fri.: 12 noon–5 p.m., weekends 2
p.m.–6 p.m.

It is only a short distance from Glasgow to the spectacular scenery
of the TROSSACHS or LOCH LOMOND and bus tours to both places –
and many others – run from Buchanan Bus Station in the city centre
(Tel. 041–332 7133). Alternatively you can head over to the Island
of ARRAN. Trains to Ardrossan Harbour leave from Central Station
and take just over an hour. The ferry takes under an hour to
Brodick and there are connecting buses there to take you to the two
hostels on the island, one in the south at Whiting Bay (Tel. 077
07–339) and the other in the more mountainous north at Lochranza
(Tel. 077 083–631).

SLEEPING

One youth hostel is near the Art Gallery. Take a train from Queen
Street low level one stop to Charing Cross and head up the hill

following the signs. It's at 11 Woodlands Terrace (Tel. 041–332 3004). Glasgow's newest Youth Hostel, formerly the Beacons Hotel, has excellent facilities including en-suite facilities for all dormitories, a restaurant and good self-catering possibilities. It is open until 2 a.m. and can be found at 7/8 Park Terrace (Tel. 041–332 3004). Alternatively, try the University of Glasgow Halls of Residence, bookable through the tourist office. An unofficial hostel, run on foreign lines with a relaxed attitude to curfews and duties, it operates each summer. The Glasgow Central Tourist Hostel is situated in the Balmanno Building, 81 Rottenrow East (Tel. 041–552 2401/2). It is a few minutes' walk from George Square and Queen Street Station, close to the University of Strathclyde.

EATING AND NIGHTLIFE

In the same area are two restaurants worth seeking out. The Ubiquitous Chip, at 12 Ashton Lane, also specializes in traditional Scottish food but is better known for its wine cellar, reputed to be among the top ten in Britain. Imaginative top-grade food served at medium-grade prices makes this an essential meeting place for the young, arty crowd (Tel. 041–334 5007). Glasgow also has a fine selection of Indian and Chinese restaurants around Sauchiehall Street and university area. One definitely not to be missed is the Shish Mahal in Gibson Street, near Glasgow University. The popularity of this place makes booking more or less essential (Tel. 041–339 8256) and you'll find well-prepared Indian dishes at reasonable prices, as well as meeting a few Glaswegian students. In the city centre try Babbity Bowster, a café/bar/restaurant which is full of character. The food is excellent and reasonably priced. It is at 16/18 Blackfriars Street (Tel. 041–552 5055). Pick up 'The List', 80p from newsstands for details of nightlife.

On to Inverness

From Edinburgh or Glasgow it's a four-hour journey up to Inverness, capital of the Highlands. The route is via Perth and Aviemore and, once you're up at Pitlochry, the scenery is wonderful. Perthshire is one of Britain's most splendid regions. Majestic landscapes and pretty villages; neat, clean towns and wonderful old country houses, many of which now serve as de luxe hotels and restaurants, are some of the attractions of this area. Perth and Stirling are the two main stopping-off stations, and from there regular buses allow you to explore the hidden corners of this unspoilt part of the UK.

A quick rundown on Inverness is all that is needed, for while it's a pleasant enough place, you should really just use it as a base for the surrounding country. The left-luggage locker facilities at the station are of the excellent modern computerized variety, which are also user-friendly. There's no fine for a lost access ticket as all the lockers can be operated by the central computer which is also good for security. While in Inverness, wander (or take a guided mini-bus tour or cruise) round LOCH NESS where the elusive monster is said to live, and visit CAWDOR CASTLE (twelve miles east) where Shakespeare set *Macbeth*. There are plenty of B&Bs around Old Edinburgh Road, as is the youth hostel at No. 1 (Tel. 0463–231771), and camping down by the river on the Craig Dunain bus route (Tel. 0463–236920).

Culloden House Hotel, three miles from the town centre, where the station is located, is the recommended luxury hotel in this area of the Highlands. While it is strictly in the 'afternoon tea only' category to most Inter-Railers, those on the Adult Eurail Pass may well consider splurging on a night in sumptuous historic surroundings, enjoying traditionally prepared dishes, and relaxing in the sort of luxury you'd forgotten existed after a few weeks on the road. It's well worth the trip out, even if just to see the eighteenth-century buildings and enjoy the surrounding countryside (Tel. 0463–790461). Tourist information at 23 Church Street is open Mon.–Sat.: 9 a.m.–8.30 p.m., Sun.: 9 a.m.–6 p.m. in summer (Tel. 0463–234353). To get into the corners not covered by rail, rent a bike from Ness Motors or the youth hostel and, armed with a map, head for the north side of Loch Ness and Urquhart Castle. If you're lucky you may even see the monster here.

The Highlands and Islands

From Inverness; take the train west to KYLE OF LOCHALSH, a 170-minute journey of beautiful unspoilt scenery through the

Wester Ross mountains. From Kyle there's a frequent five-minute ferry over to Kyleakin on the ISLE OF SKYE, Britain's most dramatic island. The peace and beauty of the Black Cuillin Hills and the haunting cloud formations are quite unmatched elsewhere. POR-TREE, the island's capital, has a tourist office overlooking the harbour. Skye can also be approached from MALLAIG, and from Mallaig you're back on the main line to FORT WILLIAM and GLASGOW. At Fort William you may be tempted to walk up BEN NEVIS, Britain's highest peak. The Youth Hostel (Tel. 0397–702336) is at the start of the trail, which takes around seven hours to complete and which affords some fine views. However, this is a tough walk, even for the very fit. Never go alone, and make sure someone knows where you're going before you start. If you were thinking of heading further north, there's a line from Inverness to WICK; but it's pretty desolate up there, so think twice. If it's isolation you're after, try the ORKNEY ISLANDS. These ex-Danish colonies are well worth visiting; the easiest approach is the ferry from John O'Groats. Visit the Stone Age settlement of SKARA BRAE and the Bronze Age STANDING STONES OF STENNESS and RING OF BRODGAR. The Oban–Glasgow run is another favourite for Highland scenery, 3½ hours of it. From OBAN you can visit the beautiful ISLE OF MULL, and from there go to the smaller, more isolated islands of Iona, Staffa, Coll and Tiree. Tourist information in Oban is at Argyll Square, turn right from the station; and there's a hostel on the Esplanade (Tel. 0631–62025).

Northern Ireland

Many more tourists are now visiting Northern Ireland despite the current 'troubles'. Bear in mind that the media tend to inflate it out of all proportion, and that most of the province is safe to visit, particularly if you're obviously a tourist. However, you may lay yourself open to security-checks from the armed forces in the affected areas and you shouldn't take photos of the security forces or police stations. That said, the scenery is nice and varied for such a small area, with lots of mountains, lakes, caves, cliffs and some wonderful sandy beaches.

There are three main rail routes from Belfast Central Station (Tel. 0232–230310) – north to Londonderry via Ballymena and Coleraine, east to Bangor, and south to Dublin via Lisburn, Portadown and Newry. The Dublin–Belfast Express takes about two hours. The boat-train for Scotland leaves from York Road Station, Belfast (Tel. 0232–235282) to the ferry from Larne to Stranraer in south-west Scotland. The Northern Ireland Railways Board offer a 50 per cent discount if you bought your Inter-Rail from BR NIR or IE.

The Emerald Card and Irish Rover, valid for travel in the Republic of Ireland, are also valid in the six counties of the North. There is also the Rail Runabout, which for £25.00, during April–Oct., offers seven days' unlimited travel on all rail services throughout Northern Ireland and to Dundalk. Available from the Central Station, Belfast.

Taking the capital, Belfast, as the centre, you'll find COUNTY DOWN and the MOURNE MOUNTAINS to the south, ARMAGH to the west, FERMANAGH further west and TYRONE inland. COUNTY LONDONDERRY is in the north-west corner and COUNTY ANTRIM in the north-east. At TORR HEAD you're only thirteen miles from Scotland, and in the north-west of Antrim's coast is the GIANT'S CAUSEWAY, the famous rock formation.

The main things to see in BELFAST are in the UNIVERSITY AREA and the city centre around DONEGALL SQUARE where the Renaissance-style City Hall is. Well worth a mention are the OPERA HOUSE and the ULSTER MUSEUM and ART GALLERY in the Botanic Gardens. The Ulster Museum is especially noteworthy for its Irish antiquities and for its internationally famous treasures from the Spanish Armada. Admission is free. Open Mon.–Fri.: 10 a.m.–5 p.m., Sat.: 1 p.m.–5 p.m., Sun.: 2 p.m.–5 p.m. Tourist Information is at St Anne's Court, North Street (Tel. 0232–246609) and is open Mon.–Fri.: 9 a.m.–5.15 p.m. and also Easter–Sept., Sat.: 9 a.m.–2 p.m. The city bus tours are a good way of seeing Belfast's sights. They take 3½ hours and run from Castle Place, June–Sept. at 2 p.m. Tues.–Thurs. The fare is £4.

There's a youth hostel at 11 Saintfield Road (Tel. 0232–647865), take bus 84 from Donegal Sq. East; but a look around the university area should turn up a pleasant B&B for a more central base. YMCA Interpoint is at 12 Wellington House (Tel. 0232–327231). 500 m from Belfast City Hall.

The ULSTER FOLK AND TRANSPORT MUSEUM at Cultra Manor, Holywood, six miles from Belfast, is well worth the detour. There are reconstructions of nineteenth-century life from farms to craft centres. A trip to Northern Ireland would be incomplete without a visit to the magnificent GIANT'S CAUSEWAY, 40,000 columns of basalt steeped in Celtic legend. At Causeway Head visit the Causeway Centre, open daily 10 a.m.–7 p.m. (earlier closing off-season). The Whitepark Bay Youth Hostel (Tel. 02657–31745) is not too far away, and is situated next to St Gobhan's Church – the smallest in Ireland at 4ft × 6ft. Whilst you're there consider a visit to nearby BUSHMILLS, home of the oldest (legal) whisky distillery at 2 Distillery Road. Established in 1608, it is open for tours Mon.– Thurs.: 10 a.m.–12 noon and 2 p.m.–2.30 p.m., Fri.: 10 a.m.–12 noon (Tel. 02657–31521). The visitor centre has many creative uses for the liquid gold.

A particularly scenic excursion can be taken throughout the area on the 'Bushmills Bus', an open-topped affair which runs July–Aug. from Coleraine to the Giant's Causeway via Portstewart, Portrush, Portballintrae and Bushmills. The journey can be broken.

LONDONDERRY (or just DERRY), two hours from Belfast, is one of Northern Ireland's most attractive towns. Tourist information at Foyle Street (Tel. 0504–267284). The OLD CITY WALLS have withstood invaders for over 350 years, and while you can walk the one-mile circuit to see good views of the city, they are hardly laid out as a walk. The GUILDHALL in Shipquay Place is a neo-Gothic building whose stained-glass windows tell the city's history. The seventeenth-century Protestant cathedral is notable for stained glass showing scenes of the siege of 1688/89. To hear traditional Irish music and enjoy a pint, try one of the pubs on Waterloo Street; Dungloe Bar, Gweedore Bar or Castle Bar.

'YUGOSLAVIA' (Jugoslavija)

Entry requirements	Passport
Population	23,600,000
Capitals	Serbia: Belgrade (pop.: 1,850,000); Croatia: Zagreb;
	Slovenia: Ljubliana; Bosnia: Sarajevo;
	Montenegro: Titograd; Macedonia: Skopje
Currency	New Dinar
	£1 = approx. 343D
Political system	Socialist Federal Republic
Religions	Serbian Orthodox, Muslim, Catholic
Languages	Serbo-Croat, Slovenian, Macedonian
	(some English, German, Italian
	and French understood)
Public holidays	1, 2 Jan.; 1, 2 May; 4 July; 29, 30 Nov.
International dialling codes	From UK: 010 + 38 + number
	From USA: 011 + 38 + number
	To UK: 99 + 44 + number
	To USA: 99 + 1 + number

The name 'Yugoslavia' means Land of the Southern Slavs – a post-First-World-War creation made up of the odd bits left from the break-up of the Austro-Hungarian Empire. The six republics held together until the Second World War, when about a tenth of the country's population was killed, many by fellow Yugoslavs in the civil war which followed. From this period emerged Marshal Tito, who kept the country together as a non-aligned Communist state. It came as a surprise to many that old 'Yugoslavia' remained together as long as it did after Tito's death in 1980 – within the country there were at least eight nationalities, speaking five different languages, using two alphabets (Cyrillic and Latin), and to make things more complicated, practising four different religions.

The individual republics began to become more and more resentful of central (Serbian) control from Belgrade, and felt there was no historical basis for 'Yugoslavia'. Violent conflict followed Croatia and Slovenia's declarations of independence in June 1991, which eventually led to all-out Civil War in places. International recognition of the independence of these two states may have

Additional information on all Eastern European countries contained in the *Eastern Europe* and *Europe – the Grand Tour* factsheets (see p.13).

prompted further nationalist independence struggles in the other republics, and at the time of writing things still look far from settled. The war zone of Sarajevo being a classic case in point. To top it all, the Civil War has brought a disastrous loss of foreign revenue from tourism, which has added to the economic problems which were present before (in 1988 inflation reached a frightening 140 per cent). At the moment it looks reasonably safe to venture into Slovenia, but our advice is to check very carefully the political situation before crossing the border, and to bear in mind that much damage has been done to the beautiful towns in the country during the fighting. The nature of the Serbian regime may also put this republic on a blacklist for many. The prices mentioned in this chapter are an extremely rough guide, because of the unstable economic and political situation.

YUGOSLAV STATE RAILWAYS
(Jugoslovenske Železnica, JZ)

Most expresses are electric, but many local trains and railcars, particularly the newest ones, are diesel. The majority of JZ rolling stock consists of redundant German carriages pensioned off years ago, so if you have to travel through 'Yugoslavia' stick to international expresses and head for carriages from other countries such as Austria, France and Switzerland. Despite that, JZ has recently bought some new stock and on these trains air-conditioning means something other than a permanently open door. The afternoon express from Zagreb to Ljubljana, for instance, uses the most modern railcars, with aircraft-style seating, air-conditioning, piped music, free newspapers, soft drinks and sandwiches. Coffee, however, is extra. But like the rest of 'Yugoslavia', the railway system is full of contrasts, and your next train is likely to be an ancient carriage with blocked loos, opaque windows and hard seats. Conditions are generally OK on trains in Slovenia; Croatia is reasonable, but Serbia is decidedly nor for the faint-hearted. The young military personnel look on travellers as a source of free cigarettes and alcohol and their methods of extracting these would worry your mother!

All the major towns are linked by rail, but only a few lines go as far as the coast. Don't be misled by the impressive variety of trains operating within 'Yugoslavia', as only the international expresses are worth travelling on. Listed here in descending order of comfort and speed are the options open to the eurorailer: international expresses, inland expresses (Ekspresni), rapides (Poslovni), fast (Brzi) and the unspeakably slow trains (Putnički). Unless you plan to visit Belgrade, go for a through express, as changing trains here nearly always means no seat for the second leg of your journey. To make things easier, here are the origins and destinations of the main international expresses:

Simplon: London–Paris–Milan–Belgrade
Venezia: Venice–Belgrade–(Sofia–Istanbul)–Athens
Ljubljana: Vienna–Moribor–Ljubljana–Rijeka
Slavija: Vienna–Moribor–Zagreb–Belgrade
Acropolis: Munich–Ljubljana–Belgrade–Kosovo–Polje–Skopje–Athens
Yugoslavia: Frankfurt–Munich–Ljubljana–Zagreb
Hellas: Dortmund–Munich–Belgrade–Skopje–Athens
Tauern: London–Ostend–Aachen–Cologne–Munich–Zagreb–Knin–Split
Istanbul: Munich–Belgrade–Sofia–Istanbul
Mostar: Stuttgart–Munich–Zagreb–Sarajevo–Kardeljevo (in winter also Zagreb–Knin–Split)

It's strongly advisable to reserve a seat on any of these expresses, all of which are valid on Inter-Rail. Reservations are obligatory from stations in Germany to stations in 'Yugoslavia' and Greece. Beware guards trying to collect unofficial supplements.

TRAIN INFORMATION

English is spoken by most information staff; if not, try German. In the backwaters, rely on your ingenuity as there won't be any information staff, let alone English speakers.

• **Reservations:** Are obligatory on some internal routes. Trains from Belgrade south to Athens and north to Zagreb or Budapest are invariably packed – get a reservation if you can, otherwise you may end up in the corridor or (better) the baggage car, a practice that guards tend to tolerate. Note that reserved seats are not marked.

• **Night travel:** 'Yugoslavian' couchettes are quite comfortable but difficult to get hold of (if possible, try for a couchette from Vienna). The price of sleepers will keep you awake worrying, so you may as well forget them.

• **Buses:** 'Yugoslavia' has an extensive network of bus services linking major and minor towns. The bus station is usually next door to the railway station, and often has better facilities. The staff are generally helpful. The buses themselves, like the trains, range from the ultra-modern to the decrepit, but they serve many places where the railway doesn't run and are always faster than Putnički trains. Fares are very cheap. Inter-Railers can save money by buying green bus tokens at newsstands.

• **Eating on trains:** Most expresses and fast trains have bars and diners. Other trains may have mini-bars but the food is expensive and drink even worse. It is far cheaper and better to buy bread, cheese and meat in shops near the station. Also, go for the excellent range of Fructal carton fruit drinks. Most stations have drinking water taps on the platforms.

• **Scenic tips:** Three-quarters of 'Yugoslavia' is covered by mountains and one-third by forests, so there are plenty of options. The most spectacular route is the recently opened Belgrade–Bar line to the Montenegrin coast. A particularly breathtaking bus ride is Cetinje to Kotor.

TOURIST INFORMATION

All major cities have a tourist office (Turističko Društno); they're normally near the stations. They keep maps and leaflets on their region and help find a room if required.

• **ISIC bonuses:** Discounts are given on some museums and cultural tours. For further information contact Karavan Student Travel Agency, Takovska 2, Belgrade.

• **Money matters:** The currency is the new dinar (D). 1 dinar = 100 paras.
Banking hours fluctuate. The longest are 7 a.m.–7 or 8 p.m. Away from the tourist centres, some banks shut from 12 noon to 3 p.m. It's also possible to change money at many travel agencies, though

expect to pay 2 per cent commission on all transactions. Banks do not charge commission. Remember to keep your exchange slips for reconversion. It's the same rate everywhere so don't bother to shop around. It's illegal to take in or out more than 1,200 D. Don't change much, particularly if you are not staying long, as exchange facilities – if they exist at all – will give you a poor rate at the border. The dinar is now a convertible currency and although the black market still exists, you won't get a much better rate than at a bank, and are likely to be cheated. Restaurant waiters are usually very willing to change money. Remember, many locals hate the dinar; take hard currency everywhere. Knock four noughts off old notes.

• **Post offices:** Open Mon.–Sat.: 7 a.m.–8 p.m. Stamps can also be bought from tobacconists and Trafik shops. Glavna Pošta = poste restante.

• **Shops:** Open Mon.–Sat.: 8 a.m.–8 p.m. with an optional 12 noon–3 p.m. siesta.

SLEEPING

Tourist offices help out a bit by supplying booklets and information on camping, private accommodation and hotels, as well as running a room-finding service. Hotels are pricey, with even the cheapest C grades charging upwards of £18.75/$30 per person. Private accommodation (sobe) is a much better bet at about £6.25/$10 per person. If you're approached at the station by locals offering a room in their house you could try and negotiate but it is illegal. Student hostels are another alternative in July and August, with doubles at about £12.50/$20. Also, there are thirty-five youth hostels scattered throughout the country, most of which are very basic, though the ones in the major cities are better. For camping, pick up the tourist information booklet which gives facilities and distances from the nearest town. Prices range between £1.25–£5/$2–$8 per person.

Finally, you can be sure to be moved on if you try to sleep at the stations, as the authorities don't look too kindly on this.

EATING AND NIGHTLIFE

The endless variety of regional specialities should make eating out in 'Yugoslavia' a pleasure, but if you go for westernized restaurants you'll find prices high. Your best bets are the self-service places or take-away stalls. If you're really low on readies, try the workers' communal eating halls (large soup-kitchen-type places full of men putting away mundane meals at an incredible pace). These are very cheap but not for those of a delicate disposition, as you'll see a lot of spitting (and worse) which can lessen the appetite somewhat. As a general rule, meat dishes represent the best value, particularly from the take-aways. Try ćevapčići (grilled and spiced beef), or raznjići (grilled pork, veal or lamb, on a spit). If you're really hard up, go for a burek (a pastry with meat, cheese or vegetable filling) or just a plain pancake washed down with yoghourt, as the locals do. If you're eating out, it's best to stay with the local wines: Riesling and Smederevka are the most popular white, Zupsko and Prokupac the most popular red.

The korzo is a pre-dinner evening stroll where everyone eyes up their neighbours in the town to see who's with who and what they're wearing. It's as good a way as any to meet the locals.

Slovenia

This republic may be safe to travel in, but check with the foreign office first.

The proximity and influence of Austria over this rural republic have helped make it one of the more comfortable to travel in. Hygiene and standards are generally more westernized than further south; in fact, northern Slovenia is just like an extension of Austria, and it's not till after the Julian Alps that the scenery begins to flatten out and change. In southern Slovenia, there are some smallish beaches at KOPER and PIRAN; and some winter sports centres.

Ljubljana

This is the capital of the republic, but it's an industrial centre and not really worth special attention. However, if you are breaking a journey here, take in the OLD TOWN with its castle, cathedral and medieval streets, or the old NATIONAL MUSEUM (a good rainy-after-noon alternative). In summer, the cultural festival means there are plenty of concerts and plays going on. Sleeping and eating shouldn't put you out: get the tourist office to fix you up with private accommodation or camp at Titova 260a (Tel. 371382) on bus route 6.

TOURIST INFORMATION AND ADDRESSES

TOURIST OFFICE: Titova Cesta 11, open Mon.–Fri.: 8 a.m.–9 p.m., Sat.–Sun.: 8 a.m.–12 noon, 5 p.m.–8 p.m. (Tel. 215412).
POST OFFICE: Titova Cesta 8, open Mon.–Fri.: 8 a.m.–8 p.m., Sat.: 8 a.m.–2 p.m.
AMEX: c/o Atlas, Trg Mestni 8, open Mon.–Fri.: 7.30 a.m.–7 p.m.; Sat.: 7.30 a.m.–1 p.m.
STUDENT TRAVEL: Celovšuka 49. Pick up youth hostel lists here and let them help you out on accommodation, open Mon.–Fri.: 10 a.m.–2 p.m., 3 p.m.–5 p.m.
PHONE CODE: 061.

A great day trip from Ljubljana is to the famous POSTOJNA CAVES. Although the entrance fee is quite expensive (£7 – half with ISIC – there is a Bureau de Change next to the pay booth), it is worth every penny and the trip lasts for several hours. The caves are one of the natural wonders of Europe and the system of underground chambers, stalactites and stalagmites gets more and more breathtaking the further you go on your tour by electric train and on foot. Take some warm clothing as it can get cold. You can get to Postojna either by train or bus; although the bus service is more frequent and takes you nearer the cave entrance, there is still a 15–20-minute walk from the bus station and almost half an hour's walk from the train station.

Julian Alps

One of the most famous Slovenian tourist postcard views is of the church on an island in the middle of LAKE BLED at the foot of the Julian Alps. Bled has been a spa resort for many years and is as popular in summer as it is in winter as a ski resort. The town is situated near the Austrian border about 35 miles from Ljubljana, and there is an hourly bus service to it from the bus station in front of the train station. The fare is only around 35 D and the journey takes about 90 minutes. You could take the less regular train service, but the station marked Bled is actually about three miles away and you'll only end up waiting for the next bus to take you there. It is well worth a day's outing and you can get some spectacular views of the island from the castle and museum overlooking the lake if you decide not to take a boat trip to the island itself. The youth hostel is a few minutes' walk along the road from the bus station at Grajska 17 (Tel. 064–78230), should you be so enchanted with the place you decide to stay overnight. Food tends to be slightly dearer here than in towns like Ljubljana, but there is a market town so stock up here if you intend staying any length of time or heading on to do some climbing in the Julian Alps. Bled is a popular starting-out point for those who wish to attempt an assault on MOUNT TRIGLAV, at 2,834 metres the highest mountain in the Julian Alps.

The other republics featured in this chapter may not be safe for tourists. Check with the foreign office before venturing into Croatia, Bosnia–Hercegovina, Serbia, Montenegro or Macedonia.

Croatia

Zagreb

This, the capital of Croatia, is also its cultural centre. It's a city which is only 250 miles (but can be more than seven hours in a train – I speak from bitter experience) from Belgrade but feels like it is in another world. For 'Yugoslavia', this city really ticks and is quite sophisticated and westernized. The people are very friendly and helpful and the contrast with Belgrade is quite marked.

The station has the full range of facilities, left luggage, restaurants; Bureau de Change, Information and the city's main post office and phone office are next door, past the old steam train which is a feature of many Yugoslav stations. Although nicely painted and highly polished, many of these trains are kept in working order so they can be used if the electricity network is destroyed.

The city is divided into three main areas: the Upper Town, dating back to the thirteenth century; the Lower Town, which is nineteenth-century; and the modern, postwar New Zagreb. Concentrate your efforts on Upper Zagreb (north of the station) and see: ST STEPHEN'S CATHEDRAL, ST MARK'S, the CROATIAN NATIONAL THEATRE and some of the many galleries and museums. There are several festivals, and the nightlife here is the most cosmopolitan you'll get. Use the cheap and excellent accommodation at the Studentski Centar Turist Biro, Savska Cesta 25 (Tel. 041–278611); or the youth hostel, Petrinjska 77 (Tel. 041–434964). Near Zagreb (1 hr by bus, 1½ hrs by train) is Kumrovec, Tito's birthplace. This old home is now a museum.

Trieste–Dubrovnik

The Adriatic was fast becoming the tourist goldmine of 'Yugoslavia' before the fighting made it unsafe to visit. Trains run as far south as Split. To get to Dubrovnik, you have to bus it from Kardeljevo (Ploče). The coast is 'Yugoslavia's' main redeeming feature – in fact, it's the only part of the country where touring isn't hard work, and even here it's bad enough; but console yourself with the fact that there are over 1,000 little islands out there in the Adriatic, and that there are towns like Split and Dubrovnik, which are well worth visiting. You're bound to find somewhere to take off your shirt and relax for a day or two. If you're interested: this stretch of the Adriatic coast is *the* centre for 'naturism' in southern Europe. Though unofficial camping's illegal, you should get away with it in the less obvious places, though there are quite a few youth hostels on the coast.

Probably the easiest option, though, is to forget the train trip to Split and head for RIJEKA from Ljubljana or Trieste, depending on whether you enter the country from Austria or Italy respectively.

There is a regular ferry service by the Jadrolinija Line down the coast stopping at many of the islands. The ticket will cost around £18.75/$30 (less October–December) but you could spend several times that on a cabin on the overnight service. Don't bother, as the bench seats are very wide and comfortable, but get on early and book your space as the ship tends to get full at Rijeka, gradually emptying as it calls at the islands on the way down the coast. If you're peckish, check out the price of the restaurant meals. Depending on inflation, it should still cost less to have a blow-out on a silver service dinner in the restaurant than a hamburger and Coke in McDonald's in the West.

On the way down, stop off at HVAR. This lovely island has lots of private accommodation and the hotels are reasonably priced, even in summer. It is well worth spending a day or two discovering Hvar village, parts of it dating back to the thirteenth century, including the oldest theatre in the Adriatic. As for other islands, ask amongst eurorailers for their recommendations. Suggestions are KRK, RAB, CRES, BRAC and KORČULA (possibly the cheapest).

Jadrolinija ferries go on down the coast and call at Split, Dubrovnik and Bar, continuing to Corfu and Igoumenitsa in Greece. From Hvar it is a six-hour journey by boat to DUBROVNIK, but as with the trains, don't be surprised if it takes you twice as long as timetabled, particularly if the weather is rough.

Split

The regional capital of Dalmatia dates back to the fourth century AD and to the Romans. The magnificent PALACE built by Diocletian in the third century developed into a medieval town, and the former palatial apartments have over the years become houses, while the corridors became streets. The basement now houses several museums and galleries. Other things to look out for are the CATHEDRAL, the ARCHAEOLOGICAL MUSEUM, with many of the palace's fittings, and the BAZAAR. The city outside the walls is the new commercial centre where the hotels and nightclubs are.

Sleeping's a problem in Split as prices are high and it's a seller's market. You could try camping at Put Trstenika (Tel. 058–521971) on bus route 7 or 17, but it's usually pretty unsavoury; or for a dormitory bed you could try the student hostel at Masleśina 66 (Tel. 058–551744), bus 18. The best of the cheap hotels is the Srebrena Vrata inside the east gate at Bulićeva Poljana (Tel. 058–46869).

There are 12 ferries per day to and from Supetar on the nearby island of Brac (approx. £2.20/$3.50 each way) where there is a good natural beach.

TOURIST INFORMATION AND ADDRESSES

TOURIST OFFICE: Titova Obala 12, open Mon.–Sat.: 7 a.m.–10 p.m., Sun.: 8 a.m.–12.30 p.m., 4 p.m.–8 p.m. in season. They handle private accommodation, but it's not cheap (Tel. 058–42142).
AMEX: Atlas, Trg Preporoda 7 (just west of the palace), open Mon.–Fri.: 8 a.m.–7 p.m., Sat.: 8 a.m.–1 p.m.
UK CONSULATE: Titova Obala 10 (Tel. 058–41464).

Dubrovnik

This was undoubtedly the most attractive city the old 'Yugoslavia' had to offer, but it has suffered greatly as a result of recent fighting. It was one of Europe's leading centres in the fifteenth century – so much so that it rivalled Venice in looks and wealth, with many Renaissance palaces and churches.

• **Transport:** The railway line to Dubrovnik has disappeared. The nearest railhead is Kardeljevo on the line from Sarajevo. Buses from Kardeljevo are fairly frequent and cheap. Dubrovnik bus station is about twenty minutes' walk from the old town. Buses also run south to Bar (three to five hours) which is on the end of a new line from Belgrade. If you are thinking of heading down to Greece you can get a ferry several times a week from Dubrovnik. Check the times at the ferry terminal or with tourist information because they are liable to sudden changes. You have to pay in hard currency for travel to destinations outside the Yugoslavian republics.

TOURIST INFORMATION AND ADDRESSES

TOURIST OFFICE: Poljana Paška Miličevića 20, open daily: 9 a.m.–9 p.m. Located by the west gate, they'll arrange accommodation and hand out maps and leaflets.

AMEX: c/o Atlas, Pile 1, open daily: 7.30 a.m.–8 p.m.

MEDICAL HELP: Maršala Tita 61 (Tel. 32677).

PHONE CODE: 050.

SEEING

A wonderful introduction to the city is to walk along on top of the old city walls – don't worry, they're thick enough to be safe. This'll give you an idea of the layout (10D). Dubrovnik's actually tiny, so you can quite easily get round the sights on foot.

The most inspiring buildings are the DOGE'S PALACE, the baroque CHURCH OF ST VLAHO beside ONOFRIO'S FOUNTAIN, the FRANCISCAN MONASTERY and the DOMINICAN CLOISTER AND MUSEUM (closed Sundays). The beaches are always busy in summer and charge, so you're actually far better taking the ferry over to LOKRUM, the island offering a national park and bathing area. (The nudist beach here is known to get quite lively in peak season!)

SLEEPING

As with most commercial resorts, sleeping can be a problem: hotels are over the top and there aren't enough hostels to go round. Sleeping on the beaches seems the natural solution – only the police don't quite view it that way, and for the kind of fines they'll impose, you could have slept at the best hotel in town. The International Student Centre is very good, but unless you reserve, you don't stand a chance. It's at Ivanska 14 (Tel. 23841), bus 2 or 4 from the bus or ferry stations. There are two youth hostels, one at Oktobarske Revolucije 17 (Tel. 23241), open April–October and worth a try and the other at Vinka Sagrestena 3 (Tel. 415038). For hotels, try the Lapad (Tel. 23473) or Gruž, Gruška Obala 68 (Tel. 24777), but even they're in the £18.75/$30 per double range. There is a campsite one and a half miles east of the station (Tel. 20770). Three buses an hour to the old city (numbers 4 or 6). If you are arriving late off the ferry, and haven't booked in advance, it may be worth your while considering accommodation offered to you on the quayside.

Strictly speaking this is illegal, but in practice the police prefer this to fining people found sleeping rough on the beach. This doesn't mean to say you can't haggle to reduce the asking price of around 140 D and 210 D for a single and double respectively.

EATING AND NIGHTLIFE

Neither is a problem. To cater for the tourists there are plenty of restaurants with reasonable menus although the price of food in the old town is about twice that of anywhere else in 'Yugoslavia', or you could live out of any of the self-service Expresses. The summer festival draws top names in 'high culture' to the town, but if that leaves you cold, there's always good manwatching potential, once everyone changes at night (or gets dressed for the first time, in many cases) and parades up and down the main streets, having an occasional drink or ice-cream. There are also nightclubs, strippers, etc., in some of the flashy hotels.

Bosnia–Hercegovina

The Turkish-influenced republic of Bosnia–Hercegovina, set among the central mountains, is en route to Dubrovnik from Zagreb or Belgrade. The stretch of line from Sarajevo to MOSTAR runs through this region, and a day's stop-off in either of these towns will be an interesting experience.

SARAJEVO, 8½ hours from Zagreb and 6½ hours from Belgrade, was under Turkish rule for over 500 years and there are still minarets, mosques, and culinary reminders of this all around. There are also reminders of the 1984 Winter Olympics in the shape of Sarajevo's above-average facilities. Tourist information is at Jugoslovenske Narodne Armije 50, open 7 a.m.–9 p.m. (Tel. 071–25151), and to get fixed up with private accommodation, go to Unis Turist, Vase Miskina 16 (Tel. 071–23868). Also try Agencija Stari Grad Serači 81 (Tel. 071–535202) which is cheaper. There's a youth hostel at Zadrugina 17 (Tel. 071–36163). The campsite is at Ilidza (Tel. 071–621436), tram 3 to the end. Eat in the Turkish quarter and on your sightseeing tour look out for BEY'S MOSQUE, the bridge where Archduke Ferdinand was shot (think back to your First World War history), and the SERBIAN ORTHODOX CHURCH. Take a stroll around the restored BASCARSIJA MARKET area. It has a pleasant atmosphere, although it has obviously been reconstructed for tourists. You can get cheap snacks and cakes here.

An interesting side trip is to the new pilgrimage site of MEDU-JORDE where four young people see visions of the Virgin Mary daily. Bus 48 from Mostar costs about £1.25/$2. MOSTAR itself, although touristy, has a magnificent bridge and the old town is worth a look.

Serbia

Belgrade (Beograd)

The capital of Serbia and former capital of 'Yugoslavia' as a whole, is not one of Europe's best cities. This is probably because since its founding in the third century the city has been destroyed and rebuilt thirty-six times, and little but grey, high-rise, concrete blocks stand there today. Despite this, Belgrade is friendlier than many Eastern European cities. The station is old, but its facilities are usable, though those in the bus station next door are superior. The station does have a cafeteria, left-luggage office (obligatory passport check), tourist information office and late night bureau de change. Building work is likely to add to the noise and chaos. A new station is under construction to the south of Belgrade. Trains coming in from this direction often stop here for long periods.

Belgrade also has its Donau station which serves the daily Bucharest train. Bus number 34 connects.

TOURIST INFORMATION AND ADDRESSES

There's an information booth inside the station, open 7 a.m.–9 p.m., but the main office is in the subway at the Albanija Building on Terazije, and is open 8 a.m.–8 p.m. (Tel. 635622). All the main hotels will hand you a free map if you ask at reception.

POST OFFICE: Takovska 2, open Mon.–Sat.: 8 a.m.–8 p.m. Poste restante and telephones also here.

AMEX: Zmaj Jovina 10, open Mon.–Fri.: 8 a.m.–8 p.m., Sat.: 8 a.m.–3 p.m.

UK EMBASSY (also for NZ): Generala Ždanova 46 (Tel. 645055).

US EMBASSY: Kneza Miloša 50 (Tel. 645655).

AUSTRALIAN EMBASSY: Čika Ljubina 13 (Tel. 624655).

CANADIAN EMBASSY: Kneza Miloša 75 (Tel. 644666).

KARAVAN STUDENT TRAVEL: Takovska 2, open Mon.–Fri.: 7 a.m.–6 p.m., Sat.: 8 a.m.–6 p.m.

PHONE CODE: 011.

SEEING

Belgrade has one main attraction: the KALEMEGDAN PARK. It is a remarkable place that contains the KALEMEGDAN FORTRESS, built by the Serbs, Austrians and Turks; it now contains an observatory and the Military Museum (closed Sundays and Mondays). The fortress has a commanding view over the confluence of the rivers Sava and Danube. Come here for a picnic and to watch the locals' afternoon strolls. Apart from this, head for the NATIONAL MUSEUM at Trg Republike. The nineteenth-century Bohemian quarter, SKADAR-LIJA, is good for a stroll.

• **Excursion:** The massive fortress of SMEDEREVO on the banks of the Danube is well worth a visit. 1½ hours by bus or over 2 hours by train. A good half-day trip. The fortress, railway station and bus station are next to each other.

SLEEPING

Go to the tourist office and ask them to help you out, as there are very few affordable beds. The youth hostel at Bulevar Jug. Narodne Armije 56a (Tel. 463846) is on tram 9 or 10. University halls around 130 D a night. Studentski Grad, 11070 Novi Beograd. Bus 601 outside station. Get off at the fourth stop. You're usually deluged with offers if you hang round the station long enough, but haggle with them to reduce prices dramatically. Across from the station is

738 Europe by Train

the Pansion Centar, at Trg Bratsva i Jedinstva 17. The station closes from 12 midnight till 5 a.m., and if you try hanging around the police give you a hard time, so take bus 53 from the station, walk up Nemanijina and turn left at Kneza Miloša out to its terminus, and camp out in the forest. There are also two official sites. They're at Kneza Višeslava 17 (Tel. 555127) and Bežanijska Koza 1a (Tel. 693509).

EATING AND NIGHTLIFE

For both activities the Skadarlija district is best. There are plenty of places to eat cheaply, but avoid stopping off for just a drink in cafés, as prices are high. There are enough stalls selling snacks dotted round Skadarlija to get a meal together as you walk, and there are street performances and music and dancing in most of the restaurants in this part.

Montenegro

South of Dubrovnik is the varied republic of Montenegro. The train services are restricted, and to get to the interesting places you really have to resort to buses. However, if you want to try and see some of Montenegro, the main line to concentrate on is the one from Belgrade to Bar, which has fantastic views and runs via TITOGRAD. Titograd is a rather pleasant, fairly modern town rebuilt after almost total destruction in 1944. There isn't much to see in the town itself, but an hour's bus ride to Cetinje is worth it for the former Royal Palace of Montenegro.

Macedonia

This is one of the most backward regions of Europe, and the pleasure of seeing a primitive land such as this is greatly diminished by the many inconveniences you'll have to put up with: hardly any trains, and expect great problems with eating and sleeping. It is worth pointing out that Macedonia is also the name of the northern Greek province over the border – a much more attractive place to stop off. If you're one of the brave ones on the Belgrade–Athens run, you'll pass through SKOPJE, the capital of the republic. Unless you're feeling really grotty and don't think you could make it straight down to Athens, don't break your journey in Skopje. It is not very attractive and is unfriendly and uninteresting. If you're staying the night, try Studentski Dom, Kuzman Josifonski (Tel. 091–235360) or youth hostel at Prolet 25 (Tel. 091–233866). See the OLD TOWN at the foot of the ruined CASTLE.

The area to head for in Macedonia is LAKE OHRID, along the Albanian border. OHRID is a charming town containing medieval Serbian remains. It stands on a beautiful clear lake in which you can swim. The local fish is a speciality, especially the trout or carp. Tourist information is at Partizanska 3 (open 7 a.m.–9 p.m.), and they'll help you out with accommodation (Tel. 096–22494).

To get to Ohrid, take a bus from Kicevo or Bitola. Both of these can be reached by train from Skopje. One train per day also runs from Florina in Greece to Bitola. There is no other reason for going to Bitola, although it does have a free campsite – a field behind a restaurant; take bus 1 from the station. Private accommodation may be a better bet than the youth hostel at Goce Delčev (Tel. 096–21626).

APPENDICES

Appendix I

CIEE OFFICES

USA

Arizona
120 East University Drive
Suite E
Tempe, AZ 85281
(602) 966–3544

California
2486 Channing Way
Berkeley, CA 94704
(415) 848–8604

UCSD Price Center
9500 Gilman Drive
La Jolla, CA 92093–0076
(619) 452–0630

1818 Palo Verde Avenue
Suite E
Long Beach, CA 90815
(310) 598–3338
(714) 527–7950

1093 Broxton Avenue
Suite 220
Los Angeles, CA 90024
(310) 208–3551

394 University Avenue
Suite 200
Palo Alto, CA 94301
(415) 325–3888

953 Garnet Avenue
San Diego, CA 92109
(619) 270–6401

312 Sutter Street
Suite 407
San Francisco, CA 94108
(415) 421–3473

919 Irving Street
Suite 102
San Francisco, CA 94122
(415) 566–6222

14515 Ventura Blvd
Suite 250
Sherman Oaks, CA 91403
(818) 905–5777

Colorado
1138 13th Street
Boulder, CO 80302
(303) 447–8101

Connecticut
Yale Co-op East
77 Broadway
New Haven, CT 06520
(203) 562–5335

District of Columbia
3300 M Street NW
2nd Floor
Washington, DC 20007
(202) 337–6464

Florida
One Datran Center
Suite 320
9100 South Dadeland Blvd
Miami, FL 33156
(305) 670–9261

Georgia
Emory Village
1561 North Decatur Road
Atlanta, GA 30307
(404) 377–9997

Illinois
1153 North Dearborn Street
2nd Floor
Chicago, IL 60610
(312) 951–0585

1634 Orrington Avenue
Evanston, IL 60201
(708) 475–5070

Louisiana
Joseph A. Danna Center
Loyola University
6363 St Charles Avenue
New Orleans, LA 70118
(504) 866–1767 .

Massachusetts
79 South Pleasant Street
(2nd floor, rear)
Amherst, MA 01002
(413) 256–1261

729 Boylston Street
Suite 201
Boston, MA 02116
(617) 266–1926

Cart S. Ell Student Center
Northeastern University
360 Huntingdon Avenue
Boston, MA 02115
(617) 424–6665

1384 Mass. Avenue
Suite 201
Cambridge, MA 02138
(617) 497–1497

Stratton Student Center
MIT, W20–024
84 Mass. Avenue
Cambridge, MA 02139
(617) 225–2555

Michigan
1220 S. University Drive
Suite 208
Anne Arbor, MI 48104
(313) 998–0200

Minnesota
1501 University Avenue, SE
No. 300
Minneapolis, MN 55414
(612) 379–2323

New York
205 East 42nd Street
New York, NY 10017
(212) 661–1450

35 West 8th Street
New York, NY 10011
(212) 254–2525

New York Student Center
895 Amsterdam Avenue
New York, NY 10025
(212) 666–4177

North Carolina
703 Ninth Street
Suite B-2
Durham, NC 27705
(919) 286–4664

Ohio
8 East 13th Avenue
Columbus, OH 43201
(614) 294–8696

Oregon
715 S.W. Morrison
No. 600
Portland, OR 97205
(503) 228–1900

Pennsylvania
3606 A Chestnut Street
Philadelphia, PA 19104
(215) 382–0343

Rhode Island
171 Angell Street (corner
of Thayer), Suite 212
Providence, RI 02906
(401) 331–5810

Texas
2000 Guadalupe Street
Austin, TX 78705
(512) 472–4931

6923 Snider Plaza
Suite B
Dallas, TX 75205
(214) 363–9941

Washington
1314 Northeast 43rd Street
Suite 210
Seattle, WA 98105
(206) 632–2448

219 Broadway Avenue East
The Alley Building
Suite 17
Seattle, WA 98102
(206) 329–4567

Wisconsin
2615 North Hackett Avenue
Milwaukee, WI 53211
(414) 332–4740

EUROPE

France
12, rue Leydet
13100 Aix-en-Provence
(42) 38.58.82

36 quai Gailleron
69002 Lyon
(78) 37.09.56

20 rue de l'Université
34000 Montpellier
(67) 60.89.29

37 bis, rue d'Angleterre
06000 Nice
(93) 82.23.83

31, rue St Augustin
75002 Paris
(1) 42.66.20.87

49, rue Pierre Charron
75008 Paris
(1) 43.63.19.87

51, rue Dauphine
75006 Paris
(1) 43.25.09.86

16, rue de Vaugirard
75006 Paris
(1) 46.34.02.90

Germany
18, Graf Adolph Strasse
4000 Düsseldorf 1
(211) 329.088

UK
28A Poland Street
London W1
(071) 437 7767

Appendix II

INTER-RAIL 1993
DISCOUNTS AVAILABLE TO INTER-RAILERS UNDER 26

SEA OPERATORS

Sealink Stena Line	Dover-Calais	30%
Sealink Stena Line	Folkestone-Boulogne	30%
Sealink Stena Line	Harwich-Hoek van Holland	30%[4]
Hoverspeed (Hovercraft/Sea Cat)	Dover Hoverport-Calais/Boulogne	50%
Hoverspeed (Sea Cat)	Folkestone-Boulogne	50%
Sealink Stena Line	Harwich-Hoek van Holland	30%[4]
P&O (European Ferries)	Dover-Calais/Boulogne	30%
P&O (European Ferries)/RMT	Dover-Oostende	30%
P&O (European Ferries)	Portsmouth-Le Havre	30%
Sealink Newhaven–Dieppe	Newhaven-Dieppe	30%
Scandinavian Seaways (DFDS)	Harwich/Newcastle-Esbjerg	50%[1]
Scandinavian Seaways (DFDS)	Harwich/Newcastle-Gothenburg	50%[1]
Scandinavian Seaways (DFDS)	Harwich-Hamburg	50%[1]
Sealink Stena Line	Fishguard-Rosslare	30%
Sealink Stena Line	Holyhead-Dun Laoghaire	50%
Sealink Stena Line	Stranraer-Larne	33%
B&I Line	Holyhead-Dublin	50%
Irish Continental Line	Cork/Rosslare-Le Havre	50%[3]
Irish Continental Line	Rosslare-Cherbourg	50%[3]

AUSTRIA

Puchberg Schneeberg-Hochschneeberg	50%
St Wolfgang Schafbergbahnhof-Schafbergspitze	50%
OeBB Wolfgangseeschiffahrt	50%
Vereinigte Schiffahrtsverwaltungen fur den Bodensee und Rhein	50%
Erste Donau-Dampfschiffarhrts-Gesellschaft-Passau-Wien	50%
Chemins de fer regionaux de la Styrie (Steiermark) Feldbach–Bad Gleichenberg	50%
Chemins de fer regionaux de la Styrie (Steiermark) Gleisdorf–Weiz	50%
Chemins de fer regionaux de la Styrie (Steiermark) Peggau Deutsch-feistritz-Ubelbach	50%
Chemins de fer regionaux de la Styrie (Steiermark) Unzmarkt–Tamsweg	50%

NOTES

1 The reduced fare available to Inter-Rail card holders is inclusive of a couchette.

2 The reduced fares available to Inter-Rail card holders is inclusive of a rest chair.

3 In June, July and August the reduction available to Inter-Rail card holders is 65%. Reservations are compulsory during July and August.

4 Reservations are compulsory on night sailings. Accommodation must be reserved in advance.

DENMARK

Det Forenede Dampskibsselskab (DFDS)	Kobenhavn–Oslo	50%[2]
Hjorring Privatbaner (HP)	Hjorring–Hirtshals	50%
Flyvebadene (Hovercraft)	Kobenhavn–Malmö	50%

FINLAND

Oy Vaasanlaivat	Vassa-Umea	50%[2]

GERMANY

Schauinslandbahn GmbH, Freiburg (Breisgau)	All	50%
Vorwohle-Emmerthaler Verkehrsbetriebe GmbH, Bodenwerder	All	50%
Kahlgrund-Verkehrs-GmbH, Schöllkrippen	All	50%
Oberrheinische Eisenbahn-Gesellschaft AG, Mannheim	Rail sections only	50%
Regentalbahn AG, Viechtach	All	50%
Lokalbahn Lam-Kötzing, Lam		50%
Tegernsee-Bahn AG, Tegernsee		50%
Verkehrsbetriebe Peine-Salzgitter GmbH, Salzgitter-Hallendorf		50%
Kreisbahn Aurich GmbH, Aurich		50%
Eisenbahn-Gesellschaft Altona-Kaltenkirchen-Neumunster, Hamburg	Kaltenkirchen-Neumunster	50%
Regionalverkehr Munsterland GmbH	All coach lines	50%
Regionalverkehr Ruhr-Lippe GmbH	All coach lines	50%
Verkehrsgesellschaft.Kreis Tecklenburg – Techlenburger Nordbahn – AG	All coach lines	50%
Verkehrsgesellschaft Kreis Unna GmbH	All	50%
Vereinigte Schiffahrtsunternehman für den Bodensee und Rhein	All	50%
Frankfurt (M) Postal and Railway buses	All	50%

MOROCCO

Cie Limadet Ferry	Malaga-Tanger	30%
Cie Marocaine de navigation	Tanger-Sete	20%

NORWAY

Fred Olsen Lines/KDS	Hirtshals-Kristiansand	50%
Ofotens Bilruter-Autobus	Narvik-Bodo	50%
Larvik Line A/S	Larvik-Frederikshavn	50%

SWEDEN

Stena Sessan Line	Goteborg-Frederikshavn	50%
Silja Line	Stockholm-Helsinki	50%
Silja Line	Stockholm-Turku S	50%
TT-Saga Line	Trelleborg-Lubeck-Travemunde	50%
Swedish State Railways	Haparanda-Boden	50%
	Storuman-Haellnaes	50%

SWITZERLAND

All these companies give a 50% reduction:

AB	Appenzellerbahn
BAM	Biere-Apples-Morges
BGF	Grindelwald-First
BLM	Lauterbrunnen-Murren
BOB	Berner Oberland-Bahnen
BOW	Oberdorf-Weissenstein
BrS	Brienzersee
BTI	Blei-Tauffelen-Ins
BVB	Bex-Villars-Bretaye
BVZ	Brig-Visp-Zermatt
CEV	Chemins de fer du Veveysans
CJ	Chemins de fer du Jura
CMN	Chemins de fer des Montagnes-Neuchateloises
EBT	Emmental-Burgdorf-Thun
FB	Forchbahn
GBS	Gurbetal-Bern-Schwarzenburg
GFM	Chemins de fer Fribourgeois
GFM/VMC	Vevey-Chatel-St Denis-Bossonnens
GGB	Gornergratbahn
GN	Glion-Rochers-de-Naye
JB	Jungfraubahn
LAF	Adliswil-Feisenegg
LAS	Les Avants-Sonloup
LEB	Lausanne-Echallens-Bercher
LLB	Leuk-Leukerbad
LLPR	Lenzerheide-Parpaner Rothorn
LSE	Luzern-Stans-Engelberg
LSM	Stockalp—Melchsee-Frutt
LSMS	Stechelberg-Schilthorn
LWM	Wengen-Mannlichen
MC	Martigny-Chatelard
MGI	Montreux-Glion
MO	Martigny-Orsieres
NStCM	Nyon-Sant-Cergue-Morez

SWITZERLAND

OeBB	Oensingen-Balsthal
OJB	Oberaargau-Jura
PBr	Pont-Brassus
RBS	Regional Verkehr Bern-Solothurn
RVT	Regional du Val-de-Travers
SBN	Beatenberg-Niederhorn
SGA	St Gallen-Gais-Appenzell-Altstatten
SGV	Vierwaldstattersee
SMB	Solothurn-Moutier
SMtS	St Imier–Mont-Soleil
SNB	Solothurn-Niederbipp
STB	Sensetalbahn
STI	Steffisburg-Thun-Interlaken
SZU	Sihital-Zurich-Uetliberg-Bahn
TB	Trogenerbahn
TBB	Thunersee-Beatenberg
Ths	Thunersee
URh	Untersee und Rhein
VCP	Vevey-Mont-Pelerin
VHB	Vereinigte Huttwil-Bahnen
WAB	Wengernalpbahn
WB	Waldenburgebahn
WSB	Whynental-und Suhrentalbahn
YSteC	Yverdon-Ste-Croix
ZSG	Zurichsee

Details of discounts are compiled according to information provided to British Rail by the operators concerned. However, this information may be subject to change without notice.

TRANSPORT MUSEUMS

The following Transport Museums offer free or reduced admittance to holders of Inter-Rail cards:

Belgium	Railway Museum, Gare de Bruxelles Nord Station
Denmark	Railway Museum, Jernbanemuseum, Odense
France	French Railway Museum, 2 rue Alfred de Glehn – Mulhouse
Germany	Transport Museum, Lessingstrasse 6, Nurnberg
Finland	Railway Museum, Hyvinkää
	Narrow Gauge Railway Museum, Jokioinen (Minkio Station)
Hungary	Transport Museum, Varosligeti, Korut II, Budapest XIV
	Metro Museum, Metro Station Deak Ferenc tér, Budapest
	Horse Carriage Museum, Paradfurdo

Norway	Railway Museum, Hamar
Portugal	Railway Museum, Santarem Station
Rumania	Railway Museum – Bucuresti (Nord) Station
Spain	Railway Museum, San Cosmey y San Damien – 2 Madrid
Sweden	Jarnvagsmuset, Museum of Transport, Ralsgaten 1, Gavle
Switzerland	Swiss Transport and Communications Museum, Lidostrasse, Luzern

The following museums offer reduced price admittance to holders of Inter-Rail cards:

France	Museum of waxworks, 10 Boulevard Montmarte, 75009 Paris
	New Museum Grevin du Forum des Halles, rue Pierre-Lescot, Niveau 1, Grand Balcon, 75001 Paris
	History of 'Touraine' museum, Chateau Royal, Quai d'Orleans, 37000, Tours
	Museum Grevin Rochelle, 38 cours des Dames, 17000, La Rochelle
	Museum Grevin, Mont-Saint-Michel, 50116, Mont-Saint-Michel
Austria	Museum of Industry (including Railway Museum), Mariahilferstrasse 212, 1140 Vienna

INTER-RAIL CENTRES

KOBENHAVN

A special Inter-Rail centre is open from 15 June until 20 September, between 7 a.m. and 12 midnight, at Kobenhavn Central Station (Hovebanegard) and provides information, refreshments and showers. Overnight sleeping is not allowed.

OSLO

An Inter-Rail centre is available at Oslo Station. The centre offers a lounge, showers, toilets, telephones, information and the sales of sandwiches and beverages. The centre is open from 15 June until 15 September between 7 a.m. and 11 p.m. each day. Overnight sleeping is not allowed.

TRONDHEIM

An Inter-Rail centre is also available at Trondheim Station. This centre provides a lounge, showers, toilets, information, a train reservation service, cooking facilities and the sale of beverages. The centre is open from 25 June until 1 September between 7 a.m. and 9.30 p.m. each day. Overnight sleeping is not allowed.

IMPORTANT INFORMATION

1. Replacement cards cannot be issued under any circumstances. You are advised to take out insurance to cover you in the event of loss or theft of your Inter-Rail card.

2. Inter-Rail card holders must pay the usual reservation fees for seats, couchettes and sleeping berths.

3. When returning your completed card for rebate, please ensure that you take it to the office which issued it, with a complete record of the journeys you made.

INTER-RAIL +26
DISCOUNTS AVAILABLE DURING 1993

SEA OPERATORS

P&O (European Ferries)/RMT	Dover-Oostende	30%
B&I Line	Holyhead-Dublin	50%
Irish Continental Line	Cork/Rosslare-Le Havre	50%[2]
Irish Continental Line	Rosslare-Cherbourg	50%[2]

AUSTRIA

Puchberg Schneeberg-Hochschneeberg	50%
St Wolfgang Schafbergbahnhof-Schafbergspitze	50%
OeBB Wolfgangseeschiffahrt	50%
Vereinigte Schiffahrtsverwaltungen fur den Bodensee und Rhein	50%
Erste Donau-Dampfschiffarhrts-Gesellschaft-Passau-Wien	50%
Chemins de fer regionaux de la Styrie (Steiermark) Feldbach-Bad Gleichenberg	50%
Chemins de fer regionaux de la Styrie (Steiermark) Gleisdorf-Weiz	50%
Chemins de fer regionaux de la Styrie (Steiermark) Peggau Deutsch-feistritz-Ubelbach	50%
Chemins de fer regionaux de la Styrie (Steiermark) Unzmarkt-Tamsweg	50%

DENMARK

Det Forenede Dampskibsselskab (DFDS)	Kobenhavn–Oslo	50%[1]
Hjorring Privatbaner (HP)	Hjorring-Hirtshals	50%
Flyvebadene (Hovercraft)	Kobenhavn-Malmö	50%

FINLAND

Oy Vaasanlaivat	Vassa-Umea	50%[1]

GERMANY

As for under 26s

NOTES

1 The reduced fare available to Inter-Rail card holders is inclusive of a rest chair.

2 In June, July and August the reduction available to Inter-Rail card holders is 65%. Reservations are compulsory during July and August.

NORWAY

North Norway Express (except on ferry services)	Narvik-Bodø/Fauske	50%
North Norway Express	Narvik-Tromsø/Atta	50%
North Norway Express	Narvik-Hammerfest/kirkenes	50%
Larvik Line	Larvik-Frederikshavn	50%
Fylkesbaatane/Sogan-Og Fjordane	Express ferries and fjord ferries	50%
Buses in the district of Nordland		50%

SWEDEN

Stena Sessan Line	Göteborg-Frederikshavn	50%
Silja Line	Stockholm-Helsinki	50%
Silja Line	Stockholm-Turku S	50%
TT-Saga Line	Trelleborg-Lubeck-Travemunde	50%
Swedish State Railways	Haparanda-Boden	50%
	Storuman-Haellnaes	50%

SWITZERLAND

All these companies give a 50% reduction:

AB	Appenzellerbahn
BAM	Biere-Apples-Morges
BGF	Grindelwald-First
BLM	Lauterbrunnen-Mürren
BOB	Berner Oberland-Bahnen

SWITZERLAND

BOW	Oberdorf-Weissenstein
BrS	Brienzersee
BTI	Biel-Täuffelen–Ins
BVB	Bex-Villars-Bretaye
BVZ	Brig-Visp-Zermatt
CEV	Chemins de fer du Veveysans
CJ	Chemins de fer du Jura
CMN	Chemins de fer des Montagnes-Neuchâteloises
EBT	Emmental-Burgdorf-Thun
FB	Forchbahn
GBS	Gürbetal-Bern-Schwarzenburg
GFM	Chemins de fer Fribourgeois
GFM/VMC	Vevey-Châtel-St-Denis-Bossonnens
GGB	Gornergratbahn

GN	Glion-Rochers-de-Naye
JB	Jungfraubahn
LAF	Adliswil–Feisenegg
LAS	Les Avants-Sonloup
LEB	Lausanne-Echallens-Bercher
LLB	Leuk-Leukerbad
LLPR	Lenzerheide-Parpener Rothorn
LSE	Luzern-Stans-Engelberg
LSM	Stöckalp-Melchsee-Frutt
LSMS	Stechelberg-Schilthorn
LWM	Wengen-Männlichen
MC	Martigny-Châtelard
MGI	Montreux-Glion
MO	Martigny-Orsières
NStCM	Nyon-Sant-Cergue-Morez
OeBB	Oensingen-Balsthal
OJB	Oberaargau-Jura
PBr	Pont-Brassus
RBS	Regional Verkehr Bern-Solothurn
RVT	Régional du Val-de-Travers
SBN	Beatenberg-Niederhorn
SGA	St Gallen-Gais-Appenzell-Altstätten
SGV	Vierwaldstättersee
SMB	Solothurn-Moutier
SMtS	St Imier-Mont-Soleil
SNB	Solothurn–Niederbipp
STB	Sensetalbahn
STI	Steffisburg-Thun-Interlaken
SZU	Sihital-Zürich-Uetliberg-Bahn
TB	Trogenerbahn
TBB	Thunersee–Beatenberg
Ths	Thunersee
URh	Untersee und Rhein
VCP	Vevey–Mont-Pèlerin
VHB	Vereinigte Huttwil–Bahnen
WAB	Wengernalpbahn
WB	Waldenburgebahn
WSB	Whynental-und Suhrentalbahn
YSteC	Yverdon-Ste-Croix
ZSG	Zurichsee

Details of discounts are compiled according to information provided to British Rail by the operators concerned. However, this information may be subject to change without notice.

Appendix III

BASIC VOCABULARY

Although it is sometimes possible to get by in English, often it's not. We've kept it pretty simple as there's no point getting too involved in a language you don't know the basics of. German can often be used in Eastern Europe. Useful books are the Berlitz *European Phrase Book* (14 languages, £3.95) and the Pan *Traveller's Multilingual Phrase Book* (8 languages, £3.99).

ENGLISH	CZECH	DANISH	DUTCH
Yes	Ano	Ja	Ja
No	Ne	Nej	Nee
Please	Prosím	Vaer så venlig	Alstublieft
Thank you	Děkuji	Tak	Dank u
Good morning	Dobrý den	Godmorgen	Goedemorgen
Goodbye	Na shledanou	Farvel	Tot ziens
Where is/are...	Kde je/jsou...	Hvor er...	Waar is/zijn...
Excuse me	Promiňte	Undskyld	Pardon
How much?	Kolik to stojí?	Hvor meget?	Hoeveel?
Can I have...	Chtěla bych...	Kan jeg få...	Mag ik...hebben
I don't understand	Nerozumím	Jeg forstår ikke	Ik begrijp het niet
Do you speak English?	Mluvíte anglicky?	Taler De engelsk?	Spreekt u Engels?
My name is...	Jmenuji se...	Mit navn er...	Mijn naam is...

ENGLISH	FINNISH	FRENCH	GERMAN
Yes	Kyllä	Oui	Ja
No	Ei	Non	Nein
Please	Olkaa hyvä	S'il vous plaît	Bitte
Thank you	Kiitos	Merci	Danke
Good morning	Hyvää huomenta	Bonjour	Guten morgen
Goodbye	Näkemiin	Au revoir	Auf Wiedersehen
Where is/are...	Missä on/ovat...	Où se trouve/trouvent...	Wo ist/sind...
Excuse me	Anteeksi	Excusez-moi	Entschuldigung
How much?	Kuinka paljon?	Combien?	Wieviel?
Can I have...	Voinko saada...	Je voudrais...	Kann ich...haben
I don't understand	En ymmärrä	Je ne comprends pas	Ich verstehe nicht
Do you speak English?	Puhutteko englantia?	Parlez-vous anglais?	Sprechen Sie Englisch?
My name is...	Nimeni on...	Je m'appelle...	Ich heisse...

ENGLISH	HUNGARIAN	ITALIAN	NORWEGIAN
Yes	Igen	Si	Ja
No	Nem	No	Nei
Please	Kérem	Per favore	Var så god
Thank you	Köszönöm	Grazie	Takk
Good morning	Jó reggelt	Bongiorno	God morgen
Goodbye	Viszontlátásra	Arrivederci	Ha det godt
Where is/are...	Hol van/vannak...	Dov'è/Dove sono...	Hvor er...
Excuse me	Elnézést	Mi scusi	Unnskyld
How much?	Mennyi/Mennyit?	Quanto?	Hvor mye?
Can I have...	Kaphatok...	Posso avere...	Kan jeg få...
I don't understand	Nem értem	Non capisco	Jeg forstår ikke
Do you speak English?	Beszél angolul?	Parla inglese?	Snakker Du engelsk?
My name is...	Nevem...vagyok	Mi chiamo...	Mitt navn er...

ENGLISH	PORTUGUESE	SPANISH	SWEDISH
Yes	Sim	Sí	Ja
No	Não	No	Nej
Please	Faz favor	Por favor	Varsågod
Thank you	Obrigado	Gracias	Tack
Good morning	Bom dia	Buenos días	God morgon
Goodbye	Adeus	Adiós	Adjö
Where is/are...	Onde está/estão...	Dónde está/están...	Var är...
Excuse me	Descuple	Dispénseme	Förlåt
How much?	Quanto?	¿Cuánto?	Hur mycket?
Can I have...	Pode dar-me...	Puede darme...	Kan jag få...
I don't understand	Não comprendo	No comprendo	Jag förstår inte
Do you speak English?	Fala inglês?	¿Habla usted inglés?	Talar Ni engelska?
My name is...	O meu nome é...	Me llamo...	Mitt namn är...

ENGLISH	TURKISH	YUGOSLAVIAN (SERBO-CROATIAN)
Yes	Evet	Da
No	Hayir	Ne
Please	Lütfen	Molim
Thank you	Teşekkür ederim	Hvala
Good morning	Günaydin	Dobro jutro
Goodbye	Güle güle/Allahaismarladik	Zbogom
Where is/are...	Nerede/Neredeler...	Gde je/su...
Excuse me	Affedersiniz	Izvinite
How much?	Ne kadar?	Koliko?
Can I have...	...rica edebilir miyim	Mogu li dobiti...
I don't understand	Anlamiyorum	Ne razumem
Do you speak English?	Ingilizce Biliyor musunuz?	Gavorite li engleski?
My name is...	Adim...'dir	Ja se Zovem...

Appendix IV

BRITISH, IRISH AND CONTINENTAL FERRIES

From	To	Operator	Type	Time hours	Average frequency
Ramsgate	Dunkerque	Sally Ferries	Ship	2½	5 daily
Dover	Calais	P&O European Ferries	Ship	1¼	15 daily
Dover	Boulogne	P&O European Ferries	Ship	1¾	6 daily
Dover	Oostende	P&O European Ferries	Ship	3¾	5/8 daily
Dover	Oostende	P&O European Ferries	Jetfoil	1¾	2/6 daily
Portsmouth	Le Havre	P&O European Ferries	Ship	5¾	2/3 daily
Portsmouth	Cherbourg	P&O European Ferries	Ship	4¾	1/4 daily
Felixstowe	Zeebrugge	P&O European Ferries	Ship	5¾	1/2 daily
Cairnryan	Larne	P&O European Ferries	Ship	2¼	4/6 daily
Dover	Calais	Sealink Stena	Ship	1½	10–16 daily
Stranraer	Larne	Sealink Stena	Ship	2½	4/8 daily
Fishguard	Rosslare	Sealink Stena	Ship	3½	1/2 daily
Holyhead	Dun Laoghaire	Sealink Stena	Ship	3½	2/4 daily
Southampton	Cherbourg	Sealink Stena	Ship	6	1/2 daily (summer only)
Newhaven	Dieppe	Sealink Stena	Ship	4	2/4 daily
Harwich	Hoek van Holland	Sealink Stena	Ship	6½	2 daily
Southampton	Cherbourg	Sealink Stena	Ship	6	1 daily
Dover	Calais	Hoverspeed	Hovercraft	35 min	12 daily (summer only)
Dover	Calais	Hoverspeed	Seacat	40 min	7 daily
Dover	Boulogne	Hoverspeed	Seacat	40 min	3/4 daily
Folkestone	Boulogne	Hoverspeed	Seacat	40 min	3/7 daily
Belfast	Stranraer	Hoverspeed	Seacat	1½	4/5 daily
Plymouth	Roscoff	Brittany Ferries	Ship	6	1/3 daily summer, 1 weekly
Plymouth	Santander	Brittany Ferries	Ship	24	2 weekly
Portsmouth	St Malo	Brittany Ferries	Ship	9	1/2 daily, not Jan./Feb.
Portsmouth	Caen	Brittany Ferries	Ship	6	1/3 daily
Harwich	Esbjerg	Scandinavian Seaways	Ship	19¾	1 daily
Newcastle	Esbjerg	Scandinavian Seaways	Ship	21½	2 weekly (summer)
Newcastle	Goteborg	Scandinavian Seaways	Ship	23	1 weekly (summer)
Harwich	Goteborg	Scandinavian Seaways	Ship	23	5/6 weekly

From	To	Operator	Type	Time hours	Average frequency
Harwich	Hamburg	Scandinavian Seaways	Ship	21½	1 daily
Cork	Le Havre	Irish Ferries	Ship	22½	1 weekly (summer only)
Rosslare	Cherbourg	Irish Ferries	Ship	18	1/3 weekly
Rosslare	Le Havre	Irish Ferries	Ship	21	2/5 weekly
Sheerness	Vlissingen	Olau Line	Ship	6	2 daily
Hull	Rotterdam	North Sea Ferries	Ship	13	1 daily
Hull	Zeebrugge	North Sea Ferries	Ship	13½	1 daily
Holyhead	Dublin Ferryport	B&I Line	Ship	3½	2 daily
Pembroke	Rosslare	B&I Line	Ship	4¼	1/2 daily

Appendix V

EURAIL AID OFFICES

AUSTRIA
ÖBB
Wien Westbahnhof
A–1150 **Vienna**

ÖBB
Salzburg Hauptbahnhof
A–5010 **Salzburg**

ÖBB
Innsbruck Hauptbahnhof
A–6010 **Innsbruck**

BELGIUM
Société Nationale des
Chemins de fer
Belges
Salon d'Accueil
Service International
Gare de Bruxelles-Midi
Brussels 1070

DENMARK
DSB Travel Agency
Central Station
Banegärdspladsen
DK–1570 **Copenhagen**

FINLAND
Valtionrautatiet
Rautatieasema
VR Lipputoimisto
SF–00100 **Helsinki**

FRANCE
Société Nationale des
Chemins de fer
Français
Guichets Internationaux
Galerie des Fresques (or
Bureaux
Informations-Réservations)
Gare de Paris-Lyon
F–75012 **Paris**

Société Nationale des
Chemins de fer
Français
Service International
Gare de Paris-St Lazare
F–75008 **Paris**

Société Nationale des
Chemins de fer
Français
Bureau Information-
Réservation
Gare de Paris-Nord
F–75010 **Paris**

Société Nationale des
Chemins de fer
Français
Bureau SNCF d'Orly
Aéroport
Cedex A 222
F–94396 **Orly-Airport**

Société Nationale des
Chemins de fer
Français
Bureau SNCF de Roissy
Aéroport Charles de Gaulle
BP 20215
F–95712 **Roissy Aéroport
Charles de Gaulle**

Société Nationale des
Chemins de fer
Français
Guichet 'Billets
Internationaux'
Gare de Marseille
St Charles
F–13232 **Marseille**

Société Nationale des
Chemins de fer
Français
Gare de Nice-Ville
F–06000 **Nice**

GERMANY
Deutsche Bundesbahn
Fahrkartenausgabe
Hauptbahnhof
D–6000 **Frankfurt/Main**

Deutsche Bundesbahn
Fahrkartenausgabe
Hauptbahnhof
D–6900 **Heidelberg**

Deutsche Bundesbahn
Fahrkartenausgabe
Hauptbahnhof
D–8000 **Munich**

Deutsche Bundesbahn
Fahrkartenausgabe
Hauptbahnhof
D–5000 **Cologne**

Deutsche Bundesbahn
Fahrkartenausgabe
Hauptbahnhof
D–7000 **Stuttgart**

Deutsche Bundesbahn
Fahrkartenausgabe
Hauptbahnhof
D–2000 **Hamburg**

Fahrkartenausgabe
Berlin Zoologischer
Garten
Jebenstrasse 8–10
D–1000 **Berlin** 12

Dresden Hauptbahnhof
Verkehrstelle am
Hauptbahnhof
D–8010 **Dresden**

Leipzig Hauptbahnhof
Fahrkartenausgabe
Georgring 14
D–7010 **Leipzig**

GREAT BRITAIN
French National
Railways
179 Piccadilly
London W1V 0BA

GREECE
Chemins de fer
Hélléniques
Bureau des Voyages et
du Tourisme No.2
1 rue Karolou
Athens 107

Chemins de fer
Hélléniques
Gare Centrale des
Voyageurs
Thessaloniki

HUNGARY
Magyar Államvasutak
Közönsegszolgolati
Iroda
Nep Kòz Earsasag
Utjah 35
H–1061 **Budapest** VI

IRELAND (Republic of)
Coras Iompair Eireann
International Rail Ticket
Sales Office
35 Lower Abbey Street
Dublin 1

ITALY
Ferrovie Italiane dello
Stato
Stazione Santa Maria
Novella
Ufficio informazioni
Florence

Ferrovie Italiane dello
Stato
Stazione Centrale
Milan

Ferrovie Italiane dello
Stato
Stazione Santa Lucia
Venice

Ferrovie Italiane dello
Stato
Stazione Termini
Rome
Ferrovie Italiane dello
Stato
Stazione Centrale
Naples

Ferrovie Italiane dello
Stato
Stazione Centrale
Bari

Ferrovie Italiane dello
Stato
Stazione Centrale
Palermo

LUXEMBOURG
Société Nationale des
Chemins de fer
Luxembourgeois
Bureau des
renseignements
Gare de Luxembourg
Luxembourg (GD)

NETHERLANDS
N.V. Nederlandse
Spoorwegen
Bureau Ep 3-32-2
Katreinetoren (in the
Hall of Utrecht
Central Station)
Utrecht

NORWAY
NSB
Billettekspedisjonen/
Oslo Sentralstasjon
0154
Oslo 1

PORTUGAL
Companhia dos
caminhos
de ferro portugueses
Bilheteira Internacional
Estaçao de Santa
Apolonia
Avenida Infante D.
Henrique
P–1100 **Lisbon**

Companhia dos
caminhos
de ferro portugueses
Estaçao de S. Bento
Praça Almeida Garret
P–4000 **Porto**

Companhia dos
caminhos
de ferro portugueses
Estaçao de Caminho
de ferro
Largo de estaçao
P–8000 **Faro**

SPAIN
Red Nacional de los
Ferrocarriles
Españoles
Alcala 44
Madrid

Officina de Viajes
RENFE
Madrid–Barajas
International
Airport
Madrid

Red Nacional de los
Ferrocarriles Españoles
Estación central de
Barcelona Sants
Barcelona

Red Nacional de los
Ferrocarriles Españoles
Calle Zaragoza 29
Seville

Red Nacional de los
Ferrocarriles Españoles
Plaza Alfonso el
Magnanimo 2
Valencia

SWEDEN
Swedish State Railways
Ticket Office
Stockholm Central Station
S–105-50 **Stockholm**

SWITZERLAND
Schweizerische
Bundesbahnen
Reisebüro
Hauptbahnhof
CH–4051 **Basel**

Schweizerische
Bundesbahnen
Auskunftsbüro
Hauptbahnhof
CH–3000 **Bern**

Chemins de fer fédéraux
Suisses
Gare de Genève
CH–1211 **Geneva**

Chemins de fer
fédéraux Suisses
Bureau de
Renseignements CFF
Geneva Airport
CH–1215 **Geneva**

Schweizerische
Bundesbahnen
Auskunftsbüro
Bahnhof
CH–6000 **Lucerne**

Schweizerische
Bundesbahnen
Auskunftsbüro
Hauptbahnhof
CH–8021 **Zürich**

Schweizerische
Bundesbahnen
Auskunftsbüro
Zürich Flughafen
CH–8058 **Zürich**

Appendix VI

COMMON CONVERSIONS

Length

1 inch = 2.54 centimetres

1 foot = 0.305 metre

1 mile = 1.609 kilometre

1 centimetre = 0.39 inch

1 metre = 3.281 feet

1 kilometre = 0.621 mile

Volume

1 cubic foot = 0.028 cubic metre

1 gallon (UK) = 4.546 litres

1 gallon (US) = 3.785 litres

1 cubic metre = 35.315 cubic feet

1 litre = 0.22 gallon (UK)

1 litre = 0.264 gallon (US)

Weight

1 pound = 0.454 kilogram

1 ounce = 28.35 grammes

1 kilogram = 2.205 pounds

1 gram = 0.036 ounce

Speed

1 m.p.h. = 1.609 kilometre/hour

1 kilometre/hour = 0.621 m.p.h.

Temperature

zero °C	=	32°F
25°C	=	77°F
50°C	=	122°F
75°C	=	167°F
100°C	=	212°F

Dates

UK/European format: dd/mm/yy

American format: mm/dd/yy

where dd = day

     mm = month

     yy = year

Times

In the 24-hour clock times after noon are as follows:

1 p.m. = 13:00, 2 p.m. = 14:00, 3 p.m. = 15:00 etc.

until midnight, which is 00:00.

ACKNOWLEDGEMENTS

I would like to thank the following people for their support and cooperation throughout this project: Gill Edwards, Julie Mitchell, Peter Lyons, Philip Wilks and Rupert Brown of British Rail who have been invaluable with their up-to-date information and late-night checkings, Janet Ennor of Eurotrain. Last but not least, thanks to my family for their kindness and encouragement.

Each year I receive dozens and dozens of letters from you, the readers, telling me of your eurorailing experiences, and how you found the book. Without your help I would find it very difficult to keep abreast of all the changes in all 27 countries, so please keep up the good work. Please, however, keep these letters brief, typed, insert relevant page nos, be concise and go for under two pages! I can't cope with any more 15-pagers! I try to acknowledge each letter individually, but sometimes it gets hard, and between trips, meeting publishing deadlines and organizing future research trips some people may wait longer than I'd ideally like for their personal 'thank you'. This year your response has been great, and to those of you who wrote especially detailed letters I'd like to take this opportunity to acknowledge your contributions: Graeme Garson, Edinburgh; Mike Zimmerman, Broadstairs; Gill Stafford, Clwyd; Tim Ryder, Oxford; Jeff Liston, Edinburgh; Damien McSweeney, Ireland; Kevin Fuller; Edward McPhillips, Ireland; Ray Furlong, Swansea; John Campbell, Glasgow; Robin Gummer and Samantha Elmhurst, Herts; Catherine Davie, Leicester; Jonathan Davis, Leeds; Helen Ford, Honiton; Sarah Jane Brooks, Oxford; Rosie McAuley, Belfast; Ian Barker, Croydon; James Knowles, Ulverston; Eva Røher, London and Luxembourg; Veronica Hessing, Notts; Gwenda Pearson and Garesh Nana from Wellington, New Zealand; Sharon and Adam Kovalevsky from London; Mr S. P. Green, Nottingham; Elizabeth Lord, Halifax; Kenneth Bell, Glasgow; John Pinder, London; Joan Michelson, London; Jon Beck, Spondon; Konstantinos Markantonatos, Athens; Nick Power, Walsall; Dr Nigel Malcolm-Smith, Edinburgh; Ruth Parkyn, Ottery St Mary; Frances Uebergang, N.S. Wales; Jonathon Ginns, Leicester; Rosemary Harley, Harbury; Monica Meary, Dublin; Matthew Shaw and Jamie Taylor, Summerton; James May,

Wiltshire; Susan Walter, Middlesex; Stephanie Smith, New Zealand; Per Johansson, Goteborg, Sweden; and M. R. Davis.

To you all, a sincere thank you.

Katie Wood, 1993.

INDEX

INDEX